COMMON DESTINY

COMMON DESTINY

A Comparative History of the Dutch, French, and
German Social Democratic Parties, 1945–1969

by

Dietrich Orlow

Berghahn Books
NEW YORK • OXFORD

Published in 2000 by

Berghahn Books

© 2000 Dietrich Orlow

Library of Congress Cataloging-in-Publication Data

Orlow, Dietrich.
    Common destiny : a comparative history of the Dutch, French, and
German social democratic parties, 1945–1969 / by Dietrich Orlow.
        p.   cm.
    Includes bibliographical references and index.
    ISBN 1-57181-185-0 (alk. paper)
    1. Socialist parties—Netherlands—History. 2. Socialist parties—
France—History. 3. Socialist parties—Germany—History.
4. Socialism—Europe Case studies. I. Title.
JN5981.075   2000   99–35021
324.2'172'094—dc21   CIP

British Library Cataloguing in Publication Data

A catalogue record for this book is available from the British Library.

CONTENTS

ACKNOWLEDGMENTS

I t is a pleasant duty to acknowledge the many institutional and personal debts which I have incurred in the process of researching and writing this book.

First and foremost, I am grateful to The Netherlands Institute of Advanced Studies (NIAS), which granted me a Fellowship for the academic year 1993–1994. My nine-month stay in Wassenaar, The Netherlands, enabled me to complete most of the research and begin the writing of the manuscript. NIAS is a delightful institution with an administration dedicated to facilitating the work of the Fellows in every way possible.

In addition, the NIAS Fellows for 1993–1994 were a singularly congenial group, providing a degree of intellectual stimulation that scholars often hope for, but seldom find. I would especially like to mention two of the Fellows, Prof. Hans Blom, now the Director of the Rijksinstituut voor Oorlogsdocumentatie, Amsterdam, and Prof. Piet de Rooy, of the University of Amsterdam, who were always ready to answer questions on the often difficult details of Dutch political history. I am also grateful to NIAS' director in 1993–1994, Prof. Dirk J. van de Kaa, and the NIAS librarian, Mevr. Dinny Young. Prof. van de Kaa combined managerial efficiency with a genuine interest in the Fellows' projects, while Mevr. Young worked tirelessly to fulfill the Fellows' many requests for interlibrary loan materials.

Much of the archival research for this project was done in three depositories, the Archiv der Sozialen Demokratie of the Friedrich-Ebert-Stiftung in Bonn, the Internationaal Instituut voor Sociaalgeschiedenis in Amsterdam, and the Office universitaire de recherche socialiste (OURS) in Paris. I am grateful to the staffs of each of these institutions, and especially to Dr. Wolfgang Gröf at the Archiv der Sozialen Demokratie and M. Denis Lefebvre at OURS. In addition, the history bibliographer at the Mugar Memorial

Library of Boston University, Mr. Donald Altschiller, provided helpful leads on a number of esoteric items.

Over the years several colleagues encouraged me to pursue this project and helped me to define and refine its conceptualization and *Fragestellung*. I am especially grateful to Prof. Maarten Brands, now the Director of the Duitsland-Instituut of Amsterdam, as well as Prof. Hans Blom.

Two colleagues were kind enough to read substantial portions or the entire manuscript. Prof. Piet Rooy subjected the parts dealing with the PvdA and Dutch politics to close scrutiny. His alertness saved me from several embarrassing errors, and I am grateful for his help. My colleague, Prof. Lancelot Farrar, in Newton, Massachusetts, volunteered for the onerous burden of reading the entire manuscript. I gratefully acknowledge his numerous suggestions for stylistic improvements. He also deserves credit for proposing the main title of the book.

As always, my wife, Maria, has been my most active supporter and collaborator. Without her work as co-researcher, word processing specialist, and stylistic watchdog this project would certainly not have been completed as soon as it was.

Needless to say, any errors or shortcomings that remain are my responsibility.

ABBREVIATIONS

Amb. Bonn	Ambassade française à Bonn, French embassy in Bonn
AN	Assemblée Nationale, French national parliament
AOFAA	Archive d'occupation française en Allemagne et l'Autriche, Colmar
Arch.SD	Archiv der sozialen Demokratie, Bonn
BB	Berlin Berichte, Willy Brandt's 1947–1948 reports as the Berlin representative of the SPD's executive committee
BHE	Bund der Heimatlosen und Entrechteten, Association of the Homeless and Dispossessed, German refugee party
Best.	Bestand
CAP	Common Agricultural Policy of the European Common Market
CAP/SFIO	Commission administrative permanente, Permanent Administrative Commission, forerunner of the CD
CD	Comité Directeur, executive committee of the SFIO
CDA	Christen-Democratisch Appèl, Christian Democratic Call
CGT	Confédération Générale du Travail, General Federation of Labor
Comisco	Committee of the International Socialist Conference, forerunner of the SI
CPN	Communistische Partij van Nederland
D'66	Democraten '66, Dutch Liberal Party

DAG	Deutsche Angestellten Gewerkschaft, German Union of White Collar Employees
DGB	Deutscher Gewerkschaftsbund, German Association of Labor Unions
DS'70	Democratische Socialisten '70, PvdA splinter group
ECSC	European Coal and Steel Community
EDC	European Defense Community
EEC	European Economic Community
ERP	European Recovery Program, the formal name of the Marshall Plan
FEN	Fédération d'Enseignement national, French National Teachers' Union
FGDS	Fédération de la Gauche démocrate et socialiste, Federation of the Democratic and Socialist Left
FO	Force Ouvrière, Workers' Force, French non-Communist labor union
For.Hbg.	Forschungsstelle für die Geschichte des Nationalsozialismus in Hamburg now: Forschungsstelle für Zeitgeschichte in Hamburg
GVP	Gesamtdeutsche Volkspartei, All-German People's Party, German left-liberal party
GP	Groupe parlementaire, parliamentary delegates of the SFIO
IISG	Internationaal Instituut voor Sociale Geschiedenis, Amsterdam
IRA	The International Ruhr Authority
JS	Jeunesses socialistes, SFIO youth organization
Jusos	Junge Sozialisten, SPD youth organization
KPD	Kommunistische Partei Deutschlands, Communist Party of Germany
KVP	Katholieke Volkspartij, Dutch Catholic People's Party
MAÉ	Ministère des Affaires étrangères, French Ministry of Foreign Affairs
MRP	Mouvement Républicain Populaire, Republican Popular Movement, French Christian Democratic Party
MSEUE	Mouvement Socialiste pour les États-Unis d'Europe, Socialist Movement for the United States of Europe
NL	Nieuw Links, New Left, oppositional group in the PvdA

NPD	Nationaldemokratische Partei Deutschlands, National Democratic Party of Germany, neo-Nazi organization
NSB	Nationaalsocialistische Beweging, National Socialist Movement, Dutch fascist party
NVB	Nederlandse Volksbeweging, Dutch People's Movement, forerunner of the PvdA
NVV	Nederlands Verbond van Vakverenigingen, Dutch Association of Labor Unions
OURS	Office universitaire de recherche socialiste, Paris
PA	Parteiausschuss, advisory committee of the SPD
PAK	Progressief Akkord, Dutch left-wing electoral alliance
PB	Partijbestuur, executive committee of the PvdA
PBO	Publieke Bedrijfsorganisatie, Public Enterprise Organization, Dutch industrial policy agency
PCF	Parti communiste français, French Communist Party
PKK	Parteikontrollkommission, party control commission of the SPD
PME	Plan de Modernisation d'équipment, French plan of modernization and resources
PR	Parteirat, party council of the SPD
PS	Parti socialiste, French Socialist Party
PSA	Parti socialiste autonome, French Independent Socialist Party
PSP	Pacifistisch Socialistische Partij, Dutch Pacifist Socialist Party
PSU	Parti socialiste unifié, French Unified Socialist Party
PV	Parteivorstand, executive committee of the SPD
PvdA	Partij van de Arbeid, Dutch Labor Party
RDR	Rassemblement démocratique révolutionnaire, Revolutionary Democratic Rally, French left-wing socialist group
RKStP	Rooms-Katholieke Staatspartij, Dutch Roman Catholic State Party, predecessor of the KVP
RPF	Rassemblement du Peuple français, Rally of the French People, Gaullist party
SD	*Socialisme en democratie*, theoretical organ of the PvdA

SDAP	Sociaaldemocratische Arbeiderspartij, Dutch Social Democratic Workers' Party, predecessor of the PvdA
SDC	Sociaal-Democratisch Centrum, Social Democratic Center, left-wing Marxist group in the PvdA
SDS	Sozialistischer Studentenbund, Socialist University Student Association
SFIO	Section française de l'internationale ouvrière, French section of the Workers' International, French Socialist Party
SHB	Sozialistischer Hochschulbund, Socialist University Association, successor to the SDS
SI	Socialist International
SMIC	Salaire minimum interprofessionel de Croissance, French minimum wage
SPS	Sozialdemokratische Partei der Saar, Social Democratic Party of the Saar
UDSR	Union démocratique et sociale de la Résistance, Democratic and Social Union of the Resistance, early political affiliation of François Mitterrand
UGCS	Union des groupes et clubs socialistes, Union of Socialist Groups and Clubs
UGS	Union de la Gauche socialiste, Union of the Socialist Left
UNR	Union pour la nouvelle République, Union for the New Republic, Gaullist party
USPD	Unabhängige Sozialdemokratische Partei Deutschlands, Independent Social Democratic Party of Germany
VVD	Volkspartij voor Vrijheid en Democratie, Popular Party for Freedom and Democracy, Dutch liberal party

INTRODUCTION

❦

A few years ago the editors of *Die Zukunft*, a periodical published by the Austrian Social Democratic Party, invited Lord Ralf Dahrendorf, the former director of the London School of Economics and former warden of St. Anthony's College, Oxford, and the then Austrian chancellor Kurt Vranitzky to discuss the future of European Social Democracy. As a sort of sweeping introduction to his analysis of the problems the Continent's Socialists would face in the future, Dahrendorf began with the good news: The twentieth century was the age of Social Democracy. The West European Social Democratic parties had succeeded in translating their ideas and programs into policies and legislation to a greater extent than their political rivals.[1]

Until recently that conclusion was shared, in a rather self-congratulatory manner, by many contemporary socialists, who also offered a ready explanation for their political achievements. Typical was a comment which the present-day leader of the Dutch *Partij van de Arbeid* (PvdA), Wim Kok, made at a retrospective conference in the mid-1980s: "The success of West European Social Democracy ... was primarily the success of choosing democracy, discussion, and compromise; it is based upon ... concrete reform projects."[2]

The optimism in the socialist ranks increasingly turned to pessimism in the 1990s. Until the triumph of the New Labour party in Great Britain and the Socialists in France lifted the self-confidence of Europe's left-wing parties,[3] Europe's social democrats seemed to have reached political dead ends. Conservatives and neoliberals on both sides of the Atlantic held them responsible for the failure of the welfare state and the chronic structural problems of the Continental European economies. Reaganism and Thatcherism were the new watchwords. Even the Social Democrats themselves seemed to have lost faith in their cause. Assessments like "deep-seated pessimism" and "ill adapted to their century" contrasted sharply with the earlier promulgations of decades of triumph.[4]

Neither deterministic triumphalism nor blanket condemnation is warranted, of course, and the present work is an attempt to present a more reasoned analysis of the history of three West European social democratic parties, the Dutch PvdA, the French *Section Française de l'Internationale Ouvrière* (SFIO), and the German *Sozialdemokratische Partei Deutschlands* (SPD), for a pivotal period of their lives, the quarter century after the Second World War.

Wim Kok's contention that the social democrats readily chose the road to pragmatic reformism (a conclusion many scholars share[5]) does little justice to what was in fact a difficult process of adjustment for West European social democracy in the post-1945 era. As this comparative analysis will show, the Social Democratic parties began their political life after the Second World War with visions of revolutionary euphoria, although twenty-five years later all three had become reformist, pragmatic, broadly based catch-all parties. But their paths to reformism did not proceed smoothly along parallel lines. Each addressed the challenges of postwar politics in its own way, meeting a broad spectrum of needs with quite different responses.

Despite the vast number of treatments of virtually all aspects of European Socialism—including a number of studies of the three parties discussed in this book—most scholars agree that the pivotal period examined here, has been curiously neglected.[6] There are a number of reasons for this. In West Germany the larger than life figure of Konrad Adenauer and the Christian Democratic party he headed dominated politics and the history of politics until the early 1960s. The PvdA's genuine political successes in the 1940s and 1950s were pushed into the background when a group of young leftists temporarily took over the party in the 1960s and attempted to rewrite its history. In France another oversized figure, Charles de Gaulle, the disappearance of the SFIO, and the triumphs of its successor organization, the *Parti Socialiste* (Socialist Party, PS), in the 1980s overshadowed the SFIO's contributions to French political life in the earlier postwar period.

The need for comparative analyses of political parties has been routinely endorsed in theory by many scholars[7] although the practical results have been rather less impressive. One genuine practitioner of the art, Angelo Panebianco, laments that since the classic studies of Robert Michels and Maurice Duverger the field has lain largely fallow.[8] Panebianco's own groundbreaking study, *Political*

Parties, has placed into a comparative context the importance of the circumstances of the parties' founding, their early history, and their interaction with the political environment, although the author's conceptualization and methodology is rather more abstract than historical.

The need for a comparative history of West European Socialism is, I believe, particularly appropriate for the period after 1945. Politics in western Europe became increasingly Europeanized, not only literally with the creation of caucuses within the European Parliament, but in a wider, political sense as the parties had to deal with Europe-wide issues. In the case of the Social Democrats these developments complemented longstanding traditions of bilateral and international contacts among the Socialist parties. Since the founding of Social Democracy various Socialist Internationals had brought the Socialist parties together in an ongoing effort to forge common positions on a variety of issues.

The three parties which are covered in this study were not chosen at random, although the choices may need a little explanation. First of all, they share a common ideological heritage: all three began their organizational life with programs based upon the classic tenets of Marxist dialectical materialism. Equally important, their postwar organizational and ideological problems were remarkably similar: all three needed to respond to the domestic and foreign policy challenges that accompanied western Europe's transformation into a tertiary industrial society and the intensifying Cold War. The three parties were also unique because of the particularly intense contacts they had with each other. Both on the bilateral and multinational level the three parties felt a constant need to interact with each other, to explain their positions to the other two "sister parties," and to attempt—by no means always successfully—to arrive at common positions, particularly on "European" issues.[9]

The question must be asked, of course, why other potential choices for a comparative analysis were excluded. Perhaps the most obvious additional candidate would be the British Labour Party, but two major factors speak against this. One is the lack of the Marxist ideological heritage. As we shall see, shedding the vestiges of a Marxist teleology was a painful process for many Dutch, French, and German Social Democrats, and while for a time Labour would become even more "left" than the Continental parties, Labour never had to overcome a formal program of determinist Marxist teleology, as the French, Dutch, and German socialists did. To the consternation of many Continental socialists, the

Labour Party also decided to opt out of Europe, with the result that the British socialists were neither particularly interested in the problems of a united Europe, nor especially anxious to discuss these issues with the Continental sister parties. For these reasons including Labour in the study would give the analysis a somewhat asymmetrical character.

Some of the same considerations speak against the Scandinavian parties. True, the history of Swedish Social Democracy in particular foreshadowed many developments in West European social democratic politics after 1945, but the Northern parties also remained somewhat aloof from West European affairs. Sweden was not a belligerent in the Second World War, and the country attempted to maintain its neutrality in the Cold War as well. As a result, the Swedish Social Democrats rejected membership in the European Community and the European Union until the 1990s.

As for the Belgians, there is no doubt that their long-time leader, Paul Henri Spaak, played a crucial role in the European unification movement. However, as a party the Belgian Socialists were at this time still very much within the ideological orbit of the French Socialists. In the period under review here the Belgian Social Democrats developed relatively few autonomous positions.

The Italians socialists, too, are less than ideal candidates for a comparative study. Unlike the Dutch, German, and French socialists, the Italians were not a major force in national politics. While the SPD, the SFIO, and the PvdA, at various times, acted as both coalition partners and key opposition elements, the Italian socialists did not play either role. Moreover, the split of the Italian socialist party into warring factions reduced the socialists' political influence still further.

The chronological parameters of the study are dictated both by developments in the larger realm of German, French, and Dutch politics and by watershed events in the history of the three parties themselves. Although it is now clear that the end of the Second World War was less of a watershed in the history of western Europe than either contemporaries or early postwar analysts thought, it is nevertheless true that most of the contemporaries were convinced an era had ended, and nowhere was that more true than in politics. The rise of the Christian Democratic parties, the exclusion of the communists from the consensual political spectrum, the elimination of fascism as a political force, the Cold War—all these factors presented West European socialists with unprecedented problems and challenges. At the other end of the time span, it is now apparent that the years 1967–1968 marked the end of the postwar era.

Western Europe was no longer a predominantly secondary industrial society; the upheavals of 1968 were a symptom of a profound shift that brought new values and new structures to the Continent's societies.

The major changes in Dutch, German, and French society were paralleled by dramatic events in the lives of the three parties at the end of the 1960s. For the SPD, life as West Germany's major opposition party at the federal level came to an end. The grand coalition of 1966 brought the German socialists into the national government for the first time since 1930, and Willy Brandt's election as chancellor of the Federal Republic in 1969 completed the Socialists' triumph.

In contrast, for the PvdA the 1960s brought political impotence and bitter infighting. At the end of the decade the party experienced an internal revolt as a group of self-styled "New Leftists" took control of key leadership positions. The victory of the radicals was temporary—in the 1970s the moderates recaptured the party—but for the contemporaries the shift of power represented a traumatic experience, which they either celebrated or lamented. A few right-wing leaders were so shocked that they left the party and formed a new, short-lived, social democratic group.

The end of the 1960s brought especially dramatic changes for the French SFIO; the party disappeared from the political landscape. After many years of political decline the venerable "French Section of the Workers' International" dissolved itself, and most of its members joined the new *Parti socialiste* (PS), but it was not a smooth transition. Under the leadership of François Mitterrand the new group would eventually become a major success story, but for many proponents of *socialisme pur et dur* (pure and hard socialism) the PS represented a travesty of the Socialist tradition in France.

The aim of this book is not to present a narrative history of the three parties, but to focus on providing a comparative analysis of their organizational life, leaders, and policies. To this end, the analysis begins with a thumbnail overview of the three parties' histories from their founding to the end of the Second World War. This is followed by a sketch of the major changes which Dutch, French, and German society underwent after the Second World War. The process was complicated, but the most salient development was the accelerating bourgeoisification of western Europe (what Helmut Schelsky in a famous book described as the "levelled middle class society").[10] For parties that had based their political outlook on the permanent existence of antagonistic classes, this disappearance of their core constituency and its absorption into the bourgeoisified society undoubtedly confronted them with what was perhaps the greatest challenge in their history. It was very much a situation of "we have met the enemy, and he is us."

The realization that the new postwar Europe had little resemblance to the old lay well in the future when the war came to an end. For the moment all three parties saw the dawn of the era of socialism. It was a brief moment of euphoria, followed quickly by disillusionment, and, more slowly, by the acknowledgment that the parties would have to adapt to new forms of politics.

The three parties spent much of the first decade after the war attempting to reinvent themselves organizationally and ideologically. At the same time, their domestic and foreign policies had to take into account revitalized capitalism at home and the reality of the Cold War abroad. As we shall see, their efforts to meet these challenges had widely varying results.

In the second half of the 1950s new challenges emerged, or rather were added to the ongoing developments. In all three countries the political landscape was subjected to major convulsions. The most dramatic events took place in France. The collapse of the Fourth Republic and the establishment of de Gaulle's Fifth Republic radically altered the rules of the political game. The SFIO, which was proud of its position as the "hinge party" (*parti charnier*) of the Fourth Republic, found itself increasingly marginalized in the Fifth. In Germany the SPD also had legitimate grounds for fearing permanent political impotence, though the reasons were different. Here the electoral successes of the Christian Democrats under their perennial leader Konrad Adenauer threatened to condemn the Social Democrats to a role as permanent opposition party. While sitting on the opposition benches had a long but increasingly unwelcome tradition in the German SPD, it was a new experience for the PvdA. Accustomed to being members of the Dutch government coalitions since the end of the Second World War, the Dutch socialists suddenly found themselves excluded from the corridors of power. Charting a way that would bring the party back to power became the subject of a sometimes bitter debate.

In the 1960s the paths of the three parties increasingly diverged. Unable to solve its internal disputes over the future political makeup and direction of the party, the SFIO essentially self-destructed. At the end of the decade a new Socialist party emerged in France, forged in the crucibles of the presidential elections of 1965 and 1968, the upheavals of May, 1968, and the dramatic departure of de Gaulle a year later. In Holland the Socialists experienced their own form of self-paralysis as a self-styled *Nieuw Links* (New Left) group succeeded—for a few years—in gaining control of the party. The German Social Democrats, on the other hand, were an unmitigated success story in the 1960s. The personnel and programmatic reforms of the 1950s finally paid off. The SPD first joined and then led the West German federal government.

While the political fortunes of the three parties after 1945 were quite different, there was an undeniable constant as well. In 1969 the Dutch, French, and German social democratic parties bore little resemblance to their predecessors twenty-five years earlier. The last quarter century had brought profound organizational, ideological, and personnel changes. Analyzing these from a comparative perspective is the central aim of this book.

– Chapter One –

PARALLEL PASTS

Founding to 1945

❧

Early History

The Dutch, German, and French Socialist parties were products of the rising political consciousness among Europe's industrial workers in the second half of nineteenth century. The three parties saw themselves as the political arm of the industrial working class, and all three adopted programs that were based upon the principles of a democratic Marxist teleology. Especially in the years leading up to First World War the number of members and voters of the three parties grew rapidly, leading the Socialists to engage in euphoric expectations about the rapid demise of capitalism, and the establishment of socialist societies. Preparations for that longed-for day included international cooperation among the Socialist parties; in addition to maintaining a wealth of bilateral and multilateral contacts, all three parties belonged to the prewar Socialist International.[1]

The illusion of capitalism's demise set up a chronic contradiction between theory and practice that was to plague the three parties until after the Second World War. One difficulty was the concept of the red family. As the pioneers of the socialist society to come, the industrial workers and their families were expected to spend their political and social lives as much as possible within a self-contained world of Socialist organizations untainted by the values and structures of the dying capitalist society around them.[2] For a number of reasons the concept was politically counterproductive, and some perceptive socialist leaders recognized early on that the workers themselves were in fact not immune to the influence of the values of the capitalist society around them, nor did they wish to be. Moreover, as democratic organizations the socialist parties rejected establishing socialism by violent means. Yet, as self-proclaimed single class organizations committed to the Marxist concept of class antagonism, they would not be able to attract sufficient support to come to power through the ballot box.

The socialists recognized the problem and attempted to deal with it in a variety of ways, none entirely successful. Although the parties' propaganda bureaus sent out a steady stream of revolutionary slogans that delighted the militants while frightening the middle classes, the revolutionary rhetoric could not obscure that this sort of *Vulgärmarxismus* (populist Marxism) had increasingly less relationship to the day-to-day political practice of the three parties. The result was a variety of attempts to revise Marxist determinism and bring it into line with the three parties' actual political work.[3]

The most famous of these was, of course, Eduard Bernstein's effort to show that socialism was above all a set of ethical principles that was perfectly compatible with political democracy and evolutionary social change. While Bernstein's ideas did not become official party doctrine in any of the three parties before 1945, they had considerable influence not only in the ranks of his own party, the SPD, but in France and Holland as well. In The Netherlands, especially, a variety of revisionism known as religious socialism would also become important. Like Bernstein, religious socialism stressed the ethical dimensions of Socialism, arguing that the precepts of "scientific" Socialism were not incompatible with the ethical principles of Judeo-Christian thought.[4]

Another, largely unacknowledged, strain of revisionism was a concept associated with the name of Ferdinand Lasalle. Although the Lasalleans had been officially defeated by the Marxists when the two wings of German Socialism merged in 1869, Lasalle's central idea—that the modern state was more than a component of the superstructure of capitalism and could be used to further the advance of a socialist society—remained influential in all three parties.[5] The Lasallean concept of the state was also related to the difficulties which the concepts of nation and nationalism presented for the three parties. As good Marxists, the socialists technically denied the significance of nationalism as a force among the laboring classes. Nationalism was yet another invention of the bourgeoisie, a part of the superstructure of values which capitalism used to oppress the working class. In actuality, matters were not that simple. Nationalism was alive and well among many industrial workers; its influence helped prepare the way for what Dieter Groh has called the "negative integration" of the laboring classes into the capitalist societies.[6] Among the three parties, the SPD found it most difficult to accept the compatibility of the nation and socialism. Before the First World War Germany's ruling circles proudly identified German nationalism with Wilhelminian authoritarianism and Prusso-German militarism. They saw both as part of the bulwark against the triumph of political democracy and the growing influence of Socialism in Germany. In response it was inconceivable to the SPD's leaders that the German working class could see anything positive in the dominant forms of contemporary German nationalism. Rejecting the Bismarckian and Wilhelminian varieties of nationalism, the SPD celebrated the democratic ideals of the unsuccessful German revolution of 1848–1849 and the glories of the socialist society to come.[7]

The SDAP and the SFIO had an easier time establishing a positive relationship to the French and Dutch nations as they existed at the end of the nineteenth century. The Dutch Socialists recognized that The Netherlands were a political democracy, albeit an incomplete one from their perspective. As a result, while the SDAP complained about oppressive class rule and the need for fundamental constitutional changes—including the abolition of the monarchy and the establishment of a republic—the party was willing to acknowledge that as democrats the Dutch Socialists could effectively work for change within the context of the Dutch political system.[8]

The SFIO developed the most positive attitude toward state and nation. The party's charismatic leader, Jean Jaurès, combined elements of Marxism and German idealist humanism to form an intellectual construct that included a decidedly positive view of French republican nationalism. While the SFIO prided itself on its Marxist positions, held high the banner of international socialist cooperation, and insisted on major changes in the French constitution (including the vote for women), the SFIO also firmly aligned itself with those forces in France that defended the republic and its ideals as a unique French contribution to the progressive evolution of mankind. Socialism for Jaurès was the fulfillment of the ideals of the French Revolution.[9]

Nevertheless, even the Dutch and French Socialists rejected full-scale integration into the political fabric of their time. Although for the most part this was not a realistic option in the years before the First World War, the three parties refused to join with bourgeois parties in multiparty coalitions as a matter of principle. The French Socialist leader Alexandre Millerand annoyed many socialist militants when he served (in a personal capacity, not as a representative of his party) as minister of commerce in the cabinet of Réné Waldeck-Rousseau from 1899 to 1902, and he was expelled from the party in 1904 after he opposed the SFIO's stand on anticlericalism and antimilitarism. The three parties also consistently voted to reject the national budgets when they were presented to parliament, although here, too, practice was eroding principle. To the consternation of the national SPD leaders, the Bavarian Socialists in 1893 abstained on a vote on the state budget. Even more dramatic, perhaps, a number of SFIO delegates did not cast ballots when the French national budget came before parliament in 1911.[10]

1914 to the Depression

The outbreak of the First World War destroyed many illusions for Europe's Socialists, chief among them that the Socialists would be able to prevent the outbreak of war and, if that proved impossible, that the workers would not participate in a fratricidal conflict. Instead, socialists had little influence over the belligerents' decision to go to war, and once hostilities began, most socialists rallied readily to the national cause.

Since The Netherlands remained neutral in the conflict, the Dutch Socialists were spared the agony of choosing between nation and class, a factor that may explain why a surprisingly large number of SDAP militants exhibited considerable sympathy with the antiwar stand of Vladimir Lenin and the Zimmerwald movement. Both the SFIO and the SPD became part of their countries' wartime coalitions, although neither party did so with great enthusiasm; both were "profoundly uncomfortable" as partners of their longstanding political enemies. While the majority in the SFIO and SPD justified its decision by the need to defend liberty— against the threat of Russian Czarism in case of the SPD, against German aggression in the case of the SFIO—minority opposition to supporting the war effort also surfaced early. In Germany this led to a split of the party in 1917 and the creation of the USPD. The French party remained unified during the war, although the influence of a pacifist *tendance* was growing.[11]

The revolutions of 1917 and 1918 in Russia and Central Europe came as a complete surprise to the leaders of the three parties.

Initially enthusiastic about the overthrow of the Czar, the leaders of all three parties soon became profoundly uneasy about the developments in Russia. The undemocratic nature of the Bolsheviks' seizure of power, and the Russian Communists' unwillingness to create democracy even after they were in control of Russia, violated, as far as the West European Socialist leaders were concerned, a key tenet of democratic socialism.[12]

Alone among the three parties the Dutch SDAP launched a revolutionary initiative in its own country. In France no revolutionary upheavals took place, and in Germany the SPD would have much preferred an evolutionary path to political democracy; the German party leaders were forced to channel a revolutionary movement from above in order to contain it. In Holland, however, the SDAP's leader, P.J. Troelstra, was briefly convinced that the hour of revolution had struck for The Netherlands. But his "revolution" amounted to little more than the party leader's paper proclamation. The episode eventually entered into the party's annals as "*de vergissing van Troelstra*" ("Troelstra's lapse"). Troelstra's call for revolution was answered neither by other party leaders, nor the party's members. The affair had no lasting effect except to isolate the SDAP from the other political parties in The Netherlands for much of the next decade.[13]

The success of the Bolshevik Revolution and Lenin's subsequent demand that the Communist party of Russia must be recognized as the model for all Socialist revolutionary organizations confronted the socialist parties with a new dilemma. The Bolsheviks created the Third (Communist) International and insisted upon specific and stringent prerequisites before a Socialist party was accepted for membership in the new organization. These included the adoption of the Russians' organizational principle of democratic centralism for each national affiliate. In addition, all members of the Communist International had to purge leaders whom the Russians and their left-wing allies identified as revisionists and right-wing deviationists.

These demands were immediately and overwhelmingly rejected by the leaders of the SDAP and the SPD. In Holland, Bolshevik sympathizers founded a new party, the CPN, but it remained an insignificant organization. The SDAP, for its part, adopted and retained a virulently anti-Communist stand. The SPD, too, rejected the Communist overtures. When the German Socialists split in 1917, the moderate Socialists had retained the majority of the party's membership, and the SPD had no intention of joining the Third International. In December, 1918 the minority USPD itself split, and a left-wing faction founded the Moscow-dominated KPD. For a time both the KPD and the USPD were members of the Communist International, but in 1922 the USPD's leaders decided to rejoin the majority Socialists. That decision left the German labor movement deeply divided, since most of the USPD members refused to follow their leaders' choice, and transferred their allegiance to the KPD.[14]

For the SFIO the question of affiliating with the Third International led to a traumatic split of the party. At the party's national congress in Tours in December, 1920, a majority of the delegates voted to join the Communist International, leaving the SFIO a shadow of its former self. Most of the leaders stayed loyal to the old house, as Léon Blum called it in his famous speech at Tours arguing against affiliation with the Communist International, but the majority of the members, especially the younger elements, went over to the newly founded PCF.

The SFIO was decimated, and the party spent much of the next decade rebuilding its organizational structure. Most of the party's remaining membership was concentrated in a few federations, particularly those of Nord, Paris, Haute Vienne, and Bouches du Rhône, although then and later, members and leaders complained that the SFIO was dominated by its Parisian organization. There were other problems as well, including persistent financial deficits, difficulties with the party's newspaper, *Le Populaire*, and ideological rifts which led to increasingly open antagonisms between various *tendances*. But all was not gloomy. The membership was growing, although it remained relatively old, particularly when compared to that of the Communists. The most visible sign of the party's resurgence, however, was the its growing electoral support, which increased steadily throughout the 1920s, with a noticeable shift from Paris and the north to southern and south-eastern areas. (In 1928 Blum was defeated in his Paris parliamentary district by the PCF leader, Jacques Duclos.) The change was also reflected in the increasing "bourgeoisification" of the party's parliamentary delegation: In 1936 fully 52 percent of the SFIO members of parliament were professionals, teachers, journalists, retailers, and artisans, while workers constituted only 8.4 percent.[15]

The break with the Communists left the SFIO with a difficult relationship that would persist until the end of the party's existence; the French Socialists wavered between nostalgia for reunion with their estranged brothers and virulent anticommunism. While the SDAP and the SPD took consistently anticommunist stands, the SFIO attempted to preserve a more left-wing image. As part of this effort the SFIO joined the Austrian Socialists and a few other groups to form the short-lived "Vienna International" (the Bolsheviks called it the "2 1/2 International") before returning to the reorganized Socialist International that included, as the French Communists gleefully noted, the "reactionary" SPD.

The 1920s confronted both the SFIO and the SPD with other challenges as well. They were invited to become members of their countries' governing coalitions, but *ministérialisme* was only part of a larger set of ideological contradictions confounding both the SFIO and the SPD. Ideological subtleties were not a major concern for the rank-and-file membership. As far as the average SFIO member was concerned, the party's ideology had the function of explaining in laymen's terms why the socialist revolution was coming. The party leaders, however, worried about the contradiction inherent in the parties' self-image as revolutionary organizations and their day-to-day practice as parliamentary and reformist groups. The SFIO adopted a domestic policy program that proposed fundamental changes for French society—such as large-scale socializations of economic assets—but also demanded piecemeal improvements in the lives of the party's supporters. Even while the party worked hard to form parliamentary coalitions which would put the program's reformist aspects into effect, the party's leaders also issued periodic cautionary admonitions that the SFIO needed to avoid excessive involvement in parliamentary politics. The SPD, too, while serving in the national government felt more comfortable outside than inside the cabinet.[16]

After the brief shock of Troelstra's call for revolution, the SDAP settled down in the 1920s to take its place on the center-left of the Dutch party spectrum. Formally, the SDAP retained a Marxist ideology, and, like the SFIO, demanded the socialization of Holland's utilities and mining industries, but in actuality the leaders devoted most of their efforts to practicing the art of the possible, a skill that would become increasingly characteristic of the Dutch Socialists. Pragmatism brought rewards: The party's membership increased from forty thousand in 1920 to sixty-nine thousand a decade later, and to eighty-eight thousand by 1935. The SDAP was also ready to enter into coalitions with bourgeois parties, although for the moment there was no corresponding willingness on the bourgeois side.

A portent of things to come was the increasing significance of "religious Socialists" in the SDAP. Also active in Germany, although it was less influential there, this group focussed on the ethical dimension of Socialist ideology, denying the exclusively materialist determinism and especially the necessity of the class struggle as prerequisites for the creation of a socialist society. In Holland the leading figures in this movement were Willem Banning, a Protestant minister who was to become the intellectual leader of the PvdA in the years immediately after Second World War, and Koos Vorrink, the head of the SDAP's youth organization in the 1920s, and the party's chairman in the 1930s and 1940s.[17]

Even before the Great Depression created unprecedented dilemmas for the three parties, they found themselves in an increasingly difficult situation. They were edging their way into the political mainstream of France, Holland, and Germany, yet many militants and leaders wanted to maintain the red family as protection against the malevolent influence of bourgeois values and institutions. At the same time there were demands, especially among younger militants, that the parties had to go beyond Marxist materialism to create an ethically motivated socialist man. In this view, since the ethical precepts of socialism were universal, the new socialist man need not come only from the ranks of the industrial proletariat.

Depression and Fascism

The parties' attempts to deal with the Great Depression and the rise of Fascism were not very successful. While the Depression confirmed the three parties in their longstanding belief that capitalism was a failed system, none was able to offer answers to the problems of the Depression that went beyond variations on the contradictory themes of fiscal responsibility and public works programs. For some leaders and many rank-and-file members the ideas of the controversial Belgian Socialist, Hendrik de Man, seemed to offer a way out of Socialism's dilemma. De Man, who already had a well-deserved reputation as a Marxist revisionist, argued that coping with the Depression required neocorporatist solutions in the form of an overall national industrial plan subscribed to by all forces in the society. Although such a proposal all but eliminated the class struggle as a central tenet of socialist thinking, there was tremendous enthusiasm for *le Plan*, especially in Holland and France.[18]

The Dutch and French Socialists escaped the fascist takeover of their countries until the outbreak of the Second World War, although in the 1930s they, too, had to cope with significant domestic fascist movements. The SPD was not only unable to stop Hitler from coming to power but, with few exceptions, the party leaders also proved singularly ineffective in dealing with German Nazism on either a theoretical or practical level. For too long the German Socialists failed to recognize the revolutionary and atavistic nature of Nazism; even after Hitler had been appointed chancellor, many SPD leaders continued to harbor illusions about continuing the party's activities as a legal opposition in the Third Reich. In part the SPD's failures were derived from an exaggerated sense of its own political and parliamentary influence—especially in Prussia—but, more important, the party's downfall can be attributed to its inability to understand the force of integral nationalism that the Nazis had unleashed.[19]

The German Socialists soon recognized, of course, that the Nazis would not tolerate a loyal opposition. Those SPD members and leaders who remained in Germany were either forced to abandon all political activities, or, if they persisted in opposing the Nazis, were executed or incarcerated in Nazi jails and concentration camps. What party activities remained took place outside of Germany. The SPD's executive committee in exile established itself first in Prague, then in Paris, and eventually in London, abandoning its first two safe havens as Czechoslovakia and France came under Nazi control.

The exiled leaders attempted to organize underground opposition to the Nazis in Germany, but quickly discovered that they were no match for the Gestapo's efficiency. Consequently, the exiled party leaders increasingly turned their attention to analyzing what had gone wrong during the Weimar years, and deriving lessons for the future from this assessment of the past. Their first reaction was a return to orthodox Marxism. The 1934 Prague Manifesto, largely the work of Rudolf Hilferding, the SPD's leading theorist, interpreted the Depression and Nazism as evidence of the impending, final crisis of capitalism, and the imminent arrival of the Socialist revolution.[20]

But the Prague Manifesto was a momentary episode. The party leadership quickly withdrew its endorsement of the document, turning instead to theoretical efforts which would have not only a profound impact on the party's future evolution, but also bring it onto a course parallel to its French and Dutch counterparts. Like the SFIO and the SDAP earlier, the SPD unequivocally recognized democracy as both means and end, the only acceptable road toward socialism. Following Jaurès, the exiled German Socialists linked nationalism and the democratic political system: to be a great nation Germany had to adopt and defend democracy. According to the SPD, the German bourgeoisie had attempted but failed to do this in 1848 and 1918, and it was now the task of the working class to give democracy firm roots in Germany. The SPD also stressed the need for European cooperation and unification. A united, democratic, socialist Europe, the party insisted, was the humanistic antithesis to the Nazis' teleology of national antagonisms and racial conflict.[21]

The SPD's identification with the political values traditionally associated with the humanistic traditions of Western Europe reinforced its antagonistic relationship with the Communists. Although the Prague Manifesto seemed to smooth the path for cooperation between the estranged brothers, the executive committee's quick abandonment of the Manifesto signaled its renewed opposition to any Communist-Socialist realignment. In fact, the Socialist leaders never seriously wavered in their conviction that Communism and Democratic Socialism were antithetical. If the longstanding ideological incompatibilities had not been reason enough, the Stalinist purges, and finally the Nazi-Soviet Pact provided additional and decisive reasons for severing relations with the KPD.[22]

In contrast to the SPD and the SDAP the French Socialists faced a serious right-wing challenge within their ranks in the 1920s and 1930s. Confronted by the disastrous effects of the Great Depression and the rise of fascism, a group of so-called Neo-Socialists questioned the SFIO's tenets of Marxist historical materialism, working class isolation, and the inevitability of the class struggle. Influenced by the ideas of Hendrik de Man, the "Neos" demanded that the SFIO abandon its Marxist orthodoxy and endorse state interventionist and corporatist solutions to France's problems. The party's leaders refused, and eventually the Neos and their leader Marcel Déat were expelled from the party. A few of the Neos, including Déat himself, went on to become fascists and eventually Nazi collaborators, but their political evolution was not typical for the Neos as a group. Most of the early Neo sympathizers remained loyal to the SFIO, and several, such as André Philip, Paul Ramadier, Jean-Louis Tixier-Vignacour, and Adrian Marquet, would go on to play leading roles in the Resistance and the post-World War SFIO. Nevertheless, for a time the Neos' challenge not only constituted a serious threat to the SFIO's unity, but rank-and-file sympathy for the Neos also led to a noticeable, if temporary, decline in the party's membership after their program had been officially condemned by the party.[23]

Among the consequences of the SFIO's firm stand against the right-wing challenge in its ranks was a better relationship with the French Communists. Unlike the Dutch and German Socialists, who consistently refused to cooperate with the Communists, the French Socialists did not rule out a political alliance with the PCF. Initially organized to combat fascist and right-wing forces in France, the Popular Front also gave its name to a government which the Socialists formed with the Radicals in 1936. The Communists did not join the cabinet, but they did support it in parliament. The Popular Front cabinet, which was headed by Léon Blum, once again confronted the SFIO with the still vexing issue of *ministérialisme*.

Always uneasy about participation in any coalition government, the SFIO had traditionally insisted it would assume executive power only if there was a realistic chance for implementing socialism in the country. This was obviously not the case in 1936 when the Popular Front cabinet of Socialist and Radical ministers took office, but Blum was able to salve the party's conscience by distinguishing between the conquest and the exercise of power. The Popular Front could not take power in France, but as the dominant party in the coalition, the SFIO, through its exercise of power, could prepare the way for realizing the Socialist program. Although Blum may not have known it at the time, he had made an important contribution to Socialist theory that would be equally, if not more, applicable to the postwar era.[24]

Neither the era of good feeling between Socialists and Communists nor the Popular Front government lasted very long. Uneasy partners in the best of times (a later analyst called the partnership "a necessary and impossible alliance"), the Socialists resented that the PCF remained outside the government and acted as a fickle partner in parliament. Above all, however, the Nazi-Soviet Pact, which the PCF perversely hailed as a triumph of Soviet statesmanship benefiting the international proletariat, caused a "profound rupture" between the two parties that was never entirely healed.[25]

Stalin's deal with Hitler touched a particularly raw nerve in the ranks of the SFIO, because by 1938 the Socialists themselves were torn apart over the issue of appeasement toward Nazi Germany. One faction in the party (the *munichois*) favored a policy of accommodating Hitler, while their opponents (the *anti-munichois*) insisted upon a policy of intransigence and firm opposition to the Third Reich's aggression. The battle split the SFIO, and became a matter of personal conflict between the SFIO's two most prominent leaders. Paul Faure headed the munichois, and Léon Blum led the anti-munichois forces. While Faure argued for the priority of pacifism as a socialist principle, Blum insisted that the preservation of democracy was a higher goal than peace at any price. On the eve of Second World War the SFIO was in a severely weakened condition. Its political enemies attacked the party for the failures of the Third Republic, and, as if to demonstrate the validity of the criticism, the SFIO was divided against itself, unable to agree on how to meet the challenge of fascism.

Compared to the SFIO, the story of the SDAP in the 1930s was remarkably free of strife and dissension. The membership remained quantitatively static, but underwent significant demographic changes. There was a noticeable shift toward white collar workers. The party was also able to attract increasing numbers of middle class voters; by the end of the decade the SDAP had become Holland's second largest party. The decade saw as well a generational shift in the leadership and a decided ideological turn to the right. A number of Dutch Socialists—including the later parliamentary leader Marinus van der Goes van Naters and the long-time member of parliament, Jacques Kadt—initially sympathized with some of the ideas enunciated by the French Neos. So did Koos Vorrink, who was elected chairman in 1934. Vorrink was an unabashed Bersteinian and a strong proponent of neocorporatism and cooperation among all democratic forces in the country.[26]

Another rising force in the party was Willem Banning, the most eloquent and outspoken of the SDAP's religious Socialists. Banning went beyond Vorrink and Jaurès in questioning the validity of the so-called *anti-these*, the concept that socialism and organized religion were incompatible forces. Banning argued that Socialism and some religious organizations might well share a commitment to progressive social change. The Dutch Socialists did not yet follow Banning and abandon the anti-these, but there was no doubt that the party's left wing was having an increasingly difficult time. A group of orthodox Marxists, who insisted the party reaffirm its commitment to revolution and materialist determinism, was expelled from the party in 1932.[27]

The SDAP vigorously criticized the SPD's failure to stop Hitler and the Nazis, and to their credit the Dutch party leaders took concrete steps to prevent indigenous fascism from establishing itself in The Netherlands. Confronted with the surprising strength of the Dutch fascist party, the NSB, the SDAP along with other democratic groups formed a multiparty alliance, *Eenheid door Democratie* (Unity Through Democracy) to combat the NSB with a united democratic front.

As its solution to the problems brought on by the Great Depression, the SDAP endorsed Henrik de Man's corporatist *Plan van de*

Arbeid (Labor Plan). Under the enthusiastic leadership of Koos Vorrink the SDAP launched a nation-wide propaganda campaign to mobilize support for the Plan. With the catchy slogan *"het moet, het kan, op met het Plan"* ("it must, it can, on with the Plan") youthful SDAP militants organized marches (complete with songs especially composed to celebrate the Plan) to rally support for a national industrial policy.[28]

The significance of all this activity was limited, certainly in the short run. The SDAP was not a member of the government, and the Dutch cabinet continued to implement supply-side economic policies; the prime minister, Hendrikus Colijn, certainly had no intention of embracing corporatist schemes. Many older leaders of the party, too, were skeptical; the colorful demonstrations struck them as a little too voluntaristic and emotional for a Socialist Party. There were, however, some significant long-term consequences. The campaign for the Plan enabled the SDAP to open avenues of communication to new constituencies, notably technocrats and left-wing Catholics, two groups that were also drawn to corporatist ideas.[29]

In 1937 the SDAP adopted a new program which represented a dramatic shift in the party's ideological position. The SDAP's earlier programs of 1894 and 1912 committed the party to orthodox Marxist ideas, but the compounded failures of the 1918 revolution, the rise of fascism, and especially the party's poor showing in the 1933 elections convinced the leaders that the SDAP's future lay in formally committing the party to revisionist ideas. The new program abandoned Marxist determinism and materialism, denied the inevitability of the class struggle, and stated that the party's aims were social reformism and the preservation of democracy. The goal of the 1937 program, according to the Dutch scholar Bertus Boivin, was "to have a little bit of Socialism in a capitalist society." The only planks in the new program that remained to remind the militants of the old party were the celebration of the red family and the anti-these, which despite Banning's best efforts, the party activists could not yet bring themselves to abandon.[30]

Armed with its 1937 program, the SDAP moved into the mainstream of Dutch politics. With almost ninety thousand members organized into 780 locals the party transformed itself from a Marxist *Klassenpartei* (class party) to a genuine *Volkspartei* (mass party). There is some doubt whether the rank- and-file members were following quite as enthusiastically along this path as the leaders, but in the last years of the decade the SDAP crossed a few more symbolic hurdles on its way to the center-left of the political spectrum.

Party leaders expressed their loyalty to the Dutch nation and monarchy, and, despite some intense opposition within the party, the SDAP's parliamentary delegates began to vote for the national defense budgets. The culmination of this evolution came in 1939, just before the outbreak of Second World War, when the SDAP became a member of the Dutch national cabinet.[31]

The Second World War and the Resistance

Although the Socialists could do little to influence the conduct of military operations against Nazi Germany or the formulation of the Allies' goals for the postwar order, they were certainly not inactive during the conflict. Members and leaders of the three parties took part in the national and international resistance efforts. Seeing themselves as an embryonic Socialist International, they were determined to draw up and coordinate plans that would enable the Continent to recover from the ravages of war while creating conditions that would prevent future conflicts. To this end the three parties envisioned a united Europe and a democratic Germany, although they differed on when Germany would be accepted as an equal partner in the new Europe.[32]

The SPD's wartime activities took place both in Germany and abroad, although resistance at home had little effect on the fate of the Third Reich, and wartime contacts between the exiles and the home forces were sporadic at best. Remarkably, however, when the exiled leaders and the underground militants in Germany were able to meet after the war, their views on the future of Germany and the party turned out to be quite similar. In addition, the struggle against Nazism had healed the rifts and personal animosities that had emerged among Germany's Socialists during the 1930s. By the end of the war all had returned to the fold—those who had broken with the party for its toleration policy of the Neo-Conservative chancellors, as well as those, like the founders of *Neu Beginnen* (Begin Anew), who had attempted to formulate a Third Way concept between Communism and Democratic Socialism. There were neither significant ideological divisions nor organized *tendances* (factions) among the German Socialists in 1945.[33]

Most of the Socialist leaders who chose to remain in Germany became what in France were known as *attentistes* (watchful waiters) rather than active resisters. Convinced it was futile to take direct action against the Nazis, they attempted to survive as private citizens, waiting for better times. A small number of activists, however, were unwilling to remain passive, and most of them paid a heavy price for their courage. These included a number of the younger militants, some of whom had been on the threshold of assuming significant leadership positions in the party when the Nazis came to power. Julius Leber, a major force in the SPD in Schleswig-Holstein and editor of the party's newspaper in Lübeck, was executed by the Nazis for his part in the 20 July 1944 plot against Hitler. Kurt Schumacher, in 1933 a member of the Reichstag from Stuttgart, spent more than ten years in a series of Nazi concentration camps. Fritz Erler, one of the founders of Neu Beginnen, was given a ten year prison sentence in 1938 for anti-Nazi activities, but he escaped in the final days before the end of the war.

While the active resisters at home languished as ineffective martyrs in prisons and concentration camps, their exiled comrades had somewhat better opportunities to make their voices heard. The focal point of SPD activism abroad was the executive committee in exile. The group was headed first by the party's last Weimar chairman, Otto Wels, and, after his death in 1939, by Hans Vogel and his deputy, Erich Ollenhauer. Although the committee spent the war years in London, by no means all exiled leaders chose Great Britain as their place of refuge. Some prominent postwar leaders, such as Willy Brandt and Herbert Wehner, escaped to Scandinavia (in the case of Wehner after a sojourn in Moscow), while the future mayor of Hamburg, Max Brauer, went to the United States.[34]

The London group had two major goals: reestablish the organizational unity of the party, and convince the Allies that there was another, democratic, Germany. The executive committee succeeded in accomplishing its first aim, but was far less effective in establishing good relations with the governments in the Allied countries. While the German Socialists maintained good contacts with other Socialist groups in exile and with some of the Labour Party leaders in London, the Allied governments and most prominent Labour representatives had no intention of recognizing the German Socialists as the representatives of the "other" Germany.[35]

All German Socialists were fully committed to political democracy and the establishment of a socialist society, but there was considerable disagreement among them on the best means of implementing these goals. Vogel and Ollenhauer tended to emphasize the need for large-scale socialization as the best means of destroying the political and economic power of Germany's capitalist ruling class, whereas Willy Brandt, like the SDAP leaders, stressed the need for cooperation with all progressive forces, including bourgeois groups. In contrast, some members of the former Neu Beginnen insisted true democracy meant working class domination, and it might well be necessary to institute a period of *Erziehungsdiktatur* (educational dictatorship) to convince the other elements in German society that they had to accept the leading role of the working class.[36]

Such ideas, which sounded suspiciously like a return by the back door of the dictatorship of the proletariat, never had widespread support in the party, but all of the SPD leaders were concerned about the future relationship of the Socialists and the German middle classes. The key to establishing better relations, they were convinced, was the party's new attitude toward nationalism. Independent of each other, both the SPD leaders in London and Kurt Schumacher in Germany decided that the party needed a more positive attitude toward the nation and nationalism if the German bourgeoisie was to be persuaded to accept the SPD as Germany's leading political party after the war. In addition, the London group wanted to use the historically positive accomplishments of the "other" Germany as an antidote to the so-called Vansittartism, which had considerable influence in British official circles.[37]

The Nazis' attack on the Soviet Union led to a temporary reexamination of the SPD's relationship to the Communists. As the Communists moved to the front ranks of the Resistance and the Soviet Union bore the brunt of the fighting against the Nazis, some German Socialists hoped for future cooperation with the KPD. Fritz Erler, for example, thought briefly that there might be a common basis in what he called "Marxist voluntarism." Hope of future cooperation also underlay the Buchenwald Manifesto, which was drafted jointly by socialist and communist inmates of that infamous concentration camp. However, such views were held by only a small minority of the leaders, and even for this group it was little more than a fleeting sentiment. The London group consistently emphasized the incompatibility of communism and democratic socialism; Erich Ollenhauer in particular was adamant that the SPD and the KPD were like fire and water. Kurt Schumacher agreed, and the similarity of the two leaders' views on this issue helped pave the way for the future close relationship of Schumacher and Ollenhauer.[38]

At the end of the war, the German Socialists found themselves in an ambivalent situation. The party's organization had been destroyed by the Nazis; many leaders had died during the Third Reich, others remained in exile. At the same time, the experience of the Nazi dictatorship had encouraged a great deal of reflection about the party's past errors and its future course of action. Moving along parallel lines, the exiled leadership and the resisters who had remained in Germany were determined that for the SPD there would be no second Weimar Republic.[39]

Although no one could reasonably blame the SFIO for France's military defeat, the French Socialists' record during the Second World War was marred by controversial decisions and sins of commission. It began with the vote on Marshall Pétain's decree powers. When the head of the government in the unoccupied zone of France demanded an end to parliamentary democracy and asked parliament for dictatorial authority, the Socialist members of parliament divided on this issue, with most (eighty-eight out of 117) voting to grant Pétain what he was asking. The vote partially reflected the earlier split between the munichois and anti-munichois forces in the party, and it provided a portend of the SFIO's rather inglorious role during the war. Although some Socialist leaders immediately founded a *Comité d'Action socialiste* (Socialist Action Committee, CAS), for much of the occupation period most of the Socialist militants remained attentistes, staying aloof from the French Resistance.[40]

The SFIO was not roused from its dormancy until 1943, when the Vichy government decided to put Léon Blum on trial as the man primarily responsible for creating the conditions that had caused the collapse of France in 1940. It was obvious, of course, that not only Blum—who defended himself brilliantly and was brilliantly defended by his Socialist lawyers, Paul Ramadier and Félix Gouin—was on trial, but that the Third Republic, the Popular Front, and France's Socialists were defendants in the courtroom at Riom. As a result, the former prime minister's close associates in the 1930s rallied around Blum, determined to resurrect the SFIO's reputation and organization. (Incidentally, the Riom trial did not produce the triumph that the Vichy authorities had anticipated, and soon afterward Blum was deported from France and sent to Buchenwald.)

Daniel Mayer, Blum's close intellectual and personal friend, took the lead in reorganizing the French Socialists. Mayer's first goal was to purge the SFIO of all collaborationist and attentiste elements. The new leader was adamant that the members of the SFIO who had voted for Pétain's decree powers had to be excluded from the party. The future SFIO would be a "hard and pure" party, open only to active members of the Resistance. Mayer also insisted that France's parliamentary democracy had to be reestablished after the Liberation, and that meant the reestablishment or continued existence of traditional political parties. Mayer, like Blum, rejected dissolving the SFIO to become a member of an all-inclusive Resistance Movement, which many of the Resistance leaders advocated. Like Kurt Schumacher, Blum and Mayer were convinced that there could be no political democracy without political parties.[41]

Although the purge of the attentistes left the party with a severely weakened organization, the SFIO's leaders were already giving considerable thought to future programs. Such intellectual ruminations were limited to the leadership—the rank-and-file militants seemed to show little interest in these activities—but at the leadership level discussions were intense. On some key questions a consensus readily emerged. As we saw, the SFIO's wartime leaders insisted upon the reestablishment of parliamentary democracy in France. They rejected both Communist notions of a dictatorship of the proletariat and populist concepts current in the Resistance. They insisted on the reestablishment of *laïcisme* in the new French Republic. (The Vichy regime had substantially weakened the separation of church and state in France.) There was also widespread agreement on the need for large-scale nationalizations of economic enterprises and the construction of a closely knit social net. In the area of foreign policy most French Socialists were ready to yield portions of national sovereignty to a united Europe. Most SFIO leaders, however, were not willing to follow Blum, who advocated fundamentally modifying the SFIO's Marxist determinism and single-class self-identification in order to attract a middle class constituency to the party and transform the SFIO from a *parti ouvrier* (working class party) to a *parti travailliste* (labor party), to use the French equivalents of the German Klassenpartei and Volkspartei.[42]

Like the SPD, the SFIO was confronted with the issues of nationalism and the party's relations with the Communists. For the SFIO the political question centered on an individual—the leader of Free France, General Charles de Gaulle. While most Socialists applauded his heroic stand against Vichy, they remained suspicious of his political ideas. Blum had been instrumental in getting the party to accept de Gaulle as the leader of the entire French Resistance, and in the course of the war a number of SFIO leaders, including Olivier Lapie, Adrien Tixier, and André Philip, served de Gaulle as emissaries and members of his cabinet in exile. At the same time, all SFIO leaders, including Blum, made it clear that their recognition of de Gaulle as the leader of Free France would come to an abrupt end with Liberation. The Socialists did not share de Gaulle's vision of French nationalism, and they did not want his brand of authoritarianism.

The SFIO's relationship to the Communists was rather more complicated than the SPD's. Those Socialists who were active in the early Resistance bitterly resented the Communists' unwillingness to participate in activities against the occupiers while the Nazi-Soviet Pact was in effect. Indeed, some Communists attacked the SFIO as the "war party" during this time. The SFIO did acknowledge, however, that once the Nazis invaded the Soviet Union the Communists became the most effective component of the French Resistance. At the same time relations between the two parties were not improved when the PCF insisted the SFIO was at best a minor player in the Resistance, and consequently tried to marginalize the Socialists as much as possible. As a result, while many rank-and-file Socialist militants hoped for permanent cooperation and perhaps even a reunion of the two parties after the war, the SFIO's leaders were far less enthusiastic. If they did not agree with Gaston Defferre, the SFIO's leader in Marseille, that Communists simply could not be trusted, they certainly shared Léon Blum's paradoxical conclusion that cooperation between France's Communists and Socialists was both "necessary and impossible."[43]

The SDAP, too, played what one party leader later described as a "disappointing" role in the Dutch Resistance. There were individual Dutch Socialists who were resisters from the first hour, but as a party the SDAP was more interested in cultivating contacts for political life after the Liberation, than in active resistance. Before the war the party leaders had laid the groundwork for multipartisan cooperation through the SDAP's membership in "Unity Through Democracy," and during the war they continued to maintain contacts with a variety of organizations whose common denominator was the preservation of Dutch democracy or at least national autonomy. This led to some embarrassing associations, to put it mildly. While Socialists were active in various Resistance groups, notably *Het Parool* (The Watchword, the name for both a group and an underground paper), there were also PvdA activists in the authoritarian *Nederlandse Unie* ("Dutch Union") and, very briefly, in the fascist, but anti-Nazi *Nationale Front*. Above all, however, in sharp contrast to both the SFIO and the SPD, the Dutch Socialists took the lead in organizing an all-encompassing new party, the NVB, which they hoped would go a long way toward replacing the multiplicity of parties that had characterized the prewar Dutch political system.[44]

While this project became a consuming wartime passion for many SDAP leaders, enthusiasm for the NVB was far more subdued among rank-and-file militants who remained emotionally attached to the old SDAP and the red family. The leaders tried to appease these feelings by stressing that the new party would be a logical evolution of the old SDAP. Its program would be based upon the 1937 document which had already signaled the party's renunciation of Marxist determinism. The new party would also continue to endorse certain traditional SDAP tenets, such as socialization of major parts of the economy, and opposition to Communism. As for the innovations, they, too, had their roots in the party's history: Neocorporatism was an essential component of the Plan, and abandoning the anti-these had long been demanded by the growing number of religious socialists. Still, not all SDAP members were convinced, and initially many militants did not make the transition to the NVB because they felt the SDAP was about to become a "bourgeois reform movement" rather than a Socialist action group.[45]

Conclusion

The Dutch, German and French Socialists came out of the war confronting an unanticipated dichotomy between vision and reality. Their expectation was that at the end of Second World War the Social Democrats would lead their countries and Europe into a new age of democracy, socialism, and international cooperation which would eliminate the national divisiveness and social injustices that had plagued the Continent in the past.[46]

The reality, of course, was rather different. There was no revolutionary change, certainly not as the Socialists had envisioned it. The magnitude of daily problems and the need to rebuild rudimentary societal relations left neither resources nor time for social revolutions. In addition, it soon became apparent that most Europeans did not want far-reaching systemic changes. Instead, they, including the majority of Social Democrats, wanted to return to a version of prewar normalcy, including a revival of the old party structures. In fact it can be argued that the German and French Socialists (this was not true for the SDAP) were undermining their own vision of the future. While they insisted that they were leading Europe into a new age, they also reiterated that their own party organizations needed to be preserved much as they had existed before the war.[47]

– Chapter Two –

THE MAKING OF A TERTIARY INDUSTRIAL SOCIETY, 1945–1969

಄

A t first glance the history of western Europe during the quarter century after the Second World War presents a picture of glaring paradoxes. Extremes of economic and social deprivation were unexpectedly followed by what in retrospect became the golden age of capitalism. National peculiarities and idiosyncrasies persisted alongside accelerating patterns of Europeanization.[1] As western Europe evolved from secondary to tertiary industrialism, a quiet revolution took place. Although this societal transformation proceeded at varying speeds and with significant national variations in the three countries under discussion here, it brought far-reaching economic, political, and social changes to them all.[2] The pace of urbanization, a postwar spurt in population growth, and the pent-up demand for consumer goods inaugurated a period of protracted and steadily increasing economic growth that began in the early 1950s and continued until the middle of the next decade. Most West Europeans experienced a dramatic increase in their standard of living, while impressive economic growth rates made possible what both contemporary and later observers have concluded was (and still is) the most striking feature of postwar West European society—the establishment of a closely knit net of social services.

Overlaid with the patina of time, the "long decade" of the 1950s, which contrasted so vividly with the hardships of the Depression and the war years, acquired the aura of a golden age. At first incredulous and suspicious, after a few years most Europeans became convinced that the good times would never end since postwar western Europe had apparently solved the problem of business cycles. Although in retrospect it is clear that hints of future problems were apparent by the end of the 1950s, the first major postwar crisis in the mid-1960s came as a profound shock, bringing with it far-reaching social and political consequences.[3]

Economic Developments

Nowhere was the "revolution without revolutionary consciousness"[4] more apparent than in West Germany. At the end of the Second World War Germany was a society on the brink of disintegration. Most contemporary Germans and Germany's occupiers were convinced the country faced unprecedented and virtually insurmountable problems. Generations of historians have shown that the famous *Stunde Null* (Zero Hour) never existed, but this does not change the fact that in 1945 the sense of starting from nothing was very much a part of the contemporary German consciousness.[5]

Yet ten years later what was by then the Federal Republic of Germany enjoyed unprecedented levels of prosperity, a successful democratic system, and enviable social relations. Historians are still debating whether the fledgling republic's good fortune was the result of "the normative power of massive facts,"[6] or the consequence of far-sighted decisions by Allied administrators and German leaders, but *Modell Deutschland* had been born. The key to West Germany's economic recovery was an unabashed policy of supply-side economics. Dubbed *Soziale Marktwirtschaft* (social market economy) by the country's longtime economics minister, Ludwig Erhard, the concept had many facets, but its priority was always the stimulation of capital investment.

Ironically, the initial results were not promising. Although the country's infrastructure was being rapidly rebuilt, as late as February, 1951 West Germany was beset by heavy inflationary pressures and high unemployment. However, Erhard and his associates persisted, and helped by the catalytic effect of the Korean War, trickle-down economics eventually benefited most West Germans. By the end of the 1950s the big three of Germany's postwar social legislation had become law: the Refugee Law, the *Lastenausgleichsgesetz* (Law for the Equalization of Burdens), and increases in social security payments tied to rises in the wage scale of the workforce (*dynamisierte Rente*) helped to distribute the gains from supply-side economics to the great majority of West Germans.

Unprecedented growth rates and the extended boom did not prepare the country for the shock of the first postwar recession in 1966–1967. The signs were there earlier, of course. At the beginning of the 1960s it became clear that the conditions which had prevailed during the long decade of the 1950s were an aberration, not the norm. A labor shortage (in 1961 the building of the Berlin Wall had effectively stopped the flow of East German refugees), coupled with declining rates of productivity and lower levels of technological improvement meant that the problems which seemed to have been permanently banished made their appearance again. Inflation, unemployment, and budget deficits all raised their ugly heads.

However, the doomsayers, who promptly foresaw disastrous political consequences for the Federal Republic, were also proved wrong. Although extreme right-wing groups (especially the neo-Nazi *Nationaldemokratische Partei Deutschlands* [NPD]) benefited from the economic downturn for a time, it was not a return of the 1930s. During the boom times of the 1950s West German society had undergone profound changes (more on this in a moment) which stabilized its cohesive forces and enabled it to weather the new economic storms without experiencing a rending of the social and political fabric.

If pessimism marked Germany's mood in 1945, France oscillated between overly optimistic expectation and the recognition that the country had emerged from the war in a state of profound crisis. At the time of the Liberation a sense of euphoria swept through France. After the nightmare of occupation and Vichy, most Frenchmen thought they were standing on the threshold of a new era, one which would restore France's status as a great power and offer solutions to the domestic problems that had chronically beset the Third Republic. It did not take France long to discover that Liberation did indeed restore the country to the ranks of the great powers (on paper at least), but that it had little effect on France's economic, political, and social difficulties. For much of the remainder of the 1940s, France's economy lurched from crisis to crisis. The problems included high inflation, lack of raw materials, low productivity, budget deficits, lagging exports, and tensions between capital and labor.[7]

The average Frenchman experienced the country's immediate postwar economic problems primarily in the form of seemingly uncontrollable inflation, shortages of consumer goods, and repeated bouts of labor unrest. The Nazis had left behind built-in inflation; at the time of Liberation, the amount of money in circulation vastly exceeded the level of products and productivity. Inflation was not brought under (relative) control until 1949. In the 1950s the French governments had to devaluate the franc periodically in order to keep the country's exports competitive.[8]

But the news was not all bad. To their credit, the early postwar governments were determined that the country's economy should not merely recover, but also experience dramatic modernization. Prodded by Jean Monnet and his group of planners, successive French cabinets created the conditions for *"une France moderne."*[9] That goal was met. The French population, which had stagnated for much of the last century, grew dramatically from 40.5 million in 1946 to 49.8 million in 1968. Primarily a country of peasants and small town inhabitants before the war, France rapidly evolved into a nation of city dwellers. Agriculture declined, while industry, both in the public and private sectors, flourished. The French social net, notoriously deficient before Second World War, became as closely knit as those of West Germany and Holland. By the end of the 1950s France exhibited many of the characteristics of a tertiary industrial society, and most Frenchmen enjoyed the benefits of a growth oriented, modernized economy.[10]

This was all the more remarkable because France labored under some unique liabilities. The war in Indochina, the Suez invasion, and the insurrection in Algeria left France with chronic financial problems. There was a decided asymmetry in the country's modernization program. In their haste to modernize French society, the country's planners concentrated on encouraging investments in basic industries (especially in the export oriented sector) and consumer goods, while neglecting the public service infrastructure. As a result, it was not altogether surprising that the social explosions in France in 1968 were more widespread and took more violent forms than in either Germany or Holland.[11]

Although after the initial Nazi attack on Rotterdam in 1940, The Netherlands was not a target of major bombing raids by either side, nor, until late 1944, the scene of significant ground warfare, the exploitative German occupation and the destructive operations of the retreating Nazi armies in 1944–1945 (which included opening the dikes in northern Holland) left the country with very serious problems. Like France, the Dutch initially diverted resources toward the effort to maintain control of their colonial empire in Asia. When this attempt failed, the loss of Indonesia seemed an additional blow to the Dutch economy; it was estimated that before the war (in 1938) the Dutch East Indies had contributed 7.6 percent to the Dutch GDP.[12]

Despite these challenges, Dutch decision makers also set their sights not merely on recovery, but on structural innovation and modernization of the country's economy. Resolutely adopting supply side policies in an ongoing process of "cool modernization,"[13] most Dutch indicators returned to prewar levels of in 1949, and in the 1950s the country's economy was rapidly transformed from primarily agricultural to preponderantly industrial and service-oriented.[14]

The transformation of the economy was both cause and effect of profound shifts in the Dutch social structure. Fuelled in part by explosive population growth,[15] there was a steady internal migration from rural to urban areas, especially the *randstad* triangle in northern Holland between Amsterdam, Rotterdam, and The Hague. Changes in employment patterns were no less dramatic. The focus of Dutch employment shifted to high technology industries (particularly chemicals and electrical products) and the service sector. As a result, the Dutch recognized early that the coming tertiary industrial society required a highly educated workforce, and they allocated disproportionately large resources to improvements in the country's educational system.

As was true for West Germany and France, the era following the Second World War brought a closely knit social service system to Holland. In fact, labor was willing to forego significant wage increases until the end of the 1950s (Dutch wages lagged behind other West European industrialized countries for most of the decade)in part because of the benefits that came with a national health service and social security system.[16] However, the era of good feeling came to an abrupt end in 1958–1959. At that time labor ceased its cooperation in the harmony model, and demanded major wage increases to keep pace with developments in the other European countries. The result was what critics called a wage explosion, and this was soon followed by severe inflationary pressures. These were to plague the country throughout the next decade, souring both the economic and political climate. In 1970, in the face of bitter opposition from organized labor, the government actually instituted legally binding guidelines for wages and salaries.

Changes in Social and Political Life

Life in western Europe changed profoundly after the Second World War. New political parties, American forms of labor-management relations, the development and acceptance of industrial policies, the secularization and bourgeoisification of society—these were only some of the factors that characterized the new western Europe.[17] True, there were also significant continuities. After an initial outburst of purge fever, most of those who had sympathized with fascism or the collaborationist regimes in France and Holland were quickly and rather smoothly reabsorbed into the mainstream of society.[18] In West Germany de-Nazification was actually more farce than high drama.[19]

But there certainly were changes. Among the most noticeable were the structural innovations in the European labor movement. In Germany, organized labor abandoned the pre-Nazi pattern of unions divided along confessional and political lines, and established instead a single union movement, the *Deutsche Gewerkschaftsbund* (German Labor Association, [DGB]). The new organization was not affiliated with any political party, although many of its leaders remained close to the Social Democrats. In contrast to the situation in France and Holland, the DGB was unable to organize the majority of white collar workers who, for the most part, remained loyal to a separate, but also politically autonomous union, the *Deutsche Angestelltengewerkschaft* (German White Collar Union [DAG]). In Holland confessional and "free" (i.e., Social Democratic) unions maintained their separate organizations, but they closely coordinated their activities and acted much like the DGB. In both countries there was also a significant decline in the number of industrial actions, and when strikes did occur, they tended to focus more on bread-and-butter issues than on political goals. Such a pattern of cooperation was not the case in France, where the animosity between the Communists and the non-Communists divided the union movement into antagonistic organizations. The largest French union, the CGT, was firmly under Communist control, and the Socialists' attempt to create a rival organization, the FO, was, despite substantial help from organized labor in the United States, not very successful.[20]

Perhaps even more important than the changes in labor organizations were the innovations in the political landscape. A new type of inclusive party, the Christian Democrats, made their appearance in both Germany and France. The Christian Democratic parties were able to attract voters across class lines, and in western Germany the CDU, along with its Bavarian sister organization, the CSU, quickly established itself as the controlling political force in the country. The French MRP did not dominate the political scene, but it, too, became a major force and indispensable coalition partner in the Fourth Republic. A uniquely French phenomenon was a "party against the parties." Charles de Gaulle, who resigned in January, 1946 as head of the government because of his inability to work with parliament and the parties, came out of retirement a year later to found the *Rassemblement du peuple français* (Assembly of the French People [RPF]). Essentially de Gaulle's personal following, committed to the general's vision of a strong France under a strong executive, the RPF quickly established itself as a major political force, drawing voters primarily from the Radicals and MRP constituencies. The Dutch political parties remained divided along confessional lines until the 1970s, but they had no difficulties forming coalitions throughout the 1940s and 1950s.[21]

These political changes were part of what has been described as the increasing pragmatization of European society. Changes in social relations were perhaps even more far-reaching. Europe was becoming an increasingly secular society, and gender relations became more complex as increasing numbers of women expected to (and did) work outside the home. Above all, however, what had long been accepted as the typically European class structure became considerably modified. This did not (yet) mean the wholesale transference of the American model in which virtually everyone was supposedly a member of the middle class, but there is no doubt about the growing bourgeoisification of western Europe. This process, the result of the progressive improvements in the quality of life and changes in employment patterns, affected most dramatically the traditional working classes. Abandoning their status as self-conscious blue collar proletarians, they increasingly adopted the possessions, life habits, and expectations traditionally associated with the bourgeoisie.[22]

National Peculiarities

In West Germany perhaps the biggest surprise was the lack of unique national developments. The end of the German *Sonderweg* (if it had ever existed) came far more painlessly than had been expected. Despite the humiliation of defeat and the total destruction of any recognized political entity, the concept of a *Staatsnation* took hold quickly, inaugurating an era of unexpected political stability. The same was true for social relations; the social climate in Germany became remarkably free of tensions. After a wave of large-scale strikes at the beginning of the 1950s, the trickle-down effects of supply-side economics defused labor-management altercations for most of the long decade. What the Dutch called the harmony model became "*freiheitlicher Korporatismus*" (democratic corporatism) on the other side of the Rhine. It was not until the recession of the mid-1960s, which brought low wage increases and severe inflationary pressure, that labor unrest again became a serious problem, leading to a series of mostly wildcat strikes.[23]

Tensions and altercations characterized the social climate in France during the first decade after the war for a number of reasons. De Gaulle's early vision of restoring France's grandeur saddled government budgets with heavy deficits. Most Frenchmen experienced a perceptible, if not dramatic, decline in their standard of living, and the Cold War added political antagonisms to the social tensions. One manifestation of the malaise was a series of politically motivated strikes that repeatedly paralyzed the country. In 1947, as a Socialist commentator was to write later, "since May labor actions have hardly ceased," but things were to get even worse. In August, 1953 there were weeks of general strikes, "the largest such developments since 1936."[24] In the early 1950s another challenge to social stability arose from the political Right. Supported by a large following of small-scale farmers and businessmen—the forces that traditionally dominated French economic and social life[25]— and led by a demagogic shopkeeper, Pierre Poujade, the Poujadist Movement presented the most dramatic technophobic challenge to the developing tertiary industrial society in France.[26]

Yet this picture of a society tottering toward disintegration is misleading. Behind the unrest and upheavals, even in France control, stability, and progress persisted. Despite the superficial picture of a country racked by constant labor unrest, the governments of the Fourth and Fifth Republics never lost control of the situation. In 1947, when the Communists undertook what appeared to many to be a serious effort to seize political power through syndicalist mobilization, the SFIO minister of the interior, Jules Moch, broke the strike wave, and in 1953 the calm fortitude of Robert Schuman (MRP) prevailed. Equally important, while de Gaulle was proclaiming his visions of grandeur, many French government and business leaders were far more realistic about the country's future prospects. Their goals were economic expansion and European unity, not chauvinistic pomp. Even the Poujadist movement was something of a tempest in a teapot. Although dramatically successful at the polls for a while, Poujadism was little more than a rearguard action of frustration.[27]

In fact, France was undergoing rapid modernization. By the mid-1950s the results were apparent even to superficial observers. The standard of living for most Frenchmen was rising continuously.

With each year, as the social net became more tightly knit, differences in life style between the classes became less marked. Individual possessions and habits previously associated with the haute bourgeoisie—especially cars and vacations—became increasingly commonplace. Frenchmen of all classes, white and blue collar workers no less than the middle classes, generally adopted a bourgeois life style.[28]

If at first glance unrest and instability characterized French social relations in the decade following the war, in The Netherlands contemporaries and scholars alike were impressed by the seemingly unchanging patterns of continuity, even nostalgia. Levels of social mobility remained low throughout the 1950s. Strikes were relatively rare and seldom politically explosive. Despite strenuous efforts by the Dutch Social Democrats (more on this in Chapter III) the political spectrum reemerged much as it had existed in the 1930s, and social relations were still largely governed by the phenomenon of *verzuiling*, the division of the country's political and social life along confessional and ideological lines.[29]

However, as in France, the superficial picture was deceptive, and more so as the decade wore on. A veneer of political and social cooperation hid rising levels of dissatisfaction and demands for social change in Holland. Pressures for modernization—continuous since the end of the war—led to a veritable social explosion by Dutch standards in the 1960s. Not only did labor abandon its willingness to accept the particularly meager rewards of supply-side economics in The Netherlands and demand higher wages, but more important, the social changes loosened the grip of the *verzuiling* on Dutch society. Arend Lijphart dates the end of the phenomenon in the year 1967, and while such precision may be an exaggeration, it is certainly true that by the end of the 1960s Holland, too, had become a tertiary industrial society, characterized by secularization, increased social mobility, and widespread bourgeoisification.[30]

Seeking an Industrial Policy

One of the more remarkable features of West European economic and social life after Second World War was the relative ease with which neocorporatist policies for managing the postwar economies were adopted. Again, there were national variations, but the ubiquity of the phenomenon was striking. This agreement on neocorporatism as the preferred form of industrial policy was by no means a foregone conclusion. In fact, it was rather surprising, since it was contrary to most of the wartime plans and discussions by the various Resistance forces.

The Resistance groups associated capitalism and corporatism with the economic and industrial policies of the fascist and collaborationist regimes. If there was any common denominator among the West European Resistance, it was a pervasive mood of anticapitalism. Even Christian Democrats talked about the end of the capitalist and bourgeois age.[31] It soon became clear, however, that neither the old elites nor the old structures would be swept away as the Resistance had expected. On the contrary, reinforced by the transatlantic partnership, capitalism and neoliberalism proved remarkably resilient.

The debate over a future industrial policy was settled first in West Germany, in part because the Germans themselves were not the only, nor even the primary, factor in the decision-making process. Although, as we shall see, the Social Democrats produced detailed plans for a full-scale socialization of the economy after the war, neither a majority of the West German voters, nor the Western Allies—and that meant especially the Americans—had any interest in putting these ideas into effect. Employing a variety of subtle and not so subtle pressures, the American and the British occupation authorities left no doubt that they preferred the restoration of some sort of free enterprise system in Germany.[32]

Instead, aided by surprisingly intact business structures and tirelessly promoted by Ludwig Erhard, West Germany's social market economy inaugurated a set of policies that combined investor-friendly legislation with neocorporatist structures. The neocorporatist practices became institutionalized in the 1960s under Erhard's Social Democratic successor, Karl Schiller, who labeled the concept *konzertierte Aktion* (concerted action), but the system was established almost immediately after the Federal Republic was founded. Chaired and guided by officials from the economics ministry, representatives from government, business, and organized labor met almost continuously to discuss policies and policy implementation—and these were not mere public relations gestures. The system was a genuine form of democratic corporate self-government.[33] Implementation did not, to be sure, come about without tensions. The coal industry's 1951 *Betriebsrätegesetz* (Law on Factory Councils), which the DGB demanded in return for labor's acceptance of supply-side economics, was bitterly opposed by the mine owners and the chancellor, Konrad Adenauer, precisely because it instituted the principle of *Mitbestimmung* (codetermination) in German economic life.[34]

France entered the Second World War as a nation divided against itself. Before the outbreak of hostilities, the Popular Front government's attempt to give France a modern social net had stirred up fierce opposition from business and farmers' groups. These forces in turn had a revenge of sorts during the Vichy years, when the collaborationist regime pursued policies that benefited primarily business and agricultural interests. However, the numerous technocrats who staffed Vichy's offices were also convinced France should not return to a nostalgic pre-industrial era, although much of the regime's propaganda seemed to promise just that. By war's end an unacknowledged confluence of ideas about France's future had emerged: Groups as politically disparate as the Gaullists, Vichy's technocrats, and the Communists all agreed that France had to undergo a crash course in modernization.[35]

Unfortunately, there was little agreement on the best means for achieving this end. Throughout the early postwar years decision-making was hampered by a variety of factors. Persistent political instability plagued the Fourth Republic no less than the Third. Contemporary observers were uncomfortably reminded of conditions in the last years of the Weimar Republic. Entrenched interest groups that had traditionally benefited from protectionism—such as the alcohol lobby—fought bitter rearguard actions against the program of modernization.[36]

Above all, however, the decision makers were themselves divided on which course of action to take. As we shall see, the Socialists, led by André Philip, the first postwar minister for industries, wanted to inaugurate a full-scale socialized economy, with centralized planning and a massive program of nationalization as its twin foundations. In contrast to Germany and Holland, France did nationalize some key sectors of the economy,[37] including the Bank of France, the electricity and gas enterprises, and some large insurance companies. These measures had widespread public approval (in part because big business was reputed to have been a mainstay of support for the Vichy regime), but the results were not what the original advocates had hoped for. The nationalized enterprises were not subjected to political control, but rather run according to traditional management principles by state-appointed technocrats.[38]

Planning, too, traveled along its own path. To be sure, the state played a key role in France's industrialization after 1945. The government provided much of the capital investment in the postwar era (the amount rose from five percent in 1938 to between twenty to thirty percent in the period 1947–1958) and a state agency developed a series of multiyear modernization plans. Rooted in ideas articulated during the Depression and projects developed by Vichy's technocrats, the initial *Plan de modernisation et d'équipement* (Modernization and Equipment plan [PME]) was enthusiastically supported by a wide spectrum of interest groups, including the Socialists.[39]

However, under the energetic guidance of Jean Monnet and his associates, the PME became less a directing agency than a coordinating one. The Plan soon developed distinctly neocorporatist features. Prodded by government officials, France's major economic interest groups, and especially those representing large-scale enterprises, matched goals and resources in order to increase the efficiency of the French capitalist system. France's industrial policy became a coordinated economy rather than a directed economy. By the middle of the decade, as one author put it, planning "lost much of its coercive character and all of its Socialist inheritance."[40]

While French neocorporatism exhibited many features also found in Germany and Holland, it had some characteristics unique to France. One was the leading role played at all levels of the planning process by technocratic civil servants. Known familiarly as *énarques*, graduates of the elite École Normale d'Administration headed not only the major desks at the ministry of finance (the superior agency of the PME), but they also held important staff positions in all of the neocorporatist planning commissions. The managers of the nationalized enterprises were also drawn from this group, while other technocrats participated in what became a revolving door syndrome in French industry: After some years in government service, a number of énarques moved to high-level positions in private enterprise.[41]

In contrast to the high profile of government officials, organized labor played a far less prominent role in France than in Germany or The Netherlands. The reason was primarily political. The French unions, dominated by the Communist CGT, refused to participate in a process which they saw (quite correctly) as stabilizing and strengthening capitalism in France. As a result, neocorporatism in France essentially involved an alliance between the state and business, especially large-scale business. Working within the constraints of chronically adverse conditions ranging from political instability to excessive outlays for defense, French neocorporatism nevertheless produced a modernized, tertiary industrial society in a remarkably short time. The planners' aims were growth and price stability, and they accomplished the first part of their goal: France achieved unprecedented growth rates. Simultaneously the country modernized its industrial structure and institutionalized a closely knit social net.[42]

The Dutch not only adopted neocorporatism in a straightforward manner, but also led the way toward reintegrating West Germany into the West European economic system. Although the Nazis' exploitation policies in Holland were no less ruthless than in France, unlike her neighbor to the south, The Netherlands had no interest in weakening German industry, especially in the Rhine-Ruhr area. The Netherlands certainly feared renewed German aggression, but they also realized that Dutch economic recovery depended on trade with her eastern neighbor. This was especially true for the heavily industrialized German regions across the Rhine, traditionally the best customers for Dutch agricultural exports.[43]

But the governments of that led The Netherlands in the immediate postwar years also decided early on that, while agriculture would remain a key component of the Dutch economy especially during the immediate recovery phase, in the long run the country needed not only to rebuild, but also to modernize and restructure itself. The Dutch adopted neocorporatism with particular enthusiasm. The PvdA quickly abandoned its early enthusiasm for a full scale socialized and planned economy, while its bourgeois coalition partners no longer upheld the principle of an unfettered free market economy.

The relative ease with which a neocorporatist industrial policy was adopted in The Netherlands was due to the fortuitous confluence of two strains of social reformism. The two leading government parties in the early postwar years, the PvdA and the KVP, had come to embrace neocorporatism along different, but parallel, paths. As we saw, in the 1920s the PvdA's predecessor, the SDAP, had become committed to Bernsteinian reformism, and in the 1930s the Dutch Socialists had been among the most enthusiastic supporters of the Plan van de Arbeid, which contained numerous neocorporatist elements, including a call for labor and management to cooperate in developing an industrial policy. The KVP came to neocorporatism through its endorsement of Catholic social reformism, which combined the social gospel of concern for the less fortunate with the concept of Christian communitarianism.[44]

The primary instrument of Dutch neocorporatism was the *Publieke Bedrijfsorganisatie* (Public Management Organization [PBO]). Originally proposed by the PvdA as a centralized planning agency, the PBO soon lost its directive character, and became the framework for the voluntary cooperation of private management, organized labor, and government officials. Under the auspices of the

PBO, the partners determined and implemented the supply-side industrial policy that became the harmony model. Disappointing a number of Socialist leaders, who had initially hoped that the PBO would inaugurate large-scale socializations, Dutch neocorporatism actually strengthened the private sector. The partners in the harmony model targeted much of the country's public investment for improvements in the The Netherlands' infrastructure, education, and social services.[45]

Neocorporatism Triumphant

Neocorporatism, rather than some form of Socialism or the American version of freewheeling capitalism, emerged as the dominant form of industrial policy formulation in western Europe for a number of reasons. Although seldom acknowledged, the recent fascist experience cast a longer shadow than had been expected. The much trumpeted fascist ideal of cooperation among the economic partners had considerable appeal for many Europeans— once it was divorced from the political dictatorship that was the essence of fascist corporatism.[46]

Equally important was the convergence of Socialist and Christian Democratic reform ideas in the Resistance. Under the impact of the Depression both groups had already developed alternatives to the rule of the market, but mutual distrust of each others' motives had prevented widespread cooperation and coordination between them. Here the Resistance was a major catalyst for change. Working together against the Nazi oppressors, Socialists and left-wing Catholics discovered that their visions of the future were far more compatible than they had expected. The Socialists abandoned their revolutionary ambitions, while the Catholics de-emphasized the sanctity of private property and embraced reforms and neocorporatist steering mechanisms as part of their social doctrine.[47]

There is also no doubt that the Cold War played a major role in the triumph of neocorporatism. Lutz Niethammer undoubtedly exaggerates when he sees the Marshall Plan as blocking the road to a Socialist Third Way, but it is certainly true that the US role in the recovery of western Europe helped to tilt the decision-making process in favor of free enterprise. Equally important, the Marshall Plan strengthened those forces that had already decided the future prosperity of western Europe depended on international cooperation, not a return to national protectionism. Here neocorporatism acquired an important international dimension that prepared the way for the subsequent supranational institutionalization of European unity.[48]

The West European countries fared remarkably well under neocorporatism for the quarter century that followed Second World War. Moreover, even when long years of investment-oriented policies soured the social climate in the 1960s, the policies were successfully adapted to meet the emerging crises. The expectation of crisis-free, indefinitely sustained periods of growth proved to be an illusion, but the systems that were variously called coordinated economy, the harmony model, and concerted action stood the test of time.

Chapter Three

EUPHORIA, DISILLUSIONMENT, AND ADAPTATION, 1945–1949

W estern Europe's Socialists perceived the Continent at the end of the Second World War as a place of both devastation and opportunity. The very magnitude of the problems facing Europe in 1945 convinced them that they were standing on the threshold of a new era, the age of Democratic Socialism. They came to this conclusion through an historical analysis of the developments that in their view had led to Europe's present sad state of affairs. The Socialists were convinced that the cumulative effect of First World War, the Great Depression, the rise and rule of fascism and the destruction wrought by Second World War—in short the course of twentieth-century European history—had finally and convincingly demonstrated the political, economic, and moral bankruptcy of nineteenth-century liberalism, conservatism, and capitalism. At the same time, the rise of Stalinism showed that the Soviet model of dictatorial one-party rule and state capitalism was not a viable alternative. With "dialectical near-certainty" they concluded the only answer to Europe's problems was Democratic Socialism.[1]

Leaders (and rank-and-file activists) of the three parties did not tire of reiterating that the Socialist parties would be given a democratic mandate to effect fundamental changes in European society. The Dutch PvdA spoke of a "societal restructuring " in The Netherlands. The SPD insisted even more dramatically that unless the Social Democrats became the decisive voice in Germany, the country and Europe would remain a center of violence and decay. After Léon Blum, the leader of the French Socialists, returned to France from Buchenwald, his first major speech was entitled, "*Le social-isme, c'est le maître de l'heure*" (Socialism is the master of the hour). Even Guy Mollet, soon to be elected as the SFIO's secretary general and a man often portrayed as the quintessential political tactician, saw as the Socialists' goal not to attain power, "but to change [the nature] of power."[2]

But what did "socialism" mean to the three parties? There was, of course, no coherent, binding program common to all three, but it is possible to delineate something like a minimal set of common beliefs immediately after the war. To begin with, virtually all Socialists insisted political democracy was an end in itself. The concept included both respect for individual civil rights and adherence to a system of political decision making founded on free, universal suffrage. Most Social Democrats favored parliamentary democracy as a constitutional system. Politically, therefore, the Socialists saw themselves as the executors of the liberal heritage. (Kurt Schumacher, the leader of the SPD, once said the Socialists had taken over what was valuable in liberalism and the rest belonged on the scrap heap of history.[3])

However, the Socialists also insisted political democracy had to be supplemented by another form of popular rule, something they called economic democracy. For the Social Democrats the political ancien régime died in 1789 and the economic old order in 1940. The concept of economic democracy involved public ownership and control in the form of socialization or nationalization of the commanding heights of the economy (such as basic industries, financial institutions and raw materials resources), and some form of planned, directed economy subject to democratic political controls.[4]

"Socialism" also meant a positive attitude toward the state and the nation as a set of historically evolved cultural values. Putting it in terms of past controversies, western Europe's Socialists after 1945 followed Jean Jaurès and Ferdinand Lasalle, not Jules Guèsde or Rosa Luxemburg. The long debate over *ministérialisme* was over; all three parties were eager to accept government responsibility in their respective countries.[5] The Continent's Socialists also favored European unity and were—at least in principle—prepared to yield portions of national sovereignty to supranational European institutions.

Finally, ethical and moral goals—since Eduard Bernstein an increasingly important, if unacknowledged, competitor for Marx's deterministic structuralism in Continental socialism—permeated postwar socialist thinking. The concept came with a variety of labels—personalist socialism, ethical socialism, religious socialism—

but it invariably involved the insistence that there was a need for the ethical self-transformation of European society. Immanuel Kant and Karl Barth, not to mention more faddish thinkers like Denis de Rougemont, achieved prominent places in the pantheon of socialist guides for moral improvement. Concretely, western Europe's socialists were convinced the democratic socialist society to come would resolve contradictions between individualism and collectivism. The citizens of the new Europe would voluntarily accept service to the collectivity as a way of realizing individual self-fulfillment.[6]

The Breakthrough

If there was considerable agreement on the "what" of socialism among western Europe's Social Democrats, this was not true for the "how" of obtaining a democratic mandate to put socialism into effect. Everyone agreed that the socialist parties needed to achieve what the Dutch called the *doorbraak* (breakthrough), a way which would enable the Social Democrats to overcome their traditional status as minority parties. Limiting their appeal before 1945 primarily to a single societal interest group, the industrial proletariat, the three Socialist parties had never obtained more than thirty percent of the popular vote in national elections, clearly not a level of support that provided a democratic mandate for revolutionary change.

Theoretically, three breakthrough scenarios offered themselves to the Social Democrats. One was some sort of national union under Social Democratic leadership. The SFIO leader André Philip, in particular but others as well, would later insist that the antifascist resistance was so permeated with socialist idealism that the Social Democrats would only have needed to tap into this desire for fundamental change to create a new political vehicle for building democratic socialist societies in western Europe.[7] Actually, this concept was never realistic. In Germany, no national resistance movement existed, and in Holland and France, where *verzet* and *Résistance* were major forces, the Resistance as a unified movement quickly disintegrated after the end of hostilities, and the traditional parties reestablished themselves.

A second possibility was a new form of working class unity. Under this scenario, the Social Democrats would spearhead a union of old and new working class voters, thus achieving victory at the polls. The new working class unity concept was based upon the assumption that the "bourgeois age had collapsed" (to quote the German Christian Democratic leader Jakob Kaiser). As a result it would be possible for the Social Democrats to mold the traditional working class and large parts of the new working class (the now proletarianized middle class) into what would in effect be a united workers' party. André Philip, who endorsed this concept as a corollary to his vision of the Resistance as a revolutionary force, would later argue that, if the SFIO had ceased chasing after the chimera of institutional union with the French Communist Party and softened its anticlerical stand to attract Catholic workers, the Socialists could have prevented the founding of what was to become the largest political party in postwar France, the Christian Democratic *Mouvement républicain populaire* (Popular Republican Movement [MRP]). Guy Mollet, who firmly rejected Philip's arguments on *laïcisme*, nevertheless agreed that the MRP "should not exist"; Christian workers belonged in the SFIO.[8] (By analogy, the same would have been true as well for the KVP in The Netherlands, and the CDU in Germany.) In retrospect, it is clear that this road to the breakthrough also had no chance of success in the immediate postwar era. The political attitudes of the potential components of any new working class party were not yet compatible, a fact of political life that was not lost on prescient contemporary observers.[9]

A variation of the new working class scenario was old working class unity. This essentially involved an institutional merger of the estranged Communist and Socialist parties. Despite siren calls from the Communists (and initially strong rank-and-file sentiment for old working class unity), leaders of the Dutch and German Social Democratic parties firmly rejected any institutional ties between Socialists and Communists. They advanced ideological, tactical, and foreign policy reasons for their decision. Most important was the incompatibility of the Communists' goal of a Marxist-Leninist Party serving as the vanguard of the dictatorship of the proletariat with the Socialists' firmly held belief in political democracy. The Socialists were also convinced any union between the two parties would benefit primarily the Communists; Schumacher feared that the Social Democrats would merely provide them with a "blood transfusion." Finally, there was the link between the Communists and the Soviet Union. The forced union of Communists and Socialists in the Soviet Zone of Occupation in Germany provided the SPD with final proof that the Communists were little more than a political standing army supporting the foreign policy aims of the Soviet Union.[10]

At the beginning of 1945 all signs seemed to point to working class reunification for the French Socialists in the form of a merger of the Communist and Socialist parties. During the war the SFIO and the *Parti Communiste Français* (PCF) had established a *Comité d'entente* to work out the terms of union between the two parties. But the unity talks, never very cordial to begin with, broke down completely when in June, 1945 the PCF presented the SFIO with a *Charte d'unité* that contained a number of unacceptable conditions. The Communists demanded that the reunited French working class party had to adopt as its ideology Marxism, as improved upon by Lenin and Stalin, and as its organizational principle the norms of democratic centralism. Finally, the PCF wanted Socialism in France to be modeled on that of the Soviet Union. As the Communists had undoubtedly expected, the SFIO rejected all of these demands.[11]

After the fact, it is obvious that neither a reunion of the two working class parties, nor their leading the way to Democratic Socialism was a politically realistic scenario. Even if the Communists and Socialists had been able to compromise their fundamental differences, such a reunited revolutionary Marxist party would have alienated both middle class voters and Catholic workers. This was not the road to the breakthrough to majority status.

A third opportunity was the transformation of the Socialist parties into Social Democratic Volksparteien—"labor parties" rather than workers' parties. Behind this seemingly insignificant semantic difference lay a major change in political conception. At first glance the Volkspartei concept appeared to have much in common with the new working class unity scenario. Both concepts assumed that not only industrial workers, but also many but also many members of the bourgeoisie would now recognize that their future lay not in the revival of capitalism, but in the establishment of Democratic Socialism. Consequently, both strategies sought the Socialist breakthrough in an alliance of industrial workers and a substantial part of the middle classes. But here the similarities ended. Unlike the proponents of the new working class unity, supporters of the Volkspartei concept were willing to accept the middle classes into the ranks of the party without asking them to undergo a change in self-image. The middle classes could support Social Democracy while retaining a bourgeois mentality; they did not need to see themselves as late-comers to the ranks of the proletariat.

In essence, as Volksparteien the Social Democratic parties would become genuine multiclass organizations, in many ways similar to the typical American parties for which Otto Kirchheimer coined the label catch-all parties.[12] This road to the breakthrough was clearly most promising in terms of potential voter support and in attracting those middle class elements for whom Social Democracy meant primarily ethical renewal rather than class solidarity.[13] But it also involved a radical break with many of the traditional tenets that had bound the red family together. As successful Volksparteien the Social Democrats needed to shed the vestiges of Marxist ideology and symbols, abandon Social Democracy's traditional anti clericalism, and, by no means least among the things dear to a traditional socialist, cease the singing of revolutionary songs.[14] This scenario for the breakthrough also closed the door on any institutionalized merger or cooperation with the Communists.

The Dutch Socialists traveled the most direct road to the Volkspartei. In February, 1946, the old *Sociaal Democratische Arbeiderspartij* (SDAP) voted to dissolve itself, and become part of a new party, the PvdA. Open to socialists, liberals, Protestants and Catholics alike, the new group was intended to be a political home for all left-of-center, progressive forces in The Netherlands. The PvdA's founders had far-reaching ambitions: They hoped their new party would destroy the traditional verzuiling of Dutch politics. That hope turned out to be illusionary. The confessional parties quickly reestablished themselves, and the PvdA became little more than a successor organization to the SDAP, augmented only by a few, rather insignificant, liberal groups. However, if the PvdA was dominated by former SDAP members, it exhibited little resemblance to a traditional socialist party. Its program deliberately rejected both Marxist determinism and any form of anticlericalism. In fact, the guiding light of the new party (who also gave the keynote address at its founding convention) was Willem Banning, a Protestant minister and fervent religious socialist.[15]

In sharp contrast, the SPD, under its charismatic, but arrogant and stubborn leader Kurt Schumacher, refused to become a Volkspartei.[16] True, party leaders talked incessantly about *"Neubau, nicht Wiederaufbau"* (constructing a new party, not rebuilding the old one), and Schumacher, in a much quoted phrase, said it did not matter whether someone came to Democratic Socialism by way of Marx or the Sermon on the Mount.[17] Nevertheless, contemporaries as well as later analysts realized that the early postwar SPD was little more than a revival of its Weimar predecessor.[18]

The reason was partly the rank-and-file's and especially the middle level functionaries' desire for a return to the familiar, and partly Schumacher's specific vision of the SPD as a modern German Social Democratic Party. The party leader was proud that the postwar SPD had been able to absorb all of the various Social

Democratic groups and *tendances* that had emerged after 1933. Free of factions, the new SPD would become the unified party of all Democratic Socialists. Schumacher also talked a great deal about attracting the middle class voters to Democratic Socialism, but he insisted they would have to come as "new workers," willing to accept the leadership of the older, more experienced victims of capitalism, the industrial proletariat.[19]

Since there was no significant support for Schumacher's vision of a new-style, anti-Communist workers' party among the French Socialists, the failure of the SFIO-PCF merger talks should have left the Volkspartei (or *parti travailliste*) scenario as the only viable alternative. Indeed, this was the path vigorously advocated by Léon Blum and his supporters, whose concept of a French Volkspartei would have transformed the SFIO into a political home open to all wage and salaried employees regardless of class identification or religious affiliation.[20] However, a majority of the old activists of the newly reorganized SFIO refused to follow Blum's bold vision, and turned instead to Guy Mollet, the mayor of Arras, secretary of the party's Pas-de-Calais federation, and one of the leaders of the Socialist teachers' union. In August, 1946 the SFIO's national congress elected Mollet secretary general of the party to replace Daniel Mayer, the man who had led the SFIO during the war, and who was generally regarded as Blum's dauphin.[21]

The vote was at least in part a referendum on Mayer's abrasive style of leadership (especially his insistence on purging the party of all elements which had not remained pure during the Vichy years[22]), but there is no doubt that Mollet's vision of the party's future was more appealing to the "foot soldiers"[23] than Blum's and Philip's ideas for a parti travailliste. Although the SFIO's quasi-official historian, Roger Quilliot, insisted that the difference between the two men was one of style rather than substance, Blum's own reaction to Mollet's attacks on Mayer's *rapport moral* (keynote report) speaks another language. In a reply that was "quite long and of high quality" the SFIO's grand old man bitterly accused the congress majority of taking the easy way out and refusing to face the difficult challenges of the future:

> You are afraid of the voters, afraid of the men you will or will not designate as candidates, afraid of public opinion, afraid of failure; but more than anything else, you are afraid of anything that is new. You are nostalgic for everything that might recall this party as you knew it in other days... And the nostalgia takes you back to this past, even though it is no longer relevant ... even though everything around you has been renewed...[24]

Mollet's recipe for the breakthrough was a mixture of revolutionary Marxist rhetoric ("sentimental Marxism," one critic called it[25]), political naïveté, and organizational acumen. The new secretary general essentially suggested that the SFIO could combine the breakthrough scenarios of working class unity and Volkspartei. He claimed that, if the party remained true to its revolutionary Marxist heritage, the SFIO would win over large numbers of Communist voters and sympathizers who were momentarily attracted to the PCF because of its leading role in the Résistance, but who would soon reject the Communists' single-minded devotion to the interests of the Soviet Union. At the same time, emphasizing such traditional, French middle class, republican values as the separation of church and state (laïcisme) and Jacobin nationalism would attract voters and members from the French bourgeoisie, in effect making the SFIO the dominant party in French politics.[26]

Disillusionment

The Social Democrats had to realize very quickly that all of their breakthrough scenarios were paper constructs. The Socialist leaders called for revival and renewal, but most West European voters were primarily concerned about revival, not renewal.[27] The results of the early postwar elections provided dramatic evidence that the parties' exaggerated hopes[28] for voter support would be severely and rapidly disappointed (see Table 1). The Social Democrats were still unable to break through the 30 percent barrier. The revitalized middle class parties and the Communists remained formidable rivals. In France the PCF did better than the SFIO in every election from 1945 to 1956. In Holland the PvdA obtained only 28.3 percent of the popular vote in the first postwar legislative elections, and in West Germany the SPD did only marginally better (29.2 percent). In fact, the West German Socialists had to acknowledge that not they, but their Christian Democrats rivals had become the first successful, democratic German Volkspartei.[29]

Politicians would not be politicians if they did not have ready answers for their failures. The Socialist leaders blamed both external and internal factors for the disappointing choices of the voters; needless to say, the parties preferred to attribute their problems to external causes. These were certainly eclectic, if not always convincing. They included the Catholic Church's opposition to Democratic Socialism; remarkably, all three parties were unanimous in attributing tremendous influence to the Vatican. (Schumacher and

TABLE 1. National Elections, 1945–1956

I. The Netherlands
Tweede Kamer

	Parties (popular vote in percent)					
Date	PvdA	CPN	Lib.	KVP	ARP (Prot.)	CHU (Prot.)
5/16/46	28.3	10.6	6.4	30.8	12.9	7.8
7/7/48	25.6	7.7	7.9	31.0	13.2	9.2
6/25/52	29.0	6.2	8.8	28.7	11.3	8.9
6/13/56	32.7	4.8	8.8	31.7	9.0	8.4

Source: Juriaan Woltjer, *Recent Verleden: De Geschiedenis van Nederland in de Twintigste Eeuw* (Amsterdam, 1992), p. 518.

II. West Germany
Bundestag

	Parties (popular vote in percent)			
Date	SPD	KPD	FDP	CDU/CSU
8/14/49	29.2	5.7	11.9	31.0
9/6/53	28.8	2.2	9.5	45.2
9/15/57	31.8	—	7.7	50.2

Source: Gerhard A. Ritter and Merith Niehuss, *Wahlen in Deutschland, 1946–1991: Ein Handbuch* (Munich, 1991), pp. 100–101.

III. France
Assemblée Nationale

	Parties (popular vote in percent)				
Date	SFIO	PCF	Radicals	MRP	Gaullists
10/21/45	23.4	26.2	10.5	23.9	—
11/10/46	17.8	28.2	11.1	25.9	3.0
6/17/51	14.6	26.9	10.0	12.6	21.6
1/2/56	15.2	25.9	11.3	11.1	2.7

Source: François Goguel and Alfred Grosser, *La Politique en France* (Paris, 1964), pp. 330–32.

the French prime minister Félix Gouin complained in almost identical words that the CDU and the MRP had a party office in every Catholic church, and that every priest was a volunteer functionary for the Christian Democratic parties.[30]) The effect of the Cold War was often cited. The leaders claimed the atmosphere produced by the East-West conflict led middle class voters to confuse Social Democracy and Communism and to see both as manifestations of the red enemy.[31] French and Dutch Socialists also noted that leaders who occupied government positions in coalition cabinets were lost to the parties, thereby weakening the Socialists' campaign efforts.[32] In France, where women had just obtained the right to vote, "irrational" voting behavior by women was a popular explanation in SFIO circles. Finally, for those who liked conspiracy theories, there lurked the influence of American finance capital.[33]

In closed party meetings the Social Democrats cited other reasons for their failures, factors that might be classified under the category of self-criticism. These included ineffective campaigning, and the recognition that for many party activists and even more voters "Democratic Socialism" remained an excessively vague and diffuse concept. Above all, however, there was the contradiction inherent in the idea of a democratic, socialist revolution. Perceptive critics pointed out that to win a democratic mandate, the Socialist parties had to appeal to and balance the often antagonistic interests of a wide array of societal groups. But the very success of that effort precluded the hoped-for revolution. A Social Democratic party might well obtain a mandate for wide-ranging reforms, but it was unlikely to become a vehicle for the revolutionary transformation of society.[34]

Adaptation

For historians of comparative politics the three parties' reaction to the end of euphoria is of particular interest. Western European Socialism would find its future role as a viable political movement by adapting to its failures. The reaction of the PvdA's leaders was honest, radical, consistent and, at least until the end of the 1950s, eminently successful. The party's leadership admitted that the original scenario for the breakthrough was unrealistic—then and for the foreseeable future.[35] The party leaders concluded unequivocally that to be politically successful the PvdA had to abandon its vision of a democratic Socialist revolution. Instead, it needed to reinforce its image as a Volkspartei, and work for piecemeal reforms as a partner in coalitions with bourgeois parties.

For a time, it appeared that the decision to embrace reformism and abandon hopes for a social democratic revolution would lead to a serious rift in the party. Many of the PvdA's rank-and-file members were far more reluctant to embrace reformism and coalition compromises than the leadership was. The PvdA's support of the Dutch cabinet's Indonesian policies specially aroused ire among the activists. In the last half of 1947 the PvdA suffered a net loss of some eight thousand members, a drain that was largely attributed to the "Indonesian factor." But there was also criticism that the party had given up on the ideal of societal restructuring too easily. The PvdA's parliamentary leader would later write in his memoirs that, when cynics complained the only thing the PvdA managed to nationalize was itself, they were essentially right.[36]

Still, the PvdA's leaders held their ground, and in the end most of the rank-and-file members followed the leadership. There was no significant permanent loss of voters and supporters to the Communists, although for a time the CPN made significant inroads into the PvdA's traditional working class constituency; this was a temporary setback. Not only did most working class voters return to the fold, they were joined by increasing numbers of middle class voters.

There are a number of reasons why the Dutch Socialists played a pioneering role in embracing what one scholar has called *gas- en waterleidings-socialisme* (utilities Socialism).[37] To begin with, as we saw, the PvdA's predecessor had already traveled a long way in this direction before the end of Second World War. The SDAP's 1937 program had all but abandoned Marxism as a deterministic system of social change, and the Plan van de Arbeid had contained numerous corporatist elements. After 1945 the PvdA's leaders continued and intensified the earlier trends.

There were also some traditions of Dutch constitutional practice which reduced the influence of second-rung leaders, particularly in the parliamentary delegation, and permitted the party's leaders greater autonomy in pursuing their course of action. In contrast to the custom in France, most Dutch cabinets were extra-parliamentary, which is to say, they were formed by agreement among the leaders of the coalition parties with relatively little involvement by the parliamentary groups. (With a clear eye toward France, one Dutch political leader—not a Socialist—noted with satisfaction that in The Netherlands "*de ministers zijn geen mandatarissen van een partij*" [the ministers do not have a mandate from a party].[38]) In addition, cabinet members could not be members of the legislature (and were thus not subject to party discipline in parliament), and there were no formal votes of confidence; Dutch cabinets were (and are) inaugurated if the second chamber of the *Staten Generaal* does not formally disapprove of the new government's composition or program.

The German Social Democrats dealt with the end of euphoria in a far less straightforward manner. The party reacted to the setback in the Bundestag election of 1949 with a set of contradictory policies which increasingly pitted the party's central executive against a group of reformers who had their base of power in the German Länder and the SPD's caucus in the Bundestag. The SPD's chairman and his close associates in the *Büro Dr. Schumacher* (who included Schumacher's successor, Erich Ollenhauer) insisted the election results of 1949 were a temporary defeat that did not require a change in either the party's program or strategy.[39]

According to Schumacher, to reach its goals the party needed to continue "intransigent opposition" (a controversial strategy the party chairman had begun in West Germany's first quasi-parliamentary body, the *Wirtschaftsrat* [Economic Council]), rejecting everything Konrad Adenauer and the CDU stood for.[40] Unlike the PvdA, the SPD would not join in a national coalition. (Actually, this was a moot point. Adenauer, too, resolutely rejected any national or great coalition.) In terms of domestic policies, the SPD would contrast the virtues of a democratic planned economy with the inevitability of social despair and economic crises that would result from the CDU's social market economy.[41] In the area of foreign policy, the chasm between the Christian Democrats and the opposition was, if anything, even wider. The SPD contemptuously dismissed Adenauer's tireless efforts to further West European integration and make West Germany part of the Western Alliance. In stridently nationalistic tones the SPD's national leaders insisted that national unification (including recovery of the lost territories east of the Oder-Neisse Line) and the restoration of full national sovereignty had to precede any agreements on European integration.[42]

Confronted with clear evidence that Schumacher's path increasingly condemned the SPD to fruitless opposition, the reformers in the party presented an alternative road for the SPD's future. The Young Turks recognized that only as a genuine Volkspartei could the SPD successfully challenge Adenauer and the Christian Democrats. Significantly, the reformers' efforts began even before the establishment of the Federal Republic and the disappointment of the 1949 election. A milestone on the road to a new party image was the Ziegenhain Conference in August, 1947. The resolution that emerged from the meeting showed the far-reaching influence of Carlo Schmid, the SPD's leader in Württemberg. The document rejected Marxist economic determinism, emphasized ethical socialism, and, as we shall see, in many ways foreshadowed the 1959 Bad Godesberg Program. Moreover, the reformers were fully aware of the political bombshell they were producing; they made sure that comrades in Great Britain and France received copies of the resolution.[43]

In the light of the CDU's continuing successes the reformers intensified their efforts to change the party's fundamental image and policies. They argued that, like the PvdA, the SPD had to abandon its time-honored Marxist rhetoric and the symbols associated with the red family.[44] As for policies, the Young Turks insisted the party had to do more than *"das ewige Nein-Sagen"*(perpetual naysaying). Stressing what would later be called *Gemeinsamkeiten* (commonalities) with the CDU, the SPD should acknowledge the successes of the social market economy and work for reforms within the context of neocorporatism.[45] The reformers also wanted to place the goal of West European integration alongside the party's primary aim of national reunification.[46] Finally, in contrast to Schumacher, who rejected all coalitions with bourgeois parties as explosive combinations, the reformers had no fear of sharing government responsibility in the Länder. In fact, they welcomed a share of executive power in order to demonstrate to potential swing voters that the SPD could govern effectively if given the chance.[47]

The conflict between the SPD's central executive and the reformers was subdued and at first glance the outcome rather one-sided. Until his death in August, 1952, Schumacher and his supporters seemed to retain complete control of the party executive and even the national congresses, where resolutions routinely endorsed the positions of the executive. (Nevertheless, Schumacher heartily disliked and distrusted the reformers; he suspected they wanted to replace him as party chairman.[48])

This picture, however, was deceptive. Taking advantage of Germany's federal structure, the reformers built camps of their own in the states. Here the Social Democratic prime ministers, or *Landesfürsten* (territorial princes), as they came to be known, were protected from Schumacher's wrath by a direct mandate of the voters, precisely what the party leader lacked. Leading critics like Max Brauer in Hamburg, Ernst Reuter in Berlin, or Wilhelm Kaisen in Bremen were all elected Länder executives who did not owe their power and status to party headquarters. And the voters continued to strengthen their positions. Using the 1949 Bundestag election results as a base of comparison, the SPD did considerably better in many state elections before 1949, and this trend continued after the establishment of the Federal Republic (see Table 2). The strong position of the state executives also allowed them to protect and nurture the next generation of SPD leaders, such as Willy Brandt. In the late 1940s and early 1950s Brandt, for example, gained prominence as Ernst Reuter's "young man."

Much to its dismay, party headquarters never succeeded in controlling the Landesfürsten. Symptomatic of the power relationship was the conflict between the mayor of Bremen, Wilhelm Kaisen, and Kurt Schumacher. To punish Kaisen for his supposed *"parteischädigendes Verhalten"* (activities harmful to the party) in opposing Schumacher's stand on the Schuman Plan, the party leader insisted that the mayor not be reelected to the SPD's executive committee at the party's 1950 national congress. Schumacher prevailed, but his personal vendetta had no effect upon Kaisen's further political career or his control of his home base in Bremen. With Kaisen heading the ticket, the SPD compiled a voting record in Bremen in the 1950s that made the party's national office both envious and frustrated.[49] The mayor remained in office until the 1960s, becoming one of the party's grand old men and a much respected father figure in Bremen.

A second nucleus of reformist activity emerged in the Bundestag delegation. Here men like Carlo Schmid, Herbert Wehner, Willy Eichler, and Fritz Erler—all influential leaders on the road to what was to become the 1959 Bad Godesberg Program—prepared the way for quietly disengaging the SPD from Schumacher's strategy of blanket opposition to the Adenauer government.

Erler had emerged as one of Schumacher's leading critics even before the first Bundestag was elected. In a long, private comment on the party leader's keynote address at the SPD's 1948 congress in Düsseldorf, Erler complained that Schumacher's speech demonstrated that the party leader was spending too much time with his circle of close associates, and had too little contact with day-to-day politics, including representatives from the other political parties. Carlo Schmid, to whom Erler had sent a copy of his letter, added that he agreed completely with Erler's assessment.[50]

Schumacher tried to enforce the dictum that the SPD's elected representatives were subject to instructions from the party's executive,[51] but he did not get his way. Not only was such a policy clearly unconstitutional, but once again the German federal system came to the aid of the delegates. The Bundestag members could defy party headquarters because of their political power

TABLE 2. West Germany: Landtag Elections, 1945–1956

Note: The CDU does not field candidates in Bavaria; the CSU runs only in Bavaria.

		Parties (popular vote in percent)			
Land	Date	SPD	KPD	FDP	CDU/CSU
Bavaria	6/30/46	28.8	5.3	2.5	58.3
	12/1/46	28.6	6.1	5.6	52.3
	11/26/50	28.0	1.9	7.1	27.4
	11/28/54	28.1	2.1	7.2	38
Hessen	6/30/46	44.3	9.7	8.1	37.3
	12/1/46	42.7	10.7	15.7	30.9
	11/19/50	44.4	4.7	31.8	18.8
	11/28/54	42.6	3.4	20.5	24.1
Württem-Baden	6/30/46	32.3	10.0	16.8	40.9
	11/24/46	31.9	10.2	19.5	38.4
	11/19/50	33.0	4.9	21.1	26.3
	3/9/52	28.0	4.4	18.0	35.9
	3/4/56	28.9	3.2	16.6	42.6
Hamburg	10/13/46	43.1	10.4	18.2	26.7
	10/16/49	42.8	7.4	13.3	34.5
	11/1/53	45.2	3.2	—	50.0
	11/10/56	53.9	—	8.6	32.2
W. Berlin	10/20/46	51.7	13.7	10.3	24.3
	12/5/48	64.5	—	16.1	19.4
	12/3/50	44.7	—	23.0	24.6
	12/5/54	44.6	2.7	12.8	30.4
Lower-Saxony	4/20/47	43.4	5.6	8.8	19.9
	5/6/51	33.7	1.8	8.4	23.8
	4/24/55	35.2	1.3	7.9	26.6
NRW (1)	4/20/47	32.0	14.0	5.9	37.6
	6/18/50	32.8	5.5	12.1	36.9
	6/27/54	34.5	3.8	11.5	41.3
R-P (2)	5/18/47	28.6	6.2	15.8	49.1
	4/29/51	34.0	4.3	16.7	39.2
	5/15/55	31.7	3.2	12.7	46.8
S-H (3)	4/20/47	43.8	4.7	5.0	34.1
	7/9/50	27.5	2.2	7.1	19.7
	9/12/54	33.2	2.1	7.5	32.2
Bremen	10/12/47	41.7	8.8	5.5	22.0
	10/7/51	39.1	6.4	11.8	9.1
	10/9/55	47.7	5.0	8.6	18.0

(1) NRW=Northrhine-Westphalia; (2) R-P=Rhineland-Palatinate; (3) S-H=Schleswig-Holstein

Source: Ritter and Niehuss, *Wahlen*, pp. 158ff.

base in the Länder. The provisions for individual candidacies (half of the members of the Bundestag are elected on this basis) in the West German constitution, and the fact that no German electoral district crosses Land boundaries increased the significance of association with a specific Land for Bundestag candidates.

Germany's federal structure, then, gave the reformers a viable power base from which to develop an alternative to the rigid line of the party executive. Almost a decade passed before the leadership acknowledged that the original scenario for the breakthrough would not succeed, but when it did, the reformers were ready to provide the party with new leaders and fresh ideas. It was no accident that the SPD's transformation from "new style workers" party to Volkspartei was made possible primarily by the efforts of the party's leaders in the Bundestag and the Länder. The fathers of the Bad Godesberg Program of 1959 were for the most part leaders of the SPD's parliamentary group, and Willy Brandt, the symbol of the party's rejuvenation in the 1960s, had been a charismatic Landesfürst of Berlin before he moved into the national spotlight.

While the German federal structure undoubtedly was a major catalyst in the SPD's self-transformation, historical factors played a role as well. Interestingly, many of these paralleled those instrumental in the PvdA's postwar successes. The German party, too, had a long—if seldom acknowledged—tradition of alternatives to Marxist determinism. (It was, after all, Eduard Bernstein who "invented" revisionism.) There were also clear parallels between the SPD's 1921 Görlitz Program and the PvdA's 1937 platform. And if communal administrative experience had pragmatized the SDAP, the success of Länder coalitions during the Weimar Republic, especially in Prussia,[52] had demonstrated the political usefulness of joining multiparty cabinets to many German Social Democrats. Finally, historical accident played a role in the evolution of the SPD as well. There is no doubt that Schumacher's death at the relatively early age of fifty-six removed a major obstacle to change.

If the SPD was saved from political isolation by the German federal structure, and the PvdA had the advantage of a forward-looking leadership, the SFIO possessed neither asset. As a result, the French Socialists confronted programmatic paralysis, strategic contradiction, and eventual political disaster. To begin with, the SFIO's organizational structure was not designed to permit ideological and strategic innovations. As we saw, in the 1930s the party had been torn apart by organized factions (the so-called *tendances*). These battles between "Néos," "Blumists," "Faurists," *munichois* and anti-*munichois* culminated in the split of the party in 1940. To preserve the party from a repeat of these factional battles after the Liberation, the anti-Vichy leaders decided to prohibit organized *tendances* in the postwar SFIO. They also attempted to strengthen the executive committee (the Comité directeur [CD]) as a way of concentrating more decision-making authority at the top. But these reforms turned out to be something of a pyrrhic victory.

Into the vacuum left by the *tendances* moved the district organizations (the *fédérations*),[53] and with their dominance of party affairs came new problems. The northern districts, particularly the two largest ones, Nord and Pas de Calais, exercised decisive influence in party affairs for the next twenty years. They were also the SFIO's only territorial units with heavy concentrations of industrial worker activists, and they wanted to keep the party as much as possible as a red family. However, the party's voting support increasingly came from lower middle class elements, especially public service employees, in southern and central France, a constituency that had far less interest in becoming part of the tradition-laden red family.[54]

At the same time, Guy Mollet, the party's new general secretary, was heavily dependent upon the support of the federations in the north. (Especially the Pas de Calais *fédération*, which was Mollet's power base.) They had been instrumental in his election as party leader, and for the next twenty-five years they continued to back him against his increasingly numerous critics. One party insider remembered "the cooperation of the two sister federations will be an essential ingredient of what one calls Molletism."[55]

The territorial organizational problem was compounded by frequent disputes between the CD and the SFIO's parliamentary delegation, the *groupe parlementaire* (GP). In sharp contrast to the situation in The Netherlands, cabinets in France were indeed "mandatories" of the parties' parliamentary delegations. Almost invariably multiparty coalitions with few shared programmatic or policy goals, the cabinets of the Fourth Republic were short-lived, weak entities. Governmental success, as André Philip noted, meant not that a party had translated its program into legislation, but that it had prevented its coalition partners from doing so.[56] Moreover, in another misguided effort to prevent too much concentration of power in any segment, the party's organizational statutes severely restricted the number of parliamentarians who could be members of the CD. Consequently, most members of the two bodies had no direct, personal knowledge of the deliberations that had guided the decision-making process in the other body.

Complaints by the members of the GP that they were asked to support policies and positions in whose formulation they had little part were often justified.[57]

When the short period of postwar euphoria ended, the party clearly lacked a grand strategy. There was no lack of proposals to lead the SFIO away from dead center, but none was able to obtain consensual support from the party's leaders. One group or another invariably denounced its rivals' initiatives. The objections varied from violating the party's revolutionary heritage to playing into the Communists' hands, and, if all else failed, "the time was not ripe." The outcome was always the same: The SFIO remained inactive, or reacted feebly, while its rivals took the initiative.

Typical was the debate over a proposal in 1948 by the left wing to attract "soft" Communist voters by giving them an institutional home in a new organization which some SFIO leaders hoped to affiliate with the SFIO, the *Rassemblement démocratique révolutionnaire* (Democratic Revolutionary Assembly [RDR]). The left argued that an organization committed to a program of Democratic Socialism and critical of France's colonial policies could serve as a funnel to the SFIO for left-wing sympathizers who were unhappy with the PCF's subservience to Moscow. It is doubtful that the RDR (whose most prominent member was Jean Paul Sartre) would have served its intended purpose, but this was not the focus of the debate within the CD. Rather, the SFIO's right wing rejected the RDR as a back-handed way of reestablishing the prewar *tendances*. Opponents of the RDR also criticized the left wing's colonial strategy as a "me too" maneuver that would attract few Communist supporters, while alienating far more middle class voters.[58]

Initiatives by the right wing to get the party off dead center by establishing better relations with left-wing Catholics fared no better. Mollet and the left wing insisted that unless the party maintained its traditional, firm stance on laïcisme, it would lose what was left of its constituency of industrial workers, without whose support no Socialist revolution was possible.[59]

The result was a policy that Mollet's right-wing critics characterized as "the worst policy". They argued that insisting the SFIO was just as revolutionary and laïciste as the PCF, only democratic, failed to attract significant numbers of Communist supporters,[60] in part because the SFIO's equivocal stance on French colonialism left the PCF as the only critical voice of France's colonial policies, especially in Indochina.[61] At the same time, the SFIO's call for social revolution and laïcisme kept many MRP voters, the only reservoir of voting strength that might have given the SFIO the status of a genuine Volkspartei, from supporting the Socialists.

Were there realistic alternatives for the SFIO? To the end of his career Mollet and his supporters insisted that there were none. Attacked by the antidemocratic forces of the Communists on the left and later the Gaullists on the right, the SFIO had to concentrate on preserving France's constitutional system. Far from pursuing the worst policy, Mollet claimed, the SFIO had prevented the worst: the destruction of democracy in France.[62]

Mollet, like Schumacher, rejected transforming the SFIO into a parti travailliste because he was still fighting the battles of the past.[63] For Mollet and his left-wing supporters any opening to the right evoked memories of the party's slide to the split of 1940. By concentrating ostrich-like on these earlier conflicts the opponents of a parti travailliste failed to see the opportunities which postwar French politics opened for this type of political entity. As election after election showed, the best hopes for reversing the party's fortunes at the polls lay politically among the middle and lower middle classes, and geographically in the southern and central France—groups and areas that even in the 1930s had favored an opening to the right.[64] Instead the SFIO absorbed the Radical tradition, which was not where the voters necessary for a party breakthrough resided.

Guy Mollet himself was part of the problem. In many ways the secretary general was imprisoned by his own rhetoric. Having promised that the SFIO could achieve a breakthrough as a revolutionary, democratic workers' party, he found himself immobilized when he could not produce the desired results. His solution to the dilemma was to escape into doing what he did best, administering the party apparatus and convincing the dwindling number of activists that, while the status quo was not good, any alternative would be far worse.[65]

In retrospect, there is considerable evidence to show that Mollet and his allies were guilty—perhaps without recognizing it—of living in the past. A number of leaders in the SFIO pointed out that the issues of social revolution, Jacobin nationalism, and laïcisme, which the secretary general saw as the bedrock foundations of the party's positions, were becoming increasingly irrelevant to the political life of France after the Second World War. Similarly, Philip pointed out as early as 1947 what the events of 1954 were to confirm: The loss of Indochina would not produce a great up welling of alienation from the Fourth Republic since the French middle classes were not nearly as intransigent on national and colonial questions as Mollet thought.[66]

Perhaps most tragically, the SFIO's insistence on pursuing its illusionary revolutionary goals did not allow the party to take credit for its real accomplishments as a genuine force for political and social reforms. As we shall see, in many ways the French Socialists were actually a political success story. They were instrumental in reversing de Gaulle's chauvinist policies in Germany, and they helped to create the modern French social net. In 1947, with Jules Moch serving as minister of the interior, the SFIO played a key role in thwarting the Communists' most serious attempt to paralyze French society. And, last but not least, the French Socialists were pioneers in creating a united western Europe.

The example of the social security system may serve to illustrate the Socialists' unnecessary defensiveness. Here was a major piece of legislation, passed into law while a Socialist was prime minister of France. The party's rhetoric, however, described this key ingredient of the reformist social net as inadequate because it had not revolutionized French society. (The Communists gleefully agreed, of course.) In contrast, the party trumpeted the half-hearted measures for a planned economy, which brought few or no direct benefits to the SFIO's voting constituency, as revolutionary change in French life.[67]

Conclusion: The Compulsion for Change

Any balance sheet of the first five years after the Second World War clearly showed that none of the three parties obtained a mandate to create revolutionary, democratic, Socialist societies as they defined those terms in 1945. In retrospect, we can identify a number of reasons for the Socialists' failure. To begin with, the contradiction between the rhetoric of revolution and the practice of reformism had a long tradition in European Social Democracy. In the 1920s and 1930s the SPD and the SFIO maintained their revolutionary programs while working hard to implement practical reforms. Most of these remained unrealized or were undone by the end of Second World War. The links in the social net which the SPD had been able to forge in the Weimar Republic were perverted by the Nazis. Across the Rhine the social legislation of the Popular Front had been repealed even before the outbreak of the war and the Vichy regime had embarked on an entirely different social agenda. In Holland before Second World War the SDAP had never been able to breach the supply side policies of keeping the Dutch currency on the gold standard which the Colijn government had consistently followed in the 1930s.

It was not surprising, then, that much of the discussion in the antifascist Resistance focused on the need to establish socialism after the war. But despite the rhetoric often employed by the Socialists, "socialism" for them did not mean revolutionary Socialism, but social responsibility and ethical concerns, in short, "humanity applied to modern society."[68] In practice the concern with societal restructuring really meant repairing or constructing the net of social services which the Social Democrats had been demanding since the beginning of the century.

It is somewhat ironic that the Socialists could legitimately claim to have both identified many of the problems Europe faced at the end of the war, and offered concrete solutions for these problems. Unfortunately for the Social Democratic parties, however, while they had correctly identified the political agenda, they needed to recognize that the political landscape in which they were now operating had changed profoundly. This meant that they, too, must change if they were going to be successful players in the politics of the new Europe.

The PvdA recognized the need for self-transformation first, and acted resolutely and consistently on it. The SPD delayed the decision, but in the course of the 1950s, it also adopted a program and policies that made it a successful Volkspartei in the 1960s. The SFIO refused to acknowledge the need for change and paid a heavy price. It took the destruction of the party to teach the reorganized Parti socialiste in the 1970s the lessons of the late 1940s.

Chapter Four

PARTIES IN FLUX, 1946–1957

The end of postwar euphoria confronted the West European Social Democrats with new challenges for which neither their history nor their ideology had prepared them. Once convinced that Democratic Socialism was the master of the hour, the Social Democrats came to realize that a majority of voters in France, West Germany, and Holland did not share their teleological expectations. As a result, the Socialists' sense of unrealistic optimism was replaced by a mixture of self-delusion, pessimism, and efforts to meet the unforeseen challenges with new ideas and new structures.[1]

Party Profiles

Changes in membership patterns provided one of the first indications that European Socialism had entered a new era. Historically the three parties were mass membership organizations whose activists were committed to practice and propagandize socialism. After the war, all three parties, viewing themselves as the institutionalization of democratic progressivism had expected a sharp rise in members, but the reverse was true. Both the SFIO's and the SPD's membership dropped dramatically. The SFIO's membership declined continuously and precipitously from 335,700 in 1945 to 91,100 in 1955. The number of SPD members, which had been 875,000 in 1947 had fallen to around 600,000 in 1953. The PvdA was the only one of the three parties which was able to increase the number of its activists in the 1950s, its membership growing from 109,600 in 1950 to 142,140 in 1956.[2]

The parties also experienced fluctuations in the socio-economic makeup of their militants. No matter how adamant the leaders of the SFIO and the SPD were that their parties must remain workers' organizations (the PvdA was not compulsive on this point), all three parties were becoming bourgeoisified. Specifically, the percentage of members in public service increased steadily, and it is only a slight exaggeration to say that by the end of the decade the French and German parties had become political interest groups dominated by lower rank civil servants.[3]

The generational character of the membership changed as well. Both the PvdA and the SFIO had considerable difficulty attracting younger activists. Neither the Dutch nor the French Socialists had a very active youth organization, and in the case of the SFIO, the problem was compounded by ideological friction between the party executive and the leaders of the SFIO's official youth organization, the *Jeunesses socialistes* (Socialist Youth [JS]). The latter tended to embrace extreme left positions with a decidedly Trotskyist flavor. The SPD was more successful in attracting younger members. The postwar party appealed to a substantial number of the "Hitler Youth generation." (The later German chancellor Helmut Schmidt was among this cohort.) Raised on the Nazi propaganda of the Volksgemeinschaft, these younger Germans found the party's programmatic coupling of Democratic Socialism and nationalism quite attractive. (In these early postwar years the generational problem was of little concern for the SFIO and the PvdA. Both the French and the Dutch Socialists insisted fascism had no lingering appeal for their constituencies.) There was little change in the gender structure of all three parties; women remained heavily underrepresented among the members of all three parties.[4]

The geographic foci also shifted, though this was less true for the SPD: most of its members continued to reside, as they had throughout the SPD's history, in the large cities of northern, Protestant Germany. The PvdA, whose membership before the war had been heavily concentrated in Amsterdam, cast its net wider to include all areas of the *randstad* in the northern Netherlands, and in the second half of the decade it began to attract members from the Catholic areas of southern Holland as well. The SFIO experienced a more dramatic change than the other parties. Except for the two federations of Nord and Pas-de-Calais, most of the party's membership was increasingly concentrated in the less industrialized eastern and southern parts of France. The party's largest federation was Bouches du Rhône, which included the region around Marseille. In fact, for the most part, the SFIO was becoming an organization whose members resided in small towns and even rural areas.[5]

The Social Democratic parties had never been wealthy organizations. Their activities were financed by dues from the members, and since most activists came from the lower end of the economic scale, the dues were very modest. There was also a direct correlation between the size of the membership and the financial health of the party. After the war, the Dutch and German Socialists had relatively few financial problems, but for the SFIO, with its rapidly declining membership, financial problems became a permanent fact of life and the party lurched from one fiscal crisis to the next.[6]

Another major change in the Social Democratic parties was the rapid disappearance of the so-called red family. This plethora of party-affiliated organizations—ranging from red kindergartens to workers' burial societies—had traditionally been a major part of working class social life as well as a means of ideological indoctrination. All efforts by the party leaders to revive the red family failed. Postwar West Europeans increasingly preferred leisure and social activities sponsored by apolitical organizations, or, when private car ownership increased rapidly in the second half of the decade, as individual or family activities. Not surprisingly, along with the decline of the red family, local party life atrophied in many areas. Virtually everywhere the traditional weekly propaganda and ideological study sessions ceased for lack of interest.[7]

With the disappearance of the red family the party-controlled press rapidly declined. A traditional means of communication between the party leadership and its working class constituency, the party press, with its well-deserved reputation for stodginess and lack of journalistic punch, could no longer compete with radio, well-produced commercial newspapers, and, later, television. The SFIO's *Populaire* and *Populaire Dimanche* ran chronic and growing deficits; by 1966 circulation had fallen to around 10,000. The SPD's venerable daily, *Vorwärts*, renamed *Neuer Vorwärts* after the war, became a weekly and eventually ceased publication altogether. Only in The Netherlands, where the *zuilen* remained intact for most of the decade, did *Het Vrije Volk* remain a viable enterprise until the 1970s.[8]

The parties' reaction to these various difficulties ranged from denial (in his history of the SFIO Roger Quilliot wrote, "how does one wake up a party that doesn't think it's asleep?") to far-reaching reform efforts.[9] The latter invariably included a central aim of reconstructing the organization to streamline decision-making.

Concretely this meant concentrating more decision-making power at the top, while reducing the autonomy of organized minority groups within the parties.[10]

These efforts were only partially successful. Complaints that the new organizations were top heavy, stifled internal democracy, or were dominated by the parties' middle-level organizations were ubiquitous.[11] Even the *tendances* did not disappear altogether. All three parties quickly developed ideologically oriented wings, if not organized factions. In the SPD the Marxist old guard and the rejuvenators (*Erneuerer*) fought low key but persistent battles with each other until the latter emerged victorious with the adoption of the Bad Godesberg Program in 1959. In the PvdA a Marxist left-wing organization, the *Sociaal Democratisch Centrum* (Social Democratic Center, [SDC]), remained a constant thorn in the side of the PvdA's leadership until the group was expelled from the party in 1959. Among the French Socialists proponents of "social democratism" (the term was used by its critics to underline the concept's German origins) stood against supporters of *socialisme pur et dur*, paralyzing the party for much of the decade until its formal split at the end of the 1950s.[12]

The parties attempted to deal with their organizational problems in a variety of ways. There was a stream of disingenuous proposals to create think-tanks as adjuncts to the national executive committees to generate new programs and ideas. There were also calls for modernized organizations that would transform the parties from ideological spearheads of the red family into vote-getting machines. The PvdA was probably most successful in this endeavor. It encouraged the creation of intraparty organizations—the so-called *werkgemeenschapen* (working groups) to focus attention on issues of particular interest to specific segments of Dutch society. Reflecting the still intact *zuilen* structure in The Netherlands, the most active working groups were those representing Catholic, Protestant, and non-church affiliated members in the party.[13] All three parties insisted—without much success—that ideological disagreements should not be aired in public. The parties' executive committees were particularly adamant that dissidents not publish their views in the nonparty press.[14]

Leaders and Leadership

At least in the early years of the decade the Social Democratic parties faced new problems with old leaders. Virtually all of the major figures in the three parties were men (there were no significant women leaders) who had played a major role in the politics of the 1930s and 1940s. The pattern of leadership continuity was particularly pronounced in the SFIO. With few exceptions the men who led the party in the 1950s were veterans of the Third Republic. None personified the bridging of the Third and Fourth Republics more than the most revered figure in the party, Léon Blum. Intellectual leader of the SFIO since the 1920s, prime minister in the 1930s, Blum resumed his leadership role after the war, enhanced with a martyr's glow. Neither Vichy's attempt to try him for treason nor his subsequent incarceration by the Nazis destroyed his spirit or his intellectual acuity. As we saw, Blum was easily the party's most fertile mind, supplying the SFIO with ideas for far-reaching reforms and envisioning for France and Europe a Socialist future. Unfortunately, in the rough and tumble of French postwar politics, Blum was more venerated than followed. He himself complained that the party seemed to expect him to work miracles, while at the same time rejecting his programmatic ideas.[15]

Blum died in March, 1950, and as a group his successors were an undistinguished lot. One of the grand old man's closest associates, Vincent Auriol, was elected president of the Republic in 1946. He remained in office until 1953, and did not take an active part in party affairs when he returned to private life. Other older leaders were political apparatchiks, who had remained in Blum's shadow. The political prestige of men like Daniel Mayer, Jules Moch, and François Tanguy-Prigent was based upon their activities in the Resistance and their loyalty to Blum. Léon Boutbien and Salomon Grumbach, two other close associates of Blum from the 1930s, were largely relegated to the sidelines after the war.

The man of the decade and beyond was Guy Mollet. Elected general secretary in 1946, he was to dominate the SFIO for the next 25 years. For his critics, Mollet and *"Molletisme"* personified what was wrong with French Socialism: ideological dogmatism and one-man rule.[16] In contrast, for his many supporters in the party he represented precisely what the SFIO needed: An able administrator and convinced socialist, who could keep a divided and frustrated party on an ideologically true course. In the CD, whose membership remained remarkably consistent, the general secretary's most prominent supporters included Pierre Commin, for many years the party's deputy general secretary; Marcel Naegelen, a veteran leader of the party's Alsatian federation; Victor Provo, the party's perennial treasurer; and Augustin Laurent, the head of Mollet's home federation.[17]

It is also true, however, that the number of Mollet's critics was growing, and they included some of the party's intellectual heavyweights. Mollet's predecessor, Daniel Mayer; Marcel Pivert, a former Trotskyite who acted as the party's socialist conscience; and Jules Moch all accused the general secretary of sacrificing the SFIO's soul on the altar of coalition politics and party administration for its own sake. In contrast, SFIO leaders like Félix Gouin and Paul Ramadier, both of whom served as prime minister in the 1940s, argued that Mollet neglected the SFIO's relationship to governmental power. A third group of critics, which included André Philip, Eduard Depreux, and Oreste Rosenfeld concentrated their attacks on Mollet's colonial and military policies, and on his unwillingness to open the party to new ideas and new voters. Still, the critics' combined efforts had little effect on Mollet's control of the party machinery, in part because the reformers were divided among themselves. As a group they found themselves "on the margins," and some of the most prominent among them eventually left the party.[18]

At first glance, the leadership question in the German SPD was considerably less complicated. Until his death in August, 1952, Kurt Schumacher's status as intellectual, political, and administrative head of the party was, at least in public, unchallenged. Herbert Wehner, a former Communist who became Schumacher's close associate after the war and who was to emerge as a leader of the reform movement in the 1950s and the 1960s, remembered (with slight exaggeration) "in those days, Schumacher was the party."[19]

Schumacher left no doubt that he wanted Erich Ollenhauer to succeed him, and the party respected his wishes. Ollenhauer was the epitome of a "decent" politician and a genuinely popular figure in the party: jovial, fond of people, honest. He lacked his predecessor's skills as an orator, but he also avoided Schumacher's habit of routinely insulting political opponents individually and collectively. In terms of personality, then, Ollenhauer presented a sharp contrast to Schumacher. This was not true of his policies, since Ollenhauer saw as his primary task preserving and continuing Schumacher's legacy, which he was convinced was the only correct path for the party.[20] "Schumacher has already said what needed to be said," was Ollenhauer's standard reply to innovative proposals. The new leader also retained his predecessor's circle of close associates as the SPD's general staff.

The new chairman's critics came primarily from two groups. On the one hand there were the Länder chieftains, who had already raised their voices, albeit in muted fashion, against Schumacher's leadership style. After Schumacher's death, men like Waldemar von Knoeringen in Bavaria, Wilhelm Kaisen in Bremen, Erwin Schöttle in Baden-Württemberg, Max Brauer in Hamburg, and the team of Ernst Reuter and Willy Brandt in Berlin became increasingly unhappy with the party's administrative and political paralysis. With the establishment of the Federal Republic in 1949, the SPD's Bundestag delegation emerged as another critical faction. Prominent members of the party's parliamentary delegation, such as Carlo Schmid, Fritz Erler, and Herbert Wehner, became increasingly critical of Ollenhauer's unwillingness to change Schumacher's policy of intransigent opposition in the Bundestag. Ollenhauer, however, was supported by the party cadres, and behind the scenes some of the old guard militants let the reformers know of their displeasure. In 1953 Carlo Schmid was refused a place on the Württemberg-Baden Land list of candidates for the Bundestag, and a year later Fritz Erler, although a deputy leader of the SPD's parliamentary delegation, failed in his bid for election to the party's executive committee.[21]

Many of the PvdA's leaders in the 1950s had also risen to prominence in the 1930s. The party's chairman after the Second World War, Koos Vorrink, had been the leader of the SDAP's youth organization in the 1920s and party chairman in the 1930s. (Incidentally, Vorrink and Ollenhauer knew each other well, and Vorrink was instrumental in helping Ollenhauer escape from Nazi Germany.) However, in contrast to the chairmen of the French and German parties, Vorrink and his successor (after 1954), Evert Vermeer, lacked real power. Powerlessness did not mean immunity from criticism, however. Vorrink's sharpest critic was the party's parliamentary leader in the 1940s and early 1950s, Baron Marinus van der Goes van Naters. He accused the party chairman of practicing "awful German ways of leadership."[22]

The real loci of power in the party lay with the PvdA's spiritual and ideological guide, Willem Banning,[23] and Willem Drees, who served as Dutch prime minister for more than a decade. Drees epitomized the "solid, sober, socially concerned" attributes that contemporaries applied to the PvdA's entire leadership group.[24] Drees insisted that as long as the PvdA was a member of the cabinet—a state of affairs he worked hard to perpetuate—the primary function of the party and its parliamentary delegation was to support the government and its policies. Not all members of the executive committee and the parliamentary delegation were entirely happy with this role. The prime minister's tactics were part of the problem. He had a pronounced tendency to play things close to his chest, and he seldom took either the executive committee or the party's members of parliament into his confidence. Some members of the PB and the parliamentary delegation objected on principle, however, claiming that Drees had reduced the party to a "government-support machine."[25] Nevertheless, for the period under consideration here, the critics were a distinct minority among the party's leaders. The undeniable fact that with "Vader Drees" at the head of the ticket, the PvdA was able significantly to increase its share of the popular vote in the 1950s, meant that the prime minister had little difficulty in getting his party to align itself behind him.

Program and Ideology

The years after Second World War presented Democratic Socialism with major ideological challenges. Traditionally, of course, Socialist ideology used Marxist dialectical materialism to explain the past, present, and future role of its primary constituency, the industrial proletariat. That bedrock foundation was already eroding before the war as ethical voluntarism gained influence in the Social Democratic parties at the expense of Marxist determinism. After 1945 the workers' declining faith in Marxism hastened the process. The Social Democrats were well aware that they had to adapt, but they also wanted to square the circle by being simultaneously Volksparteien and working class parties.[26]

The dilemma was most acute for the SPD and the SFIO. Both had elected postwar leaders determined to hold on to inherited ideological positions. From 1945 to his death in 1952 Schumacher insisted the mix he had developed in the 1920s of Enlightenment liberalism, Lasallenism, and Marxism was sufficient for the party; the SPD needed neither a new program nor novel analytical methods. The party had the right ideas, the problem was to convince the voters. Erich Ollenhauer agreed with Schumacher's positions and initially did everything in his power to have the party follow Schumacher's guidelines.[27]

A unique aspect of the SPD's postwar ideological position was its stand on the national question, which Schumacher and Ollenhauer saw as key to the SPD's political success. Based upon the party's experience in the Weimar Republic and the success of Nazism, Schumacher had concluded that the SPD could not succeed as a Volkspartei unless it could demonstrate a positive attitude to German nationalism, or as Schumacher insisted on calling it, German national feeling. He was convinced the party had failed to become a majority party in the Weimar era because its opponents were able to pin the label *"vaterlandslose Gesellen"* (rabble without a country) on it. Schumacher argued that the SPD needed to capture the "Hitler Youth generation" to be successful in the post-1945 era, and that could be done only by channeling the Nazis' chauvinism into healthy, democratic nationalism before the neofascists or the Communists seized hold of the issue. According to Schumacher and Ollenhauer this meant that the party needed to make national unification its permanent priority issue. Schumacher's argument lacked neither intellectual sophistication nor political goodwill. His aim was to do for Germany what Jaurès and Blum had done for Socialism in France: to link nationalism and democracy, so that the political system of democracy became an element of national pride.[28]

But there were problems as well. In addition to some elements of sophistry (the SPD rejected nationalism, but endorsed national feeling), Schumacher had a habit of absolutizing black and white, friend and foe. He would have it that the SPD supported healthy national feeling, democracy and Germany's right to national sovereignty, while the party's political opponents wanted to destroy democracy and acted as lackeys of the occupying powers. Schumacher did not have to wait long for domestic and foreign criticism. Not only Allied officials complained, but Schumacher's fellow Socialists in France and Holland criticized what they saw as a resurrection of German chauvinism. Vorrink declared that Schumacher was playing with fire, and André Philip remarked that obviously the SPD had not yet rediscovered its true Socialist character. (In response, Schumacher insisted that Philip not be permitted to speak at the SPD's national congress in 1950.)[29]

Setbacks in both Bundestag elections during the decade[30] led to increased criticism of the old guard's ideological and programmatic rigidity.[31] As the Cold War seemed to seal Germany's division, the number of critical voices within the party increased. The Länder leaders, most of whom saw the Allied occupation officials as partners rather than as enemies, complained that Schumacher's and Ollenhauer's position served to alienate the party from those western leaders who were genuinely interested in rebuilding German democracy. Others pointed out that fears the Communists would successfully exploit the national issue were exaggerated. Above all, however, Schumacher's prediction that the national issue would produce political benefits for the SPD was not borne out. Although the party made German reunification a central issue of its 1953 and 1957 Bundestag election campaigns, most West German voters found the CDU's promise of economic prosperity and integration into the Western Alliance more appealing.[32]

Ollenhauer's and the old guard's reaction to all this was a combination of rejection, evasion, and accommodation. After the 1953 election the party chairman still insisted no changes were needed; the party merely had to reaffirm its well-known positions. As the volume of criticism rose, the Parteivorstand pursued a dual course. It attempted to shift the focus of the debate (the 1956 national party congress was to concentrate its attention on the problems of the coming tertiary industrial society), but also tolerated a program commission, assembled by Willi Eichler, that in 1951 began discussions of what was to become the Bad Godesberg Program. Still, as a number of scholars have pointed out and some of the reformers realized at the time, it required the shock of the 1957 election losses to persuade Ollenhauer and his allies to abandon the old ways and the old ideas.[33]

The SFIO's situation was strikingly similar to that of the SPD. Like the SPD, the French party had not adopted a new program since the 1920s, and, echoing Kurt Schumacher, Guy Mollet saw no need for a new set of programmatic guidelines.[34] However, while pressure for ideological innovation in West Germany came primarily from the Länder organizations and the party's Bundestag delegation, in France the federations and local organizations tended to resist reform. Most of the party's (declining) rank-and-file members were not interested in ideological debates, and those who were split into two wings: one saw the party as a vehicle for social reform and professional advancement (this group included the large number of Socialist mayors and municipal counselors), and the other still looked upon the SFIO as the political organization that would end the rule of capitalism.[35]

In the SFIO initiatives for innovation came from within the central leadership, notably some members of the Comité Directeur. The proponents of a new party program, who dominated the program commission which the CD established in June 1950,[36] raised a variety of concerns. Perhaps the most basic complaint was that the party was standing still while French society moved on. Jules Moch, for example, pointed out that France was becoming a tertiary industrial society, but the SFIO's program assumed that secondary industrialism was a permanent state of affairs. Others noted that rank-and-file members were confused about the direction of the party as the SFIO participated in a series of ever changing coalitions.[37]

The opponents of innovation, who represented a majority of the CD members, also advanced arguments of theory and tactics. The concept of *socialisme pur et dur* was for most of the SFIO's leaders a principle that did not need constant adaptation. Moreover, and here Mollet and his supporters were undoubtedly correct, the party's rank-and-file members overwhelmingly rejected the critics' implicit goal, an opening of the party toward new constituencies. The proponents of the status-quo also argued that for a party with declining membership, already divided on any number of policy issues, it was political suicide to create additional fissures with new ideological debates.[38]

The consequence was precisely the state of affairs which the reformers criticized: programmatically and ideologically the party stood still. True, the CD and the national councils appointed several commissions to study a variety of ideological and programmatic issues, but neither the commission members nor the party as a whole showed much interest in their deliberations. Moreover, when the reports appeared (after much delay) they focused on the propagandistic aspects of the issues, rather than substantive problems.[39] The CD finally adopted a set of programmatic guidelines with a decidedly traditional slant. Disappointing the reformers, the document insisted "socialists cannot accept a society based on the profit motive," and devoted an entire section to "preparing for the disappearance of the capitalist order."[40]

The PvdA's ideological and programmatic positions contrasted strikingly to those of the SFIO. While a majority of the French Socialists were proud that they had maintained *socialisme pur et dur*, the leaders of the Dutch party congratulated themselves that they had abandoned all fossilized concepts of Marxist socialism. The PvdA, they insisted over and over again, was not simply the SDAP moved slightly to the right. The new party's pragmatic reformism and personalist Socialism was inspiring programmatic discussions even beyond the Dutch borders because they provided answers that Marxist materialism had failed to give.[41] To be sure, waving the flag of reformism and personalist Socialism did not remove all question marks. The idealist, ethical dimension remained rather vague, and, in any case, reformism and personalist Socialism did not add up to Social Democracy. Drees wrote in his memoirs that the concept of personalist Socialism, *"is mij nooit duidelijk geworden"* (never did become clear to me). This did not bother Drees, who was an unabashed pragmatist and saw little use in ideological theories. Others, however, were unwilling to follow Drees and embrace utilitarianism wholesale. They argued this would turn the PvdA into a Dutch version of the British Labour Party.[42]

Therefore the PvdA's ideological dilemma in the early 1950s lay in the relationship between Social Democracy and reformist modernism. The party had clearly abandoned Marxist materialism (including such key concepts as the inevitability of the class struggle), and in the course of the decade the PvdA cut itself off even more from its Marxist roots.[43] The head of the party's research bureau, Joop den Uyl (who was to become prime minister in the 1970s), wrote that for him socialism was just a way of simplifying societal processes to make them more efficient and transparent.[44] At the same time, the Dutch Social Democrats continued to insist that the PvdA would be able to create a democratic socialist society in Holland, remain true to Socialist internationalism, overcome alienation, and provide social justice for all.[45]

Outsiders were more skeptical. Fritz Heine dismissed the PvdA as a *"bürgerlich gemischte"* (bourgeois-mixed) party, that stood for little more than opportunistic reformism,[46] and he was not altogether wrong. A comparison of the PvdA's programs in the 1950s clearly show the progressive victory of pragmatic reformism. However, it is also true that this evolution corresponded with the wishes of most of the party's members and voters. Some intellectuals engaged in spirited debates in the party's theoretical journal, *Socialisme en Democratie*, but these aroused little interest among the membership at large. Even the members of the PB seemed to be bored by ideological issues, and such items seldom appeared on the executive committee's agenda. Most leaders were content with concrete reform projects that increased prosperity and tightened the social net.[47]

During the long decade of the 1950s Social Democracy's attitude toward governmental responsibility also changed. Rarely members of the national governments before the war, French, German, and Dutch Socialists routinely held executive responsibility after 1945. In Holland and France, the PvdA and the SFIO were members, and in the case of the PvdA, the leader of the national government for most of the period. In Germany the SPD formed the opposition at the federal level, but the party was responsible, or shared responsibility, for governing a number of the Länder. Not surprisingly, government responsibility brought a shift in the focus of power within the party. Traditionally, the parties' administrative functionaries had exercised final decision-making authority, but as the Socialists' political success became increasingly linked to the performance of their spokesmen in government and parliament, the legislators and ministers, rather than the cadres, shaped the parties' policies. Although there was some overlapping membership, and in the SPD the party leader chaired both the executive committee and the Bundestag caucus, the two groups quickly developed different priorities. Tensions between the executive committees and the parties' parliamentary and government representatives increased significantly.[48]

The shift in power from the executive committee to the party's representatives in parliament and its cabinet members was most pronounced in the case of the PvdA. The focal point of this shift was the prime minister, Willem Drees. Until the end of the decade the members of the PB were for the most part content to follow Drees' leadership; only very infrequently did the party's executive committee insist on formal consultations. This was not true, however, of the PvdA's parliamentary delegation. Tensions between the Socialist cabinet members and the party's legislators were endemic. Although the party's legislators never questioned Drees' overall leadership, they did not like to be taken for granted. While Vorrink had the reputation of supporting Drees *"door dik en dun"* (through thick and thin), the parliamentary group saw itself as more *"kritisch-constructief"* (constructively critical).[49]

There were a number of reasons for the strained relationship. With the focal point of influence shifting to the governmental side, ambitious younger party leaders sought seats in parliament, populating the group with less pliant Young Turks.[50] As we saw, they complained that Drees refused to consult with them and assumed they would vote to support whatever policies he and his cabinet had decided upon. Drees himself strenuously denied these accusations, but there is no doubt that he tended to act in a rather autocratic manner.[51]

The responsibility was not entirely Drees'; the personality of van der Goes van Naters, the PvdA's caucus chairman until 1951, helped exacerbate the situation. Goes was an ineffective administrator with an easily bruised ego. Relations between the ministers and the parliamentary delegates improved under his successor, Jaap Burger ("The best leader ... that I ever served with," remembered Jacques de Kadt[52]), although the complaints that Drees was acting too much on his own persisted until the PvdA dropped out of the cabinet.

The relationship between party executive and parliamentary delegation should have worked more smoothly in West Germany. The SPD was not a member of the governing coalition, and both Kurt Schumacher and his successor, Erich Ollenhauer, combined the functions of party chairman and head of the SPD's Bundestag caucus. Despite some politically costly missteps,[53] Schumacher was able to impose his iron will on both the party's executive committee and the parliamentary delegation.[54] Ollenhauer, however, had a more difficult time with the federal parliamentarians. The new party chairman and the old-style party functionaries, who dominated the Parteivorstand and with whom Ollenhauer was most comfortable, did not mesh well with the parliamentary delegates. As a group the SPD members of the Bundestag were better educated, younger, and more representative of the society at large than the party's functionary corps.[55] It came as no surprise that the delegation quickly developed a profile of its own, or that the old-guard functionaries attempted to limit the group's autonomy.[56] By the mid-1950s a trio of leaders in the SPD's Bundestag caucus—Herbert Wehner, Fritz Erler, and Carlo Schmid— had established major national profiles of their own, and in many ways were beginning to eclipse Erich Ollenhauer as the leading spokesman for the party.[57]

Relations between the cadres and the governmental wing of the party were particularly complicated in France. While the SFIO was a member of most governments during the Fourth Republic (21 out of 26), many party leaders as well as rank-and-file militants remained uneasy about participating in cabinets that were not committed to bringing democratic socialism to France. As with the SPD, the SFIO's parliamentary delegation, the *Groupe parlementaire* (GP) had a significantly different social profile than the CD. The GP's social profile reflected the changing patterns of the party's activists in the federations producing the bulk of the SFIO's electoral votes.[58] These were the smaller eastern and southeastern federations, which tended to be dominated by public school teachers and *petits fonctionnaires* of public enterprises. They were also areas in which Mollet's support was relatively weak. In contrast, the CD was controlled by the Nord and Pas-de-Calais districts, whose membership, as we saw, was still largely composed of industrial workers.

As a result, relations between GP and CD were, to put it mildly, difficult. In theory, the lines of authority between the two bodies were clear and unequivocal. Like Kurt Schumacher and the German Parteivorstand, Mollet and the CD insisted the SFIO's ministers and parliamentary delegates were subject to the CD's directives. The theoretical chain of command, however, did not work well in practice. Part of the problem was the misguided postwar organizational reform. In an effort to prevent the party from being dominated by the GP, as had happened in the 1930s, the number of members of parliament who could sit on the CD was limited after 1945 to ten out of thirty-one. (The rule was not changed until 1956, when the membership of the CD was enlarged as well.) In addition, the party bylaws stipulated that whenever a member of the CD was elected to parliament, he or she had to resign from the executive committee.

There was also the perennial problem of the parliamentary delegates' political autonomy. Were the members of the GP (or the CD for that matter) free to criticize the government if the SFIO was part of the coalition? Even more important, who determined the GP's stand on parliamentary votes of confidence, a frequent occurrence in the course of the Fourth Republic? The CD insisted that, as the arm of the party responsible for carrying out the mandates of the national congresses, it had the right to decide the fate of the cabinets. The GP, noting that governments were constitutionally responsible to parliament, insisted with equal vehemence that the responsibility for votes of confidence lay with the parliamentary delegates. The result of these altercations was chronic friction between the two bodies. The members of the GP complained that they were not being sufficiently consulted, and that the CD made decisions without a clear understanding of the parliamentary problems involved. The CD in turn accused the parliamentary members of lack of discipline when they voted contrary to the CD's instructions.[59]

At the end of 1951, in an attempt to clarify the lines of authority, Mollet proposed that the CD would limit itself to determining a "general line," which the GP was expected to follow. Within those parameters the GP would be free to determine its balloting in parliament, except for votes of confidence and censure, which would still be determined by the CD.[60] But the problem did not go away, in part because the GP lacked discipline and was difficult to lead. In 1951 the first postwar leader, Charles Lussy, resigned because he was unable to control the GP or to establish a good working relationship with the CD. Four years later, his successor, Eduard Depreux, also threw in the towel. He cited *"ennui"* as his reason for resigning, a unique, if rather unconvincing motivation.[61]

The most dramatic milestone in the self-destructive relations of the party's executive committee and the GP was not a disagreement over a vote of confidence, but the deputies' vote on the European Defense Community Treaty (EDC) in August, 1954. Since substantial majorities at the SFIO's 1952 national congress, various national councils, and the CD itself had all voted in favor of the

EDC's ratification, there should have been no problem. Mollet put his personal prestige on the line and promised to deliver a positive vote. However, the minority of the party that opposed the European army—or more precisely, West German rearmament—included some of the most prominent and respected figures in the party in addition to a growing number of backbenchers within the GP. Among the die-hard opponents were Daniel Mayer, Mollet's predecessor; Oreste Rosenfeld, the editor of *Populaire Dimanche*, and Jules Moch, the chairman of parliament's committee on foreign affairs and the *rapporteur* (spokesman) for the treaty when it was reported to the full assembly.

In August, 1954, the EDC was defeated in the French parliament on a procedural vote. Most of the opposition came from the Communists and Gaullists, who cast a solid block of votes against the EDC, but the decisive votes cast for defeat were by those Socialists who voted with the Communists and the Gaullists: the GP split down the middle; fifty voted in favor of ratification, fifty-three against. Those casting "no" votes had violated party discipline, and the CD was determined to punish them. Although far-reaching measures, such as dissolving the GP, were quickly discarded as impractical, Mollet and the majority of the CD suspended the party membership of the most prominent "antis"—Moch, Mayer, Lejeune, and Rosenfeld—until the next national council. Rosenfeld was also dismissed as editor of *Populaire-Dimanche*. In addition, the CD determined that backbenchers in the GP who had voted against the EDC would be barred for a time from working on parliamentary committees.[62]

Later the executive committee instituted some administrative reforms to improve cooperation between the CD and the GP. The membership of the CD was enlarged from thirty-one to forty-five, with a corresponding increase in the membership of the parliamentary delegation. Since this larger body would also be more unwieldy, the SFIO also created a sort of inner circle of the CD, the *bureau*, consisting of the general secretary, the deputy secretaries, and the treasurer. This inner circle was to handle the party's day-to-day administrative duties. None of these reforms changed the political make-up of the CD; the bureau, like the CD itself, was dominated by Mollet's supporters.

With the benefit of hindsight many commentators noted that the EDC controversy marked the beginning of the end of a united SFIO. Mollet's own reputation suffered, and the personal animosities which the debate aroused fed into an exacerbated battle over France's Algerian policy. Ironically, with the same benefit of hindsight, the EDC drama also seems as something of a tempest in a teapot. A West German army, which the "antis" had passionately opposed until August, 1954, seemed much less controversial a few months later. When the Treaties of Paris, providing for German national armed forces and the Federal Republic's membership in NATO, came up for ratification in the French parliament in May, 1955, the GP overwhelmingly approved the agreements. Die-hard opponents of German rearmament, including Jules Moch, now provided the margin of victory for ratification. Only a relatively small minority of the GP, eighteen members in all, continued their intransigent opposition.

Wartime developments in both Germany and France had invalidated the countries' prewar national constitutions. In a referendum French voters decisively rejected reinstituting the constitution of 1875, preferring to have a new constitution drafted for the new Republic. Germany, of course, no longer existed as a political entity, but was simply a territory under occupation until the Western Allies decided to create a new state out of the western zones. The Germans, under the control of the Allies, wrote a new democratic constitution for their new state as well. (In The Netherlands all major political groups, including the PvdA, agreed to reinstitute the prewar constitution.)

Chronologically, the French constitution came earlier than the German one. The constitution of the Fourth Republic was drafted in 1945 and 1946, as Raymond Aron has noted, *à froid* (in a coolheaded atmosphere); the deliberations of the Constitutional Assembly aroused little passion either among the public at large or even most of the parties' militants.[63] At the same time the first postwar elections in France provided the Communists and Socialists with a majority in the constituent assembly. Mollet was elected head of the Assembly's drafting committee.

The French Socialists were particularly concerned that parliament and political parties become the decisive elements in the country's political life. They were not insensitive to the problem of political instability which had plagued the Third Republic, but insisted that this was the result of a multitude of weak parties rather than the constitutional role of the parties. The problem would be solved by the presence of fewer and more powerful parties. André Philip, like some of his colleagues in Germany and Holland, hoped that France would develop a two party system, with a progressive Social Democratic party opposed by a more conservative, bourgeois group. He also suggested a constitutional provision for new elections if parliament toppled a government.

Resembling the similar article in the later German constitution, this proposal was designed to prevent frivolous votes of no confidence. A strong parliament, influential parties, and universal suffrage (including female suffrage for the first time in French history) were the pillars upon which a system of political democracy should rest.

To streamline legislative authority, the Socialists and Communists agreed that France needed a unicameral rather than a bicameral legislature. Some Socialist leaders, notably Léon Blum, were concerned about the weakness of the executive, but the majority of the CD opted for a weak executive, in part to preserve the cooperative arrangement with the Communists. (Initially, the CD rejected by a vote of ten to nine even the establishment of a president of the Republic.) Auriol, Boutbien, and Philip also argued for single-member districts, while Mollet and most SFIO leaders favored continuing the system of proportional representation. Recognizing that proportional representation encouraged splinter parties, some supporters of proportional representation, but not Mollet, suggested that it should be coupled with a threshold provision, so that only parties receiving more than ten percent of the national vote should be represented in the legislature.[64]

The document produced by the constituent assembly provided for a weak executive, a strong, unicameral legislature, and provisions for economic democracy, including far-reaching socialization and collectivization measures. However, in a referendum in May, 1946, the French voters decisively rejected the proposed constitution. To their credit, most of the French Socialists accepted the defeat gracefully, and ceased their efforts to proceed in lockstep with the Communists. Instead, they now worked loyally with other political groups, notably the MRP (which had emerged as the strongest party in the first postwar legislative elections) to fashion a constitution that was acceptable to the French people. Actually, the second document, except for the provision of a bicameral legislature, was not radically different from the first, although the new constitution strengthened the authority of both the prime minister and the president. In practice these provisions were to have little impact on the history of the Fourth Republic. In October, 1946, the second draft was approved in yet another referendum.[65]

In West Germany the issues confronting the makers of the new constitution were not very different from those in France, but the drafting process was. As in France, the Germans were attempting to fashion a viable parliamentary democracy, but unlike the members of the French Constituent Assembly, the Germans could not act on their own. The Allies retained a veto power over anything the Germans worked out. The occupying powers, however, could not agree on what they wanted to see in a German constitution. The Americans and the British favored a democratic and federal political entity with strong states' rights, but also a viable central government. In sharp contrast, a majority of the French cabinet wanted a truncated, extremely decentralized confederation. (In the early postwar years de Gaulle liked to talk not about "Germany," but "the Germanies.") However, by the time the West German constitutional convention, called the *Parlamentarischer Rat* (Parliamentary Council [PR]) began to meet in May, 1948, the French had accepted most of the Anglo-Saxon positions. Ignoring de Gaulle's vehement opposition, the French government agreed to the 1948 London Accords—the basis for the Western Allies' guidelines to the PR—a decision which the SFIO enthusiastically welcomed. The French Socialists had consistently rejected any territorial dismemberment of Germany, and they favored a democratic and federal, rather than confederal, structure for the new German state.[66]

Like their comrades in France the German Socialists had done considerable preparatory work before the PR met. The party's official draft was worked out by Walter Menzel, the minister of the interior in the new state of Northrhine Westphalia. In 1946 Schumacher formally asked Menzel to submit a draft constitution for what was then still expected to be a united Germany. Menzel's and all other documents were also based on the assumption that the process of drafting a constitution would be the work of the Germans themselves, free from Allied interference.[67]

Following Schumacher's guidance, Menzel submitted a draft constitution that looked very much like a new edition of the SPD's proposals for the Weimar constitution. Reflecting the Social Democrats' long-standing support for political democracy and distrust of German federalism, the document provided for civil liberties, parliamentary democracy with a unicameral legislature, the establishment of social and economic democracy by means of a socialized and planned economy, and a strong central government with correspondingly weak states. Fritz Henssler, the mayor of Dortmund and one of the party's leaders in Northrhine Westphalia, expressed the party's traditional attitude toward federalism when he insisted, "federalism in Germany has always been the cover under which reactionary forces fought against the movement for German freedom." Schumacher added a national argument to this condemnation when he noted that the line between federalism and separatism had always been fluid and never more so than in the chaotic times after the Second World War. Like the SFIO leaders, the Schumacher-Menzel team also insisted on the central role of political parties in a parliamentary democracy. The SPD leadership rejected any notion that apolitical interest groups—such as the churches or civil servants—should exercise political influence.[68]

Needless to say, on a number of these points Menzel and Schumacher were on a collision course with the Western Allies, but criticism came from within the party as well. The Allies would have vetoed any German unitary state, but they did not have to, since the strong position of the states' leaders destroyed any hope Schumacher and Menzel had for putting an end to the German tradition of federalism.

In practice, the party's official views on federalism had never been accepted by the Länder leaders. This was true in the Weimar era, and even more so after 1945. Moreover, the Allies had already created new facts by the time the PR met. In the years 1945 and 1946 they implemented what amounted to major territorial reforms in West Germany. The British created the new states of Northrhine Westphalia, Lower Saxony, and Schleswig-Holstein out of what had been Prussian provinces, while they left the city state of Hamburg as a separate Land. The Americans did the same for the city state of Bremen, and the French created the new state of Rhineland-Palatinate. With the exception of Rhineland-Palatinate, the regional SPD organizations welcomed these Allied-imposed territorial changes, while Schumacher and his close associates strongly, but impotently, opposed them.[69]

The SPD formally approved the outline of a draft Reich constitution at its 1947 Nuremberg congress. The document still reflected the Schumacher-Menzel line, but it was already under attack. Much to the dismay of Kurt Schumacher, Carlo Schmid, the justice minister of the state of Württemberg and a strong proponent of federalism and liberal democracy, used the forum of the 1947 party congress to express his conviction that excessive centralism was as detrimental to a viable democracy as unlimited particularism. The continued existence of strong Länder also meant that the new West German state would have a bi-cameral legislature. Throughout modern German history the states had always insisted upon a separate chamber to represent their interests, so it was not surprising that Carlo Schmid increasingly eclipsed Walter Menzel in the constitutional convention. Elected chairman of the PR's Main Committee, the body that coordinated the work of all other committees, Schmid would be responsible for some of the most innovative features of the new constitution, including the constructive vote of no confidence.[70]

Although the London Accords hardly fit the SPD's vision of ideal constitutional guidelines, the party welcomed them and the formation of the PR as the beginning of the restoration of German sovereignty. The members of the PR, who were elected by the states' legislatures because the Allies still distrusted direct national elections, included twenty-seven SPD delegates. (The same number as the CDU/CSU.) As was to be expected, the document that emerged from the PR's deliberations was a compromise. The SPD was pleased that the *Grundgesetz* (Basic Law, GG) as the constitution was called to emphasize its temporary and provisional character, provided for a democratic state that assigned political parties a constitutionally mandated role, contained strong guarantees of civil liberties (another Carlo Schmid specialty), and included a clear statement of financial *Kompetenzkompetenz* (the power of the national legislature to define competency limits of the states). Some members of the party's executive committee were disappointed, however, that the GG did not provide for a catalogue of "social rights," such as the right to work, to complement the list of classic civil rights.[71]

Along with the overwhelming majority of the PR, the SPD voted for the draft GG, but the document had to run two more gauntlets before it could go into effect. One was ratification by the state legislatures (the Allies prohibited a national referendum), and, prior to that, approval by the zonal commanders. The altercation with the zonal commanders became part of the SPD's mythology as the party's victory over the Allies. The American and French zonal commanders, General Lucius Clay and General Pierre Koenig, felt the draft GG left too much financial power in the hands of the federal government. They consequently demanded that the document be revised to shift more authority to the Länder. The CDU/CSU and the Liberals, traditionally more favorable to states' rights than the SPD, readily agreed, and some Social Democratic state leaders were willing to be accommodating as well, but Schumacher, throwing the entire weight of his personality into a rhetorical tour de force before the SPD's executive committee and the party's PR delegation, insisted that the party stand firm: The SPD would not vote for the GG unless the Allied commanders removed their objections. The Allied generals, anxious that the GG have broad support among the German polity, blinked and approved the draft as originally written by the PR.[72]

The SPD's leader and his supporters insisted their firm stand had made it possible for West Germany to have a viable and workable constitution, but their triumph could not disguise that the GG also represented a major defeat for Schumacher's and Menzel's ideas on a new German constitution. The GG provided for neither a unitary state nor Socialist collectivism. Rather, it reflected the views of those in the party who saw Social Democracy's political future in the context of a federal structure and liberal, rather than a class-dominated democratic system.

Elections and Coalitions

Since West Germany, France, and The Netherlands were parliamentary democracies, much of the parties' political activity centered on doing well in legislative elections. To be sure, the contests did not have the same significance in each of the three countries. In The Netherlands national elections were (and continue to be) "public opinion polls." They determine the relative strength of the parties in parliament, but in view of the Dutch multiparty system and the coalition compatibility of most of the parties, decisions on the composition of the cabinets are made after the elections by the party leaders, and not always with a great deal of regard for the voters' choices. In France the SFIO's declining share of the national vote throughout the 1950s was somewhat compensated for by the party's continuing strength in local elections. And in West Germany, where the SPD never won (in the sense of getting more votes than any other party) a national election until 1972, the party dominated politics in some of the most important Länder, which in turn gave it considerable clout in the German federal system.[73]

As noted earlier, in France the SFIO experienced a persistent decline in its electoral fortunes. The Socialists' share of the popular vote in national elections fell by one third, from 23.4 percent in October 1945, to 15.2 percent in January, 1956. In contrast, the French Communist party, which the SFIO regarded as its primary rival, retained the allegiance of a quarter of the French electorate: 26.2 percent in 1945 and 25.9 percent in 1956.[74] At first glance these figures suggest a fierce battle between SFIO and PCF for the same voters, and the Socialist leaders sometimes daydreamed that if the PCF had not existed, the SFIO could come close to getting 50 percent of the popular vote. Actually, the days when the SFIO could effectively compete with the Communists had long passed. The Socialists failed to recognize that the voters (including many workers) who cast ballots for the SFIO did so precisely because the party was not revolutionary. Their interest was "especially in reforms that could be quickly implemented." The real key to the SFIO's electoral future lay in the recognition that the red family was dead, and that the party needed to cultivate and enlarge the reservoir of petty bourgeois voters who had become the party's primary voting constituency. The disappearance of the red family was indicated by the extremely low (4 percent) correlation of active members to voters. Studies also showed that most of the SFIO's ballots came from lower middle class voters. Moreover, the majority of industrial workers who cast their ballots for the party thought of themselves subjectively as petty bourgeoisie or even middle class. Finally, all but ignoring the new women's vote certainly did not help the SFIO's cause.[75]

The German SPD had expected an overwhelming mandate from the voters in the first Bundestag election in August, 1949. Underestimating the appeal of the Christian Democrats—most Social Democratic leaders were convinced the CDU was a party divided against itself that would soon fall apart—the SPD was shocked when the final returns demonstrated that the CDU/CSU was the clear victor (31 percent to 29.2 percent).[76] The SPD's initial reaction to the defeat was to deny its significance. Conveniently blaming the Allies for favoritism toward the CDU, and convinced that once in power the Christian Democratic government would quickly reveal the bankruptcy of its policies, Schumacher insisted that reiterating the SPD's message would result in a Social Democratic victory in the next Bundestag election.[77]

That expectation received a degree of vindication from the results of Länder elections in the years after 1949; the SPD did much better in state elections than in the national contests. But much like the SFIO's simplistic and misleading analysis of the French election returns, Schumacher ignored the fact that in the Länder the SPD presented itself rather differently than in the Bundestag campaigns. In states like Northrhine Westphalia, Berlin, Bremen, and Hamburg, where the party consistently did well, its campaign image was that of a reformist, pragmatic party, worthy of being trusted with executive responsibility.[78]

Although by modern standards the SPD ran an amateurish campaign (Schumacher refused to commission polls because he thought the party knew the mood of the voters better than the pollsters), on the eve of the 1953 Bundestag election the SPD had high hopes. After all, since 1949 the SPD had increased its popular vote in state elections by 5.1 percent, while the CDU/CSU had lost 6.7 percent in these contests. The country was experiencing serious economic and social problems—the benefits of the "economic

miracle" had not yet reached large numbers of West Germans—
and the combination of widespread dissatisfaction with the Christian Democratic government's domestic policies and the SPD's
insistence on prioritizing national reunification promised to deliver substantially more votes for the SPD than the party had
received four years earlier.[79]

The results of the 1953 Bundestag election were a shock and
severe disappointment for the Social Democrats. The party's share
of the popular vote fell from 29.2 percent in 1949 to 28.8 percent in
1953, and the CDU/CSU increased its share dramatically from 31.0
percent to 45.2 percent. The leadership's initial postmortem analysis was not very helpful. While Fritz Heine identified the party's
central problem as "a frightening discrepancy between our views
and those of the majority of the people," both he and other leaders
preferred conspiracy theories, fatalism, and stonewalling to taking
concrete steps to correct the problem. Heine himself compared
Konrad Adenauer to Franz von Papen, and expressed the fear that
the 1953 election was probably the last democratic contest in West
Germany. Others blamed the defeat on a combination of pressure
from Catholic Church leaders and American government officials.
If the party had been at fault at all, its campaign workers had been
"ineffective in selling the SPD's program." Voices that called for
rejuvenation and a general overhaul of the party's program and
electoral strategy were overruled by the SPD's old guard. No new
initiative was needed. Schumacher, repeated Erich Ollenhauer,
had already told the party what had to be done.[80]

Besides, things were looking up for 1957. A number of developments on the larger political landscape seemed to pave the way
for a much better showing in the next Bundestag elections. The
BHE, the refugee party, had dissolved itself and disappeared as a
potential rival, while a small, left-liberal group, the *Gesamtdeutsche
Volkspartei* (All German People's Party [GVP]), had merged with
the SPD. The Communists were no longer a threat; in 1956 the
KPD had been prohibited as an antidemocratic organization. Finally, in 1957 the SPD was for the first time running a "scientific"
campaign which included the use of professional pollsters, and
their initial soundings were very promising.[81]

These hopeful indicators made the actual results all the more
discouraging. The SPD's popular vote did rise (from 28.8 percent
in 1953 to 31.8 percent in 1957), but this was overshadowed by the
Christian Democratic triumph: the CDU/CSU became the first
party in German history to obtain a majority of the popular vote in
a free election (50.2 percent). The reasons for the SPD's relatively

poor showing were not difficult to find. On domestic issues the party had run a "me too" campaign, while its attacks on Adenauer's foreign policy priorities appealed even less to the voters in 1957 than four years earlier. The disaster of 1957 confirmed the SPD's reputation as "the great loser," but it also convinced the party's leaders, including Erich Ollenhauer, that to go back to business as usual would condemn the party to a role as permanent opposition. In that sense, 1957 marked the turning point for the reformers in the SPD.[82]

As we saw, the first postwar national elections were a severe disappointment for the PvdA: The new party had expected a 40 percent share of the popular vote, but obtained only 28.2 percent. There was, however, even worse to come. New elections in 1948 brought further setbacks; the party obtained only 25.6 percent of the popular vote. Nevertheless, the PvdA's leaders decided to stay the course, changing neither the party's reformist program nor its attempt to appeal to constituencies outside the traditional working classes. Quite correctly as it turned out, they argued that the 1948 vote was heavily influenced by two factors that would not be important in the future. Indonesia's independence in 1949 had settled that divisive issue, and the Communists, with their unswerving loyalty to Stalin and the USSR, had used up whatever bonus of good will remained from the CPN's Resistance activities.[83]

The 1952 election brought a small but important shift. The PvdA increased its share of the popular vote to twenty-nine percent, becoming the largest party in the Dutch multiparty spectrum. Understandably, the party's leaders were *"verheugd"* (delighted). And they had good reasons for their optimism. Both the party's stand on social welfare issues and Willem Drees' personal popularity had made the PvdA attractive to voter groups that until then had been beyond its reach. The party's emphasis on the compatibility of Social Democracy and organized religion, coupled with the first signs of what was to become an accelerating process of secularization, even enabled the PvdA to make some significant inroads into the confessional camp.[84]

But the success of 1952 also brought a counterattack from Holland's Catholic hierarchy. In response to the perceived threat to its solid confessional camp, the leaders of Dutch Catholicism took one of the most controversial steps in postwar Dutch political history. In May, 1954, the country's bishops issued a so-called *mandement* (pronouncement). (More about this in the next chapter.) The aim was to retrench and fortify the Catholic *zuil* (pillar). Under pain of ecclesiastical penalties, Dutch Catholics were prohibited or at least discouraged from joining, voting for, or supporting the PvdA and its political program. It was extremely gratifying to the Dutch Social Democrats that the mandement did not achieve its purpose—in fact, it backfired. In the June 1956 elections the PvdA not only achieved its best result ever (32.7 percent of the popular vote), but a significant portion of the increase came from traditionally Catholic electoral areas. The 1956 result demonstrated that the PvdA had become an accepted Dutch Volkspartei. Joop den Uyl called the results "a political earthquake," while Jacques de Kadt wrote triumphantly that in 1956 the Dutch voters had accepted the PvdA as a "progressive, moderate, and decent party." This was certainly true, but that very acceptance demonstrated the naivety of Kadt's additional claim that the elections had provided a mandate for the construction of "Dutch Socialism, nothing more, but also nothing less."[85] Once the backlash to the mandement had run its course, the PvdA's vote declined. In the 1958 elections the party obtained 28.7 percent of the popular vote, almost the same percentage as in 1946 (28.3 percent).

In both Holland and France after the Second World War the Socialists were frequently members of their countries' governing coalitions, but as Blum had said of the Popular Front in the 1930s, the Socialists were exercising power, not conquering it. The response of the three parties to this fact of political life was quite different. The PvdA accepted government participation with the greatest enthusiasm. Until the end of the 1950s the PvdA was a member of every Dutch national cabinet, and for a decade after 1948 Willem Drees served as prime minister in four separate governments. The SFIO's presence in French cabinets was almost as ubiquitous, but unlike its Dutch counterpart, the party remained profoundly uneasy about its governmental role. On the occasion of each of the frequent cabinet crises in the Fourth Republic a substantial minority of the party's leaders argued a return to the opposition benches would leave the SFIO unsullied by coalition politics and able to regain its Socialist soul. The SPD did not become a member of the national coalition until the next decade, partly because the Socialists were not invited, but also because the SPD continued its intransigent opposition, insisting that the voters would give the party a mandate to govern on its own. In the meantime the SPD was honing its executive skills by sharing governmental responsibility in a number of Länder.

The traditions of Dutch cabinet formation were unique in several respects. Coalition agreements were usually vague; despite some complaints from parliamentary leaders, no Dutch cabinet ever presented itself before the legislature with a detailed program. A set of policy principles was the best the *Tweede Kamer* could hope for.[86] As we saw, because of the peculiar nature of *verzuiling* politics[87] cabinet formation in The Netherlands was also a job for insiders, and in the case of the PvdA that meant a starring role for Willem Drees. The longtime prime minister left no doubt about his priorities, arguing that as long as the tendency of the cabinet was recognizably progressive, the PvdA should remain in the government.[88]

In the years from 1945 to 1959 the PvdA participated continuously in two types of coalitions. As we saw, until May 1946 Holland was governed by a *rooms-rode* (Romish-red) combination, that is to say, a coalition between the PvdA and the Catholic KVP. After the PvdA's poor showing in the 1946 election, the KVP insisted on taking the Liberals and later various combinations of Protestant confessional parties into the government in order to dilute the PvdA's influence. As a result, the coalition became virtually a grand coalition or, as the Dutch called it, a *brede basis* (broad basis) coalition. The PvdA was sorry to see the end of the rooms-rode coalition. In it PvdA members had controlled the office of prime minister as well as the majority of cabinet portfolios, including such key posts as the ministry of economics. Moreover, in the early postwar years the Catholic party was dominated by its left wing, with the result that the PvdA and the KVP had relatively few disagreements on policy issues.[89]

The advent of the brede basis meant a reduction of the PvdA's influence in the cabinet, including, for a time, the loss of the prime minister's office as well as the ministries of economics and foreign affairs. As a result, many of the party's rank-and-file members were opposed to the party continuing as a member of the coalition. The party's leadership nonetheless made a firm, quick decision to remain in the government. Approaching bathos, Schermerhorn argued that in the new coalition the PvdA would still be able to safeguard its "*zedelijke ideale*" (spiritual ideals).[90]

The actual reasons for remaining in the cabinet were rather more pragmatic. The PvdA was a reformist party, and, as long as the party stayed in the cabinet, it could hope to realize at least part of its reform program, while as a member of the opposition it was essentially condemned to political impotence. The party held firm to its coalition decision for the rest of the decade, although the relationship of the governmental partners became increasingly acrimonious. Beginning about 1952, the focus of power within the KVP shifted to the right, resulting in frequent conflicts within the cabinet, especially in the area of economic and social policy. Meanwhile, criticism within the PvdA also grew. The opposition, which included some members of the PB, such as Hein Vos, Goes van der Naters, Willem Thomassen, Johannes Scheps, and Jan Willems, argued that the party's presence in the brede basis cabinet was used as a fig leaf behind which the KVP and its allies were enacting their increasingly reactionary policies. The opposition pleaded for a clean break from coalition membership so that the PvdA could rejuvenate itself as the leader of the opposition. However, the critics were neither united nor numerous. A large majority of the PvdA's leaders stood behind Drees (remarkably, even the opposition never attacked him personally) and, as the prime minister put it with a touch of self-satisfaction, had "no objection to staying in the coalition." In addition, the leaders' coalition decision had widespread support among the party's activists, and, as the election returns of the 1950s demonstrated, among the voters.[91]

Still, the opposition's arguments seemed to acquire some retrospective validity after the brede basis coalition finally collapsed in 1959. While the party leaders who had clung to the coalition for more than a decade continued to defend their decision, some academics, notably the Dutch political scientist Hans Daudt, added their critical voice. In a number of publications Daudt advanced the theory of the "*uiterste noodzaak*" (utmost necessity), postulating that the PvdA been duped by its coalition partners, who never accepted the Dutch Socialists as an equal partner. The other coalition members, led by the KVP, included the PvdA in the government coalition only to persuade the Social Democrats' supporters to accept policy decisions contrary to their interests. When the PvdA's fig leaf function was no longer necessary, the Socialists were unceremoniously dismissed from the cabinet.[92]

On balance, Daudt's criticism is off the mark. As we shall see in the next chapter, the PvdA was far more than a dupe for its bourgeois partners. Membership in the cabinet helped the Social Democrats to push through the reforms that became the foundation of the modern Dutch welfare state, and this was the key to the PvdA's coalition decision. Like its coalition partners, the PvdA had no interest in revolutionary change; the party's leaders of the 1950s wanted reforms, and they knew that these could be obtained only by participation in the coalition.[93]

If the PvdA's attitude toward coalition politics was pragmatic, the SFIO was torn between pursuing an illusionary, long-term ideal and working hard to accomplish short-term, reformist goals. In theory, the party continued to believe that its mission was to mastermind France's transition to socialism, a goal that could be reached only by an all-Socialist cabinet or in cooperation with the other proletarian party, the PCF.

For this reason, the high points of the Socialists' governmental experience were the coalitions from 1944 to 1947 that included the Communists and the brief interlude of an all-Socialist cabinet, headed by Léon Blum, which held office for one month at the end of 1946. Immediately after the war the prospect of Communist-Socialist cooperation did not seem out of the question. The left-wing parties cooperated in writing the constitution, and they were committed to laïcisme and a program of far-ranging socializations and collectivizations.[94]

But the glitter had no substance. The Blum government was clearly transitional, and whatever programmatic ideals Socialists and Communists shared, there was an unbridgeable gulf between them: the SFIO was committed to parliamentary democracy and the PCF was not. Certainly by 1947 at the latest, it was clear that the Communists, following orders from Moscow, were doing everything possible to help the USSR's interests abroad, including de-stabilizing parliamentary democracy in France. For this reason a number of SFIO leaders, including Blum, were not displeased when in May, 1947, the Socialist prime minister, Paul Ramadier, cut the Gordian knot and dismissed the Communist ministers. Others, including Mollet, felt Ramadier had violated the SFIO's axiom that the Socialists should not be a partner in any coalition that excluded the Communists. Mollet, for one, felt this principle remained valid because it prevented giving the Communists a target for their anti-SFIO propaganda.[95]

Ramadier, on the other hand, was convinced continuing the coalition with the PCF put the country and the party in an impossible position. Although in the end a majority of the CD and the GP (and a much smaller one on the *Conseil National*) agreed that the Socialists should remain in the government after the dismissal of the Communists, there is little doubt that many of the party's militants would have preferred that the SFIO return to the opposition, untainted by government participation. Olivier Lapie, one of the CD members who supported Ramadier's decision, noted laconically in his memoirs that the 1950 national congress was a rather boring affair, because for the moment there were no Socialist ministers to attack. Mollet had his revenge a few months later. Refusing to support Ramadier at the time of the next cabinet crisis, he allowed a Christian Democrat, Robert Schuman, to become prime minister.[96]

At the same time it was clear, however, that in the political constellation of the 1950s returning to the opposition for any length of time was not realistic for the SFIO. In view of the growing strength of the antisystemic forces in France and persistent rumors that they intended to overthrow the Republic by force,[97] the SFIO was compelled to act as pivot in all of the coalitions that supported parliamentary democracy, a situation that exposed the contradiction between the party's "ideological preoccupations and governmental requirements." For most of the first half of the decade France was governed by *troisième force* (Third Force) coalitions, combinations that united the SFIO, the MRP, the Radicals, and various smaller groups around the cabinet table. (The name was used to distinguish it from the other two forces, Communists and Gaullists, that dominated French political life.) While some SFIO leaders, like Ramadier and Blum, worked hard to make the Third Force succeed, others repeatedly sabotaged it.[98]

At first glance the conflict over the Third Force seemed to lack political logic. The SFIO and its main coalition partner in the Third Force, the MRP, were both committed to preserving parliamentary democracy in France, and, like the Dutch KVP, the French MRP had an influential left wing that shared many of the SFIO's policy goals, especially in the area of social legislation. Léon Blum, perceptive as ever, even suggested that the parties cooperating in the Third Force should agree on a general program, rather than negotiate an ad hoc temporary cooperation arrangement for each government.[99]

However, in the 1950s the MRP, like the KVP, came to be dominated by its right wing, and this led to increasing conflicts with the SFIO. The most emotionally divisive issue was the separation of church and state, or, more specifically, the prohibition of state subsidies for "free," Catholic schools. (More on the substantive aspects of this issue in the next chapter.) Support for laïcisme had a long tradition in French Socialist and liberal circles, it was an issue of great importance to the powerful contingent of public school teachers among the SFIO's militants, and it was a passionate article of faith for Mollet. Unfortunately, some sort of revision of the laïcist legislation was also a sine qua non for the leaders of the MRP. Consequently the Third Force was stillborn as a viable political partnership.[100] While seemingly accepting Blum's suggestion for a full-scale agreement with the MRP, Mollet insisted the crux of any agreement with the MRP had to be the Catholics' commitment to laïcisme. (This was another point of contention between Mollet and Ramadier. The latter was soft on laïcisme, and an enthusiastic proponent of genuine cooperation with the MRP.)

Mollet's stand, which was supported by a majority of the CD, was motivated partly by genuine conviction, and partly by tactical considerations in the SFIO's continuing propaganda battle with the Communists. Mollet feared, quite correctly, that the PCF would put the SFIO on the defensive for its partnership with the "reactionary" Catholics.

While Mollet's animosity to the MRP was understandable in light of the SFIO's history and its postwar political difficulties, it was not a particularly practical response. The Third Force was "impossible and necessary" because there was no alternative to it, at least until a shining white knight seemed to appear in the person of Pierre Mendès-France. In practice, then, the SFIO continued to participate in most of the Third Force cabinets from 1947 to 1951, but its back-handed and lukewarm support weakened the coalition and, with it, the entire system of parliamentary democracy. Moreover, even out of the government the SFIO could not escape responsibility for the constitutional system. Unwilling to become fellow travelers of the Communists and the Gaullists in the opposition, the Socialists had little choice but to give "conditional parliamentary support" to the cabinets they officially opposed. As a result the party was unable either to control the political agenda or effectively market its own and the coalition's accomplishments.[101]

The presidential election of 1954 added elements of political farce to the Socialists' role in Republican politics. Under the terms of the constitution the president of the Republic was elected by a special assembly consisting of the members of both houses of the legislature and some additional notables. The president had no real power, except to nominate the prime minister, but he had the right to participate in cabinet meetings and could use his office as a moral force in the country. The incumbent since 1947, Vincent Auriol, was a much-respected figure who had used his office effectively in very trying times, but he was not eligible for reelection, and there was no outstanding successor candidate in sight. The consequence was what one observer described as a "sinister comedy."[102]

The election came at a time when political disputes were at a fever pitch. The conflict over France's role in Indochina was coming to a climax and the debate over Algeria was beginning to heat up. In addition, the extremely divisive struggle over the ratification of the EDC had left wounds that were still raw. The SFIO's candidate was Réné Naegelen, whom the party had never officially nominated; Naegelen had nominated himself. In fact, a significant faction within the SFIO was very much opposed to his candidacy because of his policies when he served as governor of

Algeria from February, 1948 to April, 1951. Naegelen was a fierce supporter of continued French control of Algeria, a policy that by 1954 was coming under increasing attack within the SFIO.

Naegelen's close friendship with Mollet (although they split over the EDC) and party discipline prevented any public criticism of Naegelen by his colleagues within the SFIO, but the candidate was a red flag for the MRP. The Catholics did not object to his views on Algeria, quite the contrary, but Naegelen, an Alsatian, was a vocal opponent of the modified laïcisme rules that prevailed in the province. Legislation allowing public subsidies for Catholic schools was one legacy from the days when Alsace was part of Germany. In order to smooth the transition of the province back to France, after both World Wars the French government agreed to leave these laws in force. Naegelen passionately opposed this decision; he demanded *laïcisme pur et dur* in his native province. As the later foreign minister Christian Pineau put it, with Naegelen in the race the SFIO faced two major risks. One was that the Communists and the Gaullists, for different reasons, would vote for Naegelen, and the other that a substantial part of the SFIO would not. In any case, the MRP, the SFIO's coalition partner in the Third Force, would certainly oppose him.[103] After twenty-three ballots Naegelen lost out to a colorless Radical, Réné Coty, and for many observers the farce of the presidential election had dealt the Fourth Republic itself a mortal blow.

The successor to the Third Force was the *Front républicain* (Republican Front). Actually the Republican Front was little more than a partnership between the SFIO and the Radicals, or, even more specifically, a personal agreement between Mollet and one of the most charismatic figures in the history of the Fourth Republic, who happened to be a Radical at the time, Pierre Mendès-France. Formally, the cooperation agreement also involved another element just emerging on the French political scene: François Mitterrand and the *Union Démocratique et Social de la Résistance* (Democratic and Social Union of the Resistance [UDSR]). Most of the SFIO's rank-and-file activists were far more comfortable with the Republican Front than with the Third Force. Here, it appeared, was a perfect vehicle for the SFIO to have revenge on the MRP and regain the initiative in French politics. (The Socialists' 1955 congress, for example, passed a resolution committing the SFIO not to join any coalition that included the MRP.)[104]

The key to the success of the Republican Front was the symbiotic relationship between the organizational strength of the SFIO and the charisma of PMF, as the French pundits soon dubbed the

Radical leader.[105] As envisioned by Mollet, PMF would head the cabinet of the Republican Front, but the locus of political power would be with the SFIO as the senior partner in the coalition. Unfortunately for Mollet, theory and practice did not mesh. Mendès-France's charisma proved to be so strong that it threatened to eclipse not only the potential SFIO ministers, but also Mollet himself. And PMF's personal appeal did not stop there, but extended to the party's militants. There was clear evidence that a number of the SFIO's rank-and-file members were tempted to leave the party and become personal followers of PMF.[106]

As a result, Mollet and the SFIO's leaders delayed until June of 1954 before finally agreeing to support PMF as candidate for prime minister. Supporters of the Radical leader in the party bitterly resented what they saw as the SFIO's sabotage of the French non-Communist Left's greatest hope; Depreux, the head of the GP in 1955 and soon to be one of Mollet's most vehement opponents, spoke of "a year lost." One sticking point then and later was that Mendès-France always insisted on the right to name the members of his cabinet without securing the prior approval of the party caucuses. Another problem was that Mollet never really liked Mendès-France. Once PMF had been elected head of the government, an unlikely alliance of EDC supporters, who resented prime minister's lukewarm endorsement of that treaty, and the *lobby indochinois* combined to cut short Mendès-France's tenure as prime minister. The charismatic politician was allowed to remain in office less than a year, just enough time for PMF to extricate France from the Vietnamese quagmire.

The Republican Front, then, was not a political success story. The new coalition could not break the pattern of cabinet crises in the Fourth Republic, and, perhaps even more important, the episode soured personal relations between Mollet and Mendès-France, a factor that was to have serious consequences for the ongoing attempts to restructure the French Left during the Fifth Republic. Even those SFIO activists who had hoped that the fall of the Republican Front cabinet would enable the party to return to the opposition benches were disappointed.[107] Less than a year after the fall of the Mendès-France cabinet the Socialists were not only back in the government, but Mollet had become prime minister. In fact, in 1956 the SFIO found itself in much the same position that it had struggled with since the advent of the Fourth Republic: responsibility without power. This was not, as some scholars have contended, primarily because the SFIO clung to cabinet positions or because Mollet liked to play a role as king-maker and king-breaker. Instead programmatic ossification and an illusionary self-image made it impossible for the party to exercise influence corresponding to its political weight in the reformist, non-revolutionary atmosphere of French politics in the first half of the 1950s.

At first glance, the SPD's relationship to governmental responsibility in the 1950s seems simple and straightforward. In contrast to the SFIO's convolutions, the German Socialists trumpeted intransigent opposition: whatever the Christian Democrats proposed, the SPD opposed. In practice, things were not quite so clear-cut. The SPD exercised governmental responsibility in many of the Länder, and the national executive committee seldom interfered with plans for a Land coalition. Only when the national leadership felt a specific Land combination would be highly detrimental to the party's national stature did the executive committee pressure the state organizations to forego entering a multiparty coalition.

In a way, Schumacher himself implicitly acknowledged the party's contradictory stand. On September 6, 1949, in a keynote address to the party's executive organs and the newly elected members of the Bundestag, the party leader argued against any coalition with the Christian Democrats: The CDU's commitment to the principles of *Grosskapitalismus* (high capitalism), clericalism, and federalism precluded the SPD's entry into a coalition. He quickly added, however, that the SPD should not take the initiative in dissolving any existing coalitions in the Länder.[108]

In practice, multiparty coalitions were the rule rather than the exception in the Länder. Only in a few states, such as Bremen and Berlin, was the SPD able to obtain a majority of the popular vote and govern on its own. Even then some SPD leaders, like Wilhelm Kaisen, the mayor of Bremen, preferred coalitions with the CDU to a government composed only of Socialist ministers. He argued this would underline the SPD's image as a Volkspartei able to work together with other democratic groups.[109] Some of the SPD's leaders in the national parliament hoped to use Länder coalitions as models for breaking up the Christian Democrats' hold on federal power. This was particularly the case in Northrhine Westphalia, West Germany's largest and most populous Land. When the SPD succeeded in forming a coalition with the Liberals there in 1956, pushing the CDU into the opposition, Fritz Erler in particular, expressed the hope that the coalition in Northrhine Westphalia would be a portent of a future SPD-FDP coalition at the federal level.[110]

That expectation proved premature. At the federal level Ollenhauer and a majority of the executive committee continued to uphold the principle of intransigent opposition.[111] There is little doubt that the bulk of the party's activists supported this line, but it is also true that the strategy was an increasing political liability. Franz Haas, a member of the executive committee, put his finger on the weakest point of the SPD's strategy: Intransigent opposition was not producing votes for the party.[112] Led by Fritz Erler, the reformers in the Bundestag delegation were determined to chart a new path. They were concerned with simultaneously establishing the SPD as a Volkspartei and strengthening West Germany's parliamentary democracy. They stressed that, in view of the embryonic state of political democracy in Germany, all democrats should work together against the antidemocratic forces of the extreme left and right. Since the CDU/CSU and the FDP were democratic parties, the SPD should, in principle, put itself in a position to be able to form coalitions with them.[113]

At first glance the reformers seem to have had little success. Not until the disastrous elections of 1957 were the rejuvenators able to persuade Erich Ollenhauer and the old guard that it was necessary to modify Schumacher's legacy. But as so often in the SPD's history, theory and practice were not in alignment. As we shall see, the SPD's opposition had long been much less intransigent than the party's rhetoric pretended.[114]

Conclusion

In 1956 Joop den Uyl offered a remarkably prescient assessment of West European Socialism. He recognized that not only were all of the Social Democratic parties changing rapidly, but they were also changing in essentially similar ways. All were evolving from class-oriented workers' parties to Volksparteien. Ideologically, this meant abandoning whatever remnants of teleological determinism remained, and embracing pragmatism and reformism, becoming what den Uyl called *"levensbeschouwelijk open"* (open world views) parties. Once synonymous with concepts like class struggle and collective action, Socialism increasingly defined itself in terms of individual fulfillment, equality of opportunity, and a sense of *Gemeinschaftssinn* (sense of community) that reached beyond the members of the traditional red family.[115]

However, while the direction of the evolutionary path was universal, there were significant differences in the rate of speed and the degree of enthusiasm with which the individual parties accepted their common destiny. The PvdA stood at one end of the spectrum, having embraced reformism and pragmatism with unabashed enthusiasm since its founding in 1946. As the PvdA's leaders tended to reiterate with more than a touch of self-righteousness, the decisions they had made in 1946 continued to be right. By the mid-1950s the PvdA was an accepted and integrated Dutch Volkspartei. The party's most popular politician, Willem Drees, served as prime minister until the end of the 1950s. Affectionately known as Father Drees, he achieved the stature of national hero and was a symbol of national unity and stability. With good reason the PvdA's chairman, Koos Vorrink, noted proudly in June, 1952 that the pessimists of 1946 had been proven wrong.[116]

The SPD's road was rather more tortuous. Here the new, politically successful course was initiated not by the central leadership, but by forces of renewal concentrated in the party's Länder organizations and the SPD's Bundestag delegation. The party's national leaders tended to put roadblocks in the path toward pragmatism and reformism. The tactics of the old guard were heavy-handed under Kurt Schumacher and rather more subtle under Erich Ollenhauer, but it took the defeat of 1957 to convince a reluctant Ollenhauer to let a new generation of leaders with new ideas take over the party.

The SFIO had the most difficult time adjusting to the new ways, although it must be admitted that the French Socialists also faced the most difficult macropolitical circumstances. In contrast to Holland and Germany where, despite the wailings of some German Social Democrats, the parties' political opponents were not attempting to destroy parliamentary democracy, in France the constitutional system was under constant attack. As parliamentary democracy's *parti charnier* (hinge party) the SFIO was forced to play a key role in defending the constitutional system. When Mollet became prime minister at the beginning of 1956, it appeared that the effort to save parliamentary democracy had been a success, and it is understandable that the SFIO's leaders congratulated themselves no less ebulliently than their Dutch comrades for their triumphs.

Unfortunately, the French Socialists failed to realize that theirs was a pyrrhic victory. Concentrating on saving the system of parliamentary democracy, the party did not see that its lack of programmatic innovation and its internal difficulties weakened both the SFIO and the constitutional system. The battles over the EDC and the farce of the presidential election were symptoms of a deeper malaise. At the beginning of 1956, when the SFIO seemed to have reached the pinnacle of its success, the party also faced a very serious political image problem. In February, 1956, just after the SFIO's general secretary had assumed his new office as prime minister, Georges Brutelle, at that time one of the party's deputy general secretaries, offered a telling critique of the SFIO's political fortunes. Brutelle described the party's situation as "rather bad, because the party was unable to explain to itself" why it was acting as it was. In other words, the SFIO was about to confront the most severe crises to face both the party and French parliamentary democracy without a clear idea of its programmatic or policy priorities.[117]

Chapter Five

DOMESTIC AFFAIRS, 1945–1955

❦

The long decade of the 1950s was a difficult time. The parties' strategies and structures, as well as their policies and programs faced unprecedented challenges. Dutch, German and French Social Democrats found themselves in unfamiliar territory, and the classic teleological guidelines of European Socialism offered little help in charting a way through it.

This was true of both foreign and domestic affairs, but the shock was perhaps greater on the domestic front. Domestic issues had been the traditional priority of Socialist planning and programs, and as the war ended Social Democrats claimed they had the right programs to implement fundamental changes in the areas of economic and social policies, "cultural" affairs (i.e., education and church–state relations), colonialism, and the role of the military in domestic affairs. Taken together these policies would advance societal life to a higher, socialist level.

Economic Policies

In no field of domestic affairs were the Socialists surer of their ground, and nowhere was that certainty more called into question than in the area of economic policies. It was a traditional axiom of all Socialist programs that political democracy had to be coupled with economic democracy, which is to say, the people should control the commanding heights of the production process and the major economic policy decisions. The Socialists argued that without some form of economic democracy capitalism would continue its familiar pattern of periodic crises, and true, general prosperity would be impossible. As we saw, all three of the parties had anticipated widespread, if not universal, support for the establishment of economic democracy in their countries. Convinced that the disastrous state of the European economy at the end of the war had demonstrated the bankruptcy of the capitalist system for all to see, the Socialists counted on a powerful Zeitgeist to give them a clear mandate for instituting far-ranging changes in the European economies.[1]

In the course of the late 1940s and 1950s, the Socialists had to recognize, however, that the reports of capitalism's demise were decidedly premature. Led by the economic powerhouse of the postwar United States, Western Europe became part of an interdependent and increasingly prosperous, market-oriented Atlantic system. Not only that, but the revived capitalist system, far from bringing constant crises and increased destitution, became associated with an unprecedented period of sustained growth which resulted in a steadily rising standard of living for most Europeans. These were developments which few Socialists had anticipated. Consequently, the parties either had to revise policy proposals based upon their traditional teleological assumptions, or see themselves condemned to the sidelines, attempting to sell increasingly irrelevant policies for guiding Europe's economic future.

The process of adapting and modernizing Social Democratic economic policies was neither easy nor straightforward. Remarkably different in the three countries, the outcome was determined by a variety of factors that ranged from the macro-determinants of the international economic system to the specific politico-economic context in the three countries, and the charisma and sophistication of the party leaders involved. It is also well to remember that none of the three parties spoke with a single voice on economic or any other policy issues. Western Europe's Socialist parties were democratic, open institutions that invited internal debate and discussion.

It is perhaps best to begin this analysis of Social Democracy's changing view on economic policies with West Germany. Nowhere was the contrast between theory and reality greater, nowhere the party's path of self-transformation more tortuous or more complete. Initially the key figures formulating the SPD's economic policies were Viktor Agartz and Kurt Schumacher. Always more interested in politics than economics, the party chairman did not claim expertise in this area. Instead, Schumacher relied heavily on Agartz, an orthodox, democratic Marxist, who quickly emerged as the SPD's leading (and very popular) economic policy theorist and administrator in the early postwar years. Until 1947 Agartz also held a key government post as the director of the office of economic policy in the British zone.

Agartz's and Schumacher's explanation of the destitute state of Europe's economic life placed all of twentieth century European history neatly into an orthodox Marxist teleology. According to Agartz, both the First and Second World Wars were the result of monopoly capitalism's imperialist ambitions. It had been a grievous error on the part of the SPD during the Weimar era not to have recognized the link between the bourgeoisie's economic interest and its exercise of political power. Schumacher added that as a result of this omission the German capitalists were able to use Nazi totalitarianism as a last-ditch effort to keep capitalism alive.[2]

That effort had clearly failed, but the result was the collapse of Germany's and Europe's economies. There was no hope of recovery except for Democratic Socialism. Fritz Erler, later one of Agartz's most outspoken critics, but in the early postwar years still a believer, said efforts to combine bourgeois capitalist policies with socialism would be like crossing a herring and a pig. But more than questions of efficacy were involved. Schumacher and Agartz argued that economic decisions also determined political power relationships. If Germany were to become a true democracy, the Socialist workers' movement had to control the levers of economic decision making as Democratic Socialism was implemented.[3]

Such sentiments evoked rousing cheers at party rallies, but it was rather more difficult to explain what Democratic Socialism meant as a set of concrete economic policies. Schumacher emphasized the political dimension of the issue since economic democracy for him essentially meant stripping away political power from the capitalists. Agartz offered a more sophisticated answer. As formulated by the 1947 report of the SPD's socialization commission (of which Agartz was the primary author), economic democracy meant the *Vergesellschaftung* (socialization) of the commanding heights of the economy, which included energy and raw material sources, insurance, banking, heavy industry, and (curiously) advertising. Exempted were family-run agriculture (although large estates were to be divided into family farms, since their owners were presumed to have been political allies of the Nazis), retail trade, and small businesses. In contrast to the SFIO, the SPD was flexible on the means that should be used to create economic democracy. For the Germans socialization did not necessarily mean nationalization; public ownership might well involve control by a municipality or a Land. This was not, however, a syndicalist model: Public control was to be exercised through politico-parliamentary channels, not factory councils or union managers.[4]

Socialization was always coupled with the concept of a *Planwirtschaft* (planned economy), but the Social Democratic leaders emphasized that their planned economy bore no resemblance to either the Nazi or the Soviet model. (For Schumacher economic Stalinism was monopoly capitalism.) Subject to parliamentary, democratic controls, the planned economy of the Socialists would introduce rationality in decision making and eliminate the inevitable inefficiencies of the capitalist market economy. At the same time Democratic Socialism did not mean bureaucratic rigidity. Publicly owned companies were to compete in the marketplace, and the aim of the national planning effort was to regulate, rather than put the economy into a straight jacket. Schumacher used the classic nineteenth century metaphor "*Dampfdruck regulieren*" (to regulate steam pressure) to characterize the goal of Democratic Socialist planning.[5]

In view of the Social Democrats' professions of flexibility and rationality in the system of economic democracy to come, it is legitimate to ask how much difference existed between the CDU's *gelenkte Marktwirtschaft* (guided market economy) and the SPD's *marktwirtschaftliche Lenkungswirtschaft* (market-oriented guided economy). Actually, there was a great deal, and it lay in the political motivation of economic policies. The Christian Democrats did not link their proposals to changes in the distribution of political power, while Schumacher and Agartz assigned priority to the political consequences of a socialized and planned economy.[6]

There was, of course, a wide gap between theory and practice. The SPD's economic policy plans presumed the existence of a national government, which Germany did not have. Policy implementation was for the moment limited to the Länder. Still, for a brief moment it appeared the SPD would actually have the opportunity to put much of its economic program into practice. At the end of 1946 all of the economics ministries in the Länder governments in the Western zones were headed by Social Democrats, and when the Bizone was created at the beginning of 1947, Agartz became its first economic director. Moreover, all of the early Länder constitutions contained provisions permitting socialization measures as well as the framework for a planned economy, and these articles seemed to enjoy widespread, multipartisan support.

It was symptomatic that the provisions for economic democracy in the Hessian constitution of 1946 received praise from Oswald Nell-Breuning, the Jesuit priest who was then the CDU's most prominent social theorist.[7]

But reversals were not long in coming. In July, 1947, Agartz, disliked both for his authoritarian manner and his high- handed policies, was voted out of office by a majority of the delegates in the Bizone's quasi-parliamentary body, the *Wirtschaftsrat* (Economic Council). His successor was Ludwig Erhard, the CDU's chief spokesman on economic matters. This step might have been avoided if Agartz had agreed to modify his policies, but Schumacher was already putting the concept of intransigent opposition into practice. Although a number of Länder leaders disagreed, the SPD's leader insisted that his party's delegation in the Wirtschaftsrat refuse any compromise.

The loss of this key position weakened the SPD's ability to put its economic plans into practice, but the rapidly changing contours of the overall economic conditions in West Germany were even more significant for the eventual failure of a socialized economy. Less than a year after Agartz's dismissal, the success of the currency reform and the arrival of Marshall Plan aid combined to strengthen the hand of the proponents of a market economy, while decreasing public interest in the Socialists' economic democracy.[8]

Seeking to explain what happened to the dreams of 1945, the SPD's leaders understandably looked first to the Allies. Although the party leaders had supported the currency reform and the Marshall Plan as important and much appreciated steps toward German economic recovery, they also insisted (or persuaded themselves) that these were neutral factors not intentionally designed to revitalize the capitalist system. In contrast, they argued, General Clay's decision to suspend the socialization clauses of the Hessian constitution and General Robertson's order to delay the socialization of the coal and steel industries in the Ruhr were deliberate attempts to halt the advance of Democratic Socialism.[9]

Actually, the move away from economic democracy involved German far more than Allied factors. General Clay's decision, for example, had the backing of a majority of the Hessian Landtag delegates. All of the Christian Democrats and a substantial portion of the Social Democrats had serious reservations about putting the highly complicated constitutional provisions into practice. The unions, too, changed their stand. Under the impact of the currency reform and the Marshall Plan, Hans Böckler, the chairman of the DGB, and other union leaders increasingly emphasized

Mitbestimmung (codetermination), the right of the unions to be represented on the boards of directors of major enterprises, rather than socialization of the commanding heights as the labor movement's primary goal for structural change. As Böckler pointed out, the DGB saw itself as an economic interest organization, not as an instrument to change political power relationships. (Agartz opposed focussing attention on codetermination precisely because, he argued, it was not an effective way to destroy the power of the capitalist owners.)[10]

In retrospect, it is clear that the SPD seriously underestimated the ability of modern capitalism to reform and reorganize itself in the context of the postwar political and economic climate. There is little doubt that by the time the Federal Republic was founded, Erhard's concept of a social market economy had triumphed politically over the SPD's proposals for a socialized economy, and the boom years that began with the outbreak of the Korean War merely reinforced an already existing condition. The party leaders had anticipated that the economic upsurge caused by the Korean War would be a brief episode, followed by the inevitable crisis. To prepare for that day, Ollenhauer and Hermann Veit (the economics minister in Baden-Württemberg and since 1948 the chairman of the party's committee on economic policy) urged party militants to study Marx more diligently and become more sophisticated in presenting the SPD's alternative program to what would soon be disillusioned and receptive voters.

However, criticism of the "just you wait" strategy set in early as well. Increasingly, the SPD's economic policy planners had to recognize that the question was not how to implement economic Socialism, but how to adapt the party's policies to the reality of the prevailing social market economy. Slogans diluted from "scientific" Socialism might be very useful propaganda items for the red family, but they were irrelevant in analyzing the situation of the 1950s and developing appropriate responses. Erwin Schöttle's outburst in a meeting of the party's executive committee in September, 1956, that "he had had it with this Marxist nonsense (*marxistischer Quatsch*)" may not have been very politic, but it was heartfelt. In addition, that beacon of Marxist analysis, Viktor Agartz, was fast losing his luster. Without any government job after 1947, Agartz became head of an institute for economic analysis sponsored by the DGB, but his views were increasingly at variance with those of his employer and the SPD. Agartz moved ever further to the left, becoming an admirer of the GDR's system of Socialism. Revelations in 1956 that he was secretly receiving East German funds thoroughly discredited him and his positions.[11]

The critics could also use the party's own rhetoric against the old guard. The anticipated crisis did not materialize, and, since the SPD had always argued *"Sozialisierung ist nicht Selbstzweck"* (socialization is not an end in itself),[12] the continuing boom of the 1950s made the question asked by many party activists and voters, "how will a socialized economy improve my life?" increasingly difficult to answer. Moreover, if private control of economic activity did not automatically result in growing destitution, then perhaps the question of ownership as the key to economic policy was not as important as it seemed. Finally, all of the party's policy proposals for a socialized economy were predicated on the continuation of secondary industrialism, so that the advent of the tertiary industrial society, whose contours were emerging by the mid-1950s, left the old guard with a whole new set of unanswered questions. In a tertiary industrial society, traditional Marxist concepts like power and influence acquired radically different meanings.[13]

As the orthodox camp became confused, the reformers became increasingly vocal. If the SPD wished to become a genuine Volkspartei, the critics argued, it had to appeal to constituencies—both workers and members of the middle classes—which were benefiting from Erhard's social market economy. Although for political reasons the SPD could not simply adopt the social market economy wholesale, the set of ideas the reformers offered under the general label of *"freiheitlicher Sozialismus"* (liberal Socialism) was not fundamentally different from Erhard's policies.

Under the impact of the reformers' criticism and the party's electoral setbacks, the old guard retreated, albeit slowly and grudgingly. After the 1949 election the party published the "Dürkheimer 16 Points," a compendium that included as one of its items *"Planwirtschaft ist keine Zwangswirtschaft"* (a planned economy is not a coercive economy). While this was clearly meant to reassure the voters that a democratic, planned economy was not like the model that was being installed across the Elbe, it nonetheless suggested that the party was holding fast to the goal of a planned, socialized economy in some form. The reformers scored a more significant triumph at the party's 1952 national congress with the adoption of the so-called Dortmund Action Program. The SPD now placed an industrial policy at the center of its economic program, and abandoned the earlier plans for a full-scale planned and socialized economy. Socialization projects were limited to the raw materials sector. The Dortmund Action Program also contained for the first time the phrase that was to become the key sentence of all subsequent Social Democratic economic policy statements: *"Wettbewerb soweit möglich, Planung soweit nötig"* (as much competition as possible, as much planning as necessary).[14] After the 1953 Bundestag election the old guard retreated still further. Clearly at a loss, the old functionaries left the initiative to the reformers. The party's executive committee simply decided not to publish an already prepared, modified program of socializations.

The reformers were not slow to press their advantage, insisting it was time to throw out Marx and Marxism as a guide to economic policy. The always outspoken Erwin Schöttle demanded during a meeting of the party's executive committee that the SPD finally abandon its *"platter Vulgärmarxismus"* (shallow and superficial Marxism). By the middle of the decade the old guard had caved in. The SPD accepted the social market economy as the prevailing economic system in West Germany, and focused its concerns on concrete reforms that would improve the functioning of that system. The SPD no longer insisted that only the abandonment of free market economics would bring prosperity to the Federal Republic. On the contrary, by 1956 Schöttle warned his party to avoid even appearing to favor a planned economy.[15]

The Dutch PvdA traveled much the same path as the SPD, but with far fewer internal tribulations. The historic and personal factors were different in Holland than in Germany. The Dutch had rejected Marxism as a set of guiding principles for their economic policies as early as 1937, and there was no Viktor Agartz in the PvdA to bring back Marxist orthodoxy. Instead, as we saw, the PvdA had embraced with particular enthusiasm Hendrik de Man's 1935 Plan of Labor, which contained a variety of neocorporatist elements. Yet there were similarities to the German Socialists as well. The Dutch Social Democrats were also Lasalleans, who envisioned a strong state that should play a major role in guiding national economic activity. However, and in this sense proposals in the Dutch party paralleled the thinking among some SFIO leaders, the PvdA emphasized the technocratic rather than the political aspects of a national industrial policy.[16]

Like the Germans, the Dutch Socialists found themselves confronted with a completely unexpected set of postwar macro-economic conditions. The absence of Germany as Holland's major trading partner, the loss of the East Indian empire, a massive spurt in population growth, the new relationship with the United States under the Marshall Plan—none of these development had been foreseen by the party's wartime theorists. The PvdA was also surprised by the new direction of the Dutch NVV, which had maintained close political ties to the SDAP before the war, but now severed all institutional links with the PvdA and embraced economic reformism.[17]

In view of the PvdA's deliberately cultivated reformist and pragmatic image, the party's initial stand on economic policy sounded surprisingly radical. An early postwar party document proclaimed unabashedly "we reject capitalism." Using this premise, the party emphasized the contrast between the "spirit of socialism" and the "spirit of capitalism," and concluded Socialism was a necessity for postwar Holland.[18] To this end the PvdA envisioned a full program of socializations or nationalizations to be implemented by a powerful, democratically controlled state. Among the sectors to be socialized were the mining industry, banking, transportation, and all major industrial enterprises. As in Germany, agriculture and small businesses were exempted, although some party leaders, including Hein Vos, the PvdA's leading expert on economic policy and the country's first postwar economics minister, also wanted to socialize the country's cinemas (because of their educational and cultural potential) and the Dutch dairy industry.[19]

In addition to socialization projects, the PvdA made the institutionalization of national planning the centerpiece of the Dutch version of economic democracy. This came as no surprise. Planning had been the heart of the Plan of Labor, and the SDAP leaders who had led the effort to publicize Hendrik de Man's ideas in the 1930s were now in charge of administering Dutch economic policy. They included Hein Vos, an engineer by profession, and Jan Tinbergen, an economics professor and Nobel Prize winner who had long advocated econometric planning as the key to a rational economy.

Lack of enthusiasm for major structural changes among the unions and many of the party's leaders as well as opposition from the PvdA's coalition partners, meant that the party's socialization program was essentially stillborn (only the Dutch National Bank was nationalized[20]), but the PvdA appeared to be successful in realizing its ideas on planning. Following Tinbergen's view on the importance of statistical data, the Dutch government vastly enlarged the functions of its central statistical bureau (Tinbergen headed the enlarged office), and coupled it with a new agency, the *Publieke Bedrijfsorganisatie* (Public Enterprise Organization [PBO]). Vos, Tinbergen, and most of the PvdA leaders envisioned the PBO as an active central planning agency, which, subject to parliamentary oversight, would determine the overall direction of the Dutch economy, as well as exercise control over prices and wages.[21]

Paralleling developments in Germany, disappointment came quickly for the proponents of Dutch economic socialism. Although the party had campaigned hard on economic issues, the 1946 and 1948 elections did not provide the PvdA with a mandate for its economic program. Partly in reaction to these setbacks, there was growing scepticism within the party itself about the socialized economy. The most important critical voice was that of Willem Drees. The prime minister, never a friend of large-scale theoretical projects, advanced a number of pragmatic arguments against the Dutch version of economic democracy. He pointed out that, in view of the destitute state of the Dutch economy, socialization essentially meant taking over the bankrupt sectors of the economy and saddling the taxpayers with paying for both the restructuring and a new set of bureaucrats. There were political considerations as well. Drees, like the German reformers, pointed out that neither the Dutch voters, nor even the members of the PvdA, were particularly interested in economic Socialism.[22]

There was also the problem of the prevailing Dutch societal structure. Economic democracy presumed that a society was divided essentially along horizontal, class-based lines, but in Holland the confessional zuilen were still very much intact. And these zuilen, which the PvdA was unable to dent until 1952, divided the country not along horizontal, but along confessional, vertical lines. Finally, as we saw, the prime minister's first priority was always to keep the PvdA in the government, and he was convinced this would not be possible if the party insisted on pushing its socialization ideas. (Drees' critics countered by accusing him of doing nothing to stimulate public interest in the party's socialization projects and abandoning the PvdA's Socialist *beginselen* [basic premises]).[23]

In contrast to the socialization program, there was widespread support for the PBO as a central planning agency within the party, but here, too, the PvdA's activists encountered setbacks. At first glance, the PvdA's problem was simple electoral arithmetic. After the 1946 election the Socialists lost control of the economic ministry to the KVP and Hein Vos' successor as economics minister, Piet Lieftinck, did not share his predecessor's enthusiasm for a planned economy. Under Lieftinck the PBO essentially lost its institutionalized planning functions, becoming instead a coordinating agency that assembled statistics and arranged meetings of interest group representatives. In one sense, then, the decision to stay in the coalition sealed the fate of the Socialists' planning effort. In retrospect, however, it is also clear that not all party leaders were displeased by this development. Although he did not say so at the time, Willem Drees, a firm proponent of neocorporatism, was no more enthusiastic about centralized planning than about socializations.[24]

The planning enthusiasts made one more attempt to adapt the essentials of economic democracy to the rapidly emerging the neocorporate market economy in The Netherlands. In 1951 the party published an economic manifesto entitled *Weg naar de Vrijheid* (The Way to Freedom). Written by Vos, den Uyl, and J.G. Suurhoff (Vorrink's successor as party leader) and reflecting the ideas of Keynes and Lasalle rather than Marx, the document waved the banner of state interventionism in the face of the country's enthusiasm, stimulated by the Korean War boom, for a free enterprise economy. It was a largely stillborn effort, *"verouderd ... op het moment dat het gepubliceerd werd"* (out of date ... the moment it was published) as den Uyl later remembered. Significantly, Drees neither participated in the project nor publicly endorsed it.[25]

The publication of *Weg naar de Vrijheid* ended the PvdA's attempts to establish economic democracy in Holland. For the remainder of the decade the party was an essentially junior partner in the management of Dutch economic policy. Although Socialists were among the first to recognize the impact of the coming tertiary society,[26] the Catholic ministers of economics, not the PvdA's leaders, were the economic policy activists. Like the SPD a little later, the Dutch Socialists accepted the neocorporatist management of the free market economy and focused on intrasystemic reforms to benefit its potential voting constituency. None of the party's leaders called for renewed efforts to draft an alternative economics policy program.[27]

Discussions of postwar economic policies in France had to start with much the same givens as those in Holland and Germany; four years of war had left the economy devastated. France was experiencing shortages in every area, and worthless currencies flooded the country. In addition, the harvests of 1944–1945 were unusually poor. Even before the war, the French economy had been badly in need of modernization, and the war had exacerbated these difficulties. Finally, postwar France, unlike Germany and Holland, was subjected to chronic political and social upheavals. During the *tripartisme* coalition the Communists had joined in the general cry for increased productivity, but by 1947 they had become social revolutionaries again. The Communist-controlled CGT staged a number of politically motivated strikes in 1947 and 1948, and wildcat actions added to the general confusion. The strikes became "virtually general." Rumors of Communist coups

surfaced almost every other week. Vincent Auriol noted dispirit-
edly in his diary at the end of 1947, "We are at the center of a political, economic, and social crisis."[28]

There is some doubt as to whether the PCF was seriously attempting to take power, but the Communists were certainly trying
to destabilize the country. The man who stood in their way was
the Socialist minister of the interior, Jules Moch. Alluding to the
Communist coup in Czechoslovakia in 1948, the minister himself
later wrote he was convinced that the French Communists were
trying to stage the "Czechoslovakization" of France. His vigorous
countermeasures defeated the Communist efforts, but the price
was a significant increase in the already bitter animosity between
the PCF and the SFIO. Whenever Moch appeared in parliament
after 1947, he was greeted by cries of "workers' assassin" by the
Communist deputies.[29]

Paradoxically, despite the fierce political battles, France entered
the postwar era with a "veritable consensus" among all the major
political groups that the country needed a program of large-scale
nationalizations and a socialized economy. True, most members of
the SFIO's CD showed little interest in the details of economic policy. The Socialists left that to Léon Blum and André Philip, who
did have a clear, if overly idealistic, vision of the future: "There
was an indissoluable link," said Blum, "between social transformation and the happiness of mankind, democracy, and the peaceful organization of the world."[30]

It was axiomatic for the French Socialists, no less than for their
German and Dutch comrades, that economic democracy had to be
built upon the twin pillars of socialization and planning. And,
given the centralist tradition of French administration, socialization meant nationalization, and planning a national planning
bureau. The list of economic sectors subject to socialization was
also familiar: banking, insurance, utilities, mining and raw materials, and key industries. Agriculture was exempted; like the Germans, the French Socialists endorsed family farms.[31]

For their ideas on administering the socialized sector the French
Socialists used as a model the reforms recently inaugurated by the
Labour Party in Great Britain. The SFIO also favored a series of
industry-wide, autonomous national management boards. Although subject to governmental control, the individual managers of
the socialized businesses were to be largely independent and able to
run their enterprises according to market principles. Lest this
sound as though the SFIO was in complete agreement on its economic program, it should be noted that there were some significant

disagreements on fundamental questions among the party's lead-ers. Differences arose, for example, over the basic purpose of the socialization effort. Were the aims primarily political—in line with Schumacher's and Agartz's arguments—or was the main purpose the achievement of rationality in economic life—as Vos and Tinbergen insisted? In the case of some major industrial enterprises the two motivations came together. Everyone agreed, for example, that the Renault Auto Works should be nationalized because their own-ers had collaborated with the Nazis.[32]

In contrast to developments in Holland and Germany, in France large-scale socializations were actually implemented. In 1945 and 1946 a tidal wave of nationalizations swept through the country as banks, insurance companies, utilities, and some key industries were all nationalized. However, in practice socialization did not fulfill the Socialists' expectations. The nationalizations were car-ried out by the tripartisme government, which meant that the spe-cific implementation measures had to have the support of the PCF and the MRP as well as the SFIO. In fact, at this time the major production ministries were headed by PCF representatives. The Communists, not surprisingly, rejected the British model of dem-ocratic and pragmatic management boards, preferring instead heavy-handed, centralized bureaucracies under the direct control of government ministries. This was not what the Socialists had wanted, but in the interest of tripartisme unity, they accepted the Communists' lead.[33]

The second pillar of economic democracy, national planning, seemed to have even more universal support than the program of socializations. Everyone, it appeared, agreed that to increase the country's productivity and modernize its economy, France needed national planning. Among the SFIO leaders André Philip took the lead in developing large-scale proposals for a national planning agency. He envisioned that Le Plan should be developed and implemented by a "super-ministry" of economics, which would combine the functions of the existing departments of economics and finance and be in charge of drafting the Plan and assuring its implementation. Philip, who served as minister of economics (but not finance) in the early postwar cabinets, clearly saw himself as head of the new super agency. Opposition to Philip's initiative arose almost immediately in various quarters. The PCF rejected his proposals because they would deprive the Communist mem-bers of the cabinet of much of their authority. The French unions, with their syndicalist traditions, felt that the plan would not pro-vide for enough direct worker input. Private entrepreneurs did not wish to be subjected to the detailed dictates of a government planning agency run by a Socialist. And the technocrats at the ministry of finance, the most prestigious of French government agencies, feared the loss of their elite status.[34]

Before any of these factors could come into play, however, Philip's proposals were cut down by France's fiscal problems, or, more precisely, by the coalition's inability to agree on a solution. While the German currency reform of 1948 curbed inflation by tying the new Deutsche Mark to the American dollar, and the Dutch took the painful step of confiscating the money that was in circulation at the end of the war and issuing a new, stable currency, the French were unwilling to implement full-scale revaluation. Pierre Mendès-France, the first postwar finance minister, did propose confiscating the money in circulation much as the Dutch were doing, and he had the support of the SFIO ministers, notably Philip, but de Gaulle and a majority of the cabinet refused to take this painful step. They feared the wrath of the peasants, who were the primary beneficiaries of the black market economy of scarcity. As a result, inflation continued to be a major problem until the end of the decade, dooming any national planning effort along the lines envisioned by Philip.

To their credit, the French Socialists worked hard, if unsuccessfully, to solve the country's fiscal difficulties even after Mendès-France failed. The SFIO consistently advocated as steps to fight inflation a decrease in military expenditures coupled with vigorous measures to control prices. Their proposals did not meet with success. De Gaulle rejected spending less money for the army, and the Communists preferred the politically popular, but economically illusionary step of raising wages to keep pace with prices. In the end the American connection provided some relief, and here, too, the Socialists played a major role. It was Léon Blum who arranged for a crucial US loan in 1946, and the SFIO, as we saw, enthusiastically welcomed Marshall Plan aid for France.[35]

By the early 1950s the balance sheet of the Socialist economic program was decidedly mixed. True, on paper France had instituted a program of large-scale nationalizations, and the ouster of the Communists ended the attempt at centralized government control of the public sector of the economy. The alternative, however, was not economic democracy, but neocorporatism. In October, 1947 André Philip lost his position as minister of economics when Ramadier reshuffled his cabinet, and the Socialists never regained control of this key post. Nationalizations and Le Plan were alive and well in France, but they had become devices to advance a neocorporatist order. "By 1952," Stephen Cohen has written, "it was no longer possible to believe that the Plan would bring Socialism to France."[36]

Why did the Socialist vision of economic democracy fail in France? Unlike the SPD, the SFIO could not blame the Allies, and in contrast to The Netherlands, there was no Willem Drees in France to dampen the visionaries' enthusiasm. Some French Socialists did think they had found a French Willem Drees in Paul Ramadier, the prime minister who had forced both the Communists and the two left-wing Socialist ministers, André Philip and François Tanguy-Prigent, out of the cabinet. According to these critics, Ramadier was not really a Socialist, but a closet Radical.

This attempt to make Ramadier a scapegoat was not very convincing. Although hardly a passionate Marxist, Ramadier had been a Socialist for more than twenty years. In reality the factors blocking economic democracy in France were similar to those in Germany and Holland. With the PCF out of the cabinet, the SFIO's more conservative coalition partners, the MRP and the Radicals, were able to increase significantly their influence in the cabinet. Neither the SFIO's rank-and-file activists nor the party's potential voters showed much interest in the intricacies of a socialized economy, at least in part because, like the SPD, the SFIO was better at developing catchy slogans than at elucidating what economic democracy would mean in practice. The SFIO leaders, notably Mollet, were also anxious not to offend potential voters among the small business community, many of whose members remained suspicious of the Socialists' directed economy. Most important, however, was the success of an economic policy alternative. Led by the remarkable talents of Jean Monnet, neocorporatism, the cooperative economy, was able to guide France to recovery and prosperity.[37]

As we saw, in Holland and Germany the Socialists' reaction to the failure of their vision of economic democracy was eventually to accept neocorporatism and work within its systemic parameters. The SFIO's response was rather different. Some prominent Socialists, notably Guy Mollet, attempted to escape the party's dilemma by shifting the party's focus to other priorities, especially the battle for laïcisme. (Vincent Auriol noted in his diary in August, 1948, it was all very well for Mollet to trumpet laïcisme, but what the people were really interested in were prices and wages.[38]) Others insisted the SFIO should leave the government and agitate for a Socialist France and Europe as part of the opposition. To be sure, there were more realistic voices as well. Francis Leenhardt,

Victor Provo, and Ramadier urged the party to abandon its verbal radicalism as well as the illusion that class-based economic policies could obtain a democratic mandate for the SFIO.[39]

Unfortunately, neither most of the party's leaders nor its rank-and-file activists were willing to accept the reality of defeat. Instead, they attempted to live with the contradiction between theory and practice. While recognizing that for the moment some objective (as Marxists used the term) problems stood in the way, the SFIO's rhetoric insisted the end of capitalism was near, and a united Socialist Europe was the way of the future. In fact, on most economic issues the party felt compelled to align itself alongside the Communists.[40]

In practice, of course, the party worked to further the interests of its constituency within the prevailing system of neocorporatism. The party's demands for paid vacations, an increase in the minimum wage, old-age pensions, and subsidies for public housing constituted a reform program that did not differ substantially from those advanced by the SPD and the PvdA. Albert Gazier acknowledged as early as November, 1950 that the conditions and hopes of 1946 were no longer relevant. Economic democracy, as the French Socialists envisioned it, was not a politically realistic goal. This was also clear to Guy Mollet. When he became prime minister at the beginning of 1956, he chose the much-maligned Paul Ramadier, the man who embodied the Radical temptation for many leftists in the SFIO, to be his minister of finance. The admission that economic democracy was unrealistic did not, however, prevent the party leaders—including Mollet—from insisting that the SFIO's economic policy goal would never change: It remained the institutionalization of *socialisme pur et dur*.[41]

Social Policies

Postwar European Social Democracy is probably most closely identified with the plethora of social policies that established the modern West European welfare state. Ralf Dahrendorf's famous assessment that the twentieth century was the Social Democratic century rests primarily upon the Socialists' success in creating the tightly knit net of public services that includes social security, national health insurance, paid vacations, job security, and generous unemployment benefits for all residents. Ironically, some Socialist leaders always remained uneasy about their triumphs in this area. To begin with, Social Democrats disagreed on the purpose of the social net. Was the goal of social policy primarily political, a mechanism to level off income distinctions and thus transfer resources and power from the well-to-do to the less well-to-do? Or was the purpose essentially ethical, that is to say, all citizens should be able to maintain a decent standard of living, especially during periods of personal crisis? Some Socialists were also concerned about the consequences of the welfare state for the red family. True, the Social Democrats' constituents became more prosperous, but did not increased prosperity also bring with it a more bourgeois life-style and a diminution of class consciousness?[42]

Before the Second World War reduced the country to a subsistence standard of living, Germany had the most developed social net. Begun in the nineteenth century under Bismarck, it was significantly enlarged during the Weimar Republic and, except for being limited to "Aryan" and politically approved members of the society, essentially maintained by the Nazis. France and The Netherlands had very underdeveloped social service systems before 1945. In Holland the supply-side oriented programs of the Colijn governments in the 1930s had largely ignored social policy concerns. In France the Popular Front government had attempted to legislate some important benefits, such as paid holidays, but most of these laws had been undone by the Popular Front's immediate successors and the Vichy regime.

The impact of fascism on social policies has been hotly debated. At issue here is the degree to which the concept of the *Volksgemeinschaft* (the national community), became accepted as a social policy ideal. Although the Fascists' motivation was clearly propagandistic and political, and opponents of the regimes were specifically excluded from the benefits of any social policies, the impact of such Fascist programs as Strength Through Joy, Winter Relief, and Family and Fatherland may have had a long-term impact that went beyond mere propaganda. In this connection, it is ironic, but perhaps also symptomatic, that the beginnings of a modern social net in The Netherlands were initiated during the years of the NSB regime and the Nazi occupation.[43]

In West Germany, the SPD feared that excessive enthusiasm for the free market economy would force concerns for social legislation into the background. Instead, the Social Democrats wanted to preserve the social legislation of the Weimar era, while avoiding the mistakes of those years. During the years of hyperinflation in the early 1920s wage earners and owners of liquid wealth lost virtually everything, while owners of real property, at least in relative terms, benefited from the decline of the Mark's value. The Second

World War had created an infinitely worse situation. Years of fighting and bombing had resulted in vast numbers of homeless and millions of refugees, who constituted a potential threat to any democratic postwar order, but also a potential block of SPD votes. For this reason the SPD was adamant that there had to be a genuine *Lastenausgleich* (equalization of burdens) to cushion the consequences of the Second World War.

As was true for many aspects of public and private affairs, the Germans for some years after the war could not make social policy decisions on their own. The Allied occupation powers took an active part in determining the parameters of social legislation, and, as was to be expected, they had their own priorities. The Americans were least sympathetic toward building (or rebuilding) the social net, preferring to leave things to the market. The British, under the influence of Labour's quiet revolution at home, were more supportive of recreating the social net. Surprisingly, this was an area in which the French were most active. Much of what was later enacted as social legislation in the Federal Republic, including improved provisions for universal health insurance and better social security payments, originated in the French zone of occupation.[44]

Although the SPD was committed to intransigent opposition, this strategic concept was largely suspended when it came to social policy legislation. The SPD's delegates actually voted with the government coalition on 86 percent of all domestic policy bills that came before parliament, including such crucial pieces of legislation as the *Lastenausgleichsgesetz* (Equalization of Burdens Law) and the *dynamisiertes Rentengesetz* (Law on Accelerated Pension Payments). At the end of the "long decade of the 1950s" West Germany had a social service system in place that largely reflected the ideas of the right wing of the Social Democrats and their allies within the Christian Democrats' left wing. As far as the Social Democrats were concerned, the party's cooperative stance represented a clear victory for the reformers and a defeat for the die-hard supporters of full-scale social restructuring. Ludwig Erhard and his associates at the ministry of economics were not particularly enthusiastic about much of the legislation, but during the boom years there were sufficient funds available so that the social policies did not pose a danger to fiscal stability or Erhard's supply-side priorities.[45]

As noted earlier, Holland entered the postwar era with a very underdeveloped social service system. Not surprisingly, then, social legislation was high on the PvdA's list of priorities. Modeling their ideas on the British Beveridge Plan, even those Dutch

Social Democrats who were skeptical about socialization and government-controlled planning saw the social net as the *"voedingsbodem voor socialisme"* (nurturing ground for Socialism). In his memoirs Willem Drees, prime minister for almost a decade but social services minister for only a few months, lovingly detailed his accomplishments as minister for social services, while downplaying his role as chief of the government.[46]

The Dutch Socialists' faced both intra-party opposition and conflicts with their coalition partners in attempting to realize the PvdA's social policy program. Within the party there was a small group of orthodox Marxists who feared that a well-developed social net would lead to the bourgeoisification of Holland's workers. They were right, of course, but their concerns were not shared either by most of the party's leaders or the vast majority of its rank-and-file members. Within the coalition matters went smoothly as long as the KVP remained dominated by its left wing, which, like its counterpart in West Germany, was heavily influenced by the Catholic social gospel. As the conservatives within the KVP gained ground, however, their concerns about the costs of the social legislation led to increased friction among the coalition partners. As we shall see, the final break of the coalition in 1959 came about because the PvdA and the KVP were unable to agree on the funding of rent subsidies.[47]

Still, by that time the government, led by Willem Drees, had succeeded in putting a tightly knit social net in place. In the course of the decade every Dutch citizen became entitled to social security, national health insurance, paid vacations, and unemployment and accident insurance. The PvdA was justifiably proud of its part in creating what the party called *"socialisme van de daad"* (practical Socialism). In fact, in retrospect it is clear that social legislation played a major role in preserving social and political peace in Holland. Throughout the 1950s Dutch wages lagged significantly behind those of other West European countries, but the PvdA was able to point out that despite the government's supply-side economic policies, the country's social legislation brought significant improvements in the standard of living of most Dutch citizens.[48]

The relationship of social peace and social legislation was perhaps even more acute in France. The debate over social policy had sharply divided the country in the 1930s, pitting the advocates of improved social services against the fiscal conservatives. In fact, for the latter, social legislation was associated with illegal, revolutionary action. After all, the social policy program enacted by the

Popular Front government had been largely forced upon the cabinet by wildcat action of industrial workers, sanctioned neither by the government nor the unions.

True, the climate of opinion shifted considerably during the war. Virtually every Resistance group insisted that social service improvements become a top priority of the postwar government, at least in part because the Vichy regime's record in this area was particularly bleak. However, at the end of the war France's chronic fiscal problems forced further delays. In contrast to Germany, there was no surplus of government funds available to finance the construction of the social net. Moreover, during the revolutionary upheavals of 1947–1948 the Communist-controlled CGT insisted for political reasons on instant gratification for its constituents in the form of wage increases rather than improved social services. Nevertheless, it was indicative of the widespread support for social policy legislation that even under these adverse conditions the government in 1946 created a social security system.

By 1949 the fiscal situation had improved considerably, and during the next decade the Third Force and the Republican Front governments were able to enact significant improvements in France's social net. As in Germany and The Netherlands, cooperation of the Socialists and left-wing Catholics in the MRP provided the primary base of political support for the reforms. The specific pieces of legislation that became law included a minimum wage automatically adjusted according to the cost of living (*Salaire minimum inter-professionnel de croissance* [SMIC]), a national health service, and mandated annual paid vacations.[49]

The SFIO had every reason to be proud of its accomplishments in the area of social policy, but instead the party's self-image as a revolutionary organization put it on the defensive. French social policies, like those of Germany and Holland, did not call into question the prevailing capitalist system. As was to be expected, the Communists jeered on the sidelines that the SFIO had become reformist. There was uneasiness in the Socialist ranks as well. The critics complained that France's postwar social legislation had not gone far enough; the laws had merely reestablished the accomplishments of the Popular Front cabinet. The SFIO would have done well to ignore both charges. Competing with the Communists on the field of revolutionary fervor was politically counterproductive, and the comparison with the Popular Front was patently unfair. The critics ignored that the legislation of the 1930s had had no lasting impact; most of it was repealed within a few months after the Popular Front left office.[50]

On balance, the Social Democrats' achievements in the area of social policy profoundly changed societal relationships in Europe after the Second World War. It laid the foundation for the bourgeoisification of the industrial proletariat, and, not incidentally, changed the nature of the Socialist parties and with it their constituents' values and expectations. The social legislation of the 1940s and 1950s was certainly reformist, and the critics within the parties who bemoaned the rise of consumerism and the loss of proletarian consciousness were quite right. However, they ignored the fact that without these developments West European society would have enjoyed far less social peace, while Social Democracy would have been doomed to the role of political outsider.[51]

Church and Party

Throughout modern European history the role of organized religion in public life has been much debated. The forces that dominated political life after the French Revolution sought to reduce the influence of the churches, while organized religion combated liberalism and Marxism as dangerous manifestations of modernism and secularism. By the end of the Second World War variegated patterns of relationships between church and state had been established in the three countries. France had instituted a system of complete separation of church and state, while in The Netherlands public and private life still revolved largely around the confessional zuilen. In Germany the situation varied from state to state, although a national concordat, which the Nazis had concluded with the Vatican in 1933, was officially still in force.

Historically, relations between the Christian churches and the Social Democratic parties had been marked more by antagonism than cooperation. The churches generally supported the Socialists' political opponents, while the Social Democrats looked upon organized religion as one of the pillars of the capitalist system. Mutual distrust was especially characteristic of relations between the Socialist parties and the Catholic Church. Beginning with Pope Leo XIII's 1878 encyclical *Rerum Novarum*, Catholics had been warned that Marxism in any form was a dangerous and erroneous doctrine, while the Socialists looked upon the Catholic Church as an opposing organization. In a famous quip Kurt Schumacher claimed every parish priest acted as local party secretary for the CDU.[52]

To be sure, the estrangement between church and party had never been complete. There had always been a minority of Socialist leaders—after the Second World War they included men such as André Philip, Willi Eichler, Hinrich Kopf and Willem Banning—who were practicing church members, although their affiliation was usually with a Protestant denomination rather than with the Catholic Church.[53] Common persecution by the Nazis had also helped to break down the walls of distrust as both church leaders and Socialists found themselves incarcerated side by side in the same concentration camps.[54] Shared experiences in the emerging battle with Communism convinced yet more Social Democrats and church activists that they had to join forces to prevent the resurrection of totalitarianism in Western Europe. Finally, in the aftermath of the destruction wrought by the war, many left-wing Catholics supported various forms of Christian Socialism as an answer to Europe's destitution, and these ideas were quite compatible with concepts advanced by the personalist brand of Democratic Socialism.

The PvdA pioneered the efforts to overcome the historic antithese between the Socialists and the churches. Under the leadership of Willem Banning the Dutch Socialists set out to realize what the French Socialist leader Salomon Grumbach quite accurately called a "new concept of Socialism." The PvdA and especially Banning hoped to link Christian ethics and democratic socialism on the basis of what Banning called their common *"zedelijke pathos"* (spiritual emotion). As a consequence the traditional confession-based verzuiling of Dutch society would disappear and be replaced by a political duality of progressives and conservatives. The PvdA, of course, saw itself as the leader of the progressive forces in the country. To smooth the way for left-wing church activists to enter the progressive camp, the party not only rejected Socialism's traditional anticlerical stance, and encouraged the churches to play a larger role in Dutch political and public life, but also established Catholic and Protestant *werkgemeenschapen* (caucusses) within the organizational framework of the PvdA.[55]

The success of this effort was mixed. On the one hand, as we saw, the PvdA was not able to break up the traditional zuilen nor marginalize the confessional parties. The society envisioned by the Dutch Socialists in 1946 was not to emerge for another decade. On the other hand, it was also clear that the zuilen were beginning to weaken; in the 1950s significant numbers of practicing Protestants and, somewhat later, Catholics as well were voting for the PvdA in national if not yet in local elections. From the Socialists' perspective, time was on their side. In addition, the party's rejection of the anti-these certainly helped it to be accepted as a coalition partner by the Catholic KVP.

While the PvdA looked confidently to the future, the Dutch Catholic hierarchy fought back to keep the Catholic zuil intact. On Sunday, May 30, 1954 an episcopal *mandement* (pronouncement) was read in every Catholic church in The Netherlands. The lengthy document was a three-part missal. The first two sections were devoted to expressions of concern about the decline of morality among Dutch Catholics. It was the third part, entitled *"onchris- telijke stromingen"* (un-Christian tendencies), which had a direct impact on the relations between the PvdA and Dutch Catholics: the bishops attempted to isolate their flock from the influence of liberal and Socialist organizations and ideas. Under the threat of ecclesiastical sanctions Catholics were prohibited from joining Socialist labor unions or listening "regularly" to radio programs sponsored by the Socialist broadcast organization, VARA. The mandement did not specifically prohibit Holland's Catholics from joining or voting for the PvdA, but the document left no doubt that the bishops felt to do so was incompatible with the religious well-being of a loyal member of the Catholic Church.[56]

Although the bishops insisted the mandement had to be con- sidered in its entirety, both the media and the PvdA's leaders focussed their attention on the third part. They immediately rec- ognized the mandement's basic aim: to restore the traditional zuilen in Dutch politics and to marginalize the PvdA as a political force. There was no disagreement within the party on this point nor on the seriousness of the situation. The party's executive com- mittee devoted the bulk of five meetings of to a discussion of the mandement. The leaders disagreed, however, on how the PvdA should react to the challenge. The proposals for the party's reac- tion ranged from reasoned response to open confrontation. The party's parliamentary chairman, Jaap Burger, and Willem Thomas- sen, a veteran leader of the SDAP and now one of the PvdA's three secretaries, advocated a full-scale counterattack, including a polit- ical mobilization campaign and an immediate end to the coalition with the KVP. Drees, Vos, and one of the party's vice-chairmen, G. Ruygers, argued for a more subtle approach. They felt an open confrontation would be politically counterproductive. Instead, they urged the PvdA to stay in the government coalition, and to mount an educational, rather than a confrontational, public rela- tions campaign. The soft line won out. The PvdA remained in the coalition and its political response was deliberately moderate. The party organized a national conference which enabled a number of speakers to stress that the PvdA's program and Catholic thought were not incompatible. The party also asked Willem Banning to write a pamphlet conveying the same message.[57]

The party's reformist leadership was gratified by the results of this measured, almost appeasing response. The PvdA avoided being blamed for a government crisis, most Catholic members of the PvdA remained loyal to the party, and in the 1956 national elections the PvdA obtained the best results in its history. There was no doubt that at least in the short run the Catholic bishops' attempt to marginalize Dutch Social Democracy had failed.[58]

At the end of the war relations between church and party in Germany were far more antagonistic than in Holland, and neither the SPD nor the churches were doing much to improve the situation. Schumacher and his associates welcomed "Christian Socialism" as a potential support base for Democratic Socialism, but they continued to look upon organized religion, and especially the Catholic Church, as a political opponent. Walter Menzel put the SPD's point of view succinctly when he accused the Catholic Church of wanting to "clericalize German society." Even the shared resistance experience did not help much in bringing the two sides together. Schumacher admitted that some church leaders had been active in the anti-Nazi opposition, but he insisted their motivation had been to serve the particular interests of the Church, not German democracy.[59]

The issues that divided the SPD and organized religion were long-standing, although they now appeared in a new, postwar guise. The school question had been around since the days of the *Kulturkampf* (battle of cultures) at the end of the nineteenth century. While France's public schools were strictly secular and in The Netherlands confessional schools were the rule, in Germany three types battled for supremacy: secular schools, so-called *Simultanschulen* ("common" schools), which were attended by both Protestant and Catholic pupils, and confessional schools. The Catholic hierarchy insisted upon public schools strictly segregated by confession, with religious instruction as part of the regular curriculum. The Social Democrats preferred secular schools, but were willing to accept common schools. (It should be noted, that in practice only elementary schools were at issue; most high schools were common institutions.) With the support of the Christian Democrats Germany's Catholic bishops were able to defeat Socialist (and Allied) attempts to deconfessionalize the school system. Instead, the right of parents to choose confessional public schools for their children became part of the West German constitution.

Frustrated by the defeat on the school question, the SPD became additionally infuriated by the churches' ill-disguised support of Adenauer and the CDU/CSU in the 1949 and even more the 1953 Bundestag elections. As far as Schumacher and the party's old guard were concerned, church and party would remain open enemies. That sentiment was undoubtedly shared by most of the rank-and-file membership, but there were also some within the SPD who recognized early on that continuing altercations between the party and organized religion would benefit neither the stability of the German political system nor help the party overcome its marginalization. In addition, reformers like Carlo Schmid and Willi Eichler shared the churches' concern for the ethical and moral renewal of Germany. As we saw, Eichler, for one, had been active in the ranks of the Religious Socialists during the Weimar years.[60]

For the minority of ethical Socialists within the SPD the PvdA became an openly acknowledged model on how to improve party-church relations. A series of bilateral conferences with Dutch Socialist leaders produced a number of papers and statements emphasizing the similarities in the ethical and moral goals of Christianity and Democratic Socialism. At the same time, these SPD leaders also attempted to establish better relations with individual church leaders. The efforts met with considerable success in the case of the Protestant churches, but for the SPD and the Catholic Church the 1950s were "the years of animosity." Even the mild mannered Carlo Schmid noted with exasperation that the Catholic Church welcomed only capitalists into its ranks.[61]

At least some Social Democrats recognized, however, that the party was not entirely blameless in creating this state of affairs. The anticlericalism, both latent and open, of many party activists certainly remained a major barrier blocking improved relations between the party and the churches. As Adolf Arndt, the party's judicial expert and one of the leaders in the drive for better relations with the Catholic church, noted in a private letter to the SPD's leader in the heavily Catholic state of Bavaria, Waldemar von Knoeringen, "as long as individual Social Democrats believe that it is good form to *anpinkeln* (piss on) the Catholic Church, we shouldn't expect that talks with the hierarchy will result in anything positive." The PvdA was disappointed that the SPD did not follow the Dutch model and establish confessional caucuses as part of its organizational structure. But long-established attitudes changed slowly. The Protestant minister Heinrich Albertz, a leader of the SPD in Berlin and mayor of the city in the 1960s, lamented that "we will have to overcome considerable resistance to achieve better church-party relations." It required the party's programmatic shift in the Bad Godesberg Program for the situation to improve significantly.[62]

Traditionally, relations between organized religion and the SFIO were as bad as those between the SPD and the churches. French Socialists, along with other Republicans, insisted upon strict separation of church and state. Laïcisme, said André Philip, a practicing Protestant, was "the common foundation of practical humanism which defines French civilization." Much like Schumacher and his supporters, most SFIO leaders looked especially upon the Catholic church in France (which was, of course, the dominant form of organized religion in the country) as a Europe-wide political force determined to halt the advance of Democratic Socialism. Specifically in France, the Church had, from the SFIO's perspective, both a tainted past and present. The French Socialists contended that during the Nazi occupation the Catholic hierarchy had, with a few notable exceptions, cooperated with the Vichy regime, and after the war the Church supported both de Gaulle and the MRP.[63]

In terms of concrete politics, the issue of laïcisme focused on the public schools. The SFIO fully endorsed the view of the teachers' unions that France's public schools must remain secular institutions; the Socialists vigorously rejected religious instruction as part of the regular curriculum, and they vehemently opposed any state subsidies to "free" or Catholic schools. Laïcisme was for many Socialists a *question de coeur* (a question of essential beliefs), but the issue also had tactical significance for the party. As noted earlier, the members and leaders of the French teachers' union were the most passionate defenders of laïcisme (Guy Mollet himself had been a *lycée* teacher before he became the party's general secretary), and many of these public school teachers traditionally served the party as local and regional secretaries.[64]

If laïcisme provided part of the glue that bound the SFIO's activists together, the issue had rather less positive results for the party's political fortunes. The party's passionate attachment to laïcisme prevented the party from attracting left-wing Catholic voters and members. Again echoing Schumacher, Mollet contended that the MRP really had no right to political existence because Christian workers belonged in the SFIO, but while such sentiments might have been good Marxist theory, they had little effect on the patterns of political allegiance in postwar France.[65]

In general (and admittedly with the benefit of hindsight) the SFIO's animosity toward organized religion was clearly counterproductive. Not only did the SFIO's stand create chronic frictions with its Third Force coalition partner, the MRP, but it is now clear that most Frenchmen were far less passionate about laïcisme than were the party's militants. Ironically, this was even true for the party's primary target group, France's industrial workers. Studies showed that some of the country's most industrialized areas were also most attached to Catholic traditions. Moreover, the laïcist issue prevented a clean break between the SFIO and the PCF. The PCF's constant reminders that Socialists and Communists were charter members of the *front laïque* invariably stirred sentimental hopes that the estranged brothers might join forces again after all.[66]

There was one notable attempt to find a compromise acceptable to left-wing Catholics in the MRP and the leaders of the SFIO. In 1951 the government proposed the so-called Marie and Barrangé laws. The first made possible scholarships from public funds for students attending private (i.e., Catholic) schools, and the second recognized the course of studies at some Catholic schools as sufficient preparation for taking the state examinations. Ironically, although the legislation was introduced when the SFIO was not a member of the government, the laws were based upon the recommendations of a commission headed by the Socialist former minister of education, Olivier Lapie.

The reaction of the SFIO's old guard was swift and unequivocal. The CD denounced Lapie's efforts, and in the National Assembly the GP vehemently opposed the legislation. This had no effect on the legislative outcome (the laws were passed), but the backlash of the debate over the laws helped lead the Right to victory in the June 1951 legislative elections, enabling the MRP to form a government with the Gaullists.[67]

Episodes like the battle over the Barrangé and Marie laws led a small minority of SFIO's leaders to argue for a less adamant stand on party-church relations. They pointed out that the SFIO's (and the Communists') attacks upon the Catholic Church actually strengthened the Church, while preventing more cordial relations between the Socialists and left-wing Catholics in the MRP. Some leaders, like Lapie and Edouard Depreux (ironically, in 1945 Depreux had been a laïcist firebrand) wanted the party to practice what they called *socialisme ouvert* (open socialism) toward organized religion. Their proposals came quite close to what the PvdA was doing and the reformers within the SPD were advocating, but at least for the 1950s such efforts failed in the SFIO. For both ideological and tactical reasons Mollet, his supporters in the CD, and most of the federation secretaries insisted upon continuing the battle for separation of church and state.[68]

Colonial Policies

As members of their countries' governing coalitions the French and Dutch Socialists shared responsibility for Holland's and France's postwar colonial policies. (The SPD was only indirectly concerned with the colonial dilemma. With no colonies of her own, Germany and the Social Democrats confronted colonial issues primarily in terms of reacting to France's policies in Algeria. This will be discussed in a later chapter.) "Colonial policies" is, of course, something of a misnomer. Confronted with accelerating demands for national liberation among the colonized peoples, the primary task of the Dutch and French governments became finding the means for an orderly process of decolonization. In the past the Socialists' attitude toward colonialism and imperialism had been somewhat contradictory. In theory they condemned Western imperialism for its oppressive practices and supported self-determination in the colonies, but in practice they also shared many of the Eurocentric attitudes that linked colonialism to the blessings of European civilization in the "backward" areas of Asia and Africa, and, not incidentally, brought economic benefits to European workers.[69]

The Second World War profoundly affected the relationship of colonial powers and their possessions. The global conflict boosted the liberation asperations of the colonial peoples, but the wartime developments also tainted the liberation movements in the eyes of many French and Dutch leaders. To take Indonesia as an example, the cooperative arrangement between the Japanese occupiers and the Indonesian national liberation movement indicated to most Dutchmen that the Indonesian liberation fighters were men who had collaborated with the enemy. In the case of France, much the same situation prevailed in Indochina. The Cold War created new splits, since, after a brief fling with Dutch and French chauvinism, the Communists became adamant supporters of immediate national independence for all colonial peoples.

The Socialists' ideal solution to the colonial dilemma was to square the circle. Both the Dutch and the French Socialists envisioned a future in which the non-European peoples previously under French and Dutch control would, when ready, gain increased autonomy over their own affairs, while remaining parts of a reorganized French and Dutch union of territories. This ideal picture of the future begged a number of questions, of course. Who would determine that a colonial possession was ready for political autonomy? And what if a colonial people rejected membership in a new French or Dutch union, and desired total independence instead?

The Dutch were the first to face an acute crisis over the issue of de-colonization. In 1945 the Dutch colonial empire was a far-flung entity, but its jewel was one major possession, the Dutch East Indies. Many times larger than The Netherlands itself, this area had been under Dutch control since the seventeenth century, and over the years the economic ties between Holland and its Asian possessions had become very close. The catchy phrase, "*Indië verloren, rampspoed geboren*" (which might be loosely translated as "if [the East] Indies are lost, disaster follows") was accepted as a truism by most politicians in The Netherlands. With the end of the war both Dutch public opinion and the first postwar government expected full restoration of Dutch control over the East Indies. Not only was it felt that The Netherlands needed the resources of its East Indian possessions for the country's recovery, but, because the Indonesian independence movement and its leader, Achmed Sukarno, had collaborated with the Japanese, Holland also felt morally justified in denying their aspirations.

Expecting to return in triumph to the East Indies, the Dutch government was confronted instead with an "unforeseen event," when Sukarno made a unilateral declaration of Indonesian independence. The cabinet's initial reaction was meant to be flexible, but instead it was unrealistic. The government announced its willingness to enter into negotiations to put the relations between the mother country and its colonial possession on a new footing, perhaps something like the recently created *Union française*. At the same time the cabinet indicated that because full-scale Indonesian independence was incompatible with the Dutch constitution, it was out of the question. In addition, the Dutch refused to accept Sukarno and his movement as a negotiating partner.[70]

As a member of the governing coalition, the PvdA was thrust into the center of the painful process of decolonialization. (Willem Drees devoted fully 88 of the 340 pages in his memoirs to a defense of his and the government's policies.) The Indonesian question became a traumatic experience in the life of the PvdA, and, as one member of the PvdA's executive committee observed, virtually all of its actions and decisions were taken *contre coeur*. The PvdA found itself in the unenviable position of attempting to accomplish two incompatible goals simultaneously: The Dutch Social Democrats wanted to honor their ideological commitment to colonial emancipation and national self-determination, but the party leaders were also determined not to leave the government coalition, which meant the PvdA was tied to political forces that rejected the Indonesians' right of self-determination.

The Social Democrats' first reaction was to join the united front against negotiating with Sukarno: there should be talks with indigenous Indonesian forces, but not with the Sukarno movement. This was the KVP's position, and it was shared by most of the PvdA's leaders and rank-and-file members.[71] It soon became clear, however, that the Sukarno movement could not be ignored, and the PvdA would have to choose between accepting Indonesian independence under Sukarno, or rejecting independence and remaining in the government. The party decided to stay in the coalition and support its partners' decision to suppress the independence movement led by Sukarno. In the course of 1947 the party's and the government's position became increasingly precarious. After the May, 1946, elections the PvdA lost control of the colonial portfolio, and, frustrated by the failure to achieve a negotiated settlement, the Catholic minister for colonies, E.M.J.A. Sassen, insisted upon using military force to subdue the Indonesian independence movement. In 1947 the Dutch government launched two so-called police actions, which did not succeed in putting down the independence movement, but did manage to isolate Holland in international affairs.

Although the Socialist members of the cabinet were uneasy about the use of military force, their determination to place the cohesion of the coalition ahead of all other considerations left them little choice but to support the police actions. This decision created a serious rift within the party. The critics, who included such major figures as Schermerhorn, Banning, Kadt, and Nederhorst, opposed the leadership's decision to support the police actions, not only because it was contrary to the party's commitment to colonial emancipation, but because it tied the PvdA's hands and prevented the party from advocating its own course of action.[72]

In the end it did not matter very much, because the Dutch government itself lost control of its colonial agenda. Massive American opposition to the use of the military forced the cabinet to enter into serious negotiations with Sukarno during 1948 and 1949. In 1949 the negotiations led to an agreement granting Indonesia full independence. Although not by virtue of its own wisdom, a protracted colonial conflict (such as the SFIO would confront in Indochina and Algeria) was avoided, and the PvdA's leaders promptly congratulated themselves for their role in the relatively quick and painless settlement of the Indonesian problem. Drees argued the PvdA really never had a choice: most Dutch voters, including the PvdA's constituency, fully supported the government's course of action. The prime minister claimed that by remaining in the cabinet the PvdA had hastened the settlement because it convinced the

KVP to limit the police actions and return to the negotiating table, and the Socialists' coalition loyalty helped to obtain the Catholics' agreement to the PvdA's social legislation.[73]

Drees' critics pointed out that much of this was not only self-serving but untrue. Indonesia obtained her independence because the Americans used their leverage (which included Marshall Plan aid) to force the Dutch government to yield. As for the mood of the party's constituency, while it was undoubtedly true that most of the party activists initially supported the leaders' policies, the mood changed after the government launched its military actions. The members of the party's executive committee grew increasingly frustrated and the PvdA staged a special congress on Indonesia to permit the opposition to vent its feelings. The net loss of some eight thousand members in 1946 and 1947 demonstrated that a significant minority of the rank-and-file members disagreed with the party leaders' Indonesian policy. Nevertheless, it must also be acknowledged, that the decision to stay in the coalition reinforced the PvdA's image as a genuine Volkspartei and helped to dissipate the remaining doubts about the party's commitment to mainstream Dutch patriotism.[74]

There remained only the festering sore of the future status of New Guinea, an area which was specifically not covered by the 1949 agreement. That issue was to plague the Dutch government (and the PvdA) until 1961. In fact, the New Guinea conflict illustrates well what might have happened if the Indonesia conflict had persisted. Disagreements over the future of New Guinea not only surfaced repeatedly in the discussions of the PvdA's governing bodies, but also contributed to the fall of two of the party's most prominent leaders, Goes v.d. Naters and Hein Vos. Both disagreed with the Dutch government's policy of attempting to retain control of New Guinea, but, even more important, they felt that Drees' insistence on remaining in the cabinet at all costs reduced the party to an adjunct of the cabinet.[75]

In many ways, the colonial dilemma faced by France and the SFIO was not unlike the problems of The Netherlands and the PvdA. The French Socialists, like their Dutch comrades, hoped that constructing a new relationship between France and her colonies would square the circle of colonial emancipation and French control. The SFIO was the most enthusiastic advocate of the concept of *"l'indépendance dans l'interdépendance"* (independence within interdependence) whose institutionalization was to be the Union française. Unfortunately, the Socialists' enthusiasm was not shared by the colonial peoples.[76]

In the mid-1950s Algeria was to become a major political and military battleground, but during the first decade after the war the Fourth Republic's most pressing colonial problem was what Roger Quilliot has called the "Indochinese swamp." The Indochina conflict was a particularly divisive issue because powerful sources inside and outside the government coalition pulled in opposite directions. The Communists were staunch French chauvinists until the outbreak of the Cold War, but then became unmitigating advocates of colonial independence, especially if the liberation movement was led by communists, which was certainly the case with Ho Chi Minh in Indochina. On the other side of the political spectrum, the Gaullists, supported by most of France's high-ranking military officers, were adamant that France retain complete control of Indochina. Finally, within the government coalition, the MRP, like the KVP in Holland, also insisted that some ties between France and its Asian colonies had to be maintained; independence for Indochina was out of the question.

The SFIO, much like the PvdA, was divided on the colonial issue. There was a strong strain of Jacobin nationalism among the Socialists (critics called it *molletisme national* [national Molletism] or *colonialisme petit-blanc* [petty bourgeois colonialism]) which insisted that only the liberating influence of French civilization could bring true independence to the colonies. The SFIO's involvement with French policy in Indochina was not limited to theoretical considerations. As a member of the governing coalition for most of the decade from 1945 to 1954, the French Socialists helped to create the illusions that governed French moves in Indochina. Marius Moutet, in 1947 the minister for overseas territories and a member of the SFIO's CD, established the twin constants that all of his successors retained with minor variations: a combination of negotiations with "reasonable" indigenous forces and judicious military pressure would result in a settlement that was satisfactory both to France and the people of Indochina. Elgey effectively characterized this policy as *"pas de négociation sans une victoire militaire* (no negotiation without military victory)." Other Socialist leaders fully agreed. In 1951 Léon Boutbien, so reasonable on other issues, reported to the CD after a fact-finding tour in Indochina that Ho Chi Minh and his forces were losing ground, and that a slight increase in military pressure would succeed in defeating them altogether. This scenario had two fatal flaws. It vastly underestimated the weakness of the French military position, and by excluding from the negotiating table Indochinese representatives who were not "reasonable," the French closed the door to political leaders who had the most popular support, notably Ho Chi Minh and the Indochinese Communists. Negotiating an agreement with Emperor Bao Dai looked good on paper, but it had little effect on the actual political dynamics in Indochina.[77]

Although Indochina did not turn the SFIO's leaders against each other as Algeria would later in the 1950s, the party's position was never without its critics, and, as the French position in Indochina became increasingly untenable, pressures for pulling out of Indochina also grew within the party. Marcel Pivert was an early and vocal critic. Another prescient member of the CD, Alain Savary, concluded as early as January, 1951, "politically, the situation is lost." Paradoxically, the leadership now dug in. Strains of Jacobin nationalism continued to permeate the SFIO, and altering the party's stand on Indochina had tactical implications as well. It would mean aligning the party with the French Communists who insisted on full independence for Indochina under Ho Chi Minh's leadership. Under these circumstances, the SFIO's leaders were delighted that the party was out of the government when France suffered its decisive defeat at the battle of Dienbien Phu in 1954. In fact, the party's greatest fear was that the cabinet might fall, forcing the SFIO to rejoin the government and help mop up the mess in Indochina.[78]

Unfortunately, the party's policy in Asia left a legacy that was to haunt the French Socialists when Algeria took the place of Indochina as the focal point of the divisive debate over the future of French colonialism. Personal animosities lingered and intensified, and the SFIO's inability to reconcile the principles of national self-determination with a French "presence" would become even more obvious during the bitter debate on the future of an area that, for more than a hundred years, had been closely bound to metropolitan France.

The Parties and the Military

Decolonization and the Cold War added new dimensions to another old and contentious issue, the Social Democrats' relationship to the national armed forces. (The foreign affairs aspects of this topic will be treated in the next chapter; here we are concerned with the domestic implications of the relationship.) Traditionally, relations between the armed forces and the Socialists had been characterized by mutual distrust, to say the least. For the Socialists, the armed forces and, even more, various paramilitary

groups were bastions of conservatism and authoritarianism, prae-
torian guards for capitalism. For the military, especially the professional officer corps, the Socialists represented elements of societal
destabilization, determined to destroy the established order.

After the Second World War the debate over decolonization in
France and The Netherlands added new fuel to the mutual antagonisms. The military (and their political allies) complained that
the Socialists were unwilling to give full support to the national
efforts to retain control of the colonial empires, while the Socialists
felt that the military were pursuing policies that often precluded
political solutions. Surprisingly quickly, however, the Cold War
and the fear of Russian military expansion laid the groundwork
for a more positive relationship between the military and the
Socialists. By 1948 virtually all West European Socialists acknowledged the need for a military effort to defend Western Europe
from Soviet aggression.

This change of heart was most radical in the case of the PvdA.
The SDAP, the forerunner of the PvdA, had traditionally supported
pacifism (it was the party of the *"brokken gewertje"* [broken gun]),
exposing it repeatedly to charges by the bourgeois parties that the
Socialists lacked a sense of patriotism. The PvdA broke completely
with this tradition. As we saw, the party leaders, albeit reluctantly
and somewhat *contre coeur*, supported the military's police action
in Indonesia. Joining their bourgeois coalition partners, the Dutch
Social Democrats also readily abandoned The Netherlands' customary neutrality in international conflicts, and supported Holland's full-scale integration into the Western military alliance.[79]

The leaders never wavered from this position, but a small group
of dissidents attempted to uphold the pacifist and neutralist traditions of Dutch Social Democracy. These proponents of the *Derde
Weg* (Third Way) argued that Holland neither needed a national
army nor should the country take sides in the Cold War. Support
for the Third Way was small to begin with and became even less
significant as the Cold War heated up. As we shall see, it was not
until the end of the decade, when The Netherlands and the party
were confronted with the issue of endorsing a new strategic concept for NATO which included the potential stationing of atomic
weapons on Dutch soil that the dissidents gained some strength.

The relationship between the SFIO and the French military was
more complex. The Socialists quickly became the most vociferous
critics of de Gaulle's postwar military policies. The party leaders
felt that de Gaulle had been too lenient in weeding out the many
officers who had stayed loyal to Vichy. Far from being punished,

they seemed to hold entrenched positions in the colonial armies and the French occupation forces in Germany. The Socialists also lamented the lack of parliamentary control of the military and what they considered excessive expenditures for the armed forces.[80]

The dispute over the military led to a split between the party and de Gaulle, contributing to the General's resignation at the beginning of 1946. De Gaulle's sulking at Colombey-sur-les-Deux-Églises did not improve the relationship between the SFIO and the French military. The army leaders blamed the Socialists for not giving them the resources needed to win the war in Indochina, while the Socialists regarded most of the French officer corps as personal followers of de Gaulle,[81] whose loyalty to the constitutional system of parliamentary democracy, like that of their idol, was at best doubtful. If proof of the latter were needed, the 1947 *complot bleu* (blue plot) seemed to provide it. Although poorly organized and supported by only a few middle-rank officers, the fact that army officers on active duty were contemplating the overthrow of France's parliamentary democracy did not encourage Socialist trust in the professional military. Episodes like the complot bleu and, more important, the festering sore of the Indochina conflict, left a legacy of mutual animosity that was to bear bitter fruit in the latter half of the 1950s.[82]

In the past, relations between the SPD and Germany's armed forces had been particularly acrimonious. With good reason the Socialists viewed the officer corps as the main pillar of Prusso-German authoritarianism, whose members had also been all too willing to serve Nazi totalitarianism. On the other hand, for the army the Socialists had always been *"vaterlandslose Gesellen"* (a rabble without a country) who felt no loyalty to the German nation.[83] At the end of Second World War the problem seemed to have become a non-issue; after all, the Allies had agreed upon Germany's complete demilitarization. But with the onset of the Cold War it became clear that Germany without armed forces would have a short-lived history. Prodded by the Americans, the Western Allies agreed there should be a German military contribution to the defense of the West. In return for piecemeal increases in the Federal Republic's sovereignty, the Adenauer government and the CDU were willing to accept West German armed forces in some form.

The SPD initially vehemently rejected the establishment of what was to become the *Bundeswehr*. The party insisted the creation of any new German army could come only after the country had been reunified. Until then it was up to the Allies to defend West Germany from Soviet aggression.[84] For this reason the SPD mounted a vigorous campaign against both the European Defense Community and, later, Germany's membership in NATO. At first glance, the SPD's position seemed straightforward and in line with the party's absolute prioritization of national reunification. In practice, however, the leadership soon recognized that the SPD's line on the military led to a number of undesirable consequences. To begin with, the SPD was hard put to explain the difference between its position and that of a number of pacifist organizations which attempted to co-opt the Socialists for their agenda. Some party leaders were also both surprised and concerned about the breadth and radicalism of pacifist sentiments in the party. In addition, the party found itself in the unwanted company of the East German Communists, who, albeit for entirely different reasons, also wanted to prevent the establishment of the Bundeswehr.[85]

The party's vehement "no" to remilitarization had implications for the future stability of West German democracy as well. The party traveled a narrow line between loyal opposition and demagogic irresponsibility. Convinced it had a majority of voters behind it on this issue, the SPD first insisted on new elections to let the voters decide the issue directly, and when that failed, the PV only narrowly rejected a call for a national plebiscite on German membership in NATO. The call for a national referendum was a purely demagogic tactic, since the West German Grundgesetz does not provide for either initiatives or referenda.[86]

Unable to prevent the establishment of the Bundeswehr because it did not have the votes in the Bundestag, the party ran the risk of repeating its mistake during the Weimar years when the mutual alienation of the SPD and the Reichswehr prevented the party from influencing Germany's military policy and essentially left the Reichswehr independent of parliamentary control. Although Schumacher, Ollenhauer, and the hardliners seemed unconcerned about this danger, the party and West Germany were fortunate that a group of Young Turks in the SPD succeeded in putting the SPD on a more positive path. This group was led by the party's deputy parliamentary chairman in the Bundestag, Fritz Erler, and the chairman of the party's Committee on Security Affairs, Helmut Schmidt. Together they worked hard to integrate the new Bundeswehr into the democratic system. Although Erler loyally supported the party's rejection of the Bundeswehr as a matter of principle, he also recognized that the army's establishment was a foregone conclusion, and that the party's continued "no" would isolate the SPD and make a future federal coalition all but impossible. Behind the scenes in the Bundestag the deputy chairman was instrumental in forging the legislation that put the Federal Republic's armed forces under parliamentary control.[87] As a result, the SPD was able to avoid a repetition of the Weimar disaster. In time the party developed a quite positive relationship with the Bundeswehr (symbolized by Helmut Schmidt's brief service as a reserve officer) and by the end of the decade the party had certainly succeeded in shedding its stigma of *vaterlandslose Gesellen*.[88]

Conclusion

The three parties' views of their accomplishments after a decade or so of postwar history spanned a wide spectrum. For the PvdA the course of events since the creation of the party confirmed that the founders' plans and ideas had been essentially correct. The party was a long way from breaking the continuing influence of the zuilen, but it was on the right path. The PvdA had become a fully accepted Volkspartei, its legislative program was either enacted into law or remained on Holland's active political agenda. On the whole, the decade had been a success.[89]

The SPD was rather less pleased with its political rewards. True, the party's domestic policy agenda had certainly helped to shape legislation in this area, but the electoral rewards were disappointing. In relative terms the SPD's political influence was declining at the federal level; the success stories were all confined to the Länder. As a result, the old party leaders found themselves isolated and frustrated. Facing more of the same unless the party managed a dramatic turnaround, Ollenhauer and his supporters stood ready to step aside and let younger men with radically innovative ideas take over.

The French Socialists were similarly discouraged. Although the SFIO had been instrumental in putting France's modern social net in place, and the party had played a major role in thwarting Communist attempts to destabilize French society, France's Socialists remained on the defensive.[90] The reason, of course, was the SFIO's continuing unwillingness to admit that it was a reformist party. Pursuing the chimera of *socialisme pur et dur*, the party dismissed its own domestic policy successes as insignificant preparations for the coming revolution of Democratic Socialism. Moreover, unlike the SPD, the SFIO had no powerful group of reformers waiting in the wings.

– *Chapter Six* –

FOREIGN RELATIONS, 1945–1955

❦

The prevailing view was that, when it came to foreign policy, the Social Democrats were simply out of the loop. In West Germany the occupation powers handled foreign relations for much of the decade, and in France and Holland most accounts show the Socialist parties as having little influence or interest in the conduct of foreign relations. When they did offer new ideas, they turned out to be unrealistic and impractical.[1]

This is not an altogether fair assessment; the Socialists were not uninterested in foreign relations. In Germany the SPD based much of its early postwar electoral campaign strategy on an unsuccessful attempt to establish the priority of foreign policy in German politics. As we shall see, elsewhere too, the Social Democrats were instrumental in effecting a number of important policy decisions. It was true, however, that the Socialists entered the postwar era with some quite unrealistic expectations about the future patterns of foreign relations. They were initially convinced that the horrors of the Second World War had finally demonstrated the futility of conducting foreign relations as a series of interactions between power-oriented nation states. Learning the lessons from the failure of the Versailles system, the Big Four and the nations of Europe should and would now put internationalism ahead of nationalism and moral principles ahead of Realpolitik. They would also entrust much of the process of foreign relations to supra-national bodies like the United Nations and the Socialist International.[2]

While the Cold War quickly shattered the Socialists' illusions about continuing cooperation among the Big Four, in all three parties minority groups hoped that Europe could at least avoid taking sides in the emerging global conflict, and act instead as a Third Force separating and mediating between the antagonistic superpowers. But the Third Force also proved to be a short-lived illusion. Virtually all of its proponents soon became staunch westerners, and only a few ended up as Communist fellow-travelers.

The same Cold War that destroyed the illusion of the Third Force also caused the "German problem" to remain a staple of foreign relations. The spectrum of solutions to the German problem was extremely wide, ranging from General de Gaulle's idea of a permanent division of Germany into a series of small and independent entities, to Kurt Schumacher's scenario, under which a united, democratic, centralized, and sovereign German Reich with its 1937 territorial boundaries restored would, on its own initiative, become a peaceful and cooperative partner in the international family of nations. Most of the French and Dutch Socialists, as well as an increasing number of SPD members, rejected both of these extremes and advocated instead various forms of federalism in Germany and the firm integration of a democratic Germany into a united Europe. That Europe would be unified was axiomatic in Social Democratic circles. Socialists disagreed on the details of Europeanization, but at least in principle virtually all West European Socialists envisioned the transfer of portions of national sovereignty to supra-national European institutions.[3]

International and Bilateral Contacts

Equally axiomatic was the Socialists' commitment to internationalism; "at its core socialism is international," wrote an SFIO leader, Edouard Depreux. Indeed, the Social Democrats frequently contrasted their internationalism to what they perceived as outmoded forms of bourgeois nationalism. (They refused to recognize the Communist claim to internationalism; according to the Social Democrats the Communist parties were simply a extension of Soviet nationalism.) Even regional Socialist newspapers reported regularly on developments among the sister parties, and the leaders of the old SDAP insisted they would not dissolve the SDAP unless the new party retained an affiliation with the international Socialist movement.[4]

In addition to numerous bilateral and intra-European contacts, the Social Democrats initially had high hopes for the reorganized and revitalized Socialist International. Claiming to represent some seven million Socialists in all parts of the globe at the end of the war, the new SI would be the international voice of Democratic Socialism. Actually, the history of the international Socialist movement before the Second World War did not augur well for the success of the new, postwar effort. Three previous attempts had floundered on national antagonisms and ideological differences.

The latest attempt to create an SI grew out of contacts among Socialist leaders exiled in London. Although the new Socialist International was originally intended to be open to all Socialist (not Communist) parties, the inclusiveness of the SI soon became a matter of considerable dispute. While the SFIO thought the Socialist International should function as a bridge between East and West, the PvdA (with strong backing from the Scandinavian Socialists) insisted that including the East European Socialist parties made little sense. With the establishment of People's Democracies in the Soviet orbit, the Socialist parties that existed there were nothing but front organizations for the Communists, and their admission to the SI would permit a network of Communist mole organizations to exist within the Socialist International. With East-West tensions mounting, the SI's bridge function became an illusion, and the Committee of the International Socialist Conference (Comisco), which was founded in 1946, limited its membership to western Social Democratic parties.[5]

The German Socialists could only comment on this debate from the outside. (They were vehemently opposed to East European membership.) The SPD had not yet been readmitted to the international Socialist family, and there were strong feelings against its return. A motion to accept the SPD as a member was defeated at the June, 1947 Comisco meeting in Zurich, but warm endorsement from the PvdA and the SFIO convinced Comisco's Brussels conference in November of the same year to accept the SPD into the organization. It was a fervent testimony to the Socialists' effort to heal the wounds of war in their ranks that the Socialist International selected Frankfurt, Germany, for its July, 1951, founding congress.[6]

The Frankfurt meeting was permeated by high, if unrealistic, hopes, but even then a number of European Social Democrats felt that the SI with its global focus was not the best institutional vehicle for Socialist cooperation in Europe. This role should be assigned to an organization whose membership was limited to the West European Socialist parties. The result was the creation of the

Mouvement socialiste pour les États-Unis d' Europe (Socialist Movement for the United States of Europe [MSEUE]). Largely an initiative of French Socialists (André Philip was an especially active founding member, and Marcel Pivert the first president), the MSEUE quickly became a high profile organization, sponsoring frequent congresses and conferences to promote its central goal: the creation of a West European political entity to supersede the existing nation-states. But the MSEUE also aroused controversy. While many French and Dutch Socialists enthusiastically supported the organization, the German Social Democrats were divided. Some, like Max Brauer and Wilhelm Kaisen, the mayors of Hamburg and Bremen, became active members, but the MSEUE's association with Philip and the Dutch Socialist Alfred Mozer, both of whom Kurt Schumacher heartily disliked, soured relations with the German party's leadership.[7]

Another divisive issue was the Socialists' relationship to multipartisan movements for European unity. A particular bone of contention here was the United Europe Movement (UEM). The UEM owed its organizational life to the charismatic, if short-lived, efforts of Winston Churchill. The British opposition leader issued a ringing call for the political unification of western Europe, and his initiative led to the creation of the UEM in May, 1947. The organization in turn invited all supporters of European unification to work together with the UEM to further the common goal. The response was mixed. The Labour leaders saw the UEM as little more than a political front for the British Conservatives, and rejected affiliation with it. Deferring to the wishes of the British Labour Party, the three parties in turn also officially rejected cooperation with the UEM.[8]

Although Churchill himself soon lost interest in his brain child, the UEM quickly became the largest nongovernmental lobbying effort for a united Europe, with national committees active in all of the West European counties. The UEM's high profile led a number of Continental Social Democrats to ask for a reevaluation of their party's official position. Both Fritz Erler and Carlo Schmid, at that time prominent SPD leaders in Württemberg, had been invited to attend the UEM's first major meeting on the Continent (scheduled for May, 1948, at The Hague) and both wanted to go, but they deferred to the wishes of the SPD's executive and did not attend. The prominent SFIO leader (and former prime minister) Paul Ramadier was less accommodating. He caused something of a tempest in a teapot when he defied the wishes of his party's leaders, and served as chairman at one of the sessions at the UEM's

1948 congress. In subsequent years many other Dutch, German and French Social Democrats followed Ramadier's example, working routinely, albeit unofficially, with the UEM's national and international committees.[9]

Nevertheless, the Socialists did not become entirely comfortable with multipartisan efforts to promote European unity until the founding of Jean Monnet's *Comité d'Action pour l'Europe* (Action Committee for Europe) in the early 1950s. After he left his post as administrative head of the European Coal and Steel Community (ECSC), Monnet, the mastermind of France's postwar modernization program and one of the intellectual fathers of the Schuman Plan, created the Committee as a way of advancing functional cooperative agreements like the ECSC. Monnet was particularly anxious to secure the goodwill of the West European Socialist leaders, and he succeeded. Even the SPD, until then the staunchest opponent of institutional affiliation with multiparty organizations, became an active and enthusiastic member of Monnet's multipartisan advocacy group.[10]

In contrast to multipartisan cooperation, bilateral and multilateral contacts among the Socialist parties were not controversial. On the contrary, all of the Social Democratic parties felt a continuous need to explain their stands to the sister parties, and to attempt to coordinate policy decisions with them. In the early years after the war, relations between the SFIO and the PvdA were the least complicated. Until the European Defense Community (EDC)[11] put the two parties on opposing sides of a bitterly contested issue, the Dutch and French Socialists found little to divide them. Their frequent, mostly informal, contacts were characterized by harmonious personal relations and general agreement on the issues.

Relations between the German and Dutch Socialists were more complicated. In large part the problem involved a clash of personalities. While Erich Ollenhauer, the SPD's deputy chairman, and the PvdA's leader, Koos Vorrink, got along well, the PvdA's secretary for international affairs, Alfred Mozer, was a constant irritant for the SPD. Mozer, a German refugee from the Nazis who had settled in Holland, developed a particular dislike for Kurt Schumacher, a feeling which the latter returned in full force. Nevertheless, by a variety of means, ranging from letters to conferences and mutual speaking engagements, the two parties nonetheless worked hard to establish better relations. Acrimony continued to surface from time to time, especially when the two parties took opposing positions on some major policy issues (such as the

Schuman Plan and the EDC), but by the mid-1950s a generally harmonious relationship had developed.[12]

The relationship between the SFIO and the SPD was crucial for the evolution of postwar European Socialism. The German Socialists recognized that their French comrades held the key to the SPD's rejoining the international Socialist movement. For this reason the SPD eagerly welcomed any opportunity for contact, and routinely attempted to explain its policy positions to the French comrades. An observer from the French military government commented that Salomon Grumbach's presence at the SPD's 1947 congress as the SFIO's official delegate was celebrated by the Germans as a "momentous event." Kurt Schumacher, hardly known for his gracious manners, commented in November, 1947 that "if one looks for decent and intelligent human beings, one can find them in the ranks of the French Socialists."[13]

The SFIO leaders were less uniformly enthusiastic about bilateral contacts. A minority, which included Vincent Auriol and Jules Moch, felt that the German Socialists should be isolated as punishment by for their failure to prevent Hitler's rise to power. However, a large majority of the party's leaders, including Léon Blum, argued that on the contrary, the SFIO should take the lead in welcoming the SPD's return to the international community. In fact, a flurry of bilateral contacts took place as soon as the war ended, most notably a series of lecture tours by SFIO leaders in Germany immediately after the war, and, unique among Socialist parties, the establishment of a formal SPD liaison office in Paris. The latter was headed by Günter Markscheffel, another refugee from Nazism, who had settled in France. In 1946 he was authorized by the SFIO and the SPD to establish an office to facilitate ongoing contacts between the French and German Socialists. The two parties even developed the habit of organizing summit meetings among their leaders long before these became routine for the French and German heads of government.[14]

Still, as was true for relations between the PvdA and the SPD, all was not smooth going for the German and the French Socialists. Personal animosities remained an irritant. Schumacher's abrasive personality annoyed many SFIO leaders; Guy Mollet was quoted as fearing the possibility that his German comrades might come to power in the Federal Republic would be "the supreme catastrophe." The Germans, for their part, echoed Jules Moch's characterization of Mollet as a typical *"Oberlehrer"* (school master), and Schumacher at one point characterized Philip as "the worst of them all." But above all, the parties in the early 1950s were divided on the best road to European unity, with each side accusing the other of excessive nationalism.[15]

The Socialists' internationalism certainly did not match the ideal of supranational, institutionalized cooperation and coordination, but peer pressure should also not be underestimated as a factor in the evolution of their policy stands. The parties saw isolation within the Socialist community as a significant problem. For much of the period under discussion here the SPD found itself at odds with its sister parties, and there is no doubt that the need to overcome its isolation became a significant catalyst for the dramatic foreign policy changes which the SPD adopted in the latter half of the decade.

The First Foreign Policy Test:
The Future of Germany

All three Socialist parties were profoundly concerned about the future of Germany, but their abilities to affect the decision-making process differed markedly. At least initially the SPD was little more than an object of decisions made by the occupying powers. The SFIO and the PvdA were members of their national governments, but, while France was one of the Big Four with its own zone of occupation in Germany, The Netherlands, as a small power, could do little more than submit requests and petitions to the Great Powers.

The general emphasis on inter-Allied tensions as a prelude to the Cold War tends to obscure that all of the members of the anti-Hitler coalition came out of the conflict sharing basic goals for Germany and its future. They agreed to punish those responsible for Nazi crimes, to force German restitution for the Nazis' policies of plunder and economic exploitation, to make sure that fascism would not again come to power in the country, and to create conditions that assured Germany would not be an aggressive power in the future.

These common goals could not obscure the fact that the three Western Allies (not to mention the Soviets) had quite different ideas on how to deal with their German charge. The United States set a low priority on German reparations, and seems to have determined as early as 1946 that there should be a West German state based upon the principles of political democracy, federalism, and free enterprise. The British soon decided to follow the American lead, although they set a higher priority than the Americans on the need for territorial reforms in Germany.[16]

Most scholars and contemporary observers picture France's early postwar role in Germany as obstructionist and largely ineffective. If there was a leitmotiv to French policy in Germany, it was an insistence on the dual goals of security and economic reparations, but a decided lack of clarity on how to achieve these contradictory aims simultaneously. Moreover, the French also had didactic ambitions. They wanted to build a viable democratic society in Germany that would look upon France as friend and mentor. The later French high commissioner and ambassador in the Federal Republic, André François-Poncet, characterized the problem masterfully when he noted that France's German policy simply had too many *"calculs machiavéliques"* (Machiavellian calculations). Günter Markscheffel, the SPD's liaison in Paris, was less diplomatic; he called France's German policy a "jungle."[17]

Unfortunately, the critics remained voices in the wilderness for a considerable time. Immediately after the war France's German policy was in the hands of powerful personalities who saw themselves as personal followers of the hero of the French Resistance and the chief of France's first postwar government, General Charles de Gaulle. The General's German policy was at heart a simple program which promised to remedy the problems left by the Franco-Prussian War of 1870–1871 and the First World War. Steeped in the historiographic school of Jacques Bainville and Maurice Barrès, de Gaulle insisted on far-reaching territorial changes in Germany (including the separation of the left bank of the Rhine) and the destruction of any German central authority. Germany was once again to become "the Germanies."

The General resigned as head of the French government in January 1946, but his legacy was carried on by whole teams of Gaullist officials in the French foreign ministry and the French zonal administration, notably the longtime foreign minister, Georges Bidault and General Pierre Koenig, the commander of French forces in Germany. With the benefit of hindsight, Bidault admitted that he ceased believing in the viability of de Gaulle's policies long before he left office as foreign minister in 1948, but publicly Bidault and his party, the MRP (which called itself "the party that kept the faith") attempted to remain true to what they considered to be Gaullism.[18]

Contrary to the conclusions of some analysts,[19] the SFIO was neither uninterested in France's German policy nor willing to support the Gaullist line. In the cabinet the French Socialists developed their own German policy, one that differed significantly from that supported by the Gaullists and their allies. True, the SFIO's leaders did not speak with one voice on Germany. A minority group of hawks, whose ranks included Vincent Auriol, Jules Moch, and Olivier Lapie, argued that Germany needed to be subjected to a long period of military occupation and that a return of sovereignty to Germany lay far in the future. They also agreed with the Gaullists that France's economic recovery had to take precedence over Germany's; as Salomon Grumbach put it, "we have our [reparation] rights." However, even the Socialist hawks disagreed with the Gaullists in two fundamental respects: they did not accept the ethnocultural justifications of de Gaulle's German policy (Franco-Roman civilization vs. Teutonic barbarism), and they resolutely rejected the territorial dismemberment of Germany.[20]

Although the hawkish camp contained some prominent names, the majority of French Socialist leaders were doves when it came to Germany. Their acknowledged spokesman was Léon Blum; his ideas on the future of Germany had become accepted by most SFIO's leaders as early as the end of 1942. Like the hawks, the doves insisted on no territorial annexations, but in contrast to their comrades they placed their hopes for stability in Europe on a rapid revival of German democracy, and especially on the SPD's role in hastening this process. They looked forward to a relatively short period of military occupation, and expected to solve France's security and economic problems by integrating the new, democratic Germany into a united Europe. The Socialist doves claimed they were seizing the initiative for a new era of international cooperation instead of pursuing Bidault's and the Gaullists' short-sighted and anachronistic policy of national egotism.[21]

Until the departure of General de Gaulle the French Socialists had little leverage against their coalition partners, but after the General's resignation the power relationship within the cabinet shifted, and the SFIO ministers were able to exercise greater influence on the evolution of France's German policy. The two Socialist prime ministers who followed de Gaulle, Felix Gouin and Léon Blum, undertook what in retrospect turned out to be important new initiatives. Gouin publicly announced that it was not France's aim to dismember Germany, and, while he had to backtrack in the face of sharp criticism from the Communists and the MRP, his announcement revealed that the cabinet did not speak with one voice on the question of Germany's territorial future. Léon Blum, who headed an all-Socialist transition cabinet in late 1946 and early 1947, abandoned the link between the separation of the Rhineland from Germany and the conclusion of a Franco-British alliance upon which de Gaulle had insisted. By giving up this sine qua non of Gaullism, Blum effectively ended the dream of an "independent" state of *Rhénanie* on the left bank of the Rhine.[22]

Socialist hawks and doves were agreed in their criticism of the French zonal administration. Complaints that the military administration was cumbersome, staffed with too many prima donnas and ex-Vichyites, and acted too independently, ran like a red thread through the discussions of the SFIO's CD. The Socialists certainly had a point. The French administration in Germany was characterized by institutional complexity and the presence of a number of powerful personalities working at cross purposes. General Koenig, and his chief political advisor, J. Tarbé de Saint-Hardouin, were staunch Gaullists, as were the governors of the Länder. In contrast, Émile Laffon, the chief of administration, was reputed to be a Socialist sympathizer, but Koenig and Tarbé managed to deprive him of any real influence on major decisions, and Laffon resigned in November, 1947.[23]

In the final analysis, of course, Germany's fate would be decided by a process of compromise and conflict among the occupying powers. The road to the Federal Republic of Germany involved a number of concrete policy decisions, including the territorial dimensions of the new state, its political constitution, and its economic system. The Socialist contribution to deciding these issues was by no means unimportant. Fundamental to the debate was the question of Germany's national boundaries and internal territorial arrangements. The SPD's position on this issue was clear, if naive: Germany, with its 1937 boundaries intact, was to have a strong central government and weak states. The German Social Democrats were constantly worried about what they saw as Allied (especially French) encouragement of separatist movements, and deeply suspicious of Allied (and German) attempts to create strong Länder at the expense of the Reich.

Surprisingly, the Dutch government and the PvdA played an active part in setting a precedent for deciding Germany's future boundaries. Although the Dutch were not an occupying power, there was considerable sentiment especially in the ranks of the Catholic KVP for "rectifications" along the Dutch-German border that would have transferred substantial parts of western Germany to The Netherlands. There was public support for this as well, and the prime minister, Willem Drees, took an ambivalent position, arguing that some territorial changes were morally justified and in the interest of coalition harmony, the PvdA should side with the KVP on this issue. But Drees' own party was unwilling to follow him. Led by Koos Vorrink, the Dutch Socialists refused to endorse significant territorial transfers.[24]

While all SFIO leaders rejected Germany's dismemberment, at least some prominent Socialists were not opposed to "border corrections." Auriol was perhaps the most outspoken proponent of such measures, but most of the SFIO's leaders took their cue from Blum, who repeated the principles he had enunciated after the First World War: Germany should be left intact during the occupation regime, and, once a democratic German government had been installed, territorial changes should not be effected against the wishes of this democratically elected government. The SFIO accepted these principles, and vigorously opposed the French attempts to dismember Germany by Allied fiat, or efforts to accomplish the same goal by encouraging German separatist movements in the French zone of occupation.[25]

While the SPD gratefully registered the support of its sister parties on the question of Germany's dismemberment, the three parties were at odds over the issue of German federalism and the future of the Saar, an issue which Kurt Schumacher decided was the *Gretchenfrage* (critical question) of Franco-German relations. In retrospect the Saar's significance was vastly exaggerated, but for much of the decade the debate over the future of this territory not only soured relations between the SFIO and the SPD, but put obstacles in the path to European unification as well.

Both the German and the French Socialists insisted the economic resources of the Saar were necessary for their countries' national recovery, but for the moment the French had the upper hand. With the support of the SFIO, the French government at the end of 1946 established an economic union between the Saarland and France. The Gaullists, however, had ambitions that went far beyond economic control. With the tacit agreement of the United States and Great Britain, the French cabinet established a politically "autonomous" regime in the Saar, supervised by a French resident commissioner. This official, the fanatic Gaullist Gilbert Grandval, left no doubt that he saw the Saar as a permanent part of France's sphere of influence. Political parties which advocated an eventual reunion of the Saar with Germany were not permitted to be active. As a result the SPD in the Saar split, with most of its members joining a new party, the *Sozialdemokratische Partei Saar* (Social Democratic Party of the Saar [SDS]), which, like the Saarland Christian Democrats, accepted the Saar's status as an "autonomous" territory.

The SPD concentrated its attacks on the political aspects of France's Saar policy. Schumacher did not object to France and Germany jointly utilizing the economic resources of the Saar, but he insisted on seeing the Saar's political status from a highly nationalistic perspective, claiming that only full political reunion with Germany was acceptable and that France's policies were a form of disguised colonialism. The SPD's leader frequently drew an analogy between the Oder-Neisse line in the East and the enforced separation of the Saar from the rest of Germany in the West.[26]

The SFIO was divided on the Saar's political future. Most SFIO leaders, including Blum, Rosenfeld, Mollet, Philip, and Brutelle, advocated a return of the Saar to Germany, but a few favored either an autonomous Saarland, or the eventual Europeanization of the Saar. The SFIO's leaders attempted to strike a compromise among the various positions by proposing a resolution on the Saar which the CD passed in March, 1953. The document expressed the party's support for continued links among the German, French, and Saar economies, and expressed the hope that the Council of Europe would devise a means of consulting the people of the Saar on whether they wanted to return to Germany or become a European entity. The CD firmly rejected a political union between France and the Saar. At the same time the SFIO aligned itself with its German comrades on the question of the SDS. The French Socialists would not agree to SDS representation in the SI, and unlike the MRP, the SFIO refused to officially welcome SDS delegations visiting Paris.[27]

Although the SFIO attempted to appease the German Socialists on the Saar question, it was not enough for the SPD's leadership. The much vaunted bilateral cooperation between the two parties became a victim of Schumacher's intransigence on the Saar. The SPD leader rejected SFIO complaints about the stridently nationalistic tone of his utterances on the Saar, and when Fritz Erler scheduled joint appearances with André Philip in the Saar in early 1952, the *Büro* asked Erler to withdraw from the speaking tour because of Philip's outspoken criticism of Schumacher's position on the territory.[28]

Fortunately, Schumacher's death allowed less vociferous voices in Germany to be heard. This was certainly a fortuitous development, because in the meantime the Saar issue had increasingly embittered Franco-German relations. With the enthusiastic support of the SFIO, the French government turned to the Council of Europe to take up the issue, which brought a prominent Dutch Socialist into the limelight. The Council of Europe asked Baron van der Goes van Naters, the former leader of the PvdA's delegation in the Dutch parliament and a fervent proponent of European unification (he was, however, also a passionate cultural Francophile who made no secret of his dislike of most things German) to chair a commission that would submit a plan for the future of the Saar. Goes and his colleagues proposed that, after the people of the Saar had approved their new status in a plebiscite, the Saarland would become a mandate of the Council of Europe.[29]

Reaction to the Goes plan was mixed. While the German and French governments, as well as the SFIO, accepted the proposal, the SPD bitterly attacked the plan's substance and Goes' biases. Substantively the SPD objected both to the Europeanization of the Saar and the wording of the plebiscite questions, which left the voters only the choice of casting "yes" or "no" ballots on the Council of Europe's plan. The SPD insisted—unsuccessfully—on a third choice, the territory's return to Germany. The German party was successful, however, in obtaining permission for the pro-German parties to campaign before the plebiscite.[30]

The outcome of the plebiscite, which was held on 23 October 1955, was a surprise to most observers. Grandval had expected a sixty percent "yes" vote and the Bonn government, too, thought the Saar voters would endorse the Goes plan. The French foreign minister, Antoine Pinay, however, was more realistic; he expected a rejection of the Goes proposal. The actual result was a decisive majority for the "no" forces. With 96.6 percent of the eligible voters casting ballots, 67.7 percent voted against the Europeanization of the Saar. All concerned correctly interpreted the outcome as a vote for a return of the Saar to Germany; the pro-French government in the Saar accepted the result as a vote of no confidence and resigned immediately. The French cabinet also saw the handwriting on the wall, and, to their credit, the French Socialists were genuinely gracious in accepting the outcome of the plebiscite. Although the SFIO had endorsed the Goes plan, the party now advocated the return of the Saar to German control as quickly as possible. Only Grandval permitted himself a moment of fantasizing; for a few days he argued that in rejecting the Goes plan the voters of the Saar had expressed their support for closer association with France.[31]

The solution to the Saar question was a milestone in Franco-German relations, marking the end of the last territorial quarrel between the two countries. The Saar settlement also cleared the way for the European Economic Community. Successes in politics tend to have many parents, and the solution to the Saar problem is no exception. Konrad Adenauer and Robert Schuman are entitled to considerable credit, as is Goes, who succeeded in raising the issue above the narrow confines of national antagonisms. The three Socialist parties are often forgotten in the assignment of accolades. Despite their differences, the SPD and the SFIO consistently attempted to see the European and Franco-German bilateral aspects of the Saar question, while respecting each other's sensibilities as much as possible. Goes' role was made possible by the fervently pro-European attitude of the PvdA. And, finally, it should not be forgotten that the French prime minister in 1956 who handled the successful Franco-German negotiations on the modalities of returning the Saar to Germany, was Guy Mollet.

This final settlement of Germany's frontiers (as we now know, the Oder-Neisse boundary would also remain permanent) came at the end of the decade under discussion here. The German side of the Saar negotiations was now handled by a sovereign West German government, an entity whose existence few would have predicted ten years earlier. Political life in Germany reemerged in different forms and at various levels. The British and the Americans permitted political parties relatively soon after the end of the war, and with the economic merger of their zones into the Bizone they began the process of abandoning the extreme decentralization which had characterized all early occupation policies of the Western Allies. In contrast, the French wanted to let considerable time elapse before Germany would enter a new "political phase."

It required considerable pressure from the British and the Americans before France abandoned her go-it-alone policies in 1948. In return for British and American agreement to establish an international administration of the Ruhr area, France permitted its zone to join the Bizone. Under threat of losing its share of Marshall Plan aid, the French government also agreed to participate in drafting the London Accords, the guidelines for the establishment of a West German federal state. General de Gaulle and his loyal vassal in Germany, General Koenig, bitterly protested the cabinet's decisions, but their opposition was to no avail; the French National Assembly ratified the London Accords.

The position of the French Socialists in the whirlpool of contradictory French policies was ambivalent, but most of the SFIO leaders were optimistic about the future of Germany. They based their optimism primarily on the strength of the Social Democratic tradition in Germany. A strong SPD, in their opinion, was the best foundation for a strong German democracy. Moreover, the French Socialists did not want Germany treated as a pariah. Seeing isolation as a major breeding ground for renewed nationalism, the SFIO worked hard to revive political life in Germany, and helped their German comrades to reestablish the SPD. It came as no surprise, then, that the SFIO leaders (with some notable exceptions like Auriol and

Moch) were enthusiastic supporters of the London Accords and the subsequent establishment of the Federal Republic.[32]

In the immediate postwar era questions of economic restructuring and the problem of reparations seemed to be even more acute than political concerns. This, too, was an area of policymaking beset by glaring contradictions. It proved impossible to reconcile draining Germany's economic resources to aid the victims of Nazi aggression, with encouraging German economic revival so that the territory under occupation would not become a burden to the Allies or fall victim to Communism. As a result, the Americans and the British quickly opted for German recovery instead of exploitation and reparations, while the French attempted to put their priorities on exploiting Germany's economic resources to benefit France's recovery. Again it required American pressure to effect a change in French policy. France desperately needed American credits (Blum and Jean Monnet negotiated the first of these in 1946), which would not be forthcoming if France rejected the basic contours of American economic policies in Germany.[33]

The Western Allies disagreed not only about the priority of reparations, but also about the long-range restructuring of the German economy. The Americans favored free enterprise, but wanted to dismantle Germany's traditional trusts and cartels; the British Labour government envisioned public ownership of Germany's large-scale industrial enterprises; and the French were torn between insisting upon an extreme decentralization of the German economy, and the establishment of internationally supervised centralized structures.

The SFIO leaders were also split on specific aspects of the Allies' economic policies, but consistently adhered to two principles. One was that there had to be a correlation between political and economic goals. André Philip recognized as early as 1946 that the large-scale dismantling of German industrial facilities conducted by the French might produce short-term economic benefits for France (although he doubted it), but would certainly arouse deep German resentment and lay the basis for future political instability.[34] In line with this principle, while the French Socialists advocated international control of the economic structure of the Ruhr area, they did not oppose continued German political control of this industrial heartland. The SFIO's second principle of economic policy concerned the participation of German working-class organizations in the decision-making process. The French Socialists were adamant that the German labor unions had to be involved in whatever economic policy decisions were made for, and in, Germany. The leitmotiv of the French Socialists' political goals, then, was the reintegration of Germany into the family of nations. The SFIO was prepared to shoulder the burden of the *mission civilisatrice* (civilizing mission) of French Democratic Socialism and Republicanism to guide the Germans back into the European family.[35]

Social Democracy Between and East and West

No political group was more disappointed by the end of the wartime alliance among the Big Four and the outbreak of the Cold War than Europe's Socialists. They had come out of the war hopeful that the era of big power confrontations was over, and that a socialist Europe could play a unique role as partner of both the Americans and the Soviets.

Nevertheless, when it became clear that western Europe had to choose between the Cold War protagonists, for most Socialists the choice was not difficult. Although the United States personified the capitalist system, which the Social Democrats hoped to replace with a form of Democratic Socialism, America also represented the even more essential virtues of political democracy and individual freedom. West European Socialists had long distrusted Stalinist Russia, and the series of postwar Soviet moves that culminated in the cold coup in Czechoslovakia and the Berlin blockade simply confirmed for them that Soviet Communism was not only dictatorial but expansionist as well.

For this reason virtually all Socialists welcomed the American commitment to strengthen and defend western Europe against Soviet subversion and aggression. This was true even for France's Socialists, for whom the concept of a Socialist Europe as a Third Force between Soviet Communism and American capitalism at one point had held considerable appeal. The land mass stretching from Poland to Portugal would, they hoped, be committed to "neither capitalism nor Communism." Nevertheless, the SFIO's transition to "Atlanticism" was remarkably quick and smooth. Some leaders, like Vincent Auriol, thought France was falling rather too hastily into the American arms, but virtually all SFIO leaders, including both Blum and Mollet, had no difficulty accepting the United States as leading the defense of the West against Soviet aggression. The party enthusiastically endorsed the Marshall Plan, although the motives for this decision varied. Some French Socialists saw the United States initiative as welcome evidence of American commitment to Europe, and virtually all SFIO

leaders greeted the American insistence on international cooperation in administering the aid package as a catalyst for the unification of Europe. In addition, the SFIO, like the German SPD, at least
initially convinced itself that the American aid would not interfere
with building Democratic Socialism in Europe. Some even argued
Roosevelt's New Deal was already an embryonic form of Democratic Socialism under another name. Relatively few leaders warned
that gifts usually came with strings attached, and that the Marshall
Plan aid would inevitably mean that the United States would
determine the contours of western Europe's economic life.[36]

The military dimension of Atlanticism initially evoked a less
united and positive response. The SFIO's left wing was uneasy
about both the Truman Doctrine and the North Atlantic Treaty
Organization (NATO). Daniel Mayer, for example, feared a party
split over the issue. The spectrum of opinion on the Atlantic Pact
was indeed wide. Marcel Pivert argued against any military alliance between western Europe and the United States because he
was convinced this would only deepen the Cold War divisions.
On the other side, Léon Boutbien insisted only the American military umbrella could save western civilization. Contrary to expectations, however, the party decided the issue with surprising
solidarity. Against the backdrop of Soviet moves in Czechoslovakia and Berlin, which raised the specter of the Red Army marching
into western Europe, the CD voted to support NATO by a lopsided majority of 18:2. Only Marcel Pivert and Albert Gazier continued to oppose the pact.[37]

The SPD's path to the Western Alliance was more convoluted.
To be sure, the SPD was never neutral in the Cold War. Fear of
Soviet expansion and identification with the political and cultural
values of the West integrated the SPD into the Western Alliance
even before that term had been coined. But the SPD also insisted
that cementing West Germany into the Western Alliance would
make reunification, the party's absolute priority, more difficult. As
long as the West was unwilling to take military action to drive the
Soviet Union from German soil (something no Allied statesman
was prepared to do), Germany should take no action that would
bind the country irrevocably to the Western Alliance.[38]

The traditionally Europe-oriented SPD also recognized rather
late—certainly much later than the party's Christian Democratic
rivals—that the Americans were the key players in the developing Cold War. The *Büro Schumacher* initially looked upon the
British Labour government as its natural ally, failing to appreci-
ate that the British decided rather early to let the Americans take

the lead. Eventually most SPD spokesmen accepted the American predominance, although in Southwestern Germany some prominent regional leaders, such as Erwin Schöttle, continued to see the Franco-German relationship as the key to Germany's future. In a conversation with the French High Commissioner, François-Poncet, Schöttle criticized Konrad Adenauer's "blind following" of the Americans, and insisted there would be no solution to the German question "without France, but especially ... against France!"[39]

When the party did acknowledge the predominant role of the United States, it still saddled itself with a number of illusions about America and American policies. Like many European Socialists, Schumacher admired Roosevelt's New Deal, considering it a sort of prototype of Democratic Socialism as he envisioned it, but the party leader also felt that John Foster Dulles' announced aim of "rolling-back" Communism in Europe meant that the Americans would take concrete steps to help the SPD achieve its goal of a reunified Germany with its 1937 borders intact. When it became clear that the Americans had no intention of using military force to push the Soviets out of the country, relations between the German Social Democrats and the Americans soured. Personal animosities between Kurt Schumacher and the United States commander in Germany, General Lucius Clay, as well as Secretary of State Dean Acheson, only reinforced the disagreements on policy issues.[40]

While the SPD and the Americans were (and would remain for some time) divided on the big questions of Germany's future, they were remarkably close on a number of important short-term—especially economic—decisions. Despite grumblings among some militants that a dollar-backed currency would present a barrier to the implementation of socialism, most party members and virtually all leaders welcomed the currency reform initiated by the United States that established the Deutsche Mark in the Bizone. A positive decision on the Marshall Plan was similarly quick in coming. Although, much like their French comrades, the German Social Democrats deluded themselves that the American aid package came with no strings attached, they also recognized the concrete economic advantages which the Marshall Plan would bring for the destitute German economy, including the integration of the western zones into a revitalized international economic system. Scholars sympathetic to the party later criticized that the ERP was a neo-imperialistic venture, but this criticism did not reflect the views of contemporary party leaders.[41]

The era of cooperation between the SPD and the western powers came to an abrupt end with the series of treaties (the Ruhr Statute, the General Treaty, the Schuman Plan, the EDC, and NATO) that paved the way for the Federal Republic's economic, political, and military integration into the Western Alliance. What the Adenauer government saw as important steps for increasing West German sovereignty, accelerating West European unification, and establishing a close partnership between the Federal Republic, France, and the United States, Kurt Schumacher chose to interpret as a betrayal of German interests. Using language that reminded contemporary observers of the "stab in the back" campaign of the Weimar era (symptomatic was another outburst that Adenauer was "the chancellor of the Allies"[42]), the SPD's leader attacked each new pact and the Adenauer government in increasingly vehement terms.

A number of factors came together to lead the SPD—or, more, precisely Schumacher—to take this obstinate stand. It was consistent with Schumacher's concept of intransigent opposition to everything the Christian Democrats proposed. The SPD's chairman was convinced the Western Allies, and especially the Americans, were not impartial bystanders, but working hand in glove with Adenauer to give the Christian Democrats an edge in domestic politics. During the debate on the EDC Schumacher was also deathly ill and desperately determined to retain control of the party line. Finally, 1951 and 1952 were the time of the "Stalin notes" which briefly raised hopes that the Soviets would permit free, all-German elections and subsequently the country's reunification.[43]

The price of intransigent opposition was high: electoral setback at home and isolation abroad. This became especially apparent during the debate on West Germany's remilitarization. The issue was not a West German army as such: although the SPD had always had a strong pacifist wing, the leadership, and particularly Kurt Schumacher himself, rejected pacifism and endorsed the need for national defense. But it had to be on the party's own terms. The German armed forces were to be under the control of a sovereign German government. As long as the Western Allies refused to agree to this condition, the SPD insisted a reunified Germany should be guaranteed by an arrangement among the Four Great Powers.

This position enabled the party to take a consistent stand against the proposals for integrating West Germany's military into supranational western treaty systems, but an increasing number of critics in the SPD recognized that the party's position was unrealistic and politically counterproductive. Leaders like Willy Brandt, Erwin Schöttle, and Carlo Schmid pointed out that the party's constant *nein sagen* was alienating the SPD from the German voters, the Western Allies, and its West European sister parties, while—falsely—associating it with the Communists and their fellow-travelers. For the moment, however, the critics' success was severely circumscribed. With a last burst of energy Schumacher was able to commit the party to continue intransigent opposition for several years after his death.[44]

Integration into the Western Alliance did not present problems for the PvdA. Although, like the SPD, the old SDAP had had a strong pacifist wing and the Dutch Socialists had long supported the country's neutrality in international affairs, after the Second World War the PvdA played a major role in helping to integrate The Netherlands into the western camp. Of the three parties, the PvdA was by far the most enthusiastic westernizer. The party's consistent foreign policy goals were to align Holland and the party with the Western Allies, and to assure that West Germany was also firmly embedded in this alliance structure. The PvdA welcomed the Marshall Plan; virtually none of the party's leaders expressed doubts about the American aid package. The PvdA also welcomed Dutch membership in NATO and the presence of American troops in Europe. In fact, the Dutch Socialists' support of western military and political integration was so straightforward, that the SPD criticized its sister party for the PvdA's extreme pro-American attitude.[45]

The counterpart of the Socialists' relations with the West was the parties' attitude toward the Communists in their own countries and in the Soviet bloc. The rapid emergence of the Cold War tends to obscure that immediately after the war, the Soviet Union and the West European Communist parties were not yet the embodiment of all that Social Democracy opposed. Although the image of the Soviet Union had been severely tarnished by the experience of Stalinism and especially the purges in the 1930s, many Socialists readily acknowledged the Soviet Union's heroic role in the struggle against Nazism, and the leading part the Communists had played in the West European resistance movements. From this perspective it is not surprising that many French Socialists welcomed the 1944 Friendship Treaty between France and the Soviet Union no less enthusiastically than the French Communists.

Within months after the end of the Second World War mounting antagonisms between the United States and the Soviet Union destroyed the illusion of Four Power cooperation, and the Soviets lost no time in making it clear that they had no interest in any European Third Force. In fact, the Soviet press (and the organs of the PCF) singled out Léon Blum for particularly venomous attacks, denouncing the Socialist leader as a lackey of American capitalism.[46]

The Socialists' high expectations for the Moscow foreign ministers' conference in the spring of 1947 (with slight exaggeration Grumbach called it, "the most important [meeting] for centuries") were severely disappointed. Still, for a brief moment many European Socialists professed to see another ray of hope: ironically, it was the Marshall Plan. Since the offer of American aid was extended to all European countries, including the Soviet Union and its satellites, and the aid package ostensibly had no political strings attached to it, surely here was a chance for Europe to go its own Democratic Socialist way. Understandably, the Social Democrats who held on to this illusion were shocked when the Soviet Union not only refused the aid for itself, but forced its satellites to reject it as well. Even Léon Blum, hardly a starry-eyed and naive politician, wrote that he simply could not believe that the Soviet Union would reject Marshall Plan aid.

Despair followed disillusionment. Europe's Social Democrats watched helplessly as the Soviet Union initiated a series of aggressive moves designed to solidify her hold over eastern Europe. The Prague coup in February, 1948 (which Vincent Auriol compared to the Nazi takeover of Czechoslovakia in March, 1939), the Berlin Blockade only a few months later, and the beginnings of the purges of "native" Communist leaders in eastern Europe quickly convinced the Socialists not only that the Soviet Union was intent upon territorial aggression, but that it had replaced Germany as the primary danger to stability on the European Continent. For most Socialists this view of the Soviet Union persisted even after Stalin's successors introduced some modest liberalization measures. Only a few Social Democrats felt the Soviet Union under Khrushchev was a fundamentally different country, and that the western European Social Democrats should make a renewed effort to establish better relations with the Soviet Union.[47]

The SFIO was particularly disappointed by the changing East-West relations. During the war the French Socialists had predicated their foreign policy on the continuation of the anti-Hitler alliance and their domestic program on cooperation with the French Communists. By 1948, however, the SFIO had abandoned any hopes for improved relations with the Soviet Union under Stalin. There was a brief glimmer of hope for detente after Stalin's death, but the brutal suppression of the East German revolt in June, 1953, quickly dampened any feelings of optimism.[48]

In the immediate aftermath of the war some SPD leaders—such as Carlo Schmid and Wilhelm Kaisen—briefly hoped the Third Force concept might become reality. There was also a very small group of neutralists in the party who argued that good relations with the Soviet Union was the price Germany had to pay for achieving a reunited, demilitarized, and Socialist country. But for Kurt Schumacher and most of the SPD leaders a good relationship to the Soviets and the German Communists was an oxymoron. The Soviet Union and its satellites constituted an evil empire whose values were antithetical to true Socialism. Ernst Reuter, the mayor of West Berlin, insisted as early as 1946 that the Continent was already divided and that West Germany and the SPD had no choice but to take their stand with the West. The Third Force proponents quickly agreed, while the small band of neutralists, unable to gain a foothold in the party, either abandoned their position or drifted off to become Communist fellow travelers. By 1948 the SPD was firmly committed to a policy of opposition to the Soviet Union and—especially—its East German satellite.[49]

The pattern of consistent animosity was briefly interrupted by the episode of the so-called Stalin Notes in 1951 and 1952. This initiative by the Soviet Union and the East German regime, which remains the subject of much scholarly controversy, seemed to couple the promise of free elections and German reunification with the permanent demilitarization of the country. Since the Soviet proposal came out during the Korean War and in the midst of the debate over the European Defense Community, the West German and American governments decided that the Stalin notes were a propaganda ploy designed to achieve recognition for the East German regime while preventing West Germany's military and political union with western Europe. They rejected the Soviet initiative out of hand.[50]

The SPD's response was more complicated. The Social Democratic leaders trusted the Soviet Union no more than Konrad Adenauer did, and they were even more suspicious of the East German regime. At the same time national reunification remained the SPD's absolute priority. After a period of "embarrassed silence" the party's official reaction to the Stalin notes was to urge the Adenauer government and the Western Allies to take the Soviet initiative at face value, and make every effort to discover the Communists' true intentions.

This public response hid deep divisions within the party. A sizable portion of the leadership clearly felt that Stalin's offer represented a genuine chance for reunification, as well as an opportunity for embarrassing the Adenauer government. Others were not far from the Christian Democrats' position that Stalin's offer was a sham. The formulation bridging the opposing points of view was found by Herbert Wehner, who insisted that while the party should demand a fuller exploration of the Stalin notes, it should also make sure that genuine free elections in all of Germany were a sine qua non of any reunification process. He knew, of course, that this was the Achilles heel of the Soviet offer, since such elections would undoubtedly mean the end of the East German Communist regime. In practice, while Wehner was able at once to satisfy both the optimists and the pessimists in the party, he actually moved the SPD closer to the American position.[51]

As was true for the SFIO, there were at least some in the SPD who held out hope for improved relations with the Soviet Union after Stalin's death. Never more than a small minority in the party, these elements argued that the new Soviet leaders had inaugurated a genuine revolution in the Soviet Union, and that they were more interested in good relations with a reunified, but neutral Germany than in keeping control of the GDR. The optimists' illusions were quickly dashed. The brutal suppression of the 1953 uprisings in East Germany demonstrated that the Soviet Union was determined to keep the Communists in power in East Germany, and more direct confirmation of the Soviets' long-range aims was forthcoming. Carlo Schmid was a member of the parliamentary delegation which accompanied Konrad Adenauer to Moscow in 1955, when the chancellor negotiated both the establishment of diplomatic relations between the Soviet Union and the Federal Republic and the return of the German prisoners of war still held by the Soviets. In the course of the negotiations the new Soviet leadership made it unequivocally clear that, as far as the Soviet Union was concerned, German reunification was not an item on the international relations agenda.[52]

A controversy unique to the SPD was the issue of contacts between the SPD and the ruling party in East Germany. The SED repeatedly attempted to inaugurate official party-to-party dealings and some Social Democratic leaders, including Herbert Wehner, were willing to explore these overtures. ("There are patriots in the GDR as well," argued Wehner.) Most SPD leaders, however, rejected autonomous contacts with the SED, agreeing with the Adenauer government, that the GDR and its ruling party had no standing of their own, but existed only as puppets of the Soviet Union. Reunification, they insisted, could come only by an agreement of the Four Powers, not as a result of negotiations between the two German states or the political parties.[53]

The PvdA's attitude toward the Soviet Union and its satellites was consistent and unwavering. The Dutch Socialists had a long tradition of anti-Communism, and even the Dutch Communists' role during the Resistance did little to dispel the distrust of the Soviet Union or the CPN. The PvdA and the Dutch labor unions had been instrumental in persuading the International Association of Labor Unions to expel from the organization the Communist-controlled labor unions in the Soviet satellites. There was a small, but vocal minority in the PvdA which supported the Third Force concept, but the party leadership acted swiftly to contain this challenge. The executive committee did not permit the supporters of the Third Force to establish an organizational foothold in the party, and in 1952 the PvdA officially condemned the Third Force concept as contrary to the party program.[54]

The Dutch Socialists were equally clear about their position on the Stalin Notes. The PvdA quickly threw its support behind the United States and the Adenauer government. According to the Dutch party the Soviet initiative had no other aim than to prevent West Germany's integration into the Western Alliance. From this perspective it was only logical that the PvdA had little sympathy for either the SPD's equivocal attitude or its absolute prioritization of national reunification. As far as the Dutch Socialists were concerned, if there was to be a reunified Germany, it had to be firmly anchored in the Western Alliance.[55]

In essence, then, the three Social Democratic parties held similar views on the Soviet Union and international Communism. Neutralist or Third Force sentiments had for all practical purposes disappeared by the middle of 1948. Thereafter all three parties saw the Soviet Union and its Communist allies as the primary enemy of both democracy and Social Democracy. Neither Stalin's rather clumsy charm offensive nor the considerably more subtle efforts by his successors were able to lure western Europe's Social Democrats away from their identification with western values and the Western Alliance.

Social Democracy and European Unity: The Political Dimension

European unification was one foreign policy aim on which all Socialists agreed. During the war an endless stream of newspaper articles and position papers articulated the Social Democrats' determination that after the defeat of the Nazis, Europe must not again become a collection of warring nation states. Instead, the Continent was to be reconstructed as a federal entity with supra-national institutions overseeing the construction of Democratic Socialism in Europe. Yet, as we know, the actual construction of European unity was to be largely the work of bourgeois politicians. There were exceptions, of course—Guy Mollet was justifiably proud that he was often called one of the fathers of Europe—but for the most part the unification of Europe is associated with men like Adenauer, Schuman, and Monnet—none of them Social Democrats. This is actually surprising, since, as we shall see, the three parties' ideas on European unification were not very different from the plans which their bourgeois rivals advanced.

The Socialists' dilemma lay in their expectation that they would be able to combine goals which, in practice, turned out to be incompatible: the new Europe was to be unified, Social Democratic, and vast, stretching from Poland to the Pyrenees. (Spain and Portugal were deliberately excluded from the Socialists' plans since they were regarded as Fascist states whose political systems were incompatible with Social Democracy.) The Cold War forced the Socialists to lower their sights to western Europe, but even then their geographic vision remained too large. Virtually every West European Socialist accepted as axiomatic that both Great Britain and the Scandinavian countries would be part of the united western Europe, and they were especially disappointed that not only the Conservatives, but the British Labour Party also decided to remain aloof from Continental affairs. And no one was more saddened than Guy Mollet, who worked tirelessly well into the 1950s to entice Labour to change its mind. Wilfried Loth has noted that the French Socialists exerted a "virtually desperate energy" on this project.[56]

Although some Socialists recognized early that in view of La-bour's attitude there was no alternative to the "Europe of the Six," most Social Democrats were reluctant to lower their sights. In 1950 André Philip, frustrated by the Labour Party's unwillingness to support the European unity movement, proclaimed that he was willing to work with those who wanted a united Europe and ignore those who did not. His fellow CD members immediately denounced their iconoclastic comrade for abandoning what they claimed was the Socialists' longstanding conviction that a united Europe had to include Great Britain.[57]

While the Socialists had considerable difficulty with the geo-graphic dimensions of a unified Europe, they readily agreed on the political and economic goals. The watchwords were political democracy and a socialist economy. Social Democrats repeatedly voiced their fears of a Europe dominated by Catholics and Conservatives. Since a Socialist Europe should be more than a confederation of sovereign states, Social Democrats consistently demanded the establishment of truly supranational institutions that would exercise many of the powers previously reserved to the nation states.[58]

Virtually all Socialist leaders were enthusiastic Europeanists (the rank-and-file members were decidedly more lukewarm, but they allowed themselves to be pulled along by the emotions of their leaders), but there were important differences among the three parties in motivations and priorities. The SFIO's enthusiasm for a united Europe can be traced back to the 1920s, and specifically to the ideas of Léon Blum. The Socialist leader had already proclaimed after the First World War that only a supranational Europe could overcome the national divisions which had plagued Europe throughout much of its history: the experiences of the Second World War only strengthened his convictions. Not all of his comrades shared these sentiments, but most did, and by war's end the SFIO proudly claimed that not only did it have genuine European credentials, but it was also the only French party actually willing to yield national sovereignty in favor of European institutions.[59]

While all of the SFIO's leaders assigned high priority to supranationality in the new Europe, they were sharply divided on a number of other aspects of the unification process. One group insisted that the SFIO should work only for projects that advanced a Socialist Europe, while others believed functional agreements—like the Schuman Plan and the EDC—were important steps on the way to realizing the goal of a Social Democratic European society, even if the projects as such had no immediate socialist dimensions. The disagreement over tactics had organizational implications as well. Some French Socialists insisted that the party should work with all democratic organizations that favored a united Europe. Initially Mollet and his supporters disagreed and wanted to limit the SFIO's activities to cooperation with other Socialist groups. However, by the mid-1950s the integrationists had won out, and the SFIO became an enthusiastic institutional member of the UEM and Jean Monnet's multipartisan Action Committee for Europe.[60]

The German Social Democrats' European policy in the first decade after the war was beset by contradictions. As a matter of principle, no party was more enthusiastic about European unity or more willing to yield national sovereignty to supranational institutions. One SPD leader even announced that the SPD would be happy to become the SPE once the Socialist Europe had been created.[61] However, there remained the matter of timing and practice. The SPD insisted that only after Germany had been reunited and accepted as a fully sovereign and equal partner would the country of its own free will enter into the European compact. The party was not willing to associate itself with the vision for European unity espoused by Adenauer, de Gasperi, and Schuman, since, according to the SPD, the implementation of their plans was designed to prevent the emergence of a true Socialist Europe.[62]

Criticism of the SPD's obstinate stand came not only from the Christian Democrats, but also from within the party and from its sister organizations in the other European countries. The critics pointed out that the SPD's vision of a united Socialist Europe was becoming increasingly unrealistic and was driving the party into isolation and ineffectiveness. Instead of holding out for the unattainable the party should join multipartisan movements for European unity and work toward the two-tiered goal of unity first and Social Democracy later. Willy Brandt would later recall bitterly that Schumacher "lacked sufficient understanding of Europe and the world."[63]

The divergence between theoretical purity and practical possibility (a longstanding tradition in the SPD) became glaringly apparent in the battle between the old guard and its critics over the establishment of the embryonic European parliament, the Council of Europe. In principle, all factions in the party welcomed a European parliament, but they were sharply divided on this specific deliberative body. The reformers, who were led by the mayors of Bremen and Hamburg, Wilhelm Kaisen and Max Brauer, welcomed the Council as a forum in which the party could join forces with other democratic groups to advance the cause of European political unification. Working within the Council, they noted, would in no way prevent the Social Democrats from attempting to further their specifically socialist agenda for the new Europe. In sharp contrast, Schumacher and his allies argued that the Council of Europe would do nothing except create the "Catholic, capitalist, and cartel-dominated" Europe of Konrad Adenauer's and Robert Schuman's design. For this reason the SPD should reject the Council's establishment, and refuse to participate in its work if it were established.[64]

For the moment Schumacher and his allies triumphed. By a large majority (350:11) the party's annual congress, held in Hamburg in May, 1950, passed a resolution condemning the Council in its proposed form. For good measure the party leader also insisted that Kaisen not be reelected to the SPD's executive committee.[65] This was an empty victory, because Schumacher's wrath did not weaken the reformers. Secure in their Land basis, both Kaisen and Brauer retained their influence; Kaisen was reelected to the *Parteivorstand* at the next congress. The SPD's stand on the Council of Europe was also the swansong for Schumacher's obstinacy on the organizational aspects of European political unification. The SPD did not boycott the Council of Europe after its establishment. Contrary to his initial position, Schumacher himself urged the SPD delegates selected by the Bundestag (at this time the members of the Council of Europe were selected by the national parliaments) to go to Strasbourg. Beginning with the quasi-parliament's initial meeting, the German Social Democratic delegates participated fully and enthusiastically in the Council's deliberations.[66]

The Dutch Socialists also exhibited a somewhat schizophrenic attitude toward European unification. At first glance the PvdA and its leaders were in the forefront of the unity movement in both theory and practice. Like the SFIO, the PvdA expressed its willingness to yield national sovereignty in favor of European institutions, and Dutch Socialists had fewer qualms about cooperating with multipartisan organizations than their comrades in Germany and France. Alfred Mozer, the party's international secretary, traveled tirelessly around Europe under a variety of sponsorships promoting the unity movement. Moreover, important PvdA leaders held long-term responsible positions in the European supranational institutions once they were established. As we saw, van der Goes van Naters was instrumental in designing the Council of Europe's plan for the Europeanization of the Saar, and another PvdA leader, Sicco Mansholt, served for many years as commissioner for agriculture in the Common Market.[67]

However, there were also counteractive tendencies toward skepticism and hesitation. As was true for the SFIO, the PvdA's Euro-enthusiasm had little vertical impact; the party's rank-and-file members were far less interested in European unification than their leaders. But a minority of leaders had doubts as well. Some feared that Continental European unity would take the place of trans-Atlantic cooperation, causing the specter of a "little Europe" dominated by Germany. Here the Dutch Socialists did not find the SPD's attitude reassuring, and they repeatedly criticized the German Socialists' nationalistic stand as contrary to true socialist principles. Others, including the party's most popular politician, Willem Drees, were concerned about the unknown financial consequences of European unification. Nevertheless, the skeptics always remained a minority, and most PvdA leaders joined their comrades in the other parties in supporting the European unification process, with some even demanding the merger of the West European Socialist parties into a single Progressive European Party. By the mid-1950s the Dutch Socialists, rather than the bourgeois parties, were leading the organizational drive for European unification.[68]

Social Democracy and Military Cooperation

The prospect of supranational military cooperation caught Europe's Socialists in a serious dilemma. Traditionally suspicious of military establishments, they almost instinctively rejected military solutions to societal problems. At the same time, they confronted the reality of the Cold War and American pressure for a greater West European military effort to counter the threat of Soviet aggression. With the outbreak of the Korean War the stakes became even higher. The Americans added the demand for a West German military contribution to the defense of the West, raising the specter of a new German army, a prospect that before 1950 had not even been seriously considered by Europe's Socialists.

The three parties' answers to the dilemma differed widely. The SPD appeared at first glance to be closest to the American position. As we saw, the party did not reject a German army as such, demanding only that the German armed forces had to be the national army of a fully sovereign Germany.[69] The PvdA, while hardly enthusiastic about a new *Wehrmacht*, did not raise objections as long as the German armed forces were placed under the American military umbrella.[70] In principle the SFIO's position was clear and unequivocal: the French Socialists were opposed to a German army in any form. With few exceptions—André Philip was one— the SFIO leaders argued new German armed forces so soon after the war would be controlled by the wrong people and used for the wrong purposes. Even the SPD was no help in this instance. Citing some of Schumacher's more strident speeches, Mollet feared that any new German army would be used not to defend western Europe, but to reunite Germany by military force.[71]

The Socialists might be concerned about the dangers of new German armed forces, but there remained the reality of American pressure to do something fast. The solution seemed to be the European Defense Community (EDC). This proposal was the brainchild of the French defense minister and Radical politician, René Pleven, although almost simultaneously Philip and, ironically, Winston Churchill presented similar ideas. Under Pleven's proposal the member nations of the EDC would transfer all or a portion of their military forces to a joint European command; all of West Germany's new military establishment would be fully integrated into the EDC. Pleven was particularly determined to prevent the reestablishment of a German general staff, because it was especially this institution that instantly evoked fears of renewed German militarism among the country's neighbors. Instead, the EDC would have a general staff composed of officers from all member countries. Pleven also fervently hoped for British membership in the EDC, but such hopes were again dashed when Great Britain still decided to stay out of Continental affairs. Membership in the EDC was limited to the six core nations.[72]

From its inception the EDC aroused political passions. For more than two years supporters and opponents in the intended member countries battled each other in the press and in parliament. Emotions and personal animosities ran high, and ideological affinities counted for little in the debate. The Socialist International and the Socialist parties of the Six tried valiantly, but unsuccessfully, to arrive at a common response to the EDC. As Erwin Schöttle, one of the SPD's leaders in Württemberg, put it, "sometimes we have to recognize that other parties reach other conclusions."[73]

Throughout the debate, which continued undiminished until the French National Assembly voted against ratification (or, more precisely, tabled a motion to ratify the draft treaty) in August, 1954, the SPD's official position remained consistent: The EDC was not acceptable. As far as Kurt Schumacher and his close associates were concerned, the EDC limited German sovereignty, did not commit the West to a forward defense strategy, and solidified the division of Germany by creating yet another supra-national structure that bound West Germany to the confines of *Kleineuropa*. And if that were not enough, the German Social Democrats once again raised the Saar question, claiming that, since the EDC also treated the Saarland as an entity separate from Germany, creation of the EDC would seal the fate of the Saar as a French protectorate. As an alternative to the EDC the SPD proposed "collective security in a larger context," although the party did not indicate how that was to be achieved.[74]

The SPD's stand on the EDC fit in well with the party's overall strategy of intransigent opposition against Adenauer and the CDU, but Schumacher and his allies were also convinced that opposition to the EDC would be popular with the voters. Consequently, the party and especially Schumacher himself mounted a massive campaign to embarrass the Adenauer government and win the battle of public opinion. Schumacher gave full vent to his considerable demagogic talents, asserting that the EDC would "put German youth at the disposal of Allied generals." The party's executive also decided to thrust the young Federal Republic into its first constitutional crisis over the EDC. The SPD brought suit against the EDC proposal in Germany's Constitutional Court, claiming the treaties needed to be ratified in the Bundestag by a two-thirds majority, not a simple plurality, because the terms of the agreements changed the Basic Law's provisions against a military establishment in West Germany.[75]

The party's campaign against the EDC polarized the German political scene, but it neither derailed the ratification process in West Germany, nor did it bring the party the expected political rewards. The federal elections of 1953 and 1957 demonstrated that most West German voters did not see defeating the EDC as an issue of vital concern. At the same time, as we saw, the campaign brought the Social Democrats several unwanted allies, including the East and West German Communists and the pacifist *Ohne mich* (Count Me Out) movement. On the international scene the results of the SPD's staunch opposition were at best mixed. True, the party accomplished its larger goal when the French parliament rejected the treaty, but the SPD's nationalistic rhetoric against the EDC also aroused deep resentments and disappointment among its sister parties. The German Social Democrats had reinforced their image as unreliable supporters of a united Europe.[76]

For this reason, some party leaders within the party regarded the entire campaign as counter-productive. Their efforts had little immediate effect on the party's official position, but from a larger perspective this most recent failed campaign of intransigent opposition increased the old guard's defensiveness. It was not altogether surprising, then, that the SPD's reaction to the EDC's alternative, West German membership in NATO, was far more moderate. The SPD, now under the leadership of Erich Ollenhauer, continued to reject the terms of West German rearmament, but its opposition was remarkably low key. The SPD acknowledged that ratification of the Paris Accords (which specified the terms of German membership in NATO) was a foregone conclusion and turned its attention instead to parliamentary control of the new Bundeswehr.[77]

In contrast to the SPD's convoluted arguments and counter-productive stand, the PvdA seemed to have no hesitation in endorsing the EDC. In fact, one commentator noted that there was "deadly unanimity" in the party, but that was an overstatement. The PvdA's left-wing *tendance*, the SDC, which consistently advocated a neutralist foreign policy for The Netherlands, thought the EDC would unnecessarily provoke the Soviets. Two members of the PB, including a former prime minister, Schermerhorn, did not go this far, but they, too, feared a further acceleration of the Cold War. Drees was also skeptical of the military proposals, objecting on financial grounds and claiming—tongue-in-cheek—that as part of the EDC the Dutch military would demand fancy uniforms like the Italian *carabinieri*.[78]

Still, except for the vocal opposition of the SDC, all of these misgivings were expressed behind closed doors. Drees' skepticism in particular, which might have influenced the party's stand, remained muted. The prime minister's first priority was always to preserve the government coalition, and he knew that the bourgeois parties, and especially the Liberal foreign minister, Dirk Stikker, enthusiastically supported the EDC. Moreover, the skeptics were at all times a small minority within the party. As a result, the Dutch Social Democrats were severely disappointed when the French parliament defeated the EDC, although they also readily accepted the alternative proposal of West German membership in NATO.

Paradoxically, the party that was most closely involved with the inception of the EDC was to have the most difficulty with it. The French Socialists were members of the government coalition that had advanced the EDC proposal, but the subsequent debate on the EDC was to become a dramatic and wrenching experience for the SFIO. With the benefit of hindsight this is not altogether surprising. The question of German rearmament only five years after the war raised profound fears among the French, Socialists included, especially when it became clear that Great Britain would not join the EDC and provide an additional counterweight to the Germans. There was also the persistent problem of French nationalism, as expressed by the Alsatian leader Marcel Naegelen, who objected to the EDC because for him there could be no France without a national French army. Additional complications arose from shifts in France's domestic political alignments during the course of the debate on the EDC. The SFIO was not a member of the cabinet when the debate over the EDC reached its highest intensity, and the temptation to use opposition to the EDC against the government was great.[79]

This was the background to what became the most intensely fought controversy in the SFIO since the party's division into munichois and anti-munichois in the 1930s. In the course of the EDC's long incubation period from proposal to defeat, the SFIO's rank-and-file as well as its leaders became deeply divided on virtually all aspects of the EDC, including whether they should hide their intraparty fissures from public view. The issue also made for strange bedfellows and shifts in political alliances. The leader of the powerful Bouches du Rhône federation and mayor of Marseille, Gaston Defferre, who was usually a vocal critic of Guy Mollet, became temporarily reconciled with the secretary general because both were fervent *Cédistes*. (In France the EDC was known under the acronym CED.) On the other hand, many SFIO members of parliament refused to vote for Marcel Naegelen as the Socialist candidate for president of the Republic in December, 1953 because Naegelen was a passionate anti-Cédiste.

The party's deep schism was unexpected when the EDC was first proposed. The CD's initial reaction was simply to reject the EDC; Mollet even announced he would resign as general secretary if the party were to support the European army. But then political pressures set in. The SFIO was a member of the government that had proposed the EDC, and, as the negotiations on the treaty progressed, many of the party's original concerns about German rearmament were negated by changes in the draft treaty. As a result, in February 1952, as part of a resolution recommending confidence in the cabinet, the CD voted overwhelmingly (twenty-two to four) to support the EDC. The party had made an about-face, but the majority was confident of widespread agreement with its new stand, especially as the Social Democratic parties of the other signatory states (except for the SPD) had also indicated their support for the treaty. In addition, the CD majority expected a quick affirmative ratification vote in the Assembly.[80]

A quick parliamentary vote, however, was not forthcoming. The government feared a bitter and divisive debate on the EDC, and delayed submitting the draft treaty for almost two years, hoping that a series of requests for "clarifications" from France's treaty partners would result in terms acceptable to a majority of the National Assembly. Instead, the government's tactic worked against ratification because it gave the opposition time to get organized and put its arguments before the public.

In the SFIO the arguments for and against the EDC presented almost mirror images of each other. The Cédistes (including Philip, Mollet, and Christian Pineau) insisted the treaty offered a number of advantages. The party's conditions for safeguards against the potential dangers of a new national German army had been met. The EDC would also help Socialist cooperation and European unification by creating a second vehicle (after the Schuman Plan) for functional cooperation. They were even confident that the success of the EDC would demonstrate the viability of a united Europe to the British and persuade them to join the unification effort.[81]

The anti-Cédistes were always a minority among the SFIO's leaders (although probably not among the rank-and-file members), but the group included some of the SFIO's most prominent and charismatic spokesmen. Particularly active in the anti-Cédistes cause were Jules Moch, the hero of the 1947 battles with the Communists; Daniel Mayer, the party's wartime general secretary; Oreste Rosenfeld, Blum's son-in-law and editor of the party's newspaper *Populaire Dimanche*; and Edouard Depreux, a former minister of education. (Not incidentally, all of them were also critics of Mollet and his style of administration.) The EDC's opponents advanced tactical and ideological arguments. They claimed it was incompatible with the SFIO's role as an opposition party to support an important government-sponsored measure. The anti-Cédistes also professed to be concerned about the split between the SPD and the SFIO on this issue; they worried that this disagreement would deal a major blow to the cause of Socialist unity. The opposition argued the EDC was the wrong way to go about European unity, since the EDC provided for no political or parliamentary control structure. For good measure the opponents added that the EDC would complicate detente with the post-Stalin leaders of the Soviet Union, and, knowing how important this consideration was for Mollet and some of the other Cédistes, they insisted the SFIO should object to any military alliance that did not include Great Britain.[82]

Throughout 1953 and 1954 the anti-Cédistes forces were making headway in parliament and the party, and the dramatic split of the party's parliamentary delegation in August, 1954 did not come as a complete surprise. The subsequent ratification of the Paris Accords was an anticlimax. As we saw, a large majority of the SFIO's parliamentary delegates, including Jules Moch, the leading opponent of the EDC, voted for ratification of the Paris Accords. The anti-Cédistes' change of heart resulted from a mixture of motivations, but foremost among them was the fear that another debate over German rearmament would lead to a split of the party. This was something which neither the Cédistes nor the anti-Cédistes wanted.[83]

The Parties and European Economic Unification

In contrast to their traditional distrust of military affairs, the Social Democrats were enthusiastic proponents of European economic unification. The parties started with the conviction that economic cooperation was the cornerstone of a united and Social Democratic Europe. With its vast market the new, united Europe would bring about efficiencies of scale and social justice reforms that could only be effected in a planned economy subject to democratic supranational control mechanisms. In short, an economically united Europe was the prerequisite for inaugurating the era of Democratic Socialism on the Continent.

In the immediate postwar era it was axiomatic that the intense concentration of coal mining and steel production in the Ruhr Valley would play a key role in both German and West European economic recovery. At the same time there was widespread agreement that the Ruhr should not again become the center of the armaments industry for a new Reich. The SPD's answer to what the French called the twin goals of *sécurité* (security) and *charbon* (coal) was to institute public ownership of the coal mines and heavy industrial facilities of the Ruhr. Control by a democratically elected German government would ensure that the resources of Europe's industrial heartland would not be misused. The German Social Democrats accepted international control of the distribution of the Ruhr's products, but they vehemently rejected all schemes that envisioned a political separation of the Ruhr area from Germany, or the transfer of ownership of the area's economic resources to foreign proprietors. This included internationally supervised socialization measures, which some of the SPD's sister parties advocated.[84]

The SPD, of course, had no power to put its plans into effect without permission of the Allied occupation authorities, specifically the British, who occupied Germany's industrial heartland. On this score the SPD was initially optimistic. Since the party's proposals showed considerable affinity with the nationalization projects which the Labour government had carried out in Great Britain, the SPD expected the British to support the German Socialists' Ruhr proposals.[85] The Western Allies, however, had rather different priorities: All three were determined to establish some sort of international control over the area. This in itself did not yet preclude public ownership and control of the Ruhr resources, but by 1947 the Americans weighed in with decisions that essentially blocked major structural changes in the Ruhr. The United States authorities now gave first consideration to the revival of the German economy, which, in the eyes of the Americans, was best left in the hands of private entrepreneurs. At least for the foreseeable future there would be no large-scale socialization or nationalization in the Ruhr area.

The result was a series of Allied decisions in 1948 and 1949 that effectively blocked any implementation of the SPD's Ruhr plans. On November 10, 1948 the British promulgated Law Number 75, which confirmed that the Ruhr would remain politically part of Germany, specifically the Land Northrhine Westphalia (a decision that ended French hopes for the separation of the area from Germany), but at the same time prevented the Germans from implementing the socialization measures then under consideration by the Northrhine Westphalian *Landtag*. Law Number 75 determined that structural changes could only be effected by a future German national government. Until then ownership of the Ruhr factories and mines remained in private hands, subject to the controls already imposed by the British authorities.

The next day, November 11, representatives of the Western Allies met in London to work out a permanent solution to the Ruhr problem, and after a month of tough negotiations the three western powers agreed on a Ruhr Statute. Its terms essentially confirmed the provisions of Law Number 75, but also established an International Ruhr Authority (IRA) to determine quotas for mining and steel manufacturing, and oversee the equitable distribution of the products of the Ruhr industry to both Germany and her western neighbors. Membership in the IRA included the three western occupation powers as well as the Germans, although in practice for the moment the IRA was limited to Allied representation. Until the formal establishment of a new German political entity the occupation powers represented the Germans as well as themselves.[86]

The reaction of Europe's Socialists to this novel experiment in supranational administration was mixed. Once again, the Socialists had to acknowledge a "real disagreement" among themselves.[87] (The PvdA remained in the margins of this debate, since Holland had no way of directly influencing occupation policies in Germany.) The SPD vehemently rejected the Ruhr Statute and the IRA because it did not meet the party's minimum conditions for the future economic regime of the Ruhr, i.e., that the area had to remain under exclusive German control, and the mines and heavy industrial plants had to become German public property. In the eyes of Kurt Schumacher and his associates the IRA blocked the road to true European unity, prevented democracy from taking root in Germany; gave verisimilitude to the German Communists' claim that the Western Allies, especially France, were exploiting Germany's resources for their exclusive benefit; and established the rule of foreign capitalists over German workers. With his usual habit of "rhetorical clear cutting" the party leader attacked the newly installed Adenauer government (which had accepted the Ruhr Statute as the best that could be obtained under the circumstances), for selling out Germany's national interest. Almost as an anticlimax the SPD demanded an immediate and full-scale renegotiation of the terms of the Statute, whose purpose should be a "plan of higher Socialist order."[88]

The party's official reaction, which Schumacher and other party leaders reiterated in an unending series of ever more strident speeches and articles, was supported by most party activists, but a small group of insightful critics recognized even at this time that the party's stand was politically counterproductive. Fritz Erler, Carlo Schmid and the economics minister of Northrhine-Westphalia, Erik Nölting, were among those who were unhappy with both the tone and the substance of the SPD's attack on the Ruhr Statute.[89] In intra-party discussions they pointed out that Schumacher's Francophobic appeals to German nationalism and his attacks on the personal integrity of the Federal Republic's governmental leaders neither served the causes of European unification and Franco-German rapprochement, nor helped create a democratic consensus in the young West German republic. Several of the SPD's popular Landesfürsten argued that in spite of its shortcomings, the Statute brought important concrete advantages. The Ruhr regime was a step on the road to European unification, it sharply curtailed the Allied program of dismantling German industrial facilities, and the IRA initiated Germany's reintegration into the family of nations. Schumacher rejected all of these substantive considerations as irrelevant, asserting that the Ruhr Statute "exceeded [the party's] worst fears."[90]

In sharp contrast, the SFIO (and the PvdA) enthusiastically welcomed the Ruhr Statute. Léon Blum, the grand old man of the French Socialist party, greeted the London decisions as the beginning of a new era of Franco-German rapprochement, and the SFIO's general secretary, Guy Mollet, welcomed international control of the Ruhr as an important first step in the creation of an industrial Euro-region. He looked forward to the day when the iron fields and industrial facilities of Lorraine would be similarly deposited in the industrial bank of Europe. With slight hyperbole, Oreste Rosenfeld celebrated the pact as the triumph of parliamentarism and Socialism. International control of the area would prevent future wars, said Jules Moch.

The SFIO's response was not surprising since the terms of the Ruhr Statute embodied many of party's proposals for the future of Europe's industrial regions. The idea that national political control of an area could be combined with an international regime over its economy had been articulated by Léon Blum in the 1920s. At that time Blum was speaking of Alsace-Lorraine, but the Ruhr situation was clearly analogous. It is also understandable that the SFIO was profoundly disappointed by the SPD's vehement opposition to the Statute. Especially Schumacher's unbridled criticism of the French policymakers led to a decided cooling of relations between the two parties, even though the German leader took care not to attack his French comrades specifically.[91]

In retrospect, the German Socialists were fighting a phantom. The Ruhr Statute did not solidify the Allies' colonial regime in Germany's heartland, as the SPD insisted, but laid the foundation for cooperation on an increasingly equal basis between the Germans and the occupying powers. Nor did the Statute represent a setback to European unification. On the contrary, it prepared the ground for the next stage of the process: limited, functionally oriented projects.

In many ways the Ruhr Statute was the precursor of the Schuman Plan, formally the European Coal and Steel Community (ECSC). Like the Ruhr regime, the ECSC created a supra-national administration for a specific economic activity and made no effort to achieve full-scale political integration. But there were also significant differences between the IRA and the ECSC. The Federal Republic was now treated as an equal partner in the supranational authority. Moreover, the Schuman Plan fulfilled the implicit European promise of the Ruhr Statute by extending the area subject to supranational economic control to the heavy industrial regions of France, Italy, and the Benelux countries in addition to those of West Germany. Finally, the ECSC added a significant political and judicial dimension to the supranational regime. Unlike the Ruhr Statute, the ECSC established a rudimentary legislature and a High Court of Justice with binding jurisdiction alongside the administrative institutions.

The ECSC was to become one of the major success stories on the path to European unification (even the Gaullists, who fiercely opposed the Schuman Plan when it was proposed, would later argue that it was very much in line with their leader's ideas for a united Europe[92]), and it is not surprising that a multitude of politicians rushed to claim authorship. It is now generally agreed that, if there was a father of the Schuman Plan, it was Karl Arnold, the Christian Democratic prime minister of Northrhine West-phalia, although both Carlo Schmid and André Philip had offered proposals along the same lines.[93] Nevertheless, it was Arnold who publicly launched the idea of the ECSC in a New Year's Day address in 1949.

Six months later another and far more influential Christian Democrat, the French foreign minister Robert Schuman (who had in turn been influenced by Jean Monnet) took up the idea and formally proposed the ECSC on 9 May 1950. Europe's political leaders took immediate notice. Schuman's timing was not accidental. Growing international tensions (the Korean War was to begin in June, 1950) had led the Americans to put pressure on western Europe to increase its industrial output. This inevitably meant greater industrial strength for West Germany, and the Schuman Plan was initially designed to assure that Germany's revitalized industrial power was permanently contained and subjected to supra-national controls. To achieve this goal the French foreign minister was willing to agree that the heavy industries of France and the other members of the ECSC would be subjected to the same supranational authority.

While Schuman's proposals undoubtedly reflected France's traditional fear of Germany's economic prowess, they were also a bold and daring new initiative on the road to European unification. In view of the Social Democrats' avowed interest in the creation of a large-scale, cross-national market and supra-national controls, it might have been expected that all of the parties would welcome the Schuman Plan and even claim credit for the idea. But unanimity eluded them. Despite a flurry of international and bilateral conferences, the three parties were unable to formulate a compromise position acceptable to all of them.[94]

Among the three parties, the PvdA was the most enthusiastic, although Drees remained something of a Euroskeptic. However, in view of his party's enthusiasm and widespread support for the ECSC among the Dutch people, the prime minister was careful to restrict expressing his doubts to closed-door meetings. The other PvdA leaders did not share Drees' skepticism, and, along with the Dutch labor unions, they were convinced that the ECSC used the right combination of free enterprise initiative and governmental planning and control to create an efficient mechanism for increasing Europe's heavy industrial production. On this score they were right, but other conclusions were more naive. The Dutch Socialists

insisted the Schuman Plan in no way precluded the later socialization of the member countries' iron and steel resources, and, in
a bit of equally wishful thinking, they convinced themselves that
Great Britain would quickly join the Community.[95]

The SFIO was initially less enthusiastic. The party was suspicious in part because the initiative came from its political opponents, but a number of spokesmen voiced substantive objections
as well. Mollet complained that the segmental integration blocked
the road to full-scale political unification, and worried about "a
Europe organized against Labour Great Britain." Others shared
some of the French industrialists' concerns about German economic competition, and Jules Moch, much like Kurt Schumacher,
worried about the excessive influence of the Vatican on what
many Socialists saw as an emerging Catholic Europe of the Six.[96]

However, after some hesitation, the SFIO rallied to become a
fervent supporter of the Schuman Plan. There were a number of
reasons for its attitude shift, some pertinent, others illusionary.
The French Socialists liked the Schuman Plan because it extended
the Ruhr solution to additional areas of Europe. The party had
always insisted that the internationalization of the Ruhr economy
was the beginning not the end of economic integration, and Euro-
peanizing the steel plants and the coal fields of Lorraine alongside
those of the Ruhr advanced a process the French Socialists had
long favored. That the French *patronat* opposed the scheme only
added to its appeal. In addition, the ECSC with its High Court and
embryonic parliament did advance western Europe's political
integration, albeit at a snail's pace. There still remained, however,
the disappointing British reaction. Here some SFIO leaders took
the same line as the Dutch: The British will come around in due
course. Others were by now willing to give up on the British.[97]

Although the German Social Democrats' first reaction had
been guardedly optimistic, over the course of several months
the party decided the Schuman Plan was detrimental to European unification and Democratic Socialism; neither the endorsement of the ECSC by the West German labor unions nor the
support of the Schuman Plan by the other West European Socialist parties was able to change the SPD's stand. The party advanced tactical and ideological reasons for its position. There
was, of course, Schumacher's perennial concern with maintaining the SPD's intransigent opposition. Since the Schuman Plan
was a Christian Democratic proposal, the SPD would oppose it,
as it opposed everything the CDU and Adenauer supported.
(Guy Mollet claimed to know that if the SPD had been in the

government in West Germany, Schumacher and the party would have endorsed the ECSC.[98])

Schumacher himself insisted there were substantive reasons for his opposition to the Schuman Plan. With the benefit of hindsight none of these sound very convincing, but all were rooted in the party leader's longstanding and deep-seated distrust of France, capitalism, and political Catholicism. Most important, Schumacher claimed, was the ECSC's negative impact on the SPD's absolute political priority, German reunification. By integrating West Germany into the little Europe of the Six, the ECSC would solidify Germany's division. That in turn meant that political extremists in West Germany—Communists and neo-Nazis—could use the national issue in their campaigns against democracy in the young republic. In his address to the party's *Soziale Arbeitsgemeinschaft* on 24 May 1951 Schumacher insisted, "I told the Americans privately, the Schuman Plan is the birth certificate of a new Communist movement." According to Schumacher only the SPD's drive against the ECSC served Germany's national and democratic interests. Even after the bitter campaign on the ECSC was over and the treaties had been ratified by the Bundestag and the Bundesrat, Schumacher recalled in discussions with representatives of the US High Commissioner's office that only the SPD's opposition to the project had saved West German democracy.[99]

In addition, the party leader was convinced that the Schuman Plan, like the Ruhr Statute, was primarily designed to keep Germany politically impotent while her neighbors, especially France, exploited the country for their own economic benefit. As evidence for this conclusion he cited, in addition to the continuing barriers to Germany's regaining her full sovereignty, the planned status of the Saar. Under the Schuman Plan the Saarland, whose future the SPD's leader had decided was the *Gretchenfrage* of Franco-German relations, was to be treated as a separate political entity, economically tied to France. For Schumacher this was clear proof of French imperialism and neocolonialism. Finally, Schumacher insisted, and here he was on firmer ground, the ECSC would put an end to any realistic hopes for the socialization of Europe's coal and steel industry. Instead, it would lock in place a Europe that, in an alliteration which Schumacher repeated many times, would be "conservative, clerical, and dominated by cartels."[100]

Schumacher's convoluted reasoning allowed most party leaders as well as rank-and-file activists to live with the illusion that once the Schuman Plan had been defeated, the party and Germany would regain the initiative in foreign relations. When a member of the *Parteivorstand* asked what would actually happen if the ECSC failed, another answered blithely that the party and Germany would be free of all obligations for the next 50 years.[101] However, a significant and growing minority of party leaders was not convinced and pointed to the negative consequences of isolation at home and abroad. This group was not large, but among its ranks were most Socialist union leaders and some powerful Landesfürsten. Many of the latter (including Kaisen, Brauer, and Reuter) were familiar from the debate on the Ruhr Statute, but this time at least some of them did not limit their opposition to the internal discussions of intraparty councils.

Spearheading the public criticism was Wilhelm Kaisen, the SPD's popular leader in Bremen. Convinced that the party's stand on the Schuman Plan would be disastrous for Bremen's and the Federal Republic's economic future, the mayor of West Germany's second largest seaport sent a long article critical of the Schumacher line to the SPD's official paper, *Vorwärts*. When the paper's editors, responding to pressure from the *Parteivorstand*, refused to print the piece, Kaisen turned to *Het Vrije Volk*, the official newspaper of the PvdA, which printed the article. (The Dutch comrades, of course, were enthusiastic supporters of the Schuman Plan.)

Schumacher and his allies were furious and insisted on punishing the mayor for his *"parteischädigendes Verhalten"* (behavior damaging to the party). Other leaders, like Carlo Schmid, loyally supported the Schumacher line in public, but lamented the party leader's immoderate tone in private. Despite his fuming Schumacher was unable to prevent a spectacular and public split in the party's leadership ranks during the ratification vote on the ECSC treaty. Subjected to the full impact of Schumacher's forceful charisma, the SPD's parliamentary delegation in the Bundestag voted unanimously against ratifying the ECSC treaty, but when it came up before the Bundesrat, the SPD-governed Länder joined the states with Christian Democratic cabinets to vote for ratification, thereby assuring West German ratification of the Schuman Plan.[102]

The SPD's vehement and demagogic rejection of the Schuman Plan had largely disastrous consequences. The party was subjected to massive criticism from the Socialist parties of the other ECSC member countries, especially the SFIO.[103] Equally important, the SPD was unable to gain political advantages from its stand. The party made the ECSC a major campaign issue in the 1953 Bundestag election, but the disappointing results showed clearly that most West German voters were not convinced by the

SPD's argument that rejection of the ECSC would improve the chances for national reunification. As Rolf Steininger has aptly put it, the party's stand on the Schuman Plan was a *"schwere Wunde"* (severe blow) to the Social Democrats.[104]

Conclusion

In the decade after the end of the Second World War, the West European Socialists had to give up a number of cherished illusions about their role in the conduct of foreign relations. Contrary to their expectations, Socialists neither set the agenda for the early postwar foreign policy priorities, nor took the lead in implementing foreign policy decisions. These were left primarily to the Christian Democrats and their political allies. The Social Democrats could not even formulate common stands on the most important foreign policy questions. In spite of sincere efforts to coordinate their positions, national rivalries and mutual suspicions remained, and on some crucial issues, like the EDC and the Schuman Plan, the three parties were bitterly divided. And yet the ideal of Socialist cooperation remained a factor in shaping the policies of Europe's Socialists. The fear of isolation in the ranks of the SI was certainly a catalyst in leading the SPD, after Schumacher's death, to abandon its obstructionist stand on foreign policy questions. By the mid-1950s the West German Social Democrats had moved much closer to their sister parties in France and The Netherlands. Moreover, as in the case of the Council of Europe, once the Schuman Plan became effective, the SPD cooperated fully in the institutions set up by the ECSC. In fact Fritz Erler wrote that cooperation among the Socialist delegates to the ECSC's advisory parliament was making "gratifying progress."[105]

At the same time the Socialists did make some important contributions to postwar foreign relations. This was particularly true for the surprisingly swift Franco-German rapprochement. Socialists acted as catalysts for reducing tensions between the two countries. Closely connected with improved Franco-German relations was the issue of West European unification. The Socialists had hoped to shape this issue to their specifications, and when that proved to be yet another illusion, the PvdA and the SFIO cooperated with their political opponents to advance what became the latter's agenda for European unification. It was particularly remarkable that the SFIO, badly shaken by the aftereffects of the EDC debate, was able to put personal animosities aside and take a leading role in creating the conditions that made the Common Market and Euratom possible. The SPD, partly for domestic tactical reasons and partly because of Kurt Schumacher's myopic vision, remained aloof for a time, but by the mid-1950s the German Social Democrats, too, were on their way to acknowledging that even in foreign affairs *Gemeinsamkeiten* (commonalities) rather than incompatibility characterized the goals of the Christian Democrats and the Social Democrats. In fact, a decade after the war the torch of leadership for European unification had passed from the bourgeois parties to the Socialists.

Chapter Seven

THE END OF THE LONG DECADE

Crisis and Response, 1955–1961

$\mathcal{S}$

There were clear signs toward the end of the 1950s that the postwar era was coming to an end. The West European countries were undergoing rapid qualitative and quantitative changes, becoming tertiary industrial, bourgeoisified societies. Critics disdainfully called the new phenomenon a "consumerist society," but they could not prevent the Socialists' core constituency, the industrial workers, from enthusiastically embracing their increasingly bourgeoisified status.[1] At the same time the Social Democratic parties seemed ill-prepared to deal with the new challenges. The Club Jean Moulin, one of a number of new left-wing political groups that emerged in France at the end of the decade (a development that was itself evidence of changing political patterns), commented derisively that both the Communists and the non-Communist French Left had lost touch with reality, and become irrelevant for the groups that really mattered in the new society.[2]

While this conclusion might be dismissed as a polemical assessment, it is true that the three parties were facing serious organizational, ideological and political problems at the end of the decade. Everywhere members took little interest in party activities, leading to calls for overhauls of the parties' organizational structures to make them more open and pluralistic. In Germany and France the Social Democrats had to find ways of coping with the rise (or continued success) of bourgeois catch-all parties—the Christian Democrats in Germany and the Gaullists in France. (In Holland the establishment of a single Christian Democratic party was still some years away.) At the same time the Social Democrats had to recognize that their own hopes for the breakthrough had become illusionary since their share of the popular votes either stagnated or declined.[3]

The end of the decade also saw important developments in coalition politics. The *brede basis* coalition, which had governed The Netherlands since the end of the war, broke up amid much mutual recrimination from its former components. For the first time since its founding, the PvdA was an opposition party. This was a situation long familiar to the SPD, and the German Socialists were increasingly frustrated by their inability to share political power at the national level. The SFIO headed a government coalition with Guy Mollet as prime minister at the beginning of 1956, but the party's new governmental experience had disastrous consequences for the SFIO. The Dutch scholar S.W. Couwenberg, whose political sympathies lay with the Catholic KVP, noted with some satisfaction that while the Socialists had dominated all West European governments immediately after the war, by the end of the 1950s they had been forced into the opposition virtually everywhere.[4]

Although all three parties confronted significant challenges in the second half of the decade, this story cannot avoid a certain asymmetry: the problems of the PvdA and the SPD paled in comparison to those facing the SFIO. Self-proclaimed guarantors of the Fourth Republic, the French Socialists had to endure the charge that they had helped to destroy that same Republic. The Fifth Republic presented the SFIO with the challenge of a new constitutional system that sharply reduced the party's political influence in France. The experience sent shockwaves through the SFIO, leading the German Socialist leader Herbert Wehner to conclude at the beginning of 1959 that, "we are witnessing the collapse of the SFIO."[5] That prediction was overly pessimistic (or at least premature), but there is little doubt that of the three parties the SFIO was subjected to the most formidable internal and external challenges.

Internal Party Developments

All three parties felt a sense of growing frustration as the nature of West European politics changed and the fulcrum shifted to the right. Signs of crisis were abundant, beginning with membership problems. The Social Democratic parties traditionally viewed a large and multi-generational membership as a sign of political health, and, measured by that indicator, the parties were not well. The PvdA's membership figures were actually rising (from 105,609 in 1950 to 147,074 in 1959), but the party leaders were worried nonetheless, observing that the new militants were primarily older people who had benefited from the postwar social reforms. In fact, in 1958 the PvdA dissolved its youth organization, traditionally a funnel for younger workers into the party, because there were not enough members to sustain a viable organization. The SPD had a slightly different problem. Although *Die Falken*, the SPD's answer to the Boy Scouts, was also virtually moribund and the party's overall membership was declining, the Social Democrats were able to attract an increasing number of the thirty-something genera-tion. The SFIO, finally, had the worst of both experiences. Its over-all membership was stagnating, the French Socialists were not attracting a significant share of the growing youthful contingent in the society, and the members who remained took virtually no part in party activities. Moreover, in the SFIO membership problems were coupled with perennial financial difficulties. The members' lack of interest in party affairs led to chronic tardiness in dues payments. At the end of the 1950s fully one-third of the SFIO's budget came from the mandatory salary deductions of the party's parliamentary delegates. (Finances were less of a concern for the PvdA and the SPD, since in both Germany and Holland political parties received public funds.[6])

The parties were also beset by a lack of internal dynamics. Critics complained that the PvdA had become a *regentenpartij* (caretaker party), whose overage leaders saw themselves pri-marily as government and party administrators rather than po-litical innovators. They clung to their executive posts and led the party much as they presided over a government department. Party congresses, again according to the critics, were ritual dis-posals of a predetermined agenda. There was little opportunity for genuine political debates.[7]

The problems of a regentenpartij did not pose itself for the SPD; the German Socialists were in the opposition throughout the 1950s. The SPD's major difficulty was the power of the *Apparat*, its corps of functionaries, which rested like a mortmain on the life of the party. As a large party the SPD had a formidable corps of full-time functionaries (some 400 in 1956) who were for the most part con-tent to administer the status quo, and reluctant to yield power to the innovators among the elected political leaders in the Länder[8] and the party's parliamentary delegation in the Bundestag. Fortu-nately, the party had Herbert Wehner. A former Communist who broke with the KPD during the Second World War, Wehner had been one of the few newcomers to the party who was welcomed into Kurt Schumacher's inner circle. Consequently, he was persona grata with the party's functionaries. At the same time, as deputy chairman of the Bundestag delegation, he was also a singularly effective parliamentary leader whose rhetorical skills and legislative competence enhanced the party's governmental ambitions. Wehner himself, never a modest man, would later claim he single-handedly rescued the party from becoming a permanent opposition fixture.[9]

The SFIO was permeated by an atmosphere of continuing crisis, and the party wavered between recognition of the malaise and self-delusion. Conscious of its intraparty difficulties, the SFIO took several steps to reactivate the life of the party. Membership of the CD was enlarged to reflect more accurately the various strands of opinion in the party. The party also created a new post, the *assistant fédéral* (federation administrator), to revive the often completely moribund party activities in the provinces. At the same time Mollet and his supporters insisted fundamentally all was well with the party. The leadership celebrated the SFIO's triumph over the PCF in Pas-de-Calais in 1956, and announced that the party's good showing in the municipal elections of April, 1958—which came less than a month before the collapse of the Fourth Republic—demonstrated "the loyalty of the workers to the Socialist party which remains more than ever the only left-wing force that is capable of preserving the future of French democracy."

But bombast could not hide the increasing doubts about the SFIO's future. While Guy Mollet and his allies kept a firm grip on the party, on several occasions the secretary general also questioned out loud whether he was still representing the views and feelings of the party as a whole.[10] A growing, but far from united, group of opposition leaders answered this question with a resounding "no." They blamed *Molletisme* and *personnalisme* (Mollet's personal rule) for the decline of the SFIO and the crisis in French Socialism. As evidence they presented a long litany of failed opportunities and wrong decisions, but for the critics the last straws were the conduct of the war in Algeria and the general secretary's role in returning de Gaulle to power.

The critics were a curious group of old and new faces. Mollet's longtime enemies, such as Daniel Mayer, Oreste Rosenfeld, Robert Verdier, and Marcel Pivert, saw new opportunities to weaken the general secretary. (Pivert played a minor role in the final drama; he died at the beginning of 1958.) In 1957 André Philip, the party's perennial curmudgeon, publicly demanded that the SFIO adopt a new and more modern program. Mollet and his supporters refused.

Expelled for violating party discipline, Philip took his revenge in a series of publications arguing that Mollet had destroyed French Socialism to further his own personal ambitions. A somewhat surprising presence among the critics was Edouard Depreux. He had been one of Mollet's closest associates in the years following the Second World War; on a number of occasions Mollet had proposed him as prime minister. After 1955, however, Depreux broke with the general secretary over the war in Algeria, and formed a new party, the *Parti Socialiste Autonome* (Autonomous Socialist Party [PSA]).[11]

André Philip's call for a new SFIO program should not have come as a surprise; calls for ideological innovation were endemic in the three parties. The spectrum of opinion ranged from radical innovators, who thought ideological statements were anachronisms in the era of catch-all parties, to the traditionalists, who insisted the truths of Social Democracy had been written down long ago and there was no need for opportunistic tinkering with the classic formulations. In between stood the majority which acknowledged the continuing need for ideologically based programs, but was also determined to fit the Social Democrats' ideological premises to the reality of a tertiary industrial society.

In both the SFIO and the SPD the ideological debate centered on an issue which the PvdA had confronted (and resolved) in 1946: What was the role of Marx and Marxism in a modern Social Democratic party? For the postwar Dutch Socialists the answer had been little or none, but matters were not as clear cut in the other two parties. The French and German traditionalists argued that there was no socialism without Marx, while the reformers, citing internal party problems and declining electoral support, countered that holding fast to Marx and Marxism would perpetuate the contradiction between theory and practice, and condemn the parties to the status of political sects. Speaking specifically of the SFIO, the French political scientist Jean-Paul Cahn commented bitterly that the party represented the "dichotomy between the rhetoric of pure and hard Socialism and the petty bourgeois actions of Mollet and those close to him."[12]

In this struggle for the soul of socialism, the PvdA had the most secure stand. The party accepted the pervasive bourgeoisification and radically altered politics of a tertiary industrial society. The Dutch Socialists recognized that concrete reform proposals, not doctrines of class struggle, would motivate voters in the new Europe. In the late 1950s Joop den Uyl, who was to become the PvdA's leader and Dutch prime minister in the 1970s, told his comrades that there was nothing wrong with *verburgerlijkt social-isme* (bourgeoisified Socialism). Most of his fellow party leaders shared this sentiment. As we shall see, oppositional groups, who protested the PvdA's continuing departure from the paths of the traditional Left, had little support in the party.[13]

The SPD, too, responded positively to the swift and far-reaching changes in West German society. The party opened itself up in precisely the ways Kurt Schumacher had rejected in 1945. It proclaimed itself a party of labor, whose target group was all wage earners, regardless of socioeconomic status. The party also made strenuous efforts to improve relations with a variety of apolitical interest groups, acknowledging their positive contribution to societal life. This was especially true for the Protestant churches. Here the SPD's merger with the GVP had a catalytic effect. The GVP was a small group of left-wing Liberals led by Gustav Heinemann, an active lay leader with excellent contacts to Protestant church dignitaries. (Parallel effort to reach out to organized Catholicism did not come until the 1960s.) At the same time some critics lamented the loss of the party's identity as a true workers' party and criticized the leadership for its ostensible opportunism, although, as we shall see, such sentiments were largely limited to a few prominent intellectuals and the party's university student affiliate.[14]

The SFIO seemed not so much opposed to the trend toward tertiary industrialization and bourgeoisification as it was unconcerned. It appeared that the party leaders felt no response from them was required because the future of socialism was assured, whatever gyrations capitalism might undergo. Some critics within the SFIO did call for adapting the party's stand to the new French societal realities, but most of them were expelled or resigned. Freed from the bonds of party discipline, they joined the throng of critics who pressured for change from outside the party. Although their prescriptions for the future varied considerably, the clubs and new parties like the PSA, as well as individual critics, all agreed that while the SFIO was indispensable if the French Left was to have a future, in its present form the party was unable to fulfill the role as kingpin of the left.[15]

The proclamation of new programs was traditionally one of the most important means by which Democratic Socialists responded to societal changes. In these periodic documents the Socialist parties attempted to link the permanent ideological verities of Democratic Socialism to specific proposals for policies and legislative initiatives. In 1959 both the Dutch and German Socialists adopted new programs. The PvdA's program committed the party to the *"strijd tot verwerkelijking van het democratische socialisme"* (struggle toward the realization of Democratic Socialism), but the concept of Democratic Socialism was a far cry from Marxist determinism. The PvdA insisted Democratic Socialism meant individual freedom and responsibility, equality of opportunity, political democracy, and a sense of solidarity. Most important, all of these goals could be accomplished within the capitalist system by means of democratically sanctioned reforms. In fact, the party recognized the benefits of capitalism. As its economic policy the 1959 program specifically adopted (with attribution to the author, Karl Schiller), the most famous phrase of the German Socialists' new program, *"Wettbewerb so weit möglich, Planung so weit nötig"* (as much competition as possible, as little planning as necessary). No wonder that a small group of left-wing critics complained that in the PvdA's 1959 program "the red heart [was] cut out of the party."[16]

The SPD's Bad Godesberg Program has been the subject of a great deal of scholarly and contemporary analysis, and there is no need to discuss the contents in any great detail here. Rather, it will be put into the comparative context of the late 1950s. Calls for an overhaul of the SPD's ideological premises had been endemic ever since the party's rebirth after the Second World War, and they became more strident as the SPD suffered successive defeats in the two Bundestag elections of the 1950s. The reformers, foremost among them Willi Eichler,[17] insisted that the SPD's last formal program, the 1925 Heidelberg document, was simply out of date. Schumacher, however, had resisted demands for a new program as premature, and his successors as well as the cadres remained unenthusiastic. Part of the reason was nostalgia for the traditional image of the SPD, but the old guard also recognized that the party activists showed far less interest in a new program than the voters.

The disastrous 1957 election brought a new sense of urgency to the work on the new program. The margin of the CDU's victory in 1957 persuaded the leadership—Erich Ollenhauer now pushed the program commission to get the job done—that a new program was crucial for the SPD's political future. The decision was a clear victory for Willi Eichler and the reformers. Even so, the leadership was careful to guard its flanks against expected attacks from the traditionalists. In a move heavy with symbolism the party executive asked Benedikt Kautsky, the son of Karl Kautsky, the primary author of the party's famous 1891 Erfurt Program, to evaluate the draft of the new document.

Despite such symbolic nods to the past, the Bad Godesberg Program represented a radical break with German Social Democratic tradition. The SPD renounced Marxist determinism, replacing it with ethical Socialism (*"der Mensch ist ein Wert an sich"* [a human being is a value in itself]). The program also stressed that the party was a democratic and pragmatic reform party, fully cognizant of the benefits of entrepreneurial initiatives. Finally, the SPD endorsed German federalism, the Western Alliance, and European unification. The SPD, in other words, redefined itself as a pragmatic, reformist Volkspartei.[18]

Reaction from the party militants to the draft document, which the executive committee had sent to all locals for discussion, was sharply divided. From the resolutions initially adopted by the locals and districts, it was expected that fully one-third of the delegates would vote against the new program at the Bad Godesberg congress. Abandoning the party's traditional stand on socializing key industries especially angered many delegates. Surprisingly, when the final vote came the opposition had been reduced to a handful of delegates. One reason for this was the reformers' persuasive arguments and the care with which they answered the opposition's concerns; another was the surprising role which Herbert Wehner played at the Bad Godesberg congress. Respected by both the traditionalists and the reformers, Wehner waited until the last moment to take a position, but when he did he threw his full political and rhetorical weight behind the draft program.[19]

The reaction from the sister parties was mixed. The SFIO was divided and took no official stand. The PSA rejected the Bad Godesberg Program as a "renunciation of Socialism," an opportunistic reaction to concerns about continuing electoral defeats. Such sentiments were unworthy of a true socialist party. The PvdA, as might be expected, enthusiastically welcomed the SPD to the ranks of Social Democratic pragmatists and reformers.[20]

Although the SFIO confronted many of the same problems that beset the SPD, the French party showed remarkably little interest in programmatic discussion, let alone innovation. A small minority of CD members felt the Bad Godesberg Program should become a model for French Socialism, but they were unable to persuade their comrades to move the SFIO in this direction. Most French Socialist leaders feared a move to the right would pervert the party's true heritage. The CD did ask Jules Moch to chair a commission charged with drafting a new program, but Moch did not take his task very seriously, and the members of the executive committee discussed the resulting document with an equal lack of enthusiasm. This was not surprising, since what emerged from the commission's deliberations in December, 1960, was essentially a restatement of traditional Franco-Marxist verities, augmented by a few references to the current political situation in the country. What the draft called de Gaulle's dictatorship was explained as a predictable stage in the evolution toward true Social Democracy, a stage which Marx had already alluded to.[21]

Since in politics severe problems routinely prompt calls for new leaders, it was not surprising that the SPD replaced a number of the veterans in its leadership team. The second half of the 1950s saw the ultimate triumph of the reformers, which entailed a shift of power from the party executive to the Bundestag delegation, and, a novelty in the history of the party, the nomination of candidates for chancellor and the members of a shadow cabinet. With the defeat in the 1957 Bundestag election still fresh in their minds, the delegates at that year's national congress refused to reelect a number of the old guard members of the Parteivorstand, turning instead to the reformist leaders of the Bundestag delegation, Fritz Erler, Carlo Schmid, and Herbert Wehner. A year later the reformers solidified their position. The party changed its organizational structure, creating a presidium (a sort of inner circle of the Parteivorstand), and the reformers dominated this body as well. The triumph of reformism was also reflected by the membership of the SPD's campaign commission, the group that was in charge of preparing the party for the 1961 Bundestag election. It was headed by Willy Brandt, an energetic reformer who in 1958 had replaced the oldline Marxist Franz Neumann as head of the party's West Berlin organization. All of the commission's members were committed to the concept that only if the SPD ran as a reformist Volkspartei could the party hope to improve its fortunes at the ballot box.

The final eclipse of the old guard was marked by the formal selection of a shadow chancellor for the 1961 campaign. Since 1949 it had been axiomatic that the party leader would also serve as head of the government if the party won the election, but now the reformers argued that Erich Ollenhauer, for all his qualities as a decent man, was insufficiently charismatic for the age of television politics. In the end the party leader himself came to the same conclusion. The party's 1961 candidate for chancellor was Willy Brandt, the "German Kennedy" and youthful mayor of West Berlin.[22]

Did the old guard yield power without a struggle? Essentially, yes. Ollenhauer was clearly uneasy about the political and personnel changes, and the speed with which they were enacted, but the reformers were grateful that the party leader recognized that he had reached the twilight of his career and decided to smooth the way for change rather than attempt to stand in its way. Herbert

Wehner, who had no intention of taking a back seat in the future party, also looked upon Willy Brandt with considerable misgivings. While recognizing Brandt's skills as a campaigner, he continued to see the West Berlin mayor as an outsider, insufficiently molded by the party's heritage.[23]

Still, the SPD settled its leadership problems with a minimum of acrimony. Things did not go as smoothly in the SFIO. In the latter half of the 1950s the party was bitterly divided over a number of policy and personnel issues and, not surprisingly, the critics concentrated their attacks on Guy Mollet as the man who had led the SFIO down the wrong path. The general secretary gave as good as he received. Unlike Erich Ollenhauer, Mollet was not prepared to be pushed into honorable retirement. Instead, in addition to issuing ritual calls for party unity, Mollet and his supporters used a carrot and stick approach to retain control of the party. The carrots included Mollet's agreement that minority views should be represented on the CD, and that he hoped to keep the lines of communication open to those members who had left the SFIO for the PSA. The CD also voted that the SFIO's biannual congresses should have the opportunity to discuss fundamental questions facing the party. (Mollet's critics had long charged that the party's old guard stifled genuine political debates at party meetings.) The sticks included expulsion from the party for the most vociferous critics, such as Oreste Rosenfeld and André Philip. This dual tactic succeeded in reinforcing Mollet's and his supporters' control of the SFIO; oppositional leaders who were not expelled for the most part gave up the fight and resigned from the party.[24]

To outsiders perhaps the most visible symptom of the crisis confronting European Socialism was the appearance of a plethora of new parties, party splits, and extra-party groups among the non-Communist left. The phenomenon was most pronounced in France, but the first party to be challenged in this manner was the PvdA. In 1957 a new party, the *Pacifistisch-Socialistische Partij* (Pacifist Socialist Party [PSP]) made its appearance in The Netherlands. Ostensibly a completely new political group, the PSP actually resulted from a split in the PvdA. As we saw earlier, a left-wing minority in the PvdA had always remained profoundly uneasy about the pragmatic direction of Dutch Socialism. By the end of the 1950s these misgivings needed only the spark provided by two decisions made by the PvdA's leadership to erupt into open flames. The party executive committee first rejected the demand by members of the left-wing opposition that they be allowed to organize themselves as a *daklozenraad* (Council of the Homeless).

(They chose this name to indicate that they could not feel at home in the already existing Protestant, Catholic, and humanistic werkgemeenschapen.) The Dutch Left also vehemently opposed the PvdA's decision to endorse the stationing of American atomic weapons in western Europe. Actually, the men who created the PSP objected to the entire evolution of Dutch Socialism since the Second World War, and it was not surprising that the party's founding proclamation listed not only all of the standard demands of the traditional Socialist Left, including large-scale socializations, but also Holland's return to a foreign policy of nonalignment.[25]

The PvdA initially decided to treat its new rival as an unimportant splinter group. This was not pure arrogance. Until the 1960s the PSP was far less successful than its leaders had hoped. Although the party attracted some young intellectuals, the PSP was unable to draw a significant number of members or voters away from the PvdA, and only in Amsterdam was the PSP a serious concern for the old party. The PvdA's leadership was actually more worried about an intra-party opposition group, the *Socialistisch-Democratisch Centrum* (Socialist Democratic Center [SDC]). More or less tolerated by the party's leaders, the SDC had led an uneasy organizational existence almost since the party's founding. Seeing itself as the Marxist conscience of Dutch Socialism, the SDC issued a steady stream of publications criticizing the PvdA's leadership for abandoning the red family and leaving the path of true Socialism. Like the PSP, the SDC also advocated a neutralist foreign policy. In June 1959 the peaceful coexistence of the party and the SDC came to an end. The PB expelled the SDC, officially for violating party discipline, but actually because the PvdA's coalition partners in the cabinet were using the SDC's existence to question the PvdA's commitment to reformism. With the expulsion of the left-wing *tendance* the PvdA hoped to make it clear that it would not tolerate groups within its ranks that might lead to doubts about the party's future as a pragmatic Volkspartei and a *ministériable* coalition partner.[26]

In Germany the Bad Godesberg Program sparked a left-wing backlash in the SPD. Although the new program was adopted with overwhelming support at the party's 1959 national congress, the opposition was able to use the SPD's university student affiliate, the *Sozialistischer Studentenbund* (Socialist Student Association [SDS]) as its organizational base. Under the influence of some of its professorial mentors, notably Wolfgang Abendroth and Ossip Flechtheim, the SDS became a rallying point for those who wanted to preserve the SPD's Marxist heritage. Both Abendroth and Flechtheim wrote a number of polemical publications, insisting that with the Bad Godesberg Program the SPD had left the path of true socialism and adapted itself to capitalism. The party, that is to say, was guilty of opportunism.[27]

The SPD's leadership reacted vigorously and issued polemical statements of its own, attacking Abendroth and Flechtheim. The PV also attempted to convince the SDS to moderate its oppositional stance. When this failed, the party used its heavy guns. Abendroth and Flechtheim (as well as Viktor Agartz, who had also joined the fray[28]) were expelled from the SPD, and the party declared membership in the SDS incompatible with membership in the SPD. The party also created a new student organization, the *Sozialistische Hochschulbund* (Socialist University Association [SHB]), which was to cause problems as well, but that lay in the future. For the moment order had been restored and the left-wing agitation would not hinder the triumph of reformism.[29]

The phenomenon of organized opposition, party splits and new party formations was most pervasive in France. In the SFIO itself the Mollet government's conduct during the war in Algeria and the Suez invasion led to the revival of organized *tendances*. Mollet's role in bringing de Gaulle back to power added further fuel to the intraparty rivalries, and in 1959 a group of opposition leaders left the SFIO and founded the PSA. But the altercations within the SFIO were in some ways of rather less significance than developments taking place outside the party. While Mollet insisted that parliamentarism would soon return to France, the popular approval of the de Gaulle constitution, and the General's ability to settle the Algerian problem, made it clear that the French Left would have to accommodate itself to the new presidential constitutional system.

Many of the politically interested young were especially convinced the old parties, including the SFIO, had become anachronisms.[30] They turned instead to the bewildering array of new political clubs that made their appearance in the late 1950s. The name "club" was meant to evoke images of grass-roots politics during the French Revolution, and some of the names (e.g., the Club Jacobin) tried to reflect this heritage directly. Others recalled the days of the French Resistance—another era in which the contours of French politics had presumably been wide open to fundamental change—and named themselves after Resistance heroes from the Second World War. This was the case with one of the most important of the new organizations, the Club Jean Moulin. Ideologically, the clubs covered a wide spectrum, from left-wing

Catholics to forlorn Trotskyites without a home. As a phenomenon, the clubs thought they were the yeast that would rejuvenate the deflated French Left, creating a modernized, united alternative to de Gaulle and Gaullism. Typical was the statement by the Club Jean Moulin, that the clubs represented a synthesis of the ideas of Jaurès and Bernstein and therefore they were the true foundation of a French labor movement.[31]

The second half of the decade also saw the emergence of a number of new parties with varying significance. Some, like the *Union de la Gauche Socialiste* (Union of the Socialist Left [UGS]) were little more than discussion forums for a few intellectuals with a laudatory if naive aim, in this case the amalgamation of Marxist and left-wing Catholic social ideas. Others, like the *Tribune de Socialisme* were essentially groups of subscribers to the periodical of the same name, a phenomenon that had a long tradition in French politics. In a different league, at least as far as its ambition was concerned, was the PSA; it hoped to replace the SFIO as the true voice of French Socialism. Michel Rocard, secretary general of the PSA's successor organization from 1967 to 1973, and in 1990 the French prime minister, wrote that the party's founders wanted to "create a *genuine* [sic] Socialist party, purer, more loyal to the tradition of true Socialism."[32]

The PSA's founders had hoped that the party would attract a sizable number of militants away from the SFIO, but these hopes were quickly dashed. The party never had a mass following, and virtually all of its members resided in the Paris region. The PSA did have a relatively youthful membership, however. In addition, the PSA became a new political home for a number of disaffected SFIO leaders—including Tanguy-Prigent, Mayer, Philip, and Auriol. (The former president of the Republic published a bitter open letter to Mollet explaining his break with the SFIO.) Depreux could also celebrate a genuine triumph: Pierre Mendès-France joined the PSA. But the democratic Left's most charismatic figure proved to be a disappointment; he took little active part in the PSA's affairs. Recognizing its numerical insignificance, the PSA merged in April, 1960 with a number of small left-wing groups, including the *Tribune de Socialisme*, to form a new group, the *Parti Socialiste Unifié* (Unified Socialist Party [PSU]). The new grouping, however, could not fulfill the promise of its name; it also remained a numerically small component of the French Left.[33]

Pointing repeatedly to their lack of significant membership (less than one percent of the SFIO's membership switched its allegiance to the new groups), Mollet and the SFIO treated the PSA and PSU with contempt. The membership figures were certainly correct, but what the PSA and PSU lacked in quantity, to some extent they made up for in quality. Virtually all of Mollet's opponents eventually found their way to the PSU; the party's executive committee included no less than twenty-one former SFIO members of parliament, and their departure weakened the SFIO's role as the dominant force among the French non-Communist Left. Wilfried Loth has written the departure from the SFIO of long-time leaders like Auriol, Grumbach, Philip, Verdier, Tanguy-Prigent, Gouin, and Mayer demonstrated "that there existed a democratic Left in de Gaulle's France which no longer felt at home in the SFIO, or did not yet feel at home there."[34]

National Politics: Elections and Coalitions

The second half of the decade saw a number of dramatic political developments in all three countries, with the Socialists experiencing electoral triumphs and defeats in quick succession. In The Netherlands the longtime coalition that had governed the country since 1945 fell apart, and the PvdA was forced into the unfamiliar role of parliamentary opposition. In Germany the SPD succeeded in getting closer to its goal of assuming national governmental responsibility when, in an unexpected move, the Social Democrats joined forces with the liberal *Freie Demokratische Partei* (Free Democratic Party [FDP]) to form a coalition in West Germany's largest state, Northrhine Westphalia. In France Guy Mollet became prime minister in 1956, but his appointment also marked the beginning of the end for the Fourth Republic. Less than a year after Mollet left office, Charles de Gaulle had given France a new cabinet and a new constitutional system.

On 13 June 1956, the Dutch voters went to the polls in the fourth national elections since the end of the Second World War. The results were a triumph for the PvdA; the party achieved the best showing in its history: 32.7 percent of the popular vote. In Dutch terms this represented a dramatic increase over the 29.0 percent in the 1952 elections. (The victory appeared even larger, because the membership of the legislature had been increased from 100 to 150 delegates.) As far as the PvdA was concerned, the voters had rejected the Catholic bishops' *mandement* and the attempt to preserve the Catholic *zuil* by ecclesiastical fiat. There were renewed hopes that the day of the *doorbraak* had finally dawned. Equally important, the outcome seemed to provide a vote of confidence to the governing coalition and its Socialist prime minister, Willem Drees.[35]

The feelings of triumph were short-lived, and a closer look at the 1956 results reveals why. The PvdA eclipsed the KVP, but just barely. The Catholics scored 31.7 percent of the popular vote (1952: 28.7 percent) and the KVP's setback (in relative terms) spurred the Catholics to work harder in the next contest, the elections for *Provinciale Staten* (regional parliaments) on 6 March 1958. In a vigorous and, at times, demagogic campaign (the KVP claimed the PvdA's "reign" in Holland since 1945 had been worse than the German occupation), the Catholic party succeeded in blaming the PvdA for the economic problems that were beginning to make their appearance in The Netherlands. The Dutch Socialists' share of the popular vote was reduced to 28.7 percent, while that of the KVP climbed to 32.9 percent. The outcome of the provincial elections had no direct effect on national politics, but the PvdA's analysts were clearly worried. Rightly convinced that without middle class swing voters the PvdA was doomed to stagnation, the party's leaders were particularly concerned about the PvdA's lack of firm support among these voters.[36]

They were right. A year later, on 12 March 1959 new national elections confirmed the results of the regional contests. In the meantime the coalition had come to an end, and the campaign was characterized by mutual attacks of the former coalition partners. Although for the first time the party attempted to run a professional campaign, the outcome was a severe disappointment. The Catholics obtained 31.6 percent, eclipsing the Socialists' 30.3 percent. It was not difficult to pinpoint the Socialists' problems. The PvdA had clearly failed to penetrate the middle class constituency in sufficient numbers. The party did attract votes from all segments of society, but its appeal remained concentrated among the lower and lower middle classes. In addition, the Socialist leaders had always expected that they would be the primary beneficiary of increasing secularization, what the Dutch called *ontzuiling*. By the end of the decade evidence of secularization was widespread, but the reward did not go to the PvdA. Rather, it went to a new liberal grouping, the *Volkspartij voor Vrijheid en Democratie* (Popular Party for Liberty and Democracy [VVD]), which obtained 12.2 percent of the popular vote.

In analyzing these disappointing results the PvdA's leaders offered a number of explanations, not all of them consistent with each other. Some commentators pointed to technical problems, arguing that the PvdA's campaign methods were still too old-fashioned for the age of television. Willem Drees, not surprisingly, thought the problem was the breakup of the coalition. The former prime minister strongly urged his party to abandon the tactics of confrontation, and return to the government as quickly as possible. Finally, there were some perceptive voices who noted the primary problem was the PvdA's failure to attract younger middle class voters. They argued this was the rapidly growing core constituency of the new tertiary industrial society, and the PvdA needed to concentrate its political mobilization efforts on the newly secularized and educated segments of Dutch society.[37]

In West Germany between 1953 and the end of the decade there were 19 contests for state legislatures and the Bundestag election of 15 September 1957.[38] (The Saarland is excluded from this calculation since the area did not become a Land until 1957.) In the state contests the SPD's share of the popular vote increased steadily, and in some cases spectacularly. As a result, the party had high hopes for the 1957 national contest. This was the first time that the SPD mounted a scientific campaign, complete with commissioned polls and posters designed by media experts. The party also hoped that the merger with the GVP would enable the SPD to tap into a larger share of the middle class voting constituency.[39] But the results were devastating. True, the SPD increased its share of the popular vote to 31.8 percent (1953: 28.8 percent), but these figures meant little in comparison with the Christian Democrats' triumph. For the first time in German history a single party had obtained a majority of the popular vote in a free election: the combined share of the popular vote for the CDU and CSU was 50.2 percent (CDU: 39.7 percent, CSU: 10.5 percent)

The initial reaction of the party's leaders was, as might be expected, shock and despair. Herbert Wehner briefly returned to the jargon of his days as an orthodox Marxist and attributed the outcome to the power of capitalism and authoritarian restoration. Others lamented that the party's scientific campaign had not been scientific enough. But perhaps the most perceptive analysis was provided by a young party member, Erhard Eppler, who had just switched his allegiance from the GVP to the SPD. In a long memorandum to Carlo Schmid, Gustav Heinemann, and Fritz Erler, entitled "After the Lost Election," Eppler emphasized that while the party had certainly committed tactical campaign errors, the SPD's central problem was its inability to sell itself as an inclusive, non-ideological, left-of-center Volkspartei. Eppler reminded the party that the SPD's core constituency of industrial workers had been reduced to about twenty percent of the overall electorate.

Eppler's concrete remedies for the future sounded like predictions of what was to come: a new program, a forceful statement of the party's modern outlook, presentation of a shadow cabinet, and a "party chairman who to members and voters alike most convincingly embodies the rejuvenated SPD." Erler's marginal comments on Eppler's analysis indicated that he agreed with his young colleague, and fortunately for the future of the SPD, eventually so did the other party leaders. As we saw, the 1957 defeat provided the final piece of persuasive evidence which allowed the reformers to take control of the party.[40]

The SFIO's electoral history was also a roller coaster experience, but in contrast to their German and Dutch comrades the French Socialists had to contend with fundamental changes in the French electoral system. The Fourth Republic had used a system of proportional representation in legislative elections. Under the Fifth Republic this was changed to a system of single-member districts, with run-off elections between the two top vote getters in multiparty districts in which no candidate obtained the majority of the popular vote. Since candidates seldom obtained a majority of the popular vote in the first contest, electoral alliances for the run-off elections became a crucial element of French campaign strategy.

The SFIO's (relative) triumph came in the last legislative elections of the Fourth Republic in January, 1956. The party obtained 15.2 percent of the popular vote, an increase over its 1951 result of 14.6 percent. The party leaders were elated, especially since the SFIO's increase was coupled with a slightly larger decrease in the Communist vote (1956: 25.9 percent; 1951: 26.9 percent). The CD promptly attributed the party's success to increased working class votes and the SFIO's promise to find a solution to the Algerian problem. The party leaders conveniently ignored that the good showing of the democratic Left was primarily the result of Pierre Mendès-France's charisma. Independent analysts noted that the SFIO was riding the coattails of PMF as titular leader of the Republican Front. Still, as a result of the 1956 elections, the SFIO became the strongest party in the Republican Front coalition, and Guy Mollet was elected prime minister—with PMF's lukewarm support.[41]

It is difficult to describe the SFIO's electoral experience in the first years of the Fifth Republic as anything but lurching from disaster to disaster. Sensing the problems ahead, the party was deeply divided on de Gaulle's new constitution. The SFIO's national congresses traditionally cast lopsided votes in favor of positions endorsed by the leadership, but at the 1958 meeting the leaders' recommendation for a affirmative vote on the forthcoming referendum passed by only 2687:1176 votes. As had been true during the EDC debate, some strange alliances emerged among the party's leaders. The traditional rivals Guy Mollet and Gaston Defferre both favored a yes vote on the constitutional referendum, while Mollet's long-time ally Francis Leenhardt (the head of the *Fédération Nord*) urged a negative vote.[42]

The first legislative elections of the Fifth Republic were held shortly after the referendum, in November, 1958. It was not one of the SFIO's stellar performances. The party launched a poorly orga-nized, largely negative campaign, attacking the Communists and the PSA rather than attempting to present the Socialists' positive goals. The SFIO's share of the popular vote, 11.8 percent, was con-siderably less than the 1956 result (15.2 percent). True, its tradi-tional rivals also lost: the PCF obtained 14.3 percent (1956: 25.9 percent) and the MRP 8.3 percent (1956: 8.8 percent). But none of this changed the essential fact that the SFIO was losing ground. Prominent Socialist leaders, such as Defferre and Lacoste, tem-porarily lost their parliamentary seats. In addition, the SFIO was increasingly becoming a party whose members and voters were concentrated in the small towns of southern and eastern France, rather than in the "dynamic zones of the north and the north-east." The SFIO was also unable to attract a significant number of young voters. The only positive of the result was a slight improvement of the SFIO's traditionally poor showing among women voters.[43]

Not surprisingly, the SFIO's own analysis of the 1958 results was more optimistic. Guy Mollet noted the PCF's heavy losses with considerable *Schadenfreude*. Although it was clear that the bulk of the disaffected Communist voters had turned to the Gaull-ists, in a bout of wishful thinking the general secretary concluded that, next time, they would vote for the SFIO. Such musings were fanciful at best, but in any case, as the more perceptive party lead-ers pointed out, there was a far more important problem. In the Fifth Republic, parliamentary representation was not the key to political power, capturing the presidency was. Accomplishing that feat would require a revitalized Left united behind a charismatic leader to challenge de Gaulle and Gaullism. The party's task ahead in the 1960s, then, was to adjust its politics and campaigns to the new presidential constitution.[44]

In European politics there is traditionally a close connection between governmental coalitions and elections, with coalition agreements coming in two basic varieties, electoral pacts and agreements to form multiparty governments. Electoral pacts, in which the parties agree to cooperate in running election campaigns or back each other's legislative candidates, are especially important for electing a president and legislative delegates if the constitution provides for run-off elections. In parliamentary democracies, which France was before 1958 and Germany and Holland were throughout the period, post-election agreements to form multi-party governmental coalitions were more important than electoral pacts.

The Netherlands was the epitome of a successful parliamentary democracy.[45] The Dutch political system was characterized by a multiplicity of parties representing the major zuilen of the society; neither the Socialists nor any other single party was ever able to form a government on its own. As we saw, since 1945 the PvdA had been a partner in every Dutch government coalition, and a majority of the party's leaders—Willem Drees foremost among them—saw no reason to change. Others were less happy with the arrangement, and their numbers, and unease, was growing. The bishops' 1954 mandement, the increasingly aggressive tone of the KVP's campaigns and a number of ill-considered legislative proposals by the KVP led to a growing feeling among some of the PvdA's leaders that the party was being taken for granted and treated as junior partner in the coalition. The insurrection was concentrated among the PvdA's parliamentary delegation, and headed by that group's leader, Jaap Burger, who in a series of moves and speeches took the lead in attempting to distinguish the PvdA's political profile more clearly from that of its Catholic coalition partner. The KVP in turn accused Burger of destroying the harmony of the coalition.[46]

In December, 1958 the cabinet fell, and for more than five months The Netherlands were governed by a caretaker cabinet as the parties scrambled to create a new coalition. The ostensible reason for the government's fall was a disagreement over a taxation measure, but the PvdA's leaders immediately proclaimed that the KVP had pushed the Socialists out of the government. Actually, the coalition had pretty much exhausted its store of agreements.

The PvdA's leaders were deeply divided about the party's future course. While Drees urged his colleagues to help him patch up the old coalition, Burger and his allies insisted upon prior agreement by all of the coalition partners to a formal governmental program. The KVP rejected that demand as a form of subtle blackmail. In the altercation the PvdA had the weaker hand.(The Catholics had tradition on their side in this argument. It was not customary for Dutch cabinets to come before parliament with a full-fledged government program.) The KVP joined forces with the liberal VVD, which posed no preconditions for entering into a coalition with the KVP, except that the new government must not include the PvdA. Drees, forced to end his long tenure as prime minister, blamed Burger for sabotaging a new coalition agreement and forcing the Socialists to take their place on the opposition benches. Others, including the former prime minister Schermerhorn, took a more philosophical view: western Europe in general was moving toward the political Right and Holland was just part of the overall trend.[47]

Fear that this trend might become a permanent fixture throughout western Europe led the SPD to accelerate its efforts to attain a share of governmental power. Fortunately for the party, Germany's federal system allowed the Socialists to pursue their goal with parallel strategies at the national and state levels. Developments in the Länder were particularly important because for the moment the barriers against joining a national coalition appeared virtually insurmountable; after the 1957 election the Christian Democrats seemed more solidly in control of the federal government than at any time since the founding of the Federal Republic.

The coalition dynamics in the Länder were, however, more fluid, a fact of political life which the SPD's judicial expert, Adolf Arndt, gratefully recognized. In a meeting of the executive committee he commented, "we should be thankful that we live in a federal state, otherwise it wouldn't look good for the SPD." Arndt was right. As we saw, in 1956 the SPD succeeded in capturing a major state. Taking advantage of the breakup of the longtime coalition between the Christian Democrats and the Liberals (FDP) in West Germany's largest state—Northrhine Westphalia—the Socialists formed a new coalition with the FDP. The reasons for the fall of the old coalition had more to do with friction between the CDU and the FDP in Bonn than disagreements over state issues, but the new partners were also aware of the larger implications of their coalition agreement. The FDP was sending a message to the CDU that the Liberals had an alternative to the alliance with the Christian Democrats, while the SPD leaders saw their triumph in Düsseldorf as a stepping stone toward becoming partners in a national coalition.[48]

The last few years of the Fourth Republic were characterized by a series of cabinet crises. Between January, 1956 and May, 1958 four separate governments held office. Ironically, the cabinet with the longest tenure (February 1956 to May 1957) and the strongest political base was the coalition headed by Guy Mollet. Backed by the Socialists, the Radicals, and the MRP, it had the initial support of a solid majority of the National Assembly. But these figures were deceptive. The most influential figure in the Republican Front coalition was Pierre Mendès-France, and he stayed outside the cabinet. PMF had demanded the foreign ministry portfolio, but Mollet refused, preferring that Mendès-France become prime minister instead, a post the Radical leader rejected because the parties would not give him the freedom to choose the members of his cabinet. There were also problems with the relationship between the SFIO as a party and the Mollet government. Critics complained that, like Willem Drees, Guy Mollet wanted to transform the party into a handmaiden of the government. Gaston Defferre and André Philip bitterly criticized Mollet's decision to serve as prime minister while continuing to control the party. Here, they argued, was clear evidence of the general secretary's galloping *personnalisme*. (Officially, Mollet had yielded the administration of the party to Pierre Commin, but it was an open secret that Commin did what Mollet told him to do.[49])

The Republican Front government fell in May, 1957, ostensibly, as in the case of the Dutch coalition eighteen months later, because of disagreements on tax policies. In fact, the cabinet had already lost most of its credibility as a result of its participation in the Suez invasion of October, 1956, and its failure to end the "dirty war" in Algeria. The SFIO was directly involved in both debacles. The Suez invasion was a personal decision made by Guy Mollet, and the man responsible for implementing the cabinet's Algerian policy, the resident general in Algeria, Robert Lacoste, was a prominent SFIO member and close ally of the prime minister. At its fall the cabinet left behind a pervasive sense of crisis. Michel Winnock smelled *"l'odeur de la peste"* (vapors of pestilence), André Philip felt he was living in a prefascist era, and Eduard Depreux called 1956 "a year that I marked as a black spot [*pierre noir*] in the history of French Social Democracy."[50]

The SFIO was sharply divided on the role it should play to halt the spreading malaise that engulfed France until it became a constitutional crisis in the spring of 1958. The party proclaimed that, as always, France's Socialists stood firm in support of democracy and Socialism, but some leaders recognized that this was not enough. Philip called for a cooperative effort of the entire Left—a new edition of the Popular Front—to counter the subversive activities of the army and the administration in Algeria. Mollet wished for a government that "we do not join, but which is dependent on our votes." Others insisted that the SFIO become part of a grand coalition of parties favoring parliamentary democracy. A few farsighted leaders, like Gaston Defferre, recognized that a grand coalition was also not enough; the problem was the constitutional system itself. The Fourth Republic was identified with parliamentarism, and after the seemingly unending series of cabinet crises, the French people had lost faith in parliamentarism. The SFIO, the staunchest pillar of the Fourth Republic, was unable to save the Republic or stay out of the government. (Mollet was vice-prime minister and Moch minister of the interior in the last cabinet of the Fourth Republic.) Symptomatic of the party's self-paralysis was the CD's decision, in the fall of 1957, to appoint a commission to look into recommendations for possible constitutional changes, but then to defer any action on the commission's report.[51]

The SFIO was not alone with its problems. The entire French Left was unprepared for the final crisis when it came in May, 1958. Although the signs of the Republic's implosion had been apparent for some time, neither the cabinet nor parliament acted to prohibit the illegal and extra-legal activities of the civilian and military authorities in Algeria, and, later, in France itself. The eventual solution to the crisis was, of course, de Gaulle's return to power, an outcome in which the SFIO and especially Guy Mollet played a key role. Although in the course of the Fourth Republic's troubled life the general secretary had often expressed his determination to prevent de Gaulle and Gaullism from returning to power in France,[52] it was Mollet, who, after a secret visit to Colombey-les-deux-Églises, paved the way for the general's return to the Elysées Palace.[53]

Explanations for this stunning turnabout vary. Mollet's critics once again saw clear evidence of his personal ambitions. They claimed, during his meeting with the general the secretary general was seduced by the prospect of a post in the new de Gaulle government; the Socialist leader already saw himself as prime minister again. Mollet himself always stressed his fear that the alternative to de Gaulle was civil war, which would inevitably have led to either a military dictatorship or a Communist revolution. In addition, Mollet seems to have felt that, much as had been the case in 1946, once de Gaulle had mastered the acute emergency, France would return to its normal constitutional system of parliamentary democracy.[54]

The party was not united behind Mollet's position. Notably the leaders of the Seine Federation argued the entire Left, including the Communists, should have united to oppose de Gaulle's return to power at all costs. For these left-wing leaders de Gaulle was the French Franco, determined to install a quasi-fascist regime in France. The CD actually voted 17:9 to join the CGT and other left-wing groups in organizing a mass demonstration against de Gaulle's return. As in the case of the EDC, the GP, initially opposed to de Gaulle, eventually split into virtually equal camps: forty-two deputies voted for de Gaulle's investiture, forty-nine against. Among those voting for de Gaulle, Mollet, Max Lejeune, and Eugène Thomas also agreed to serve as state secretaries in the new de Gaulle government.

De Gaulle's return to power was not, of course, a brief episode, but the beginning of the Fifth Republic, and at the outset of the new era, it was not Mollet and the French Socialist leaders, but Pierre Mendès-France and a young Radical, François Mitterrand, who spearheaded the non-Communist effort against de Gaulle and his regime. They were the Left's "shield of honor."[55] But the political marriage of de Gaulle and the majority of the SFIO was also not of long duration. If, as Depreux noted, Mollet *"y a cru"* (was a Gaullist believer), he did not remain one for long. The party soon resumed its oppositional role. However, there is no doubt that Mollet's and the party's role in smoothing de Gaulle's return to power accelerated the SFIO's decline as a major force among the French non-Communist Left. As we saw earlier, for a number of prominent SFIO leaders the party's stand in May, 1958, was the reason for their final break with the old organization. But even many of the militants who remained loyal to the party were unhappy with the actions of Mollet and his supporters. At the national congress of September, 1958, tempers ran high, and for the first time since 1946 some delegates openly demanded Mollet's resignation.[56]

Unity in what remained of the party seemed to have been restored when, for both tactical and political reasons, Mollet joined the opposition to de Gaulle. Disagreements with the general's domestic and foreign policies and the disastrous results of the November, 1958, legislative elections persuaded the SFIO that its political future was not as an ally of de Gaulle. However, even then the Mollet wing of the party continued to support the general in at least some of his policies, notably his efforts to reach a settlement in Algeria. In fact, the SFIO's opposition was focused more on the constitutional system—presidentialism instead of parliamentarism—than on de Gaulle's concrete policies.[57]

Clearly, the SFIO's fate was intricately linked to the constitutional system of the Fourth Republic. More than any other political group the SFIO was identified (and saw itself) as *the* political foundation of the Fourth Republic. Consequently, the collapse of that regime and the decline of the French Socialists moved along parallel lines. Moreover, the end of parliamentary democracy in

France also significantly weakened Guy Mollet's position as leader of the party. His support of de Gaulle's return to power and his initial acceptance of a part in the new government alienated many of the SFIO's militants. The opposition, already vocal in 1958, flexed its muscles even more at the next year's congress. In the elections for members of the CD at the July, 1959, national congress Mollet sank to ninth place in the balloting. A similar portent of the growing split was the revival of *tendances* in the party. In 1959 six of the forty-five members of the CD formally identified themselves as an anti-Mollet minority.[58]

Domestic Policies

The three parties placed rather different priorities on domestic and foreign policy issues. Although the SFIO insisted that its goal continued to be to "transform the society and prepare it for the passage from political democracy to Socialist democracy," in the assessment of his government's record Mollet devoted twenty pages to domestic affairs and sixty-eight (quite defensive) pages to foreign policy.[59] In the PvdA and the SPD the priorities were reversed. The Dutch Socialists were facing growing challenges to their domestic program, but they did not question the long established multi partisanship in Dutch foreign policy. The SPD, for its part, had already made peace with many of the CDU's domestic policies. As a result the party had an increasingly difficult time defining what was specifically Social Democratic about its domestic program. Yet, despite their differing priorities, the parties' domestic policy concerns were remarkably similar: the relationship of government and the economy; public expenditures for the social net; relations between the parties and the churches; and, in Germany and France, the armed forces' role in society.

The PvdA had to address domestic concerns first because some unique problems faced Holland at the end of the decade. In a sense, the party found it had been too successful. The Dutch version of the welfare state was by now well-established, and even the PvdA's political rivals (and coalition partners) accepted the social net as a given; observers spoke of the Socialists' "intellectual breakthrough" on this score. At the same time, tertiary industrialism brought major structural changes to the Dutch economy, and these adversely affected some of the PvdA's traditional voting constituencies. Coal mining became increasingly obsolete, and in 1957 a major strike of coal miners in Southern Holland destroyed the postwar

pattern of generally harmonious labor relations in The Netherlands. The PvdA claimed the strike had been fomented by KVP
agitators, but the party could not deny that there were serious
problems to agitate about. At the same time, in other sectors of the
economy the successful supply-side policies, which had made the
boom of the 1950s possible, gave way to increasing problems of
wage and income differentials. Full employment and a growing
labor shortage allowed skilled workers to make a mockery of the
official wage scales. By the end of the decade, extralegal wage
agreements were the norm rather than the exception.

The PvdA had a difficult time formulating concrete policy proposals to deal with the new challenges. Sharply divided over the
desirability of shifting over to a demand-side economic program,[60]
the Socialists left new initiatives to the bourgeois parties. True, the
long-range goal remained as lofty as ever. In a commentary on the
PvdA's 1959 congress (which had adopted the party's new program) Willem Banning tried to distinguish between the welfare
state, in itself a laudable accomplishment, and true Democratic
Socialism, which he defined as "whenever welfare is distributed
in a just way and when no other chains (for example political dictatorship) have replaced the chains of poverty." However, neither
Banning nor any other PvdA leader was able to state how the
PvdA's lofty aim was to be accomplished in the context of the late
1950s. While a majority of the party leaders reiterated their rejection of policies associated with the old Socialism—nationalizations
and centralized planning—for the last decade they had convinced
themselves that wage controls were the keys to a successful industrial policy. When the Dutch Socialists were confronted with the
collapse of this steering mechanism, they could think of nothing
except to endorse Karl Schiller's catchy principle "as much competition as possible, as little planning as necessary."[61] It fell to the
KVP to offer specific proposals that would increase the wealth of
the salaried classes.

The SPD, for whom Karl Schiller had formulated his famous
dictum, found itself in a rare position. Theory and practice did not
contradict each other. The victory of the reformers over the traditionalists meant that the party could formulate specific policy proposals that realistically addressed the societal conditions prevailing
at the end of the decade. Concretely, the SPD abandoned large-
scale planning as an essential part of Democratic Socialism. The
party also attempted to endow the concept of *Gemeineigentum*
(community ownership) with new meaning. Traditionally, this had
meant public ownership of the means of production, but in the

new SPD the debate focused on issues like profit sharing and stock options for wage earners. Rather than demanding fundamental structural changes, the SPD's economic proposals were designed to reduce income maldistribution and preserve genuine competition, while preventing excessive concentrations of power in private hands. In line with its new thinking, the party discovered the middle class was a positive force in the economy, and, not incidentally, a source of potential SPD votes.[62]

As a government party the SFIO's domestic accomplishments were overshadowed by its foreign policy disasters, but in retrospect Guy Mollet was proud of his cabinet's domestic policy record. The prime minister remembered that he had inherited a difficult economic and financial situation, but that his government had been successful in dealing with the problem. It is true, when the cabinet fell, France had one of the lowest unemployment rates among the Common Market countries, but Mollet's government had accomplished this by continuing the policies that virtually all French cabinets had pursued since the end of the war: massive investment in the public sector of the economy and expansion of the social net. There was nothing specifically Socialist about these policies since the program was quintessential postwar French statism, and critics from the left and right lost no time in attacking the Mollet government's economic policies. The left, as always, criticized the cabinet's lack of revolutionary vision and action, while right-wing critics, who included some of the SFIO's coalition partners, focused on the fiscal consequences of Mollet's program. That issue was becoming increasingly acute as severe strains on the French budget raised legitimate fears of renewed, uncontrolled inflation.[63]

As if to answer both groups of critics, the SFIO in July, 1957, appointed a commission, headed by Francis Leenhardt, to formulate a new economic program. The result was a stunning contrast to the document that would be adopted at Bad Godesberg two years later. Although the draft emphasized the values of managerial initiative and competition, the SFIO commission also called for further nationalizations, beginning with the banking system, and increased investment in the public sector. The commission's report aroused little interest among the rank-and-file membership; the dramatic events of 1958 pushed discussions of economic programs to the margins. Still, domestic policy concerns led to the SFIO's break with de Gaulle. The Socialists accused de Gaulle of shifting resource priorities toward private enterprise and neglecting investments in the public sector, the segment of the economy

which the Socialists saw as the key to France's continuing modernization. As Mollet put it, "governmental stagnation" had led to
his resignation.[64]

Economic policy issues, of course, are closely related to questions of taxation and budgetary priorities, and, while the economies
of the three countries were still vigorous, financial difficulties were
beginning to present some acute challenges. In Holland the cabinet was sharply divided over the most effective means of contain-
ing the budget deficits, with the debate focusing on the costs of
state-subsidized housing construction. That program had been
one of the PvdA's major initiatives after the Second World War,
and by all accounts it had done a great deal to alleviate Holland's
chronic problem of substandard housing in many of the country's
urban areas. While the PvdA argued for continued investment in
public housing, to be financed by a two-year one percent surcharge on the income tax levied on higher incomes, its bourgeois
partners insisted on limiting the surcharge to one year. It was this
clash over the budget for 1959 which led to the fall of the coalition
at the end of 1958.[65]

Since the SPD was not in a position to set government policy, its
proposals were reactions to the consequences of the Christian
Democrats' decade-long practice of supply-side economics. Ludwig Erhard's social market economy, while certainly raising the
standard of living for virtually all West Germans, had also significantly increased income disparities among the various segments
of West German society. Interestingly, the SPD did not propose to
address the problem via changes in the tax structure. (German
taxes were already high and steeply graduated.) Rather, the party
advocated a combination of strengthening the social net for those
at the lower end of the economic scale, and creating greater opportunities for all employees to participate in the wealth of private
enterprise. The traditionalists were shocked, but in the aftermath
of Bad Godesberg the SPD actually endorsed the concept of *Volksaktien*, shares of stock in private or privatized companies which
wage earners could acquire for relatively little money. (The Christian Democratic government had introduced such Volksaktien as
part of the privatization of the government-controlled Volkswagen
auto company.[66])

France faced particularly formidable financial problems. The
Suez expedition, the continuing war in Algeria, and the Mollet
government's increased allocation for social services had raised
inflationary pressures. There seemed to be only two solutions to
the problem: Either a devaluation of the French franc (in these

days currency exchange rates were still fixed under the Bretton Woods Agreement) or the imposition of what Mollet called *sévérité fiscale* (fiscal severity). The first meant increased prices for virtually all imported goods, the second severe curtailments of social expenditures and investments in the public sector. It was especially disappointing to a party that prided itself in pursuing Socialist policies, that both solutions were standard capitalist answers to capitalist problems. Christian Pineau commented sadly at a CD meeting that there really was no Socialist answer to France's fiscal problems. In the end the Mollet government devalued the franc, but the measure was not successful; inflation began galloping again.[67]

The debate over social policies took on a different character as western Europe began to encounter the challenges of the tertiary industrial society. Traditionally the Social Democrats had focused their social policy demands on measures that cushioned wage earners against the uncertainties of the market place. Suddenly the focus shifted to such novel topics as increased opportunities for education and quality of life issues. It was clear that the coming tertiary industrial society would need a well-educated workforce, which meant a vast expansion of educational facilities, especially at the university and technical college levels. But the new society would also provide more leisure time and more disposable income, and this brought issues like commercial television and state-run lotteries to the fore.

The PvdA played a major role in addressing the educational issues head-on. One of the last major reform acts of the *brede basis* cabinet was the so-called *mammoetwet* (mammoth law) which led to profound changes throughout the entire Dutch educational system. The reforms, characterized by increased educational opportunities at all levels and more chances for students to cross over between school types, have stood the test of time. In its essentials the mammoetwet is still in effect today, meeting well the needs of Dutch tertiary industrialism. Although the driving force behind the educational reforms was the KVP politician J.L.M.Th. Cals, the PvdA enthusiastically backed the reform package.

The party's leadership was divided, however, on the establishment of commercial television and state-run lotteries. For many Social Democrats both concepts ran counter to their longstanding beliefs that public control of the airwaves was necessary to fulfill the educational and informational mission of radio and television, and that the state should not promote gambling and games of chance. In the end, the PvdA agreed to both proposals in a futile attempt to preserve coalition harmony.[68]

The SPD had an easier time with social issues. Anxious to present itself as a coalition partner, many of its proposals were of the "we can do more of the same, and we can do it better" variety. Financial concerns were not yet a major concern in Germany, so the SPD could offer a catalogue of expanded social services without arousing fiscal worries. As in Holland, commercial television was a matter of controversy. The government had proposed that a second network, which had (and still has) the pedestrian name *Zweites Deutsches Fernsehen* (Second German Television channel [ZDF]) should be a commercial channel. The SPD was opposed to this, and in cooperation with a number of Christian Democrats, who also raised objections, the party was able to defeat the government proposal. There was no opportunity for a mammoetwet in Germany, since educational issues are handled by the Länder. However, the SPD-governed states did recognize the needs of the future, and laid the groundwork for what was to be a massive expansion of educational offerings in the 1960s.[69]

The SFIO had the most difficult time coming up with a viable social policy. As the war in Algeria became an increasingly large budgetary item, none of the French governments at the end of the Fourth Republic had funds to invest in domestic programs. But there was a lack of vision as well. The SFIO tended to look upon France's future as an expanded and modernized secondary industrial society. Insisting on "economic expansion coupled with social solidarity," the party saw little need for addressing educational reforms, for example. That neglect, which the de Gaulle governments continued, was to have profound and bitter consequences in the 1960s. (Commercial television was not yet an issue in France.[70])

There were important developments as well in another long-standing controversy—relations between organized religion and the parties. The PvdA set out to repair the damage as old antagonisms between Catholics and Socialists seemed to flare up again toward the end of the decade. Lingering resentment of the 1954 mandement and deteriorating relations between the KVP and the PvdA stirred dormant resentments between Catholics and PvdA militants. (Relations between the party and the Protestant churches were not a problem.) Remarkably, both the PvdA's leadership and the Catholic Church hierarchy worked hard to confine the antagonisms to the political organizations. The PvdA made sure that its campaign attacks were directed against its political rival and not the Catholic Church, while the bishops made no effort to give ecclesiastical support to the KVP. It was as though they had exhausted their ammunition after the mandement.

While the PvdA worked to preserve the ground already won, the SPD had to set out on a new campaign. In the earlier part of the decade the party had made some headway in improving contacts with the Protestant churches, and in the late 1950s the party began a concerted effort to put relations with the Catholic Church on a new footing. After the Bad Godesberg Program had formally recognized organized religion for its valuable contributions to societal life, a number of party leaders attempted to engage members of the Catholic hierarchy in a series of dialogues. On a more concrete level, several SPD-governed Länder agreed to Church demands for making religious instruction a part of the curriculum in the public schools—traditionally a major sticking point for the Social Democrats. It must be remembered, of course, that there was movement on the Catholic side as well. The liberalizing trends that culminated in the encyclicals of Pope John XXXIII and the Second Vatican Council, began in the late 1950s.[71]

Not surprisingly the men in the forefront of the SPD's effort were the same reformers who had led the party to the Bad Godesberg Program: Fritz Erler, Willy Brandt, Carlo Schmid, Waldemar von Knoeringen, and Willi Eichler. Remarkably, most of them came from a Protestant religious background. (Two exceptions were Waldemar von Knoeringen, the head of the Bavarian SPD, and Hans-Jochen Vogel, in the 1960s and 1970s the lord mayor of Munich.) The policy of improving relations with organized religion evoked surprisingly little opposition from the party's rank-and-file, which was symbolic of the changing times and the changing party.

While the SPD and the PvdA were traveling in the same direction, the SFIO took a different path. By the end of the 1950s secularization, but also new ideas among church leaders, were common phenomena in France, as they were in the rest of western Europe. The SFIO, however, appeared to take little note of these developments. It was continuing to fight the laïciste battles of the Third and Fourth Republics, which was a politically counterproductive stand, to put mildly. Since France needed a united Left to counter Gaullism and by no means all of the French Left was committed to laïcisme, the concept and the SFIO's support of it had a divisive rather than a uniting effect. Nor were all SFIO leaders committed to laïcisme. Olivier Lapie, usually on the left side of the party spectrum, made something of a career of trying to soften the party's stand on laïcisme. In 1959 de Gaulle asked him to head yet another government commission charged with finding a compromise between the antagonistic standpoints of church and state. The commission's work resulted in the Debré Law which for the first time in a century permitted an institutional role for the churches in public education.[72]

Although the Mollet government had attempted (unsuccessfully) to open channels of communication to the Vatican, Mollet and the traditionalists—who constituted a majority of the party—insisted there could be no French Republic and no Socialist program without a firm commitment to laïcisme. An angry majority of the CD demanded that Lapie resign his membership in the mediating commission because the group's goals were contrary to party doctrine. Still, the eternal nay-sayers did not go unchallenged. Among the minority of CD members Jacques Brutelle spoke of the "hypocrisy of the laïques." Equally important, there was movement among the groups and leaders of the New Left outside the SFIO. For the PSA, which saw itself as the keeper of the Left's holy grail, laïcisme was not an indispensable precondition of the future socialist society. In his bitter polemic *Le Trahi de Socialisme* André Philip insisted that the old version of laïcisme simply had no place in a modern Social Democratic ideology. It was increasingly clear, then, that on this issue the SFIO's rigidity isolated the party within the French non-Communist Left.[73]

Both the SPD and the SFIO had to deal with another chapter in the perennial story of relations between the parties and the armed forces. The SPD had to determine its position on the new Bundeswehr, and in France the army's challenge to the constitutional system ultimately brought down the Fourth Republic.

Despite the SPD's long (and justified) tradition of distrust of the German armed forces, the party's reaction to the establishment of the Bundeswehr was remarkably unemotional and positive. The German Social Democrats were fortunate to have Fritz Erler as their expert on military affairs in the Bundestag. In cooperation with a number of other reformers, notably the youthful Helmut Schmidt, Erler was able to convince both the party and the legislature that the Bundeswehr should be firmly embedded in the fabric of West German democracy.[74]

In some ways, Erler had an easier time with his Christian Democratic colleagues in the Bundestag than with many of his comrades in the party. Old traditions die hard, and there was a significant minority within the SPD that felt the party should continue its opposition to any West German armed forces. Such sentiments were particularly widespread among the SPD's youth organizations, the SDS and what was left of the Falken. Erler repeatedly complained to the party's executive committee that he was the target of unfair attacks from these organizations. However, as would be the case in the Bad Godesberg Program a couple of years later, the opposition represented more noise than substance. At the 1958 party congress a large majority of the delegates affirmed the SPD's positive stand on national defense and the need for a democratic Bundeswehr. Subsequently, the party's executive committee urged party members to serve in the Bundeswehr, and encouraged party organizations to establish positive relations with Bundeswehr units stationed in their vicinity.[75]

The SFIO's position on the role of the army at the end of the decade was far less clear cut. What at first glance appeared to be a simple problem of the army's growing independence of civilian control, was, in the view of Mollet and his close associates, a more complicated matter. As a result the SFIO did not condemn the growing autonomy of the armed forces outright, as one might have expected, but equivocated. The reason was not cowardice or naiveté, but the secretary general's recognition that the French army was traumatized by the defeat in Indochina and in the midst of an identity crisis. Mollet and the party majority hoped to resolve the crisis by yielding to the army's demand for peace with honor in Algeria, while rejecting its request for a French atomic bomb and a greater role for the military in internal affairs. As we shall see in the next section, Mollet and the party would fail on all counts.[76]

Foreign Policy

Although the three parties shared a number of foreign policy concerns—the Atlantic Alliance, East-West relations, and European unification—they differed considerably in their ability to influence the conduct of foreign affairs. The PvdA was a member of the government for almost the entire period, but the Socialists did not control the foreign affairs ministry. In France a Socialist prime minister, Guy Mollet, and a Socialist foreign minister, Christian Pineau, directed the country's foreign relations during a crucial period of a year and a half. In contrast, the SPD could articulate its ideas only from the opposition benches.

The Atlantic Alliance was subjected to a number of strains during these years. American proposals to station tactical atomic weapons in western Europe divided the Socialist parties. Among the three parties the PvdA was least concerned about these issues. Even in the face of challenges from the PSP, the PvdA maintained its policy of consistent support for the Alliance. The Dutch Socialists rejected any Dutch military disengagement from NATO, welcomed German membership in NATO, and accepted the necessity of stationing US tactical atomic weapons in Europe. Only at the end of the decade did the party express doubts about the need to place a new generation of medium-range missiles on European soil.[77]

In the SPD there was a clear shift toward accepting Germany's membership in the Atlantic Alliance. The change was part of the SPD's move to the political center, but personal relations also played a part. As a group the reformist leaders had a much better relationship with American policy makers than had Schumacher and his close associates. At the same time, the SPD led the fight in the Bundestag to prevent the Bundeswehr from having an atomic arsenal of its own. This pleased the Americans and the other Western Allies, underscored the SPD's new reputation as a moderate and reasonable force in German foreign relations, while it represented a defeat for the nationalist defense minister, Franz-Josef Strauss.[78]

Over the years the SFIO had consistently supported France's close cooperation with the Atlantic Alliance, and it was ironic that during the Mollet government's term of office relations between France and the Atlantic Alliance reached their nadir. The principal cause of the tensions was France's precipitous action during the Suez Crisis in the fall of 1956. In retrospect, the Suez adventure was a disaster from beginning to end. Jules Moch called it a "monument of errors and hypocrisies." If putting severe strains on the Atlantic partnership were not enough, the failed policy also further alienated the French military from the Fourth Republic, deepened divisions within the SFIO, turned many French intellectuals and students from the party, and isolated the party within the SI. Oreste Rosenfeld blamed Suez for the end of European Socialism and the coming of de Gaulle.[79]

The long-simmering fuse of the Suez bomb was the ambition of the Egyptian dictator Gamal Abdel Nasser to become a major player in Near East affairs. Guy Mollet was actually less concerned about Nasser's nationalization of the Suez Canal Company (the official justification for the military action), than about Nasser's support for the Algerian independence movement. The prime minister and the resident general in Algeria, the Socialist Robert Lacoste, were convinced that without Nasser's support the Algerian rebels would quickly agree to an armistice on France's terms. Beyond that they saw Nasser as the new Hitler in international affairs, determined to create and control a vast empire. From this perspective, letting the Egyptian leader fulfill his ambitions was tantamount to another Munich.[80]

The actual operation was a military success followed by diplomatic humiliation. On 29 October Israeli troops attacked Egyptian positions. (Israel participated in the invasion partly because it, too, regarded Nasser as a menace in international affairs, but primarily because the reward for Israeli involvement was access to the results of French atomic weapons research.[81]) On the following day the British and French governments sent an ultimatum to the Egyptians, demanding they rescind the nationalization of the Suez Canal Company. When the ultimatum was ignored, the British and French bombarded Port Said. Within days the Americans, who had not been consulted about the Anglo-French action, weighed in with massive pressure on the British and the French to cease their operations. The British prime minister Anthony Eden yielded first, and Mollet had no choice but to follow suit.

The fallout among the SFIO leaders was intense and bitter. While Mollet's supporters loyally defended the prime minister and accepted his explanation that removing Nasser from the scene was the key to a settlement in Algeria and tranquility in the Middle East, the critics, led by André Philip, vigorously attacked everything about the Suez operation. They insisted that the Suez debacle had isolated the SFIO from its sister parties, alienated France from its principal ally, and made negotiating a peaceful settlement in Algeria all but impossible. All this, according to Philip and his fellow critics, because Guy Mollet was pursuing the impossible dream of returning France to superpower status and holding on to its colonial empire. Philip was certainly exaggerating, but there is little doubt that the Suez affair had profound repercussions for the future of the SFIO and Mollet's position within the party.[82]

Mollet and his supporters were convinced not only that they had the winning formula for settling the Algerian conflict, but that the elections of 1956 had demonstrated the French voters thought so too. After all, a few months before becoming prime minister Mollet had claimed "we [the French Socialists] are the only ones capable of proposing a solution that keeps North Africa linked to France."[83] (Although the Mollet government had granted Morocco and Tunisia independence in March, 1956, the cabinet and Mollet himself felt Algeria presented an entirely different case.) Underlying the mantra that the party and government would repeat incessantly—armistice, negotiations, elections—was the concept of

France's *mission civilisatrice* (civilizing mission). Algeria might well enjoy a considerable degree of political and cultural autonomy, but some sort of continuing French presence was needed to guide Algeria to a higher level of civilization. For good measure the Socialists added that an independent Algeria was also unacceptable because it would inevitably be controlled by Moscow.[84]

Needless to say, the Algerian rebels did not accept the French government's goals, and neither, for entirely different reasons, did the French settlers in Algeria, the French army, or French public opinion. Partly to appease these constituencies, and partly because Mollet himself attached a more narrow, nationalistic significance to French control of Algeria, the Mollet government pursued an essentially repressive rather than an emancipatory policy. After the loss of Indochina and the granting of independence to Tunisia and Morocco, Algeria remained "the last bastion of a great France."[85]

Guy Mollet was undoubtedly right in feeling that his government had been extended a considerable advance credit when it came into office. The National Assembly readily voted decree powers which allowed the cabinet and Lacoste considerable latitude in pursuing their policies. The party's official line was also routinely endorsed by large majorities at the SFIO's national congresses.

However, expectations of success were soon replaced by disappointment and disillusionment. On his first visit to Algeria, shortly after becoming prime minister, riots and a shower of rotten tomatoes showed Mollet what the French settlers thought of his attempt to find a peaceful and equitable solution. After that, the situation rapidly deteriorated. Lacoste, increasingly convinced that only a military solution was possible, allowed the armed forces to operate as they saw fit. The results were widespread tortures and other atrocities, and, in the most famous episode of military highhandedness, the kidnapping of the Algerian rebel leader Ben Bella while he was traveling over Moroccan airspace. In Paris the government, despite mounting media exposure of these activities and criticism from the SI, drew the wagons together and denied what it could not control or prevent. Mollet and his supporters became defensive and determined to succeed. Algeria became a "veritable trauma" for them. Mollet himself thought "France was playing out her destiny in the Algerian drama."[86] True, the SFIO vigorously condemned the open rebellion of the Algerian settlers and the army, but by then it was too late. Mollet and the Fourth Republic had demonstrated that they could not find a solution to the Algerian problem.

While the SFIO and the government were losing credibility, the critics at home and abroad found a ready target. Not surprisingly, the same leaders who had attacked the Suez expedition were equally critical of Mollet's Algerian policy. What was to become in the 1960s the new French Left crystallized around the issue of opposition to Mollet's Algerian policy. Disagreement with the Mollet line was a major catalyst for the founding of the PSA, and the immediate inspiration for André Philip's influential polemic, *Le Trahi de Socialisme*. In addition to Philip, Courtois and Defferre joined the attack on the general secretary in the CD, while Rosenfeld submitted a long and bitter report to the Socialist International. In addition to the familiar faces in the SFIO, a number of leaders outside the party, such as François Mitterrand and Pierre Mendès-France, as well as numerous figures in the club scene joined the growing throng of critics.

The reaction of the other two parties to France's Near East policy was muted in public (it also became customary to attack Robert Lacoste as a substitute target for Guy Mollet and his government) and angry in private. Alfred Mozer, usually a friend of the SFIO, called the Suez expedition "especially disappointing." For the SPD tactical considerations as well as issues of Socialist solidarity came into play. The Mollet government was in charge of negotiating the modalities of the return of the Saar to Germany, and for that reason alone the German Social Democrats were anxious not to annoy the SFIO's leaders. With a touch of cynicism Herbert Wehner noted, "the return of the Saar has its price." In private, however, the German Socialists sided with Mollet's critics. Fritz Erler thought that Mollet was pursuing a goal—colonialism—that had been condemned by history.[87]

There was a connection between the French failures in the Middle East and major advances in the process of West European unification—the Common Market and Euratom. The by now well-established success of the ECSC and the obvious need for larger markets of Europe's expanding economy undoubtedly played a part in the move toward the Common Market, but the French Socialists especially felt a need for a success to offset their failures in the Middle East.

The significance of the Common Market for the history of the three Social Democratic parties can hardly be overestimated. The Common Agricultural Policy (CAP) that became an integral part of the Treaty of Rome, forced the German, Dutch, and French parties to focus on the problems of farmers and agriculture, a topic and constituency that they had until now largely neglected. The Common Market also brought the German Social Democrats out of European isolation; the European Economic Community (EEC) and Euratom were the first West European unification projects which the SPD formally endorsed. As for the SFIO, the Common Market was consistent with its long-established efforts to advance European unification, but, by agreeing to expose France to the progressive implementation of free trade, it also forced the party (as well as France itself), to "enter into modernity."[88]

Although all three parties would eventually become enthusiastic supporters of the EEC, at the outset of the often difficult negotiations they were more skeptical. The SFIO was once again divided. Some leaders, following the majority of French public opinion and the *patronat*, felt that France was not yet ready to give up her traditional trade barriers. Mollet disagreed, but for political reasons was reluctant to assume a leadership role in this case, leaving it to his foreign minister, Christian Pineau. Both in the cabinet and the party Pineau supported the Common Market as enthusiastically as he had the EDC.

In Holland Drees remained a Euro-skeptic. In fact, the usually even-tempered and reasonable prime minister suspected a Popish plot behind the whole idea.[89] But the majority of the PvdA's leaders saw only benefits in the EEC. They welcomed the advantages of an expanded market for Dutch industry and agriculture and the promise of stable prices under the CAP. The key man here was Sicco Mansholt, from 1945 to 1957 the Dutch minister of agriculture and, beginning in 1958, the EC's commissioner for agriculture. The formulation of the CAP was, to a large extent, his work. The PvdA also thought the provisions in the draft treaty for Community-wide planning and financial integration would propel the European economy to new levels of prosperity and sophistication.

The reasons for the SPD's dramatic shift on European unification were partly tactical and partly ideological. Tactically the reformers wanted to signal that the SPD had abandoned intransigent opposition and become a cooperative Volkspartei. Ideologically, the party since its founding had advocated eliminating tariffs in Europe. In fact, some leaders, like Helmut Schmidt, initially opposed the Rome Treaties because they felt the EEC left too many trade barriers in place. In addition, there was the link to Euratom. A number of SPD experts on energy shared the concerns about the imminent shortage of fossil fuels, and consequently welcomed the accelerated development of atomic energy promised in the Euratom treaty.[90]

The Socialists' contribution to the establishment of the EEC was profound, even greater than they realized at the time. Christian Pineau forced the pace of the negotiations, ignoring the objections of the French patronat and pulling along the more cautious Guy

Mollet. The SPD's endorsement of the Common Market meant that the treaty was ratified quickly in the Bundestag, unhindered by the parliamentary maneuvers the SPD had put in the way of the Schuman Plan and the EDC. As it turned out the Europeanists managed to create the Common Market just in time. Had Charles de Gaulle been in power in France when the Treaty of Rome was negotiated, he certainly would not have accepted the supranational decision-making elements built into the EEC agreement.[91]

There was also movement on the East-West front at the end of the decade; detente with Nikita Khrushchev's Soviet Union was in the air. To be sure, the messages coming from Moscow were contradictory. On the one hand the new Soviet leaders had denounced Stalin's crimes, and they talked incessantly about peaceful coexistence. On the other hand, Soviet troops brutally suppressed the Hungarian Revolution in the fall of 1956, and in 1958 the Soviet Union issued an ultimatum to the Western Allies which began another Berlin crisis, culminating in the construction of the Berlin Wall three years later.

The three parties viewed the prospect of improved relations with the Soviet Union from different perspectives. Initially the SFIO leaders had high hopes for detente after Khrushchev's speech denouncing Stalin, and these sentiments were shared by the PSA and some other French left-wing leaders, including Pierre Mendès-France. Their optimism was quickly dashed, however, when a delegation of party dignitaries visited Moscow in July, 1956. In their meetings with Khrushchev the French Socialists quickly learned the limits of detente: better relations did not mean changes in the prevailing power contours in Europe. The Soviets insisted the West recognize the realities of 1945, including the permanent division of Germany. Khrushchev attempted to persuade his French guests that the existence of two separate German states was in France's as well as the Soviet Union's interest, and he dismissed Mollet's spirited defense of the Federal Republic as a different, democratic Germany that did not threaten its neighbors. The SFIO delegation came back disillusioned, and reaffirmed its commitment to the Western Alliance. The party also condemned unequivocally the Soviet moves in Hungary. The PvdA moved in tandem with the SFIO. The Dutch Socialists, too, insisted NATO remained the bedrock of East-West relations, and they used particularly harsh language to denounce the Soviet brutalities in Hungary.[92]

The SPD remained optimistic rather longer. The proposal that became known as the *Deutschlandplan* (Germany Plan) was an integral part of the SPD's continuing quest for German reunification, but it was triggered by proposals from the Polish foreign minister Adam Rapacki. In October, 1957, the minister urged that the Great Powers should negotiate a military disengagement pact. He specifically suggested that the United States and Soviet Union remove some of their troops from Central Europe, and create a zone in Central Europe, including Poland, Czechoslovakia, and both Germanies, in which no atomic weapons would be stationed.

A number of SPD leaders, foremost among them Herbert Wehner, argued that the "Rapacki Plan" signaled the Soviets' willingness to negotiate a comprehensive settlement to reduce tensions in Central Europe.[93] (Wehner and everyone else assumed, of course, that Rapacki would not have launched his initiative without prior Soviet approval.) Since the SPD had always stressed the key to reducing tensions in Europe was a reunified and democratic Germany linked to a security pact among the Big Four, the party presented a plan of its own—the Germany Plan—which coupled the essentials of the Rapacki Plan with the SPD's proposals for German reunification. Concretely, a committee headed by Wehner proposed that the Soviets permit German reunification on the basis of free elections in all of Germany. The reunified country would then agree not to join any military alliance or to have atomic weapons stationed on its soil.[94]

The ideas contained in the Germany Plan were not new. In fact, they represented the last hurrah of the old SPD's persistent efforts to link reunification with military non-engagement. Although both the executive committee and the party's parliamentary delegation loyally supported the plan in public, privately many leaders were skeptical. One of these was Willy Brandt, who described the proposal as *nicht wirklichkeitsnah* (not realistic) especially in view of the Soviets' Berlin ultimatum. A number of parliamentarians, including some members of the commission which drafted the plan, had serious reservations. One SPD Bundestag delegate, Karl Mommer, even voiced in public what others thought privately: the plan was too risky, because without the West's military umbrella a reunified Germany would be easy prey for the Soviets.[95]

The SPD launched the Germany Plan with considerable media fanfare, but it aroused little interest in West Germany or among the Western Allies. French and Dutch Socialist leaders were also unenthusiastic, and warned against weakening NATO.[96] The USSR praised the SPD's initiative as a positive development, but it soon turned out that the Soviets deliberately misinterpreted the thrust of the Germany Plan as a willingness on the part of the SPD to recognize the legitimacy of the GDR. In line with this interpretation the Communist regime in East Germany welcomed the

SPD's ideas, and promptly suggested the sovereign East and West German governments should now negotiate the future of Germany as equal partners.[97]

The death blow came from Nikita Khrushchev himself when he met in March, 1959, with a high-level SPD delegation that included Fritz Erler and Carlo Schmid. Khrushchev gave the German Social Democrats the same message he had given the French Socialists earlier: the West would have to recognize the realities of 1945, and accept the division of Europe into two power blocs. As far as Germany was concerned, the realities of 1945 included the permanent existence of two separate German states. Ironically, the Germany Plan was officially released one day after, as Willy Brandt put it, the delegation came back "with less than empty hands."

As a result, to quote Willy Brandt again, "the Germany Plan was taken off the table faster than it had been put on the table." Undoubtedly, no one was more disappointed than Herbert Wehner, who seems to have genuinely believed that the SPD's initiative had a realistic chance of advancing the prospect of German reunification. Wehner had not only expected Soviet support, but also hoped that the East German Communists would agree to German reunification. He was convinced that "there were patriots in the SED as well." Fritz Erler, less optimistic on this score, replied that "Ulbricht is no Gomulka, but a quisling." When the failure became obvious, Wehner's first reaction was to disassociate the party from the plan, but Brandt and Erler quickly persuaded him that after the media circus surrounding the original publication, the SPD had lost its chance for "deniability."[98]

In the end, Wehner, as he so often did at crucial moments in the party's history, not only acknowledged the naivete of the Germany Plan, but turned the SPD's failure into an advantage. Shocking the press, his comrades, and the Christian Democrats alike, Wehner on June 30, 1960, delivered what became known as his *Gemeinsamkeiten* (commonalities) speech in the Bundestag. In a brilliant address that held parliament spellbound, Wehner acknowledged the failure of the party's past foreign policies and stressed the commonalities that bound the Social Democrats and Christian Democrats to all facets of the Western Alliance. The speech was far more than a mea culpa. Wehner was keeping his major political goal, a national coalition between the SPD and one or more of the bourgeois parties, firmly in sight. He hoped (correctly, as it turned out) that what the Bad Godesberg Program had done for domestic policies, the *Gemeinsamkeiten* speech would do for foreign relations.[99]

Conclusion

In a number of ways the second half of the 1950s was a watershed in the postwar history of the Social Democratic parties. Although the SFIO might not acknowledge it, what Piet de Rooy has called "the red dream" was over.[100] Visions of the breakthrough had become unrealistic, and indeed the political trend in western Europe was toward conservatism. For the PvdA these were perhaps the most disappointing years since its founding. The party discovered that despite a decade of hard work, the verzuiling of Dutch society remained a fact of political life. Moreover, when the beginnings of ontzuiling did become apparent, the Social Democrats were not the primary political beneficiaries. Compounding these problems, the party had considerable difficulty adjusting to its new role as an opposition party. Although a growing minority saw the PvdA's future as leading a new bloc of progressive Dutch parties, most leaders were uncomfortable out of the government and clearly wanted to get back into the coalition as quickly as possible. (Politicians have short memories, but the minority's vision was, of course, what the leaders of the NVB had articulated when they founded the PvdA back in 1946.)

The SPD found itself in almost the reverse situation. After the shock of the electoral setback of 1957, the party set out to lay the foundations for its final transformation from Klassenpartei to Volkspartei. The Bad Godesberg program, the party's acceptance of the Common Market, and Wehner's *Gemeinsamkeiten* speech were important milestones along the way. By the end of the decade the party's efforts were bearing fruit; the West Germans were reacting positively to the SPD's new image.[101]

The SFIO was clearly in the least favorable position. Despite the urgings of a number of leaders, the party as a whole had failed to modernize either its structure or program. In addition, the undoubted successes of the Mollet government, ranging from the return of the Saar to Germany to the EEC, were overshadowed by the Suez debacle and the festering sore of Algeria. When the Mollet government left office, the SFIO's general secretary was, for many on the French Left, the man they most loved to hate, and this alienation was compounded by Mollet's role in helping de Gaulle return to power. On the threshold of the Fifth Republic the SFIO was a severely weakened organization unable to take the lead in rejuvenating the French non-Communist Left.

Chapter Eight

THE TROUBLED 1960S

❦

The 1960s were a decade of paradoxes, contradictions, and upheavals. The amount of disposable income and leisure time available to most Europeans continued to increase, while the processes of bourgeoisification and secularization accelerated. As a result the concept of "working class" took on new meaning. "The worker as consumer" was Albert Détraz' characterization of the French industrial proletariat. At the same time, Europeans were reminded that the "golden age of capitalism," as Eric Hobsbawn recently called it, would not continue indefinitely. For the first time since the early 1950s there was a noticeable downturn in the economy, and that, together with a series of studies issued by the Club of Rome, gave rise to (decidedly exaggerated) pessimistic visions of the future among intellectuals, who seemed to delight in hearing messages of gloom and doom.[1]

Politics, too, were changing rapidly and radically. The 1960s were marked by a profound generational shift, most dramatically manifested in the upheavals of 1968. At first glance the revolutionaries of 1968 seemed just what the Socialists needed to recoup their political fortunes. However, while most members of the 1968 generation described themselves as leftists, they had little interest in the established Social Democratic parties. The young radicals talked about societal revolution and grass-roots democratization—concepts that by this time had little place in the vocabulary of the established parties. The young revolutionaries also questioned long-established postulates of postwar Social Democracy. Was the continuation of the Cold War really inevitable? Why not recognize the German Democratic Republic? Should not western

Europe's relationship to NATO be reexamined in the light of American involvement in Viet Nam? Was continued economic growth really desirable as an end in itself?

Yet, while the young rushed to new forms of leftism, the classic workers acted more like the middle class they were becoming. Tory workers in France voted for de Gaulle and the Gaullist party. In Holland the PvdA noticed that *ontzuiling* weakened not only the confessional interest groups, but also the traditional working class institutions. The Socialists' core constituency was getting soft along with those of the other parties. In 1967 the PvdA cut all formal ties between the party and its newspaper, *Het Vrije Volk*. Five years later the paper ceased publication as a national press organ altogether, becoming a Rotterdam local instead.[2]

All three parties acknowledged that something new was in the air and that they would have to do something about it, but their responses differed substantially. The SPD continued on the road begun at Bad Godesberg, promising to find a middle ground between the excesses of freewheeling capitalism and the tendencies toward anarchy and utopianism inherent in the visions of the youthful revolutionaries.

In contrast, the SFIO had a difficult time adjusting to the new era. In 1962 French voters approved a change in the country's constitution to provide for the election of the president by direct popular vote. This meant that if the Left were to have any hope of displacing de Gaulle from the Elysée Palace, the opposition parties would need to agree on a candidate who had a realistic chance of winning against the general. It was also necessary to provide the candidate with an effective campaign organization. The search for a leader and a left-wing organization that could be an effective player in the politics of the Fifth Republic led to a bewildering array of party splits, brief electoral pacts, and personal posturing. The SFIO was at the center of it all, though the party was increasingly unable to control the dynamics of the game.[3]

The PvdA was also subjected to severe internal strains in the 1960s. In the last half of the decade a group of young rebels who called themselves *Nieuw Links* (New Left) fought a fierce battle with the PvdA's old guard for control of the party. Ironically, many of Nieuw Links' visions echoed sentiments voiced by the PvdA's founders in 1946. Frans Grosfeld's 1969 definition of socialism as "the striving after a society in which all individuals can completely fulfill themselves so that the total effect of this individual fulfillment is the achievement of the collective goal" could have been written by Willem Banning. The rebels' hope that the PvdA could spearhead a progressive bloc to counter Holland's "reactionary" forces was also reminiscent of the PvdA's early *doorbraak* theories. In contrast to the PvdA's founders, however, Nieuw Links rejected integration and coalition as the bases of political success, favoring polarization and confrontation instead. Rather than smoothing the way for a return of the *brede basis* coalition, the radicals wanted the PvdA to pursue a strategy of unabashed opposition to the bourgeois parties, especially the Catholic KVP.[4]

The State of the Parties

In the rapidly changing political circumstances of the 1960s all three parties recognized the need for organizational streamlining and increased efficiency of communication. The SPD made relatively few changes in its established structures, but they were important ones. In 1958 the party had established the office of the *Präsidium* (presidium), a sort of steering committee of the executive committee, and in the 1960s the presidium and the leaders of the SPD's parliamentary delegation increasingly assumed a policymaking role, with the Parteivorstand acting as an approbation agency.[5]

While the PvdA's old guard was comfortable with the party's traditional organizational format, Nieuw Links voiced a number of criticisms. Above all they complained that the PvdA's parliamentarians acted too independently in party affairs. According to the radicals the regentenpartij had been treating the rank-and-file members for too long as ciphers whose acceptance of the parliamentary leaders' decisions was taken for granted. The reformers also argued that the on-going process of ontzuiling had made the PvdA's traditional *werkgemeenschapen* obsolete. Nieuw Links's organizational proposals included shifting power within the party to the *Partijbestuur*—the organ Nieuw Links claimed better reflected the views of the party's militants—and providing for more grass-roots democracy throughout the PvdA's organization. The outcome of the Dutch organizational debates was a draw. Nieuw Links would eventually gain control of the PB, and the group's supporters dominated some of the party's locals, but the old guard was able to retain its influence in the parliamentary delegation as well as that body's predominance in party affairs. The werkgemeenschapen, too, did not disappear.[6]

The SFIO faced a variety of difficulties. The party was chronically short of money, and, like the PvdA, had to watch its newspaper wither away. By the end of the 1960s *Le Populaire* existed primarily to inform France's political leaders about the SFIO's official line; most of the party members neither read nor subscribed to the paper. The party's election campaigns were notorious for their technical incompetence. The GP and the federations paid little attention to edicts issued by the CD, but the CD was also increasingly incapable of formulating a clear line. No wonder Georges Guile, newly elected to the CD and appalled by the organizational chaos around him, feared in March, 1962 that "the party is going to die for lack of discipline."

The SFIO's leadership did attempt to implement some reforms. To counteract the impression that the party majority (i.e., Mollet and his supporters) were ignoring the growing rifts within the party, in 1962 the minorities were accorded formal representation on the CD. Unity within diversity was the new (and old) watchword. In July, 1967, as the meetings of the enlarged CD were becoming interminable, the executive committee created an eleven-member *Bureau du Parti*, an office that was the equivalent of the SPD's Präsidium. Finally, the CD decided that the party's national congresses should be held biannually rather than annually. The aim was to reduce the opportunity for acrimony and mutual backbiting which increasingly characterized these gatherings. Unfortunately, the reforms had little effect; the party's organizational difficulties persisted.[7]

Of the three parties only the SPD was pleased with its membership profile. The party's membership was growing, expanding into new socioeconomic groups, and getting younger. In 1973 the party had one million members; two-thirds of these had joined since 1963. In 1963 43.9 percent of the membership was thirty-five years old or younger, and six years later that figure had risen to 54.6 percent.[8]

In contrast, the PvdA's overall membership was steadily declining and aging rapidly. The party had 154,188 members in March, 1959; ten years later that figure had sunk to 122,000. Moreover, the party, unlike the SPD, was unable to attract a significant portion of the cohort born after the Second World War generation. At first glance this may seem surprising since the Nieuw Links radicals were members of the 1968 generation. The explanation lay in the nature of the Nieuw Links phenomenon. Nieuw Links was essentially a self-proclaimed leadership elite which, except for a few areas like Amsterdam and Groningen, had little influence among the rank-and-file members.[9]

The SFIO's membership patterns largely paralleled those of the PvdA, but the numbers were even more disappointing. The party had 95,670 members in November, 1962, and 89,417 in June, 1965. Since France had a population about four times that of The Netherlands, this meant that by the 1960s the SFIO had ceased to be a mass party. It was also an old and male-dominated party. In 1963 less than three percent of the members were twenty-five years of age or younger, while more than one-third were older than fifty-five. Only 9.2 percent of the members were women. The SFIO was also increasingly becoming a small town party. The party's parliamentary delegation had always had a large number of mayors in its ranks, and in the years from 1956 to 1967 there was a twofold shift among this group. The number of mayors in the GP not only increased (from forty-nine percent to fifty-nine percent), but the group had far more small town municipal leaders. The GP included twenty-five mayors of towns with fewer than 40,000 inhabitants in 1956 and forty-four in 1967. At the end of its institutional life the SFIO's declining corps of militants was drawn increasingly from the small towns of rural France.[10]

The SPD experienced the most dramatic turnover in its leadership ranks. Erich Ollenhauer's announcement in July, 1959 that he would not be the party's candidate for chancellor in 1961 had already foreshadowed the end of an era. Elections to the presidium confirmed the shift. Of the nine members of the presidium elected in May, 1962 only two—Ollenhauer, who remained party chairman until his death, and Alfred Nau, the party's longtime treasurer—were identified with the old guard. The others were Länder politicians and leaders of the party's Bundestag delegation. (Guy Mollet, recognizing that Ollenhauer was retiring from active national political engagement, proposed him as president of the Socialist International. The SPD leader was elected in September, 1963, but died only three months later.)

The SPD's new candidate for chancellor, Willy Brandt, was the most visible embodiment of the party's youth and vigor. Even some of his fellow reformers felt of the cult of personality being constructed around Brandt was a little too much. In a private letter Fritz Erler commented Brandt "is no monument." The candidate's shadow cabinet was dominated by prominent state politicians; the Länder leaders, of course, had long been the driving force in the SPD's transformation to a Volkspartei. Some were familiar faces, like the longtime prime minister of Hessen, August Zinn, but others were newcomers. This was the time when Helmut Schmidt and Karl Schiller moved from Land politics in Hamburg to the national scene. Schmidt would become head of the SPD's Bundestag delegation in the 1960s, and German chancellor in the

1970s. Schiller was one of the party's most popular figures in the 1960s, and was to be credited with solving the problems created by the recession of 1966–1967. In 1964 Brandt also took over the reins as head of the SPD.[11]

While the torch passed relatively smoothly in the SPD, developments in the PvdA were more acrimonious. The rise of Nieuw Links brought additional complications, but even without this new factor the party had to realign its leadership contours. After the PvdA's move to the opposition benches both the PB and the parliamentary delegation had to find new roles for themselves. Traditionally, the PvdA had a weak chairman who did little more than preside over the meetings of the PB. Since the early 1950s the party's strongman had been Willem Drees, but unlike Guy Mollet, he had no ambition to administer the party. Before the election of the Nieuw Links leader André van der Louw as vice-chairman in 1969 and leader in 1971 brought some drama to the chairman's office, the post had been filled by a succession of relatively colorless individuals: Evert Vermeer from 1960 to 1965, and Sjeng Tans from 1965 to 1971. In addition, the PB was a notoriously self-perpetuating body. Formally chosen by the party congress, there were virtually no contested elections, since all members who wanted to remain on the PB were automatically reelected.[12]

That should have left the field free for the parliamentary delegation, especially since its leader, Jaap Burger, had precipitated the fall of the *brede basis* coalition. Unfortunately, Burger was better at tearing down than at building up. Once the party was out of the government Burger had difficulty leading his parliamentary group as an effective opposition. As a result of widespread dissatisfaction with his leadership style, he was voted out of office in March, 1962, and replaced by Anne Vondeling. The new leader was accommodating rather than abrasive, but Vondeling soon developed problems of his own. During the brief period in the mid-1960s when the PvdA was back in the government,[13] Vondeling resigned to take a position in the cabinet. His successor as legislative leader was G.M. Nederhorst, one of the party's venerable old men, a left-wing Socialist whom no one could accuse of being too soft. Unfortunately, Nederhorst was also notoriously unwilling to subject himself to party discipline, and his managerial abilities left a great deal to be desired. The PvdA's parliamentary group finally found an effective leader in Joop den Uyl, who was elected chairman of the PvdA's parliamentary delegation in December, 1966, but by that time much damage had been done.[14]

The SFIO, too, had its leadership problems, although they were of a different character. The German Socialist Günter Markscheffel, who had headed the SPD's Paris liaison office and who knew the party's leaders well, wrote that the party was a seething cauldron of factional in-fighting, incapable of any real political decision-making. Mollet, according to Markscheffel, retained power largely through his control of the cadres. That characterization was not entirely fair. It is certainly true that Mollet was very skillful at controlling the party's *Apparat*, but the secretary general also remained a charismatic figure who enjoyed immense respect among the admittedly dwindling number of activists. There were no successful challenges to Mollet's position from within the party because after almost twenty years as leader of the party, Mollet's stature in the SFIO was comparable to what Kurt Schumacher's had been earlier in the SPD: Mollet was the party.[15]

The Socialist parties' self-image also encountered difficulties. By the beginning of the decade both the PvdA and the SPD presented themselves as progressive, multiclass, catch-all parties, and in the 1960s the SPD developed the enthusiasm of a recent convert to the new religion. Both leaders and members were now enthusiastically committed to being a Volkspartei, and while the party insisted it was still the representative of the working class, that group was redefined to include virtually everyone who earned a wage or ran a small business. The party's ideal constituency was a fluid continuum ranging from industrial and white collar workers to the middle classes. Social Democrats and Christian Democrats, the SPD proclaimed, wanted the same things for mostly the same people, but the Social Democrats could do a better job of realizing these common goals.[16]

Ironically, the PvdA, which had pioneered this image in the late 1940s, had more difficulty with its self-identification in the 1960s. The party leaders were deeply divided on the party's role in the tertiary industrial society. They agreed with Joop den Uyl that the PvdA needed to be a democratic, socialist, future-oriented Volkspartei, but that left a great deal of room for specifics. The debate on these simmered all through the 1960s, with at least three scenarios for the party's future crystallizing out of the discussion. Jaap Burger was convinced The Netherlands were headed for a period of "enlightened dictatorship" under the bourgeois parties, and the PvdA needed to assert itself as the voice of oppressed democrats. (He later withdrew the statement about a bourgeois "dictatorship.") Willem Thomassen, who became mayor of Rotterdam in 1965, and Anne Vondeling insisted the Dutch Social Democrats should return to their roots. The PvdA needed to model itself on the British Labour Party, and become an all-encompassing left-of-center progressive Volkspartei. And Nieuw Links opted for a rejuvenated PvdA that would serve as the yeast for the democratic revolutionary transformation of all of Dutch society.[17]

The SFIO lived through a similar, decade-long identity crisis.[18] In December, 1964 the CD appointed a blue-ribbon commission to look into the party's self-image. It was given a grandiose mandate, to "study ways of giving the distribution of the party's ideas a new image and assured efficiency,"[19] but the commission's work was buried with little publicity. This was largely because Mollet felt any change in the party's image would destroy the SFIO's true character. The secretary general's aim in the 1960s was to prevent what became a matter of course in the 1970s: the creation of a modern French *Parti travailliste* instead of a party of *socialisme pur et dur*.[20]

Yet the politics of the 1960s made modernization imperative if the Socialists wanted to continue to be a major political force. This meant reaching out to other organized political groups or to segments of society that were not part of the Socialists' traditional core constituency. In the 1960s the SPD set out to do this in earnest. The target groups included professionals and intellectuals (Willy Brandt was especially successful in animating a coterie of prominent authors, including Günter Grass, to support his national campaigns), yet the most promising and most difficult partner was the Catholic Church.[21]

The party made a concerted effort to persuade the church hierarchy and Catholic voters that the programs and policies of the new SPD were compatible with Catholic social and political doctrines. In the spring of 1962 the party issued a much-discussed pamphlet entitled *Katholik und Godesberger Programm*. It pointed to many parallels between the SPD's program and the thoughts which Pope John XXIII had enunciated in his encyclical *Mater et Magister*. A series of meetings between party leaders and high church dignitaries followed, culminating, in March, 1964, in Fritz Erler's private audience with Pope Paul VI. Simultaneously, a number of SPD-governed Länder concluded successful new concordats with the Catholic Church.

Despite some grumbling among the old guard about appeasing the Catholic Church, there was no doubt that the charm offensive was a political success. In the latter half of the 1960s two prominent Social Democratic politicians, Hermann Schmidt-Vockenhausen and Georg Leber, were elected members of the central committee of the Organization of German Catholics. More important, the

SPD's vote in Catholic areas increased significantly. The party won almost a majority of the popular vote in the 1966 state election in the heavily Catholic Land of Northrhine Westphalia, and in the 1969 Bundestag election the SPD for the first time since the founding of the Federal Republic did better than the CDU in urban areas with a predominantly Catholic voting population.[22]

In Holland discussions of the party's new image centered on the desirability and possibility of having the PvdA spearhead the creation of a left-of-center catch-all party. Proponents of a Dutch *Progressieve Partij* envisioned a formation that ideally would absorb the old PvdA, D'66, left-wing elements in the KVP, the PSP, and possibly some moderate elements among the Communists. Hopes for a new party proved unrealistic, but for the 1969 national elections some of the potential partners took tentative steps to create a so-called *Progressieve Akkoord* (Progressive Accord [PAK]), a loose working group designed to negotiate a campaign agreement for the 1969 contest. However, even these modest plans fell apart. D '66 refused to participate, and while some PvdA leaders continued to push the project, they eventually concluded that Dutch politics were not yet ready for an inclusive left-wing organization. The potential partners did agree on a joint campaign platform and a shadow cabinet for the 1972 elections, but plans for a new progressive party were definitely abandoned in 1975. (Ironically, the bourgeois confessional parties accomplished what the left-wing groups failed to do. In 1970 they created a new party, the *Christelijk Democratisch Appel* [Christian Democratic Call, CDA], the Dutch equivalent of the German CDU.)[23]

Implementation of the popular election of the president after 1962 and single-member legislative districts made a new image for the SFIO even more imperative in France than in The Netherlands. Indeed, the possibility of a united Left looked more hopeful than it had in the 1950s. Influenced by the ideas of John XXIII, French left-wing Catholics looked for ways to lower the ideological barriers between Marxism and Catholic social thought, raising expectations that the MRP might join the French version of the New Left. There were also hopes that after Khrushchev's denunciation of Stalin's crimes, the PCF might come out of its cocoon and be more open to overtures from the non-Communist Left.

The SFIO was not, in principle, averse to cooperating with other left-wing groups; in January, 1962 the CD appointed another commission charged with finding ways of "making contact" with such organizations. However, there remained the questions of with whom to make contact and to what end. Guy Mollet, for one, insisted the SFIO would either dominate the union of left-wing groups, or would remain outside it. Clearly the established parties—the MRP, the Radicals, and the PCF—were candidates for cooperative action, but in the 1960s there were also the clubs which had become centers of political activism outside the established parties.[24]

And high on the clubs' agenda was a rejuvenation of the old non-Communist Left. A number of prominent politicians, such as Gaston Defferre, the head of the SFIO's largest federation and the mayor of Marseille, agreed and eagerly sought contact with the clubs. Defferre recognized that here was a potential constituency of the New Left that was not attracted to the traditional parties. The Club Citoyen '60, for example, had a largely left-wing Catholic membership. However, the bulk of the SFIO's leadership, including the general secretary, was disdainful of the clubs and unwilling to accord them a major, let alone dominant, role in left-wing politics.[25]

The SFIO was in more familiar territory when dealing with the Communists. A number of Socialists argued that as long as the Communists remained a formidable force, it would be difficult to challenge Gaullism successfully without their cooperation, and for this reason the SFIO leaders should be willing to explore some sort of tactical alliance between the estranged brothers. However, by no means all prominent Socialists accepted this line of argument. Gaston Defferre and most leaders of the Southern and eastern federations wanted the Communists excluded from any left-wing alliance. They were convinced an agreement with the PCF would alienate moderate leftists and doom the New Left to failure.

The debate took a dramatic turn in November, 1962 with "Mollet's coup." The general secretary concluded an electoral pact with the Communists for the upcoming legislative elections. The agreement provided that whenever a run-off contest was necessary in a legislative district (under the French constitution this was the case if no candidate won a majority of the votes in the initial balloting) the Socialist and Communist candidates would agree to step aside in favor of the candidate who had done better in the first round of balloting. Reactions to the agreement in the CD were mixed. Mollet's most enthusiastic supporter was Claude Fuzier, the leader of the Seine Federation, a traditionally leftist organization in the SFIO. But all members of the CD were unhappy that Mollet had acted without putting the proposal before the CD first (Mollet argued there was not enough time), and many remained unconvinced by his argument that the 1962 pact would aid the party in achieving its first priority, defeating Gaullism. In the final vote the secretary general won grudging support from the CD for his coup. The party's National Council, which was dominated by the northern federations, was more enthusiastic: the delegates endorsed the pact by a large margin.[26]

Despite this vote of confidence the SFIO/PCF electoral alliance was implemented successfully only in the Paris region. Most other federations ignored the agreement during the campaign, convinced that their militants would not vote for a Communist candidate in any case.[27] But the issue went beyond tactical considerations. Opposition to Mollet's high-handed action erupted into the open at the 1963 national congress, with the result that in the balloting for members of the CD at the congress Mollet dropped from tenth to twenty-sixth place.[28]

The issue arose again in October, 1966, this time in connection with the 1967 *Assemblée Nationale* elections. In the meantime a new organization, the *Fédération Gauche Démocrate et Socialiste* (Left Federation of Democrats and Socialists [FGDS]), had entered the arena. The FGDS was a confederation of various left-wing organizations, including the SFIO. During its relatively brief life the FGDS was at various times virtually all things to all men. Gaston Defferre had envisioned it as the union of all non-Communist Left and moderate forces (and perhaps as a vehicle to wrest control of the SFIO from Mollet), while François Mitterrand, who eventually became president of the FGDS and used it as the organizational base for his 1965 presidential campaign, set out to coopt the Communists as electoral allies of the FGDS. Mollet and his allies saw the FGDS as either a rival that needed to be combated or a vehicle that would permit the SFIO to control the New Left. For the secretary general the FGDS had to be a "new instrument in the service of Socialism." In order to retain the initiative for the SFIO, Mollet proposed at the party's Suresnes congress in October, 1966, that the FGDS negotiate an electoral accord with the PCF. The delegates gave unanimous approval to the resolution, but they insisted that the basis of discussions with the Communists had to be the FGDS' (decidedly moderate) program. This was clearly meant to preclude any far-reaching ideological alliance, a point on which Mollet had been somewhat unclear. While he emphasized that the aim of the negotiations with the PCF was an electoral agreement, not a political agreement, he also talked cryptically about hopes for "erasing 1920," a reference to the split of the PCF and the SFIO at the congress of Tours.[29]

Programs and Policies

Although programs and policies were frequently at variance with each other in the history of European Socialist parties, they were (and are) essential components of the parties' images and self-images. The evolution from ideologically based to catch-all parties made programmatic distinctions all the more important. Joop den Uyl, the most philosophically oriented of Europe's Socialist leaders, noted in 1967 that the rise of catch-all parties would make it increasingly difficult for the voters to distinguish between the mainstream parties.[30]

As a recent convert to catch-all pragmatism, the SPD saw as its major task translating the Bad Godesberg Program into concrete policy proposals and explaining how these would benefit virtually all segments of West German society. The party's 1961 campaign platform was a ten point catalog of all-encompassing, if piecemeal, reforms. The SPD promised improvements in the legal provisions for paid vacations, health insurance, social security, veterans' benefits, public housing, municipal planning, environmental protection, and transportation.[31]

Like the SPD, the PvdA had adopted a new program in 1959, but unlike the Bad Godesberg document, the Dutch effort aroused fervent criticism from the rising, albeit as yet unorganized, Nieuw Links forces. According to the young radicals a catalogue of *biefstuk* (bread-and-butter) reforms might have been suitable for a regentenpartij of the 1950s, but not for a revolutionary party of the 1960s.

To answer this criticism, while simultaneously defending the PvdA's traditional concerns, Joop den Uyl, on behalf of the Wiardi Beckman Stichting, presented his influential paper *Om de Kwaliteit van het bestaan* (On the Quality of Existence) at the PvdA's 1963 congress. Leaning heavily on the ideas of John Kenneth Galbraith, den Uyl expressed agreement with Nieuw Link's concerns about the growing gap between private wealth and public poverty and the excesses of materialism. He also demanded a greater role for government in influencing private expenditures and consumption, increased investment in the public sector, and what he called "organized leadership for economic growth." Finally, den Uyl endorsed a particular concern of Nieuw Links, and urged the PvdA to commit itself to increase Dutch foreign aid to the Third World. At the same time den Uyl did not repudiate the PvdA's earlier programs. He did not urge the abandonment of biefstuk Socialism, and the proposed expanded role for government was limited to guidance, not control. There was no demand for large-scale socializations or a central planning apparatus. In fact, the PvdA's 1964 guidelines on economic and social policies were little more than a Dutch translation of the equivalent sections of the Bad Godesberg Program.[32]

Even so, den Uyl's conciliatory efforts aroused considerable opposition both within the party and from its political rivals. The KVP insisted *Kwaliteit* was another step in the PvdA's polarization campaign; the Socialists wanted to diminish private freedoms and increase state controls. Some major figures in the PvdA agreed, noting that even if this had not been den Uyl's intent, it was certainly the impression he evoked. Both Jaap Burger and Willem Drees, not usually on the same side of an argument, agreed that den Uyl's initiative had contributed to the PvdA's defeat in the 1963 elections by scaring off middle class voters. These criticisms missed the intraparty significance of *Kwaliteit*, however, for by successfully merging the concerns of the Young Turks with the established priorities of the PvdA, den Uyl had demonstrated his qualities as compromiser, which would make him the key figure in the second half of the decade and beyond.[33]

The SFIO also began the decade with what appeared to be a serious effort to adapt its programmatic principles to the new circumstances of the 1960s. In June, 1960 a commission headed by Jules Moch and composed primarily of members of the Bureau de parti presented a draft *programme fondamentale* (basic program) to the CD. The document began by recognizing that much had happened since 1945 to challenge some longstanding axioms of Marxist Socialism. Neither the expected series of economic crises nor the pauperization of the working classes had come about. The draft also acknowledged that in the face of these developments most of the SFIO's sister parties had given up the traditional demands for socialization of the means of production and centralized planning of the economy.

Despite these nods in the direction of the SPD and the PvdA, the draft emphasized that human progress was not possible under either capitalism or Soviet Communism and that only political democracy, full-scale planning, and socialization could produce a society that "was free of class [struggle] and war." For good measure, the draft program also contained the reminder that a socialist society was not possible without laïcisme. The CD accepted the draft in March, 1963, showing the majority of the leaders was convinced the party had to remain true to the time-honored principles of *socialisme pur et dur*. Some members of the executive committee did object that the draft was written as if in a vacuum, ignoring the impact of modern forces like the market, but they could not prevail against the majority of old believers. Ideological innovations of French Socialism were going to come not from within, but from outside the SFIO.[34]

Although the SPD was not in a position to translate its program into policies, the party did its best to demonstrate that the new Social Democrats had something important to contribute to the debate on Germany's future. The party's primary vehicle was a series of large-scale, well publicized meetings bringing together experts from various fields and party leaders to discuss domestic affairs. Some advocates of the old policies (like economic planning) raised their voices at these sessions, but most party spokesmen emphasized that the SPD endorsed the social market economy, and wanted only to shift some priorities to emphasize stable families, profit sharing, educational reforms, and an independent peasantry. In the area of security policies, the party firmly supported NATO and a democratic Bundeswehr, while spearheading the opposition to providing the German armed forces with atomic weapons.[35]

Nevertheless, all was not smooth sailing. The so-called emergency laws confronted the party with a particularly thorny domestic policy issue. This was a package of legislation assigning to the German federal government many of the rights which the Allies had reserved for themselves under the Occupation Statute. The Adenauer government had introduced the legislation in the mid-1950s, after the FRG became formally sovereign, but the laws languished in the Bundestag for more than ten years. By the 1960s the SPD was caught between the labor unions' fierce opposition to the legislation (which would have prohibited strikes during periods of a declared emergency), and the party's desire to avoid a confrontation with the Christian Democrats in order not to endanger the chances for a coalition. When the legislation finally became law in 1968, the Social Democrats were members of the federal government. In this capacity they accepted a watered-down version of the emergency legislation which did not please the labor unions or the party's left, but which did add to the SPD's reputation as a responsible force for law and order.[36]

The German Social Democrats also faced some formidable problems in the area of intra-German affairs. The East German decision to build the Berlin Wall created an entirely new situation in Germany, leading at least some party leaders to conclude that the SPD needed to rethink its traditional policies toward the Communist East. Although the specific treaties implementing the *Ostpolitik* did not came into force until the 1970s, the intellectual foundations were laid in the 1960s. The key individuals here were Willy Brandt and his intellectual alter ego, Egon Bahr. Both concluded that after the construction of the Berlin Wall, Germany and Europe would remain part of separate, antagonistic power blocs for the foreseeable future. As a result, the SPD and West Germany had to base their relations to the East on two premises. One was that the Federal Republic was and would remain firmly anchored in the Western Alliance. The second postulated that West Germany needed to find ways of maintaining contacts between the peoples of the two German states and the two halves of Berlin that did not, in the eyes of the Communist rulers, threaten the existence of the Communist regime. That is to say, West Germany and the SPD would need to accept the realities of 1945. Bahr first aired the ideas underlying the new policy in a speech at the Tutzing Academy in July, 1963, provocatively entitled, *Wandel durch Annäherung* (change by coming together). Brandt's and Bahr's ideas ran into immediate opposition, but the embryonic Ostpolitik was also showing its first, very tentative results. An agreement, negotiated by the mayor's office in December, 1963, permitting limited visitation rights for West Berliners in East Berlin was the first (and for many years the last) crack in the Berlin Wall.[37]

The SPD's policies toward European unification and the Atlantic Alliance were unequivocal. The party was committed to European unification and British membership in the EEC, and led the opposition to the German Gaullists, who sought closer ties between West Germany and France, even if that meant weakening the special relationship with the Americans. Largely due to the tireless efforts of the SPD's delegation in the Bundestag, the German parliament added a preamble to the 1963 Franco-German consultation treaty which, much to de Gaulle's disappointment, removed the pact's anti-American sting.[38] Although disappointed that the United States took no action to prevent the building of the Berlin Wall, the reformers continued to seek closer relations with Washington, ignoring criticism from some left-wing elements that the party should be more critical of United States policies, especially in Vietnam. Here the change in leadership was a decidedly positive development. Willy Brandt was very much persona grata in the White House of John F. Kennedy, and Fritz Erler had a particularly good relationship with the American ambassador in Bonn, George McGhee.[39]

In trying to formulate specific policy proposals, the PvdA was caught between the desire to get back into the government and its ambition to suggest genuine alternatives to the present coalition's policies. For the most part "me-tooism" won out. The

PvdA accepted the end of wage controls, and Willem Drees even agreed with the bourgeois parties that investment in the public sector had to be curtailed. In fact, Drees offered ringing praise of neocorporatism as the economic policy that in the long run was best for both labor and management. A few left-wingers demurred, objecting notably to the party's endorsement of profitsharing schemes, but the conflicts that really aroused the party's passions involved social and cultural policies. The PvdA remained sharply divided over the introduction of commercial television, and the proposed engagement of Crown Princess Beatrix to the German aristocrat and diplomat Claus von Amsberg stirred passions as few issues had before or since.

A sizable segment of the PvdA, including G.M. Nederhorst, the head of the party's parliamentary delegation, was resolutely opposed to the union of the future Dutch monarch with a German. At work here were visceral emotions that included at least subconsciously the Socialists' feelings that they had not been anti-German enough in the Second World War. (Nieuw Links was also opposed to the marriage, although in view of the radicals' concern about increased aid to the Third World their objection to Amsberg made little sense. As a German diplomat von Amsberg, who had spent much of his career posted in Africa, he had been an effective advocate of increased western aid to Third World countries.) Nederhorst went so far as to write a letter detailing his objections. The letter was not meant to be made public, but Nederhorst sent it to so many people that the contents were soon leaked to the press. Most party leaders were not, however, willing to go public with their unease about the royal union. Keeping their party's goal of not alienating potential future coalition partners firmly in mind (the bourgeois parties had agreed not to oppose the marriage), the PB reprimanded Nederhorst for his unauthorized action.[40]

Although, as we shall see, Nieuw Links attempted to alter the party's traditional priorities, the PvdA's foreign policies did not change substantially. The party leaders rejected any loosening of Holland's ties to NATO and the Atlantic Alliance. The PvdA also remained steadfastly pro-European. Like the SPD, the Dutch Socialists were severely critical of de Gaulle's successful attempts to keep the British out of the Common Market, and their demand that there should be no atomic weapons under the control of any Continental West European nation was an indirect criticism of the French *force de frappe*. In contrast to the bourgeois parties, the PvdA also favored turning New Guinea, the last remnant of the Dutch East Indies empire, over to Indonesia.[41]

Among the three parties the SFIO was least interested in developing concrete policy proposals of its own. The party was simply too concerned with its own internal problems and what it regarded as the indispensable prerequisite before any Socialist policies could be implemented: *"sortir de Gaulle"* ([to make] de Gaulle leave). As a consequence, the SFIO limited its domestic policy proposals to criticizing the president for destroying the social net which the SFIO had laboriously constructed, and insisting that the general's preference for private enterprise solutions would drive France to economic ruin. Some leaders pointed to the SPD's success in attracting new voters with its Bad Godesberg Program and complained that the SFIO's ritualistic demand for more nationalizations hid a fundamental *"nudité doctrinale"* (ideological nakedness), but the majority of the CD insisted only socializations and nationalizations would bring about continued prosperity. The party leaders also blamed de Gaulle for dismantling laïcisme. During the 1959 debate on the Debré Law and at the 1962 party congress Mollet and other party leaders pulled out all of the rhetorical stops fighting this issue.[42]

On foreign policy questions the French Socialists acknowledged that the general had successfully solved the Algerian problem, but the SFIO's attitude on the French *force de frappe* was ambivalent. While the party officially rejected independently controlled French atomic weapons, in practice the Mollet government had laid the groundwork for the *force de frappe* in 1956, and the party's opposition to de Gaulle's atomic weapons program was never more than lukewarm. On the other hand, the party vigorously condemned the general's European and Atlantic policies. The SFIO opposed the decision to loosen France's ties to NATO, and the Socialists were especially critical of de Gaulle's veto of the British entry into the Common Market. Mollet also thought the Franco-German consultation treaty was little more than "an exchange of compliments between two old men." The SFIO continued to stress the need for full-scale, integral European unity, although it insisted on *socialisme pur et dur* here as well: Europe needed an economy that was "organized, coordinated, planned."[43]

Internal Party Opposition and Extraparty Challenges

All three parties were confronted with a variety of internal and external oppositional movements during the turbulent 1960s. In the SPD the critics continued to focus on the Bad Godesberg Program and the SPD's evolution toward a catch-all party, but in the course of the 1960s they found additional targets as well. They lamented what they saw as the SPD's uncritical acceptance of American policies in Vietnam, and the party's the grand coalition in 1966 particularly embittered the critics. Geographically the opposition was concentrated in the party districts of Frankfurt, Munich, and Berlin, and organizationally in the *Junge Sozialisten* (Young Socialists [Jusos]) and the *Sozialistischer Studentenbund* (Association of Socialist Students [SDS]).[44]

Membership in the oppositional groups overlapped, but after 1965 the party leaders were most concerned about the SDS. In the 1940s and 1950s the student organization had been a major nurturing ground for future SPD leaders (Helmut Schmidt was president of the organization in 1947), but by the 1960s the party leaders and the SDS' spokesmen looked upon each other with barely disguised animosity. The right wing of the party saw the SDS as vulnerable to Communist influence, while the leaders of the SDS regarded themselves as part of the revolutionary, but non-Communist, new European Left. In their view the SPD was being drawn from the true path of socialism by its reformist leaders; from the SDS' perspective Erler was the evil genius of the post-Bad Godesberg party.[45]

The SPD's executive committee first tried negotiations with the SDS to bring the organization back in line, and then moved to take disciplinary action. As we saw, in November, 1961 the executive committee expelled the political scientists Wolfgang Abendroth and Ossip Flechtheim, whom the party leaders regarded as the intellectual mentors of the revolt against Bad Godesberg, and cut all ties to the SDS. Instead, the party recognized a dissident group within the SDS, the *Sozialistische Hochschulbund* (Socialist University Association [SHB]) as its new university affiliate.

The SDS radicals were never a serious threat to either the SPD's reformist course or the party's organizational unity. The complaints of a group of university students and professors, usually couched in incomprehensible Marxist jargon, meant little to most activists. At the same time there was an undeniable feeling among a number of rank-and-file members that all was not well with the party. This did not lead to party splits or organized *tendances*, but on occasion it did erupt into the open. This was the case at the March, 1968, party congress in Nuremberg. The executive committee had introduced a resolution asking the delegates to give retroactive approval to the leaders' decision to enter the grand coalition. It passed, but only by a vote of 302:129; not exactly a rousing vote of confidence for the leadership. Nevertheless, the opposition's significance should not be overrated. The reformers remained in firm control of the party at all times, and the opposition was steadily diluted. The party membership was growing rapidly, and most of the new and younger members were attracted to the SPD precisely because it presented itself as an open, reformist organization that wanted to take its place in the center of the political spectrum.[46]

The PvdA faced oppositional challenges from both inside and outside the party. The outside force, represented primarily by the PSP, was not particularly worrisome. Founded in 1957 as a "home for left-wing Socialists," the PSP, too, saw itself as part of the new revolutionary, but non-Communist Left. Until the mid-1960s the PvdA had essentially ignored the PSP as an unimportant heckler on the sidelines, but in 1965 the PSP seemed to draw additional adherents from those members and voters of the PvdA who opposed the party's consistent support of NATO, and especially the PvdA's endorsement of the stationing of more American atomic weapons on European soil. As a result, the Dutch Socialists were determined to marginalize the PSP; PvdA members were officially warned not to cooperate with the PSP in any form. Actually, this step proved unnecessary since the left-wing party's rise to political prominence was short-lived.[47]

The internal opposition, Nieuw Links, represented a far more serious problem. The group was not tightly organized, and its membership fluctuated, but the adherents shared a number of common sentiments and aims. To begin with, the PvdA's Young Turks were literally, as Hans van der Doel put it, "young and angry." But they also made every effort to fit the image of respectable politicians. At party meetings they wore "dark blue suits," rather than torn jeans, and they exhibited *beschaafde manieren* (Emily Post manners). They neither created organized *tendances* nor did they threaten to split the party. Rather, saw the PvdA as a stodgy regentenpartij, which the radicals were going to transform from within into a dynamic force for revolutionary change.

Most supporters of Nieuw Links were students, academics at the beginning of their careers, or young professionals; several were facile writers and gifted speakers. The geographical centers of their activities were Amsterdam and Groningen. Few had any political experience (one exception was Han Lammers, who was a member of the Amsterdam city council), but they wrote for a number of periodicals that circulated widely among students and young professionals. These included *Politeia*, a periodical that was very popular among Dutch university students, *Tijd en Taak,* a left-wing Christian Socialist organ, as well as *Links* and *Vera,* two journals that attempted to mobilize opposition to the apartheid policies in South Africa. In addition Nieuw Links issued a steady stream of its own publications.

Nieuw Links knew what it did not like about the PvdA, and its publications spelled this out in considerable and provocative detail. The opening salvo was *Tien over rood,* (Ten [Authors] Writing About What it Means to be Red) which appeared just as the short-lived, second version of the brede basis coalition was breaking up. Between August and November, 1967 Nieuw Links offered three more programmatic pamphlets: *Een Partij om mee te werken* (A Party in Which to Work Cooperatively) demanded more internal democracy within the PvdA, *De macht van de rooie ruggen* (The Power of the Red Back) argued for nationalizations and a planned economy, and *De meeste mensen willen meer* (Most People Want More) laid out a scenario for true equality and opportunity for education in the society to come. In addition to its publications, in February, 1967, Nieuw Links sent a letter to the PB telling the party executive what had gone wrong in the past and needed to be corrected in the future.[48]

There was a consistent leitmotiv in all of these publications: Nieuw Links wanted the PvdA to abandon its (successful) quest to be accepted as a coalition partner by the bourgeois parties. Nieuw Links demanded specifically that the PvdA announce that under no circumstances would the party enter into a coalition with the KVP. Instead, Nieuw Links advocated constant, negative campaigning to take advantage of the fact that the Dutch political spectrum, as Nieuw Links saw it, was moving rapidly to the left. According to this scenario the PvdA could win a majority of the Dutch electorate by concentrating its appeals on "old working-class supporters and culture-sensitive voters."[49]

Nieuw Links also offered specific recommendations for the party's domestic and foreign policies. In domestic affairs they wanted a truly socialist society, which they defined as one which had succeeded in eliminating obstacles to total human freedom: material want, insecurity, injustice, and lack of opportunity for self-realization. This was to be accomplished by increasing government intervention to remove barriers to freedom, although here Nieuw Links was rather short on specifics. (As if to prove that the radicals, too, were not free from self-interested motivation, they insisted that income taxes on academic salaries needed to be reduced.) Nieuw Links also could not agree on its foreign policy aims. A minority advocated a more neutralist position for The Netherlands, and some even demanded Holland's withdrawal from NATO. Most, however, remained loyal to the Western Alliance, although they thought Portugal, as a "fascist" state should be expelled from NATO, while Holland should extend diplomatic recognition to East Germany and the Vietcong. There was agreement on one demand, however: a massive increase in foreign aid to developing countries. The Leftists thought The Netherlands should devote two percent of its gross domestic product to this purpose.[50]

The reaction of the PvdA's old guard to the challenge of the young rebels was not unanimous. Burger, Tans, and a few old radicals like Johannes Scheps were at least sympathetic toward the idea that the party needed some shaking up. Others, Drees foremost among them, saw Nieuw Links as little more than immature troublemakers. (One of Nieuw Links' slogans was *mooi rood is niet lelijk* [beautiful red is not ugly]. Drees wrote that he agreed, but added *lelijk is niet mooi rood* [ugly is not beautiful red].) In general, sentiment within the party was shifting in favor of Nieuw Links, especially after the fall of the Cals cabinet in October, 1966, had again embittered relations between the PvdA and the KVP. Vondeling probably best represented this middle line. In contrast to Drees, he thought Nieuw Links's concerns were legitimate.

The new attitude was reflected not only in Nieuw Links' growing influence in the party's Amsterdam and Groningen locals, but also in the PB's increased toleration for its activities. When Nieuw Links first became active, the PB had attempted to prevent the radicals from using the party's membership lists to distribute their publications, but that prohibition was lifted in September, 1966. Still, sympathy for Nieuw Links' general aims was one thing, but agreement with its specific ideas quite another. For the most part the party's established leaders remained critical of the group's substantive policy proposals. Unlike Nieuw Links, the PvdA's establishment saw no evidence of a deep-seated crisis in Dutch and European society that required a social revolution. As far as the foreign policy proposals were concerned, the old leaders were sympathetic toward helping the Third World, but they unanimously rejected any moves toward neutralism or the loosening of Holland's ties to NATO and the Atlantic Alliance.[51]

By 1968 Nieuw Links' growing strength and the right wing's opposition to it led to a party split. The decisions to permit Nieuw Links to proselytize among the members and to participate in the PAK was the last straw for the right wing. Led by William Drees, Jr., the former prime minister's son, a number of dissidents, including

Willem Drees, Sr., left the PvdA to form a new party, *Democratische Socialisten '70* (Democratic Socialists '70 [DS '70]). Other leaders, like Johannes Scheps, Jacques de Kadt, and the PvdA's longtime treasurer, Eibert Meesters, resigned from the party, although they did not join DS '70. (De Kadt went to the liberal D '66 party.[52])

DS '70 was, however, a short-lived and insignificant effort. It attracted few militants from the PvdA, a fortuitous development that owed much to the efforts of Joop den Uyl, the party's new parliamentary leader. (He was elected in December 1966.) Although some would later criticize den Uyl for allowing Nieuw Links too much influence, he was by no means uncritical of the rebels. He thought *Tien over rood* "hopelessly superficial," opposed the idea of an absolute commitment not to enter into a coalition with the KVP, and rejected the polarization strategy, especially if it involved mobilizing forces outside the established parties. (Some Nieuw Links leaders had suggested the models of German APO and the French student mobilizations should be applied to Holland.[53]) Den Uyl did think, however, that a soft approach was more effective in dealing with the Young Turks than frontal opposition. Consequently, while he rejected their demand that the PvdA refuse to join any coalition with the Catholics, he agreed that the party should not make government participation its primary goal. The parliamentary leader was also sympathetic toward shifting some steering functions from the parliamentary delegation to the PB. But he drew a firm line on Nieuw Links' demands for virtually unlimited internal democratization in the party, responding that "a multifaceted party must be subject to some direction."[54]

Den Uyl was to become the key figure in the PvdA's future, but at the end of the 1960s his success in taming Nieuw Links seemed decidedly limited. Nieuw Links' most visible triumph came in March 1969: André van der Louw was elected vice-chairman of the PvdA. He was so overjoyed that he burst into spontaneous dancing, an episode that entered the party's annals as van der Louw's "bear dance." (Van der Louw, who had long hair and a rather corpulent figure, was physically well suited to the performance.) Two years later he became chairman. The 1969 congress also adopted a resolution committing the PvdA not to enter into a coalition with the KVP.

Nieuw Links' sense of triumphant victory was matched by the right wing's despair. Even for those who had not left the party, van der Louw's bear dance remained a nightmarish memory. Contemporary and subsequent analyses did not help much to bridge the gap between the two sides. For the sympathizers of Nieuw

Links the twenty year history of the PvdA from 1946 to 1966 was a sort of misguided prelude, from 1966 to 1969 the party struggled to find itself, and only in 1969 with Nieuw Links' triumph had it finally found its true identity. For the opponents of Nieuw Links the rebels were irresponsible radicals, who had no sense of political reality and alienated potential voters.[55]

A more balanced reflection yields a less black-and-white picture. Nieuw Links' victory was more symbolic than real, for the PvdA under its new leadership was not about to lead the revolutionary transformation of Dutch and European society. Most members of Nieuw Links eventually admitted that this had been a utopian goal anyway. A few left for more extreme groups outside the established parties, but the vast majority of the radicals became moderates quickly after they achieved positions of responsibility. In addition, to their dismay, Nieuw Links never controlled the party's parliamentary delegation, where the real political decision making continued to take place. In the legislature Nieuw Links remained a relatively small group of outsiders. Of forty-five PvdA members of parliament in 1972 only twelve identified themselves as sympathizers of Nieuw Links. In the end it was den Uyl, not the rebels who triumphed. The PvdA remained a genuine Volkspartei; it never disavowed the 1959 program. In den Uyl the PvdA had found an effective leader who not only kept the party together in difficult times, but made the PvdA ministériable again in short order.[56]

All serious challenges to the SFIO's leadership team came from outside the party. To the end of its existence Mollet and his supporters remained in control of a dwindling party. The secretary general's critics had no illusions that they could drive Mollet from power. Their only choices were to leave the party or accept Mollet's continued leadership. Some, like Gaston Defferre, the mayor of Marseille, stayed in the party. Others, who included the founders of the PSA and the PSU, argued that under Mollet the SFIO had *se sclérose* (atrophied) as a political force, and efforts at reform from within were useless.

The founders of the PSA/PSU had long complained that Mollet used the SFIO as an instrument of personal power. They promised their creation would be different. Provided they accepted the party's goal of working to attain Socialism, all *tendances* were accorded formal representation on the executive committee. In this way the founders had hoped to build a mass organization that attracted dissatisfied members and voters from the SFIO as well as other elements of the French *gauche nouvelle*.

The grandiose plans failed, and the attempt to open the party to a virtually unlimited number of *tendances* turned out to be counter-productive. Supporters of right-wing Social Democracy and Trot-skyites had little appreciation of each other, and their presence in the same organization confused the voters. On the other hand, attempts to rein in the free-for-all of opinions led to charges of broken promises. André Philip, a founding member of the PSU, resigned from the party at the beginning of 1961, because he felt the PSU restricted his freedom of expression.

The PSU was never able to attract a mass membership. At the time of its founding in 1961 the PSU had some sixteen thousand members (virtually all of them lived in the Paris region, inciden-tally), but that figure dropped to ten thousand by 1963/64. As Michel Rocard, its secretary general (and a future prime minister of France) remembered, in 1963 the PSU was struggling "with ... serious internal difficulties." The party's disastrous showing in the 1967 legislative elections persuaded a number of PSU leaders that it was time to dissolve the organization altogether. Rocard left the party and joined Mitterrand's circle. The PSU struggled on, and the upheavals of 1968 gave the party a surge of popularity (the membership rose to some 15,500), but it was a brief moment of illusionary glory. A year later the PSU became part of the PS.[57]

In contrast to its modest membership, the PSA/PSU always boasted a relatively large number of prominent leaders, including the most charismatic figure in French left-wing politics, Pierre Mendès-France. Unfortunately for the PSA/PSU, Mendès-France continued his habit of remaining aloof from direct involvement in party affairs. Nevertheless, the PSU's concentration of prominent leaders permitted it to play a role as an ideological bridge between the SFIO's rigid *socialisme pur et dur* and the future PS's more eclec-tic program. Although the PSU thought of itself as truly socialist and continued to endorse economic planning, the leaders' concept of socialism also included a flexibility in traditional Franco-Marx-ist concepts, such as opposition to the SFIO's knee-jerk commit-ment to laïcisme.[58]

The SFIO's attitude toward the PSU's challenge oscillated be-tween appeasement and disdain. Initially concerned about the loss of prominent leaders and some younger militants to the new party, the Socialists attempted to lure back the dissidents. This failed, but the SFIO also quickly recognized that the PSA/PSU was not a serious threat. The French Socialists now simultaneously ignored the rival, and sought to preempt the PSU's intended role as mediator between the Communists and the non-Communist Left by establishing better relations with the Communists. (This was part of the motivation for "Mollet's coup.") On balance, the Socialists thought they had been quite successful, and by the end of 1967 Mollet was convinced the PSU was about to fall apart.[59]

While that prediction was not wrong, only premature, the SFIO had little reason to gloat over the PSU's decline. By 1969 the SFIO was itself confronting terminal problems. *Socialisme pur et dur*, which the party insisted was the correct centrist position between Dutch and German Social Democratic reformism and Soviet Communism, had failed to provide answers for the problems of the 1960s. The party was ignored by the students of 1968, and it played no part in bringing down de Gaulle. By the end of the decade most French left-wing activists concluded that the SFIO was existing as its own raison d'être, a charge that Mollet and his supporters vehemently rejected. To the end, the Molletists were convinced that they had something valuable to bring to the gauche nouvelle: They were the guardians of the grail; true French Socialism had always resided in the SFIO.[60]

The man who was to give the SFIO its coup de grace was François Mitterrand, the "unifier of the Left."[61] Mitterrand was no Socialist ideologue. He had a "very believing and very open" Catholic upbringing,[62] and he obtained a membership card in the Socialist party only after he became its leader. His reputation as a man of the Left rested upon his fervent and consistent opposition to Charles de Gaulle. Unlike the SFIO's leaders, most of whom oscillated between cooperation and opposition to de Gaulle, Mitterrand never wavered in his conviction that the general had established an extralegal regime in France.[63] Mitterrand was also a superb tactician, who outflanked Mollet's efforts to retain control of his dwindling number of supporters. Starting with a group of politicians personally loyal to him, Mitterrand secured the agreement of the eclectic forces that had emerged in the late 1950s and 1960s to form a new party that included remnants from the now largely defunct clubs, a majority of the PSU, what was left of the Radicals, and, most important, the anti-Mollet forces within the SFIO.[64]

The new party was officially launched in July, 1969 at the two-part congress of Issy, where the SFIO first dissolved itself, and then the SFIO delegates joined Mitterrand's supporters to create the PS with Mitterrand as president. At first glance it appeared that the new PS was little more than the SFIO under another name. Always something of a political loner, Mitterrand never had a large-scale organization of his own, so it was natural that he would draw upon the SFIO's apparatus for the new party. The PS's first secretary general, Alain Savary, an ex-SFIO member who had spent several years in the club scene, was actually Mollet's choice. In addition, all of the PS's original federation secretaries came from the old SFIO. Mitterrand's shadow cabinet also included a majority of ex-SFIO figures, although they were primarily men who in various stages of their career had broken with Mollet: Gaston Defferre, Pierre Mauroy, Michel Rocard, Charles Hernu.

Appearance was deceptive, however. The PS was a quite different organization from the SFIO, and it would be dominated by Mitterrand, not Mollet. Savary was quickly dismissed as secretary general, and replaced by Pierre Mauroy. Most of the holdover federation secretaries rapidly made way for Mitterrand loyalists. Above all the new party was intended as a vote-getting machine, not a limping and nostalgic red family. Jules Moch, who left the PS in 1971, wrote rather plaintively, "I did not recognize my old party anymore."[65] The party attracted a larger, younger membership, drawn from a much wider segment of French society. Its program was highly eclectic, abandoning *socialisme pur et dur,* and substituting what one analyst called "Socialism à la Austria," which is to say, Socialism in name, but not in practice. Mitterrand also did not hesitate to abandon old shibboleths, such as laïcisme or cooperation with the Communists. In fact, it was Mitterrand's ability to unite opposites that assured his later success. His admiring biographer Franz-Olivier Giesbert noted that in the spirit of Jaurès and Blum, Mitterrand found a home in the PS for "social-centrism ... techno-progressivism ... pink Socialism, and ... Jacobin Marxism."[66]

Remarkably, better relations with the Communists did not prevent the PS from rejoining the mainstream of European Social Democracy. While the SFIO after 1956 had been increasingly alienated from the rest of the European Socialist movement, the PS developed excellent relations with both the SI and the sister parties in Holland and Germany.[67]

Elections

Elections are the lifeblood of democracies, and in the 1960s they seemed to come at a fast and furious pace. Actually, this was not true. The number of Dutch contests was not usually large, and in Germany the federal system had always made the Bonn Republic "the land of perpetual elections." In France, however, the presidential and plebiscitary system of the Fifth Republic scheduled a seemingly unending series of legislative and presidential elections, interspersed with frequent national referenda.

The SFIO did not do well in these contests. Since the party's election campaigns were models of technical inefficiency, it was not surprising that the 1960s brought a steady decline in the French Socialists' electoral fortunes. The first legislative elections of the Fifth Republic were held on 18 and 25 November 1962, two months after France's new constitution had been approved in a national referendum by a vote of 61.7 percent to 38.2 percent. The results were a severe disappointment for the SFIO; the 12.7 percent of the popular vote (1958: 15.7 percent) was the party's worst showing since the end of the Second World War. The leaders found small comfort in the destruction of the party's traditional centrist rivals and partners (Radicals: 7.5 percent; MRP: 8.9 percent). Worrisome for the SFIO was not only the Gaullist steamroller (31.9 percent), but the Communists' continuing strength, which increased from 19.2 percent in 1958 to 21.7 percent in 1962. In addition, the results showed that the SFIO was no longer a significant political force in many areas of northeastern France (Ardennes, Meurthe-et-Moselle, Vosges). Its geographic focal point was the Midi, where it "was becoming a party of aged functionaries and rural folk voting Left out of habit."[68]

The presidential election of June, 1965, was the first one in which the head of state would be elected by direct popular vote. The French Left, that is to say, would need a candidate who could put up a credible showing against de Gaulle in a straight popularity test. The search for alliances and candidates resulted in a bewildering process of negotiations, self-nominations, and intrigues. These will be covered in more detail later in this chapter. Here it will be sufficient to note that the most successful left-wing candidate was not a Socialist, but the maverick François Mitterrand. Surprising virtually everyone (except himself), Mitterrand obtained 32.2 percent in the first round of balloting, forcing de Gaulle, who had obtained 43.7 percent, into a run-off. In the second round de Gaulle won handily (54.5 percent), but Mitterrand increased his vote to a respectable 45.4 percent, demonstrating that the Left could be a real factor in the era of presidential politics.

The problems of the Left became even clearer during the legislative elections of 5 March 1967. Under Mitterrand as president, the FGDS fielded a common list of candidates who obtained 18.7 percent of the popular vote in the first round of balloting, a respectable showing behind the Communists 22.4 percent. The FGDS did less well in the second round of balloting. Mitterrand and the

FGDS had negotiated an electoral accord with the PCF in December, 1966, obligating the FDGS to support the Communist candidate in districts where the PCF had placed first among the left-wing groups. It was clear, however, that many SFIO voters refused to vote for the Communist candidates. Tony Judt estimates that some forty percent of the SFIO's supporters deserted the united Left ticket in the second round of balloting.[69]

The *Assemblée Nationale* elections in June, 1968, came at a particularly dramatic time in France's history, barely a month after the events of May had pushed the Fifth Republic to the brink of collapse. The elections revealed, for the last time as it turned out, the full strength of de Gaulle's charisma. The government successfully linked the student unrest with left-wing political opposition to Gaullism, and the elections became a Gaullist tidal wave. The Gaullist parties obtained 46 percent (1967: 37.7 percent) of the popular vote in the first round of balloting. The Communists sank to 20.0 percent (1967: 22.4 percent) of the popular vote and the FGDS to 16.5 percent (1967: 18.7 percent). Among the left-wing groups only the PSU benefited from the May riots: the party's share of the popular vote rose to 3.9 percent (1967: 2.2 percent).

The presidential election of June, 1969, was held less than a year after the legislative contest of 1968, but in the meantime the French political scene had changed dramatically. Mitterrand had resigned as head of the FGDS, and the federation essentially ceased to exist. But de Gaulle, too, had left the scene. Mortally wounded by the events of May, 1968, the general used the results of a defeat in a referendum on a relatively minor issue for his decision to resign from the presidency and retire, once again, to Colombey-les-deux-Églises.

The Gaullist candidate in 1969 was Georges Pompidou, de Gaulle's last prime minister. The scrambling for a viable candidate among the left-wing groups to oppose Pompidou was not an edifying spectacle, and neither were the results. Gaston Defferre, who ran again, obtained a very disappointing 5.0 percent of the popular vote in the first round of balloting on 1 June. The colorless president of the senate, Alain Poher, who had Mollet's support, did much better. He received 23.4 percent, forcing Pompidou into a run-off election. This time Poher obtained 42.4 percent, not far behind Mitterrand's showing of 45.4 percent in 1965. But the Left still failed to elect a president of the Fifth Republic; Pompidou won the run-off contest with 57.6 percent. The Socialists would need to wait another decade before one of their number would move into the Elysée Palace.[70]

Dutch elections in the 1960s were significantly affected by the accelerating processes of secularization and ontzuiling. A growing number of voters were no longer committed to a specific political party, but prepared to switch their votes between parties, depending on the various groups' candidates and programs. This phenomenon of vote switching was familiar in American and British elections, but large numbers of uncommitted voters represented a new challenge for the PvdA.[71] (Unlike the SFIO, neither the Dutch nor the German Socialists had to worry about the Communists as rivals. The German KPD had been outlawed since 1956, and while the members of the PB were concerned about Communist inroads among the generation of 1968, in fact the Dutch CPN was not a significant political force.)

There were five major national contests in The Netherlands in the course of the decade: elections for the second chamber of the national parliament in March 1959, May 1963, and February 1967, and contests for the provincial parliaments in March 1962 and March 1966. The basic question facing the PvdA in all of these contests was whether to campaign as a potential coalition partner of the bourgeois parties, notably the KVP, or whether to polarize the electorate in the hope that the PvdA would lead a left-wing coalition to victory at the polls. Most of the PvdA's campaigns emphasized polarization, especially as Nieuw Links increased its influence in the party, but the results were decidedly mixed.

The parliamentary elections of 12 March 1959 were a severe setback for the PvdA, with the party obtaining only 30.3 percent of the popular vote (1956: 32.7 percent). The results were all the more disappointing because the PvdA had placed high hopes in its polarizing campaign, designed to present the PvdA as a new and dynamic party, ready to cure the ills left by the old coalition. Instead, most voters obviously agreed with the KVP's position that the PvdA was primarily to blame for the country's problems. Moreover, it was difficult to see the Socialists as young and dynamic. With three exceptions, all of the PvdA candidates for parliament were incumbents; and the three exceptions were all over 65 years of age. The downward trend continued with the regional elections of March, 1962 (overall the PvdA obtained 29.9 percent), and the legislative elections of 1963. This time the PvdA's share sank to 28 percent (1959: 30.3 percent) while its major rival, the KVP, was able to increase its share to 31.9 percent (1959: 31.6 percent). The setback of 1963 was particularly bitter since the PvdA was convinced this time it had put together a winning combination to regain its position as the strongest party in the Dutch parliament.[72]

But worse was to come. The subsequent regional contests brought no improvement and neither did the national elections of February, 1967. Although the party's ticket was now headed by a new and charismatic leader, Joop den Uyl, the 1967 contest was an unmitigated disaster, the PvdA obtaining by 23.5 percent, its worst result since 1946. The party's chairman, Evert Vermeer, estimated that in 1967 some 14 percent of the voters had no permanent political home, but the PvdA captured relatively few of these. Particularly worrisome was the party's continuing failure to attract younger voters; most of these cast their ballots for one of the Liberal parties. (The VVD obtained 10.7 percent, and a new liberal grouping, *Democraten '66* [Democrats '66, D'66] 4.5 percent.) Nieuw Links lost no time in blaming the PvdA's old leaders for the election debacle, and the 1967 election results played a catalytic role in enabling the radicals to capture control of the party.[73]

In Germany, there were twenty-one state elections and three Bundestag contests during the decade. The Social Democrats had high hopes for the September 1961 national election. The party's campaign was professionally prepared and run, the building of the Berlin Wall had embarrassed the bourgeois government, and the SPD's new, younger campaign team under the leadership of Willy Brandt contrasted vividly with the Christian Democrats led by the now eighty-nine year old Konrad Adenauer. Most party leaders were convinced this time the SPD would eclipse the CDU/CSU as West Germany's strongest party. That was an exaggerated hope, but the 1961 elections were certainly a relative success for the SPD. The CDU/CSU lost its absolute majority, declining to a 45.4 percent share of the popular vote (CDU: 35.8 percent; CSU: 9.6 percent), while the SPD increased its share to 36.2 percent (1957: 31.8 percent). Pursuing its "me too" campaign tactics (ironically, just at the time that the PvdA was engaged in its polarization strategy), compared to the 1957 result the party gained an additional two million popular votes. The trend continued in the state elections that took place between 1961 and 1965. There were eleven of these, with the SPD gaining an average share of 45.6 percent of the popular vote. The highest was 61.9 percent (Berlin in December, 1963) and the lowest 35.3 percent (Bavaria in November 1962).[74]

It is not surprising, then, that the SPD was full of optimism for the 1965 Bundestag election. The party presented a full-fledged shadow cabinet, and the campaign was skillfully handled by a professional consulting firm. Above all, the elusive momentum factor which had helped the Christian Democrats so often before, seemed to be with the SPD this time around. Party militants felt it in their bones that *"Genosse Trend"* (comrade trend) was on their side. The actual results were disappointing in that the SPD still could not overtake the CDU/CSU (SPD: 39.3 percent; CDU/CSU: 47.6 percent), but the party's share of the popular vote had increased by another 3.1 percent, and the party strategists noted with particular satisfaction that the SPD continued to do better in heavily Catholic areas.[75]

The state elections that followed the 1965 contest demonstrated that the voters are a fickle component of the democratic process. Overall the SPD's share of the popular vote dropped to 44.7 percent, a decrease of 0.9 percent from the period 1961–1965. The main reason, of course, was the 1966–1967 recession, but there were repercussions from the SPD's headlong pursuit of political commonalities as well: Some voters, and especially a number of militants, felt the party had lost its political identity. To be sure, there were also some bright spots: The party won 59.0 percent in the Hamburg elections of March, 1966, and 51.0 percent in the Hessen contest of November, 1966. But the Social Democrats were particularly proud of their showing in the July, 1966 state election in Northrhine Westphalia. In this largest and heavily Catholic German state the SPD almost obtained a majority of the popular vote: 49.5 percent. The victory in Northrhine Westphalia was capped by the heady triumph of the national election of 1969. The CDU was embroiled in leadership battles, and its share of the popular vote sank to 36.6 percent (1965: 38.0 percent), while the CSU maintained its strength at 9.5 percent (1965: 9.6 percent). The popularity of the SPD's charismatic young team brought the SPD its best result since the end of the Second World War, 42.7 percent of the popular vote (1965: 39.3 percent).

The Parties and Governmental Participation

A somewhat facetious comparison of the three parties' relationship to governmental power might run as follows: The SPD spent the first half of the decade trying to share governmental responsibility and the second half working to keep it, the PvdA debated throughout the entire decade whether it was worthwhile to return as a member of the coalition partner of the bourgeois parties, and the SFIO spent ten years deciding if it recognized the French constitutional system as legitimate.

The SPD's case was clear. The meager results of a decade of intransigent opposition had convinced the new party leaders that the SPD must try to become a member of the national coalition. The choice of coalition partner—the Christian Democrats or the liberal Free Democrats—was less important than becoming a member of the coalition itself, because the Socialists were convinced that once the SPD had demonstrated its ability to share responsibility for governing the country, the voters would give the party a mandate to govern without the need of partners.

From a firm and growing base of SPD-dominated Länder governments, and led by a dynamic new team, the party set out to capture the national prize. Fortunately for the SPD, developments among its political opponents and potential partners helped the party's cause. Relations between the Christian Democrats and the Liberals were becoming more acrimonious, and there was pressure from both the CDU and the FDP on Adenauer to resign as chancellor and make room for his heir apparent, Ludwig Erhard. The old chancellor, however, was convinced Erhard would be a disaster as head of the national government. Consequently, Adenauer approached the SPD with an offer to explore forming a grand coalition after the 1961 elections, with Adenauer continuing as chancellor.

A number of SPD leaders—among them Erler and Mommer, but especially Wehner—were prepared to take up the offer, but most party leaders raised serious political and tactical objections. It was obvious that the chancellor was using the SPD to fight his own intra-coalition and intraparty battles. In their haste to finalize the project, the supporters of the coalition, Wehner foremost among them, had also failed to involve the SPD's Bundestag delegation and the parliamentarians resented being left out of the loop. Complaints that Herbert Wehner was acting as though he were still in the Communist party surfaced quickly. Most important, however, the rank-and-file membership was viscerally opposed to any coalition headed by Konrad Adenauer, the man who personified the political enemy for the SPD's activists. Despite Wehner's valiant efforts, the 1961–1962 negotiations failed.[76]

In the meantime the federal government stumbled through the last months of the Adenauer era. The *Spiegel* affair (which the SPD deliberately did not exploit to embarrass its potential coalition partner[77]) demonstrated the government's ineptness and the defense minister's highhandedness. The resulting public outcry forced Franz Joseph Strauss to resign. There was no national election to test the voters' mood between 1961 and 1965 (although it was obvious from the polls and the Länder contests that the government's popularity had sunk to unprecedented lows), but the election of the federal president in 1964 provided a new opportunity for coalition testing. The German president, who has largely ceremonial duties, is elected by a so-called Federal Assembly (*Bundesversammlung*), a body made up of all members of the Bundestag and an equal number of parliamentarians from the state legislatures chosen in proportion to the parties' strength in the Länder parliaments. Because of its showing in the recent state elections the SPD had a pivotal position in the Bundesversammlung.

The incumbent in 1964 was the Christian Democrat Heinrich Lübke. The president was not a particularly distinguished holder of the office, but he was a strong supporter of a grand coalition between the CDU/CSU and SPD. (As a member of the Catholic Center party and a delegate in the Prussian Landtag before 1933 Lübke remembered affectionately the longstanding and generally harmonious relationship between Catholics and Social Democrats in Prussia during the Weimar years.) The SPD leaders were sharply divided on whether the Socialists should nominate their own candidate to run against Lübke. Erwin Schöttle and Helmut Schmidt argued that the party had to nominate one of its own even if he could not win, because not to do so would be an indirect admission that the SPD had no suitable candidates. (In 1959 Lübke had defeated Carlo Schmid.) Supporters of the grand coalition, who included most of the party's right-wing leaders, argued instead that giving Lübke the party's votes would create a sense of good feeling that might hasten a future coalition with the CDU/CSU. Subjected to Herbert Wehner's rhetorical bravura, a majority of the party's executive committee agreed to pursue the second strategy, and Lübke was reelected.[78]

The president was grateful for the SPD's support, and he continued to favor a grand coalition, but for the moment the goal of Socialist governmental participation remained as elusive as ever. Konrad Adenauer had left the chancellor's office, and as we saw, in the 1965 Bundestag elections the voters had given his successor, Ludwig Erhard, a clear mandate.[79] The new chancellor much preferred continue the coalition with the FDP rather than make an arrangement with the Social Democrats. However, shortly after his election victory Erhard began to self-destruct. He was neither able to deal successfully with the 1966 recession, nor tame the rebellious regional chiefs in his own party. A number of these felt a government of national unity with the SPD was the best way to deal with Germany's first major postwar recession, and, not incidentally, drive Erhard from power. The Erhard cabinet fell on October 27.

In 1966, then, the SPD was finally in the position of a bride surrounded by suitors. But whose offer to take? A small group of party leaders suggested refusing marriage altogether, arguing the SPD should remain unattached because early national elections would undoubtedly give the party a clear mandate to govern alone. But that course of action had few supporters, and the Social Democrats were left with the choice of accepting an offer from the CDU/CSU or working with the Liberals. Initially, a majority of the party's executive committee and most of the members of the Bundestag delegation favored a social-liberal cabinet. Such a combination had the advantage that the SPD and FDP were about to form a coalition in Northrhine Westphalia with the Social Democrat Heinz Kühn as prime minister. In addition, in a federal cabinet with the FDP, the SPD would have been entitled to the chancellor's office as the stronger partner. But there were drawbacks as well. Without new national elections such a cabinet would have had a very weak parliamentary base. Finally, the Social Democrats and Liberals were traditionally far apart on the role of the government in the economy, and the new cabinet would need to make some immediate economic policy decisions.[80]

In contrast to the sentiment of the party majority, the triumvirate of post-Bad Godesberg leaders, Herbert Wehner, Fritz Erler, and Willy Brandt, while welcoming the social-liberal coalition in Northrhine Westphalia, favored a grand coalition with the CDU/CSU at the federal level. They, and especially Herbert Wehner, who at this time stood at the zenith of his influence in the party, were honestly convinced that the 1966–1967 crisis required strong government intervention, backed by broad parliamentary support, to be effective. In addition, there were personnel considerations. In the battle for power in the CDU, Kurt Georg Kiesinger, the prime minister of Baden-Württemberg, had emerged as the Christian Democrats' nominee for chancellor. Over the years, Kiesinger and Erler, who represented the same district, Reutlingen, in the Bundestag, had developed a particularly good working relationship. Finally, for some Social Democrats, the CDU/CSU's offer contained another tempting morsel: The grand coalition would have the votes to change the electoral laws so as to create a two party system in Germany. (After reflection the SPD rejected this ploy.)

The combination of arguments eventually convinced most of the skeptical party leaders and Bundestag delegates, and on December 1, 1966 the grand coalition cabinet with Kurt Georg Kiesinger as chancellor and Willy Brandt as foreign minister took office. Lübke, who exaggerated his part in the outcome, said it was the happiest day of his tenure as president, but a number of SPD back-benchers in the Bundestag, as well as many rank-and-file members, were less delighted. Some sixty-two Social Democratic delegates abstained when the Bundestag voted on Kiesinger's nomination as chancellor.[81]

There is no doubt that the grand coalition served the SPD's primary and immediate purpose of demonstrating its ability to act responsibly and effectively as a member of the national cabinet. The man who mastered the economic problems of the recession was Karl Schiller, the Social Democratic economics minister, while Willy Brandt in his role as foreign minister took the first steps on the road to the Ostpolitik. Still, the critics were never entirely silenced. Without using these terms, they saw the grand coalition as the German version of the Dutch Socialists' *uiterste noodzaak* (extreme necessity) experience: the bourgeois parties were in trouble, and so they invited the Social Democrats to bail them out.[82]

A significant proportion of the rank-and-file membership and a number of backbenchers in the Bundestag delegation also felt, much as their comrades in Holland did, that they were being asked to act primarily as a support group for decisions made by the cabinet. In addition, the grand coalition had a third drawback familiar from the Dutch experience: it seriously distorted the workings of the parliamentary system by eliminating any effective opposition in the Bundestag. As a small party, the FDP was clearly unable to play this role, and this led to a widespread feeling among the 1968 generation that the political system needed an opposition outside of parliament. The result was the *Ausserparlamentarische Opposition* (Extra-Parliamentary Opposition [APO]), an umbrella designation for a number of mostly student-led groups that, much as in France albeit on a smaller scale, organized demonstrations and riots in the summer of 1968.[83]

Although many party leaders greeted the grand coalition as the answer to the SPD's and Germany's immediate problems, the coalition partners had agreed that they would not conclude an electoral pact for the federal elections scheduled for September, 1969. In fact, as the legislative contest approached, relations between the coalition partners grew increasingly acrimonious, a factor that also had an impact on the election of a new federal president in March of that year. (Lübke was not eligible for reelection.) This time the SPD was determined to nominate its own candidate to run against the Christian Democrat Gerhard Schröder. Willy Brandt especially pushed for the candidacy of Gustav Heinemann, a former Christian Democrat and Protestant lay leader who joined the SPD in the 1950s. In 1969 Heinemann was the minister of justice in the grand coalition.

Neither the CDU/CSU nor the SPD had enough votes to carry its own candidate, which meant that both needed the support of the Liberals. The SPD's systematic campaign to cultivate the goodwill of the Liberals had short-term and long-term goals. In the short run it clearly pleased the significant minority in the party that had never liked the grand coalition, and it would help to elect a Social Democrat as federal president for the first time. Looking further into the future, the strategy might prepare the ground for a social-liberal coalition. The SPD's strategy was aided by fortuitous developments within the Liberal party. The old, decidedly right-wing leadership had been replaced by a much younger and more left-liberal group which welcomed cooperation with the post-Bad Godesberg SPD. The FDP was also resentful, of course, that the Christian Democrats had been behind the proposal to change the electoral laws so as to eliminate a role for the Liberals in national politics. The SPD's tactic worked, and on 5 March 1969 Gustav Heinemann was elected federal president.[84]

After the SPD had done spectacularly well in the 1969 federal elections the question was not whether the party would remain part of the government coalition, but who would be its partner. Despite the problems of the old coalition, Herbert Wehner and Helmut Schmidt (now the chairman of the SPD's Bundestag delegation) favored a continuation of the coalition with the CDU/CSU. This time, however, they were unable to overcome the objection of their colleagues. The issue was settled by Willy Brandt, who arranged "the fastest cabinet formation" in the history of the Federal Republic. As soon as the polls were closed and the early projections indicated that the SPD and the FDP would have a— very small—majority in the new Bundestag, he phoned the leader of the Liberals, Walter Scheel, to suggest forming a coalition. Scheel readily agreed, and the result was the creation of the social-liberal coalition, which remained in office from 1969 to 1982. On 21 October 1969 Willy Brandt became the first Social Democratic chancellor in the history of the Federal Republic.[85]

The PvdA, which had been part of the governmental coalition in Holland for virtually all of its history, found itself in the unfamiliar role of being the leading opposition party after the breakup of the *brede basis* coalition. Even before the rise of Nieuw Links complicated the situation even further, the party leadership disagreed on a future course of action. There were three factions, which can be personified by their principal spokesmen—Willem

Drees, Joop den Uyl, and Jaap Burger. Drees wanted a new edition of the grand coalition, arguing that the PvdA would not obtain majority support on its own or as part of an alliance of progressive parties. In addition, he felt the whole concept of a progressive-reactionary dichotomy was alien to Dutch politics. In one of his polemical contributions he wrote, "polarization [is] a faddish concept that doesn't solve anything." Joop den Uyl also thought the PvdA should attempt to get back into the government. He praised the grand coalition in West Germany as a "good example," and emphasized the importance of the *"smalle marge"* (small [but important] difference) between exercising influence within the cabinet, and sitting on the opposition benches. In the long-run, however, den Uyl was not willing to discard the prospect of an alliance of progressive parties, which had been the aim of the abortive PAK. He had less faith in a long-term partnership with the KVP than Drees, and preferred a left-wing coalition. Burger went even further. He did not trust the Catholic leaders at all, and argued the PvdA should join a new coalition only after the partners had agreed to a detailed government program before the new cabinet took office. Burger thought it unlikely that the KVP would agree to such a demand, but without such a pact, he insisted, the Socialists would do better as an opposition party.[86]

These theoretical considerations assumed practical significance after the elections of 1963. As we saw, the PvdA did not do well in the elections, giving additional weight to the arguments for a new partnership with the KVP. Although the PvdA would obviously be a junior partner in any new alliance with the KVP, Vondeling, now the PvdA's parliamentary chairman, and Drees pressed for rejoining the coalition, while Burger and the party's chairman, J.G. Suurhoff, were opposed. Actually, at this time the Socialists' discussions were moot; polarization had become a dominant sentiment within the KVP as well. The party's longtime parliamentary chairman, C.P.M. Romme, who had been Drees' partner and counterpoint for more than a decade, favored a new coalition with the PvdA, but in February, 1961, Romme had been replaced by a far more abrasive parliamentary leader, Norbert Schmelzer. The new leader vehemently opposed a coalition with the PvdA, and he prevailed in the KVP caucus. In June, 1963, the KVP delegation voted thirty to seven not to extend a coalition offer to the Socialists.[87]

The coalition question became acute far sooner than most political leaders had expected. After less than two years in office, the Catholic-Liberal cabinet under the Catholic prime minister V.G.M. Marijnen fell as a result of internal disputes. Against Schmelzer's wishes and without new elections the KVP now turned to the PvdA with an offer to renew the *brede basis* coalition. The driving forces for a revival of the old coalition were the new Catholic prime minister-designate, J.L.M.Th. Cals, and, the PvdA's Anne Vondeling. The latter turned out to have rather grandiose ministerial ambitions of his own, namely the foreign affairs portfolio. The PB and most of the PvdA's parliamentary delegation were not involved in the negotiations.

The PvdA accepted the Catholics' offer, but the Cals cabinet was not a happy experience for any of the participants. Vondeling did not become foreign minister, but finance minister, a position he neither wanted nor was qualified for. The cabinet faced severe budgetary problems, with the unfortunate Vondeling at the center of the fiscal controversies. On the sidelines the right wing of the KVP, backbenchers in the PvdA (who resented having been presented with a fait accompli), and Nieuw Links clamored for polarization and an end to the coalition. And if all these factors were not enough, Norbert Schmelzer, the leader of the KVP's parliamentary delegation, and the prime minister had a particularly poor relationship.[88]

This was the background to what became known in Dutch political history as "Schmelzer's night." In the course of a meeting of the KVP's parliamentary delegation on October 13, 1966, which lasted until dawn of the following day, Schmelzer, overcoming the objections of the prime minister and the KVP's left wing, persuaded the Catholic parliamentarians to issue an ultimatum to the PvdA. The Socialists would either agree to the KVP's domestic (especially fiscal) policies, or the Catholics would bring down the cabinet. The PvdA refused (Vondeling felt particularly insulted) and later that same day the Cals cabinet resigned.

Schmelzer's night was a watershed in Dutch postwar political history. The long era of postwar cooperation had come to an end; polarization seemed to be the wave of the future. In fact, many observers feared a return to the political habits of the 1930s when the bourgeois parties systematically kept the Socialists out of the government. Nieuw Links, of course, was delighted with the fall of the cabinet since a break with the KVP had been their goal all along. The old guard in the PvdA and Joop den Uyl were far less pleased. The PvdA's poor showing in the 1967 elections demonstrated that Drees had been right: The party could not attain a mandate to govern on its own. Den Uyl subsequently tried to put together a left-wing coalition with D'66, but the Liberals refused and for the moment, the PvdA had to resign itself to the role of opposition. It required all of den Uyl's skills to change the party's status, but that would be the story of the 1970s.[89]

The SFIO's relationship to governmental power was a contradiction in terms. In the final analysis, attaining governmental responsibility in the Fifth Republic meant capturing the presidency. This required building a coalition to support a candidate who could appeal to a broad spectrum of voters. However, like many left-wing groups and politicians, the majority of SFIO leaders refused to accept either the viability or the legitimacy of the Fifth Republic's constitutional system. One of those reductionist conclusions that contain a kernel of truth might be relevant here. Political scientists have often commented that while the West German parties were uneasy about acting as opposition, preferring instead a harmony model of inter-party cooperation, French political groups relished the role of opposition. Opposition for the French, as suggested here, does not mean waiting in the wings to become the next government, but concentrating on battling and blocking the incumbent, the very opposite of the harmony model.[90]

The SFIO's self-destructive attitude became especially important during the 1965 presidential election. By this time it should have been clear that the Fifth Republic would not be a brief episode, as the SFIO had hoped and assumed. Equally obviously, General de Gaulle would run for reelection in 1965. At the same time Mollet and others who feared that France would be subjected to "Gaullist fascism," were clearly wrong.[91] France would remain a democracy, and the voters would judge de Gaulle and his challengers in a free election.

Recognizing that the new constitutional system was here to stay, some SFIO leaders, foremost among them Gaston Defferre, the mayor of Marseille and a longtime leader of the SFIO's largest federation, Bouches du Rhône, thought the moderate French Left should field a common, viable candidate. Defferre was also convinced he should be that candidate. In cooperation with a close friend, the editor of the French news magazine *L'Express*, Jean-Jacques Servan-Schreiber (quickly dubbed JJSS by the media), Defferre laid the groundwork for his own candidacy. Beginning in September, 1963 a series of articles appeared in *L'Express* detailing the qualities of "Homme X," the man who would be the successful presidential candidate of the Left. It did not take readers very long to note that "Homme X" was in fact Gaston Defferre, and it was hardly a surprise when in December he announced his candidacy for president.

Although Defferre did not have the official endorsement of his party when he threw his hat in the ring, there was no doubt that he was trying to force Mollet's and the SFIO's hand. Georges Suffert, a supporter of Defferre's candidacy and, in 1965, the secretary of the Club Jean Moulin, wrote that the mayor of Marseille wanted to end the paralysis of the Left and shake up the old Socialist party. Defferre was also convinced that the drive for the presidency would be successful only if he were able to move his own party and the entire French non-Communist Left toward reformism. To that end he offered himself as a "bourgeois socialist" candidate with a platform of "democratic Socialism à la Scandinavia." His campaign platform, which had the catchy title *Horizon 80*, was decidedly reformist, and in all essential points a French version of the Bad Godesberg Program. Defferre emphasized his commitment to European unification and the need for domestic reforms, especially improved housing and modernization of the educational system. The candidate rejected a planned economy, and all but abandoned the Left's traditional laïcisme. The last point was clearly meant to appeal to the MRP and left-wing Catholics in the clubs. The PSU, which refused to support Defferre's candidacy, was right in claiming that the mayor of Marseille represented the *"tentation centriste de la SFIO"* (centrist temptation of the SFIO).

For a time momentum seemed to carry Defferre forward. True, the Communists announced immediately that the PCF would, under no circumstances, support him, but Defferre had not counted on them. In fact, he rejected the Communists as partners in his coalition. On the other hand, Defferre was a popular figure among both left-wing Catholics and the club scene. He was also the leader of the SFIO's largest federation and the only one whose membership continued to grow. In addition, Defferre had a number of important members of the CD—including Gazier, Jacquet, Brutelle, Changeragor, and Pineau—and most of the GP on his side. Finally, twenty-nine of the SFIO's ninety-three federations supported him even before, in April, 1964, the SFIO declared Defferre its official candidate. A month later the optimistic candidate himself was convinced momentum and the country were with him.[92]

Gaston Defferre had hoped that with the support of his own party and a coalition of left-wing, non-Communist groups he would be the next president of France, but he had seriously underestimated the opposition to his candidacy within the SFIO. The Communists' refusal to support him had implications for the 1962 electoral pact between the SFIO and the PCF. As a result, Claude Fuzier, the leader of the Seine Federation and the most enthusiastic supporter of the pact, came out against Defferre. More important, Mollet also recognized the centrist temptation that Defferre personified, and he was determined to resist it. Mollet did not oppose Defferre's candidacy outright, that was not his way. Instead, to use Suffert's metaphor, he threw a number of banana peels in Defferre's path.

The most damaging of these was the perennial laïciste controversy. Although Defferre was a popular figure in the SFIO, his position on Church-state relations aroused the opposition of many SFIO militants. The National Federation of Teachers, an organization that traditionally had close ties to the SFIO, expressed serious misgivings about Defferre's lack of firm support for laïcisme. Publicly Mollet only complained that Defferre's candidacy had been launched from the outside rather than inside the party, but behind the scenes Mollet staged one of the tactical maneuvers for which he was famous. In cooperation with the leaders of the teachers' union the general secretary managed to push through a resolution at the SFIO's June, 1965 national congress that clearly contradicted Defferre's position on laïcisme. As a result, the MRP, which had earlier endorsed *Horizon '80*, withdrew its support from Defferre, leaving him without a key component of his planned coalition. He formally withdrew as a candidate on June 18, 1965.[93]

As far as Mollet and the traditionalists were concerned, the destruction of Defferre's candidacy had solved a major problem for the party. The SFIO had avoided the centrist temptation. That the moderate Left no longer had a viable candidate was not a significant concern for Mollet and his supporters because Mollet did not want his party to accept presidentialism in any case. The secretary general rejected Defferre's vision of the French *Gauche nouvelle* because it would have transformed the SFIO into an nondescript member of a vague alliance of Social Democratic reformist groups.

Although Mollet and his allies were victorious in 1965, it was a short-lived triumph. An increasing number of SFIO leaders did not share the old guard's vision for the party. They complained that the SFIO had become the institutionalization of "social[ist] mediocrity," and, like the Bourbons, the party "had neither learned nor forgotten anything." Moreover, Defferre's forced withdrawal from the presidential race left the door open for François Mitterrand, a politician who was cast from much the same ideological mold as Defferre. Mitterrand had no part in Defferre's debacle. He was one of the first to endorse Defferre's candidacy, and Mitterrand loyally waited until the mayor withdrew before announcing his own candidacy. Moreover, the two men remained close allies, and in future years Defferre would be routinely included among the members of Mitterrand's shadow cabinet.[94]

While Mitterrand and Defferre were ideological soul mates, the two men had rather different ideas on the role of the FGDS and the composition of the *Gauche nouvelle*. Defferre wanted to build the FGDS into a coalition of left-wing groups that would neither need nor ask for Communist support, whereas with a "revolutionary audacity" Mitterrand attempted to entice the Communists into cooperating with the FGDS. André Philip wrote in a post-election analysis that while Defferre planned to use the weight of public opinion to force the moderate parties to support him, Mitterrand used the parties to create a personal power base that was then beyond the control of these same parties. This was particularly true for the SFIO, on which Mitterrand was determined not to become dependent. Mollet, on the other hand, saw the relationship in precisely the terms Mitterrand rejected. Since Mitterrand had no significant organizational base when he announced his candidacy, Mollet was convinced the SFIO would be able to dictate its terms to the new candidate. According to the general secretary, as the largest group within the coalition the SFIO was entitled to at least one-third of the seats on the FGDS's executive committee, giving the Socialists an effective veto power over all major decisions. But Mitterrand surprised the master tactician. By the end of September he had transformed the FGDS into an alliance of groups encompassing the entire left spectrum from the MRP to the Communists, with the exception of the PSU.

But the alliance functioned as a support group for Mitterrand, not as a federation of autonomous organizations. Mollet (who disliked Mitterrand about as much as Defferre) and the SFIO were essentially marginalized in the presidential campaign.[95] The alliance with the Communists gave Mitterrand's FGDS a more left-wing coloration, but no one who had followed the candidate's career should have been surprised that Mitterrand ran on a platform of reformist Social Democracy. The candidate, who would later define his idea of Socialism as simply "justice for all," was impatient with ideological debates, professing not to see a great deal of difference between the various left-wing programs.

As we saw, Mitterrand ran an effective campaign, astonishing virtually all pundits by his good showing. For the SFIO there were three lessons in Mitterrand's success. One was clearly that he had persuaded the Communists to support a Social Democratic candidate. (In December, 1966, fresh from his good showing in the presidential election of the previous year, Mitterrand in his capacity as president of the FGDS again negotiated an electoral pact with the Communists, this time for the legislative elections in March, 1967.) The second demonstrated that Mitterrand's pragmatic approach had succeeded in capturing voting constituencies which the SFIO had long targeted without success: left-wing Catholics, urban areas in the South, the Parisian *banlieue*, and increasing numbers of independents. And the third was the strength of Mitterrand's electoral alliance, the FGDS, which rapidly eclipsed the SFIO as the fulcrum of left-wing political activity. In the 1967 legislative elections many Socialist candidates enthusiastically ran on the FGDS ticket and happily appropriated Mitterrand's campaign slogan "[a] free, fraternal, and happy France."[96]

To be sure, there were limits to Mitterrand's political golden touch. After a brief honeymoon, the Communists withdrew from the alliance. Both sides recognized that their pact was based upon the same false premises as the earlier agreement between the PCF and the SFIO. It was essentially an agreement between rivals who had little in common except a desire to defeat Gaullism. As André Philip pointed out, Democratic Socialism and French Communism, at least as constituted in the 1960s, were fundamentally incompatible: "A Socialist party and a Communist party have nothing in common." Nevertheless, before the events of 1968 took the wind out of the FGDS' sails, Mitterrand's claim that his organization was the *"axe et armature de toute majorité nouvelle* (the fulcrum and arsenal of the whole new majority) was not without foundation.[97]

Mitterrand's and the FGDS' 1967 success persuaded even Mollet that if the French Left was to be a player in French politics, some sort of reorganization was inescapable. The SFIO's general secretary now shifted his priorities to making sure that whatever new organization was created, it did not adopt the wrong program and elect the wrong leaders. Mollet left no doubt what and whom he had in mind: "I have been sorely tried by the Socialists who call themselves modernists," and by "modernists" he clearly meant Mitterrand, Defferre, and their associates. The secretary general was determined that the SFIO would not be submerged by the FGDS' modernism. If necessary, the SFIO would risk a complete break with the FGDS, though for tactical and public relations reasons Mollet wanted Mitterrand and the FGDS to initiate the divorce. In the meantime, as Mitterrand put it, Mollet "invented" ever more complicated procedural difficulties to delay a final fusion of the FGDS and the SFIO.[98]

The 1968 upheavals and their aftermath dramatically altered the relationship of the French Left to governmental power. Except for the PSU none of the traditional parties or leaders had any contact with the young rebels, and when they rallied to show their belated support, the results were more farcical than convincing. A contemporary description of one of the largest demonstrations "shows at the head of the procession [the charismatic student leader] Daniel Cohn-Bendit and far behind, very far behind in the crowd [the Communist leader] Waldeck-Rochet, [the Radical] Réné Billères, Guy Mollet and François Mitterrand."

The legislative elections which followed in June, 1968 completed the picture of the traditional Left's irrelevance. If the students disdained the old Left in May, the voters sent the same message in June. Except for the PSU, the Gaullist landslide buried all of the left-wing parties, and especially the FGDS, which the Gaullist government successfully tainted with the brush of Communism, anarchy, and riots. Mitterrand, who resigned as president of the FGDS, described himself as the most hated man in France. Mollet should have remembered the description well, since it had been applied to him when he left office in 1957. (Incidentally, what was left of the FGDS remained firmly *moderniste*; Defferre was reelected chairman of the parliamentary group.[99])

For a few weeks after the June, 1968 elections it appeared that Mollet had been able to seize the initiative again. For some time the secretary general had been eyeing a closer agreement with the Communists, partly to counter similar moves by the newly strengthened PSU, but primarily to undercut the *modernistes* in his own party and among Mitterrand's followers. That road was closed by the PCF's positive reaction to the Warsaw Pact's military intervention in Czechoslovakia in August, 1968. As a result, a number of former allies of the secretary general in the CD now joined those who had always been opposed to dealing with the Communists, and demanded a clean break with the PCF. Mollet had no choice but to yield.

The only option now remaining was a union of the non-Communist Left. But what program and which leaders? Mollet and his supporters continued to insist that the new formation be committed to revolutionary *socialisme pur et dur*. (The secretary general thought "revolutionary" was a word Mitterrand and his allies feared.) Mollet also reiterated that the constituent components of the new party should be represented in the new organization's executive committee according to their institutional strength. This would have given the SFIO, still the largest organized force among the non-Communist Left, a position of decisive influence. Mollet agreed that he should not head the new party (and thought neither should Mitterrand), but he did hope that as a member of the new organization's executive committee he would still be able to fight against *les gens des clubs* (the guys from the clubs).[100]

Ironically, these maneuverings took place against the background of what appeared to be a rejuvenated Gaullist regime once again firmly in control of France. It therefore came as something of a shock when in April, 1969 the president staked his political career on the outcome of a referendum on a relatively minor reorganization of the French Senate. As we know, the voters rejected the government's proposition, and the French political scene became unexpectedly and dramatically open. There would have to be new presidential elections, and for the first time in the history of the Fifth Republic the Left and its opponents would play on a more or less even playing field. With de Gaulle out of the picture, it was by no means certain that the Gaullist candidate, Prime Minister Georges Pompidou, would be able to carry the election. For once, the Left had a good chance of winning the race, provided it had a viable candidate and an efficient organization to back him.

As it turned out the Left had neither, and the 1969 presidential election became the Left's *gâchis*, a missed opportunity. The SFIO bore a large part of the responsibility for the debacle. As if to underline the "Balkanization" of the Left, a whole bevy of candidates declared themselves ready to take de Gaulle's place. Michel Rocard ran for the PSU, Jacques Duclos for the Communists, and the Trotskyite Alain Krivine was the candidate of the "Gauchistes."

The SFIO's contribution to the 1969 presidential race would have been a farce, if it had not been a tragedy. The party supplied not one, but two candidates. Mollet had originally hoped to find a candidate who would favor changing the constitution to restore parliamentary democracy, but that proved impossible. Gaston Defferre ran again, but Mollet was no more supportive of the mayor in 1969 than in 1965; the secretary general continued to regard Defferre as a Social Democrat rather than as a Socialist. At a meeting of the CD on April 29, Mollet had suggested that Christian Pineau would be a better Socialist candidate than Defferre, but both Pineau himself and the other members of the CD backed Defferre. (Mitterrand, still smarting from the FGDS' poor showing in the 1968 legislative elections, decided not to run.[101])

Defferre's campaign received virtually no help from the SFIO organization, which was still controlled by Mollet loyalists in the party, and at the last moment Mollet muddied the waters even further by endorsing a candidate whom he had rejected at the end of April, the president of the French Senate, Alain Poher. This decision, of course, destroyed whatever viability Defferre's candidacy might have had. (Ironically, Poher and Defferre were close personal friends.) Although the mayor of Marseille never expected to become president, he had hoped that by obtaining more votes than the Communist candidate, he would be able to shift the balance of power among the Left to the non-Communist forces. Instead, he obtained a mere five percent of the popular vote in the first round of balloting, while the Communist leader Jacques Duclos obtained 21.5 percent. Mollet could also celebrate a triumph of sorts: in the first round Poher did the best of any of Pompidou's challengers (23.5 percent), and in the run-off contest he was able to increase his percentage to 42.4 percent. (Pompidou won with 57.5 percent.[102])

Still, for Mollet the 1969 election campaign was a pyrrhic victory at best. The Left had been "profoundly traumatized" by the 1969 election campaign, and while the secretary general remained, as one observer put it, "mistress of the party," there was not much of party left to be mistress of. While Mollet was convinced that he had saved the SFIO from the contagion of Social Democracy and modernism, by 1969 very few Socialists were willing to rally around the flag of *socialisme pur et dur*. Appalled by Mollet's obvious sabotage of the Defferre campaign, the mayor of Marseille and a large number of longtime SFIO leaders, including Brutelle, Gazier, Jacquet, Leenhardt, and Pineau, felt that they could no longer work with Mollet. They resigned from the CD as a group. Mollet had prevented Defferre from making the SFIO into a Social Democratic party, but unwillingly he had also prepared the way for Mitterrand and the "modernistes". In the end, the SFIO failed because it was never able to develop a viable relationship to governmental power in the Fifth Republic. The hinge party of the Fourth Republic could not find a way to open the door to power in the Fifth.[103]

Conclusion

The 1960s witnessed the final triumph of reformism, modernism, and Social Democracy, although the victory also left some victims in its wake. The triumph of reform was most complete in the case of the SPD. The organizers of a recent meeting to assess the history of the SPD in the years 1966 to 1982 had good reasons to give their conference the overall title, "Breakthrough [*Durchbruch*] to a Modern Germany." In the PvdA the antics of Nieuw Links threatened to derail reformism for a while, but after a few years Dutch Social Democracy was back on the path it had pursued since the founding of the PvdA in 1946. For the SFIO the price of modernism was the death of the old organization and the failure of its political strategy. A number of former SFIO notables remained bitter about Mitterrand's destruction of their party; Mitterrand's defeat in the 1974 presidential election was attributed in part to the refusal of many former SFIO militants to support him. In fact, analysts writing in the mid-1970s were not optimistic about the future of the French Left.[104]

Such pessimism was not warranted. The triumph of reformism, which poised the SPD and PvdA for success in the 1970s, was, in the case of the PS only delayed until the 1980s. At the same time even the political successes left a lingering, slightly bitter aftertaste—what Oskar Pollak called the *Enttäuschung der Erfüllung* (disappointment of fulfillment). The European Socialists had won their political battles, but, as it seemed to many, lost their ideals.[105]

Sentiments of self-flagellation and doom saying should not obscure, however, that Social Democratic reformism helped to preserve stable and democratic societies in western Europe during some very trying times. The Social Democrats succeeded in reintegrating the 1968 generation into the political mainstream. In France Mitterrand began the process of eroding the Communists' strength, while attracting youthful militants to the PS. In Holland, den Uyl succeeded in taming the youthful radicals of Nieuw Links without alienating them from the PvdA. In Germany Willy Brandt and Gustav Heinemann were instrumental in bringing most of the former APO leaders into the party. It is no surprise that many of the present-day SPD leaders were youthful APO militants in the late 1960s.[106]

At the same time, the youthful radicals did have a positive impact upon the priorities of Social Democracy, although not quite to the extent they had hoped. The Social Democrats' concern with the problems of the Third World, which later found its most concrete expression in the work of the North-South Commission headed by Willy Brandt and the on-going projects of such institutions as the German Friedrich Ebert Foundation, had their origins in the demands by the 1968 generation that Social Democracy look beyond the Atlantic axis.

The triumph of reformism at the end of the decade also gave new impulses to the international cooperation of Social Democracy. Since all three parties now shared essentially similar ideas on what Social Democracy meant, their multilateral and bilateral communications became more intense and more fruitful. After the SPD had adopted the Bad Godesberg Program, relations between the Germans and the traditionalist wing of French Social

Democracy had become increasingly strained. From Mollet's perspective the SPD had succumbed to the temptation of modernism, and, not incidentally, provided additional ammunition for his opponents in the SFIO. The PS under Mitterrand established far more cordial relations with the neighboring Socialists than Mollet had been able to do. One important concrete result was the development of a common European program by the Socialist parties. It was a sign of the coming new times that in 1965 Mollet's longtime critic Gérard Jacquet became chairman of the coordinating bureau for the Social Democratic parties in the European Community.[107]

CONCLUSION

⌒⤳⌒

It may be appropriate to end this analysis of the Dutch, German, and French Socialist parties with another reference to Ralf Dahrendorf's postulate that the twentieth century was the era of Social Democracy. It is now clear that if that assessment has any validity at all, it should be limited to the second half of the century. Only after the Second World War were the Socialist parties able to influence and sometimes dominate the political agenda of western Europe.

The Socialists' new role became possible only after the parties remade themselves and honestly addressed their historic shortcomings and failings. Here the SPD faced a particularly formidable challenge. Before the Nazis came to power it had been the largest and best organized of the West European Socialist parties. But the SPD's much vaunted organizational strength failed to prevent the Nazi *Machtergreifung* (seizure of power). Like the SPD, the Dutch SDAP was also an outsider in the Dutch zuilen-dominated politics for most of its history, although in the course of the 1930s the party was making its way into The Netherlands' political mainstream. The SDAP was still rejected as coalition partner by the dominant bourgeois parties until the last weeks before the war, but the Dutch Socialists were accepted as full partners in the national effort to combat Holland's indigenous Fascists. The French SFIO was traumatized by the split of 1920. The party was torn between the desire to carve out a position independent of the Communists and the hope that the estranged brothers might come together again. The Popular Front and their joint Resistance activities against the Vichy regime and the Nazi occupation perpetuated illusions about a reunited French working class party even beyond 1945.

After the Second World War virtually nothing was the same. The three parties had to adapt all aspects of their institutional lives—organization, leadership, ideology, domestic and foreign policies—to new realities. The most profound impact on the parties' organization was the disappearance of the red family. Some of the signposts were the decline of readers and subscribers to the party press, the disappearance of the party affiliates that had been the core of the activists' social life, and, most important, the dwindling membership and the increasing miscorrelation between voters and militants.

The three parties reacted in quite different ways to their organizational challenges. The SFIO essentially watched its own disappearance. Although the party leaders took note of the declining number of activists, lamented the problems of the party press, and bemoaned the lack of party activity in many areas of the country, they took only sporadic action to deal with the problems. Rather, they insisted the SFIO gained in depth what it lost in breadth: the ever smaller number of activists who remained true to the party assured the SFIO's continued commitment to *socialisme pur et dur*.

In contrast, the Dutch and German Socialists, with a significant time differential to be sure, recognized that the red family was a thing of the past, and that the Social Democratic parties had to transform themselves into what were primarily vote-getting machines. The PvdA led the way in acknowledging this priority, and a decade later the SPD followed the Dutch lead. Surprisingly, the shift in emphasis actually had a positive effect on membership. The number of SPD and PvdA members actually stabilized or increased, although the new members for the most part joined the Dutch and German Socialist parties precisely because these parties had abandoned efforts to bind their activists into the constraints of the red family.

Traditionally, the leaders of Europe's Socialist parties could be divided into two broad categories: charismatic, spell-binding orators and cadre functionaries. Many of the leaders in the founders' generation—Bebel, Troelstra, Jaurès—typified the first group. After the First World War the administrators predominated, although Banning, Schumacher, and Blum proved there were exceptions to the rule. Politics after the Second World War called for different leaders altogether. The spellbinding orator of outdoor rallies was much less effective in the age of radio, and administrators like Ollenhauer and Mollet found themselves increasingly out-of-place in the era of the disappearing red family and declining membership rolls.

The new Socialist leaders had to appeal primarily to voters and be campaign managers, government administrators, and legislative specialists. The new political conditions enabled men like Willem

Drees, Jules Moch, and the German Landesfürsten to become regional and national leaders. Similarly, the parties' parliamentary leaders, Fritz Erler, Jaap Burger, Edouard Dépreux, increased their influence at the expense of the cadres. In contrast, Guy Mollet, the quintessential party functionary, was never able to achieve the status of a genuine national leader.

In the 1960s the advent of television added yet another dimension to the demands of political leadership. François Mitterrand and Willy Brandt were masters of the new medium, Mollet and Ollenhauer much less so. In Holland the young leaders of Nieuw Links were decidedly telegenic, while the PvdA's old guard looked awkward and, yes, old on the screen.

Changes in the ideology of Social Democracy were even more dramatic than the shifts among the leaders. The founders of the three parties committed their organizations to programs of Marxist determinism, and while pragmatic reformism and Bersteinian ethical Socialism had largely eroded Marxist determinism by 1945, there still persisted remnants of the perennial contradiction between practice and theory. In the postwar era the SFIO continued to try to square the circle. It held fast to the old ways, although its Marxist traditions had long been diluted by Jacobin nationalism and the Jaurèssian links between revolutionary Marxism and France's Republican culture. Still, the French Socialists insisted they were a revolutionary party, committed to *socialisme pur et dur*. This stand had some unfortunate consequences. On the one hand the SFIO's rhetorical commitment to the proletarian revolution prevented a clean break with the Communists, and on the other hand the Socialists' insistence on the indissoluble link between Socialism and laïcisme strained relations with the Christian Democrats and alienated potential left-wing Catholic voters.

The SPD and the PvdA experienced fewer ideological problems. Prodded by Willem Banning and Koos Vorrink, the PvdA abandoned Marxism and adopted reformism and ethical socialism when it was founded in 1946. The SPD followed, although Schumacher, Ollenhauer, and the old guard delayed a full-scale commitment to Bernsteinian ethical Socialism for more than a decade. Only the impact of the electoral setbacks of the 1950s finally made it possible for Willi Eichler and the party's program commission to persuade the party leaders that the SPD needed a new ideological foundation. The result was a dramatic break with the party's past, the Bad Godesberg Program.

Ironically, just about the time that the Germans adopted the Bad Godesberg Program, Nieuw Links was challenging the PvdA's longstanding commitment to pragmatic reformism with a program of radical ethical-anarchical humanism. The adoption of such a program would have meant the end of the PvdA as a Volkspartei, and it required the considerable tactical skills of Joop den Uyl to save the party from political marginalization.

The parties had to adapt not only their ideologies and programs, but also their domestic policy expectations. At the end of the war all three parties proclaimed the need for a Social Democratic revolution in Europe. Economic democracy would parallel political democracy, the commanding heights of the economy would be subject to public ownership and control, and economic life would be steered by some sort of state planning apparatus. In the area of social policies the Socialists demanded a closely knit net of social services, and an end to what they identified as clerical privileges.

The Socialists soon recognized that they had to abandon their dreams of a Social Democratic revolution. There would be no full-scale public control of economic life, and social policies would be limited to important, but piecemeal reforms. The SFIO had the hardest time adjusting. Although the party was instrumental in creating the postwar French social net, it insisted that these victories were not ends in themselves, but stepping stones on the road to the full-scale triumph of Democratic Socialism. As the prospects for that triumph receded, Mollet and his allies insisted on maintaining laïcisme as the last remnant of the dream that had been Socialism. It was a politically disastrous position, and it was increasingly challenged by Mollet's critics, notably Pierre-Olivier Lapie and Gaston Defferre, but the old guard persisted. Until the demise of the party in 1969 Mollet and his allies reiterated there was no *socialisme pur et dur* without laïcisme.

In contrast, the SPD and the PvdA became increasingly enthusiastic supporters of piecemeal domestic reforms. Long before the Bad Godesberg Program signalled the SPD's final acceptance of Ludwig Erhard's social market economy, the German Social Democrats had quietly abandoned their strategy of intransigent opposition in the area of domestic policies. The closely knit system of social services in West Germany was the result of cooperative efforts by the SPD and left-wing forces among the Christian Democrats.

Until Bad Godesberg the SPD remained somewhat defensive about its abandonment of intransigent opposition in the area of domestic policies, but the PvdA enthusiastically pursued the goal of piecemeal reform throughout the 1940s and 1950s. The Dutch Socialist leaders endorsed *biefstuk socialisme*, by which they meant that the PvdA's domestic policies were primarily intended to improve the quality of life for all Dutch citizens. Willem Drees and his colleagues were unabashedly proud that the PvdA had been instrumental in creating the postwar system of social services in Holland.

It was not until the end of the 1950s that the Nieuw Links radicals questioned the essential goals of *biefstuk socialisme*. In a sense they wanted the party to reaffirm its revolutionary goals. However, they had little success in turning the PvdA away from pragmatic reformism, in part because the Young Turks had considerable difficulty articulating their concept of revolution.

The three parties also had to abandon some cherished foreign policy positions, although here the changes came rather more easily. The obvious need for armed struggle against fascism and Nazism had already rendered the Socialist traditions of pacifism and neutrality obsolete, and the rapidly intensifying Cold War forced the Socialists to take sides again. For most of them it was not a difficult choice. Already committed to western political and ethical values, the three parties readily endorsed collective security and the Atlantic Alliance as the best means of defending western Europe. They also became enthusiastic supporters of West European unification.

Remarkably, despite its persistent dream of closer cooperation with the French Communists, the SFIO led the way in becoming an enthusiastic supporter of NATO and European unification. The PvdA, unburdened by any love-hate relationship with the Dutch Communists, jumped on the bandwagon. The SPD was the last to come on board. Although it never wavered in its commitment to western values and interests, the party's priority of German national unification led it to pursue the chimera of Four-Power cooperation, and consequently reject West Germany's full-scale integration into the Western Alliance for much of the first decade after the war. After 1955, however, the SPD increasingly abandoned its earlier position and, after a brief throwback during the episode of the Germany Plan, emphasized its commitment to a bi-partisan German foreign policy. The culmination of this evolution was Herbert Wehner's *Gemeinsamkeiten* speech in June, 1960.

To be sure, the parties' shift in foreign policy orientation was not without some painful and costly errors. The SPD's dogged insistence on the priority of national reunification not only misjudged the mood of the West German electorate and cost the party votes, but alienated its sister parties for a time. For the first decade after the war the SPD found itself in the role of outsider. On the other hand, the PvdA and the SFIO faced some problems that the SPD did not have to confront. The French and Dutch parties pursued colonial policies that a were a temporary setback for the Dutch Socialists, but proved fatal for the French. The PvdA's willingness to support the Dutch police actions in Indonesia cost it both votes and members, and in retrospect it was a fortuitous development for both Holland and the PvdA that the Dutch were forced to grant independence to their East Indies possessions in 1949. For the SFIO the nightmare of French decolonization dragged on much longer. Already divided over the response to Ho Chi Minh's revolt against French rule in Indochina, the party was all but torn apart by the leaders' stand on the war in Algeria. Although the SFIO endorsed independence for Morocco and Tunisia (a step that was implemented while Mollet served as prime minister), Mollet and his allies insisted Algeria presented different problems that could only be solved by the territory's continued association with France. The result of this obstinate decision was the Suez debacle, the party's split, and the SFIO's isolation in the ranks of the SI.

Still, these setbacks should not obscure that in the quarter century after the Second World War the three Social Democratic parties scored more triumphs than failures. The SPD and the PvdA made successful transitions to modern catch-all parties, and while that evolution would be left to the SFIO's successor organization, the PS, the French Socialists, like their Dutch and German comrades, were instrumental in guiding Holland, West Germany, and France into socio-economic modernism. In that sense Ralf Dahrendorf was right: The social net and the structures of neocorporatism that laid the basis for Europe's golden age of capitalism were largely the work of Social Democrats.[1]

The Socialist contribution to the evolution of foreign relations, too, should not be underestimated. In the 1950s the Social Democrats helped to establish the multipartisan foreign policies that fully integrated western Europe into the Western Alliance, while simultaneously advancing European unification. In the 1960s the Socialists took some pioneering steps toward East-West detente. Though long in the future, German reunification has been called a day of triumph for the Ostpolitik that originated during the great coalition in West Germany. In that same decade the Socialists were also the first to call attention to the problems of the Third World and the consequences of the income discrepancies between the Northern and Southern hemispheres.

As the troubled 1960s came to an end, West European Socialism faced variations of the challenges that had led to Social

Democracy's transformation since 1945. For the Social Democrats, that is to say, there was no turning back. For the SPD the 1970s represented the culmination of its efforts to become the dominant force in German politics. As often happens in politics, official party histories were rewritten to reflect the new verities. Echoing Wim Kok and invoking Ferdinand Lasalle and Eduard Bernstein, the keepers of the SPD's official historiography emphasized that pragmatism, reformism, and ethical Socialism had always been the leitmotiv of the party's actions. Herbert Wehner in later years complained that Schumacher and Ollenhauer had lacked "political sensitivity and saw the party as a community of faith." All this was certainly true, but for much of its history the party worked hard to hide its pragmatic side beneath thick layers of Marxist determinism. The new historiography also celebrated the social-liberal coalition of 1969 as a "historic breakthrough," although it was hardly the breakthrough that Schumacher and his associates had in mind when they rebuilt the shattered party after the Second World War.[2]

To be sure, for the SPD there was much to celebrate in the 1970s. For a dozen years two Social Democratic chancellors, first Willy Brandt and then Helmut Schmidt,[3] led a social-liberal government in the Federal Republic. The coalition fell in 1982, forcing the Socialists back to the opposition benches. They remained there until September, 1998, burdened by both personnel and ideological problems. No new leader with the stature of Schumacher, Brandt, or Schmidt has emerged. The struggle for leadership is, at least in part, a result of deep ideological divisions within the party. While the SPD remains committed to a market economy, some of its leaders, like the past chairman Oskar Lafontaine, favor demand-side economic policy, while others, such as the present German chancellor and party chairman Gerhard Schröder, advocate more emphasis on supply-side decisions.

Part consequence, part cause of the SPD's internal turmoil, the party has been losing voters and members. Although all German parties face the problems of what the Germans call *Politikver-drossenheit* (being tired of politics), the SPD has a special difficulty. Many younger voters, the main source of the party's successes in the 1960s and 1970s, became disenchanted with the Social Democrats, and turned to the new Green party which emerged as a viable political force in the 1980s.[4]

The PvdA's history in the 1970s evoked memories of the SPD's path in the 1950s. For much of the decade the Dutch Social Democrats experienced a decline in their political fortunes, and it was not until the 1977 elections that the PvdA, now under the firm leadership of Joop den Uyl, was able to reverse the trend.

In the 1980s, however, the party once again found itself in the political wilderness. In vivid testimony to the weakening of the traditional *zuilen* the Dutch confessional parties succeeded in creating a center-right umbrella organization. They agreed to dissolve themselves and form a new party, the *Christelijk-Democratisch Appel* (Christian Democratic Call, [CDA]).[5] Paralleling to some extent the success story of the German Christian Democrats, the new organization became a formidable vote-getting machine that dominated Dutch politics for much of the decade. The PvdA returned to the cabinet as partner in several *brede basis* coalition, but it was always in the role of junior partner. There was no return to the days of *Vader* Drees.

Ironically, the 1990s brought a combination of electoral setbacks and governmental successes. Although the 1994 national elections brought the "greatest defeat" in the party's history, the vagaries of Dutch coalition-building enabled the PvdA to become the dominant player in the cabinet formation. Much like the SPD twenty-five years earlier, the Dutch Socialists formed a coalition with the Liberals. Since 1994 the leader of the PvdA, Wim Kok, has been the Dutch prime minister.[6]

In France the successor organization to the SFIO, the Parti Socialiste was, as Angelo Panebianco has noted, less a successor than a replacement.[7] Abandoning *socialisme pur et dur*, François Mitterrand made the PS into an eclectic amalgam of seemingly disparate, if not contradictory, elements. Former SFIO members, but also disillusioned Communists, left-wing Catholics, and, in particularly large numbers, previously unaffiliated members of the new professional and technical classes, found a political home in the PS. Comparing Mitterrand to Helmut Schmidt, one of the French leader's biographers wrote "Mitterrand [was] the man who brought France politically into the modern age and the French Left to its senses."[8] These efforts, too, were crowned with success. If the 1970s were a triumphant decade for the SPD, the 1980s were the same for the PS. François Mitterrand became the Fifth Republic's first left-wing president, serving for two terms from 1981 to 1995.

Despite these triumphs, in the heady days of Thatcherism, Reaganism, and the collapse of Communism most analysts saw little ground for optimism about the future of European Social Democracy in France or elsewhere. The fate of the Social Democrats was predicted to be "decline and maladaptation," because the Socialists were unable to adjust to an era that saw the forces of the market as the answer to all of Europe's problems. Some Socialists readily joined the throng of pessimists. Exhibiting much hand-wringing—something Socialists have always been good at—they seemed to have a great deal of difficulty carving out a realistic alternative to the conservative-liberal juggernaut.[9]

Yet, such pessimistic conclusions were also decidedly premature. Only two years after the Socialists lost the presidency in France, the PS triumphed in the 1997 legislative elections, forcing the Gaullist president Jacques Chirac to appoint the new leader of the PS, Lionel Jospin, as prime minister. This and the Social Democrats' even more recent electoral victories in Great Britain and Germany have demonstrated that there is life in Europe's democratic Left after all. A genuine alternative to the conservative-liberal agenda is emerging. The Socialist leaders and parties are not agreed on specific elements of their future agenda, but they have identified the political enemy as well as their own priorities. Social Democracy rejects neoliberalism, or, in more personalist polemical terms, the American model. Socialists are convinced that relying only on private initiative and the market to produce a better society is a political, economic and above all ethical dead end.

From the perspective of Europe's Social Democrats the alternative is a return to the past, but not the Marxist past. Rather, it is the final triumph of Bernsteinian ethical and pragmatic socialism. This programmatic tradition of the Left was well summarized recently by Friedhelm Farthmann, the longtime minister of labor and social services in the German state of Northrhine Westphalia. In the spirit of Banning, Schmid, and Philip—as well as Bernstein—Farthmann described the priorities of modern Social Democracy as follows: the right to work, maintenance of the social net, peaceful internationalism, and emancipation coupled with democracy. To these very Bernsteinian principles Farthmann and others add the need for solidarity in the face of postmodern alienation, and the continuing progress of European unification.[10] It remains to be seen whether the voters of western Europe, too, see this paradoxically traditional and modern program as a clear and welcome alternative to the conservative-liberal model.

NOTES

Introduction

1. Franz Kreuzer (ed.), "Die Zukunft der Sozialdemokratie: Ein Streitgespräch zwischen Franz Vranitzky und Ralf Dahrendorf," in *Die Zukunft* 8 (1990): 5. Dahrendorf had earlier articulated this thesis in his book, *Die Chancen der Krise: Über die Zukunft des Liberalismus* (Stuttgart, 1983).

2. Wim Kok, "Het verleden van de Sociaal-Democratie en haar opdracht voor de toekomst," in Jan Bank et al. (eds.), *In dienst van het gehele volk: De Westeuropese sociaal-democratie tussen aanpassing en vernieuwing, 1945–1950* (Amsterdam, 1987), p. 150. In July, 1994 Kok became prime minister of The Netherlands, the first Social Democrat to hold that position since the 1970s.

3. See *Der Spiegel* (5 May 1997), "Nach Tony Blairs Wahlsieg: Modell für den Machtwechsel?" pp. 22ff.

4. Piet de Rooy, *"Van uit een nieuwe wereld": Over de periodieke somberheid en het utopisch verlangen in de Nederlandse sociaal democratie* (Amsterdam, 1993), p. 21; and Philip M. Williams, *Crisis and Compromise: Politics in the Fourth Republic* (Hamden, CT, 1964), p. 439.

5. Rolf Steininger, "Die Linke Europas nach dem Zweiten Weltkrieg, 1943–1949: Ein Tagungsbericht," *Internationale Wissenschaftliche Korrespondenz* 16 (1980): 248.

6. Kurt Klotzbach, *Der Weg zur Staatspartei: Programmatik, praktische Politik und Organisation der deutschen Sozialdemokratie 1945 bis 1965* (Bonn, 1982), pp. 32ff; Hans Daalder, "Zestig jaar Nederland," in *Politiek en Historie: Opstellen over Nederlandse Politiek en Vergelijkende Politieke Wetenschap*, J.Th.J. van den Berg and B.A.G.M. Tromp (eds.), (Amsterdam, 1990), p. 453 n. 13; J.Th.H. van den Berg, "Het miskende tijdvak: De eerste twintig jaar van de Partij van de Arbeid," *Zevende jaarboek*, p. 14; François Lafon, "Des principes du Molletisme," in *Guy Mollet: Un camarade en République*, ed. by Bernard Ménager (Lille, 1987), p. 60; and Horst Lademacher, "Frühe Versuche zur Änderung der Parteienlandschaft nach 1945," in *Auf dem Weg zum modernen Parteienstaat: Zur Entstehung, Organisation und Struktur politischer Parteien in Deutschland und den Niederlanden*, Hermann W. von der Dunk and Horst Lademacher (eds.), (Melsungen, 1986), p. 318.

7. See, for example, Hans Daalder and Peter Mair, *Party Systems in Denmark, Austria, Switzerland, The Netherlands, and Belgium* (New York, 1987); and Daalder, "Parties, Elites, and Political Development in Western Europe," in *Political Parties*

and Political Development, ed. by Joseph La Palombara and Myron Weiner (Princeton, NJ, 1966), pp. 43–77.

8. Angelo Panebianco, *Political Parties: Organization and Power* (New York, 1988), pp. xii [sic], and 163–65; Robert Michels, *Political Parties* (Glencoe, IL, 1951); and Maurice Duverger, *Political Parties*, tr. Barbara and Robert North (London, 1964).

9. Günther Markscheffel to Erich Ollenhauer, 6 June 1963, Best. Ollenhauer/376 (Arch.d.SD).

10. Helmut Schelsky, *Wandlungen der deutschen Familie in der Gegenwart* (Stuttgart, 1955).

Chapter 1

1. For a history of European Socialism see Jacques Droz, et al., *Histoire Générale du Socialisme*, 4 vols. (Paris, 1978). Some general histories of the three parties include Susanne Miller, *Die SPD vor und nach Godesberg* (Bonn, 1974); Daniel Ligou, *Histoire du socialisme en France (1871–1961)* (Paris, 1962); Piet de Rooy, *De rode droom: Een eeuw social-democratie in Nederland* (Nijmegen, 1995); H. de Vos, *Geschiedenis van het socialisme in Nederland in het kader van zijn tijd* (Baarn, 1976).

2. Panebianco, *Parties*, p. 11; and Peter Steinbach, "Die SPD zwischen Tradition und Neubeginn: Programmatische Grundlinien im zeitgeschichtlichen Wandel," in *Die Kapitulation von 1945 und der Neubeginn in Deutschland*, ed. by Winfried Becker (Cologne, 1987), p. 300.

3. Klotzbach, *Weg*, pp. 25–27; Panebianco, *Parties*, p. 16; and Erich Matthias, *Sozialdemokratie und Nation* (Stuttgart, 1952), pp. 54–55. To paper over the contradictions the three parties routinely passed compromise resolutions that were known in the SFIO as "nègre-blanc" documents. See Ligou, *Socialisme*, p. 192.

4. Eduard Bernstein, *Die Voraussetzungen des Sozialismus und die Aufgaben der Sozialdemokratie* (Stuttgart, 1899); Percy B. Lehning, "Socialisten tussen plan en macht," in *De ideologische driehoek: Nederlandse politiek in historisch perspectief* J.W. de Beus et al. (eds.), (Meppel, 1989), p. 190.

5. Willy Albrecht, "Einleitung," in Kurt Schumacher, *Reden, Schriften, Korrespondenzen, 1945–1952*, ed. by Willy Albrecht (Bonn, 1985), pp. 35–38; and Kurt Schumacher, *Der Kampf um den Staatsgedanken in der deutschen Sozialdemokratie* (Ph.D. diss., Münster, 1926).

6. Dieter Groh, *Negative Integration und revolutionärer Attentismus* (Frankfurt a.M., 1973); and Matthias, *Nation*, pp. 53 and 170.

7. The best account of the SPD's struggle with the concepts of nation and nationalism is still Matthias, *Nation*.

8. Johan S. Wijne, "Op weg naar de Partij van de Arbeid: Het beginsel van de SDAP van 1937 en het streven naar een democratisch-socialistische volkspartij," in *Het vierde jaarboek voor het democratisch socialisme*, Jan Bank et al. (eds.), (Amsterdam, 1983), p. 164; and Willem Banning, "Bij het aftreden van Vorrink als partijvoorzitter," *Socialisme en Democratie* 12 (1955): 65–67.

9. Ligou, *Socialisme*, pp. 204, 209–11, 220, 232–37; and Iring Fetscher, "Jean Jaurès," in *Konkretionen politischer Theorie und Praxis: Festschrift für Carlo Schmid*, Arnold Arndt et al. (eds.), (Stuttgart, 1972), pp. 66–67, 70.

10. Ligou, *Socialisme*, pp. 186–87; and Joseph Rovan, *Geschichte der deutschen Sozialdemokratie*, tr. Charlotte Roland (Frankfurt a.M., 1980), p. 65.

11. Ligou, *Socialisme*, pp. 241, 246 (quotation), 257, 264– 66; Tony Judt, *La Reconstruction du Parti Socialiste, 1921–1926* (Paris, 1976), p. 4; and Rovan, *Geschichte*, pp. 105ff.

12. Judt, *Reconstruction*, pp. 126–27; Peter Lösche, *Der Bolschewismus im Urteil der Sozialdemokratie, 1903–1920* (Berlin, 1967); and Kai-Uwe Merz, *Das Schreckbild: Deutschland und der Bolschewismus, 1917 bis 1921* (Berlin, 1995).

13. The quotation is from Vos, *Socialisme*, p. 159. See also the comprehensive account, H.J. Scheffer, *November 1918: Journaal van een revolutie die niet doorging* (Amsterdam, 1968). On the consequences see Siep Stuurman, *Verzuiling, kapitalisme en patriarchaat* (Nijmegen, 1983), p. 319.

14. On the CPN see A.A. de Jonge, *Het Communisme in Nederland* (Den Haag, 1972). The best and most detailed treatment of the German Social Democrats during the Weimar years is Heinrich August Winkler, *Arbeiter und Arbeiterbewegung in der Weimarer Republik 1918–1933*, 3 vols. (Bonn, 1984–1990).

15. The most detailed account of the drama at Tours and the SFIO's history in the 1920s is Judt, *Reconstruction*. See also Ligou, *Socialisme*, pp. 304–6.

16. See in addition to Judt, *Reconstruction*, and Ligou, *Socialisme*, D.N. Baker, *Revolutionism in the French Socialist Party Between the World Wars: The Revolutionary Tendencies* (Ph.D. diss., Stanford U., 1955).

17. Henrik F. Cohen, *Om de Vernieuwing van het Socialisme: De Politieke Orientatie van de Nederlandse Sociaal-Democratie 1919–1930* (Leiden, 1974), pp. 164–67, 171ff, 197–99, 229–30; and Peter Jan Knegtmans, *Socialisme en Democratie: De SDAP tussen klasse en natie 1929–1939* (Amsterdam, 1989), pp. 25ff, 85ff, 145. In Germany the religious Socialists included Willi Eichler, who would later become the principal author of the SPD's reformist Bad Godesberg Program. See below, pp. 189–90.

18. Erik Hansen and Peter A. Prosper, "Political Economy and Political Action: The Programmatic Response of Dutch Social Democracy to the Depression Crisis, 1929–39," in *Journal of Contemporary History*, 29 (1994), 143–44; Cohen, *Vernieuwing*, p. 192; and Johannes Glasneck, "Hendrik de Man (1885–1933)," in *Lebensbilder europäischer Sozialdemokraten des 20. Jahrhunderts*, ed. by Otfried Dankelmann (Vienna, 1995), pp. 331–41.

19. For the history of the SPD in the last years of the Weimar Republic see especially, Donna Harsch, *German Social Democracy and the Rise of Nazism* (Chapel Hill, NC, 1993); and Rainer Schaefer, *SPD in der Ära Brüning* (Frankfurt a.M., 1990). For Dutch criticism of the SPD's stand see Knegtmans, *SDAP 1929–1939*, pp. 76–77. In a famous phrase Kurt Schumacher called Nazism an *"Appel an den inneren Schweinehund"* (appeal to the inner beast in man).

20. Günter Plum, "Volksfront, Konzentration und Mandatsfrage: Ein Beitrag zur Geschichte der SPD im Exil, 1933–1939," *Vierteljahrshefte für Zeitgeschichte*, 18 (1970), 420, 441–42; and Françoise Foret, "La reconstruction du SPD après la Deuxième Guerre Mondiale," *Le mouvement social* 95 (1976): 138–39.

21. Matthias, *Nation* provides the most detailed analysis of the SPD's reassessment of its ideological positions. See esp., pp. 188ff, 204–06, and 278–79. See also Klotzbach, *Weg*, p. 31; René Ponthus, "Tendances et activité de la Social Democratie allemande emigrée (1933–1941)," *Le Mouvement social* 84 (1973): 73, and 76; and Klaus Voigt, "Europäische Föderation und neuer Völkerbund: Die Diskussion im deutschen Exil zur Gestaltung der internationalen Beziehungen nach dem Krieg," in *Deutschland nach Hitler: Zukunftspläne im Exil und aus der Besatzungszeit, 1939–1949*, Thomas Koebner et al. (eds.), (Cologne, 1987), pp. 108–9.

22. Matthias, *Nation*, pp. 196–98; and Udo Vorholt, *Die Sowjetunion im Urteil des Sozialdemokratischen Exils 1933 bis 1945* (Ph.D. diss. U. Dortmund, 1991). Ponthus, "Tendances," pp. 72, 78, and 85–86 severely criticizes the SPD for its "rightist" positions.

23. Ligou, *Socialisme*, pp. 381ff. The most detailed, recent analysis of Déat and his ideas is Reinhold Brender, *Kollaboration in Frankreich im Zweiten Weltkrieg: Marcel*

Déat und das Rassemblement national populaire (Munich, 1992). As early as 1928 Philip had published a book supporting de Man's criticism of traditional Marxism. See *Henri de Man et la crise du socialisme* (Paris, 1928).

24. On the PF see Ligou, *Socialisme*, pp. 378ff; and Jules Moch, *Front Populaire* (Paris, 1971); and Julian Jackson, *The Popular Front in France* (New York, 1987). The literature on Léon Blum is vast. Some of the most important works include, Gilbert Ziebura, *Léon Blum et le Parti Socialiste* (Paris, 1967); Colette Audry, *Léon Blum ou la politique du juste* (Paris, 1955); Jules Moch, *Rencontres avec ... Léon Blum* (Paris, 1970); Joel Colton, *Léon Blum: Humanism in Politics* (New York, 1965); and Jean Lacouture, *Léon Blum* (Paris, 1980).

25. The quotations are from, Roger Quilliot, *La S.F.I.O. et l'exercise du pouvoir 1944–1958* (Paris, 1972), p. 199; and Ligou, *Socialisme*, p. 456 resp.

26. Knegtmans, *SDAP 1929–1939*, pp. 67ff, 93–97, 110, 117, 153; C.H. Wiedijk, *Koos Vorrink ... Een biografische Studie (1891–1940)* (Amsterdam, 1986), pp. 252, 260, 285ff, 313; Jan Bank, *Opkomst en ondergang van de Nederlandse Volksbeweging (NVB)* (Deventer, 1978), pp. 100–03; and Dick Pels, "Zaken-socialisme, of: het einde van de utopie," and Paul Scheffer, "Contouren van een ontzuilde hervormingspartij," in *Sociaaldemocratie tussen zakelijkheid en moraal*, Gees J.M. Schuyt en Siep Stuurman (eds.), (Amsterdam, 1991), pp. 48 and 85 resp.

27. H.M. Ruitenbeek, *Het ontstaan van de PvdA* (Amsterdam, 1955), pp. 59ff.

28. See esp., Gerard Nederhorst, "Het Plan van de Arbeid," in *Het eerste jaarboek voor het democratisch socialisme* Jan Bank et al. (eds.), (Amsterdam, 1979), pp. 113–14, 122, and 130, "Het moet, het kan, op voor het Plan," in *Van brede visie tot smalle marge: acht prominente socialisten over de SDAP en de PvdA*, Jan Bank and Stef Temming (eds.), (Alphen a.d. Rijn, 1981), pp. 33–45.

29. Hans Righart, "Die Demokratisierung einer Ständegesellschaft," in *Tradition und Neugestaltung: Zu Fragen des Wiederaufbaus in Deutschland und den Niederlanden in der frühen Nachkriegszeit*, Horst Lademacher and Jac Bosmans (eds.), (Münster, 1991), pp. 198ff; and Knegtmans, *SDAP 1929–1939*, pp. 160, and 176–79.

30. The quotation is from Bertus Boivin et al., *Een verjongingskuur voor der PvdA: Opkomst, ontwikkeling en betekenis van Nieuw Links* (Deventer, 1978), p. 13. See also Wijne, "Arbeid," pp. 154ff; and S.W. Couwenberg, *Modern socialisme: Achtergrond, ontwikkeling, perspectief* (Alphen a.d.Rhijn, 1972), pp. 67–68.

31. Knegtmans, *SDAP 1929–1939*, pp. 104ff, 219ff, 245; and Ruitenbeek, *PvdA*, pp. 16, 29–32.

32. Wilfried Loth, *Sozialismus und Internationalismus: Die französischen Sozialisten und die Nachkriegsordnung Europas, 1940–1950* (Stuttgart, 1977), p. 66; Walter Lipgens, *A History of European Integration* (Oxford, 1982), pp. 47ff.

33. Richard Löwenthal, "Die Schrift 'Neu beginnen!'—50 Jahre danach," *Internationale Wissenschaftliche Korrespondenz*, 19 (1983), 561–70; Werner Röder "Deutschlandpläne der sozialdemokratischen Emigration in Großbritannien, 1942–1945," *Vierteljahrshefte für Zeitgeschichte*, 17 (1969), 72–76.

34. Jan Foitzik, "Revolution und Demokratie. Zu den Sofort- und Übergangsplanungen des sozialdemokratischen Exils für Deutschland 1943–1945," *Internationale Wissenschaftliche Korrespondenz*, 24 (1988), 317–20; Willy Brandt, *Erinnerungen* (Frankfurt a.M., 1989), p. 131; and Hans-Jürgen Grabbe, *Unionsparteien, Sozialdemokratie und Vereinigte Staaten von Amerika 1945–46* (Düsseldorf, 1983), p. 70.

35. Lothar Kettenacker, "Großbritannien und die zukünftige Kontrolle Deutschlands," in *Die Britische Deutschland- und Besatzungspolitik, 1945–1949*, Josef Foschepoth and Rolf Steininger (eds.), (Paderborn, 1985), p. 40; and Rolf Steininger,

"British Labour, Deutschland und die SPD, 1945/46," *Internationale Wissenschaftliche Korrespondenz* 15 (1979): 194.

36. See in addition to the works already cited, Werner Röder, "Politische und soziale Probleme der Arbeiterklasse am Ende des Zweiten Weltkrieges und in der unmittelbaren Nachkriegszeit," *Internationale Wissenschaftliche Korrespondenz*, 22 (1986), 2–3, 8. Foitzik, "Revolution," pp. 310–15 undoubtedly overstates the anti-democratic attitudes of the SPD's leaders in exile.

37. In his work, *Black Record: Germans Past and Present* (London, 1941) Lord Robert Vansittart subjected all Germans and all German history to scathing and deterministic condemnation. For the German Socialists' activities in London see esp., Werner Röder, *Die deutschen sozialistischen Exilgruppen in Großbritannien*, (Hanover, 1968), pp. 113–14, 143–46, 153–54; Richard Löwenthal, "Konflikte, Bündnisse und Resultate der deutschen politischen Emigration," *Vierteljahrshefte für Zeitgeschichte*, 39 (1991): 626–36.

38. Röder, *Exil*, pp. 105–110, and 203; and Friedrich Heine, *Dr. Kurt Schumacher* (Göttingen, 1969), p. 56. The text of the Buchenwald Manifesto is in, Manfred Overesch, *Die Deutschen und die deutsche Frage 1945–1955: Darstellungen und Dokumente* (Düsseldorf, 1985), pp. 51–56.

39. Steinbach, "SPD," pp. 298–99.

40. The best accounts of the SFIO during the Second World War are Ligou, *Socialisme*, Sadoun, *Socialistes*; and Daniel Mayer, *Les Socialistes dans la Résistance* (Paris, 1968). See also Robert Verdier, *PS/PC: Une lutte pour l'entente* (Paris, 1976), p. 116.

41. See Mayer's letter to party members, July, 1943, in Sadoun, *Socialistes*, pp. 112–13. On the concept of a supraparty "Resistance Party," see Andrew Shennan, *Rethinking France: Plans for Renewal 1940–1946* (New York, 1989), pp. 41, 51, 85–89; and René Rémond, "Les Problèmes politique au lendemain de la Libération," in *La Libération de la France: Actes du Colloque international ... 1974*, ed. by Centre Nationale de la Recherche Scientifique (Paris, 1976), pp. 821–25.

42. B.D. Graham, "The Play of Tendencies: Internal Politics in the SFIO Before and After the Second World War," in *Contemporary French Political Parties*, ed. by David S. Bell (New York, 1982), pp. 147–48; Edouard Depreux, *Souvenirs d'un militant: De la social-democratie au socialisme—Un demi-siècle de luttes, 1918–1968* (Paris, 1972), p. 204; and Loth, *Sozialismus*, pp. 35–36.

43. The quotations are from Quilliot, SFIO, pp. 10, and 199. On the wartime relationship of the two parties see also Wilfried Loth, "Die französische Linke und die 'Einheit der Arbeiterklasse,' 1943–1947," in *Einheitsfront-Einheitspartei: Kommunisten und Sozialdemokraten in Ost- und Westdeutschland, 1944–1948*, Dietrich Staritz and Hermann Weber (eds.), (Cologne, 1989), pp. 274–75, and 283 n. 39; and Verdier, *PS/PC*, pp. 115ff, and 316ff.

44. The quotation is from Johannes H. Scheps, "Van Arbeiderspartij tot Volkspartij (1940–1945)," in Bank (ed.), *Visie*, p. 65. See also Bank, *NVB*, pp. 66, 88, 103–06, 202–03; Ruitenbeek, *PvdA*, pp. 103, 150ff, 186; and Wiedijk, *Vorrink*, p. 358.

45. The quotation is from Herman de Liagre Böhl et al., *Nederland industrialiseert! Politieke en ideologische strijd rondom het naoorlogse industrialisatiebeleid, 1945–1955* (Nijmegen 1981), p. 128. See also Willem Thomassen, "Hier: de Partij van de Arbeid," in Bank (ed.), *Visie*, pp. 95–98, 115; Ruitenbeek, *PvdA*, pp. 116–19, and 163; and Bank, *NVB*, chap. 2, p. 108.

46. Loth, *Sozialismus*, pp. 65–66.

47. Heine to Oswald Zienau, 11 July 1946, Best. Schumacher,93. See also J.C.H. Blom, "Jaren van tucht en ascese: Enige beschouwingen over de stemming in Herrijzend Nederland (1945–1950)," *Bijdragen en Mededelingen betreffende de Geschiedenis*

der Nederlanden, 96 (1981), 300–33; Lutz Niethammer, et al (eds.), *Arbeiterinitiative 1945: Antifaschistische Ausschüsse und Reorganisation der Arbeiterbewegung in Deutschland* (Wuppertal, 1976), p. 715; and Annie Kriegel, "Marxisme et réformisme dans le socialisme français au lendemain de la Seconde Guerre Mondiale," in *Réformisme et révisionisme dans les socialismes allemand, autrichien, et français*, ed. by François-Georges Dreyfus (Paris, 1984), pp. 141–44.

Chapter 2

1. Hartmut Kaelble, *Auf dem Weg zu einer europäischen Gesellschaft: Eine Sozialgeschichte Westeuropas, 1880–1980* (Munich, 1987), p. 99; Réné Girault, "Der kulturelle Hintergrund der französischen Integrationspolitik," in *Vom Marshallplan zur EWG: Die Eingliederung der Bundesrepublik Deutschland in die westliche Welt*, Ludolf Herbst et al. (eds.), (Munich, 1990), p. 562; and Frans Messing *De Nederlandse economie 1945–1980: Herstel, groei, stagnatie* (Bussum, 1981), p. 10.

2. Kaelble, *Weg*, pp. 25–27, 60ff, 108ff, 115, and 139–40; Richard F. Kuisel, *Capitalism and the State in Modern France: Renovation and Economic Management in the 20th Century* (New York, 1981), p. 267; Stanley Hoffmann, "Paradoxes of the French Political Community," in Hoffmann et al., *In Search of France* (Cambridge, MA, 1963), p. 61; and the special issue "Herrijzend Nederland 1944–1950" of *Bijdragen en Mededelingen betreffende de Geschiedenis der Nederlanden* 96 (1981).

3. The best discussion of developments in Germany is, Werner Abelshauser, *Die Langen Fünfziger Jahre: Wirtschaft und Gesellschaft der Bundesrepublik Deutschland, 1949–1966* (Düsseldorf, 1987), pp. 70–71. On the downturn of the 1960s see esp. pp. 70–71.

4. Martin Broszat, "Einführung," in Institut für Zeitgeschichte (ed.), *Nachkriegsgesellschaften im historischen Vergleich* (Munich, 1982), p. 11.

5. Rainer Hudemann, *Sozialpolitik im deutschen Südwesten zwischen Tradition und Neuordnung 1945–1953* (Mainz, 1988), p. 559.

6. Broszat, "Einführung," p. 11.

7. Georgette Elgey, *Histoire de la IVe République* (Paris, 1965), 1:56 reports an anecdote about the French minister of justice, P.H. Teitgen. The minister's reply to a journalist's comment on 8 May 1945, "Mr. Minister we are living through historic times," was a laconic, "Let's not exaggerate." On France's continuing problems see ibid., pp. 26, and 134ff.

8. Kuisel, *Capitalism*, pp. 212 and 237–38; and Stephen S. Cohen, *Modern Capitalist Planning: The French Model* (London, 1969), pp. 93ff; and Bruce Desmond Graham, *The French Socialists and Tripartisme, 1944–1947* (Toronto, 1965), pp. 54–56.

9. The quotation is from a chapter title in Elgey, *République*, 1:413ff. See also Cohen, *Planning*, pp. 113–15.

10. See Wilfried Loth, "Der Durchbruch zur Dynamisierung: Die französische Gesellschaft in den 50er Jahren," in *Modernisierung im Wiederaufbau: Westdeutschlands Geschichte in den 50er Jahren*, Axel Schildt and Arnold Sywottek (eds.), (Bonn, 1993), pp. 69–79; and, for a more popular treatment, John Ardagh, *The New French Revolution: A Social and Economic Survey of France, 1945–1967* (London, 1968).

11. François G. Dreyfus, *Histoire des Gauches en France 1940–1974* (Paris, 1975), p. 132; and Cohen, *Planning*, pp. 238–39.

12. Messing, *Economie*, p. 51.

13. J.Th.H. van den Berg, "Het miskende tijdvak:," pp. 19–20, citing Kossman.

14. C.J. v.d. Weijden, "Enige aspecten van de macro-economische ontwikkel-ing," in *Nederland naar 1945: Beschouwingen over ontwikkeling en beleid*, G.A. Kooy et. al (eds.), (Deventer, 1980), pp. 141–62.

15. Concerned about this, the government actually encouraged emigration for a time after 1945.

16. Messing, *Economie*, pp. 14, 41, and 61ff.

17. Kaelble, *Weg*, pp. 33–34; Herman W. von der Dunk, "Tussen welvaart en onrust: Nederland van 1955 tot 1973," in *Bijdragen en Mededelingen betreffende de Geschiedenis der Nederlanden* 101 (1986): 2.

18. Jean Pierre Rioux, *La France de la IVe République* (Paris, 1980–1983), 1:57–61; and J.C.H. Blom, "Jaren," pp. 187–88.

19. Charles S. Maier, "The Two Postwar Eras and the Conditions for Stability in Twentieth Century Europe," *American Historical Review*, 86 (1981), 351.

20. Jochem Langkau, Hans Matthöfer and Michael Schneider (eds.), *SPD und Gewerkschaften* (Bonn, 1994), I:51ff, 113–14; Ulrich Borsdorf, "In Kauf genommen: Der Marshall-Plan und die Zweiteilung der Einheitsgewerkschaft in Deutsch-land," in *Der Marshall-Plan und die europäische Linke*, Othmar N. Haberl and Lutz Niethammer (eds.), (Frankfurt a.M., 1986), p. 195.

21. Maier, "Eras," p. 332; William D. Irvine, *French Conservatism in Crisis: The Republican Federation of France in the 1930s* (Baton Rouge, LA, 1979), p. 232; Rioux, *IVe République*, 1:80.

22. Kaelble, *Weg*, pp. 42–44, 73, and 138; Dunk, "Tussen," pp. 19–20; Albert Détraz, "L'ouvrier consommateur," in *Les nouveaux comportements politiques de la classe ouvrière*, Leo Hamon (ed.), (Paris, 1962), pp. 184–88; and Hans van den Doel, *Het biefstuk socialisme en economie* (Utrecht, 1978), pp. 120–21.

23. Abelshauser, *50er Jahre*, p. 16; and Arnold Sywottek, "Wege in die 50er Jahre," in Schildt and Sywottek (eds.), *Modernisierung*, p. 39.

24. The quotations are from, Roger, p. 271; and Pierre-Olivier Lapie, *De Léon Blum à de Gaulle: Le caractère et le pouvoir* (Paris, 1971), p. 473. See also Wilfried Loth, "Frankreichs Kommunisten und der Beginn des Kalten Krieges: Die Entlas-sung der kommunistischen Minister im Mai 1947," *Vierteljahrshefte für Zeit-geschichte* 26 (1978): 39–40.

25. Michel Winock, *La République se meurt* (Paris, 1978), p. 24, called Poujadisme the "politics of nostalgia."

26. Kuisel, *Capitalism*, pp. 270–71; Hoffmann, "Paradoxes," p. 64.

27. Jean-Baptiste Duroselle, "Changes in French Foreign Policy since 1945," in Hoffmann, *Search*, pp. 337.

28. William James Adams, *Reconstructing the French Economy: Government and the Rise of Market Competition since World War II* (Washington, DC, 1989), p. 244; and Alain Lipietz, "Governing the Economy in the Face of International Challenge: From National Developmentalism to National Crisis," in *Searching for the New France*, James F. Hollifield and George Ross (eds.), (New York, 1991), pp. 23–24.

29. Blom, "Jaren," pp. 196 and 198; D.F.J. Bosscher, "(Niet) Naar een Christelijke Volkspartij," *Documentatiecentrum Nederlandse Politieke Partijen Jaarboek* (1977), pp. 112– 133; and Arend Lijphart, *Verzuiling, pacificatie en kentering in de Nederlandse politiek*, 2nd ed. (Amsterdam, 1979).

30. J.C.H. Blom, "De Tweede Wereldoorlog en de Nederlandse samenleving: continuiteit en verandering," in Blom, *Crisis*, pp. 171–72; Willem Verkade, *Demo-cratic Parties in the Low Countries and Germany* (Leiden, 1965), p. 246; Juriaan Wolt-jer, *Recent Verleden: De Geschiedenis van Nederland in de Twintigste Eeuw* (Amsterdam, 1992), pp. 268ff; and Lijphart, *Verzuiling*, pp. 11ff.

31. Kurt Georg Kiesinger, *Dunkle und helle Jahre: Erinnerungen 1904–1958*, ed. by Reinhard Schmoeckel (Stuttgart, 1989), pp. 339–40; and Helga Grebing, "Politische und soziale Probleme der Arbeiterklasse am Ende des Zweiten Weltkrieges und in der unmittelbaren Nachkriegszeit,"*Internationale Wissenschaftliche Korrespondenz* 22 (1986): 5–6 and 14.

32. Werner Plumpe, "Auf dem Weg in die Marktwirtschaft: Organisierte Industrieinteressen, Wirtschaftsverwaltung und Besatzungsmacht in Nordrhein-Westfalen 1945–1947," in *Neuland: Nordrhein-Westfalen und seine Anfänge nach 1945/46*, Gerhard Brunn (ed.), (Essen, 1986), pp. 75–77; Barbara Mettler-Meiboom, "Über das Verhältnis von Ökonomie und Politik beim Marshall-Plan," in *Marshall-Plan*, Haberl and Niethammer (eds.), p. 137; Edgar Wolfrum, *Französische Besatzungspolitik und deutsche Sozialdemokratie: Politische Neuansätze in der "vergessenen Zone" bis zur Bildung des Südweststaates 1945–1952* (Düsseldorf, 1991), p. 233.

33. Plumpe, "Marktwirtschaft," pp. 77–78; and Helmut Schmidt, *Weggefährten: Erinnerungen und Reflexionen* (Berlin, 1996), p. 403.

34. Abelshauser, *50er Jahre*, p. 24.

35. Kuisel, *Capitalism*, pp. 185ff and 267; and Shennan, *France*, pp. 72 and 104.

36. SFIO/CD, 8 Sept. 1948; Hoffmann, "Paradoxes," pp. 50–52 and 91; Pierre Kerleroux, "Introduction," in Vincent Auriol, *Journal du Septennat* (version intégrale), ed. by Jean- Pierre Azéma (Paris, 1974), 3:xvii [sic]; and Kuisel, *Capitalism*, pp. 202–05, and 269.

37. Jacques Chapsal, *La vie politique en France depuis 1940*, 2nd. ed. (Paris, 1969), p. 98 calls it "la vague de nationalisation."

38. Kuisel, *Capitalism*, pp. 202ff and 315 n. 9.

39. Franz Knipping, "Vichy als Kontinuitätsproblem der französischen Zeitgeschichte," in *Wege in die Zeitgeschichte: Festschrift zum 65. Geburtstag von Gerhard Schulz*, Jürgen Heideking et al. (eds.), (Berlin, 1989), p. 302.

40. Kuisel, *Capitalism*, pp. 244–47, and 266 (quotation).

41. Cohen, *Planning*, p. 39; and Quilliot, *SFIO*, pp. 367–68.

42. Cohen, *Planning*, pp. 149–53, and 183. On the Plan's achievements see Elgey, *IVe République*, 1:432–34.

43. Albert E. Kersten, "Die Niederlande und die Westintegration der Bundesrepublik," in *Vom Marshallplan zur EWG: Die Eingliederung der Bundesrepublik Deutschland in die westliche Welt*, Ludolf Herbst et al. (eds.), (Munich, 1990), p. 123; and Gerhard A. Ritter, *Der Sozialstaat, Entstehung und Entwicklung im internationalen Vergleich* (Munich, 1991), pp. 168–69.

44. Ferdinand J. ter Heide, *"Ordening en verdeling": Besluitvorming over sociaal-economisch beleid in Nederland 1949–1958* (Kampen, 1986), pp. 344ff; and Ger Harmsen and Bob Reinalda, *Voor de bevrijding van de arbeid: Beknopte geschiedenis van de Nederlandse vakbeweging* (Nijmegen, 1975), pp. 316–19.

45. Leon de Wolff, "Sociaal-democratie en neo-corporatisme," in *Het eerste jaarboek voor het democratisch socialisme* (Amsterdam, 1979), pp. 41–71; and Heide, *Ordening*, pp. 345– 46. For an overall introduction to Dutch neocorporatism see also H.J.G. Verhallen et al. (eds.), *Corporatisme in Nederland* (Alphen a/d Rijn, 1980); and A. Peper, "Socialisme en Technocratie," in *Wetenschappelijke socialisme, over de plannen van SDAP en PvdA*, A. Peper et al. (eds.), (Amsterdam, 1982), p. 26.

46. Maier, "Eras," p. 349; Lutz Niethammer, "Arbeiterbewegung im Kalten Krieg," in *Marshall-Plan*, Haberl (ed.), p. 590; Cohen, *Planning*, pp. 51–53, and 254; and Kuisel, *Capitalism*, p. 144.

47. On the wartime contacts of Socialists and Catholics in The Netherlands see especially, Madelon de Keizer, *De Gijzelaars van Sint Michielsgestel: Een elite-beraad in oorlogstijd* (Alphen a/d Rijn, 1979).

48. Niethammer, "Arbeiterbewegung," p. 585; and Hoffmann, "Paradoxes," p. 55.

Chapter 3

1. The quotation is from Sadoun, *Socialistes*, p. 269. For contemporary examples of this sentiment see also M. van der Goes van Naters, "Een jaar politieke ver-houdingen," in *Socialisme en Democratie* 4 (1947): 11; and Kurt Schumacher's speech "Wir verzweifeln nicht," 6 May 1945, in Schumacher, *Reden, Schriften, Korrespon-denzen, 1945–1952*, ed. by Willy Albrecht (Bonn, 1985), p. 232.

2. Willem Drees, *Drees 90: Geschriften en Gesprekken*, ed. by Hans Daalder (Bus-sum, 1976), p. 152; Léon Blum's address is in *L'Oeuvre de Léon Blum*, Robert Verdier et al. (eds.), (Paris, 1954–1963), 6, pt. 1, pp. 65–78; and Schumacher's keynote address to the May 1946 SPD congress, in *Reden*, p. 418.

3. SFIO, CD, 24 Oct. 1945; Schumacher, "Wir ...," and "Politische Richtlinien für die SPD ...," 25 Aug. 1945, in *Reden*, pp. 232, 272–73; and Willem Thomassen, "Hier: de Partij van de Arbeid," in *Visie*, Bank et al. (eds.), p. 109. See also Doeko Bosscher, "Die Rekonstruktion des Parteiensystems in den Niederlanden zwischen 1945 und 1952," in *Tradition*, Lademacher et al. (eds.), pp. 103–4.

4. Schumacher to Hans Vogel, 4 Aug. 1945, ibid., p. 244; and I. Opstelten,"De partijprogramma," in *Socialisme en Democratie*, 3 (1946), 65–72; and André Philip, *Les reformes de structure pour la rénovation de la République* (Algiers, 1944), pp. 6–8. In terms of their programmatic goals the Dutch and German Socialists gave priority to decentralized "socializations," while the French SFIO preferred centrally con-trolled nationalizations.

5. SFIO, CD, 13 Nov. 1944; Depreux, *Souvenirs*, pp. 256–58; Wijne, "Weg,"p. 164; and Willy Albrecht, "Einleitung," in Schumacher, *Reden*, pp. 35–38.

6. Willi Eichler, later one of the fathers of the SPD's Bad Godesberg program, put it more succinctly than most: "Socialism [is] nothing more and nothing less ... than applied ethics." (Quoted in Sabine Lemke-Müller, *Ethischer Sozialismus und soziale Demokratie: Der politische Weg Willi Eichlers vom ISK zur SPD* [Bonn, 1988], p. 223). In 1952 Joop den Uyl, later to be a Dutch prime minister, defined the Socialist perspective as "freedom which connects (*aanvaardt*) responsibility in solidarity." See "Den maatschappelijke orde in Socialistisch perspectief," *Socialisme en Democ-ratie*, 9 (1952), p. 26.

7. Sadoun, *Socialistes*, pp. 309–10, n. 34; Pierre Belleville, "'Links' in Frankrijk na de oorlog," *Socialisme en Democratie*, 11 (April, 1954), p. 236. For a brief biographi-cal note on Philip see André, Philip, *André Philip par lui-même ou les Voies de la lib-erté* (Paris, 1971), pp. 7–25.

8. SFIO, CD, 22 Dec. 1944 and 27 June 1945; Schumacher, "Politische Richtlin-ien," 28 Aug. 1945, pp. 261–62; André Philip, *Les socialistes*, 2nd ed., (Paris, 1967), pp. 111–12; and Guy Mollet, *Bilan et perspective socialiste* (Paris, 1958), p. 101. See also Dreyfus, *Gauches*, p. 32.

9. Belleville, "Links," p. 237.

10. Schumacher, "Wir ...," 6 May 1945, pp. 228–29; and Schumacher to Vorrink, 5 April 1946, in Best.Schumacher, 93 (Arch.d.SD). For a contemporary analysis by the SPD of the forced merger between Social Democrats and Communists in the Soviet zone of occupation see Gustav Dahrendorf, "Die Zwangsvereinigung der

Kommunistischen und Sozialdemokratischen Partei in der russischen Besatzungszone," 16 March 1946, in Best.Schumacher, 45a. The best and most comprehensive analysis of developments in the Soviet Zone is Norman Naimark, *The Russians in Germany…1945–1949* (Cambridge, MA, 1997).

11. The SFIO's increasing frustration with the negotiations can be followed in the CD discussions, 22 Nov., 7 and 21 Dec. 1944, 21 Aug. 1945, and 26 Sept. 1945. The best scholarly analysis is Loth, "Linke," pp. 355–76. See also Verdier, *PS/PC*, pp. 138–42.

12. Otto Kirchheimer, "The Transformation of Western European Party Systems," in *Political Parties and Political Development*, Joseph La Palombara and Myron Weiner (eds.), (Princeton, NJ, 1966), pp. 184–200.

13. See for example, Carlo Schmid's address to the founding convention of the SPD in Württemberg, 10 Feb. 1946, in Best. Schmid,1447 (Arch.d.SD).

14. Hartmut Soell, *Fritz Erler: Eine politische Biographie* (Berlin, 1976), I: 77–78 and II: 962; Bank, *NVB*, pp. 68–105; Ruitenbeek, *PvdA*, p. 63.

15. Despite its rather historicist tone the best account of the founding of the PvdA is still, Ruitenbeek, *PvdA*.

16. SPD, PV, 13 and 14 March 1947 (Arch.d.SD); and Schumacher to Max Denker, 20 Sept. 1945, in *Reden*, pp. 336–37.

17. Schumacher, "Programmatische Erklärungen," 5 and 6 Oct. 1945, in *Reden*, p. 317. References to the Sermon on the Mount were a recurrent theme among postwar Social Democrats. The left-wing PvdA leader, Johannes Scheps, described the party's goals as, "Een samenleving die naar nieuwe vormen de boodschaap van de *bergrede* [sic] als grondslag zal kennen." See Johannes H. Scheps, *Het progressieve als waardeloze pronk* (Apeldoorn, 1971), p. 52.

18. Albrecht Kaden, *Einheit oder Freiheit: Die Wiedergründung der SPD 1945/46*, 3rd. ed. (Bonn, 1990), pp. 281–83; and Klotzbach, *Weg*, pp. 63–65.

19. Schumacher, "Wir … 6.5.45," pp. 230–31, and "Politische Richtlinien," in *Reden*, pp. 261–62; and Heine to Emil Kirschmann, 19 Aug. 1946, Best. Schumacher,93.

20. Blum had already provided a blueprint for the post-war rejuvenation of French Socialism in his wartime book, *À L'Echelle humaine* (Paris, 1945). See also Loth, *Sozialismus*, pp. 73–76.

21. Depreux, *Souvenirs*, p. 245; Ligou, *Socialisme*, p. 544; Quilliot, *S.F.I.O.*, p. 113; and Bernard Ménager (ed.), *Guy Mollet: Un camarade en Republique* (Lille, 1987), pp. 183–84.

22. For a discussion of the historiography of the August, 1946 congress see Loth, *Sozialismus*, p. 130 n. 3. The most detailed account of Mollet's life and thought is, Denis Lefebvre, *Guy Mollet, Le mal aimé* (Paris, 1992). See also Quilliot, *SFIO*, pp. 35–36.

23. Quilliot entitles his chapter on the August, 1946 congress "La revolte des fantassins." See *SFIO*, pp. 170ff.

24. The quotations are from Dreyfus, *Gauches*, p. 54; and Daniel Mayer, *Pour une Histoire de la Gauche* (Paris, 1969), p. 335. Blum's address can be found in Mayer's work, pp. 321–40. See also Quillot, *SFIO*, pp. 172ff and 389–90; and Jérme Jaffre, "Guy Mollet et la conqute de la SFIO en 1946," in *Guy Mollet*, pp. 17–31.

25. Loth, "Linke," p. 370.

26. In words that echoed Schumacher's view of the relationship between Socialism and the middle classes, Mollet proclaimed, "*Si les classes moyennes se prolétarisent, c'est à elles de venir au socialisme, et non au socialisme d'aller à elles.*" Quoted in

Loth, *Sozialismus*, p. 331 n. 17. On the SFIO's love-hate relationship with the Communists, see esp. Verdier, *PS/PC*.

27. Blom, "Jaren," pp. 300–33; and Miller, *SPD*, pp. 19–20.

28. In February 1946 the PvdA was still anticipating 46 percent of the popular vote. See Woltjer, *Verleden*, p. 159.

29. The SPD's support came overwhelmingly from working class voters. In fact, most of the party's voters cast their ballots for the SPD precisely because they still saw it as a working class party. See Wolfgang Hirsch-Weber and Klaus Schütz, *Wähler und Gewählte: Eine Untersuchung der Bundestagswahlen 1953* (Berlin, 1957), pp. 179–80 and 401. For Mollet's acknowledgement of the SFIO's failure see Lefebvre, *Mollet*, p. 382.

30. Schumacher, "Wir ...," p. 223; and SFIO, CD, 4 June 1946 (Gouin).

31. Needless to say, the bourgeois parties did their best to encourage this confusion. The CDU's 1953 election slogan "All Marxist Roads lead to Moscow" was a particularly effective example of such efforts.

32. SFIO, CD, 13 Nov. 1946; Willem Thomassen, "Binnenlandse Notities," *Socialisme en Democratie* 5 (1948): 41.

33. Eberhard Schmidt, *Die verhinderte Neuordnung 1945–1952: Zur Auseinandersetzung um die Demokratisierung der Wirtschaft in den westlichen Besatzungszonen und in der Bundesrepublik Deutschland* (Frankfurt a.M., 1970), pp. 39–40. For a different and more persuasive analysis see Diethelm Prowe, "Socialism as Crisis Response: Socialization and the Escape from Poverty and Power in Post-World War II Germany," *German Studies Review* 25 (1992): 68–69.

34. SFIO, CD, 13 Nov. and 11 Dec. 1946. See also Klotzbach, *Weg*, p. 149; Philip, *Socialistes*, p. 230; and Couwenberg, *Socialisme*, p. 183.

35. A member of the PvdA's executive committee told his fellow members in Nov. 1951, "In the next fifty years we certainly cannot count on a majority [of votes] in our country." See PvdA, PB, 24 Nov. 1951.

36. The PvdA's parliamentary leader, van der Goes van Naters, was sharply critical of the party's decision to abandon full-scale economic planning. See his memoirs, *Met en tegen de tijd* (Amsterdam, 1980), pp. 157 and 239. See also PvdA, PB, 29 March 1947; and J.F. de Jongh, "Over de noodzaak van een nieuw socialistisch maaatschappijbeeld," in *Socialisme en Democratie* 3 (1946): 231–36.

37. De Rooy, *Wereld*, pp. 29–30.

38. F.J.F.M. Duynstee, *De Kabinetsformatie 1945–1965* (Deventer, 1966), p. 164. The author of the quote was Tilanus, the head of the Protestant Christelijk-Historisch Unie. On the relationship of party and parliamentary groups see Panebianco, *Parties*, p. 175.

39. Ulrich Buczylowski, *Kurt Schumacher und die deutsche Frage: Sicherheitspolitik und strategische Offensivkonzeption vom August 1950 bis September 1951* (Stuttgart-Degerloch, 1973), p. 62.

40. SPD, PV, Parteiausschuss and Kontrollkommission, 8 Sept. 1951, and 9/10 April 1952. See also Klotzbach, *Weg*, pp. 190–91; and for a theoretical-structural analysis of the SPD's attitude, Klaus Günther, *Sozialdemokratie und Demokratie 1946–1966* (Bonn, 1979), pp. 135–39; and Christoph Stamm (ed.), *Die SPD-Fraktion im Frankfurter Wirtschaftsrat 1947–1949: Protokolle, Aufzeichnungen, Rundschreiben* (Berlin, 1993), pp. XXVII and XXXIX [sic].

41. Bernhard Koolen, *Die wirtschafts- und gesellschaftspolitische Konzeption von Viktor Agartz zur Neuordnung der westdeutschen Nachkriegsgesellschaft* (Cologne, 1979), pp. 53 and 142–43.

42. For an analysis of Schumacher's attempt to link nationalism and democracy see Kurt Thomas Schmitz, *Deutsche Einheit und Europäische Integration: Der sozialdemokratische Beitrag zur Außenpolitik der Bundesrepublik Deutschland ...* (Bonn, 1978), pp. 33ff and 194.

43. Schmid to Alfred Frisch, 2 Oct. 1947, Best. Schmid,1447. On the significance of the Ziegenhain Conference see Schmitz, *Einheit*, pp. 251–52 n. 27; V. Stanley Vardys, "Germany's Postwar Socialism: Nationalism and Kurt Schumacher (1945–1952)," in *Review of Politics*, 27 (1965), 222; and Gerhard Hirscher, *Carlo Schmid und die Gründung der Bundesrepublik: Eine politische Biographie* (Bochum, 1986), pp. 37–38.

44. SPD, PV, 11 and 12 March 1949; and SPD, PV, PA, KK, District secretaries, Bundestagfraktion, Länder ministers, 17 Sept 1957 (Brandt). See also Soell, *Erler*, 1: 246–47.

45. SPD, PV, 8 Sept. 1953 (Schoettle). See also Soell, *Erler*, 1: 163, 580 n. 254, and 973; and Klotzbach, *Weg*, pp. 153–54.

46. SPD, PV and PA, 22 and 23 Jan. 1949 (Kaisen), and 5/6 Jan. 1950. See also Carlo Schmid, *Erinnerungen* (Munich, 1979), p. 474; and Soell, *Erler*, 1: 92, 135, and 564 n. 67.

47. These demands surfaced repeatedly at the meetings of the SPD's executive committee. See SPD, PV, 2/3 Nov. 1951 (Hennssler and Schoettle), and 26 Oct. 1953 (Haas).

48. Willy Brandt, *Links und frei: Mein Weg 1930–1950* (Hamburg, 1982), pp. 429ff.

49. SPD, PV, 5/6 Jan. 1950. On the character and importance of the regional leaders in the immediate postwar era see Walter Mühlhausen and Cornelia Regin (eds.), *Treuhänder des deutschen Volkes—Die Ministerpräsidenten der westlichen Besatzungszonen nach den ersten freien Landtagswahlen: Politische Portraits* (Melsungen, 1991); and Marie Elise Foelz- Schroeter, *Föderalistische Politik und nationale Repräsentation 1945 bis 1947* (Stuttgart, 1974), pp. 108ff. For the Schumacher-Kaisen controversy see Albrecht, "Einleitung," p. 160; and Renate Meyer-Braun, "'Rebell' Wilhelm Kaisen ... Briefwechsel zwischen Alfred Faust und Fritz Heine aus den Jahren 1950–1956," in *Bremisches Jahrbuch*, 67 (1989), 109–39.

50. Erler to Ollenhauer, 5 Oct. 1948 and Schmid to Ollenhauer, 14 Oct. 1948, Best. Schmid,1450.

51. SPD, PV, 14 Sept. 1952 (Ollenhauer). See also Albrecht, "Einleitung," p. 144; and Soell, *Erler*, 1: 141–42.

52. Dietrich Orlow, *Weimar Prussia, 1918–1933*, 2 vols. (Pittsburgh, 1986 and 1991).

53. On the significance of vertical and geographic factions for party stability see Panebianco, *Parties*, p. 38.

54. Pierre Rimbert, "Le Parti socialiste SFIO," in *Partis politiques et classes sociales*, Maurice Duverger (ed.), (Paris, 1955), pp. 195–207; Duverger, "SFIO: mort ou transfiguration?" in *Les Temps Modernes* 10 (numéro spécial, 1955): 1863–1885. See also SFIO, CD, 13 Nov. 1946 (Boutbien).

55. SFIO, CD, 9 Jan. 1946 (Depreux); Laurent Olivier, "La Fédération socialiste du Nord," in *Cahier et Revue de L'Ours* 2 (1994): 80; and Jean Poperen, *La Gauche française: Le nouvel age (1958–1965)* (Paris, 1972), 2: 237.

56. Philip, *Socialistes*, pp. 128 and 136; and Lapie, *Blum*, pp. 415, and 425–26.

57. See Charles Lussy, "Communication ... à la réunion du Groupe ...," 4 Dec. 1951, appended to, SFIO, CD, 5 Dec. 1951. For the relationship of the party leadership and the parliamentary groups see also Panebianco's "organograms," *Parties*, p. 175.

58. For the bitter debates on the RDR within the CD see SFIO, CD, 10 March and 7 April 1948. See also Ligou, *Socialisme*, p. 562.

59. SFIO, CD, 10 Aug. 1951. A major factor in the SFIO's fanatic support of laï-cisme was the preponderance of lacist instituteurs in the ranks of the party's middle level functionaries. See Dreyfus, *Gauches*, pp. 117ff. On the school question see also Lefebvre, *Mollet*, pp. 137ff.

60. SFIO, CD, 20 June 1951; and Günther Markscheffel, "43. Nationalkongress der ... SFIO vom 11. bis 14.5.1951 in Paris," 16 May 1951, p. 8, Best. Markscheffel, 36. See also Quilliot, *SFIO*, p. 391.

61. SFIO, CD, 13 Nov. 1946 and 20 June 1951. It should be noted that individual Socialist leaders, such as Philip and Boutbien, were among the earliest and most vociferous critics of France's attempts to maintain control of Indochina. See Markscheffel, "Eindrücke und Gespräche vom Pariser Aufenthalt vom 12.3. bis 18.3.1947," 22 March 1947, pp. 5 and 7, in Best. Markscheffel, 37a.

62. Markscheffel, "43. Nationalkongress ...," pp. 2–3 and 8; and Quilliot, *SFIO*, pp. 753– 56.

63. Sadoun, *Socialistes*, p. 277.

64. Rimbert, "SFIO," in *Partis*, Duverger (ed.).

65. See Philip's bitter criticism of Mollet's role as secretary general in, *Socialistes*, pp. 180–81. At the same time, Loth, *Sozialismus*, p. 377 n. 11 and 13 is right to point out that the SFIO's problems should not be reduced to Mollet and *molletisme*.

66. Dreyfus, *Gauches*, p. 87 is particularly critical of the role which "colonialisme petit- blanc" played in the SFIO's attitude toward the Third World.

67. For internal discussions of the SFIO's successes and failures in the area of social policy see SFIO, CD, 23 April and 11 June 1947, 10 March and 31 Aug. 1948, 8 Nov. 1950, and 11 April 1951; Depreux, *Souvenirs*, pp. 294–95, 307, and 318; and Lapie, *Blum*, p. 109–11. See also Shennan, *Rethinking*, pp. 89–90;

68. The quotation is from Matthias, *Nation*, p. 347 n. 14.

Chapter 4

1. In June 1950 Jules Moch was sure, "*Jamais le parti ne s'est si bien porté. L'espérance reprend, la propagande aussi, la fierté aussi, le parti respire, il se regonfle.*" Quoted in Elgey, *République*, 1:457. See also SFIO/CD, 13 Jan. 1954; and Ollenhauer's statement of 13 Nov. 1952 quoted in Rudolf Hrbek, *Die SPD, Deutschland und Europa: Die Haltung der Sozialdemokratie zum Verhältnis von Deutschland-Politik und Westintegration 1945–1957* (Bonn, 1972), p. 347; and Hein Vos, "Congresrede," *Socialisme en Democratie* 8 (1951): 150–52.

2. H.G. Simmons, *French Socialists in Search of a Role, 1956–1967* (Ithaca, NY, 1970), p. 278; Stephen Padgett and William E. Paterson, *A History of Social Democracy in Postwar Europe* (New York, 1991), pp. 92–93; and Scheps, *Pronk*, p. 86.

3. SFIO/CD, 19 Oct. 1955; SPD/PV/KK/PA, 9/10 April 1952; and PvdA/PB, 28 Oct. 1950. See also Mattei Dogan, "Les clivages politiques de la classe ouvrière," in *Les nouveaux comportements politiques de la classe ouvrière*, ed. by Leo Hamon (Paris, 1962), p. 127; and Panebianco, *Parties*, pp. 25ff.

4. SFIO/CD, 16 Jan. 1952; SPD/PV, 11/12 March 1949. See also Everhard Holtmann, "Die neuen Lasselleaner: SPD und HJ-Generation nach 1945," in Martin Broszat et al (eds.), *Von Stalingrad zur Währungsreform: Zur Sozialgeschichte des Umbruchs in Deutschland*, 3rd. ed. (Munich, 1990), p. 192, 195, 208–09; and Duverger, "SFIO," p. 1869.

5. Dreyfus, *Gauches*, p. 131.

6. SFIO/CD, 7 Nov. 1951 and 30 June 1957; and Alfred Nau, "Arbeitsbericht Finanzen," July, 1956, Best. SPD/Parteitage 1946–1949 [sic](For.Hbg.).

7. SFIO/CD, 27 Jan. 1954; Simmons, *Role*, p. 198; Helmut Köser, "Innovationsprozeße in der SPD," in *Politische Vierteljahresschrift* 16 (1975): 35; W. Thomassen, *Opening van Zaken: Een en ander over de voorbereiding van de PvdA* (Amsterdam, 1946), pp. 11–12. For an account of the exception to the rule see Olivier, "Nord," p. 78.

8. Erler to Walter Schütze, 25 Feb. 1954, Best. Erler, 169; SFIO/CD, 11 July 1951 and 10 Dec. 1952; and Quilliot, *SFIO*, p. 364.

9. "*Comment réveiller un parti qui ne se juge nullement endormé.*" Quilliot, *SFIO*, p. 438. Hrbek, *SPD*, pp. 347–48 describes the SPD's reaction as "*trotziges Selbstbewusstsein.*"

10. Panebianco, *Parties*, p. 204; Hartmut Soell, "Fraktion und Parteiorganisation: Zur Willensbildung der SPD in den 60er Jahren," *Politische Vierteljahresschrift*, 10 (1969), 605; Quilliot, *SFIO*, pp. 29–34. On the tradition of the *Tendances* see esp. *Cahiers et Revue de L'Ours* 2 (1994).

11. Markscheffel to Ollenhauer, 21 Sept. 1953, Best. Markscheffel, 4). See also Simmons, *Role*, pp. 3 and 170–75; Köser, "Innovation," p. 35; and Soell, *Erler*, 1:237ff.

12. Brandt to Schumacher, 23 May 1952, Best. Ollenhauer, 191; Jan Bank et al., "Profiel: Jacques de Kadt," in *Het eerste jaarboek voor het democratisch socialisme*, Bank et al. (eds.), (Amsterdam, 1979), p. 336 n. 27; Anet Bleich, *Een partij in de tijd: Veertig jaar Partij van de Arbeid, 1946–1986* (Amsterdam, 1986), pp. 97–98; and SFIO/CD, 12 Dec. 1951.

13. Johannes H. Scheps, "Van arbeiderspartij tot volkspartij (1940–1945)," in *Visie* Bank et al. (eds.), p. 79.

14. PvdA/PB, 28 June 1947; and SFIO/CD, 10 Dec. 1946. The rule was often honored in its breach. See Mollet's defense of his friend Naegelen when the latter published a piece in the conservative Parisian daily *Le Figaro*. SFIO/CD, 17 June 1953.

15. SFIO/CD, 12 Jan. 1947. See also Heinz-Gerhard Haupt, "Léon Blum," in Marieluise Christadler (ed.), *Die geteilte Utopie: Sozialisten in Frankreich und Deutschland* (Opladen, 1985), p. 256; and Ligou, *Socialisme* pp. 597–601.

16. Loth, *Sozialismus*, p. 377 n. 13; Philip, *Socialistes*; Lefebvre, *Mollet*, p. 144. See also Auriol to Fernand Donzé, 17 July 1959, in Depreux, *Souvenirs*, pp. 409–10.

17. For a sociological profile of the SFIO's leaders and the CD see Simmons, *Role*, pp. 287–88.

18. The quotation is from Philippe Alexandre, *L'Adversaire du Général: Gaston Defferre* (Paris, 1964), p. 108. On Pivert see the full-scale biography, Jacques Kergoat, *Marceau Pivert: Socialiste de Gauche* (Paris, 1994).

19. On Wehner and his relationship to Schumacher see his own unpublished autobiography in Best. Ollenhauer, 462 and Wayne C. Thompson, *The Political Odyssey of Herbert Wehner* (Boulder, CO, 1993), pp. 104–05. Erik Nölting complained that Schumacher had reduced all other party leaders to the level of expert advisors. See Claudia Nölting, *Erik Nölting* (Essen, 1989), p. 550.

20. Heine, *Schumacher*, pp. 65–66; Lewis J. Edinger, *Kurt Schumacher: A Study in Personality and Political Behavior* (Stanford, CA, 1965), p. 142; and Schmid, *Erinnerungen*, p. 536. On Ollenhauer see the rather critical biography by Brigitte Seebacher-Brandt, *Ollenhauer: Biedermann und Patriot* (Berlin, 1984).

21. SPD/PV, 29 July 1953. On Erler see the exhaustive biography, Soell, *Erler*. For Wehner's relationship to Ollenhauer see Wehner to Ollenhauer, 24 June 1957, Best. Ollenhauer, 462. For a theoretical discussion of the relationship of party executive and parliamentary groups in Socialist parties see Panebianco, *Parties*, p. 112.

22. Goes van Naters, *Tijd*, pp. 140–45. See also Wiedijk, *Vorrink*, pp. 393–94.

23. See Joop den Uyl's laudatio on the occasion of Banning's 70th birthday, "Banning 70 jaar," *Socialisme en Democratie* 15 (1958): 81–83.

24. Berg, "Tijdvak," p. 19.

25. Chris van Esterik and Joop van Tijn, *Jaap Burger: Een leven lang dwars* (Amsterdam, 1984), p. 133.

26. Willy Brandt put it this way, "We have to become *Volkspartei* without ceasing to be a workers' party." SPD/PV/PA/KK, 17 Sept. 1953.

27. SPD/PV/PA/KK, 8/9 Sept. 1951 and 9/10 April 1952. See also Kaden, *Einheit*, p. 71; Peter Merseburger, *Der schwierige Deutsche: Kurt Schumacher* (Stuttgart, 1995), p. 10; and Köser, "Innovation," p. 47.

28. Schumacher to Siegfried Aufhäuser, 27 Aug. 1946, Best. Schumacher, 29; and Berard to MAE, 21 Aug. 1952, Amb. Bonn, XP 91/XP 3/4 (AOFAA). See also Jörg Gabbe, *Parteien und Nation: Zur Rolle des Nationalbewußtseins für die politischen Grundorientierungen der Parteien in der Anfangsphase der Bundesrepublik* (Meisenheim, 1976), pp. 52 and 215; and Wolfgang Benz, "Kurt Schumacher als deutscher und europäischer Sozialist," in *Kurt Schumacher als deutscher und europäischer Sozialist,* Willy Albrecht (ed.), (Bonn, 1988), p. 27.

29. SFIO/CD, 2 Feb. 1949; and Vorrink's article in, *De Volkskrant*, 17 June 1952.

30. See below, pp. 87–89.

31. Soell, *Erler*, 1:233ff, 242ff, and 262–67; Hartmut Mehringer, *Waldemar von Knoeringen: Eine politische Biographie* (Munich, 1989), 2:376; Hirscher, *Schmid*, pp. 32–36; and Köser, "Innovation," p. 31. A particularly useful summary of the reformers' ideas can be found in a radio talk show the Südwestfunk aired on 14 July 1954. The discussants included Erler as moderator and Schmid, Brandt, Schoettle, and Eichler as participants. A copy of the transcript is in Best, Erler, 10.

32. SPD/PV/PA, 22 and 23 Jan. 1949; and SPD/PV, 5 Jan. 1950.

33. See Erler to Dieter Sternweiler, 26 Nov. 1955, Best. Erler, 169; Uwe Kitzinger, *German Electoral Politics: A Study of the 1957 Campaign* (Oxford, 1960), p. 126; and Lademacher, "Versuche," p. 316.

34. SFIO/CD, 8 Jan. 1947 and 20 June 1951. See also Shennan, *Rethinking*, p. 89; and Quillot, *SFIO*, pp. 228–34.

35. Judt, *Marxism*, pp. 251–52.

36. SFIO/CD, 21 June 1950. The members were Moch, Gazier, Rosenfeld, Tanguy- Prigent, Philip, Pineon, Defferre, and Laurent.

37. SFIO/CD 27 May 1953 and 23 Nov. 1955.

38. SFIO/CD, 31 July and 7 May 1952. See also Pierre Belleville, "Links in Frankrijk na de oorlog," *Socialisme en Democratie* 11 (1954): 235.

39. SFIO/CD, 13 March and 7 May 1952.

40. SFIO/CD, 1 June 1955.

41. Thomassen, *Opening*, pp. 22–23; Padgett, *SD*, p. 26; and Geert Ruygers, "De Katholieken en de doorbraak," *Socialisme en Democratie* 6 (1949): 280–84. Ruygers points to the influence of the PvdA's ideological innovations on the SPD's programmatic discussions.

42. See Willem Banning, "Enkele problemen der socialistische theorie," *Socialisme en Democratie* 3 (1946): 257–63; and Bart A.G.M. Tromp, "Drees en het democratisch socialisme," in *Willem Drees*, Hans Daalder and N. Cramer (eds.), (Houten, 1988), p. 32.

43. See the comparison of the 1947 and 1959 programs in, Thomassen, "Hier: PvdA," in *Visie*, Bank (ed.), p. 117; and Lademacher, "Versuche," p. 17.

44. Joop M. den Uyl, "Heroriëtering van het socialisme," *Socialisme en Democratie* 9 (1952): 282. This important article is also reprinted in den Uyl's collection of writings, *Inzicht en uitzicht* (Amsterdam, 1978), pp. 42–52.

45. H.J. Hofstra, "Over de verhouding van utopie, socialistisch ideaal en compromis," *Socialisme en Democratie* 9 (Oct. 1952): 594–99.

46. SPD/PV, 22/23 Feb. 1952.

47. See PvdA, *De weg naar vrijheid*, 2nd ed. (Amsterdam, 1951); and Willem Banning, *Kompas: Toelichting op het beginselenprogramma 1959* (Amsterdam, 1959). See also den Uyl, "Om een zuiver democratisch Bestel," *Socialisme en Democratie* 12 (March, 1955): 176–81; and for a criticism of this trend, Theo J.A.M.van Lier, "Op weg naar de vorzorgingsstaat (1950–1960)," in *Visie*, Bank (ed.), pp. 141–71.

48. SFIO/CD, 31 Aug. 1948; Simmons, *Role*, pp. 60–61; Bleich, *PvdA*, p. 122; and Vos, "Rede," pp. 45–46.

49. Marinus van der Goes van Naters, "Het 'nieuwe bestand' en de grote conflicties (1945–1950)," in *Visie*, Bank (ed.), pp. 131; and Maarten Brinkman, "Drees en de Partij van de Arbeid," in Daalder, *Drees*, p. 72.

50. PvdA/PB, 19 Jan 1956.

51. Marinus van der Goes van Naters, "Duynstee en de werkelijkheid," *Socialisme en Democratie* 24 (1967): 806 and 827ff. Drees' own view of the relationship is reflected in, Duynstee, *Kabinetsformatie*, p. XXXVII [sic].

52. Bank, "Kadt," pp. 318–21.

53. The infamous episode in Nov. 1949, when Schumacher called out in the Bundestag that Adenauer was "the chancellor of the Allies," led to widespread criticism of Schumacher by members of the SPD's parliamentary delegation and even doubt about his ability to lead the party in parliament, but in the end, as Erik Nölting wrote in his diary, "everyone knuckled under once again" (*"aber man kuscht einmal wieder"*). Quoted in, Nölting, *Nölting*, p. 40.

54. Willy Albrecht, "Einleitung," p. 144.

55. Hirsch-Weber and Schütz, *Wähler 1953*, pp. 366ff; and Harry Nowka, *Das Machtverhältnis zwischen Partei und Fraktion in der SPD* (Cologne, 1973), p. 135ff.

56. See the exchange of letters, Erler to Ollenhauer, 14 May 1952, and Franke to Erler, 5 June 1952, Best. Erler, 66 I. See also Köser, "Innovation," pp. 46–47.

57. Manfred Friedrich, "Parlamentarische Opposition in der Bundesrepublik Deutschland: Wandel und Konstanz," in *Parlamentarische Opposition: Ein internationaler Vergleich*, Heinrich Oberreuter (ed.), (Hamburg, 1975), p. 244.

58. Mattei Dogan, "L'Origine sociale du personnel parlementaire français élu en 1951," in *Partis*, Duverger (ed.), (Paris, 1955), p. 322. For a comparison of the GP's sociological profile in 1936 and after the Second World War see Sadoun, *Socialistes*, p. 243.

59. The debate runs like a red thread through the meetings of the SFIO/CD. Highlights include the sessions of 11 April, 20 June, and 4 Sept. 1951, 19 March 1952, and 12 Jan. 1955. See also Williams, *Crisis*, p. 403; Quilliot, *SFIO*, pp. 337–38; and Frédéric Cépède, "Les statuts des tendences dan le Parti Socialiste, 1905–1969," *Cahiers et Revue de L'Ours* 2 (1994): 4.

60. SFIO/CD, 3 Dec. 1951.

61. Ibid., 18 April and 30 Nov. 1955. On Lussy's resignation see his "Communication," 4 Dec. 1951, appendix to SFIO/CD, 5 Dec. 1951; and Lapie, *Blum*, p. 415.

62. SFIO/CD, 4 July 1954–29 June 1955 passim. Jules Moch, *Histoire du réarmement allemand depuis 1950* (Paris, 1965), p. 334 and 334 n. 3; Simmons, *Role*, pp. 175–76; and Depreux, *Souvenirs*, pp. 421–22. For a German Socialist's view of the controversy see Markscheffel to Mayer, 1 Sept. 1954, Best. Markscheffel, 10.

63. Aron is quoted in, Shennan, *Rethinking*, p. 137. See also ibid., pp. 121–24; SFIO/CD, 6 Feb. 1945. The most detailed history of the constitution-making process is in, Gordon Wright, *The Reshaping of French Democracy* (New York, 1948).

64. SFIO/CD, 20 June and 12 Dec. 1945; and Philip, *Réformes*, pp. 2–6, and 13ff. The results of the referendum of 21 Oct. 1945 are in, Jacques Chapsal, *La vie politique en France depuis 1940*, 2nd. ed. (Paris, 1969), p. 605.

65. The results of the referendum are in, Chapsal, *Vie*, p. 606.

66. SFIO/CD, 12 Jan. 1947. See also Frank R. Pfetsch, "Die französische Verfassungspolitik in Deutschland nach 1945," in *Die französische Deutschlandpolitik zwischen 1945 und 1949*, Institut Français de Stuttgart (ed.), (Tübingen, 1987), pp. 115–37.

67. On Menzel see Schmid, *Erinnerungen*, p. 408; and Gerhard Hirscher, *Sozialdemokratische Verfassungspolitik und die Entstehung des Bonner Grundgesetzes* (Bochum, 1989), pp. 236–38.

68. Schumacher, "Politische Richtlinien für die S.P.D. in ihrem Verhältnis zu den anderen politischen Faktoren," 25 Aug. 1945, in Schumacher, *Reden*, pp. 262–63; Michael G.M. Antoni, *Sozialdemokratie und Grundgesetz. Band I: Verfassungspolitische Vorstellungen der SPD von den Anfängen bis zur Konstituierung des Parlamentarischen Rates 1948* (Berlin, 1991), 1:126–32; Foelz-Schroeter, *Politik*, p. 122. Many of Schumacher's constitutional ideas can already be found in his 1924 dissertation, *Kampf*.

69. President of the Senate of Bremen, "Neugliederung Deutschlands," 25 May 1946, Best. Schumacher, 54; Kaisen to Ollenhauer, 17 March 1947, Best. Ollenhauer, 183. See also Katrin Kusch, *Die Wiedergründung der SPD in Rheinland-Pfalz nach dem Zweiten Weltkrieg (1945–1951)* (Mainz, 1989), pp. 104ff; Walter Mühlhausen, "Treuhänder des deutschen Volkes: Die Ministerpräsidenten im Interregnum," in *Treuhänder*, Mühlhausen and Regin (eds.), pp. 17ff.

70. Schmid, *Erinnerungen*, pp. 292–94; Petra Weber, *Carlo Schmid 1896–1979: eine Biographie* (Munich, 1996), p. 360; Hirscher, *Verfassungspolitik*, p. 128.

71. SPD/PV, 24/25 Aug. 1948; and Menzel to Ollenhauer, 17 Sept. 1948, Best. Ollenhauer/23. See also Hans-Jürgen Grabbe, "Die deutsch-alliierte Kontroverse um den Grundgesetzentwurf im Frühjahr 1949," in *Vierteljahrshefte für Zeitgeschichte* 26 (1978): 397.

72. SPD/PV, 19/20 April 1949; and Schumacher to Edith Baade, 27 April 1949, in Schumacher, *Reden*, p. 663. The party chairman's address is reprinted in, ibid., pp. 634–63. See also Albrecht, "Einleitung," pp. 140–46; Erich J.C. Hahn, "The occupying Powers and the Constitutional Reconstruction of West Germany, 1945–1949," in *Cornerstone of Democracy: The West German Grundgesetz, 1949–1989*, Detlef Junker et al. (eds.), (Washington, D.C., 1995), pp. 7–35.

73. J.A.W. Burger, "Interview …," in *Hergroepering der partijen?* G. Puchinger (ed.), (Delft, 1968), p. 18; SFIO/CD, 29 April 1953; and Simmons, *Role*, pp. 16–17 and 281.

74. Dogan, "Clivages," p. 124. A full compendium of French election statistics from 1945 to 1969 is in François Goguel and Alfred Grosser, *La Politique en France* (Paris, 1969), pp. 330–40.

75. The quotation is from Dreyfus, *Gauches*, p. 185. See also Mattei Dogan, "Le vote ouvrier en Europe occidentale," *Revue française de Sociologie* 1 (1960): 35–38.

76. Statistical information on all postwar Bundestag and Landtag elections is in, Gerhard A. Ritter and Merith Niebuss (eds.), *Wahlen in der Bundesrepublik Deutschland, 1946– 1987* (Munich, 1987). For the results of the 1949 Bundestag election see pp. 74–76. For a detailed analysis of the 1949 election see Jürgen Falter, "Alte und neue Parteiorientierungen," in *Wie neu war der Neubeginn? Zum deutschen Kontinuitätsproblem nach 1945*, Everhard Holtmann (ed.), (Erlangen, 1989), pp. 50ff.

77. Albrecht, "Einleitung," p. 148.

78. For the results of the Länder elections see Ritter and Niebuss (eds.), *Wahlen*, pp. 138–48.

79. SPD/PV, 29 July 1953; and Hirsch-Weber, *Wähler 1953*, pp. 18–20 and 396–400. Both Erler and Schmid had urged the party to commission polls. See Erler to Ollenhauer, 27 Nov. 1952, Best. Ollenhauer, 191; and Schmid, *Erinnerungen*, pp. 528–29.

80. SPD/PV/PA/KK/Fraktion/Länderminister, 17 Sept. 1953; SPD/PV, 19/20 Feb. 1954; Schmid, *Erinnerungen*, pp. 544–45; and Nitschmann, "Lehren aus dem Wahlkampf für die Arbeiterpartei," n.d. (ca. Nov., 1953), Best. Ollenhauer, 191. Heine also admitted after the election, "we just didn't believe the published polls" (SPD/PV, 7 Oct. 1953). See also Hirsch-Weber, *Wähler, 1953*, pp. 401–03. The results are in Ritter, *Wahlen*, p. 73.

81. SPD/PV, 20/21 April 1956; SPD/PV, PA, KK, 10/11 March 1956 and 24 Jan. 1957; SPD/PA, 30 March 1957; and Erler to Dieter Sternweiler, 26 Nov. 1955, Best. Erler, 169. See also Joseph Müller, *Die Gesamtdeutsche Volkspartei ... 1950–1957* (Düsseldorf, 1990), pp. 378– 81, and 393–94.

82. The results are in Ritter, *Wahlen*, p. 74. The most detailed analysis of the 1957 campaign is in Kitzinger, *Study 1957*.

83. The results are in Woltjer, *Verleden*, p. 518. The April 1949 issue of *Socialisme en Democratie* was devoted to a series of articles on the success and failure of the *doorbraak*. See also Koos Vorrink, *Verantwoording en opdracht: Vijf jaar Partij van de Arbeid* (Amsterdam, 1951), p. 5; Henk Deugd, *Tussen doorbraak en reklame: de PvdA verkiezingscampagnes van 1956 tot 1967* (Rotterdam, 1988), pp. 123–24. On the decline CPN see de Jonge, *Communisme*, pp. 89–90 and 106–7.

84. PvdA/PB, 28 June 1952. See also Rudy B. Andeweg and Ron Hillebrand, "De kiezers en de PvdA," in *Het zesde jaarboek voor het democratisch socialisme*, Jan Bank et al. (Amsterdam, 1985), pp. 20–21, 24, and 28–31. The results are in Woltjer, *Verleden*, p. 518.

85. PvdA/PB, 21 June 1956. The Kadt and den Uyl quotes are from their articles in the June/July 1956 issue of *Socialisme en Democratie*, which is devoted to a series of analyses of the elections by a number of party leaders. See also den Uyl, "De smalle marge van democratische politiek," *Socialisme en Democratie* 27 (Aug. 1970): 308; and Deugd, *Tussen*.

86. R.B. Andeweg et al. (eds.), *Politiek in Nederland* (Alphen a.d. Rijn, 1981), p. 231;Willem Drees, *Zestig jaar levenservaring* (Amsterdam, 1963), pp. 291–92, 300; and Duynstee, *Kabinet 46–65*, p. 71.

87. Arend Lijphart, *Verzuiling, pacificatie en kentering in de Nederlandse politiek* (Amsterdam, 3rd. ed., 1979), p. 11.

88. PvdA/PB, 31 May 1952; Jac Bosmans, "Drees en Romme," in *Drees*, Daalder (ed.), p. 96; Herman de Liagre Böhl et al., *Nederland industrialiseert! Politieke en ideologische strijd rondom het naoorlogse industrialisatiebeleid, 1945–1955* (Nijmegen 1981), p. 125; Frans van Baardewijk, "De PvdA van het koninkrijk 1945–1947," in *Tweede jaarboek*, Bank et al. (eds.), p. 202; and Couwenberg, *Socialisme*, p. 194.

89. Jac Bosmans, "Beide er in en geen, van beide er uit: De rooms-rode samenwerking 1945–1952," in P.W. Klein, and G.N. v.d. Plaat (eds.), *Herrijzend Nederland in de periode 1945–1950*, P.W. Klein, and G.N. v.d. Plaat (eds.), (The Hague, 1981), p. 46.

90. Willem Schermerhorn, "Na vijf jaren Partij van de Arbeid," *Socialisme en Democratie*, 8 (Jan. 1951), 5; and Bosmans, "Rooms-rode," p. 48.

91. PvdA/PB, 28 July 1951 and 27 May 1955. The quotation is from, Drees, *60*, p. 291. See also J. Bosmans, "Kanttekeningen bij de politieke en parlementaire

ontwikkeling van Nederland," in J.C.H. Blom and G.N. v.d. Plaat (eds.), *Wederopbouw, Welvaart en Onrust: Nederland in de Jaren Vijftig en Zestig*, J.C.H. Blom and G.N. v.d. Plaat (eds.), (Houten, 1986), pp. 37–61.

92. H. Daudt, "De ontwikkeling van de politieke machtsverhoudingen in Nederland sinds 1945," in G.A. Kooy et. al (eds.), *Nederland naar 1945: Beschouwingen over ontwikkeling en beleid* (Deventer, 1980), pp. 178–97. For the historiography of this scholarly controversy see Ferdinand J. ter Heide, *"Ordening en verdeling": Besluitvorming over sociaal-economisch beleid in Nederland 1949–1958* (Kampen, 1986), p. 342.

93. J. Bosmans, "Historische twijfel aan de 'uiterste noodzaak.' De onzin van Daudt," *Acta Politica* 22 (1987): 228.

94. SFIO/CD, 24 Oct. 1945; and Graham, *Tripartisme*, p. 64–65.

95. On the dismissal of the Communist ministers (according to Williams, *Crisis*, p. 24, "the most important date in the history of the Fourth Republic"), see in addition to Williams, esp. Jean-Jacques Becker, "Paul Ramadier et l'année 1947," in Serge Berstein et al. (eds.), *Paul Ramadier: La République et le Socialisme*, Serge Berstein et al. (eds.), (Brussels, 1990), pp. 221– 37.

96. Lapie, *Blum*, p. 272.

97. For an example of rumors of a Gaullist Putsch see Vincent Auriol, *Journal du Septennat* (version intégrale), ed. by Jean-Pierre Azéma (Paris, 1974), 2:523 (13 Nov. 1948).

98. Chapsal, *Vie*, p. 172 (quotation); and Poperen, *Gauche*, 1:41–42 n.1.

99. Auriol, *Journal*, 2:633 n. 85.

100. Ligou, *Socialisme*, p. 567; and Marscheffel, "43. National-Kongress der … SFIO … 11. bis 14.5.1951," p. 2, Best. Markscheffel, 36.

101. The quotations are from, Quilliot, *SFIO*, p. 329; and Loth, *Sozialismus*, p. 254. See also SFIO/CD, 10 March 1948, 12 Sept. 1951, 14 May 1952, and 20 May 1953; Verdier, *PS/PC*, p. 199 and Philip, *Socialistes*, p. 128.

102. Dreyfus, *Gauches*, pp. 137–38.

103. SFIO/CD, 2 Dec. 1953; Lapie, *Blum*, pp. 483ff; and Depreux, *Souvenirs*, pp. 410ff. On Naegelen's colonial mentality see Quilliot, *SFIO*, p. 267.

104. Dreyfus, *Gauches*, p. 161.

105. In a private letter Fritz Erler wrote, "Perhaps a miracle will happen in our country as well, because the installation of Mendès-France is certainly one for France. The man is one of the strongest forces in French politics." See Erler to Walter Schütze, 29 June 1954, Best. Erler, 169. On PMF's charisma see also Poperen, *Gauche*, 1:74–77; Depreux, *Souvenirs*, pp. 400ff; and Mayer, *Gauche*, pp. 381ff.

106. Saul Rose, "The French Election of 1956," *Political Studies*, 4 (1956) pp. 252–53; and Dreyfus, *Gauches*, pp. 135 and 142.

107. SFIO/CD, 23 Feb. and 30 Nov. 1955 (Depreux' quotation). See also Braatoy, "Bericht über Gespräche mit Jules Moch," 23 May [1955], Best. Ollenhauer, 422.

108. Rolf Steininger (ed.), *Die Ruhrfrage 1945/46 und die Entstehung des Landes Nordrhein-Westfalen* (Düsseldorf, 1988), p. 995. For structural analyses of the SPD's oppositional stance see Klaus Günther, *Sozialdemokratie und Demokratie 1946–1966* (Bonn, 1979), pp. 135ff; and Soell, *Erler*, 2:1024–25.

109. See Meyer-Braun, "Wilhelm Kaisen," p. 166. See also Erler to August Zinn, 15 Dec. 1954, Best. Erler, 170; and Wolfrum, *Besatzung*, p. 131.

110. Erler to Roderick Boetner, 20 March 1956, Best. Erler, 171. On the 1956 coalition in Northrhine Westphalia see also Gerhard Brunn, "'Jungtürken' an die Macht: Die sozialliberalen Koalitionen von 1956 und 1966 in Düsseldorf," in *NRW*, Brunn (ed.), p. 123–36.

111. N.a., "Gedächtnisprotokoll der Parteiausschussitzung am 17.9.1950 in Stuttgart," n.d., Best. Markscheffel, 21; and C. Cheysson, "Note [on a dinner with Ollenhauer]," 6 Dec. 1949, Amb. Bonn, XP65/XP3/4 (AOFAA).

112. SPD/PV, 26 Oct. 1953.

113. See Schmid, *Erinnerungen*, pp. 423–24. In the 1950s Erler and the later Christian Democratic chancellor Kurt Georg Kiesinger established a tradition of weekly joint radio appearances to discuss current issues. A selection of some of the transcripts for 1958 is in, Best. Erler/14. On the relationship of Erler and Kiesinger see also Soell, *Erler*, I:352–60; and Kiesinger, *Erinnerungen*, pp. 370–71.

114. To the end of his life Schumacher remained highly dubious about "cooperative arrangements" that involved the SPD and other parties. See his letter to the party's Hanover local, 3 April 1952, in Schumacher, *Reden*, p. 1003.

115. Joop den Uyl, "Theorie en beweging," *Socialisme en Democratie*, 13 (Feb. 1956), 158–59. This essay is also reprinted in the collection *Inzicht*, pp. 53–59.

116. PvdA, PB, 26 June 1952. See also Berg, "Tijdvak," pp. 21–23.

117. SFIO/CD, 22 Feb. 1956.

Chapter 5

1. Hans-Peter Ehni, "Sozialistische Neubauforderung und Proklamation des 'Dritten Weges,'" *Archiv für Sozialgeschichte* 13 (1973): 136; and, Maier, "Eras," p. 327.

2. See Agartz' address in Parteivorstand (ed.), *Protokoll der Verhandlungen des Parteitages der Sozialdemokratischen Partei Deutschlands, 9.-11. Mai 1946* (Hamburg, 1947 [reprint: Glashütten i. Taunus, 1976]), pp. 57–86; and Schumacher's speech to the Lower Saxon Landtag, 28 Aug. 1946, in Schumacher, *Reden* p. 447. See also Koolen, *Agartz*, pp. 49ff.

3. SPD/PV, 26 Sept. 1946. For the history of the SPD's economic policy see Helga Grebing, "Der Sozialismus," in Schildt and Sywottek (eds.), *Modernisierung*, pp. 646–58; Klotzbach, *Weg*, pp. 62–63; and Soell, *Erler*, 1:72ff and 2:974–75.

4. See the detailed discussion in Nemitz, *Marktwirtschaft*, pp. 61–62; Klotzbach, *Weg*, pp. 136ff; and Koolen, *Agartz*, pp. 142–43.

5. The quotes are from, SPD, Landesverband Hamburg, *Leitsätze ... zur Gestaltung einer sozialistischen deutschen Wirtschaftsverfassung* [Hamburg, 1946], p. 3. See also SPD, Bez. Westliches Westfalen, *Die Sozialisierung im Landtag Nordrhein-Westfalen* (Dortmund, 1947), pp. 10ff.

6. Werner Abelshauser, "Marktwirtschaft oder Planung?" in Lademacher and Bosmans (eds.), *Tradition*, p. 114.

7. Prowe, "Socialism," pp. 70–73; and Dieter Gosewinkel, *Adolf Arndt: Die Wiedergründung des Rechtsstaats aus dem Geist der Sozialdemokratie (1945–1961)* (Bonn, 1991), pp. 78ff.

8. SPD/PV, 13/14 March, and 7/8 Aug. 1947; Klotzbach, *Weg*, p. 149; and Plumpe, "Marktwirtschaft," pp. 83–84.

9. In support of the thesis see Wolfgang Abendroth, *Aufstieg und Krise der deutschen Sozialdemokratie* (Frankfurt a.M., 1964), p. 73; Reinhard Blum, *Soziale Marktwirtschaft* (Tübingen, 1969); and Hans-Hermann Hartwich, *Sozialstaatspostulat und gesellschaftlicher Status Quo* (Cologne, 1970). For a more critical assessment of the argument see Dörte Winkler, "Die amerikanische Sozialisierungspolitik in Deutschland, 1945–1948," in *Politische Weichenstellungen im Nachkriegsdeutschland 1945–1953*, Heinrich August Winkler (ed.), (Göttingen, 1979), pp. 88–110.

10. Willy Brandt, "BB" (no. 14, 24 Feb. 1948), in Best. Schumacher,126; Eberhard Schmidt, "Ohne Alternativen? Thesen zum Verhältnis der westdeutschen Gewerkschaften zum Marshall-Plan," in Haberl and Niethammer (eds.), *Marshall-Plan*, p. 216 n. 7; and Ritter, *Sozialstaat*, p. 161.

11. SPD/PV, 9 April 1948, 3 May 1954, and 17/18 Sept. 1956; Veit's address to the 1950 party congress, *Sozialdemokratische Wirtschaftspolitik* (Bonn, 1950); Nölting, *Nölting*, p. 491; and Rudolf A. Pass, "Bankrott der 'sozialen Marktwirtschaft,'" 13 April 1951, in Best. Ollenhauer, 369.

12. Prowe, "Socialism," p. 69.

13. On the party's concern with the tertiary industrial revolution see especially Carlo Schmid's address to the July 1956 party congress, which was published separately under the title *Mensch und Technik* (Bonn, 1956).

14. The text of the Dortmund action program is reprinted in, Miller, *SPD*, pp. 27–28. For comments (mostly favorable) by various party functionaries on the Dortmund document see Best. PV, 04695 (Arch.SD).

15. See SPD/PV, 29 June, and 8 Sept. 1953, and 9 and 10 March 1956. The quote is from, ibid., 18 Sept. 1954. See also SPD/PV, and SPD/PV, *Aktionsprogramm: Änderungsentwurf der Programmkommission* (Bonn, 1954), p. 19; and Heinrich Deist, *Wirtschaft von morgen*, ed. by Gerhard Stümpfig, 2nd. ed. (Bonn, 1973).

16. P.W. Klein, "Wegen naar economisch herstel 1945–1950," in *Herrijzend Nederland in de periode 1945–1950*, P.W. Klein, and G.N. v.d. Plaat, eds (The Hague, 1981), p. 101; and Lehning, "Socialisten," pp. 156–58, and 192–93. For an assessment of the most recent literature on The Netherlands in the 1950s and 1960s see J.C.H. Blom, "'De Jaren Vijftig' en 'De Jaren Zestig'"? *Bijdragen en Mededelingen van de Geschiedenis der Nederlanden*112 (1997): 517–28.

17. See Herman Jan Langeveld, "Die niederländische Gewerkschaftsbewegung und der Marshall-Plan," in *Marshall-Plan*, Haberl and Niethammer (eds.), p. 384; and Vorrink, *Verantwoording 1951*, pp. 6–7.

18. Hein Vos, "De Weg naar Vrijheid," *Socialisme en Democratie*, 9 (Jan. 1952), 9. See also Koos Vorrink, "Radiorede …, 30 Jan 1946," in *Documentatiecentrum Nederlandse Politieke Partijen—Jaarboek 1975*, p. 90; and the collection of articles in, *Socialisme en Democratie*, 9 (Sept. and Oct. 1952).

19. J. Barents, "Een Kernprogram," *Socialisme en Democratie* 8 (Feb. 1951): 89–96.

20. Bank, "Theorie," p. 115.

21. John Jansen van Galen et al. (eds.), *"Het moet, het kan! Op voor het Plan!" Vijftig jaar Plan van de Arbeid* (Amsterdam, 1985), esp. pp. 194ff.

22. Brinkman, "Drees," p. 75; and Drees, *Zestig*, p. 153; and Bank, "Theorie," pp. 111–13.

23. PvdA/PB, 31 Oct. 1953. See also Goes van Naters, *Tijd*, p. 157.

24. PvdA/PB, 27 Jan. and 24 March 1951; Willem Drees, "Polarisatie, een modebegrip dat niets oplost," *Accent* (19 June 1971), p. 12; Tromp, "Drees," pp. 44–45; and de Liagre Böhl et al., *Nederland*, pp. 108–9 and 122.

25. PvdA, *Vrijheid*. Den Uyl's quotation is from, den Uyl, *Inzicht*, pp. 11–12.

26. Joop den Uyl, "De arbeid in de wereld van morgen," in *Inzicht*, pp. 64–74.

27. F. Hartog, "Socialistische conjuntuurpolitiek, " *Socialisme en Democratie* 12 (April/May, 1955): 271–75; and Hein Vos, "De bestedingen-nota," *Socialisme en Democratie*, 14 (March, 1957), 145–53. See also Frans Boumans et al., *De PvdA en haar streven nar de verzorgingsstaat … 1945–1959* ([Amsterdam, 1984]), pp. 10ff; Pels, "Zaken," pp. 48–49 and 71– 72.

28. The quotes are from Dreyfus, *Gauches*, p. 78; and Auriol, *Journal*, 1:554 (18 Nov. 1947). See also Wilfried Loth, "Frankreichs Kommunisten und der Begin

des Kalten Krieges: Die Entlassung der kommunistischen Minister im Mai 1947," *Vierteljahrshefte für Zeitgeschichte* 26 (1978): 27–28.

29. SFIO/CD, 30 April 1947, 18 Feb. and 20 Oct. 1948, and 11 Aug. 1953; Moch, *Blum*, pp. 318–20, and Jules Moch, *Une si longue vie* (Paris, 1976), pp. 250 and 408 (quotation). Auriol described Moch as "un grand homme d'État" for his success in defeating the strikes. See *Journal*, 2:504 (29 Oct. 1948).

30. SFIO/CD, 17 March 1948; Mayer, *Gauche*, pp. 314ff; Moch, *Blum*, pp. 309–10; and Dreyfus, *Gauches*, pp. 22–23 and 62ff.

31. SFIO/CD, 24 Oct. 1945 and 22 May 1946; and [Jules Moch], *Qu'est-ce que les nationalisation?* (Paris, 1945). This pamphlet appeared anonymously under the SFIO's auspices, but Mayer, *Gauche*, p. 259 notes that it was written by Moch.

32. Shennan, *Rethinking*, pp. 256–57.

33. See SFIO, *Trois mois d'action: L'oeuvre des ministres socialistes dans le gouvernement Gouin* (Paris, 1946); and Vincent Auriol, "Le projet de memorandum du Parti socialiste sur l'unité organique," Aug. 1945, in Quilliot, *SFIO*, app. 3, pp. 785ff. See also Dreyfus, *Gauches*, p. 81.

34. SFIO/CD, 4 June 1946, 5 March 1947, and 19 Jan. 1949; André Philip, *Les reformes de structure pour la rénovation de la République* (Algiers, 1944), p. 12; and Kuisel, *Capitalism*, pp. 173ff, 201–02.

35. SFIO/CD, 29 Jan. 1947 and 8 Feb. 1951. See also Graham, *Tripartisme*, pp. 247– 48; and Kuisel, *Capitalism*, pp. 231ff.

36. The quotation is from, Cohen, *Planning*, p. 124. See also SFIO/CD, 9 April 1946; and Quilliot, *SFIO*, pp. 124–25.

37. SFIO/CD, 8 Sept. 1948 and 8 Oct. 1952; Moch, *Vie*, p. 243; and André Philip, "La pensée des partis ouvrièrs," in *Comportements*, Hamon (ed.), p. 201. On Monnet see esp. François Duchene, *Jean Monnet: The First Statesman of Interdependence* (New York, 1994).

38. Auriol, *Journal*, 2:405–06 (31 Aug. 1948).

39. The divisions within the party were reflected in the continuous—and inconclusive—debates within the CD. See for example, SFIO/CD, 10 March 1948, 8 Feb. and 11 April 1951 and 23 April 1952. See also Philip, *Socialistes*, p. 230; Quilliot, *SFIO*, pp. 344– 45, and 370; Dreyfus, *Gauches*, p. 147; Lapie, *Blum*, p. 109–11.

40. SFIO/CD, 6 Jan 1954, 4 Aug. 1954, 28 July 1954 and 27 Oct. 1954. See also Simmons, *Role*, pp. 13–14.

41. SFIO/CD, 8 Nov. 1950. See also G. Bossuat, "Guy Mollet: La puissance française autrement," *Relations internationales* 57 (spring 1989): 42; and the perceptive articles by Albert Gazier, "Frankrijks Economische Structuur," *Socialisme en Democratie* 12 (Dec. 1955): 686–91; and Joop den Uyl, "Theorie en beweging," in ibid. 13 (Feb. 1956): 155–56.

42. See the minutes of a discussion among Dutch party leaders on this topic in, "Enkele problemen van de welvaartstaat," *Socialisme en Democratie* 10 (April 1953): 231–53. The SFIO leader Gazier wanted to have it both ways; he spoke of the "working class" conquests: its purchasing power." See SFIO/CD, 4 Sept. 1957.

43. Broszat et al. (eds.), *Stalingrad*.

44. Hudemann, *Sozialpolitik*, esp. pp. 6–7, 28–29, 547; and Heinrich Küppers, *Staatsaufbau zwischen Bruch und Tradition: Geschichte des Landes Rheinland-Pfalz, 1946– 1955* (Mainz, 1990), p. 153.

45. Kitzinger, *Study 1957*, p. 95; and Friedrich, "Opposition," p. 238.

46. The quotation is from, Joop den Uyl, "Kanttekeningen bij de verkiezingsuitslag," *Socialisme en Democratie* 16 (April, 1959): 207. See also Drees, *Zestig*, pp.

282–83; and J.P. Jansen, "J.G. Suurhoff (1905–1967): Een levensbericht," in *Eerste jaarboek*, Jan Bank et al (eds), pp. 242–81.

47. PvdA/PB, 6 April 1957; and Willem Banning, "Balans van een discussie," *Socialisme en Democratie* 10 (June 1953): 16–25. See also Heide, *Ordening*, p. 340.

48. The quotation is from J.Th.H. van den Berg, "Het miskende tijdvak: De eerste twintig jaar van de Partij van de Arbeid," *Zevende jaarboek*, p. 23. See also Drees, *Zestig*, p. 284–87; and Tromp, "Drees," p. 46.

49. See Quilliot, *SFIO*, pp. 135–37; and Ritter, *Sozialstaat*, 188–90.

50. SFIO/CD, 25 Jan. 1956; Ligou, *Socialisme*, pp. 523–24; Loth, "Durchbruch," p. 74; Moch, *Blum*, pp. 333–34; and Mayer, *Gauche*, p. 306.

51. Liagre-Böhl, *Nederland*, p. 118; and Heinrich Popitz et al., *Das Gesellschaftsbild des Arbeiters: Soziologische Untersuchungen in der Hüttenindustrie* (Tübingen, 1957), pp. 169, 180–81, 226 and 241ff.

52. Kurt Schumacher, "Wir verzweifeln nicht," in Schumacher, *Reden*, p. 223.

53. André Philip was not only a leading member of the French Protestant church, he was also very active in establishing contacts with German Protestants after the war. See Jean Moreau, "Les aspects particuliers de la politique d'occupation française dans les domaines de la jeunesse et de l'éducation populaire," in *La dénazification par les vainqueurs*, Jérôme Vaillant (ed.), (Lille, 1981), pp. 25 and 33.

54. Depreux, *Souvenirs*, p. 357. See also Keizer, *Gijzelaars*; and G. Ruygers, "Christendom en socialisme," *Socialisme en Democratie* 15 (July/Aug. 1958): 463–66.

55. SFIO/CD, 21 May 1957; and Willem Banning, "Het ideologisch problem van het socialisme," *Socialisme en Democratie* 3 (June, 1946): 161–65.

56. In attempting to specify what was allowed and not allowed, the *mandement* was not without some (involuntary) humorous touches: If the VARA (the Socialist broadcasting network) broadcast a Beethoven symphony, Catholics were allowed to listen, but if the broadcast was a talk by a Socialist leader, Catholics were ordered to switch to another program immediately. On the background and content of the *mandement* see Adriaan Manning, "Uit de voorgeschiedenis van het mandement van 1954," *Jaarboek Katholiek Documentatie Centrum 1971* (Nijmegen, 1971), pp. 138–48; and Anneke Visser, *Alleen bij uiterste noodzaak? De rooms-rode samenwerking en het einde van de breide basis 1948–1958* (Amsterdam, 1986), pp. 155ff.

57. PvdA/PB, 25 May, 1, 5, 6, and 8 June, and 31 July 1954; the speeches by various party leaders at the PvdA's special *mandement* congress, reprinted in *Socialisme en Democratie*, 11 (Aug. 1954); Willem Banning, *Ons Socialisme … Een verweer en appèl naar aanleiding van het Mandement 1954 …* (Amsterdam, 1954); and Drees, *Zestig*, p. 303.

58. Theo J.A.M. van Lier, "Op weg naar de vorzorgingsstaat (1950–1960)," in *Visie*, Bank and Temming (eds.), p. 161; and Drees, *Zestig*, p. 304.

59. See Menzel's report "Die Arbeit der sozialdemokratischen Bundestagsfraktion," in SPD, PV (ed.), *Protokoll der Verhandlungen des Parteitages der [SPD]* (Bonn [1956], p. 30. See also Schumacher, "Politische Richtlinien für die SPD," in Schumacher, *Reden*, p. 271; and Schumacher to Stampfer, 18 June 1946, Best. Schumacher, 93.

60. Eichler, "Rolle," p. 171; Schmid, *Erinnerungen*, p. 262; Soell, *Erler*, 1:124–25 and 278ff; and Lemke-Müller, *Sozialismus*, p. 233.

61. SPD/PV, 7/8 Aug. 1947, 6 Jan. and 29 June 1953; SPD/PV/PA/KK/Fraktion/Min.Prä, 6 Sept. 1949; and Eichler to Brauer, 21 Nov. 1952, Best. Brauer, Schriften v. 52–58. The best short analysis of the SPD's evolving relationship to the churches is, Kurt Klotzbach, "SPD und Katholische Kirche nach 1945: Belastungen,

Mißverständnisse und Neuanfänge," in *Archiv für Sozialgeschichte*, 29 (1989), XXXVI-XLVII [sic].

62. PvdA/PB, 28 Nov. 1953; Arndt to von Knoeringen, 29 Aug. 1958 and Albertz to Schumacher, 26 Jan. 1951, Best. Ollenhauer, 368 and 189 resp.

63. SFIO/CD, 13 March 1945 and 18 July 1951. See also Jean-Claude Criqui, "Der französische Sozialismus," in *Katholizismus und freiheitlicher Sozialismus in Europa* Albrecht Langner (ed.), (Cologne, 1965), p. 124.

64. SFIO/CD, 21 April 1948 (quotation); and Dogan, "Origine," pp. 306–7.

65. Lapie, *Blum*, pp. 379–80; and D.S. Bell and Byron Criddle, *The French Socialist Party: The Emergence of a Party of Government*, 2nd ed. (New York, 1988), p. 17–20.

66. This is a recurrent concern in the CD deliberations. See SFIO/CD, 28 Jan., 26 June, 11 July, and 10 Aug. 1951, and 11 May 1955. See also Dogan, "Clivages," p. 103; and Lefebvre, *Mollet*, pp. 137ff.

67. Lapie, *Blum*, pp. 300ff and 397ff.

68. SFIO/CD, 27 June and 12 Sept. 1951; and Depreux, *Souvenirs*, pp. 201 and 357. See also the joint communiqué of the CD and GP in *Populaire*, 9 Jan. 1952.

69. Frans van Baardewijk, "De PvdA van het koninkrijk 1945–1947," in Bank, *Tweede Jaarboek*, pp. 165ff; and Shennan, *Rethinking*, pp. 141, and 159–61.

70. A. Stempels, *De parlementaire geschiedenis van het Indonesische vraagstuk* (Amsterdam, 1950), p. 37 (quotation); and Drees, *60*, pp. 218–19. The most detailed account of the history of Dutch decolonization is still C. Smit, *De liquidatie van een Imperium: Nederland en Indonesië* (Amsterdam, 1962).

71. PvdA/PB, 19 July 1947; Drees, *Zestig*, pp. 276ff; Baardewijk, "PvdA," pp. 172– 73; and Jan Bank, "Drees en de Indonesische revolutie," in Drees, Daalder and Cramer (eds.), p. 134.

72. PvdA/PB, 28 July 1947; Drees, *Zestig*, pp. 220–21 and 229. See also Smit, *Liquidatie*, pp. 46ff, 84, 90, 117–18, and 150.

73. PvdA/PB, 28 Nov. 1948 and 31 Dec. 1949; and Drees, *Zestig*, pp. 222, 234, and 278.

74. PvdA/PB, 29 April and 14 Aug 1947, and 28 Feb. 1948; and the proceedings of the party's special congress on Indonesia, PvdA, *Verslag van het Congres-Indonesië ... 7. Sept. 1946* (Amsterdam [1946]).

75. PvdA/PB, 30 Dec. 1950, 6 and 15 Jan. 1951, 6 Feb. 1957, and 2 Jan. 1958; Marinus van der Goes van Naters, "Het 'nieuwe bestand' en de grote conflicties (1945–1950)," in Bank (ed.), *Visie*, pp. 127–29, and *Tijd*, pp. 146ff; Hein Vos, "Congresrede," *Socialisme en Democratie*, 8 (March, 1951), 147; and Drees, *Zestig*, p. 265.

76. SFIO/CD, 18 Dec. 1945; and Auriol, *Journal*, 1:658 (31 Dec. 1947). See also Quilliot, *SFIO*, pp. 145, 154–56, 460 (quotation). France was the only country which gave diplomatic support to the Dutch police actions in Indonesia. See Auriol, *Journal*, 2:706 n. 82. The most complete account of the Indochina conflict is Lucien Bodard, *La Guerre d'Indochine*, 4 vols. (Paris, 1972–73). The best recent treatment of the Indochina conflict is Martin Shipway, *The Road to War: France and Vietnam, 1944–1947* (Providence, RI, 1996).

77. SFIO/CD, 3 Dec. 1946, 27 Sept. and 11 Oct. 1950; Auriol, *Journal*, 3:303–04 (20 July 1949); and Elgey, *République*, 1:171 (quotation) and 254.

78. SFIO/CD, 11 Oct. and 8 Nov. 1950, 11 Jan. 1951, 7 Jan. 1952, and 10 March 1954; Auriol, *Journal*, 1:533 (8 Nov. 1947); Depreux, *Souvenirs*, pp. 3224 and 394; Lapie, *Blum*, pp. 521–22.

79. On the relationship of Dutch society and the military in the 1950s see J.C.H. Blom, "Maatschappij en krijgsmacht in de jaren vijftig," in, *Burgerlijk en Beheerst*, Blom (Amsterdam, 1996), pp. 209–22.

80. Frank Willis, *France, Germany, and the New Europe, 1945–1967* 2nd ed. (Stanford, CA,1968), pp. 68–69 and 85; and Ligou, *Histoire*, p. 535.

81. Gouin complained (SFIO/CD, 3 Dec. 1946) that 85 percent of the regimental officers stationed around Paris were *"inféodés à de Gaulle."*

82. Complaints about the military and its independent actions were a constant theme of the CD meetings. See SFIO/CD, 13 Nov. 1944, 21 May and 1 Oct. 1947, 3 and 10 March 1948, and 3 Jan. 1951. See also Auriol, *Journal*, 3:585 n. 59 (23 June 1949); Lapie, *Blum*, p. 415; and Graham, *Tripartisme*, p. 129.

83. Dieter Groh and Peter Brandt, *"Vaterlandslose Gesellen": Sozialdemokratie und Nation, 1860–1990* (Munich, 1992), pp. 23 and 120.

84. N.a., "Gedächtnis-Protokoll der Parteiausschussitzung am 17.9.1950 in Stuttgart," n.d., Best. Markscheffel, 21. See also Buczylowski, *Frage*, pp. 168ff; and Löwke, *Wehrfrage,*.

85. Erler to Ollenhauer, 8 Dec. 1953, Best. Erler, 66 I. See also Buczylowski, *Frage*, p. 55; and Stefan Appelius, *Pazifismus in Westdeutschland: Die Deutsche Friedensgesellschaft, 1945–1968* (Aix la Chapelle, 1991), p. 1:256ff, 285–86.

86. SPD/PV, 22 and 23 Feb. 1952 and 21 Jan. 1955.

87. See Erler, "Aktenvermerk," 17 July 1952, Best. Ollenhauer, 426; and the meeting of the SPD/PV/Sicherheitsausschuss, 8 May 1954 and 11 April 1956, Best. Ollenhauer, 392 and 393. See also Brandt, *Erinnerungen*, p. 30; and Soell, *Erler*, 2:209–10.

88. See SPD/PV/Sicherheitsausschuss, 24 March 1956, Best. Ollenhauer, 393; and Erler to Julius Deutsch, 20 July 1956, Best. Erler, 171.

89. See the special edition of *Socialisme en Democratie*, 13 (Feb. 1956), "Tien jaar Partij van de Arbeid."

90. SFIO/CD, 11 May 1951. See also Ligou, *Histoire*, p. 601.

Chapter 6

1. Klaus Hänsch, *Frankreich zwischen Ost und West: Die Reaktion auf den Ausbruch des Ost-Westkonfliktes, 1946–48* (Berlin, 1972), pp. 65–66.

2. Adriaan Manning, "Die Niederlande und Europa von 1945 bis zum Beginn der fünfziger Jahre," *Vierteljahrshefte für Zeitgeschichte* 29 (1981): 6; Serge Berstein, "French Power as Seen by the Political Parties after World War II," in *Power in Europe? Great Britain, France, Italy, and Germany in a Postwar World, 1945–1950*, Josef Becker and Franz Knipping, eds (Berlin, 1986), p. 176; Auriol, *Journal*, 1:631 (18 Dec. 1947); and Lipgens, *Integration*, 215–16.

3. M. van der Goes van Naters, "De Nieuwe Partij en het federatief Europa," *Socialisme en Democratie* 13 (Feb. 1956): 103–8; Schumacher's speech in the Bundestag 9 March 1951, in Schumacher, *Reden*, pp. 934–35; Schmid, *Erinnerungen*, p. 462; Loth, *Sozialismus*, p. 18; and Buczylowski, *Frage*, pp. 37–38.

4. SFIO/CD, 23 Nov. 1948; Depreux, *Souvenirs*, p. 531; and Drees, *Zestig*, p. 177.

5. SFIO/CD, 24 March 1948; Rolf Steininger, "Der Wiederaufbau der Sozialistischen Internationale," in *Der Marshall-Plan und die europäische Linke*, Haberl and Niethammer (eds.), pp. 488ff.

6. N.a., "Die deutsche Frage auf der Konferenz in Clacton," n.d. [1946], in Best. Markscheffel, 7; and SFIO/CD, 12 Jan. 1947. On the Frankfurt congress see esp. the documentation in Best. Erler, 108.

7. See the documentation in, Best. SPD/PV, 2866 and 2867; Boutbien to Markscheffel, n.d. (ca. May, 1947) in Best. Markscheffel, 373; SFIO/CD, 30 April

1948; and Brauer's contribution to an MSEUE brochure, 25 July 1952, and "Résolution du Comité executif international du M.S.E.U.E. ...," 17/18 May 1952, Best. Brauer, Div. Korr., 1949–1967. For the founding of the MSEUE see Loth, *Sozialismus*, pp. 225ff; and for criticism of the organization see Ollenhauer to Brauer, 26 March 1952 in Best. Ollenhauer, 191; and PvdA/PB, 26 May 1954.

8. Wilfried Loth, *Der Weg nach Europa: Geschichte der Europäischen Integration, 1939–1957*, 2nd. ed. (Göttingen, 1991), pp. 55–58.

9. SFIO/CD, 17 March 1948; SPD/PV/PA, 22 and 23 Jan. 1949; and [Markscheffel], "Über die Absichten Léon Blums," n.d. [ca. Feb. 1947], Best. Markscheffel, 37a. See also Hrbek, *SPD-Europa*, pp. 86ff; and Loth, *Sozialismus*, pp. 208–9.

10. See the documentation in Best. Ollenhauer, 438–40. On Monnet's committee see Duchene, *Monnet*, pp. 284ff.

11. On the Socialists and the EDC see below, pp. 167ff.

12. SFIO/CD, 3 Jan. 1951; PvdA/PB, 22 Feb. 1947 and 31 Oct. 1953; SPD/PV, 30 March 1951, 23 Sept. 1952 and 7 Oct. 1953; Ollenhauer to Vorrink, 5 April 1946, Best. Schumacher, 93; and Friso Wielenga, "Buitenlandse politiek als splijtzwam: PvdA en SPD in de vroege jaren '50," *Socialisme en Democratie* 44 (1987): 193–94.

13. Tarbé de Saint-Hardouin to Bidault, 17 July 1947 and François-Poncet to MAÉ, 23 Nov. 1949, Amb. Bonn, XP/65/XP3/4 (AOFAA). The Schumacher quote is from Loth, *Sozialismus*, p. 334 n. 46.

14. SFIO/CD, 20 Feb. 1945, 5 March 1946, and 6 Oct. 1948. On the French Socialists' lecture tours see Loth, *Sozialismus*, p. 332 n. 27; and Raymond Poidevin, "Die Neuorientierung der französischen Deutschlandpolitik 1948/49," in *Kalter Krieg und deutsche Frage. Deutschland im Widerstreit der Mächte 1945–52*, Josef Foschepoth (ed.), (Göttingen, 1985), p. 137; and on the function of the SPD's Paris office, Markscheffel, "Die Vertretung der S.P.D. in Frankreich," 27 May 1946, Best. Schumacher, 30.

15. The quotations are from Alfred Grosser, *L'Allemagne de notre temps, 1945–1978* (Paris, 1978), p. 285; and Schumacher to Brill, 4 Sept. 1951, in Schumacher, *Reden*, p. 819. See also SFIO/CD, 12 Jan. 1947; Klaus-Jürgen Müller, "Die SPD Kurt Schumachers und Frankreich," in *Paris-Bonn: Eine dauerhafte Bindung schwieriger Partner*, Klaus Manfrass (ed.), (Sigmaringen, 1984), pp. 192–94; and Hrbek, *SPD-Europa*, p. 349.

16. John Gimbel, *The American Occupation of Germany, Politics and the Military, 1945–1949* (Stanford, 1968); Wolfgang Krieger, *General Lucius D. Clay und die amerikanische Deutschlandpolitik 1945–1949* (Stuttgart, 1987); and Martina Kessel, *Westeuropa und die deutsche Teilung: Englische und französische Deutschlandpolitik auf den Außenministerkonferenzen von 1945 bis 1947* (Munich, 1989), esp. pp. 211ff.

17. Markscheffel to Ollenhauer and Heine, 10 Aug. 1946, Best. Schumacher, 30. The François-Poncet quotation is from Küppers, *Staatsaufbau*, p. 212. See also Willis, *France*, pp. 38–39; Alain Lattard, "Zentralismus und Dezentralisierung in der französischen Deutschland- und Besatzungspolitik 1945–1947," in Becker (ed.), *Die Kapitulation*, Klaus Manfrass (ed.), pp. 181–209; and Wolfrum, *Besatzung*.

18. The quotation is from, Kessel, *Westeuropa*, p. 214. On the Gaullist German policy see also Pierre Maillard, *De Gaulle et L'Allemagne: Le rêve inachevé* (Paris, 1990), pp. 83ff and 112; Rainer Hudemann, "De Gaulle und der Wiederaufbau in der französischen Besatzungszone nach 1945," in *De Gaulle, Deutschland und Europa*, Wilfried Loth and Robert Picht (eds.), (Opladen, 1991), pp. 153–67; and Reinhard Schreiner, *Bidault, der MRP und die französische Deutschlandpolitik, 1944–1948* (Frankfurt a.M., 1985).

19. Hänsch, *Frankreich*, pp. 30, 39, and 237.

20. SFIO/CD, 9 April 1946, 12 Jan. and 30 July 1947, and 22 Sept. 1949 (quotation); Auriol, *Journal*, I:362 (entry for 22 July 1947) and subsequent.; and Wilfried Loth, "Die Franzosen und die deutsche Frage 1945–1949," in *Die Deutschlandpolitik Frankreichs und die französische Zone 1945 bis 1949*, Claus Scharf and Hans-Jürgen Schröder (eds.), (Wiesbaden, 1983), p. 36 n. 26.

21. SFIO/CD, 1 Dec. 1945 (Rosenfeld) and 14 May 1947 (Philip). See also Erling Bjøl, *La France devant l'Europe: La politique européenne de la IVe République* (Copenhagen, 1966), pp. 151–53.

22. SFIO/CD, 19 Feb. 1947. See also Raymond Poidevin, "Frankreich und die deutsche Frage, 1943–1949," in *Die deutsche Frage im 19. und 20. Jahrhundert*,Josef Becker and Andreas Hillgruber (eds.), (Munich, 1983), p. 415.

23. SFIO/CD, 1 Dec. 1945, 1 Oct. 1947, and 4 Aug. 1948. See also Alain Lattard, "Zielkonflikte französischer Besatzungspolitik in Deutschland: Der Streit Laffon-Koenig 1945–1947," *Vierteljahrshefte für Zeitgeschichte* 39 (1991): 1–35.

24. Friso Wielenga, *West-Duitsland: partner uit noodzaak* (Utrecht, 1989), pp. 391ff; and H.A. Schaper, "'Wij willen zelfs niet Mönchen-Gladbach': De annexatiekwestie 1945–1949," *Internationale Spectator* 29 (May, 1985): 261–72.

25. See Markscheffel to Ollenhauer, 15 Sept. 1946, and to SPD/PV, 8 Oct. 1946, Best. Markscheffel, 7; SPD/PV, 4 June 1946. On Blum's proposals after the First World War see Richard Gombin, *Les socialistes et la guerre: La SFIO et la politique étrangère française entre les deux guerres mondiales* (Paris, 1970), pp. 234–35.

26. See Schumacher's addresses to the Bundestag, 21 Sept. and 15 Nov. 1949, in Schumacher, *Reden*, pp. 712 and 729–30; and Erler to Werner Raberger, 12 Nov. 1954, Best. Erler, 169. For an analysis of Schumacher's position see especially, Wolfgang Benz, "Kurt Schumacher als deutscher und europäischer Sozialist," in *Schumacher*, Albrecht (ed.), pp. 32–33.

27. See SFIO/CD, 25 March 1953. See also SFIO/CD, 26 Jan. 1949 and 21 Nov. 1951; and Bjarne Braatoy, ["Gespräch mit Oreste Rosenfeld und Georges Brutelle"], n.d. [23–26 March 1953], Best. Ollenhauer, 422. See also the comment of Winfried Becker in, *Die Saar 1945–1955: Ein Problem der europäischen Geschichte*, Rainer Hudemann and Raymond Poidevin (eds.), (Munich, 1992), pp. 321–23.

28. Heine to Erler, 25 Jan. 1952, Best. Erler, 66I.

29. See the report on Goes' visit to Saarbrücken, 18 Nov. 1953, Best. Ollenhauer, 454.

30. See Mommer to Ollenhauer, 6 Oct. 1954, Best. Ollenhauer/454 and the rest of the documentation in this folder. See also Heinrich Schneider, *Das Wunder an der Saar* (Stuttgart, 1974), p. 223.

31. See Grandval's letter to Mendès-France, 15 Oct. 1955, quoted in Judith Hüser, "Frankreich und die Abstimmung vom 23. Oktober 1955," in *Saar*, Hudemann and Poidevin (eds.), p. 376 n. 62.

32. SFIO/CD, 12 Jan. and 19 Feb. 1947, 15 May 1947, 24 June 1947, 4 Aug. 1948, 2 Feb. 1949, and 6 April 1949. See also Willis, *France*, p. 58; and for a more negative view, Hänsch, *Frankreich*, p. 88.

33. On the Allies' economic policies in general see Werner Abelshauser, "Westeuropa vor dem Marshall-Plan," in *Marshall-Plan*, Haberl and Niethammer (eds.), p. 117; and on the specifics of the French variant, Willis, *France*, pp. 125–27 and 145–46; Lattard, *Gewerkschaften*, p. 2; and Wolfrum, *Besatzung*, pp. 244ff. Laffon's views are analyzed in Lattard, "Zielkonflikte."

34. SFIO/CD, 2 Feb. 1949. In fact, in 1947 and 1948 there were a number of protest actions in the French zone. See Willis, *France*, pp. 219–23.

35. Markscheffel, "Über die Absichten Blums," n.d. [ca. Feb. 1947], Best. Markscheffel, 37a; and SFIO/CD, 23 Feb. 1949. See also Poidevin, "Ruhrfrage," p. 319; and Loth, *Sozialismus*, pp. 236–37. Jules Moch, one of the SFIO's skeptics about the future of democracy in Germany, later wrote that Blum had, *"comme toujours,"* been right. Moch, *Blum*, pp. 331–32.

36. SFIO/CD, 17 and 24 March 1948; SFIO, Commission Internationale et Commission des Affaires Économiques, "Travail préparatoire pour determiner la position de la delegation française à … l'aide américaine" [hereafter: "Marshall-Plan 3/48"], 17 March 1948, Best. Ollenhauer, 451; Mollet, *Bilan*, pp. 14, 18–19; and Auriol, *Journal*, 1:138, and 2:521 (entries for 13 March 1947 and 11 Nov. 1948). See also Wilfried Loth, "Die französischen Sozialisten und der Marshall-Plan," in *Marshall-Plan*, Haberl and Niethammer (eds.), pp. 377–78 n. 19.

37. SFIO/CD, 30 March 1949, 6 April 1949, and 26 April 1950. See also Loth, *Sozialismus*, pp. 230–31.

38. See Schmid, *Erinnerungen*, p. 433; Klaus von Schubert, *Wiederbewaffnung und Westintegration: Die innere militärische und außenpolitische Orientierung der Bundesrepublik, 1950–1952* (Stuttgart, 1970), p. 179; and Buczylowski, *Frage*, pp. 149–50.

39. François-Poncet to Mendès-France, 10 Sept. 1954, Amb. Bonn, XP/91, XP/3/4 (AOFAA).

40. Grabbe, *Unionsparteien*, pp. 51–54, 60–61; and Buczylowski, *Frage*, pp. 88–89, and 137–40.

41. SPD/PV, 28 and 29 May 1948; and Hans-Peter Ehni, "Die Reaktion der SPD auf den Marshall-Plan," in *Marshall-Plan*, Haberl and Niethammer (eds.), pp. 219ff. For a critical view of the SPD's position see Erich Ott, *Die Wirtschaftskonzeption der SPD nach 1945* (Marburg, 1978), pp. 169ff.

42. See the text of Schumacher's Bundestag speech, 15 May 1952, in Schumacher, *Reden*, p. 902.

43. On Schumacher's last illness see Merseburger, *Schumacher*, pp. 507–8.

44. SPD/PV, 18 and 19 Feb. 1954; [Willy] Br[andt], "Die Ausgestaltung der aussenpolitischen Haltung der SPD," 16 Nov. 1954, Best. Ollenhauer, 422; and the documentation in this folder. See also Klaus Peter Schulz, "Resolutionen und Realitäten," *Deutsche Rundschau*80 (1954): 915–21.

45. Vorrink, *Verantwoording*, pp. 13–14; and Maurice Allais, "Atlantische Unie: De Enige Oplossing," *Socialisme en Democratie* 9 (July–Aug. 1950): 442–46. See also D.F.J. Bosscher, "De Partei van de Arbeid en het buitenlands beleid (1945–1973)," *Bijdragen en Mededelingen betreffende de Geschiedenis der Nederlanden* 101 (1986): 41–43. For the German Socialists' criticism of the PvdA see Albertz to Schumacher, 26 Jan. 1951, Best. Ollenhauer, 189.

46. Shennan, *Rethinking*, p. 50; and Loth, "Marshall-Plan," in *Marshall-Plan*, Haberl and Niethammer (eds.), pp. 372–73, 380 n. 55.

47. Hänsch, *Frankreich*, p. 139. SFIO/CD, 6 Oct. 1948; Auriol, *Journal*, 2:132 (entry for 7 March 1948. See also Jean-Baptiste Duroselle, "Changes in French Foreign Policy since 1945," in *Search*, Hoffmann et al. (eds.), p. 338; and Renata Fritsch-Bournazel, "Mourir pour Berlin? Die Wandlungen der französischen Ost- und Deutschlandpolitik während der Blockade 1948/49," *Vierteljahrshefte für Zeitgeschichte* 35 (April 1987): 175.

48. SFIO/CD, 5 March 1948, and 26 April 1950; Loth, *Sozialismus*, pp. 322 n. 19, and 355 n. 18; and Quilliot, *SFIO*, pp. 432–33.

49. SPD/PV, 14 Nov. 1947; Carlo Schmid, "Das deutsch-französische Verhältnis und der Dritte Weg," *Die Wandlung*, 2 (1947), 795ff; and Albrecht, "Einleitung," p. 138.

50. Rolf Steininger has in *Eine vertane Chance zur Wiedervereinigung? Die Stalin-Note vom 10.3.52* (Bonn, 1985) and a number of other publications maintained that Stalin's offer represented a genuine chance to unify Germany along the lines of the later "Austrian model," and that Adenauer and the Americans sabotaged this chance. For an effective rebuttal of this thesis see Hermann Graml, "Die Legende von der verpassten Gelegenheit: Zur sowjetischen Notenkampagne des Jahres 1952" *Vierteljahrshefte für Zeitgeschichte* 29 (1981): 307–41.

51. The quotation is from Graml, "Legende," p. 335. See also Manfred Kittel, "Genesis einer Legende: Die Diskussion um die Stalin-Noten in der Bundesrepublik 1952–1958," *Vierteljahrshefte für Zeitgeschichte* 41 (1993): 357; and Schubert, *Wiederbewaffnung*, pp. 169–70, and 186.

52. SPD/PV, 29 June 1953; and SPD/PV/PA/PK, 16 Oct. 1955.

53. Hartmut Soell, "Die deutschlandpolitischen Konzeptionen der SPD-Opposition 1949–1961," in *Deutschlandpolitik der Nachkriegsjahre*, Erich Kosthorst et al. (eds.), (Paderborn, 1976), pp. 32, and 49ff. The quotation is on p. 57.

54. For the arguments of the Third Way proponents see W.H. Nagel, "De Derde Weg," *Socialisme en Democratie* 9 (June, 1952): 345–49; and for the party's official condemnation, PvdA/PB, 16 Jan. 1952; and J. de Kadt, "De nieuwe Situatie," *Socialisme en Democratie* 7 (Feb. 1950): 96.

55. Hess and Wielenga, "Niederlande," p. 363ff. The PvdA also invited Schmid to report on his 1955 journey to Moscow. See PvdA/PB, 30 Sept. 1955.

56. The quotation is from Loth, *Weg*, p. 79. See also SFIO/CD, 19 Jan. 1949; Geoffrey Warner, "Die britische Labour-Regierung und die Einheit Westeuropas," *Vierteljahrshefte für Zeitgeschichte*, 28 (1980), 312ff; and René Massigli, *Une comédie des erreurs, 1943–1956: Souvenirs et reflexions sur une étape de la construction europénne* (Paris, 1978), pp. 171ff, 224, 309, and 339.

57. SFIO/CD, 13 Sept. and 13 Dec. 1950. See also Loth, *Sozialismus*, p. 214.

58. Philip, *Socialistes*, p. 220; and Mollet, *Bilan*, pp. 25–26; and Jean-Paul Cahn, "Le SPD et la Communauté Européenne de Défense (CED): Quelques aspects du problème," *Revue Allemagne* 19 (Oct.-Dec. 1987): 385.

59. See Philip's statement, 26 May 1952, Best. Brauer/Div.Korr. 1949–67; SFIO/CD, 10 March and 1 Dec. 1948; Quilliot, *SFIO*, pp. 308–10.

60. See SFIO/CD, 29 Sept. 1948 and 13 Sept. 1950; Richard T. Griffiths, "European Utopia or Capitalist Trap?" in *Socialist Parties and the Question of Europe in the 1950s*, Richard T. Griffiths (ed.), (Leiden, 1993), pp. 9–24; and Loth, *Sozialismus*, pp. 162–63.

61. This was Ernst Reuter. See T. Cohen, *Socialisten in Europa: De samenwerking van de socialistische partijen in het kader van de Europese Gemeenschap, 1952–1972* (Amsterdam, 1974), pp. 59–60 n. 12.

62. [Laloy], "Entretien entre le Dr. Schumacher et M. Laloy," 16 Feb. 1948, AOFAA/Bonn Amb., XP65/XP3/4; and SPD/PV, 17 Feb. 1948.

63. The quotation is from, Brandt, *Erinnerungen*, p. 26. See also SPD/PV, 9 April 1948 and 20/21 Jan. 1951; SFIO/CD, 7 May 1952; M. van der Goes van Naters, "Internationaal Socialisme," *Socialisme en Democratie*, 9 (May, 1952), 283–87; and A. Mozer-Ebbinge and R. Cohen (eds.), *Alfred Mozer: 'Gastarbeider' in Europa* (Zutphen, 1980), p. 39.

64. SPD/PV/Parteiausschuss, 22 and 23 Jan. 1949. Schumacher used the alliteration on this and many other occasions. See also Hrbek, *Europa*, pp. 86ff.

65. SPD/PV, 19 April 1950; and Heine, *Schumacher*, pp. 101–02.

66. SPD/PV, 24 June 1950; Erler to Brill, 7 March 1957, Best. Erler, 171 and the documentation in Best. Erler, 118.

67. Marinus van der Goes van Naters, "Een constitutie voor Europa?" *Socialisme en Democratie* 10 (Feb. 1953): 68–69. See also the special issue of *Socialisme en Democratie* 11 (Sept. 1954): 497ff.

68. See PvdA/PB, 1 Aug. 1947; and H. Vredeling, "Naar een Progressieve Europese Partij," *Socialisme en Democratie* 27 (1970): 144–51. See also Daalder and Cramer (eds.), *Drees*, p. 141; and Daalder, "Zestig," pp. 217–18.

69. The most detailed treatments of West German rearmament are, Lutz Köllner et al. (eds.), *Anfänge westdeutscher Sicherheitspolitik*, 3 vols. (Munich, 1982–1993); Schubert, *Wiederbewaffnung*; and David Clay Large, *Germans to the Front: West German Rearmament in the Adenauer Era* (Chapel Hill, ND, 1995).

70. PvdA/PB, 10 May 1950. See also Kersten, " Niederlande," p. 131.

71. SFIO/CD, 29 Sept. 4 Oct., and 6 Dec. 1950, and 12 Dec. 1951. See also the CD's resolution in ibid., 26 April 1950.

72. See Loth, *Sozialismus*, p. 282; and Takeshi Nakai, *Die deutsche Sozialdemokratie zwischen Nationalsozialismus und Internationalismus, 1945–1952* (Bonn, 1975), pp. 155, and 166. On the details of the negotiations see Massigli, *Comédie*, pp. 239ff.

73. SPD/PV, 18 Sept. 1954; and "Resolution de la Conférence européenne d'IS," 28 Feb. 1954, in Best. Erler, 108 (Arch.d.SD). See also Raymond Aron, "Esquisse historique d'une grande querelle idéologique," in *La querelle de la CED: Essai d'analyse sociologique*, Aron and Daniel Lerner (eds.), (Paris, 1968), p. 9.

74. SPD/PV, 7 and 8 Sept. 1951, and 29 July 1953; Schumacher, "Für ein starkes Europa—gegen nationalistischen Missbrauch der Macht," 22 Sept. 1951 in Best. Ollenhauer, 420.

75. See Schumacher's address to the SPD's Soziale Arbeitsgemeinschaft, 24 May 1951; and Schubert, *Wiederbewaffnung*, p. 119.

76. Quilliot, *SFIO*, pp. 512–13. See also Soell, *Erler*, 1:441; and Mozer, *Mozer*, p. 40.

77. See SPD/PV, 10 and 11 Dec. 1954, 25/26 March and 3 May 1955; the documentation in, Best. Schmid, 1403, and Best. Ollenhauer, 423; André François-Poncet to Ministère des Affaires Étrangères, 4 March 1955, Bonn Ambassade, XP 92/XP 3/4 (AOFAA); and Erler to Erich Bacher, 20 July 1956, in Best Erler, 171.

78. The quotation is from J.G. Bomhoff, "Over de EDG (een tegenstem)," *Socialisme en Democratie* 11 (March, 1954): 146. Drees' objections are cited in, Drees, *Zestig*, p. 316; and Griffiths, *Parties*, p. 136. See also PvdA/PB, 29 Dec. 1953; and A.E. Kersten, "Niederländische Regierung, Bewaffnung Westdeutschlands und EVG," in *Die Europäische Verteidigungsgemeinschaft: Stand und Probleme der Forschung*, H.E. Volkmann and W. Schwengler (eds.), (Boppard a.Rh., 1985), pp. 191–219.

79. On the French debate on the EDC, see esp. Aron and Lerner (eds.), *Querelle*; Jean-Pierre Rioux, "Französische öffentliche Meinung und EVG," in Volkmann, *EWG*, p. 163.

80. SFIO/CD, 12 Dec. 1951, 19 Feb. and 19 March 1952, and 20 Jan. 1954. The CD's vote took place on 2 Feb. 1952. See also Moch, *Réarmament*, pp. 239–44.

81. SFIO/CD, 7 Nov. 1951, 19 March 1952, 21 and 28 Jan., and 23 Sept. 1953. See also Massigli, *Comédie*, pp. 401–02, and 444–45; Hervé Alphand, *L'étonnement d'être: Journal 1939–1973* (Paris, 1977), pp. 243, and 255 (21 Jan. and 28 Oct. 1954); and Lapie, *Blum*, pp. 476, and 479.

82. SFIO/CD, 7 Nov. 1951, 4 March, 8 July, 29 Sept., and 28 Oct. 1953, 3 March and 16 June 1954; Bjarne Braatoy, ["Gespräch mit Oreste Rosenfeld und Georges Brutelle"] [23–26 March 1953], Best. Ollenhauer, 422; Markscheffel to Mayer, n.d. [July, 1954], and Mayer to Markscheffel, 23 Aug. 1954, Best. Markscheffel, 10;

Depreux, *Souvenirs*, p. 399; and Daniel Mayer, *Contre le rearmament allemand* (Paris, 1950).

83. François-Poncet to Pinay, 4 March 1955, Amb.Bonn, XP92/XP3/4 (AOFAA); SFIO/CD, 6 Oct. 1954; SPD/PV, 10/11 Dec. 1954; Bjarne Braatoy, "Bericht über ein Gespräch mit Jules Moch ...," 23 May [1955], Best. Ollenhauer, 422; Erler to Erich Bacher, 20 July 1956, Best. Erler/171; and Moch, *Réarmament*, pp. 343–44. In his memoirs Moch added, rather lamely, that he was in New York at the time of the vote, and "my political friends made me vote" for the Paris Accords. See Moch, *Vie*, p. 481.

84. See Heine to Markscheffel, 9 March 1946, Best. Kurt Schumacher, 93 (Arch.d.SD); SPD/PV, 28 and 29 May 1948; and the documentation in Best. Ollenhauer, 452 and 453; Jean Laloy, "Entretien entre le Dr. Schumacher et M. Laloy," 16 Feb. 1948, Bonn Ambassade, XP 65/XP 3/4 (AOFAA). See also Wolfgang Rudzio, "Die ausgebliebene Sozialisierung an Rhein und Ruhr: Zur Sozialisierungspolitik von Labour-Regierung und SPD 1945–1948," *Archiv für Sozialgeschichte* 18 (1978): 9.

85. Steininger, "British Labour," p. 194. Remarkably, some French statesmen had the same impression. See Auriol, *Journal*, 1:79 (13 Feb. 1947).

86. Rolf Steininger (ed.), *Die Ruhrfrage 1945/46 und die Entstehung des Landes Nordrhein-Westfalen* (Düsseldorf, 1988), p. 215–16.

87. The quotation is Grumbach's in, SFIO/CD, 1 Feb. 1950. See also SFIO/CD, 23 Nov. 1948; Auriol, *Journal*, 2:585 (30 Dec. 1948); and the SPD's resolution of 7 Jan. 1949 (and Carlo Schmid's annotations) opposing the statute in Best. Schmid, 1142 (Arch.d.SD).

88. Schumacher to Edith Baade, 1 Feb. 1949, in Schumacher, *Reden*, p. 626; and Schumacher's article, "Frankreich und die SPD," written for publication in the newspapers *Vorwärts* and *Freiheit* (Mainz), 25 Feb. 1949, in Best. Ollenhauer, 453; and Fritz Hennssler to PV, 10 May 1948, Best. Ollenhauer, 452. See also Klotzbach, *Weg*, pp. 154–58.

89. Nölting, *Nölting*, pp. 499–501.

90. SPD/PV, 21 and 22 Jan. 1949; and the press release by the Sopade Informationsdienst, 7 Jan. 1949, appended to this protocol.

91. SFIO/CD, 12 Jan. and 19 Feb. 1947, 17 and 23 Nov. 1948, and 16 Feb. 1949; *Populaire*, 17 Nov. 1948 (Blum), and 2 Jan. 1949 (Rosenfeld); Auriol, *Journal*, 2:586 (entry for 30 Dec. 1948). See also the documentation in Best. Ollenhauer, 451 and 452.

92. Maillard, *De Gaulle*, p. 98.

93. Schmid, "Verhältnis"; and Raymond Poidevin, *Robert Schumans Deutschland- und Europapolitik zwischen Tradition und Neuorientierung* (Munich, 1976), p. 18.

94. See Socialist International (ed.), "Minutes of the Francfort Conference on the Schuman-Plan, 27–28 June 1951" (hereafter: "Schuman Conference"), Best. Schumacher, 152. See also Kurt Klotzbach, "Die deutsche Sozialdemokratie und der Schuman-Plan," in *Die Anfänge des Schuman-Plans*, Klaus Schwabe (ed.), (Baden-Baden, 1988), pp. 335–37; and Horst Lademacher, *Zwei ungleiche Nachbarn* (Darmstadt, 1990), p. 245.

95. PvdA/PB, 17 May 1950; G.M. Nederhorst, "De Betekenis van de Europese Gemeenschap voor kolen en staal," and Alfred Mozer, "Het Plan Schuman," *Socialisme en Democratie*, 8 (Dec., 1951), 667–70, and 6 (June, 1950), 362–67 resp. See also Albert Kersten, "A Welcome Surprise? The Netherlands and the Schuman-Plan Negotiations," in *Anfänge*, Schwabe (ed.), p. 303.

96. "Schuman Conference," p. 3 (Grumbach); and Lapie, *Blum*, pp. 247–48. The quotation is from, Poidevin, *Europapolitik*, p. 266.

97. SFIO/CD, 23 Nov. 1948, and 10 May and 13 June 1950. See also Elgey, *République*, 1:449–51 (citing an interview with Mollet); and Loth, *Sozialismus*, pp. 262–66.

98. See SPD/PV, 19 May 1950; SFIO/CD, 27 June 1951; and Schumacher's address to the congress of the SPD's Palatinate district, 15 May 1950 in Best. Schumacher, 153.

99. The speech is reprinted in, Schumacher, *Reden*, p. 809.

100. Schumacher's famous alliteration can be found in the speech of 24 May 1951 cited in the previous note. See also Schmid, *Erinnerungen*, pp. 451–52; Miller, *SPD*, pp. 30–31; Schmitz, *Einheit*, p. 78; and Schumacher, *Reden*, p. 1010.

101. SPD/PV, PA, and KK, 8 and 9 Sept. 1951.

102. SPD/PV, 5 Jan. 1950, and 30 March 1951. See also Nölting, *Nölting*, p. 502; Brandt, *Links*, p. 448; and Schmid, *Erinnerungen*, p. 518. On the Schumacher-Kaisen controversy see Albrecht, "Einleitung," p. 160; and Meyer-Braun, "Kaisen- Briefe, pp. 113–14.

103. Koos Vorrink called the SPD's attitude "detrimental [*fataal*] to ... Socialism" (PvdA/PB, 13 April 1951).

104. Steininger, "Schumacher-SI," p. 82.

105. Erler to Brill, 7 March 1957, Best. Erler, 171.

Chapter 7

1. The quotation is from Winock, *République*, p. 18. See also Beatrix W. Bouvier, "Auf der Woge des Zeitgeistes: Die SPD seit den sechziger Jahren," in *Partei und soziale Bewegung: Kritische Beiträge zur Entwicklung der SPD seit 1945*, Dieter Dowe (ed.), (Bonn, 1993), p. 84; and Dunk, "Tussen," p. 13.

2. Club Jean Moulin, *L'État et le Citoyen* (Paris, 1961), p. 262. On the role of the Clubs see below, pp. 194–95.

3. For an analysis of the election returns, see below, pp. 196–201.

4. S.W. Couwenberg, "De ondergang van de brede basis," *Katholiek Staatkundig Maandschrift* 13 (May, 1959): 130.

5. SPD/PV, 11 Feb. 1959 (Wehner).

6. Ibid., 29/30 June 1956. See also A. Pais, "Een jonge socialist beziet zijn partij," *Socialisme en Democratie* 15 (Nov. 1958): 664–70; and Scheps, *Pronk*, p. 86.

7. PvdA/PB, 21 July 1960; Theo van Tijn, "Koude oorlog in de PvdA: Het sociaal-democratisch centrum, 1955–1959," in *Het verbleekte ideaal: De linkse kritiek op de Sociaal Democratie in Nederland*, B.W. Schaper et al. (eds.), (Amsterdam, 1982), p. 70; and Roel H. Kingma, *Nieuw Links in de PvdA: Voorspel, ontwikkeling en confrontatie (1946) 1966–1969* (Amsterdam, 1971), p. 26.

8. As late as July, 1956 Willy Brandt failed—yet again—in his bid to become a member of the executive committee. See Soell, *Erler*, 1:275.

9. Wehner's assessment of his role was made in SPD/PV, 13.1. 1964. See also ibid., 20 Nov. 1957; Soell, *Erler*,1:300–02; and Helmut Köser, "Innovationsprozesse in der SPD," *Politische Vierteljahresschrift* 16 (1975): 30, 34, 50.

10. The communiqué was voted by the SFIO/CD, 23 April 1958. For Mollet's self-doubts see for example, ibid., 1 April 1959. See also Olivier, "Nord," pp. 76–77; and Markscheffel, "SFIO-Kongress am 14. u. 15.1.1956 in Puteaux," 26 Jan. 1956, Best. Ollenhauer, 210.

11. SFIO/CD, 24 July 1957; Rosenfeld to members of the general council of the SI, 7 June 1958 (hereafter: "Rosenfeld Report"), Best. Markscheffel, 8; and Depreux,

Souvenirs, pp. 15 n. 2, 246, 457, and 480. See Philip's letter to the CD, 13 Nov. 1956, reprinted in Philip, *Voies*, pp. 168–69 and 185–88. See also Philip, *Socialistes*, and *Trahi*. For a more scholarly analysis of these polemical attacks see Ligou, *Socialisme*, pp. 604–5. On the PSA see below, pp. 195–96.

12. Jean-Paul Cahn, *Le Parti Social-Democrate Allemand (SPD) et la France, 1954–58* (Diss., Univ. Strasbourg, 1993), 2:789.

13. J.M. den Uyl, "Marxisme anno 1959," *Socialisme en Democratie*, 16 (1959), 474–83; and PvdA/PB, 12 May and 20 Oct. 1960.

14. In Jan. 1958 Wehner told the PV, "We have to abandon this ... sectarian discussion about socialization." (SPD/PV, 24 Jan. 1958).

15. Georges Lefranc, *Le Socialisme réformiste* (Paris, 1971), p. 117; Simmons, *Role*, pp. 217ff; and Winock, *Meurt*, pp. 95–96, 184–85.

16. The quotation is from, Couwenberg, *Socialisme*, p. 160. See also PvdA/PB (ed.), *Programma 1959* (Amsterdam, 1959); and PvdA/PB, 27 Sept. 1957, and 29 Aug. 1958.

17. The cooperative nature of the parties' programmatic efforts was underlined by the presence of Willi Eichler as the SPD's official delegate at the PvdA's 1957 congress in The Hague.

18. On the evolution of the Bad Godesberg Program, see the documentation in Best. Ollenhauer/388–89; SPD/PV, *Entwurf zu einem Grundsatzprogramm*, ed. by Willi Eichler (Bonn, 1958); SPD/PV, 25 April 1958; and "Vorschläge ... des Präsidiums vom 21.1.-9.2.1959," Best. PV-Protokolle 1959; Eichler's explanation of the program's historical background, Willi Eichler, "Die politische Rolle des Godesberger Programms," in Eichler, *Willi Eichlers Beiträge zum demokratischen Sozialismus*, Klaus Lompe and Lothar F. Neumann (eds.), (Bonn, 1979), pp. 158–78; and Susanne Miller, *Sozialdemokratie als Lebenssinn: Aufsätze zur Geschichte und Gegenwart der SPD* (Bonn, 1995), pp. 302–04.

19. Miller, *Aufsätze*, pp. 310–11; Klaus Schütz, *Logenplatz und Schleudersitz: Erinnerungen* (Berlin, 1992), p. 70; Brandt, *Erinnerungen*, pp. 327–28.

20. The quotation is from, Depreux, *Souvenirs*, p. 560. See also J.J. Voogd, "Van Heidelberg tot Godesberg," *Socialisme en Democratie*, 16 (Dec., 1959), 724–27.

21. SFIO/CD, 1.12.60. See also Simmons, *Role*, pp. 221–22.

22. SPD/PV, 9 June 1958, and 5 July 1959. For criticism of Ollenhauer see Eppler to Erler, 24 Sept. 1957, and Erler to Fritz Ehrle, 23 Dec. 1957, Best. Erler,172. See also Soell, "Fraktion," pp. 606–07; Helmut Köser, "Innovationsprozesse in der SPD," *Politische Vierteljahresschrift* 16 (1975): 36–37. Brandt himself had proposed Carlo Schmid as the party's shadow chancellor.

23. SPD/PV, 29 Jan. 1960 (Wehner); and Brandt, *Erinnerungen*, pp. 32–33.

24. Debates on personnel questions are a constant theme of the CD meetings from 1958 to 1960. See also [Günter Markscheffel], "Congrès extraordinaire du Parti SFIO ... 4.12.1958" (hereafter: "SFIO 12/58"), Best. Markscheffel, 36; and Markscheffel, "Parteitag der SFIO am 4. Dezember 1958," n.d., Best. Ollenhauer, 438; Panebianco, *Parties*, p. 42; and Simmons, *Role*, pp. 178–80.

25. On the PSP see Jack Hofmann, Paul den Kamp et al., *Ontwapenend: Geschiedenis van 25 jaar PSP, 1957–1982* (Amsterdam, 1982), pp. 45ff; and Lucas van der Land, *Het onstaan van de Pacifistisch Socialistische Partij* (Amsterdam, 1962), pp. 54–56.

26. PvdA/PB, 29 May and 30 Oct. 1959. See also Luuk Wijmans, "De linkse stroming: Vleugelstrijd in de Nederlandse Sociaal-Democratie," in *Ideaal*, Schaper (ed.), pp. 53 and 57.

27. Abendroth, *Aufstieg;* Ossip K. Flechtheim, "Die Anpassung der SPD: 1914, 1933 und 1959," *Kölner Zeitschrift für Soziologie und Sozialpsychologie,* 17 (1965), 584–604; and Theo Pirker, *Die SPD Nach Hitler ... 1945–1964* (Munich, 1965).

28. Viktor Agartz, *Entwurf des Grundsatzprogramms der SPD* (Munich, 1959).

29. SPD/PV, 7 Feb. 1958; and [SPD/PV], "Prof. Abendroth und das Godesberger Programm" [1961], Best. Schmid, 1408. See also Bouvier, *SPD,* pp. 107–08.

30. SFIO/CD, 29 Nov. 1957, 4 June and 6 Aug. 1958; "Rosenfeld Report"; [Markscheffel], "Unterhaltung Ollenhauer-Mendès-France ... 10.4.1959," n.d., Best. Ollenhauer/425; and Erler, "Ergebnis ... Besprechungen in Paris," 10 and 11 July 1958, Best. Erler, 67 II.

31. See esp. Janine Mossuz, "Que sont devenus les clubs," *Revue Française de Science Politique* 20 (Oct., 1970): 964–73. See also Faucher, *Clubs,* pp. 270 and 277; and Club Jean Moulin, *État.*

32. The quotation is from Michel Rocard, *Le PSU et l'avenir socialiste de la France* (Paris, 1969), p. 16.

33. Depreux, *Souvenirs,* pp. 497 and 520ff. Auriol's letter is reprinted in ibid., pp. 504–5. On the PSU's self-image see Edouard Depreux, *Le Renouvellement du Socialisme* (Paris, 1960); and Rocard, *PSU.*

34. Wilfried Loth, "Der französische Sozialismus in der Vierten und Fünften Republik," *Neue Politische Literatur* 22 (1977): 227.

35. On the overall Dutch election results see Centraal Bureau Statistiek, *Statistiek der Verkiezingen* (The Hague, 1946ff). One entire issue of *Socialisme en Democratie* 14 (Jan. 1957), was devoted to analyses of the 1956 election and its aftermath.

36. PvdA/PB, 28 March 1958; Drees, *Zestig,* p. 301; and Joop den Uyl, "Na een nederlaag," *Socialisme en Democratie* 15 (1958): 260–65.

37. Philip van Praag, *Strategie en Illusion: Elf jaar intern debat in de PvdA (1966–1977)* (Amsterdam, 1990), p. 25–28; Deugd, *Doorbraak,* pp. 125–28; and J.A.W. Burger, "De gauw-gauw-verkiezingen," *Socialisme en Democratie* 16 (1959): 193–200.

38. The full results are in, Gerhard A. Ritter and Merith Niebuss (eds.), *Wahlen in der Bundesrepublik Deutschland, 1946–1987* (Munich, 1987), pp. 158ff.

39. See above, p. 188.

40. Eppler to Erler, 24 Sept. 1957, and Erler to Eppler, 14 Oct. 1957, Best. Erler, 172; Herbert Wehner, "Sozialdemokratische Politik im geteilten Deutschland" [Feb. 1958], Best. Ollenhauer, 423; and SPD/PV, 30 Oct. 1959.

41. The results are in, Chapsal, *Vie,* p. 607; See also Rioux, *République,* 2:88–91; and Simmons, *Role,* pp. 17–18.

42. The referendum results are in, Chapsal, *Vie,* p. 608. See also Winock, *Meurt,* pp. 212–13, and 252; and Simmons, *Role,* p. 88.

43. Dreyfus, *Gauches,* pp. 207–12. The quotation is on p. 212. The election results are in, François Borella, *Les parti politiques dans la France d'aujourd'hui,* 4th ed. (Paris, 1981), p. 44.

44. [Günter Markscheffel], "Congrès extraordinaire du Parti SFIO ... 4.12.1958," pp. 1–3, Best. Markscheffel, 36; and Simmons, *Role,* pp. 97–99 and 181.

45. Panebianco, *Parties,* p. 219.

46. PvdA/PB, 31 Oct. 1958, and 2 Dec. 1958; J.C.H. Bloom and Wichert ten Haven, "De sociaal-democratie tussen doorbraak en coalitie," *Socialisme en Democratie* 43 (1986): 3–8; and Duynstee, *Kabinetsformatie,* pp. 187ff. See also Esterik, *Burger,* pp. 121–22.

47. The fall of the *brede basis* coalition produced a flurry of mutual recriminations within the party and a small library of publication by subsequent analysts. For the debate within the party see PvdA/PB, 27 Nov. 1959, and 15 Sept. and 20 Oct. 1960;

J. de Kadt, "Om de macht van onze beweging: De val van het kabinet Drees," and "Het kabinet de Quay," *Socialisme en Democratie* 16 (Jan., 1959): 1–15, and (June, 1959): 321–39 resp.; Drees, *Zestig*, p. 332; and Tijn, "Koude," p. 74. For scholarly analyses see esp., Duynstee, *Kabinet 46–65*, pp. 217–19; Couwenberg, "Ondergang"; and Heide, *"Ordening"* pp. 359–63.

48. The quotation is from SPD/PV, 28/29 Nov. 1958. See also Gerhard Papke, *Unser Ziel ist die unabhängige FDP: Die Liberalen und der Machtwechsel in Nordrhein-Westfalen 1956* (Baden-Baden, 1992), pp. 205, 212, and 227; and Arnulf Baring, *Machtwechsel: Die Ära Brandt-Scheel*, 3rd. ed. (Stuttgart, 1982), p. 52.

49. SFIO/CD, 21 Jan. 1956; and Mollet, *Bilan*, pp. 69–70. See also Quilliot, *SFIO*, pp. 548–50, and 554–55; Moch, *Vie*, pp. 493–94; and Serge Berstein, "Le Gouvernement Pierre Mendès-France et les partis," in *Pierre Mendès-France et le mendèsisme L'expérience gouvernementale (1954–1955) et sa postérité*, François Bédarida and Jean-Pierre Rioux (eds.), (Paris, 1985), pp. 110–19.

50. Winock, *Meurt*, p. 108; Philip, *Trahi*, p. 208; and Depreux, *Souvenirs*, p. 563. For a corrective reminder that France in 1958 was not Germany in 1932 see Erler, "Ergebnis … Besprechungen in Paris …," 19 July 1958, Best. Erler, 67II.

51. The quotation is from SFIO/CD, 22 May 1957. On the reform of the constitution see "Rapport sur la réforme de la constitution," and the discussion in, SFIO/CD, 23 Oct. 1957.

52. See for example, SFIO/CD, 4 Sept. 1951.

53. For a detailed description see Moch, *Vie*, pp. 528ff; and Jean-Paul Cointet, "Guy Mollet, la SFIO et l'arrivée au pouvoir du Général de Gaulle," in, *Guy Mollet: Un Camerade en république*, Ménager et al. (eds.), (Lille, 1987), pp. 335–47.

54. SFIO/CD, 15 and 26 May 1958; and "Rosenfeld Report." Mollet's own account of the events of May 1958 is in *13 mai 1958 - 13 mai 1962* (Paris, 1962), pp. 2ff.

55. See Winock, *Meurt*, p. 207; and Simmons, *Role*, p. 4.

56. Depreux, *Souvenirs*, p. 481; SFIO/CD, 4 and 18 June 1958; and Tanguy- Prigent to SFIO secretary general, 15 July 1958, quoted in, Quilliot, *SFIO*, pp. 831–33. See also Markscheffel, "Der Parteitag der französischen Sozialisten," 15 Sept. 1958 (appendix), Best. SPD/PV.

57. Mollet's letters of resignation are reprinted in, Guy Mollet, *Textes choisis … 1945–1975*, ed. by Denis Lefebvre ([Paris], 1995), pp. 146–48, and *13 mei*, pp. 23–31. See also Markscheffel, "SFIO 12/58," pp. 6–7 and 14; SFIO/CD, 1 April and 6 Aug. 1958, and 13 Sept. 1960.

58. See Markscheffel's report on the SFIO's 1959 congress, 13 July 1959, Best. Markscheffel/8; and Cépède, " Statuts,"p. 4.

59. The quotation is from, Mollet, *Bilan*, p. 73.

60. PvdA/PB, 29 Oct. 1955, 6 Feb. 1957, and 31 Jan. 1958; and H. Vos, "De sociale economische politiek," *Socialisme en Democratie*, 16 (1959), 340–49.

61. The quotation is from, PvdA, *Congres … 959*, p. 73. See also den Uyl, "Fundamentele," p. 103; and "Tussen dogmatisme en opportunisme: De economie in het nieuwe beginselprogram," and "De volgende tien jaar," *Socialisme en Democratie*, 17 (1960), 211–16, and 18 (1961), 377–89 resp.

62. Knoeringen, "Politik - Werbung - Propaganda," 25 May 1959, Best. Erler, 62.

63. Mollet, *Bilan*, pp. 71ff; and SFIO/CD, 25 Feb. 1959. For contemporary criticism of the government's record see Philip, *Trahi*, chaps. 4 and 7, and pp. 135–37.

64. SFIO/CD, 17 July 1957, 8 Oct. 1958, 25 Feb. and 30 Sept. 1959; and Mollet's letter of resignation, 27 Dec. 1958.

65. PvdA/PB, 28 June 1957; and Drees, *Zestig*, p. 328.

66. Klotzbach, *Weg*, pp. 538ff.

67. SFIO/CD, 24 July and 9 Oct. 1957. See also G. Bossuat, "Guy Mollet: La puissance française autrement," *Relations internationales* (no. 57, 1989), p. 44.

68. PvdA/PB, 27 Nov. 1959, 5 Jan. and 15 Sept. 1960.

69. Klotzbach, *Weg*, pp. 533–34.

70. The quotation is from Bossuat, "Mollet," p. 46. See also Jean-Paul Brunet, "La Politique et économique sociale du gouvernement Guy Mollet," in *Mollet*, Ménager et al. (eds.), pp. 413–43.

71. See the documentation in Best. Erler, 171 and 172. See also the proceedings of a 1958 conference between Social Democrats and Catholics, Karl Foster (ed.), *Christentum und Demokratischer Sozialismus* (Munich, 1958). For criticism of the SPD's "appeasement" policy toward the Catholic Church see R. Reventlow (chairman of the party's Munich district) to Erler, 17 Jan 1955, Best. Erler, 69.

72. See Jean-Claude Criqui, "Der französische Sozialismus," in *Katholizismus und freiheitlicher Sozialismus in Europa*, Albrecht Langner (ed.), (Cologne, 1965), pp. 125–27.

73. SFIO/CD, 8 Oct. 1958 (quotation), and 12 and 22 July 1959; and Philip, *Trahi*, pp. 214–15. See also Mollet's speech to the AN, 23 Dec. 1959, reprinted in *13 mei*, pp. 178ff.

74. [Erler], "Anregung des Sicherheitsausschusses beim PV," 3 July 1959, Best. Ollenhauer/388. See also Soell, *Erler*, 2:801ff; and Thompson, *Wehner*, p. 155.

75. SPD/PV, 23 Oct. 1958; and Erler to Frank and von Knoeringen, 21 March 1959, Best. Erler, 67 II.

76. SFIO/CD, 24 Feb. 1960; and Bossuat, "Mollet," p. 48.

77. G.J.N.M. Ruygers, "De Partij van de Arbeid en het vraagstuk van de atoomwapens," *Socialisme en Democratie* 16 (1959): 162–73; and Land, *PSP*, pp. 24, and 119–20.

78. SPD/PV, 4 March 1958. See also Soell, *Erler*, 1:413–14.

79. Moch, *Vie*, p. 502; and "Rosenfeld Report." The best full-scale account of the Suez affair is, Selwyn Ilan Troen and Moshe Shemesh, *The Suez-Sinai Crisis* (New York, 1990).

80. At the SFIO/CD meeting on 5 Sept. 1956 Mollet proclaimed, "Le vrai problèm est de savoir si on laissera un dictateur marcher à la conquête du monde.... Je souhaite que la volonté de resistance du Parti à Nasser soit entière."

81. Avishai Margalit, "The Chances of Shimon Peres," *New York Review of Books* 43 (9 May 1996): 20.

82. See SFIO/CD, 28 Nov. 1956; Mollet, *Bilan*, pp. 31–34; Philip, *Socialistes*, pp. 161–65; and Serge Berstein and Pierre Milza, "Les forces politiques françaises entre l'humiliation et la volonté de grandeur," *Relations internationales* (no. 57, 1989), 12. For criticism by the SPD and the PvdA see SPD/PV, 17/18 Sept. 1956; and PvdA/PB, 9 Nov. 1956.

83. SFIO/CD, 21 Sept. 1955.

84. On the SFIO's "Jacobin" attitudes toward French colonialism, especially in North Africa see Mollet, *Bilan*, pp. 46–47; Quilliot, *SFIO*, pp. 613ff; and Bossuat, "Mollet," pp. 26–27.

85. Dreyfus, *Gauches*, pp. 166 and 173–76 (the quotation is on p. 174).

86. The quotations are from Depreux, *Souvenirs*, p. 443; and Berstein, "Forces," p. 10 resp. For Mollet's justification of his Algerian policies see *13 mei*, pp. 85ff; and for the internal debate within the SFIO, Ligou, *Socialisme*, pp. 606ff.

87. The quotations are from SPD/PV,PA,KK, 10/11 March 1956 (Wehner), and PvdA/PB, 9 Nov. 1956 (Mozer). On Erler's position see Soell, *Erler*, 1:346. On the SPD's position see also SPD/PV, 17/18 Sept. and 7 Nov. 1956; Thomas Scheffler,

Die SPD und der Algerienkrieg (1954–1962) (Berlin, 1995), esp. pp. 79–80; and Cahn, *SPD*, 2:790.

88. The quotation is from Winock, *Meurt*, p. 111. See Cohen, *Europa*, pp. 129– 30; and Griffiths, *Parties*, p. 61.

89. Wendy Asbeck Brusse, "The Dutch Socialist Party," in *Parties*, Griffiths (ed.), pp. 125, 129. Fritz Heine also thought Jean Monnet, the driving force behind the EEC, was "tied too closely to Roman circles." SPD/PV, 13/14 Jan. 1956.

90. SFIO/CD, 21 June 1957; SPD/PV, 13/14 Jan. 1956, and 7/8 March 1957; Herbert Wehner, "Das Aktionskomitee Jean Monnets und die Entwicklung von Euratom," 21 July 1956, Best. Ollenhauer, 438; and Hrbek, *SPD*, pp. 244ff and 366–67 n. 181. On the Euratom negotiations see esp. Pierre Guillen, "La France et la négociation du Traité d'Euratom," *Relations internationales* 44 (1985): 391–412; and Peter Weilemann, *Die Anfänge der europäischen Atomgemeinschaft... 1955–1957* (Baden-Baden, 1983).

91. Loth, *Weg*, pp. 131–32; Bjøl, *France*, p. 162; Hrbek, *SPD*, pp. 360–61; and Berstein, "Forces," p. 20.

92. SI, "Rundschreiben 80/57," 31 Dec. 1957, Best. Erler, 108; and PvdA/PB, 27 Oct. 1956. See also Quilliot, *SFIO*, pp. 568–76; and Mollet, *13 mei*, p. 54.

93. SPD/PV/PR/KK, 11 July 1958 (appendix); SPD/PV/Fraktionsvorstand, 17 March 1958; and Ollenhauer's address to the PR, 5 May 1959, Best. SPD/PV-Protokolle. See also Lothar Wilker, *Die Sicherheitspolitik der SPD 1956–1966: Zwischen Wiedervereinigungs- und Bündnisorientierung* (Bonn-Bad Godesberg, 1977), pp. 41–44; and Thompson, *Wehner*, p. 137.

94. On the debate on the proposal see the documentation in Best. Ollenhauer, 423. The other members of the commission were Wehner, Erler, Prof. Meyer, Ernst Paul, Kurt Mattick, Gustav Heinemann, and Helmut Schmidt. The text of the Plan is reprinted in, Günther Scholz, *Herbert Wehner* (Düsseldorf, 1986), pp. 360–65.

95. SPD/PV, 7 Feb. and 12 Dec. 1958, and 24/25 April and 5 July 1959; SPD/PV/PR/KK, 5–7 July 1959. See also Soell, *Erler*, 1:662 n. 266.

96. SFIO/CD, 22 Jan. and 13 Feb. 1958. On the PvdA's position see "Summarized Report of the Committee on Collective Security and Disarmament... Paris," 8 Jan. 1958, Best. SPD/PV-Protokolle. For Mollet's skepticism see *13 mei*, pp. 57–64.

97. See SED (Ulbricht) to SPD-Parteivorstand, 2 April 1959, Best. Erler, 62; Kaack, *Geschichte*, pp. 249–50; and Manfred Wilke, *SED-Politik gegen die Realitäten: Verlauf und Funktion der Diskussion über die westdeutschen Gewerkschaften in SED und KPD/DKP 1961–1972* (Cologne, 1990), pp. 220–22.

98. The quotations are from Brandt, *Erinnerungen*, pp. 52 and 167; and Soell, *Erler*, 2:916 resp. For the SPD's struggle to abandon the Germany Plan without losing face see SPD/PV, 23/24 Jan., and 4 and 6 May 1959, 12 March and 1 July 1960; and Wehner's undated note to Erler, Best. Erler, 94. See also Wilker, *Sicherheit*, pp. 56–57.

99. Soell, "Konzeptionen," p. 59; and Günther Gaus, "Herbert Wehner und der Bonner Parlamentarismus," in, *Herbert Wehner: Beiträge zu einer Biographie,*Gerhard Jahn et al (eds.), (Cologne, 1976), p. 149.

100. The reference is to the title of Piet de Rooy, *De rode droom: Een eeuw sociaaldemocratie in Nederland* (Nijmegen, 1995).

101. See Ollenhauer's address to the PR, 30 Jan. 1960, Best. PV-Protokolle. Hans-Jochen Vogel, the SPD's chairman in the 1980s, credits the Bad Godesberg Program with making it possible for a man like him, a practicing Catholic from a bourgeois family, to become leader of the SPD. See Hans-Jochen Vogel, *Nachsichten: Meine Bonner und Berliner Jahre*, 2nd ed. (Munich, 1996), p. 520.

Chapter 8

1. The quotation is the title of Albert Détraz, "L'ouvrier consommateur. See also J.M. den Uyl, "Socialisme en nieuwe maatschappijkritiek," *Socialisme en Democratie* 27 (Dec., 1970): 558–62.

2. Quilliot, *SFIO*, p. 748; and R. de Rooi, "Zoekgeraakte progressieven," *Socialisme en Democratie* 23 (1966): 62–69. For criticism of the decision to close down the party's newspaper see. Scheps, *Pronk*, pp. 138ff. On the decline of the party-controlled press in Germany see SPD/PV 30 Sept. 1963;

3. See Markscheffel to Ollenhauer, 5 April 1960, Best. Ollenhauer/368; and Roy Macridis, "Wandel des Regierungssystems ... Oppositionsformen in Frankreich," in *Parlamentarische Opposition: Ein internationaler Vergleich*, Heinrich Oberreuter (ed.), (Hamburg, 1975), p. 94.

4. The quotation is from Frans Grosfeld, "Het socialistisch experiment," *Socialisme en Democratie* 26 (1969): 464. On the rise of Nieuw Links see below, pp. 242–46.

5. Wolfgang F. Dexheimer, *Koalitionsverhandlungen in Bonn: 1961–1965–1969* (Bonn, 1973), pp. 111–12.

6. PvdA/PB, 16 April and 9 Sept. 1964. See also Ed van Thijn, "De PvdA geprovoceerd (1960–1970)," in *Visie,*Bank and Temming (eds.), pp. 175–76.

7. The quotations are from SFIO/CD, 28 March 1962 and 6 June 1965. On the problems of the party press see ibid., 14 Dec. 1960, 29 Nov. 1961, 6 June 1962, and 27 June 1964; and on the party's electoral campaign, ibid., 25 March 1964. Frank Wilson, *The French Democratic Left, 1963–1969* (Stanford, CA, 1971), p. 156 described Guile as the "most vocal party patriot of the SFIO." For an outsider's impression of the SFIO's listlessness see Markscheffel, "53. Jahreskongress der SFIO, 18.-21.5.61," n.d., Best. Ollenhauer, 371.

8. Waldemar von Knoeringen, "Die Jugendpolitik der Sozialdemokratie," pp. 5–6, enclosure in, Knoeringen to Ollenhauer, 10 Nov. 1961, Best. Ollenhauer, 390. See also Karlheinz Schonauer, *Die ungeliebten Kinder der Mutter SPD* (Bonn, 1982), p. 128.

9. On the party's membership problems see PvdA/PB, 17 March 1959, 15 Nov. 1961, 25 Jan. 1963, and 26 May 1966; PvdA, *Verslag van het negende congrès ... 17, 18, en 19 januari 1963* (Amsterdam [1963]), p. 12. On Nieuw Links' numerical weakness see Bertus Boivin et al., *Een verjongingskuur voor der PvdA: Opkomst, ontwikkeling en betekenis van Nieuw Links* (Deventer, 1978), pp. 45–46.

10. Denis Lefebvre, "Guy Mollet: Un unitaire dans les Années 60—1963 L'Année charnière," in *Mollet*, Bernard Ménager et al. (eds.), pp. 108–09.

11. The quotation is from Erler to Brandt, 23 Oct. 1962, Best. Erler, 62. See also SPD/PV, 5 July 1959, 19 July 1960, and 13 Jan. 1964; and SPD/PV/PR/KK, 15 Feb. 1964. For a detailed analysis of the shift of power from Ollenhauer to Brandt and the reformers see Beatrix W. Bouvier, *Zwischen Godesberg und Großer Koalition: Der Weg der SPD in die Regierungsverantwortung* (Bonn, 1990), pp. 62ff, 273, and 278.

12. PvdA/PB, 17 Nov. 1960, and 5 June and 15 Oct. 1964.

13. See below, p. 261.

14. PvdA/PB, 18 Oct. 1961, 8 June 1962, and 11 Nov. 1965. For criticism of Burger see Esterik and Tijn, *Burger*, pp. 161ff; and Anne Vondeling, *Nasmaak en voorproef* (Amsterdam, 1968), p. 93.

15. For examples of factional conflicts in the CD see SFIO/CD, 29 May and 5 June 1963, and 28 Feb. 1968; Markscheffel to Ollenhauer, 5 April 1960, and "Bericht über den Ausserordentlichen Kongress der [SFIO] ... 21. und 22. Dezember in Puteaux (Seine)" (hereafter: "Bericht ... Puteaux"), Best. Ollenhauer, 368 and 210 resp. On Mollet's position in the party at this time see also Claude Estier, *Journal*

d'un Fédéré: La Fédération de la Gauche au jour le jour (1965–1969) (Paris, 1970), p. 15; Lefebvre, *Mollet*, p. 387; and Simmons, p. 205.

16. SPD/PV, 29 Jan. and 23 Aug. 1960, 27 April 1961, and 22 March 1963; Heinz Kühn et al., "Bundestagswahl 65," and Brandt to Erler et al., 24 July 1963, Best. Erler, 67 I. See also Bouvier, *SPD*, pp. 75–76, and 81–83.

17. The crisis of the 1960s in the PvdA produced a vast amount of analytical literature. The documentation listed here is a small sample, representative of the various points of view. On den Uyl's statement see. Couwenberg, *Socialisme*, p. 118. On Burger's standpoint, Esterik, *Burger*, pp. 141, and 192ff; on the Thomassen/Vondeling line see Vondeling, *Nasmaak*, pp. 205–06, and 217ff; and for NL's position see Bleich, *Partij*, pp. 29–31.

18. For particularly poignant discussions of the SFIO's problems see SFIO/CD, 28 Dec. 1962, and 25 March, and 16 Dec. 1964; and, from the outside, SPD/PV, 15 Nov. 1963.

19. "Bericht…. Puteaux," pp. 5–6.

20. See Claude Fuzier, "J'ai été élu fédéral sur une ligne anti-pivertiste …," *Cahier et Revue de l'Ours* (no. 2, 1994), p. 92.

21. On the contacts between the SPD and the intellectuals see the documentation in Best. Erler, 63; and Bouvier, *SPD*, pp. 268–69.

22. SPD/PV, 9/10 Jan. 1961; and the documentation in Best. Erler, 62–63, and Best. Schmid, 492–94. See also Kurt Klotzbach, "SPD und Katholische Kirche nach 1945: Belastungen, Missverständnisse und Neuanfänge," in *Archiv für Sozialgeschichte*, 29 (1989), XLIV-XLVI [sic]; and Alexander Schwan, "Katholische Kirche und deutsche Sozialdemokratie," in *Katholiken und ihre Kirche in der Bundesrepublik Deutschland*, Günter Gorschenek (ed.), (Munich, 1976), pp. 205–10. For a fuller discussion of the election returns see below, pp. 249–54.

23. For internal discussions of the elusive Progressieve Partij see PvdA/PB, 27 April, 17 Aug., and 26 Aug. 1967, and 14 Oct. 1968; the articles in *Socialisme en Democratie*, 24 (nos. 7/8, 1967); and Scheps, *Pronk*, pp. 68, 96ff, 122–24, and 165ff. For the PAK and its failure see PvdA/PB, 27 Jan. 1969; and Praag, *Strategie*, pp. 72–73.

24. SFIO/CD, 22 June 1960, 25 Jan. 1961, and 18 Sept. and 23 Oct. 1963, 24 Feb. 1965; and Markscheffel, "Der SFIO-Parteitag vom 30. Mai bis 2. Juni 1963" (hereafter: "SFIO-Parteitag 1963"), n.d., Best. Ollenhauer, 376.

25. For a sympathetic, overall analysis of the club scene see esp., Jean-André Faucher, *Les Clubs Politiques en France* (Paris, 1965); Mossuz, "Cl ubs," p. 971; and Georges Suffert, *De Defferre à Mitterrand: la Campagne présidentielle* (Paris, 1966), pp. 50–51.

26. SFIO/CD, 24 Jan. and 7 Oct. 1962, and 26 June and 7 Nov. 1963. See also Lefebvre, *Mollet*, p. 387; and Verdier, *PS/PC*, pp. 222ff.

27. SFIO/CD, 21 Jan. 1962; Markscheffel to Ollenhauer, 19 Dec. 1962, Best. Markscheffel, 2; and Verdier, *PS/PC*, 245–46.

28. Simmons, *Role*, p. 238.

29. Poperen, *Gauche*, 1:422ff, and 2:37. On Mitterrand's relationship to the FGDS and his 1965 presidential campaign see below, pp. 250–51 and 262–66.

30. J.M. den Uyl et al., *Een stem die telt: Vernieuwing van de parlementaire democratie* (Amsterdam, 1967), pp. 11, 14, 20–23, 35.

31. Many of these demands had bi-partisan support with the result that the 1960s saw a significant increase in the tightening of the social net. See Ritter, *Sozialstaat*, p. 183.

32. Joop den Uyl, *Om de Kwaliteit van het bestaan* (Amsterdam, 1963).

33. PvdA/PB, 17 Oct. 1963; Praag, *Strategie*, p. 31; and Berg, "Tijdvak," p. 18.

34. SFIO/CD, 22 June 1960. For criticism of the SFIO's ideological ossification see Claude Bruclain, *Le socialisme et l'Europe* (Paris, 1965), pp. 41–44, and 121–22; and Criqui, "Sozialismus," p. 105.

35. SPD, Wirtschaftspolitischer Ausschuss. "Stenographische Niederschrift der Wirtschaftspolitischen Tagung der SPD vom 3.-5. Oktober 1963 … Essen." Bestand SPD, PV/04696; SPD/PV, 17 Feb., 13/14 June, and 10 and 20 Oct. 1960, 13/14 April 1962, and 25 Oct. 1963; SPD/PV/PR/KK, 15 Feb. 1964; Erler to Eppler, 16 Oct. 1963, and 31 July 1964, Best. Erler, 62; and Knoeringen to Ollenhauer, 16 Nov. 1961, Best. Ollenhauer, 390. See also Bouvier, *SPD*, pp. 68–69, 142, 168–69, and 190ff; Soell, *Erler*, 1:346–49; Michael Longerich, *Die SPD als "Friedenspartei"* (Frankfurt a.M., 1990), pp. 188–89; and. Thompson, *Wehner*, p. 225.

36. SPD/PV, 16 March 1962; and Brandt to Erler, 25 Oct. 1962, and Erler to Brandt, 5 Nov. 1962, Best. Erler, 62. The most complete analysis of the evolution of the emergency laws is Michael Schneider, *Demokratie in Gefahr? Der Konflikt um die Notstandsgesetze: Sozialdemokratie, Gewerkschaften und intellektueller protest (1958–1968)* (Bonn, 1986).

37. The most detailed study of Bahr's ideas is, Andreas Vogtmeier, *Egon Bahr und die deutsche Frage* (Bonn, 1996). In a memo to Brandt, 11 Feb. 1963, Bahr wrote, "everything that deepens the Franco-German friendship is good. Everything that deepens the German-American relationship is better." Quoted in Vogtmeier, p. 75. Wehner labelled Bahr's ideas "pure nonsense." (The German is a wordplay: "Ba[h]rer Unsinn.") Quoted in ibid., p. 64. On the Tutzing speech see Brandt, *Erinnerungen*, pp. 66–67, and 73–74; and Diethelm Prowe, "Die Anfänge der Brandtschen Ostpolitik 1961–1963," in *Aspekte deutscher Außenpolitik im 20. Jahrhundert: Aufsätze Hans Rothfels zum Gedächtnis,* Wolfgang Benz and Hermann Graml (eds.), (Stuttgart, 1976), pp. 274–75. On the visitation agreements see esp. Prowe, "Anfänge"; and Hanns Jürgen Küsters, "Adenauer und Brandt in der Berlin-Krise 1958–1963," *Vierteljahrshefte für Zeitgeschichte* 40 (1992): 483.

38. On the SPD's Europe policy and the party's reaction to the Franco-German pact see SPD/PV, 10 July 1962, and 5 Feb., 8/9 March, 11 May, and 15 Nov. 1963; Seydoux to MAÉ (on a conversation with Carlo Schmid), 27 Oct. 1969, AOFAA/Amb. Bonn, XP92/XP3/4; and Markscheffel to Ollenhauer, 3 Feb. 1963, Best. Ollenhauer, 6. See also Reiner Marcowitz, *Option für Paris?: Unionsparteien, SPD und Charles de Gaulle 1958–1969* (Munich, 1996), pp. 91–92, and 97ff; Schmitz, *Einheit*, pp. 72, and 186–87; and Bouvier, "SPD," pp. 109–20.

39. On the SPD's much-improved relations with the United States, see SPD/PV/PR/KK, 28 June 1963; George McGhee, *At the Creation of a New Germany: From Adenauer to Brandt* (New Haven, CT, 1989), pp. XX [sic], and 51; and Marcowitz, *Option*, pp. 223ff and 237.

40. PvdA/PB, 21 April 1960, 20 Sept. and 15 Nov. 1962, 28 Feb. 1963, 21 Jan. and 15 Oct. 1964, and 29 Sept. 1966; and Joop den Uyl, "De volgende tien jaar," *Socialisme en Democratie* 18 (1961): 377–89. Beatrix' and Claus' marriage in March 1966 led to unruly demonstrations, esp. in Amsterdam, but the PvdA took no part in organizing these.

41. PvdA/PB, 16 March and 6 July 1961, 30 Aug. 1962, 29 Jan., 28 Feb., and 5 Sept. 1963, 21 Jan., 25 Feb., and 9 Sept. 1964; Goes van Naters, "Vijftien jaar Engeland/Europa," *Socialisme en Democratie* 20 (1963): 342; and Uyl, "Kwaliteit," p. 134. See also Cohen, *Europa*, p. 112.

42. The quotations are from SFIO/CD, 5 Sept. 1962 (Mollet); and Bruclain, *Socialisme*, p. 42. See also SFIO/CD, 12 July 1961, 30 Jan. 1963, 15 April 1964, 24 Feb. and 3 March 1965, and 6 Sept. and 11 Oct. 1967; and Mayer, *Gauche*, p. 35.

43. The quotations are from Cohen, *Europa*, p. 116; and SFIO/CD, 5 Sept. 1962. For the SFIO's stand on foreign policy issues see also Bossuat, "Mollet," pp. 35 and 41.

44. SPD/PV, 24 Oct. 1960 and 9/10 Jan. 1961; and Heinrich Oberreuter, "Parlamentarische Opposition in der Bundesrepublik Deutschland," in *Politische Oposition in Deutschland und im internationalen Vergleich*, Walter Euchner, ed (Götttingen, 1993), pp. 62–63.

45. See SPD/PV, "Dokumention zur Entwicklung des SDS," in Best.PV/Protokolle, 20 Sept. 1961; Waldemar Ritter (the PV's youth specialist), "Bericht," 7 March 1966, Best.Erler, 65; and the documentation in Best. Ollenhauer, 235, and Best. Erler, 672. See also Klaus Günther, "Die andere Meinung in der SPD 1949, 1955/56, 1958/61," *Archiv für Sozialgeschichte*, 13 (1973), 43ff.

46. SPD, *Parteitag der SPD ... 17.-21. März 1968 in Nürnberg* (Hanover, 1968), pp. 124ff and 252–54; and Bodo Zeuner, "Das Parteiensystem in der Großen Koalition (1966–1969)," in, *Das Parteiensystem der Bundesrepublik: Geschichte, Entstehung, Entwicklung*, Dietrich Staritz (ed.), (Opladen, 1976), p. 192; and Soell, *Erler*, 2:1143 n. 702.

47. The quotation is from Hofmann, *PSP*, p. 87. See also PvdA/PB, 20 May 1965.

48. The quotations are from,Doel, *Biefstuk*, pp. 155, 160. See also Ed van Thijn, "Is het PvdA-socialisme een wegwerpideologie?" *Socialisme en Democratie*, 28 (Nov. 1971), 540–53; Jan Nagel, *Ha, die PvdA!* (Amsterdam, 1966), p. 36; R. Kroes, *New Left, Nieuw Links, New Left: Verzet, beweging, verandering in Amerika, Nederland, Engeland* (Alphen a.d. Rijn, 1975), pp. 1–3, 51, and 57–58;. Kingma, *Nieuw Links*, pp. 27, and 52ff. The Dutch title *Tien over rood* also involves a word play: "tien over rood" is a form of billiard playing. For a more detailed discussion of the publications' content see Kroes, *New Left*, pp. 1–3; and Boivin, *Opkomst*, pp. 38–42, 77, 97, and 107. The Feb. 1967 letter is reprinted in, Jos van Dijk (ed.), *Nieuw Links in de PvdA* (Amersfoort, 1969), pp. 156–57.

49. Praag, *Strategie*, pp. 65–67, 91 (quotation), and 95–98.

50. PvdA/PB, 26 May 1966 and 23 Sept. 1968; PvdA, *Congrès 1/63*, pp. 34–35 and 41; Nagel, *PvdA*, pp. 65–67; Doel, *Tien*, pp. 9–10, 17ff, and 55.

51. The quotation is from Drees, "Polarisatie," p 11. The increasingly acrimonious debates between NL and the old guard dominated the meetings of the PB from 1965 to 1969. See also Vondeling, *Nasmaak*, pp. 187–91; and Scheps, *Pronk*, p. 55.

52. Willem Drees, Jr., *Taken van de sociaal-democratie in de jaren '70* [Utrecht, 1971]; PvdA/PB, 17 Dec. 1964; and Scheps, *Pronk*, pp. 68ff, 136, and 271.

53. For a discussion of these developments in Germany and France see below, pp. 258 and 266–67.

54. The quotations are from Bleich, *Partij*, p. 155; and den Uyl's statement in, PvdA/PB, 16 Dec. 1968. See also PvdA/PB, 18 May 1967; Joop den Uyl, "De smalle marge van democratische politiek," *Socialisme en Democratie*, 27 (Aug. 1970), 306, and 314; and Rooy, *Wereld*, p. 31, and Droom, p. 65.

55. For bitter criticism of the Nieuw Links "crazies" ("*gekken*") see Jacques de Kadt et al. *Afscheid van de PvdA? Van democratie naar volksdemocratie* (Amsterdam, 1969), pp. 2ff; and Drees, *Drees 90*, pp. 256–57.

56. On the successful integration of NL into the PvdA see J.M. den Uyl, "PvdA-congrès: Terug naar de werkelijkheid," *Socialisme en Democratie*, 25 (1968), 563–66, and 27 (Feb., 1970), 57–58 resp.; and Thijn, "PvdA 1960–70," pp. 197–99. See also

Boivin, *Opkomst*, pp. 73, and 102–06; Doel, *Biefstuk*, pp. 170–71; and Praag, *Strategie*, p. 61, and 71.

57. The quotations are from, Rocard, *PSU*, pp. 7 and 27. See also Markscheffel, "Bericht vom ersten Nationalkongress der ... PSU in Clichy, 24. 25. und 26. März 1961," n.d., Best. Ollenhauer, 371; and "SFIO-Parteitag .... 1963"; and Loth, " Französischer Sozialismus," pp. 228, 234–35; Giesbert, *Mitterrand*, p. 281; and Ligou, *Socialisme*, pp. 625ff. The account by Poperen, *Gauche*, esp. the chapter "La crise du PSU," I:335ff is that of a participant-observer. Poperen was a leading member of one of the PSU's *tendances*. Philip's letter of resignation, 20 Feb. 1961, is reprinted in Philip, *Voies*, pp. 191–93.

58. Depreux, *Renouvellement*, p. 36; Rocard, *PSU*, pp. 19–23; Philip, *Socialistes*, pp. 227, 232–33, 240, and "Pensée," p. 209–10; and Dreyfus, *Gauches*, p. 228.

59. Mollet's prediction was quoted by Dankert in, PvdA/PB, 14 Dec. 1967.

60. SFIO/CD, 22 May 1966. For criticism of Mollet's Franco-Marxism and his increasing isolation in the SFIO see Robert Aron, *Le Socialisme français face au Marxisme* (Paris, 1971), p. 262; François Lafon, "Des principes du Molletisme," in, *Mollet*, Ménager (ed.), pp. 86–88; and Estier, *Journal*, p. 137.

61. Franz-Olivier Giesbert, *François Mitterrand ou la tentation de l'histoire* (Paris, 1977), p. 306.

62. François Mitterrand, *Ma part de verité* (Paris, 1969), p. 17.

63. "Le gaullisme vit sans lois," wrote Mitterrand in his passionate anti-de Gaulle polemic, *Le Coup d'État permanent* (Paris, 1964), p. 271.

64. On Mitterrand as a tactician see Loth, "4. u. 5. Rep.," pp. 230 and 238; Günter Pollach, "François Mitterrand," in *Lebensbilder europäischer Sozialdemokraten des 20. Jahrhunderts*, Otfried Dankelmann (ed.), (Vienna, 1995), pp. 347–49; and Daniel Singer, *Is Socialism Doomed? The Meaning of Mitterand* (New York, 1988), p. 63.

65. Moch, *Vie*, p. 613; Mitterrand, *Ma part*, pp. 280–82; and Singer, *Mitterrand*, p. 72.

66. The quotation is from, Giesbert, *Mitterrand*, p. 264.

67. Hans-Eberhard Dingels (head of the SPD/PV's *Auslandsreferat*) to Carlo Schmid, 26 May 1977, Best. Schmid, 1444.

68. The quotation is from, Giesbert, *Mitterrand*, p. 264. The election results are in, Chapsal, *Vie*, pp. 609–11; and Borella, *Partis*, pp. 42–45.

69. Tony Judt, *Marxism and the French Left: Studies in Labour and Poltics in France, 1830–1981* (Oxford, 1986), pp. 237 and 259–60. The SFIO's leaders' unease about the alliance with the Communists came through well in, SFIO/CD, 12 Oct. 1966. On the 1965 presidential contests and the FGDS-PCF accord see below, pp. 262–66.

70. On the 1969 presidential campaign see below, pp. 251 and 268–69.

71. Bart Tromp, "Party Strategies and System Change in The Netherlands," *West European Politics*, 12 (1989), 85; and Vondeling, *Nasmaak*, p. 24.

72. The results are in Woltjer, *Verleden*, p. 519; and Duynstee, *Kabinetsformatie*, p. 277. For a rather more optimistic analysis see Joop den Uyl, "Krachtmeter zonder beslissing," *Socialisme en Democratie*, 19 (1962), 321–29.

73. E.J. Prins, "20 jaar Partij van de Arbeid - de tijd dringt," *Socialisme en Democratie*, 23 (1966), 389–92; J.G.H. Tans, "Wat nu?" and R. de Rooi, "Kenttekeningen bij de verkiezingsuitslag," *Socialisme en Democratie*, 23 (1966), and 24 (1967), 244–45 and 161–67 resp. See also Deugd, *Doorbraak*, p. 132.

74. The results for the elections analyzed below are from, Ritter and Niebuss (eds.), *Wahlen*, pp. 101, 158ff. See also Ollenhauer's address to the SPD/PR, 30 Jan. 1960; and SPD/PV/Fraktion, 19 Sept. 1961. For a less optimistic assessment of the SPD's electoral future see SPD/PV, 2 June 1961 (Schmidt).

75. See the documentation in Best. Erler, 63 and 92. See also Bouvier, *SPD*, pp. 271–72; and Thompson, *Wehner*, pp. 232–33.

76. SPD/PV, 19 July 1960, 10 July and 16 Dec. 1962, and 9 Feb. and 26 April 1963; SPD/PV/Fraktion, 19 Sept. 1961; and Erler, "Notiz," 5 Dec. 1962, Best. Erler, 93. For sentiments against any coalition under Adenauer see the collection of letters from rank-and-file members in Best. Ollenhauer, 416–18. The best and most detailed account of the road to the grand coalition is in, Baring, *Machtwechsel*.

77. In October, 1962 the influential news magazine *Der Spiegel* published an article exposing some NATO units' lack of war-preparedness. In response the minister of defense, Franz-Joseph Strauss, claiming the piece violated Germany's national security, ordered the Hamburg police to search the magazine's editorial offices and asked the Spanish police to arrest a number of the *Spiegel*'s editors vacationing in Spain—all without a search warrant. For criticism of the SPD's reticence during the affair see Soell, *Erler*, 2:745–46. For a more sympathetic view of Strauss' actions see Wolfgang Krieger, *Franz Josef Strauss: der barocke Demokrat aus Bayern* (Göttingen, 1995), pp. 49–52.

78. For the debate on the SPD's stand in the *Bundesversammlung* see SPD/PV, 14 Feb. and 5 June 1964; and SPD/PV/PR/KK, 15 Feb. and 6 June 1964. See also Soell, *Erler*, 2:777ff.

79. Alfred Grosser, usually a perceptive French observer of German politics, wrote after the election, "the future of the SPD … looks bleak. If not permanently, at least for many years [the SPD] will be condemned to play the role of opposition party." See *Le Monde*, 22 Sept. 1965.

80. Schütz, *Logenplatz*, pp. 116–17; Inge Marssolek and Heinrich Potthoff (eds.), *Durchbruch zum modernen Deutschland?: Die Sozialdemokratie in der Regierungsverantwortung 1966–1982* (Essen, 1995), pp. 29–30; and Reinhard Schmoeckel and Bruno Kaiser, *Die vergessene Regierung: Die Grosse Koalition, 1966 bis 1969* (Bonn, 1991), p. 55.

81. Marssolek, *Durchbruch*, p. 20 quotes Wehner as saying, "In these times the liberal oil is not enough for us Social Democrats, we need the [Christian] cross." See also Gerhard Brunn, "'Jungtürken," pp. 133–34. On the issue of electoral reforms see Erler to Ollenhauer, 6 Dec. 1962, Best. Erler, 93; and Eckhard Jesse, *Wahlrecht zwischen Kontinuität und Reform: 1949–1883* (Düsseldorf, 1985), pp. 169ff.

82. This is the thesis of Zeuner, "Koalition 66–69," pp. 177–78. For the leaders' post-facto arguments justifying the grand coalition see SPD, PV, *Bundeskonferenz 1967*, pp. 8ff.

83. On the mood within the party and the significance of the grand coalition for West German society see Castrup to Erler, 19 Dec. 1966, Best. Erler, 63; SPD/PV (ed.), *Parteitag … 1968*, pp. 252–54; Nowka, *Machtverhältnis*, p. 141; and Wolfgang Rudzio, "Die Regierung der informellen Gremien," *Sozialwissenschaftliches Jahrbuch für Politik*, 3 (1972), 339–66.

84. See Soell, "Fraktion," p. 622.

85. The quotation is from, Heino Kaack, *Geschichte und Struktur des deutschen Parteiensystems* (Opladen, 1971), p. 360. See also Brandt, *Erinnerungen*, p. 269; and Dexheimer, *Koalition*, p. 104.

86. The quotation is from, Drees, "Polarisatie," p. 12. See also PvdA/PB, 17 March 1959, 15 June 1961, 16 Oct. 1962, and 15 April 1965; Uyl, "Smalle," p. 320; Esterik, *Burger*, p. 187; and J.Th.J. v.d. Berg, "Democratische hervormingen, politieke machtsverhoudingen en coalitievorming in Nederland," *Acta Politica* 21 (1986): 283.

87. Robbert Ammerlaan, *Het verschijnsel Schmelzer: Uit het dagboek van een politieke tekkel* (Leiden, 1973), pp. 125ff.

88. On the cabinet formation and Vondeling's role see Ammerlaan, *Schmelzer*, pp. 190– 92; P.F. Maas, *Kabinetsformaties 1959–1973* (Den Haag, 1982), pp. 150–51 and 162ff; Duynstee, *Kabinet 46–65*, pp. 386ff; and Vondeling, *Nasmaak*, pp. 140ff and 180–81. For criticism of Vondeling's policies see PvdA/PB, 16 Dec. 1965, and 20 Jan. and 23 Feb. 1966.

89. Incidentally, the debate over Schmelzer's actual intentions continues. The PvdA was convinced his aim had been to bring down the coalition, while his defenders insist the ultimatum was intended as a shock treatment to overcome the cabinet's self-paralysis. For a sample of analyses of the much-discussed "Schmelzer's night" see Vondeling, *Nasmaak*, pp. 173–76; Maas, *Kabinet*, pp. 179ff, 221, 390–91 n. 43; Ammerlaan, *Schmelzer*, pp. 73, 194ff, 213, 226ff, and 275; and Praag, *Strategie*, pp. 33–34.

90. Claus Leggewie, "Alles andere als (parlamentarische) [sic] Opposition: Über die Grenzen der Opposition im politischen System Frankreichs," in *Opposition*, Euchner (ed.), pp. 127–36.

91. SFIO/CD, 28 Dec. 1962. For a discussion of the divisions within the SFIO on *présidentialisme* see SFIO/CD, 28 Dec. 1962, and 27 March 1963.

92. The quotations are from, Alexandre, *Defferre*, p. 8; and Rocard, *PSU*, p. 28 resp. On Defferre's political career and his circle of advisors see Alexandre, *Defferre*; Suffert, *Defferre*, pp. 63ff; Faucher, *Clubs*, pp. 144, and 287–89; and for his program, Gaston Defferre, *Un Nouvel Horizon* (Paris, 1965). For Defferre's assessment of his chances see SFIO/CD, 27 May 1964; and for the continuing skepticism of Mollet and other CD members see ibid., 18 Dec. 1963. The federation figures are a little misleading since many of the SFIO's regional organizations existed only on paper.

93. On Defferre's candidacy and the SFIO's relations with the PCF see SFIO/CD, 3 Feb., 24 Feb., 3 March, 7 April, and 12 Oct. 1965; and Lefebvre, "Unitaire," pp. 116–18, and "La 'Galaxie Defferre' et le Parti Socialiste," *Cahier et Revue de l'Ours* (no. 2, 1994), 94–99. For accounts of the 1965 SFIO congress see PvdA/PB, 17 June 1965; Wilson, *Left*, p. 128; and Simmons, *Role*, pp. 163–67.

94. For especially sharp clashes between Mollet and Defferre see SFIO/CD, 23 June and 15 Sept. 1965. The quotations are from Giesbert, *Mitterrand*, p. 305; and Dreyfus, *Gauches*, pp. 258–59 resp.

95. The quotation is from, Faucher, *Clubs*, p. 249. The debate within the SFIO on the relationship of the party to the FGDS and Mitterrand can be followed in SFIO/CD, 8 and 29 Sept., and 17 Nov. 1965. For an interesting perspective on Mitterrand's long-range significance in French politics see the interview with Olivier Duhamel in, *Der Spiegel*, 17 October 1994, pp. 184–89.

96. On the SFIO's efforts to saddle Mitterrand with a program, and the candidate's own ideological position see SFIO/CD, 5 July 1967, and 3 July 1968; Singer, *Mitterrand*, pp. 78ff; and Giesbert, *Mitterrand*, pp. 311–12.

97. The quotations are from, Philip, *Socialistes*, p. 240; and Estier, *Journal*, p. 77.

98. The quotation is from Estier, *Journal*, p. 39. For the ongoing debate within the CD on the relationship of the SFIO to the new party see SFIO/CD, 10 May, 14 June, 5 July, 11 and 25 Oct., and 22 Nov. 1967.

99. The quotations are from Giesbert, *Mitterrand*, pp. 241 and 250 resp. On the SFIO's reaction to the events of May, 1968 and the subsequent elections see SFIO/CD, 15 May and 3 July 1968.

100. The quotations are from SFIO/CD, 27 Nov. and 5 Dec. 1968. For the CD's discussions of relations between the SFIO, the PCF, and the new party see ibid., 3 and 17 July, 23 Aug., 4 Sept. (incl. appendix), 4 and 23 Oct., 27 Nov., and 5 Dec. 1968. (André Delelis [Ménager, *Mollet*, p. 194] remembered that after 1968 Mollet was a changed and increasingly bitter man, who knew that he no longer had the support of the party.)

101. The characterizations "Balkanization" and "farce" are from, Poperen, *Gauche*, 2:237 and 261.

102. On Poher's decidedly Social Democratic but lackluster platform see Alain Poher, "[Interview avec Georges Altschuler et George Leroy, 'Europe-Soir' ... 10 juin 1969]," Dossier Claude Fuzier (OURS).

103. The quotations are from, Dreyfus, *Gauches*, p. 320; and Poperen, *Gauche*, 2:10.

104. Giesbert, *Mitterrand*, p. 293; Bell, *PS*, pp. 146–47; and Wilson, *Left*, pp. 189, and 201.

105. Quoted in Franz Kreuzer (ed.), "Die Zukunft der Sozialdemokratie: Ein Streitgespräch zwischen Franz Vranitzky und Ralf Dahrendorf, *Die Zukunft* (no. 8, 1990), 8. See also Gordon Smith, "Core Persistence: Change and the 'People's Party,'" *West European Politics*, 12 (1989), 158; Wolfgang Merkel, "Niedergang der Soczialdemokratie? Sozialdemokratische und sozialistische Regierungspolitik im westeuropäischen Vergleich," *Leviathan*, 18 (March, 1990), 106ff.

106. Giesbert, *Mitterrand*, p. 304; and Werner Kaltefleiter, *Parteien im Umbruch* (Düsseldorf, 1984), p. 34.

107. SFIO/CD, 5 Feb. 1963 (appendix). See also Cohen, *Europa*, pp. 112, 121–23, and 129.

Conclusion

1. J.Th.J. van den Berg, "Het miskende tijdvak," p. 35.

2. The quotations are from Marssolek, *Durchbruch*, p. 79; and Herbert Wehner, *Staatserhaltende Opposition oder Hat die SPD kapituliert? Gespräche mit Herbert Wehner*, ed. by Günter Gaus (Reinbek, 1966), p. 34. See also, Shlomo Na'aman, "Von der Problematik der Sozialdemokratie als demokratische Partei: Zur Jubiläumsfeier des Jahres 1863," *Archiv für Sozialgeschichte* 5 (1965): 503–25; and T. Wöltgens, "Beginselen in een nieuwe context," *Socialisme en Democratie* 53, 7/8 (1996): 369–75.

3. Schmidt once described the foundations of his political outlook as Christianity, Bernsteinian ethics, and Karl Popper's doctrine of piecemeal social engineering. See, Michael Schneider, "Helmut Schmidt," in Otto Borst (ed.), *Persönlichkeit und Politik in der BRD* (Göttingen, 1982), pp. 167–68.

4. Erhard Eppler, "Mutiges Political Animal," *Der Spiegel* 47 (29 March 1993), 44.

5. Clear evidence of the accellerating process of *ontzuiling*, in 1968 the *Katholieke Illustratie* ceased publication. Since 1867 this weekly had been a staple of virtually every Catholic household in The Netherlands.

6. The quotation is from Wöltgens, "Beginselen," p. 373. See also, Rob Gollin, "Partij van wrok en een beetje nieuw bloed," *Volkskrant*, 6 Nov. 1993.

7. Panebianco, *Political Parties*, p. 311, n. 71.

8. The quotation is from Daniel Singer, *Is Socialism Doomed? The Meaning of Mitterrand* (New York, 1988), p. 294.

9. Couwenberg, *Modern socialisme*, p. 192; Scheffer, "Contouren van een ontzuilde hervormingspartij," in Gees J.M. Schuyt and Siep Stuurman (eds.), *Soci-*

aaldemocratie tussen zakelijheid en moraal (Amsterdam, 1991), pp. 88–89; and Christiane Lemke, and Gary Marks (eds.), *The Crisis of Socialism in Europe* (Durham, NC, 1992), pp. 15–16.

10. Wöltgens, "Beginselen," pp. 369, and 371–75; Friedhelm Farthmann, *Blick voraus im Zorn: Aufruf zu einem radikalen Neubeginn der SPD*, 2nd. ed. (Düsseldorf, 1996); and Erhard Eppler, "Das linke Leiden an der Wirklichkeit," *Die Zeit*, 24 May 1991.

BIBLIOGRAPHY

1. Archival Depositories

Amsterdam. Internationaal Instituut voor Sociaal Geschiedenis
   Archief PvdA, PB, Notulen van de vergadering van het Partijbestuur
   (1946–1969)
Bonn. Archiv der Sozialen Demokratie - Friedrich-Ebert-Stiftung
   Bestand Fritz Erler
   Bestand Günter Markscheffel
   Bestand Erich Ollenhauer
   Bestand Parteivorstand (1946–1966)
   Bestand Carlo Schmid
   Bestand Kurt Schumacher
Colmar. Archive de l'Occupation Française en Allemagne et Autriche
   Dossier Secretariat Général aux affaires allemandes et autrichiennes
   Dossier Berlin
   Dossier Cabinet du Haut-Commissariat
   Dossier Direction générale des affaires politiques
   Dossier Direction d'information
   Dossier l'Administrateur Laffon (1945–1947)
   Dossier Offices des nouvelles de France
   Dossier Ambassade de France à Bonn
   Dossier Direction générale des affaires économiques
Hamburg. Bibliothek der Arbeiterbewegung - Forschungsstelle für Zeit-
geschichte in Hamburg
   Bestand Max Brauer
   Bestand SPD - Bezirk Hamburg
Paris. Office universitaire de recherche socialiste
   Dossier Claude Fuzier
   Dossier SFIO, CD, Comptes-rendus du Comité directeur (1944–1969)

2. Significant Individual Unpublished Documents

Grumbach, Salomon. "Deutschland und die Probleme der Ruhr: Resolution für die
   Pariser Konferenz europäischer Sozialisten." Bestand Ollenhauer. April 1948.

Kühn, Heinz et al. "Die politisch-psychologische Situation 1965: Beiträge zur Analyse der Bundestagswahl und Ansätze zur zukünftigen Politik der SPD." Bestand Carlo Schmid. Ca. Nov. 1965.

[Markscheffel, Günter]. "Congrès extraordinaire du Parti SFIO … 4.12.1958." Bestand Günter Markscheffel. Dec. 1958.

———."Interner Bericht vom 51. Konress der SFIO vom 9. bis 12. Juli 1959 …." Bestand Markscheffel. [July, 1959].

Poher, Alain. "[Interview avec Georges Altschuler et George Leroy. 'Europe-Soir' … 10 juin 1969]." Dossier Claude Fuzier.

Schwarzenberg, Roger-Gérard. "Essai d'interprétation d'une campagne présidentielle. 18 juin/19 décembre 1965: Candidats — Programmes — Partis." Diplôme d'Etudes. Université de Paris. OURS Bibliothèque. n.d.

SFIO, Commission internationale et commission des affaires économique. "Travail préparatoire pour determiner la position de la délégation française à la conférence des partis socialistes des pays ayant acceptés le principe de l'aide américaine." Bestand Ollenhauer. March, 1948.

———. Groupe d'études doctrinales. "Avant-projet de programme fondamentale de la … SFIO." Dossier SFIO, CD. May 1960.

Socialist International, ed. "Minutes of the Francfort Conference on the Schuman-Plan, 27–28 June 1951." Best. Schumacher. [London, 1951].

[SPD,PV]. "Prof. Abendroth und das Godesberger Programm." [Bonn, 1961]. Bestand SPD, PV.

———. ed. "3. Kongress der Sozialistischen Internationale. Stockholm, 15.–18.7.1953." Bestand SPD, PV. July 1953.

———. "Entwurf für ein Grundsatzprogramm der SPD: Fassung vom 13.8.1959." Bestand SPD, PV. Aug. 1959.

———. "Die schwarz-rote Lüge: Eine Dokumentation über die Haltung der SPD während der Koalitionsverhandlungen … 17. September bis 7. November 1961." Bestand Ollenhauer. [Nov. 1961].

SPD. Wirtschaftspolitischer Ausschuss. "Stenographische Niederschrift der Wirtschaftspolitischen Tagung der SPD vom 3.–5. Oktober 1963 … Essen." Bestand SPD, PV.

3. Primary Sources

3.1. Documentary Publications

Agartz, Viktor. *Entwurf des Grundsatzprogramms der SPD*. Munich, 1959.

Bucher, Peter, ed. *Quellen zum politischen Denken der Deutschen im 19. und 20. Jahrhundert: Nachkriegsdeutschland, 1945–1949*. Darmstadt, 1990.

Club Jean Moulin. *L'État et le Citoyen*. Paris, 1961.

Deutscher Bundestag and Bundesarchiv, eds. *Der Parlamentarische Rat 1948–1949*. Boppard a.Rh., 1975ff.

Flechtheim, Ossip K., ed. *Dokumente zur parteipolitischen Entwicklung in Deutschland seit 1945*. Berlin, 1962. 9 vols.

Konstanzer, Eberhard. "Weisungen der französischen Militärregierung 1946–1949." *Vierteljahrshefte für Zeitgeschichte*. 18 (1970), 204–36.

Seelinger, Rolf, ed. *SPD—Grosser Kompromiss ohne Ende?* Munich, 1969.

Steininger, Rolf, ed. *Die Ruhrfrage 1945/46 und die Entstehung des Landes Nordrhein-Westfalen*. Düsseldorf, 1988.

3.2. Official and Semi-Official Party Publications

(*Note*: The numerous, mostly short, individual articles in the parties' official periodicals have not been separately entered in the bibliography. The official and semi-official party journals used in this study were the following:)

Bulletin intérieur du Parti Socialiste
Cahier et Revue de l'OURS
Neue Gesellschaft
Neuer Vorwärts
Nouvelle Revue socialiste
Politisch-Parlamentarischer Pressedienst
Le Populaire
Revue socialiste
Socialisme en democratie
Vorwärts

3.2.1. PvdA (including DS'70)

Banning, Willem. *Ons Socialisme ... Een verweer en appèl naar aanleiding van het Mandement 1954* .... Amsterdam, 1954.

———. *Kompas: Toelichting op het beginselenprogramma 1959*. Amsterdam, 1959.

Democratisch Centrum Nederland. *Naar nieuwe politieke verhoudingen*. Bilthoven, 1967.

Drees, Willem jr. *Taken van de sociaal-democratie in de jaren '70*. [Utrecht, 1971].

Leune, Han, et al. eds. *Mooi rood is niet lelijk*. Rotterdam, 1969.

NVV and SDAP. *Het Plan van de Arbeid: Rapport van de Commissie uit NVV en SDAP*. Amsterdam, 1935.

PvdA. *Beschrijvingsbrief ... het Congres PvdA ... maart 1969*. [Amsterdam, 1969].

———. *Verslag van het Congres-Indonesië ... 7. Sept. 1946*. Amsterdam [1946].

———. *Verslag van het Congres, 1946–1969*. Amsterdam, 1946–1969.

———. *De weg naar vrijheid: Rapport Plancommissie PvdA*, 2nd ed. Amsterdam, 1951.

———. *De weg naar vrijheid: Verkiezingscongres, 19 April 1952*. [Amsterdam, 1952].

Schermerhorn, W. and N.A. Donkersloot. *De derde weg*. Amsterdam [1952].

Thomassen, W. *Opening van Zaken: Een en ander over de voorbereiding van de PvdA*. Amsterdam, 1946.

Uyl, Joop M. den, et al. *Een stem die telt: Vernieuwing van de parlementaire domocratie*. Amsterdam, 1967.

———. *Om de kwaliteit van het bestaan*. Amsterdam, 1963.

Vermeer, Evert A. *Balans per 31.12.59. Terugblik op een jaar oppositie*. Amsterdam [1960].

Vorrink, Koos. "Radiorede ..., 30 Jan 1946." In *Documentatiecentrum Nederlandse Politieke Partijen — Jaarboek 1975*. Groningen, 1975. Pp. 84–94.

———. *Verantwoording en opdracht: Vijf jaar Partij van de Arbeid*. Amsterdam, 1951.

3.2.2. SFIO (including PSA, PSU, PS)

Defferre, Gaston. *Un Nouvel Horizon*. Paris, 1965.

Depreux, Eduard. *Le Renouvellement du Socialisme*. Paris, 1960.

———. *Servitude et grandeur du P.S.U.* Paris, 1974.

Moch, Jules. *Le Parti Socialiste au peuple de France: Commentaires sur le manifeste de novembre 1944*. Paris, 1945.

———. *Qu'est ce que le socialisme*. Paris, 1944.

Mollet, Guy. *Bilan et perspective socialiste*. Paris, 1958.

———. *Textes choisis ... 1945–1975*. Ed. Denis Lefebvre [Paris], 1995.

Philip, André. *Pour un socialisme humaniste*. Paris, 1960.

————. *Les réformes de structure pour la rénovation de la République.* Algiers, 1944.
PSA. *Le Prémier congrès nationale du Parti Socialiste Autonome.* Paris, 1959.
Ramadier, Paul. *Le Socialisme de Léon Blum.* Paris, 1951.
Rocard, Michel. *Le PSU et l'avenir socialiste de la France.* Paris, 1969.
SFIO. *L'Action socialiste à la seconde Constituante.* Paris, 1946.
————. *Congrès nationales … 1944–1969.* Paris, 1944–1969. Note: Until the 1950s
the proceedings of the national congresses were not published; mimeo-
graphed copies are available at OURS.
————. *Programme d'action du Parti Socialiste ….* Paris, 1945.
————. *Un programme, une équipe, des réalisations.* Paris, 1947.
————. *Trois mois d'action: L'oeuvre des ministres socialistes dans le gouvernement
Gouin.* Paris, 1946.

3.2.3. SPD

Deist, Heinrich. *Wirtschaft von morgen.* ed. by Gerhard Stümpfig. 2nd. ed. Bonn,
1973.
Dowe, Dieter et al. eds. *Programmatische Dokumente der deutschen Sozialdemokratie.*
2nd. ed. Berlin, 1984.
Eichler, Willi. *Willi Eichlers Beiträge zum demokratischen Sozialismus.* Ed. Klaus
Lompe and Lothar F. Neumann. Bonn, 1979.
Germer, K.J. ed. *Von Grotewohl bis Brandt: Ein dokumentarischer Bericht über die SPD
in den ersten Nachkriegsjahren.* Berlin, 1974.
Henssler, Fritz. *Das Nein der SPD zum Ruhrstatut.* Dortmund, 1949.
Löwenthal, Richard. *Jenseits des Kapitalismus.* Bonn, reprint 1978.
Nölting, Erik. *Gegen die Zwangswirtschaft.* Mannheim, 1951.
Schmid, Carlo. *Mensch und Technik.* Bonn, 1956.
Schumacher, Kurt. *Deutschlands Beitrag für Frieden und Freiheit.* Hannover, 1950.
————. *Europa oder Europa-AG?.* Hanover, 1951.
Die SPD-Fraktion im deutschen Bundestag: Sitzungsprotokolle, 1957–1966. Ed. Wolf-
gang Hölscher and Heinrich Potthoff. Düsseldorf, 1993. 2 vols.
SPD, Bez. Westliches Westfalen. *Die Sozialisierung im Landtag Nordrhein-Westfalen.*
Dortmund, 1947.
SPD, Landesverband Hamburg. *Leitsätze … zur Gestaltung einer sozialistischen
deutschen Wirtschaftsverfassung* [Hamburg. 1946].
SPD/PV. *Acht Jahre sozialdemokratischer Kampf um Einheit, Frieden und Freiheit*
Bonn, 1954.
————. *Aktionsprogramm: Änderungsentwurf der Programmkommission.* Bonn, 1954.
————. *Bestandaufnahme 1966* Bonn, 1966.
————. *Bundeskonferenz der SPD 1967.* Bad Godesberg [1967].
————. *Entwurf zu einem Grundsatzprogramm.* Ed. Willi Eichler Bonn, 1958.
————. *Die Europa-Politik der Sozialdemokratie.* Bonn, 1953.
————. *Grundsatzprogramm … Bad Godesberg.* Bonn, 1959.
————. *Der Parteivorstand der SPD im Exil: Protokolle der Sopade 1933–1940.* Ed.
Marlies Buchholz and Bernd Rother. Bonn, 1995.
————. *Protokoll der Verhandlungen des Parteitages der Sozialdemokratischen Partei
Deutschlands, 1946–1969.* Hamburg et al. 1947–1969.
SPD (Sopade). *Deutschland-Berichte.* Ed. Klaus Behnken et al. Frankfurt a.M.,
1980. 7 vols.
Stamm, Christoph, ed. *Die SPD-Fraktion im Frankfurter Wirtschaftsrat 1947–1949:
Protokolle, Aufzeichnungen, Rundschreiben.* Berlin, 1993.
Veit, Hermann. *Sozialdemokratische Wirtschaftspolitik.* Bonn, 1950.

3.3. *Memoirs and Diaries*

Acheson, Dean. *Present at the Creation.* New York, 1970.

Alphand, Hervé. *L'étonnement d'être: Journal 1939–1973.* Paris, 1977.

Aron, Raymond. *Mémoires.* Paris, 1987.

Auriol, Vincent. *Journal du Septennat.* version intégrale. ed. Jean-Pierre Azéma Paris, 1974. 7 vols.

Bank, Jan and Stef Temming. eds. *Van brede visie tot smalle marge: acht prominente socialisten over de SDAP en de PvdA.* Alphen a.d. Rijn, 1981.

Bergsträsser, Ludwig. *Befreiung, Besatzung, Neubeginn: Tagebuch des Darmstädter Regierungspräsidenten 1945–1948.* ed. by Walter Mühlhausen München, 1987.

Blum, Léon. *L'Oeuvre de Léon Blum.* Ed. Robert Verdier et al. Paris, 1954–1963. 6 vols.

Brandt, Willy. *Erinnerungen.* Frankfurt a.M. 1989.

———. *Links und frei: Mein Weg 1930–1950.* Hamburg, 1982.

Burger, J.A.W. "Interview ...." In *Hergroepering,* ed. by Puchinger. Pp. 2–27.

Depreux, Eduard. *Souvenirs d'un militant: De la social-democratie au socialisme — Un demi- siècle de luttes, 1918–1968.* Paris, 1972.

Drees, Willem. *Drees 90: Geschriften en Gesprekken.* Ed. Hans Daalder. Bussum, 1976.

———. *Zestig jaar levenservaring.* Amsterdam, 1963.

Dumaine, Jacques. *Quai d'Orsay (1945–1951).* Tr. Alan Davidson. London, 1958.

Eichler, Willi. *Weltanschauung und Politik: Reden und Aufsätze.* Frankfurt, a.M. 1967.

Eschenburg, Theodor. "Erinnerungen an die Münchener Ministerpräsidenten-Konferenz 1947." *Vierteljahrshefte für Zeitgeschichte.* 20 (1972). 411–17.

Estier, Claude. *Journal d'un Fédéré: La Fédération de la Gauche au jour le jour 1965–1969.* Paris, 1970.

Fetscher, Iring. *Neugier und Furcht: Versuch mein Leben zu verstehen.* Hamburg, 1995.

Galen, John Jansen van. ed. *"Het moet, het kan! Op voor het Plan!" Vijftig jaar Plan van de Arbeid.* Amsterdam, 1985.

Gniffke, Erich W. *Jahre mit Ulbricht.* Cologne, 1966.

Goes van Naters, Marinus van der. *Met en tegen de tijd.* Amsterdam, 1980.

Grebing, Helga ed. *Entscheidung für die SPD: Briefe und Aufzeichnungen linker Sozialisten, 1944–1948.*

———. *Lehrstücke der Solidarität: Briefe und Biographien deutscher Sozialisten, 1945–1949.* Stuttgart, 1983.

Kiesinger, Kurt Georg. *Dunkle und helle Jahre: Erinnerungen 1904–1958.* Ed. Reinhard Schmoeckel. Stuttgart, 1989.

Kissinger, Henry A. *Memoiren: 1973–1974.* Munich, 1982.

Lapie, Pierre-Olivier. *De Léon Blum à de Gaulle: Le caractère et le pouvoir.* Paris, 1971.

Marjolin, Robert. *Le Travail d'une Vie: Mémoires, 1911–1986.* Paris, 1986.

Massigli, René. *Une comédie des erreurs, 1943–1956: Souvenirs et reflexions sur une étape de la construction européenne.* Paris, 1978.

McGhee, George. *At the Creation of a New Germany: From Adenauer to Brandt.* New Haven, CT, 1989.

Mendès-France, Pierre. *Oeuvres complètes.* Paris, 1985–1990. 6 vols.

Mitterrand, François. *Ma part de verité: De la rupture à l'unité.* Paris, 1969.

Moch, Jules. *Rencontres avec ... Léon Blum.* Paris, 1970.

———. *Une si longue vie.* Paris, 1976.

Mollet, Guy. *Textes choisis ... 1945–1975.* Ed. Denis Lefebvre [Paris], 1995.

———. *13 mai 1958 - 13 mai 1962.* Paris, 1962.

Mozer-Ebbinge, Alfred and R. Cohen. eds. *Alfred Mozer: 'Gastarbeider' in Europa.* Zutphen, 1980.

Philip, André. *André Phiip par lui-même ou les Voies de la liberté*. Paris, 1971.

Pünder, Hermann. *Von Preussen nach Europa: Lebenserinnerungen*. Stuttgart, 1968.

Rossmann, Erich. *Ein Leben für Sozialismus und Demokratie*. Tübingen, 1946.

Scheps, Johannes H. *Het progressieve als waardeloze pronk*. Apeldoorn, 1971.

Schmid, Carlo. *Erinnerungen*. Munich, 1979.

Schmidt, Helmut. *Weggefährten: Erinnerungen und Reflexionen*. Berlin, 1996.

Schütz, Klaus. *Logenplatz und Schleudersitz: Erinnerungen*. Berlin, 1992.

Schumacher, Kurt. *Reden, Schriften, Korrespondenzen, 1945–1952*. Ed. Willy Albrecht. Bonn, 1985.

Strauss, Franz Josef. *Die Erinnerungen*. Berlin, 1989.

Thijn, Ed van. "De PvdA geprovoceerd (1960–1970)." In *Visie*, edited by Bank. Pp. 175–99.

Thomassen, Willem. "Hier: de Partij van de Arbeid." In *Visie*, edited by Bank. Pp. 89–118.

Uyl, Joop M. den. *Inzicht en uitzicht: Opstellen over economie en politiek*. Amsterdam, 1978.

Verway-Jonker, Hilda. "De Ideologie van de SDAP (1930–1940)." In *Visie*, edited by Bank. Pp. 13–30.

Vogel, Hans-Jochen. *Nachsichten: Meine Bonner und Berliner Jahre*. 2nd ed. Munich, 1996.

Vondeling, Anne. *Nasmaak en voorproef*. Amsterdam, 1968.

Wehner Herbert. *Staatserhaltende Opposition oder hat die SPD kapituliert? Gespräche mit Herbert Wehner*. Ed. Günter Gaus. Reinbek, 1966.

Wolff, Sam de. *Voor het land van belofte: Een terugblik op mijn leven*. Bussum, 1954 [reprint: Nijmegen, 1973].

4. Secondary Sources

Abelshauser, Werner *Die Langen Fünfziger Jahre: Wirtschaft und Gesellschaft in der Bundesrepublik Deutschland, 1949–1966*. Düsseldorf, 1987.

———. "Marktwirtschaft oder Planung?" In *Tradition*, edited by Lademacher and Bosmans. Pp. 107–20.

———. "Westeuropa vor dem Marshall-Plan." In *Marshall-Plan,*edited by Haberl and Niethammer. Pp. 99–131.

———. ed. "Freiheitlicher Sozialismus oder soziale Marktwirtschaft?" *Vierteljahrshefte für Zeitgeschichte*. 24 (1976), 414–49.

———. ed. *Konflikt und Kooperation: Strategien europäischer Gewerkschaften im 20. Jahrhundert*. Essen, 1988.

Abendroth, Wolfgang. *Aufstieg und Krise der deutschen Sozialdemokratie*. Frankfurt a.M. 1964.

Abert, J.G. *Economic Policy and Planning in The Netherlands, 1950–1965*. New Haven, 1969.

Abma, R. "Het Plan van de Arbeid en de SDAP." *Bijdragen en Mededelingen betreffende de Geschiedenis der Nederlanden*. 92 (1977), 37–68.

Adams, William James. *Reconstructing the French Economy: Government and the Rise of Market Competition since World War II*. Washington, DC, 1989.

Agartz, Viktor. *Partei, Gewerkschaft, Genossenschaft*. Ed. Hans Willi Weinzen. Frankfurt a.M., 1985.

Albrecht, Willy. "Einleitung." In Schumacher. *Reden*. Pp. 31–199.

————. *Der Sozialistische Deutsche Studentenbund*. Bonn, 1994.

————. "'Unter den Talaren …' Studentenbewegung und Sozialdemokratie bis 1968." In *Partei*, edited by Dowe. Pp. 59–80.

————.ed. *Kurt Schumacher als deutscher und europäischer Sozialist*. Bonn, 1988.

Alexandre, Philippe. *L'Adversaire du Général: Gaston Defferre*. Paris, 1964.

Ammerlaan, Robbert. *Het verschijnsel Schmelzer: Uit het dagboek van een politieke teckel*. Leiden, 1973.

Amoyal, Jacques. "Les Origines socialistes et syndicalistes de la planification en France." *Le Mouvement social*. No. 87 (1974), 137–69.

Andeweg, Rudy B. *Dutch Voters Adrift: On Explanations of Electoral Change 1963–1977*. Leiden, 1982.

———— et al. eds. *Politiek in Nederland*. Alphen a.d. Rijn, 1981.

Antoni, Michael G.M. *Sozialdemokratie und Grundgesetz. Band I: Verfassungspolitische Vorstellungen der SPD von den Anfängen bis zur Konstituierung des Parlamentarischen Rates 1948*. Berlin, 1991.

Appelius, Stefan. *Pazifismus in Westdeutschland: Die Deutsche Friedensgesellschaft, 1945–1968*. Aix la Chapelle, 1991. 2 vols.

Ardagh, John. *The New French Revolution: A Social and Economic Survey of France, 1945–1967*. London, 1968.

Arend, Peter. *Die innerparteiliche Entwicklung der SPD 1966–1975*. Bonn, 1975.

Arndt Arnold et al. eds. *Konkretionen politischer Theorie und Praxis: Festschrift für Carlo Schmid*. Stuttgart, 1972.

Aron, Raymond. "Esquisse historique d'une grande querelle idéologique." In *CED*, edited by Aron and Lerner. Pp. 1–19.

———— and Daniel Lerner. eds. *La querelle de la CED: Essai d'analyse sociologique*. Paris, 1968.

Aron, Robert. *Le Socialisme français face au Marxisme*. Paris, 1971.

Ashkenasi, Abraham. *Reformpartei und Aussenpolitik: Die Aussenpolitik der SPD* Cologne, 1968.

Audry, Colette. *Léon Blum ou la politique du juste*. Paris, 1955.

Auerbach, Hellmuth. "Die europäische Wende der französischen Deutschlandpolitik 1947/48." In *EWG*, edited by Herbst. Pp. 577–91.

————. "Die politischen Anfänge Carlo Schmids." *Vierteljahrshefte für Zeitgeschichte*. 36 (1988), 595–648.

Baardewijk, Frans van. "De PvdA van het koninkrijk 1945–1947." In *Tweede jaarboek*, edited by Bank. Pp. 164–212.

Baerwaldt, Helmut. *Das Ostbüro der SPD, 1946–1971: Kampf und Niedergang*. Krefeld, 1991.

Bahr, Egon. *Sicherheit für und vor Deutschland*. Munich, 1991.

Baker, Donald. *Revolutionism in the French Socialist Party.…* Ph.D. Diss. Stanford University, 1965.

————. "Two Paths to Socialism: Marcel Déat and Marceau Pivert." *Journal of Contemporary History*. 11 (1976), 107–28.

Bakvis, Herman. *Catholic Power in The Netherlands*. Kingston, Canada, 1981.

Bank, Jan. "Drees en de Indonesische revolutie." In *Drees*, edited by Daalder. Pp. 109–36.

————. *Katholieken en de Indonesische revolutie*. Baarn, 1983.

———— *Opkomst en ondergang van de Nederlandse Volksbeweging (NVB)*. Deventer, 1978.

————. et al. "Profiel: Jacques de Kadt." In *Eerste jaarboek*, edited by Bank et al. Pp. 283–338.

————. *Stuuf Wiardi Beckman: Partriciër en sociaal-democraat*. Amsterdam, 1987.

————. "De theorie van de vernieuwing en de praktijk van de wederopbouw: Het Nederlandse socialisme in de tweede helft van de jaren veertig." In *Dienst*, edited by Bank, Pp. 98–121.

———— et al. eds. *In dienst van het gehele volk: De Westeuropese sociaal-democratie tussen aanpassing en vernieuwing, 1945–1950*. Amsterdam, 1987.

———— et al. eds. *Het eerste jaarboek voor het democratisch socialisme*. Amsterdam, 1979.

———— et al. eds. *Het tweede jaarboek voor het democratisch socialisme*. Amsterdam, 1980.

———— et al. eds. *Het vierde jaarboek voor het democratisch socialisme*. Amsterdam, 1983.

———— and Stef Temming. eds. *Van brede visie tot smalle marge: acht prominente socialisten over de SDAP en de PvdA*. Alphen a.d. Rijn, 1981.

———— et al. eds. *Het zesde jaarboek voor het democratisch socialisme*. Amsterdam, 1985.

Banning, Willem et al. *Hedendaagse Waardering van Karl Marx*. Amsterdam, 1950.

Baring, Arnulf. *Machtwechsel: Die Ära Brandt-Scheel*. 3rd. ed.Stuttgart, 1982.

Barsalou, Joseph. *La Mal-Aime: Histoire de la IVe Rpublique*. Paris, 1964.

Becker, Josef and Andreas Hillgruber. eds. *Die deutsche Frage im 19. und 20. Jahrhundert*. Munich, 1983.

————, ed. *Die Kapitulation von 1945 und der Neubeginn in Deutschland*. Cologne, 1987.

———— and Franz Knipping. eds. *Power in Europe? Great Britain, France, Italy, and Germany in a Postwar World, 1945–1950*. Berlin, 1986.

Becker, Jean-Jacques. "Paul Ramadier et l'année 1947." In *Ramadier*, edited by Berstein et al. Pp. 221–37.

Becker, Winfried. "Die Entwicklung der Parteien im Saarland 1945–1955 nach französischen Quellen." In *Saar*, edited by Hudemann. Pp. 253–96.

Bédarida, François and Jean-Pierre Rioux. *Pierre Mendès-France et le mendèsisme: L'expérience gouvernementale (1954–1955) et sa postérité*. Paris, 1985.

Bell, Daniel. *The End of Ideology: On the Exhaustion of Political Ideas in the Fifties*. 2nd ed. Glencoe, IL, 1962.

———— and Byron Criddle. *The French Communist Party in the Fifth Republic*. New York, 1994.

———— and Byron Criddle. *The French Socialist Party: The Emergence of a Party of Government*. 2nd ed. New York, 1988.

Bell, David S. ed. *Contemporary French Political Parties*. New York, 1982.

Bellers, Jürgen. "The German Social Democratic Party, II." In *Parties*, edited by Griffith. Pp. 78–89.

————. *Reformpolitik und EWG-Strategie der SPD: Die innen- und außpolitischen Faktoren der europapolitischen Integrationswilligkeit einer Oppositionspartei (1957–1963)*. Munich, 1979.

Benz, Wolfgang. "Konzeption für die Nachkriegsdemokratie: Pläne und Überlegungen im Widerstand, im Exil und in der Besatzungszeit." In *Zukunftspläne*, edited by Koebner, Pp. 201–13.

————. "Kurt Schumachers Europakonzeption." In *EWG*, edited by Herbst. Pp. 47–61.

————."Kurt Schumacher als deutscher und europäischer Sozialist." In *Schumacher-Europa*, edited by Albrecht. Pp. 15–37.

———— and Hermann Graml. eds. *Aspekte deutscher Aussenpolitik im 20. Jahrhundert: Aufsätze Hans Rothfels zum Gedächtnis*. Stuttgart, 1976.

Berg, J.Th.J. van den. "Democratische hervormingen, politieke machtsverhoudingen en coalitievorming in Nederland." *Acta Politica*. (21 July, 1986), pp. 265–90.

————. "Het miskende tijdvak: De eerste twintig jaar van de Partij van de Arbeid." In *Zevende jaarboek.* edited by Krops et al. Pp. 14–43.

Berger, Wilhelm and Carl Hinrichs. eds. *Zur Geschichte und Problematik der Demokratie: Festgabe für Hans Herzfeld.* Berlin, 1958.

Berghahn, Volker R. *The Americanisation of West German Industry. 1945–1973.* Cambridge, 1986.

Bergounioux, Alain. "Guy Mollet et la Rupture du Tripartisme." In *Mollet,* edited by Ménager. Pp. 381–400.

————. "Le Néo-socialisme, Marcel Déat: Réformisme traditionnel ou esprit des années trente." *Revue historique.* 259 (1978), 389–412.

Bernstein, Eduard. *Die Voraussetzungen des Sozialismus und die Aufgaben der Sozialdemokratie.* Stuttgart, 1899.

Berstein, Serge and Pierre Milza. "Les forces politiques françaises entre l'humiliation et la volonté de grandeur." *Relations internationales.* No. 57 (1989), 7–24.

Berstein, Serge. "French Power as Seen by the Political Parties after World War II." In *Power,* edited by Becker. Pp. 163–83.

————. "Le Gouvernement Pierre Mendès-France et les partis." In *PMF,* edited by Bédarida. Pp. 110–19.

———— et al. eds. *Paul Ramadier: La République et le Socialisme.* Brussels, 1990.

Beus, J.W. de et al. eds. *De ideologische driehoek: Nederlandse politiek in historisch perspectief.* Meppel, 1989.

Birke, Adolf M. "Grossbritannien und der Parlamentarische Rat." *Vierteljahrshefte für Zeitgeschichte.* 42 (1994), 313–59.

Bjøl, Erling. *La France devant l'Europe: La politique européenne de la IVe République.* Copenhagen, 1966.

Bleich, Anet. *Een partij in de tijd: Veertig jaar Partij van de Arbeid. 1946–1986.* Amsterdam, 1986.

Bloemgarten, Salvador. *Henri Polak, Sociaal democraat, 1868–1943.* The Hague, 1993.

Blom, J.C.H. *Burgerlijk en Beheerst.* Amsterdam, 1996.

————. *Crisis, Bezetting en Herstel: Tien studies over Nederland 1930–1950.* The Hague, 1989.

————. "Jaren van tucht en ascese: Enige beschouwingen over de stemming in Herrijzend Nederland (1945–1950)." *Bijdragen en Mededelingen betreffende de Geschiedenis der Nederlanden.* 96 (1981), 300–33.

————. "'De Jaren Vijftig' en 'De Jaren Zestig'?" *Bijdragen en Mededelingen betreffende de Geschiedenis der Nederlanden.* 112 (1997), 518–28.

————. "De Tweede Wereldoorlog en de Nederlandse samenleving: Continuïteit en verandering." In *Verleden,* edited by Wels. Pp. 336–57.

———— and G.N. v.d. Plaat. eds. *Wederopbouw, Welvaart en Onrust: Nederland in de jaren vijftig en zestig.* Houten, 1986.

Blum, Léon. *À L'Échelle humaine.* Paris, 1945.

Blum, Reinhard. *Soziale Marktwirtschaft.* Tübingen, 1969.

Bodard, Lucien. *La Guerre d'Indochine.* Paris, 1972–73. 4 vols.

Böhl, Herman de Liagre et al. *Nederland industrialiseert! Politieke en ideologische strijd rondom het naoorlogse industrialisatiebeleid, 1945–1955.* Nijmegen, 1981.

Bogaarts, M. "'Land in zicht?'" In *Politieke Opstellen,* edited by Centrum voor Parlementaire Geschiedenis. Nijmegen, 1982.1:1–19.

Boivin, Bertus et al. *Een verjongingskuur voor der PvdA: Opkomst, ontwikkeling en betekenis van Nieuw Links.* Deventer, 1978.

Boll, Friedhelm. "Hitler-Jugend und skeptische Generation: Sozialdemokratie und Jugend nach 1945." In *Partei,* edited by Dowe. Pp. 33–57.

Borella, François. *Les partis politiques dans la France d'aujourd'hui*. 4th ed. Paris, 1981.

Borsdorf, Ulrich. "In Kauf genommen: Der Marshall-Plan und die Zweiteilung der Einheitsgewerkschaft in Deutschland." In *Marshall-Plan*, edited by Haberl and Niethammer. Pp. 194–211.

Borzeix, Jean Marie. *Mitterrand lui-même*. Paris, 1973.

Bosch, Michael and Wolfgang Niess. eds. *Der Widerstand im deutschen Südwesten*. Stuttgart, 1982.

Bosmans, J. "'Beide er in en geen van beide er uit': De rooms-rode samenwerking 1945–1952, continuïteit of discontinuïteit?" In *Nederland*, edited by Klein and Plaat. Pp. 29–54.

———. "Historische twijfel aan de 'uiterste noodzaak.' De onzin van Daudt." *Acta Politica*. 22 (1987), 227–33 and 250–51.

———. "Kanttekeningen bij de politieke en parlementaire ontwikkeling van Nederland." In *Wederopbouw*, edited by Blom and Plaat. Pp. 37–61.

Bosscher, Doeko F.J. "De Partei van de Arbeid en het buitenlands beleid 1945–1973." *Bijdragen en Mededelingen betreffende de Geschiedenis der Nederlanden*. 101 (1986), 38–51.

———. "Die Rekonstruktion des Parteiensystems in den Niederlanden zwischen 1945 und 1952." In *Tradition*, edited by Lademacher. Pp. 89–105.

Bossuat, G. "Guy Mollet: La puissance française autrement." *Relations internationales*. No. 57 (1989), 25–48.

———. "Paul Ramadier et le Plan Marshall." In *Ramadier*, edited by Berstein. Pp. 239–57.

Bottenburg, Maarten van. *"Aan de Arbeid": In de wandelgangen van de Stichting van de Arbeid, 1945–1995*. Amsterdam, 1995.

Boumans, Frans et al. *De PvdA en haar streven nar de verzorgingsstaat ... 1945–1959*. [Amsterdam, 1984].

Bouvier, Beatrix W. "Auf der Woge des Zeitgeistes: Die SPD seit den sechziger Jahren." In *Partei*, edited by Dowe. Pp. 81–99.

———. "Die SPD und Charles de Gaulle in den sechziger Jahren." In *De Gaulle*, edited by Loth and Picht. Pp. 109–20.

———. *Zwischen Godesberg und Großer Koalition: Der Weg der SPD in die Regierungsverantwortung*. Bonn, 1990.

Braun, Hans. "Helmut Schelskys Konzept einer 'nivellierten Mittelstandsgesellschaft': Würdigung und Kritik." *Archiv für Sozialgeschichte*. 29 (1989), 199–223.

Braunthal, Julius. *Geschichte der Internationale*. Hanover, 1971–74. 3 vols.

———. ed. *Sozialistische Weltstimmen*. Berlin, 1958.

Bracher, Karl Dietrich et. al. *Geschichte der Bundesrepublik Deutschland*. Stuttgart, 1981–83. 5 vols.

Brehm, Thomas. *SPD und Katholizismus 1957 bis 1966*. Frankfurt a.M., 1989.

Breitman, Richard. *German Socialism and Weimar Democracy*. Chapel Hill, NC, 1981.

Brender, Reinhold. *Kollaboration im Zweiten Weltkrieg: Marcel Déat und das Rassemblement national populaire*. Munich, 1992.

Brink, Eddy van den et al. *De PvdA is niet heilig*. Baarn, 1978.

Brinkman, Maarten. "Drees en de Partij van de Arbeid." In *Drees*, edited by Daalder. Pp. 57–94.

Broszat, Martin. et al. eds. *Von Stalingrad zur Währungsreform: Zur Sozialgeschichte des Umbruchs in Deutschland*. 3rd. ed. Munich, 1990.

———. ed. *Zäsuren nach 1945: Essays zur Periodisierung der deutschen Nachkriegs-geschichte*. Munich, 1990.

Bruclain, Claude. *Le socialisme et l'Europe*. Paris, 1965.

Brugmans, Hendrick Jr. *Denis de Rougement en het Franse personalisme*. The Hague, 1946.

Brunet, Jean-Paul. "La Politique économique et sociale du gouvernement Guy Mollet." In *Mollet*, edited by Ménager. Pp. 413–43.

Brunn, Gerhard. "'Jungtürken' an die Macht: Die sozialiberalen Koalitionen von 1956 und 1966 in Düsseldorf." In *NRW*, edited by Brunn. Pp. 123–36.

———, ed. *Neuland: Nordrhein-Westfalen und seine Anfänge nach 1945/46*. Essen, 1986.

Brusse, Wendy Asbeek. "The Dutch Socialist Party." In *Parties*, edited by Griffiths. Pp. 106–34.

Buchholz, Marlis and Bernd Rother. "Einleitung." In *Sopade 33–40*, edited by Behnken et al. Pp. XIII–IL [*sic*].

Buczylowski, Ulrich. *Kurt Schumacher und die deutsche Frage: Sicherheitspolitik und strategische Offensivkonzeption vom August 1950 bis September 1951*. Stuttgart-Degerloch, 1973.

Bührer, Werner. "Die französische Ruhrpolitik und das Comeback der west-deutschen Industriellen 1945–1952." In *Franzosen*, edited by Hüttenberger and Molitor. Pp. 27–46.

Buschfort, Wolfgang. *Das Ostbüro der SPD*. Munich, 1991.

Buttlar, Walrab von. *Ziele und Zielkonflikte der sowjetischen Deutschlandpolitik 1945–1947*. Stuttgart, 1980.

Cahn, Jean Paul. "Einige Bemerkungen zum Thema Kurt Schumacher und Frankreich." In *Schumacher-Europa*, edited by Albrecht. Pp. 113–31.

———. *Le Parti Social-Democrate Allemand (SPD) et la France, 1954–58*. Diss. Univ. Strasbourg, 1993. 2 vols. Published as a monograph. Bern, 1996.

———. "Le SPD et la Communauté Européenne de Défense (CED): Quelques aspects du problème." *Revue Allemagne* (1987), 379–98.

Campen, Samuel I.P. van. *The Quest for Security: Some Aspects of Netherlands For-eign Policy, 1945–1950*. The Hague, 1958.

Carmoy, Guy de. *Les politiques etrangères de la France*. Paris, 1967.

Centraal Bureau Statistiek. *Statistiek der Verkiezingen*. The Hague, 1946ff.

Centre Nationale de la Recherche Scientifique. ed. *La Libération de la France: Actes du Colloque international … 1974*. Paris, 1976.

Cépède, Frédéric. "Les statuts des tendances dans le Parti Socialiste, 1905–1969." *Cahiers et Revue de L'Ours*. No. 2. (1994), 1–5.

Chapsal, Jacques. *La vie politique en France depuis 1940*. 2nd. ed. Paris, 1969.

Charlot, Jean. *Le Gaullisme d'Opposition, 1946–1958*. Paris, 1983.

Christadler, Marieluise, ed. *Die geteilte Utopie: Sozialisten in Frankreich und Deutschland*. Opladen, 1985.

Claeys-van Haegendoren, Mieke. *Hendrik de Man*. Utrecht, 1972.

Cohen, Henrik F. *Om de Vernieuwing van het Socialisme: De Politieke Orientatie van de Nederlandse Sociaal-Democratie 1919–1930*. Leiden, 1974.

Cohen, Stephen S. *Modern Capitalist Planning: The French Model*. London, 1969.

Cohen, T. *Socialisten in Europa: De samenwerking van de socialistische partijen in het kader van de Europese Gemeenschap, 1952–1972*. Amsterdam, 1974.

Cointet, Jean-Paul. "Guy Mollet, la SFIO et l'arrivée au pouvoir du Général de Gaulle." In *Mollet*, edited by Ménager. Pp. 335–47.

Colton, Joel. *Léon Blum: Humanism in Politics*. New York, 1965.

Conze, Werner and Rainer Lepsius. eds. *Sozialgeschichte der Bundesrepublik Deutschland.* Stuttgart, 1983.

Couwenberg, Servatius Willem. "Christentum und moderner Sozialismus in den Niederlanden." In *Katholizismus,* edited by Langner. Pp. 155–82.

———. *Modern socialisme: Achtergrond, ontwikkeling, perspectief.* Alphen a.d.Rhijn, 1972.

———. *Naar nieuwe politieke verhoudingen.* Bilthoven, 1967.

———. "De ondergang van de brede basis." *Katholiek Staatkundig Maandschrift* 13 (1959), 121–31, and 188–93.

Cox, A. ed. *Politics, Policy, and the European Recession.* New York, 1982.

Criddle, Byron. "France: Legitimacy Attained." In *Opposition,* edited by Kolinsky. Pp. 116–36.

———. *Socialists and European Integration: A Study of the French Socialist Party.* New York, 1969.

Criqui, Jean-Claude. "Der französische Sozialismus." In *Katholizismus,* edited by Langner. Pp. 91–134.

Czernetz, K. et al. *Orientation Socialism Today and Tomorrow.* Amsterdam, 1960.

Czerwick, Edwin. *Oppositionstheorien und Aussenpolitik: Eine Analyse sozialdemokratischer Deutschlandpolitik 1955 bis 1966.* Königstein, 1981.

Daalder, Hans. "Parties, Elites, and Political Development in Western Europe." In *Parties,* edited by La Palombara et al. Pp. 43–77.

———. "Parties and Politics in the Netherlands." *Political Studie.* 3 (1965). 1–16.

———. "Polarisatie: 'Een zaak van Taktiek en Strategie.'" In Daalder. *Politiek.* Pp. 193–202.

———. *Politiek en Historie: Opstellen over Nederlandse Politiek en Vergelijkende Politieke Wetenschap.* Ed. J.Th.J. van den Berg and B.A.G.M. Tromp. Amsterdam, 1990.

———. "Zestig jaar Nederland." In Daalder. *Politiek.* pp. 203–58.

——— and Peter Mair, eds. *Party Systems in Denmark, Austria, Switzerland, The Netherlands, and Belgium.* New York, 1987.

——— and N. Cramer, eds. *Willem Drees.* Houten, 1988.

Dahrendorf, Ralf. *Die Chancen der Krise: Über die Zukunft des Liberalismus.* Stuttgart, 1983.

———. *Gesellschaft und Demokratie in Deutschland.* Munich, 1966.

Dam, M. van and J. Beishuizen. *Kijk op de kiezer: Feiten …Utrecht 15 februari 1967.* Amsterdam, 1967.

Dankelmann, Otfried, ed. *Lebensbilder europäischer Sozialdemokraten des 20. Jahrhunderts.* Vienna, 1995.

Daudt, H. *Coalitievorming in de na-oorlogse Nederlandse politiek.* Amsterdam, 1985.

———. "De ontwikkeling van de politieke machtsverhoudingen in Nederland sinds 1945." In *Nederland,* edited by Kooy. Pp. 178–97.

Dell, Edmund. *Schuman Plan and the British Abdication of Leadership in Europe.* New York, 1995.

Détraz, Albert. "L'ouvrier consommateur." In *Comportements,* edited by Hamon. Pp. 181–87.

Deugd, Henk. *Tussen doorbraak en reklame: de PvdA verkiezingscampagnes van 1956 tot 1967.* Rotterdam, 1988.

Dexheimer, Wolfgang F. *Koalitionsverhandlungen in Bonn: 1961–1965–1969.* Bonn, 1973.

Dietzfelbinger, Eckart. *Die westdeutsche Friedensbewegung, 1948 bis 1955.* Cologne, 1984.

Dijk, Jos van ed. *Nieuw Links in de PvdA.* Amersfoort, 1969.

Doel, Hans van den. *Het biefstuk socialisme en economie*. Utrecht, 1978.

———— et al. *Tien over rood: Uitdaging van Nieuw Links aan de PvdA*. Amsterdam, 1966.

Doering-Manteuffel, Anselm. "Deutsche Zeitgeschichte nach 1945: Entwicklung und Problemlagen der historischen Forschung zur Nachkriegszeit." *Vierteljahrshefte für Zeitgeschichte*. 41 (1993). 1–29.

Dogan, Mattei. "Les clivages politiques de la classe ouvrière." In *Comportements*, edited by Hamon. Pp. 101–27.

————. "L'Origine sociale du personnel parlementaire français élu en 1951." In *Partis*, edited by Duverger. Pp. 291–328.

————. "Le vote ouvrier en Europe occidentale." *Revue française de Sociologie*. 1 (1960), 25–44.

Doorn, J.A.A. van. "Corporatisme en technocratie — Een verwaardloosde polariteit in de Nederlandse politiek." *Beleid en Maatschappij* 8 (1981), 134–149.

Dowe, Dieter ed. *Partei und soziale Bewegung: Kritische Beiträge zur Entwicklung der SPD seit 1945*. Bonn, 1993.

Drees, Willem. "Polarisatie, een mode-begrip dat niets oplost." *Accent* (19 June 1971), pp. 11–14.

Dreyfus, François G. *Histoire des Gauches en France, 1940–1974*. Paris, 1975.

————. *Réformisme et révisionisme dans les socialismes allemand, autrichien, et français*. Paris, 1984.

————. "Die SPD und die Deutsche Demokratische Republik 1949–1989." In *Deutschland und Europa*, edited by Timmermann. Pp. 507–33.

Droz, Jacques et al. *Histoire Générale du Socialisme*. Paris, 1978. 4 vols.

Droz, Jacques. "Historiographie d'un siècle de la Social Democratie allemande." *Le mouvement social*. No. 95 (1976), 3–23.

Drummond, Gordon D. *The German Social Democrats in Opposition, 1949–1960: The Case Against Rearmament*. Norman, OK, 1982.

Duchene, François. *Jean Monnet: The First Statesman of Interdependence*. New York, 1994.

Dunk, Herman W. von der. "Tussen welvaart en onrust: Nederland van 1955 tot 1973." *Bijdragen en Mededelingen betreffende de Geschiedenis der Nederlanden*. 101 (1986), 2–20.

———— and Horst Lademacher. eds. *Auf dem Weg zum modernen Parteienstaat: Zur Entstehung, Organisation und Struktur politischer Parteien in Deutschland und den Niederlanden*. Melsungen, 1986.

Duroselle, Jean-Baptiste. "Changes in French Foreign Policy since 1945." In *Search*, edited by Hoffmann. Pp. 305–58.

Duverger, Maurice. *Political Parties*. Translated by Barbara and Robert North. London, 1964.

————, "SFIO: mort ou transfiguration?" *Les Temps Modernes*. 10 (numéro spécial, 1955), 1863–1885.

————. ed. *Partis politiques et classes sociales*. Paris, 1955.

Duynstee, F.J.F.M. *De Kabinetsformatie 1945–1965*. Deventer, 1966.

Earle, Edward M. *Modern France: Problems of the Third and Fourth Republics* Princeton, NJ, 1951.

Eckert, Georg." Auf dem Weg nach Godesberg: Erinnerungen an die Kulturkonferenz der SPD in Ziegenhain," In *Freiheit*, edited by Flohr et al. Pp. 49–58.

Edinger, Lewis J. *German Exile Politics* Berkeley, CA, 1956.

———— *Kurt Schumacher: A Study in Personality and Political Behavior* Stanford, CA, 1965.

Ehni, Hans-Peter. "Die Reaktion der SPD auf den Marshall-Plan," In *Marshall-Plan*, edited by Haberl and Niethammer. Pp. 217–30.

———. "Sozialistische Neubauforderung und Proklamation des 'Dritten Weges,'" *Archiv für Sozialgeschichte*, 13 (1973), 139–90.

Eldersveld, Samuel et al. *Elite Images of Dutch Politics* Ann Arbor, MI, 1981.

Elgey, Georgette. *Histoire de la IVe République, 1945–1958*. Paris, 1965 and 1968. 2 vols.

Eppler, Erhard. "Das linke Leiden an der Wirklichkeit." *Die Zeit* (24 May 1991).

Eschenburg, Theodor. "Regierung, Bürokratie und Parteien, 1945–1949," *Vierteljahrshefte für Zeitgeschichte*, 24 (1976), 58–74.

Esterik, Chris van and Joop van Tijn. *Jaap Burger: Een leven lang dwars*. Amsterdam, 1984.

Euchner, Walter, ed. *Politische Oposition in Deutschland und im internationalen Vergleich*. Götttingen, 1993.

Faas, Henry. *God, Nederland en de franje: Necrologie van het Nederlandse partijwezen*. Utrecht, 1967.

Falter, Jürgen. "Alte und neue Parteiorientierungen — Die Bundestagswahl 1949 zwischen Kontinuität und Neubeginn," In *Wie neu*, edited by Holtmann. Pp. 50–69.

Farthmann, Friedhelm. *Blick voraus im Zorn: Aufruf zu einem radikalen Neubeginn der SPD*, 2nd. ed. Düsseldorf, 1996.

Fassen, Sjoerd van. "Ten koste van de helderheid: De overgang van de 'Socialistische Gids' tot 'Socialisme en Democratie' 1938," In *Tweede jaarboek*, edited by Bank et al. Pp. 149–62.

Faucher, Jean-André. *Les Clubs Politiques en France*. Paris, 1965.

———. *13è mai 1958 - 13è mai 1968: La gauche française sous de Gaulle*. Paris, 1969.

Fauvet, Jacques. "Naissance et mort d'un 'traité,'" In *CED*, edited by Aron. Pp. 23–87.

Fetscher, Iring, "Jean Jaurès," In *Konkretionen*, edited by Arndt. Pp. 62–80.

Fischer, Alexander et al. *Die Deutschland-Frage und die Anfänge des Ost-West-Konflikts, 1945–1949*. Berlin, 1984.

Fischer, Per. *Die Saar zwischen Deutschland und Frankreich*. Frankfurt a.M., 1959.

Fischer, Peter, "Die Bundesrepublik und das Projekt einer Europäischen Politischen Gemeinschaft," In *EWG*, edited by Herbst. Pp. 279–99.

Flechtheim, Ossip K. "Die Anpassung der SPD: 1914, 1933 und 1959." *Kölner Zeitschrift für Soziologie und Sozialpsychologie*, 17 (1965), 584–604.

Flohr, Heiner et al., eds. *Freiheitlicher Sozialismus*. 2nd. ed. Bonn-Bad Godesberg, 1973.

Foelz-Schroeter, Marie Elise. *Föderalistische Politik und nationale Repräsentation 1945 bis 1947*. Stuttgart, 1974.

Först, Walter, ed. *Zwischen Ruhrkontrolle und Mitbestimmung*. Cologne, 1982.

Foerster, Roland G. "Innenpolitische Aspekte der Sicherheit Deutschlands 1947–1950." In *Anfänge*, edited by Köllner et al. Pp. 1:403–575.

Foitzik, Jan. "Revolution und Demokratie. Zu den Sofort- und Übergangsplanungen des sozialdemokratischen Exils für Deutschland 1943–1945." *Internationale Wissenschaftliche Korrespondenz*. 24 (1988), 308–42.

Foret, Françoise. "La reconstruction du SPD après la Deuxième Guerre Mondial." *Le mouvement social*. No. 95 (1976), 117–45.

Fortuyn, Pim. *Sociaal-economische politiek in Nederland, 1945–49*. Alphen a.d. Rhijn, 1981.

Foschepoth, Josef and Rolf Steininger, eds. *Die Britische Deutschland- und Besatzungspolitik, 1945–1949*. Paderborn, 1985.

Foschepoth, Josef. "Grossbritannien und die Deutschlandfrage auf den Außen-ministerkonferenzen 1946/47." In *Britische Deutschlandpolitik*, edited by Foschepoth and Steininger. Pp. 65–85.

———, ed. *Kalter Krieg und deutsche Frage: Deutschland im Widerstreit der Mächte 1945–52*. Göttingen, 1985.

Foster, Karl, ed. *Christentum und Demokratischer Sozialismus*. Munich, 1958.

Freudenhammer, Alfred and Karlheinz Vater. *Herbert Wehner*. Munich, 1978.

Friedrich, Manfred. "Parlamentarische Opposition in der Bundesrepublik Deutschland: Wandel und Konstanz." In *Opposition*, edited by Oberreuter. Pp. 230–65.

Fritsch-Bournazel, Renata. "Frankreich und die deutsche Frage 1945–1949." In *Deutschlandfrage*, edited by Fischer. Pp. 85–95.

———. "Mourir pour Berlin? Die Wandlungen der französischen Ost- und Deutschlandpolitik während der Blockade 1948/49." *Vierteljahrshefte für Zeitgeschichte*. 35 (1987), 171–92.

———. "Die Wende in der französischen Nachkriegspolitik, 1945–1949." In *Französische Deutschlandpolitik*, edited by Institut. Pp. 1–25.

Fuzier, Claude. "J'ai été élu fédéral sur une ligne anti-pivertiste ...," *Cahier et Revue de l'Ours* (no. 2, 1994), 87–92.

Gabbe, Jörg. *Parteien und Nation: Zur Rolle des Nationalbewußtseins für die politischen Grundorientierungen der Parteien in der Anfangsphase der Bundesrepublik*. Meisenheim, 1976.

Gacon, Jean. *1944–1958: Quatrième République*. Paris, 1987.

Galan, C. de. "Om de kwaliteit van het bestaan," In *Socialisme*, edited by Peper. Pp. 61–68.

Galen, John Jansen van et al., eds. *"Het moet, het kan! Op voor het Plan!" Vijftig jaar Plan van de Arbeid*. Amsterdam, 1985.

Gaus, Günther. "Herbert Wehner und der Bonner Parlamentarismus," In *Wehner*, edited by Jahn. Pp. 146–55.

Geismann, Georg. *Politische Struktur und Regierungssystem in den Niederlanden*. Frankfurt a.M., 1964.

Giesbert, Franz-Olivier. *François Mitterrand ou la tentation de l'histoire*. Paris, 1977.

Gillingham, John. *Coal, Steel and the Rebirth of Europe, 1945–1955: The Germans and French from Ruhr Conflict to Economic Community*. New York, 1991.

Gimbel, John. *The American Occupation of Germany: Politics and the Military, 1945–1949*. Stanford, 1968.

———. "Byrnes' Stuttgarter Rede und die amerikanische Nachkriegspolitik in Deutschland," *Vierteljahrshefte für Zeitgeschichte*, 20 (1972), 39–62.

———. "Die Entstehung des Marshall-Plans." In *Marshall-Plan*, edited by Haberl and Niethammer. Pp. 25–35.

Girardet, Raoul. *L'idée coloniale en France de 1871 à 1962*. Paris, 1972.

Giraud, Henri-Christian. *De Gaulle et les Communistes*. Paris, 1988, 2 vols.

Girault, Réné. "The French Decision-Makers and their Perception of French Power in 1948." In *Power*, edited by Becker. Pp. 47–65.

———. "Der kulturelle Hintergrund der französischen Integrationspolitik." In *EWG*, edited by Herbst et al. Pp. 561–76.

Gladdish, Ken. *Governing from the Center: Politics and Policy-Making in The Netherlands*. De Kalb, IL, 1991.

Glasneck, Johannes. "Hendrik de Man 1885–1933," In *Lebensbilder*, edited by Dankelmann. Pp. 331–41.

Godson, Roy. *American Labor and European Politics: The AFL as a Transnational Force*. New York, 1976.

Goes, Marinus van der van Naters. "Het 'nieuwe bestand' en de grote conflicties (1945–1950)." In *Visie*, edited by Bank. Pp. 120–32.

Goguel, François and Alfred Grosser. *La Politique en France* Paris. 1969.

Gombin, Richard. *Les Origins du Gauchisme* Paris. 1971.

———. "Socialisme français et politique étrangère. "*Études internationales*. 2 (1971), 395–409.

———. *Les socialistes et la guerre: La SFIO et la politique étrangère française entre les deux guerres mondiales*. Paris, 1970.

Gorschenek, Günter, ed. *Katholiken und ihre Kirche in der Bundesrepublik Deutschland* Munich. 1976.

Gosewinkel, Dieter. *Adolf Arndt: Die Wiedergründung des Rechtsstaats aus dem Geist der Sozialdemokratie 1945–1961*. Bonn, 1991.

Grabbe, Hans-Jürgen. "Die deutsch-alliierte Kontroverse um den Grundgesetzgentwurf im Frühjahr 1949." *Vierteljahrshefte für Zeitgeschichte*. 26 (1978), 393–418.

———. *Unionsparteien, Sozialdemokratie und Vereinigte Staaten von Amerika 1945–46*. Düsseldorf, 1983.

Graham, Bruce Desmond. *Choice and Democratic Order: The French Socialist Party, 1937–1950*. New York, 1994.

———. *The French Socialists and Tripartisme, 1944–1947* Toronto, 1965.

———. "The Play of Tendencies: Internal Politics in the SFIO Before and After the Second World War. " In *Contemporary,*edited by Bell. Pp. 38–64.

Graml, Hermann. "Die Legende von der verpassten Gelegenheit: Zur sowjetischen Notenkampagne des Jahres 1952." *Vierteljahrshefte für Zeitgeschichte* 29 (1981), 307–341.

Grebing, Helga. "Demokratie ohne Demokraten? Politisches Denken, Einstellungen und Mentalitäten in der Nachkriegszeit." In *Wie neu*, edited byHoltmann. Ppp. 6–19.

———. *Konservative gegen die Demokratie: Konservative Kritik and der Demokratie in der Bundesrepublik nach 1945*. Frankfurt a.M., 1971.

———. "Politische und soziale Probleme der Arbeiterklasse am Ende des Zweiten Weltkrieges und in der unmittelbaren Nachkriegszei." *Internationale Wissenschaftliche Korrespondenz*. 22 (1986), 1–20.

———. "Der Sozialismus." In *Modernisierung* edited by Schildt and Sywottek. Pp. 646–58.

Griffiths, Richard T. "Between Market and Planning: The Origins of Indicative Planning in The Netherlands, 1945–1951." In *Tradition*, edited byLademacher and Bosmans. Pp. 121–57.

———, ed. *Socialist Parties and the Question of Europe in the 1950s*. Leiden, 1993.

Groh, Dieter. *Negative Integration und revolutionärer Attentismus*. Frankfurt a.M., 1973.

——— and Peter Brandt. *"Vaterlandslose Gesellen": Sozialdemokratie und Nation, 1860–1990*. Munich, 1992.

Grosser, Alfred. *Affaires Extérieures: La Politique de la France 1944–1984*. Paris, 1984.

———. *L'Allemagne de notre temps, 1945–1978*. Paris, 1978.

Grosser, Dieter. "Die Sehnsucht nach Harmonie: Historische und verfassungsstrukturelle Vorbelastungen der Opposition in Deutschland." In *Opposition*, edited by Oberreuter. Pp. 206–29.

Günther, Klaus. "Die andere Meinung in der SPD 1949, 1955/56, 1958/61." *Archiv für Sozialgeschichte*. 13 (1973), 23–52.

———. *Sozialdemokratie und Demokratie 1946–1966*. Bonn, 1979.

Guillen, Pierre. "La France et la négociation du Traité d'Euratom." *Relations internationales*. No. 44 (1985), 391–412.

———. "Frankreichs Europapolitik vom Scheitern der EVG zur Ratifizierung der Verträge von Rom." *Vierteljahrshefte für Zeitgeschichte*. 28 (1980), 1–19.

———. "Frankreich und die NATO-Integration der Bundesrepublik." In *EWG*,edited by Herbst et al. Pp. 427–45.

Haberl, Othmar N. and Lutz Niethammer, eds. *Der Marshall-Plan und die europäische Linke*. Frankfurt a.M., 1986.

Hänsch, Klaus. *Frankreich zwischen Ost und West: Die Reaktion auf den Ausbruch des Ost-Westkonfliktes, 1946–48*. Berlin, 1972.

Hahn, Erich J.C. "The occupying Powers and the Constitutional Reconstruction of West Germany, 1945–1949. In *Grundgesetz*, edited by Junker et al. Pp. 7–35.

Hamon, Leo, ed. *Les nouveaux comportements politiques de la classe ouvrière*. Paris, 1962.

Hanrieder, Wolfram F. *Germany, America, Europe: Forty Years of German Foreign Policy*. New Haven, CT, 1989.

Hansel, Detlef. "Sozialdemokratische Positionen zur Remilitarisierung der BRD 1950–1954/55." *Militärgeschichte*. 29 (1990), 55–63.

Hansen, Erik and Peter A. Prosper. "Political Economy and Political Action: The Programmatic Response of Dutch Social Democracy to the Depression Crisis, 1929–39." *Journal of Contemporary History*. 29 (1994), 129–54.

Harmsen, Ger. *Nederlands Communisme: Gebundelde opstellen*. Nijmegen, 1982.

——— and Bob Reinalda. *Voor de bevrijding van de arbeid: Beknopte geschiedenis van de Nederlandse vakbeweging*. Nijmegen, 1975.

Harsch, Donna. *German Social Democracy and the Rise of Nazism*. Chapel Hill, NC, 1993.

Hartwich, Hans-Hermann. *Sozialstaatspostulat und gesellschaftlicher Status Quo*. Cologne, 1970.

Haupt, Heinz-Gerhard. "Léon Blum." In *Utopie*, edited by Christadler. Pp. 247–56.

Hauth, Ulrich. *Die Politik von KPD und SED gegenüber der westdeutschen Sozialdemokratie 1945–1948*. Frankfurt a.M., 1978.

Heide, Ferdinand J. ter. *"Ordening en verdeling": Besluitvorming over sociaal-economisch beleid in Nederland 1949–1958*. Kampen, 1986.

Heideking, Jürgen et al., eds. *Wege in die Zeitgeschichte: Festschrift zum 65. Geburtstag von Gerhard Schulz*. Berlin, 1989.

Heine, Friedrich. *Dr. Kurt Schumacher*. Göttingen, 1969.

Henke, Klaus-Dietmar "Politik der Widersprüche: Zur Charakteristik der französischen Militärregierung in Deutschland nach dem Zweiten Weltkrieg." *Vierteljahrshefte für Zeitgeschichte*. 30 (1982), 500–37.

Herbst, Ludolf et al., eds. *Vom Marshallplan zur EWG: Die Eingliederung der Bundesrepublik Deutschland in die westliche Welt*. Munich, 1990.

Herbst, Ludolf, ed. *Westdeutschland 1945–1955: Unterwerfung, Kontrolle, Integration*. Munich,1986.

Herf, Jeffrey. "Demokratie auf dem Prüfstand." *Vierteljahrshefte für Zeitgeschichte*. 40 (1992), 1–28.

"Herrijzend Nederland, 1944–1950. [special edition]," *Bijdragen en Mededelingen betreffende de Geschiedenis der Nederlanden*. 96 (1981).

Hess, Jürgen C. and Friso Wielenga." Die Niederlande und die Wiedervereinigung Deutschlands: Ein Beitrag zur Debatte um die 'verpassten Gelegenheiten' im Jahre 1952." *Vierteljahrshefte für Zeitgeschichte*, 35 (1987), 349–84.

Hildebrand, Klaus. *Integration und Souveränität: Die Aussenpolitik der Bundesrepublik Deutschland, 1949–1982*. Bonn, 1991.

Hildebrand, Klaus and Reiner Pommerin, eds. *Deutsche Frage und europäisches Gleichgewicht: Festschrift für Andreas Hillgruber*. Cologne, 1985.

Hillel, Marc. *L'Occupation française en Allemagne, 1945–1955*. Paris, 1983.

Hirsch-Weber, Wolfgang and Klaus Schütz. *Wähler und Gewählte: Eine Untersuchung der Bundestagswahlen 1953*. Berlin, 1957.

Hirscher, Gerhard. *Carlo Schmid und die Gründung der Bundesrepublik: Eine politische Biographie*. Bochum, 1986.

———. *Sozialdemokratische Verfassungspolitik und die Entstehung des Bonner Grundgesetzes*. Bochum, 1989.

Hönemann, Stefan and Markus Moors. *Wer die Wahl hat ...: Bundestagswahlkämpfe seit 1957*. Marburg, 1994.

Hoekstra, D.J., ed. *Partijvernieuwing in politiek Nederland*. Alphen a.d.R., 1968.

Hoffmann, Stanley "The Effects of World War II on French Society and Politics." *French Historical Studies*. 2 (1961), 28–63.

———. "Paradoxes of the French Political Community." In *Search*, edited by Hoffmann. Pp. 1–117.

——— et al. *In Search of France*. Cambridge, MA, 1963.

Hofmann, Jack Paul den Kamp et al. *Ontwapenend: Geschiedenis van 25 jaar PSP, 1957–1982*. Amsterdam, 1982.

Hogan, Michael J. *The Marshall Plan*. New York, 1987.

Hollifield, James F. and George Ross, eds. *Searching for the New France*. New York, 1991.

Holtmann, Everhard." Die neuen Lasselleaner: SPD und HJ-Generation nach 1945." In *Stalingrad*, edited by Broszat et al. Pp. 169–210.

———, ed. *Wie neu war der Neubeginn? Zum deutschen Kontinuitätsproblem nach 1945*. Erlangen, 1989.

Hrbek, Rudolf." The German Social Democratic Party, I." In *Parties*, edited byGriffith. Pp. 63–77.

———. *Die SPD, Deutschland und Europa. Die Haltung der Sozialdemokratie zum Verhältnis von Deutschland-Politik und Westintegration 1945–1957*. Bonn, 1972.

Hudemann, Rainer. "De Gaulle und der Wiederaufbau in der französischen Besatzungszone nach 1945." In *De Gaulle*, edited by Loth and Picht. Pp. 153–67.

———. *Sozialpolitik im deutschen Südwesten zwischen Tradition und Neuordnung, 1945–1953*. Mainz, 1988.

——— "Zentralismus und Dezentralisierung in der französichen Deutschland- und Besatzungspolitik 1945–1947." In *Kapitulation*, edited by Becker. Pp. 181–209.

——— and Raymond Poidevin, eds. *Die Saar 1945–1955: Ein Problem der europäischen Geschichte ...*. Munich, 1992.

Hüser, Judith. "Frankreich und die Abstimmung vom 23. Oktober 1955," In *Saar*, edited by Hudemann and Poidevin. Pp. 359–79.

Hüttenberger, Peter and Hansgeorg Molitor, eds. *Franzosen und Deutsche am Rhein 1789–1918–1945*. Essen, 1989.

Hulst, H. van et al. *Het roode vaandel volgen wij: Geschiedenis van de S.D.A.P. van 1880–1940*. The Hague, 1969.

Hurtig, Christiane. *De la SFIO au nouveau parti socialiste*. Paris, 1970.

Hurwitz, Harold et al. *Die Anfänge des Widerstands*. Cologne, 1990. 2 vols.

Institut Français de Stuttgart, ed. *Die französische Deutschlandpolitik zwischen 1945 und 1949*. Tübingen, 1987.

Institut für Zeitgeschichte, ed. *Nachkriegsgesellschaften im historischen Vergleich.* Munich, 1982.

Irvine, William D. *French Conservatism in Crisis: The Republican Federation of France in the 1930s.* Baton Rouge, LA, 1979.

Jackson, Julian. *The Popular Front in France.* New York, 1987.

Jaffre, Jérme. "Guy Mollet et la conquête de la SFIO en 1946." In *Mollet,* edited by Ménager. Pp. 17–31.

Jahn, Gerhard et al., eds. *Herbert Wehner: Beiträge zu einer Biographie.* Cologne, 1976.

Jansen, J.P. "J.G. Suurhoff (1905–1967): Een levensbericht." In *Eerste jaarboek,* edited by Jan Bank et al. Pp. 242–81.

Jenson, Jane. "The French Left: A Tale of Three Beginnings." In *France,* edited by Hollifield and Ross. Pp. 85–112.

Jesse, Eckhard. *Wahlrecht zwischen Kontinuität und Reform: 1949–1983.* Düsseldorf, 1985.

Jonge, A.A. de. *Het Communisme in Nederland.* The Hague, 1972.

Judt, Tony. *Marxism and the French Left: Studies in Labour and Poltics in France, 1830–1981.* Oxford, 1986.

———. *Past Imperfect: French Intellectuals, 1944–1956.* Berkeley, CA, 1992.

———. *La Reconstruction du Parti Socialiste, 1921–1926.* Paris, 1976.

Junker, Detlef et al., eds. *Cornerstone of Democracy: The West German Grundgesetz, 1949–1989.* Washington, D.C., 1995.

Kaack, Heino. *Geschichte und Struktur des deutschen Parteiensystems.* Opladen, 1971.

Kaden, Albrecht. *Einheit oder Freiheit: Die Wiedergründung der SPD 1945/1946.* 3rd. ed. Bonn, 1990.

Kadt, Jacques de et al. *Afscheid van de PvdA? Van democratie naar volksdemocratie.* Amsterdam, 1969.

Kaelble, Hartmut. *Auf dem Weg zu einer europäischen Gesellschaft: Eine Sozialgeschichte Westeuropas, 1880–1980.* Munich, 1987.

Kahn, Helmut Wolfgang. *Helmut Schmidt: Fallstudie über einen Populären.* Hamburg, 1973.

Kalma, P., ed. *Socialisme en Economische Politiek.* Amsterdam, 1977.

Kaltefleiter, Werner. *Parteien im Umbruch.* Düsseldorf, 1984.

Keizer, Madelon de. *De Gijzelaars van Sint Michielsgestel: Een elite-beraad in oorlogstijd.* Alphen a/d Rijn, 1979.

Kergoat, Jacques. "Marceau Pivert et le pivertisme." *Cahier et Revue de L'Ours.* No. 2 (1994), 67–75.

———. *Marceau Pivert: Socialiste de Gauche.* Paris, 1994.

Kerleroux, Pierre." Introduction." In Auriol. *Journal,* 3:vii–xxvii [*sic*].

Kersten, Albert E. "Niederländische Regierung, Bewaffnung Westdeutschlands und EVG." In *EVG,* edited by Volkmann and Schwengler. Pp. 191–219.

———. "Die Niederlande und die Westintegration der Bundesrepublik." In *EWG,* edited by Herbst et al. Pp. 121–38.

———. "A Welcome Surprise? The Netherlands and the Schuman-Plan Negotiations." In *Anfänge,* edited by Schwabe. Pp. 285–304.

Kessel, Martina. *Westeuropa und die deutsche Teilung: Englische und französische Deutschlandpolitik auf den Aussenministerkonferenzen von 1945 bis 1947.* Munich, 1989.

Kettenacker, Lothar. "Grossbritannien und die zukünftige Kontrolle Deutschlands." In *Britische Deutschlandpolitik,* edited by Foschepoth and Steininger. Pp. 27–46.

Kingma, Roel H. *Nieuw Links in de PvdA: Voorspel, ontwikkeling en confrontatie 1946 1966–1969.* Amsterdam, 1971.

Kirchheimer, Otto. "The Transformation of the Western European Party Systems." In *Parties,* edited by La Palombara and Weiner. Pp. 177–200.

Kittel, Manfred. "Genesis einer Legende: Die Diskussion um die Stalin-Noten in der Bundesrepublik 1952–1958." *Vierteljahrshefte für Zeitgeschichte.* 41 (1993), 355–89.

Kitzinger, Uwe. *German Electoral Politics: A Study of the 1957 Campaign.* Oxford, 1960.

Klein, Hans-Dieter. "Erich Ollenhauer 1901–1963: Jugendfunktionär und Internationalist." In *Lebensbilder,* edited by Dankelmann. Pp. 403–14.

Klein, Jean. "Frankreich und die deutsche Frage," In *Deutschland,* edited by Timmermann. Pp. 143–55.

Klein, P.W. "Wegen naar economisch herstel 1945–1950." In *Herrijzend Nederland,* edited by Klein, and Plaat. Pp. 85–101.

——— and G.N. v.d. Plaat, eds. *Herrijzend Nederland: Opstellen over Nederland in de periode 1945–1950.* The Hague, 1981.

Klink, Dieter. *Die Entwicklung des sozialistischen Denkens von Erfurt 1891 bis Bad Godesberg 1959.* Hamburg, 1960.

Klotzbach, Kurt. "Die deutsche Sozialdemokratie und der Schuman-Plan," In *Anfänge,* edited by Schwabe. Pp. 333–44.

———. "Parteien und Gesellschaft: Zu Tendenzen und Problemen der Parteienforschung nach 1945," *Archiv für Sozialgeschichte.* 13 (1973), 1–21.

———. "SPD und Katholische Kirche nach 1945: Belastungen, Missverständnisse und Neuanfänge." *Archiv für Sozialgeschichte.* 29 (1989), XXXVII–XLVII [*sic*].

———. "Tussen Ideaal en Werkelijkheid: Sociaal-Democraten in een verwoest Duitsland, 1945–1950." In *Dienst,* edited byBank. Pp. 122–46.

———. *Der Weg zur Staatspartei: Programmatik, praktische Politik und Organisation der deutschen Sozialdemokratie 1945 bis 1965.* Bonn, 1982.

Knegtmans, Peter Jan. *Socialisme en Democratie: De SDAP tussen klasse en natie 1929–1939.* Amsterdam, 1989.

Knipping, Franz. "Vichy als Kontinuitätsproblem der französischen Zeitgeschichte." In *Wege,* edited by Heideking et al. Pp. 290–304.

Knorr, Heribert. *Der parlamentarische Entscheidungsprozess während der Grossen Koalition, 1966 bis 1969.* Meisenheim am Glan, 1975.

Kocka, Jürgen, ed. *Angestellte im europäischen Vergleich.* Göttingen, 1981.

Koebner, Thomas et al., eds. *Deutschland nach Hitler: Zukunftspläne im Exil und aus der Besatzungszeit, 1939–1949.* Cologne, 1987.

Köllner, Lutz, et al., eds. *Anfänge westdeutscher Sicherheitspolitik: 1945–1956.* Munich, 1982–93, 3 vols.

Köser, Helmut. *Die Grundsatzdebatte in der SPD von 1945/46 bis 1958/59.* Ph.D. diss. Universität Freiburg, 1971.

———. "Innovationsprozeße in der SPD." *Politische Vierteljahresschrift.* 16 (1975), 29–54.

Kok, Wim. "Het verleden van de Sociaal-Democratie en haar opdracht voor de toekomst," In *Dienst* edited by Bank et al. Pp. 147–57.

Kolinsky, Eva, ed. *Opposition in Western Europe.* New York, 1987.

Koolen, Bernhard. *Die wirtschafts- und gesellschaftspolitische Konzeption von Viktor Agartz zur Neuordnung der westdeutschen Nachkriegsgesellschaft.* Cologne, 1979.

Kooy G.A. et al., eds. *Nederland naar 1945: Beschouwingen over ontwikkeling en beleid.* Deventer, 1980.

Kosthorst, Erich et al. eds., *Deutschlandpolitik der Nachkriegsjahre.* Paderborn, 1976.

Kratz, Peter. *Rechte Genossen: Neokonservatismus in der SPD*. Berlin, 1995.

Krautkrämer, Elmar. "Der innerdeutsche Konflikt um die Ministerpräsidentenkonferenz in München 1947." *Vierteljahrshefte für Zeitgeschichte* 20 (1972), 154–74.

Kreuzer, Franz, ed. "Die Zukunft der Sozialdemokratie: Ein Streitgespräch zwischen Franz Vranitzky und Ralf Dahrendorf." *Die Zukunft*. No. 8 (1990), 5–19.

Kriegel, Annie. "Marxisme et réformisme dans le socialisme français au lendemain de la Seconde Guerre Mondiale." In *Réformisme*, edited by Dreyfus. Pp. 139–47.

Krieger, Wolfgang. *General Lucius D. Clay und die amerikanische Deutschlandpolitik 1945–1949*. Stuttgart, 1987.

———. *Franz Josef Strauss: der barocke Demokrat aus Bayern*. Göttingen, 1995.

Kroes, R. *New Left, Nieuw Links, New Left: Verzet, beweging, verandering in Amerika, Nederland, Engeland*. Alphen a.d. Rijn, 1975.

Krop, Marnix, ed. *Burengerucht: Opstellen over Duitsland*. Deventer, 1978.

Krops, M. et al., eds. *Het zevende jaarboek voor het democratisch socialisme*. Amsterdam, 1986.

Küppers, Heinrich. *Staatsaufbau zwischen Bruch und Tradition: Geschichte des Landes Rheinland-Pfalz, 1946–1955*. Mainz, 1990.

Küsters, Hanns Jürgen. "Adenauer und Brandt in der Berlin-Krise 1958–1963." *Vierteljahrshefte für Zeitgeschichte*. 40 (1992), 483–542.

Kuisel, Richard F. *Capitalism and the State in Modern France: Renovation and Economic Management in the 20th Century*. New York, 1981.

Kusch, Katrin. *Die Wiedergründung der SPD in Rheinland-Pfalz nach dem Zweiten Weltkrieg 1945–1951*. Mainz, 1989.

Lacouture, Jean. *Léon Blum*. Paris, 1980.

Lacroix-Riz, Annie. "Autour d'Irving Brown: Le Free Trade Union Committee, le Département d'État et la Scission Syndicale française 1944–1947." *Le Mouvement social*. No. 151 (1990), 79–118.

Lademacher, Horst. "Zur Bedeutung des Petersberger Abkommens vom 22. November 1949." In *Kalter Krieg*, edited by Foschepoth. Pp. 240–65.

———. "Die britische Sozialisierungspolitik im Rhein-Ruhr-Raum." In *Britische*, edited by Foschepoth. Pp. 101–17.

———. "Frühe Versuche zur Änderung der Parteienlandschaft nach 1945." In *Weg,* edited by Dunk et al. Pp. 303–18.

———. "Die Kontinuität der Absicht: Die Vorstellungen des niederländischen Gewerkschaftsverbandes zur sozial- ökonomischen Neuordnung vor und nach dem II. Weltkrieg." In *Konflikt*, edited by Abelshauser. Pp. 91–115.

———. *Zwei ungleiche Nachbarn*. Darmstadt, 1990.

——— et al. "Der Weltgewerkschaftsbund im Spannungsfeld des Ost-West-Konflikts." Archiv für Sozialgeschichte. 18 (1978), 119–215.

——— and Jac Bosmans, eds. *Tradition und Neugestaltung: Zu Fragen des Wiederaufbaus in Deutschland und den Niederlanden in der frühen Nachkriegszeit*. Münster, 1991.

Lafon, François. "Des principes du Molletisme." In *Mollet*, edited by Ménager. Pp. 59–91.

Laloy, Jean. "Un tournant des relations franco-allemandes: De la crise de Berlin à la communauté européenne 1948–1950." In *Paris-Bonn*, edited by Manfrass. Pp. 179–85.

Land, Lucas van der *Het onstaan van de Pacifistisch Socialistische Partij*. Amsterdam, 1962.

Langeveld, Herman Jan. "Die niederländische Gewerkschaftsbewegung und der Marshall-Plan," In *Marshall-Plan*, edited by Haberl and Niethammer. Pp. 381–406.

Langkau, Jochem, Hans Matthöfer and Michael Schneider, eds. *SPD und Gewerkschaften*. Bonn, 1994. 2 vols.

Langner, Albrecht, ed. *Katholizismus und freiheitlicher Sozialismus in Europa*. Cologne, 1965.

———. "Die Sozialdemokratische Partei Deutschlands." In *Katholizismus*, edited by Langner. Pp. 25–90.

La Palombara, Joseph and Myron Weiner, eds. *Political Parties and Political Development*. Princeton, NJ, 1966.

Large, David Clay. *Germans to the Front: West German Rearmament in the Adenauer Era*. Chapel Hill, ND, 1995.

Larkin, Maurice. *France since the Popular Front*. New York, 1988.

Lasserre, René, Wolfgang Neumann, and Robert Picht, eds. *Deutschland-Frankreich: Bausteine zum Systemvergleich*. Gerlingen, 1980.

Lattard, Alain. *Gewerkschaften und Arbeitgeber in Rheinland-Pfalz 1945–1949*. Translated by Eva Ziebura Mainz, 1988.

———. "Zentralismus und Dezentralisierung in der französischen Deutschland- und Besatzungspolitik 1945–1947." In *Kapitulation*, edited by Becker and Manfrass. Pp. 181–209.

———. "Zielkonflikte französischer Besatzungspolitik in Deutschland: Der Streit Laffon-Koenig 1945–1947." *Vierteljahrshefte für Zeitgeschichte*. 39 (1991), 1–35.

Le Couriard, Daniel. "Les Socialistes et les débuts de la guerre d'Indochine 1946–1947." *Revue d'histoire moderne et contemporaine*. 31(1984), 334–53.

Lecourt, Robert. *Entre l'Église et l'État: Concorde sans Concordat, 1952–1957*. Paris, 1978.

Lefebvre, Denis. "The French Socialist Party, 1954–57." In *Parties*, edited by Griffith. Pp. 43–56.

———. "La 'Galaxie Defferre' et le Parti Socialiste." *Cahier et Revue de l'Ours*. No. 2 (1994), 93–101.

———. *Guy Mollet: Le mal aimé*. Paris, 1992.

———. "Guy Mollet: Un unitaire dans les Années 60—1963 L'Année charnière," In *Mollet*, edited by Ménager. Pp. 105–26.

LeFranc, Georges. *Le Socialisme réformiste* Paris. 1971.

Leggewie, Claus. "Alles andere als parlamentarische [*sic*] Opposition: Über die Grenzen der Opposition im politischen System Frankreichs." In *Opposition*, edited by Euchner. Pp. 127–36.

Lehning, Percy B. "Socialisten tussen plan en macht." In *Driehoek*, edited by de Beus et al. Pp. 147–93.

Lemke, Christiane, and Gary Marks, eds. *The Crisis of Socialism in Europe*. Durham, NC, 1992.

Lemke-Müller, Sabine. *Ethischer Sozialismus und soziale Demokratie: Der politische Weg Willi Eichlers vom ISK zur SPD*. Bonn, 1988.

Lepsius, Rainer. "Bundesrepublik Deutschland." In *Nachkriegsgesellschaften*, edited by Institut für Zeitgeschichte. Pp. 33–39.

Lettau, Reinhardt. "It's Time for a Change." In *Plädoyer*, edited by Richter. Pp. 129–31.

Lipietz, Alain. "Governing the Economy in the Face of International Challenge: From National Developmentalism to National Crisis." In *France*, edited by Hollifield and Ross.

Lier, Th. A.J.M. van. "De weg naar vrijheid." In *Socialisme*, edited by A. Peper et al. Pp. 45–59.

Ligou, Daniel. *Histoire du socialisme en France 1871–1961*. Paris, 1962.

Lijphart, Arend. The Politics of Acommodation. 2nd ed. Berkeley, 1975.

———. *The Trauma of Decolonization: The Dutch and West New Guinea*. New Haven, 1966.

———. *Verzuiling, pacificatie en kentering in de Nederlandse politiek*. 3rd ed. Amsterdam, 1979.

Lipgens, Walter. "Bedingungen und Etappen der Außenpolitik de Gaulles 1944–1946." *Vierteljahrshefte für Zeitgeschichte*. 21 (1973), 52–102.

———. *A History of European Integration*. Oxford, 1982.

——— "Innerfranzösische Kritik der Außenpolitik de Gaulles, 1944–146." *Vierteljahrshefte für Zeitgeschichte*. 24 (1976), 136–98.

Lipschits, I. "Geschiedschrijving over de Nederlandse politieke partijen: Reactie en aanvulling." *Bijdragen en Mededelingen betreffende de Geschiedenis der Nederlanden*. 91 (1976), 455–88.

Lösche, Peter. *Der Bolschewismus im Urteil der Sozialdemokratie, 1903–1920*. Berlin, 1967.

Löwke, Udo F. *Die SPD und die Wehrfrage, 1949–1955*. Hanover, 1976.

Löwenthal, Richard. "Konflikte, Bündnisse und Resultate der deutschen politischen Emigration." *Vierteljahrshefte für Zeitgeschichte*. 39 (1991), 626–36.

———. "Die Schrift 'Neu beginnen!' — 50 Jahre danach." *Internationale Wissenschaftliche Korrespondenz* 19 (1983), 561–70.

———, ed. *Die Zweite Republik — 25 Jahre Bundesrepublik Deutschland: Eine Bilanz*. Stuttgart, 1970.

Lompe, Klaus and Lothar F. Neumann, eds. *Willi Eichlers Beiträge zum demokratischen Sozialismus*. Bonn, 1979.

Longerich, Michael. *Die SPD als "Friedenspartei."* Frankfurt a.M., 1990.

Loth, Wilfried. "Die deutsche Frage in französischer Perspektive." In *Westdeutschland*, edited by Herbst. Pp. 37–49.

———. "Der Durchbruch zur Dynamisierung: Die französische Gesellschaft in den 50er Jahren." In *Modernisierung*, edited by Schildt and Sywottek. Pp. 69–79.

———. "Die Europabewegung in den Anfangsjahren der Bundesrepublik." In *EWG*, edited by Herbst et al. Pp. 63–77.

———. "Frankreichs Kommunisten und der Beginn des Kalten Krieges: Die Entlassung der kommunistischen Minister im Mai 1947." *Vierteljahrshefte für Zeitgeschichte*. 26 (1978), 9–65.

———. "Die Franzosen und die deutsche Frage 1945–1949." In *Deutschlandpolitik*, edited by Scharf. Pp. 27–48.

———. "Die französische Linke und die 'Einheit der Arbeiterklasse,' 1943–1947." In *Einheitsfront*, edited by Staritz. Pp. 355–76.

———. "Der französische Sozialismus in der 4. und 5. Republik." *Neue Politische Literatur*. 22 (1977), 221–43.

———. "Die französischen Sozialisten und der Marshall-Plan." In *Marshall-Plan*, edited by Haberl und Niethammer. Pp. 359–80.

———. "Les projets de politique extérieure de la Résistance socialiste en France." *Revue d'histoire moderne et contemporaine*. 24 (1977), 544–569.

———. *Sozialismus und Internationalismus: Die französischen Sozialisten und die Nachkriegsordnung Europas, 1940–1950*. Stuttgart, 1977.

———. *Der Weg nach Europa: Geschichte der Europäischen Integration, 1939–1957*. 2nd. ed. Göttingen, 1991.

———— and Robert Picht, eds. *De Gaulle, Deutschland und Europa*. Opladen, 1991.

Maas, P.F. *Kabinetsformaties 1959–1973*. The Hague, 1982.

Macridis, Roy. "Wandel des Regierungssystems … Oppositionsformen in Frankreich." In *Opposition*, edited by Oberreuter. Pp. 83–105.

Mahoney, Daniel J. *De Gaulle: Statesmanship, Grandeur, and Modern Democracy*. Westport, CN, 1996.

Maier, Charles S. "The Two Postwar Eras and the Conditions for Stability in Twentieth-Century Western Europe." *American Historical Review*. 86 (1981), 327–52.

Maillard, Pierre. *De Gaulle et L'Allemagne: Le rêve inachevé*. Paris, 1990.

Manfrass, Klaus, ed. *Paris-Bonn: Eine dauerhafte Bindung schwieriger Partner*. Sigmaringen, 1984.

Manning, Adriaan. "Die Niederlande und Europa von 1945 bis zum Beginn der fünfziger Jahre." *Vierteljahrshefte für Zeitgeschichte*. 29 (1981), 1–20.

————. "Uit de voorgeschiedenis van het mandement van 1954." *Jaarboek Katholiek Documentatie Centrum 1971*. Nijmegen, 1971. Pp. 138–48.

Marcowitz, Reiner. *Option für Paris?: Unionsparteien, SPD und Charles de Gaulle 1958–1969*. Munich, 1996.

Margalit, Avishai. "The Chances of Shimon Peres." *New York Review of Books*. 43 (9 May 1996), 18–23.

Marssolek, Inge and Heinrich Potthoff, eds. *Durchbruch zum modernen Deutschland?: Die Sozialdemokratie in der Regierungsverantwortung 1966–1982*. Essen, 1995.

Matthias, Erich. *Sozialdemokratie und Nation*. Stuttgart, 1952.

Matz, Klaus-Jürgen. *Reinhold Maier*. Düsseldorf, 1989.

May, James. "Is there a European Socialism?" *Journal of Common Market Studies*. 13 (1975), 492–502.

Mayer, Daniel. *Pour une Histoire de la Gauche*. Paris, 1969.

————. *Les Socialistes dans la Résistance*. Paris, 1968.

Mehringer, Hartmut. *Waldemar von Knoeringen: Eine politische Biographie*. Munich, 1989. 2 vols.

Melandri Pierre, and Maurice Vasse. "France: From Powerlessness to the Search for Influence." In *Power*, edited by Becker and Knipping. Pp. 461–73.

Ménager, Bernard, et al., eds. *Guy Mollet: Un Camerade en république*. Lille, 1987.

Merkel, Wolfgang. "Niedergang der Sozialdemokratie? Sozialdemokratische und sozialistische Regierungspolitik im westeuropäischen Vergleich." *Leviathan*. 18 (1990), 106–33.

Merseburger, Peter. *Der schwierige Deutsche: Kurt Schumacher*. Stuttgart, 1995.

Merz, Kai-Uwe. *Das Schreckbild: Deutschland und der Bolschewismus, 1917 bis 1921*. Berlin, 1995.

Messing, Frans. *De Nederlandse economie 1945–1980: Herstel, groei, stagnatie*. Bussum, 1981.

Mettler-Meiboom, Barbara. "Über das Verhältnis von Ökonomie und Politik beim Marshall-Plan." In *Marshall-Plan*, edited by Haberl and Niethammer. Pp. 132–38.

Meyer-Braun, Renate. "'Rebell' Wilhelm Kaisen … Briefwechsel zwischen Alfred Faust und Fritz Heine aus den Jahren 1950–1956." *Bremisches Jahrbuch*. 67 (1989), 109–39.

Michels, Robert. *Political Parties*. Glencoe, IL, 1951.

Middel, B. *De nieuwe elite van de PvdA*. Groningen, 1976.

Middendorp, C.P. *Ideology in Dutch Policies … 1970–1985*. Assen, 1991.

Miller, Susanne. *Sozialdemokratie als Lebenssinn: Aufsätze zur Geschichte und Gegenwart der SPD.* Bonn, 1995.

———. *Die SPD vor und nach Godesberg.* Bonn, 1974.

Milward, Alan S. *The European Rescue of the Nation State.* London, 1992.

———. *The Reconstruction of Western Europe, 1945–1951.* Berkeley, CA, 1984.

——— et al., eds. *The Frontier of National Sovereignty: History and Theory, 1945–1992.* New York, 1993.

Minderaa, J.T. "Die interessenpolitischen und weltanschaulichen Bindungen der niederländischen Parteien." In *Weg*, edited by Dunk. Pp. 227–38.

Mitterrand, François. *Le Coup d'État Permanent.* Paris, 1964.

Moch, Jules. *Histoire du réarmament allemand depuis 1950.* Paris, 1965.

———. *Front Populaire.* Paris, 1971.

Moeller, Robert. *Protecting Motherhood: Women and the Family in the Politics of West Germany.* Berkeley, CA, 1993.

Moraw, Frank. *Die Parole der "Einheit" und die Sozialdemokratie.* Bonn-Bad Godesberg, 1973.

Moreau, Jean. "Les aspects particuliers de la politique d'occupation française dans les domaines de la jeunesse et de l'éducation populaire." In *Dénazification*, edited by Vaillant. Pp. 19–35.

Morgan, Roger. *Washington und Bonn: Deutsch-amerikanische Beziehungen seit dem Zweiten Weltkrieg.* Munich, 1975.

Morsey, Rudolf. *Heinrich Lübke: eine politische Biographie.* Paderborn, 1996.

Mossuz, Janine. "Que sont devenus les clubs." *Revue Française de Science Politique.* 20 (1970), 964–73.

Mozer, Alfred. "De SPD." In *Buren*, edited by Krop. Pp. 297–335.

Mühlhausen, Walter. "Treuhänder des deutschen Volkes: Die Ministerpräsidenten im Interregnum." In *Treuhänder*, Mühlhausen and Regin. Pp. 7–34.

———. "Wandel der Entscheidungsstrukturen: Sozialisierung und Mitbestimmung in der Besatzungszeit." In *Tradition*, edited by Lademacher and Bosmans. Pp. 159–93.

——— and Cornelia Regin, eds. *Treuhänder des deutschen Volkes — Die Ministerpräsidenten der westlichen Besatzungszonen nach den ersten freien Landtagswahlen: Politische Portraits.* Melsungen, 1991.

Müller, Joseph. *Die Gesamtdeutsche Volkspartei ... 1950–1957.* Düsseldorf, 1990.

Müller, Klaus-Jürgen. "Die SPD Kurt Schumachers und Frankreich." In *Paris-Bonn*, edited by Manfrass. Pp. 191–96.

Na'aman, Shlomo. "Von der Problematik der Sozialdemokratie als demokratische Partei: Zur Jubiläumsfeier des Jahres 1863." *Archiv für Sozialgeschichte.* 5 (1965), 503–25.

Nachtmann, Walter. "Erwin Schöttle." In *Widerstand*, edited by Bosch and Niess. Pp. 153–61.

Nagel, Jan. *Ha, die PvdA!* Amsterdam, 1966.

Naimark, Norman. *The Russians in Germany...1945–1949.* Cambridge, MA, 1997.

Nakai, Takeshi. *Die deutsche Sozialdemokratie zwischen Nationalsozialismus und Internationalismus, 1945–1952.* Bonn, 1975.

Nederhorst, Gerard. "Het Plan van de Arbeid." In *Eerste jaarboek*, edited by Jan Bank, et al. Pp. 109–36.

Nemitz, Kurt. *Sozialistische Marktwirtschaft.* Frankfurt a.M., 1960.

Nicholls, Anthony J. *Freedom with Responsibility: The Social Market Economy in Germany, 1918–1963.* New York, 1994.

Niedermayer, Oskar and Richard Stöss, eds. *Stand und Perspektiven der Parteien-forschung in Deutschland.* Opladen, 1993.

Niethammer, Lutz. "Arbeiterbewegung im Kalten Krieg." In *Marshall-Plan,* edited by Haberl and Niethammer. Pp. 575–600.

——— et al., eds. *Arbeiterinitiative 1945: Antifaschistische Ausschüsse und Reorgani-sation der Arbeiterbewegung in Deutschland.* Wuppertal, 1976.

Noack, Paul. *Das Scheitern der Europäischen Verteidigungsgemeinschaft.* Düsseldorf, 1977.

Nölting, Claudia. *Erik Nölting.* Essen, 1989.

Northcutt, Wayne. *Mitterrand: A Political Biography.* New York, 1992.

Nowka, Harry. *Das Machtverhältnis zwischen Partei und Fraktion in der SPD.* Cologne, 1973.

Oberreuter, Heinrich. "Parlamentarische Opposition in der Bundesrepublik Deutschland." In *Opposition,* edited by Euchner. Pp. 60–75.

———, ed. *Parlamentarische Opposition: Ein internationaler Vergleich.* Hamburg, 1975.

Olivier, Laurent. "La Fédération socialiste du Nord." *Cahier et Revue de L'Ours.* No. 2 (1994), 75–86.

Orlow, Dietrich. "Delayed Reaction: Democracy, Nationalism, and the SPD, 1945–1966." *German Studies Review.* 16 (1993), 77–102.

———. *Weimar Prussia, 1918–1933.* Pittsburgh, 1986, and 1991. 2 vols.

———. "West German Parties since 1945: Continuity and Change." *Central Euro-pean History.* 18 (1985), 188–201.

Ott, Erich. *Die Wirtschaftskonzeption der SPD nach 1945.* Marburg, 1978.

Overesch, Manfred. *Die Deutschen und die deutsche Frage 1945–1955: Darstellungen und Dokumente.* Düsseldorf, 1985.

———. "Senior West German Politicians and their Perception of the German Sit-uation in Europe, 1945–1949." In *Power,* edited by Becker. Pp. 117–34.

Padgett, Stephen and William E. Paterson. *A History of Social Democracy in Postwar Europe.* New York, 1991.

Panebianco, Angelo. *Political Parties: Organization and Power.* New York, 1988.

Papke, Gerhard. *Unser Ziel ist die unabhängige FDP: Die Liberalen und der Machtwechsel in Nordrhein-Westfalen 1956.* Baden-Baden, 1992.

Paranque, Régis. *Le Malaise français.* Paris, 1970.

Paterson, William E. and Alastair H. Thomas, eds. *Social Democratic Parties in Western Europe.* New York, 1977.

Pelinka, Anton. *Social Democratic Parties in Europe.* New York, 1983.

Pels, Dick. "Zaken-socialisme, of: het einde van de utopie." In *Moraal,* edited by Schuyt et al. Pp. 46–79.

Peper, A. "Socialisme en Technocratie." In Peper, *Socialisme.* pp. 11–35.

——— et al., eds. *Wetenschappelijke socialisme, over de plannen van SDAP en PvdA* Amsterdam, 1982.

Peper, Bram. "The Netherlands: A Permissive Response." In *Politics,* edited by Cox. Pp. 87–110.

Petzina, Dietmar. "Von der Konfrontation zur Integration." In *Franzosen,* edited by Hüttenberger. Pp. 161–82.

Pfetsch, Frank R. "Die französische Verfassungspolitik in Deutschland nach 1945." In *Deutschlandpolitik,* edited by Institut. Pp. 115–37.

Philip, André. *Henri de Man et la crise du socialisme.* Paris, 1928.

———. "La pensée des partis ouvrièrs." In *Comportements,* edited byHamon. Pp. 199–210.

———. *Pour une communauté réelle: Le Plan Schuman.* Paris, 1951.

———. *Le socialisme trahi.* Paris, 1957.

———. *Les socialistes.* 2nd ed. Paris, 1967.

Pickles, Dorothy. *French Politics: The First Years of the Fourth Republic.* London, 1953.

Pingel, Falk. "Die Russen am Rhein? Die Wende der britischen Besatzungspolitik im Frühjahr 1946." *Vierteljahrshefte für Zeitgeschichte.* 30 (1982), 98–116.

Pirker, Theo. *Die Geschichte der sozialdemokratischen Partei Deutschlands, 1955–1964.* 3rd. ed. Berlin, 1977.

———. *Die SPD Nach Hitler … 1945–1964.* Munich, 1965.

Plum, Günter "Volksfront, Konzentration und Mandatsfrage: Ein Beitrag zur Geschichte der SPD im Exil, 1933–1939." *Vierteljahrshefte für Zeitgeschichte.* 18 (1970), 410–42.

Plumpe, Werner. "Auf dem Weg in die Marktwirtschaft: Organisierte Industrieinteressen, Wirtschaftsverwaltung und Besatzungsmacht in Nordrhein-Westfalen 1945–1947." In *NRW,* edited by Brunn. Pp. 67–84.

Poidevin, Raymond. "Die europapolitische Initiativen Frankreichs des Jahres 1950… " In *EWG,* edited by Herbst et al. Pp. 257–62.

———. "La France devant le danger allemand 1944–1952." In *Frage,* edited by Hildebrand and Pommerin. Pp. 252–67.

———. "Frankreich und die deutsche Frage, 1943–1949." In *Frage,* edited by Becker et al. Pp. 405–20.

———. "Frankreich und die Ruhrfrage 1945–1951." In *Historische Zeitschrift.* 228 (1979), 317–334.

———. "Die Neuorientierung der französischen Deutschlandpolitik 1948/49." In *Kalter Krieg,* edited by Foschepoth. Pp. 129–44.

———. *Robert Schuman: homme d'État 1886–1963.* Paris, 1986.

———. *Robert Schumans Deutschland- und Europapolitik zwischen Tradition und Neuorientierung.* Munich, 1976.

———. "Le rôle personnel de Robert Schuman dans les negotiations C.E.C.A." In *Anfänge,*edited by Schwabe.Pp. 105–15.

Pollach, Günter. "François Mitterrand." In *Lebensbilder,* edited byDankelmann, Pp. 343–55.

Ponthus, René. "Tendances et activité de la Social Democratie allemande emigrée 1933–1941." *Le Mouvement social.* No. 84 (1973), 63–86.

Poperen, Jean. *La Gauche française, 1958–1973.* Paris, 1972–1975. 2 vols.

Popitz, Heinrich et al. *Das Gesellschaftsbild des Arbeiters: Soziologische Untersuchungen in der Hüttenindustrie.* Tübingen, 1957.

Potthoff, Erich. *Der Kampf um die Montanmitbestimmung.* Cologne, 1957.

Praag, Philip van. *Strategie en Illusion: Elf jaar intern debat in de PvdA 1966–1977.* Amsterdam, 1990.

Prowe, Diethelm. "Die Anfänge der Brandtschen Ostpolitik 1961–1963." In *Aspekte,* edited by Benz and Graml. Pp. 249–86.

——— "Economic Democracy in Post World War II Germany: Corporatist Crisis Response, 1945–1948." *Journal of Modern History.* 57(1985), 451–82.

———. "Socialism as Crisis Response: Socialization and the Escape from Poverty and Power in Post-World War II Germany." *German Studies Review.* 25 (1992), 65–85.

Puchinger, G., ed. *Hergroepering der partijen?* Delft, 1968.

Quilliot, Roger. *La S.F.I.O. et l'exercise du pouvoir 1944–1958.* Paris, 1972.

Rémond, René. "Les Problèmes politique au lendemain de la Libération." In *Libération,* edited by Centre. Pp. 821–25.

Rhijn, A.A. van. *De protestants christen in de PvdA.* Amsterdam, 1956.

Richter, Hans Werner, ed. *Plädoyer für eine neue Regierung oder keine Alternative.* Reinbek b. Hamburg, 1965.

Righart, Hans, "Die Demokratisierung einer Ständegeselleschaft." In *Tradition* edited byLademacher et al. Pp. 195–214.

Rimbert, Pierre. "Le Parti socialiste SFIO." In *Partis,* edited by Duverger. Pp. 195–207.

Rioux, Jean Pierre. *La France de la IVe République.* Paris, 1980–1983. 2 vols.

———. "Französische öffentliche Meinung und EVG." In *EVG,* edited by Volkmann. Pp. 159–76.

Ritter, Gerhard A. *Der Sozialstaat, Entstehung und Entwicklung im internationalen Vergleich.* Munich, 1991.

——— and Merith Niebuss, eds. *Wahlen in der Bundesrepublik Deutschland, 1946–1987.* Munich, 1987.

Röder, Werner. *Die deutschen sozialistischen Exilgruppen in Grossbritannien.* Hanover, 1968.

———. "Deutschlandpläne der sozialdemokratischen Emigration in Grossbritannien, 1942–1945." *Vierteljahrshefte für Zeitgeschichte.* 17 (1969). 72–86.

———. "Politische und soziale Probleme der Arbeiterklasse am Ende des Zweiten Weltkrieges und in der unmittelbaren Nachkriegszeit." *Internationale Wissenschaftliche Korrespondenz.* 22 (1986), 2–8.

Rohe, Karl. *Vom Revier zum Ruhrgebiet: Wahlen, Parteien, politische Kultur.* Essen, 1986.

Rombek-Jaschinski, Ursula. *Nordrhein-Westfalen, die Ruhr und Europa, 1945–1955.* Essen, 1990.

Rooy, Piet de. *De rode droom: Een eeuw social-democratie in Nederland.* Nijmegen, 1995.

———. *"Van uit een nieuwe wereld": Over de periodieke somberheid en het utopisch verlangen in de Nederlandse sociaal democratie.* Amsterdam, 1993.

Rose, Saul. "The French Election of 1956." *Political Studies.* 4 (1956), 250–63.

Rothwell, Victor H. "Grossbritannien und die Anfänge des Kalten Krieges." In *Kalter Krieg,* edited by Foschepoth. Ppp. 88–110.

Rovan, Joseph. "Adieu à Schmid." *Documents: Revue des Questions allemandes.* 35 (1980), 50–53.

———. *Geschichte der deutschen Sozialdemokratie.* Translated by. Charlotte Roland. Frankfurt a.M., 1980.

Rudolph, Karsten et al., eds. *Geschichte als Möglichkeit: Über die Chancen von Demokratie; Festschrift für Helga Grebing.* Essen, 1995.

Rudzio, Wolfgang. "Die ausgebliebene Sozialisierung an Rhein und Ruhr: Zur Sozialisierungspolitik von Labour-Regierung und SPD 1945–1948." *Archiv für Sozialgeschichte.* 18 (1978), 1–39.

———. "Die Regierung der informellen Gremien." *Sozialwissenschaftliches Jahrbuch für Politik.* 3 (1972), 339–66.

——— "Das Sozialisierugskonzept der SPD und seine internationalen Realisierungsbedingungen," In *Britische,* edited by Foschepoth. Pp. 119–34.

Ruitenbeek, H.M. *Het ontstaan van de PvdA.* Amsterdam, 1955.

Rupieper, Hermann-Josef. *Der Besetzte Verbündete: Die amerikanische Deutschlandpolitik 1949–1955.* Opladen, 1991.

Sadoun, Marc. *Les socialistes sous l'occupation: Résistance et collaboration.* Paris, 1982.

Schaefer, Rainer. *SPD in der Ära Brüning.* Frankfurt a.M., 1990.

Schaper, H.A. "Het Nederlandse veiligheidsbeleid 1945–1950." *Bijdragen en Mededelingen betreffende de Geschiedenis der Nederlanden.* 96 (1981), 277–99.

————. "'Wij willen zelfs niet Mönchen-Gladbach': De annexatiekwestie 1945–1949." *Internationale Spectator*. 29 (1985), 261–72.

Schaper, B.W. et al. *Het verbleekte ideaal: De linkse kritiek op de Sociaal Democratie in Nederland*. Amsterdam, 1982.

Scharf, Claus and Hans-Jürgen Schröder, eds. *Die Deutschlandpolitik Frankreichs und die französische Zone 1945 bis 1949*. Wiesbaden, 1983.

Scheffer, H.J. *November 1918: Journaal van een revolutie die niet doorging*. Amsterdam, 1968.

Scheffer, Paul. "Contouren van een ontzuilde hervormingspartij." In *Moraal*, edited by Schuyt. Pp. 80–115.

Scheffler, Thomas. *Die SPD und der Algerienkrieg 1954–1962*. Berlin, 1995.

Schelsky, Helmut. *Wandlungen der deutschen Familie in der Gegenwart*. Stuttgart, 1955.

Schildt, Axel and Arnold Sywottek, eds. *Modernisierung im Wiederaufbau: Westdeutschlands Geschichte in den 50er Jahren*. Bonn, 1993.

Schmid, Carlo. "Bund und Länder." In *Zweite Republik*, edited by Löwenthal. Pp. 244–60.

————. "Das deutsch-französische Verhältnis und der Dritte Weg." *Die Wandlung*, 2 (1947), 792–805.

Schmidt, Eberhard. "Ohne Alternativen? Thesen zum Verhältnis der westdeutschen Gewerkschaften zum Marshall-Plan," In *Marshall-Plan*, edited by Haberl and Niethammer. Pp. 212–32.

————. *Die verhinderte Neuordnung 1945–1952: Zur Auseinandersetzung um die Demokratisierung der Wirtschaft in den westlichen Besatzungszonen und in der Bundesrepublik Deutschland*. Frankfurt a.M., 1970.

Schmitz, Kurt Thomas. *Deutsche Einheit und Europäische Integration: Der sozialdemokratische Beitrag zur Aussenpolitik der Bundesrepublik Deutschland ...* Bonn, 1978.

Schmoeckel, Reinhard and Bruno Kaise. *Die vergessene Regierung: Die Grosse Koalition, 1966 bis 1969*. Bonn, 1991.

Schneider, Heinrich. *Das Wunder an der Saar*. Stuttgart, 1974.

Schneider, Michael. *Demokratie in Gefahr? Der Konflikt um die Notstandsgesetze: Sozialdemokratie, Gewerkschaften und intellektueller Protest 1958–1968*. Bonn, 1986.

————. "Helmut Schmidt." In *Persönlichkeit*, edited by Borst. 2:147–70.

Scholz, Günther. *Herbert Wehner*. Düsseldorf, 1986.

Schonauer, Karlheinz. *Die ungeliebten Kinder der Mutter SPD*. Bonn, 1982.

Schreiner, Reinhard. *Bidault, der MRP und die französische Deutschlandpolitik, 1944–1948*. Frankfurt a.M., 1985.

Schröder, Karsten. *Egon Bahr*. Rastatt, 1988.

Schroeder, Wolfgang. "Christliche Sozialpolitik oder Sozialismus: Oswald von Nell-Breuning und Viktor Agartz." *Vierteljahrshefte für Zeitgeschichte*. 39 (1991), 179–220.

Schubert, Klaus von, *Wiederbewaffnung und Westintegration: Die innere militärische und außenpolitische Orientierung der Bundesrepublik, 1950–1952*. Stuttgart, 1970.

Schulz, Gerhard. *Von Brüning zu Hitler: Der Wandel des politischen Systems in Deutschland 1930–1933*. Berlin, 1992.

Schulz, Klaus Peter. "Resolutionen und Realitäten." *Deutsche Rundschau*. 80 (1954), 915–21.

Schumacher, Kurt, *Der Kampf um den Staatsgedanken in der deutschen Sozialdemokratie*. Ed. F. Holtmeier. Stuttgart, 1973.

Schunck, Peter. "De Gaulle und seine deutschen Nachbarn bis zur Begegnung mit Adenauer." In *De Gaulle*, edited by Loth and Picht. Pp. 21–43.

Schuyt, Gees J.M. and Siep Stuurman, eds. *Sociaaldemocratie tussen zakelijheid en moraal*. Amsterdam, 1991.

Schwabe, Klaus, ed. *Die Anfänge des Schuman-Plans*. Baden-Baden, 1988.

Schwan, Alexander. "Katholische Kirche und deutsche Sozialdemokratie." In *Kirche*, edited by Gorschenek. Pp. 205–17.

Schwartz, Thomas A. *America's Germany: John J. McCloy and the Federal Republic of Germany*. Cambridge, MA, 1991.

Schwarz, Hans-Peter. *Adenauer*. Stuttgart, 1986–1991. 2 vols.

———. Die Eingliederung der Bundesrepublik in die westliche Welt." In *EWG*, edited by Herbst. Pp. 593–612.

Seebacher-Brandt, Brigitte. *Ollenhauer: Biedermann und Patriot*. Berlin, 1984.

Shennan, Andrew. *Rethinking France: Plans for Renewal 1940–1946*. New York, 1989.

Shipway, Martin. *The Road to War: France and Vietnam, 1944–1947*. Providence, RI, 1996.

Simmons, H.G. *French Socialists in Search of a Role, 1956–1967*. Ithaca, NY, 1970.

Singer, Daniel. *Is Socialism Doomed? The Meaning of Mitterrand*. New York, 1988.

Smit, C. *De liquidatie van een Imperium: Nederland en Indonesië*. Amsterdam, 1962.

Smith, Gordon. "Core Persistence: Change and the 'People's Party.'" *West European Politics*. 12 (1989), 157–68.

Smith, Tony. "The French Colonial Consensus and People's War, 1946–1958." *Journal of Contemporary History*. 9 (1974), 217–47.

Soell, Hartmut. "Die deutschlandpolitischen Konzeptionen der SPD-Opposition 1949–1961." In *Deutschland*, edited by Kosthorst et al. Pp. 41–61.

——— "Fraktion und Parteiorganisation: Zur Willensbildung der SPD in den 60er Jahren." *Politische Vierteljahresschrift*. 10 (1969), 604–26.

———. *Fritz Erler: Eine politische Biographie*. Berlin, 1976. 2 vols.

———, "Kurt Schumacher," In Christadler, ed., *Utopie*, pp. 259–74.

Soutou, Georges-Henri. "La politique française à l'égard de la Rhénanie 1944–1947." In *Franzosen*, edited by Hüttenberger et al. Pp. 47–66.

Spitaels, Guy, ed. *La crise des relations industrielles en Europe: Diversité et unité, les réponses possibles*. Bruges, 1972.

Spoo, Eckart, ed. *Was aus Deutschland werden sollte: Konzepte des Widerstands, des Exils und der Alliierten*. Heilbronn, 1995.

Stammen, Theo. *Parteien in Europa: Nationale Parteiensysteme — Transnationale Parteienbeziehungen — Konturen eines europäischen Parteiensystems*. Munich, 1981.

Staritz, Dietrich and Hermann Weber, eds. *Einheitsfront-Einheitspartei: Kommunisten und Sozialdemokraten in Ost- und Westdeutschland, 1944–1948*. Cologne, 1989.

Staritz, Dietrich, ed. *Das Parteiensystem der Bundesrepublik: Geschichte, Entstehung, Entwicklung*. Opladen, 1976.

Steinbach, Peter. "Die SPD zwischen Tradition und Neubeginn: Programmatische Grundlinien im zeitgeschichtlichen Wandel." In *Kapitulation*, edited by Becker. Pp. 297–333.

Steiner, Wolfgang. *SPD-Parteitage 1964 und 1966: Analyse und Vergleich*. Meisenheim am Glan, 1970.

Steininger, Rolf, "British Labour, Deutschland und die SPD, 1945/46," *Internationale Wissenschaftliche Korrespondenz*, 15 no. 2, 1979, 188–226.

———. *Deutschland und die Sozialistische Internationale nach dem Zweiten Weltkrieg*. Bonn, 1979.

————. *Eine vertane Chance zur Wiedervereinigung? Die Stalin-Note vom 10.3.52.* Bonn, 1985.

————. "Einleitung." In *Ruhrfrage,* edited by Steininger. Pp. 12–216.

————. *Ein neues Land an Rhein und Ruhr: Die Ruhrfrage 1945/46 und die Entstehung Nordrhein- Westfalens.* Cologne, 1990.

————. "Kurt Schumacher, die Sozialistische Internationale und die Ruhrfrage," In *Schumacher,* edited by Albrecht. Pp. 61–94.

————. "Die Sozialisierung fand nicht statt." In *Britische Deutschlandpolitik,* edited by Foschepoth and Steininger. Pp. 135–50.

————. "Der Wiederaufbau der Sozialistischen Internationale." In *Marshall-Plan,* edited by Haberl and Niethammer. Pp. 481–500.

————. "Zur Geschichte der Münchener Ministerpräsidenten-Konferenz 1947." *Vierteljahrshefte für Zeitgeschichte.* 23 (1975), 375–453.

Stempels, A. *De parlementaire geschiedenis van het Indonesische vraagstuk.* Amsterdam, 1950.

Stöss, Richard, ed. *Parteien-Handbuch: Die Parteien der Bundesrepublik Deutschland, 1945–1980.* Opladen, 1983. 2 vols.

Struve, Günter. *Kampf um die Mehrheit.* Cologne, 1971.

Stuurman, Siep. *Verzuiling, kapitalisme en patriarchaat.* Nijmegen, 1983.

Suffert, Georges. *De Defferre à Mitterrand: la Campagne présidentielle.* Paris, 1966.

Sywottek, Arnold. "Die 'fünfte Zone'. Zur gesellschafts- und außenpolitischen Orientierung und Funktion sozialdemokratischer Politik in Berlin 1945–1948." *Archiv für Sozialgeschichte.* 13 (1973), 53–129.

————. "Tabuisierung und Anpassung in Ost und West: Bemerkungen zur deutschen Geschichte nach 1945." In *Zukunftspläne,* edited by Koebner. Pp. 229–60.

————. "Wege in die 50er Jahre," In *Modernisierung,* edited by Schildt and Sywottek.

Texcier, Jean. "Die ideologische Entwicklung des demokratischen Sozialismus in Frankreich." In *Weltstimmen,* edited by Braunthal. Pp. 78–107.

Thibaud, Paul. "La Philosophie Politique de Pierre Mendès-France." In *PMF,* edited by Bédarida. Pp. 45–51.

Thiébault, Jean-Louis. "La Gouvernement de Guy Mollet." In *Mollet,* edited by Ménager. Pp. 299–312.

Thompson, Wayne C. *The Political Odyssey of Herbert Wehner.* Boulder, CO, 1993.

Thoss, Bruno. "Die Lösung der Saarfrage 1954/55," *Vierteljahrshefte für Zeitgeschichte.* 38 (1990), 225–88.

Tijn, Theo van. "Koude oorlog in de PvdA: Het sociaal-democratisch centrum, 1955–1959. " In *Ideaal,* edited by Schaper. Pp. 69–77.

————. *De macht van de rooie ruggen.* Amsterdam, 1967.

Timmermann, Heiner, ed. *Deutschland und Europa nach dem 2. Weltkrieg.* Saarbrücken-Scheidt, 1990.

Tormin, Walter. *Die Geschichte der SPD in Hamburg, 1945–1950.* Hamburg, 1994.

————, ed. *Der Traum von der Einheit.* Hamburg, 1990.

Troen, Selwyn Ilan and Moshe Shemesh. *The Suez-Sinai Crisis.* New York, 1990.

Tromp, Bart A.G.M. "Drees en het democratisch socialisme." In *Drees,* edited by Daalder et al. Pp. 26–56.

————. "Party Strategies and System Change in The Netherlands." *West European Politics.* 12 (1989), 82–97.

Turner, Ian D., ed. *Reconstruction in Post-War Germany: British Occupation Policy and the Western Zones, 1945–1955.* New York, 1989.

Uschner, Manfred. *Die Ostpolitik der SPD.* Berlin, 1991.

Vaillant, Jérôme, ed. *La dénazification par les vainqueurs.* Lille, 1981.

Vaillant, Jérme. "Frankreichs Kulturpolitik in Deutschland. 1945–1949." In *Franzosen,* edited by Hüttenberger. Pp. 203–17.

Vandenbussche, Robert. "Guy Mollet et le groupe parlementaire Socialiste sous le IVe et Ve République." In *Mollet,* edited by Ménager. Pp. 263–84.

Vansittart, Robert. *Black Record: Germans Past and Present.* London, 1941.

Vardys, Stanley V. "Germany's Postwar Socialism: Nationalism and Kurt Schumacher 1945–1952." *Review of Politics.* 27 (1965), 220–44.

Veenstra, W.J. "De Partij van de Arbeid en Europa." *Internationale Spectator.* (no. 4, 1977), 246–55.

Verdier, Robert. *PS/PC: Une lutte pour l'entente.* Paris, 1976.

Verhallen, H.J.G. et al., eds. *Corporatisme in Nederland.* Alphen a/d Rijn, 1980.

Verkade, Willem. *Democratic Parties in the Low Countries and Germany: Historical Origins and Development.* Leiden, 1965.

Visser, Anneke. *Alleen bij uiterste noodzaak? De rooms-rode samenwerking en het einde van de brede basis 1948–1958.* Amsterdam, 1986.

Vogtmeier, Andreas. *Egon Bahr und die deutsche Frage.* Bonn, 1996.

Voigt, Klaus. "Europäische Föderation und neuer Völkerbund: Die Diskussion im deutschen Exil zur Gestaltung der internationalen Beziehungen nach dem Krieg." In *Zukunftspläne,* edited by Koebner et al. Pp. 104–22.

Volkmann, H.E. and W. Schwengler, eds. *Die Europäische Verteidigungsgemeinschaft: Stand und Probleme der Forschung.* Boppard a.Rh., 1985.

Voorhoeve, J.J.C. *Peace, Profits, and Principles: A Study of Dutch Foreign Policy.* The Hague, 1979.

Vorholt, Udo. *Die Sowjetunion im Urteil des Sozialdemokratischen Exils 1933 bis 1945.* Ph.D. Diss. University of. Dortmund, 1991.

Vos, H. de. *Geschiedenis van het socialisme in Nederland in het kader van zijn tijd.* Baarn, 1976.

Wall, Irwin M. *French Communism in the Era of Stalin The Quest for Unity and Integration, 1945–1962.* Westport, CT, 1983.

Walter, Karin. *Neubeginn-Nationalsozialismus-Widerstand: Die politisch-theoretische Diskussion der Neuordnung in CDU und SPD 1945–1948.* Bonn, 1987.

Wansink. D.J. *Het Socialisme op de Tweesprong: de Geboorte van de SDAP.* Haarlem, 1939.

Warner, Geoffrey. "Die britische Labour-Regierung und die Einheit Westeuropas." *Vierteljahrshefte für Zeitgeschichte.* 28 (1980), 310–30.

Wassenberg, Arthur. "Neo-Corporatisme: de carriere en de schutklappen van een begrip." In *Corporatisme,* edited by Verhallen. Pp. 337–69.

Weber, Hermann. "Der ewige Kommunist? Die Instrumentalisierung der Vergangenheit des Politikers Herbert Wehner." In *Geschichte,* edited by Rudolph. Pp. 401–13.

Weber, Petra. *Carlo Schmid 1896–1979: eine Biographie.* Munich, 1996.

Weijden C.J.v.d. "Enige aspecten van de macro-economische ontwikkeling," In *Nederland,* edited by Kooy et al. Pp. 141–62.

Weilemann, Peter. *Die Anfänge der europäischen Atomgemeinschaft... 1955–1957.* Baden- Baden, 1983.

Weisenfeld, Ernst. *Welches Deutschland soll es sein? Frankreich und die deutsche Einheit seit 1945.* Munich, 1986.

Wels, C.B., ed. *Vaderlands verleden in veelhoud.* The Hague, 1980.

Wiedijk, C.H. *Koos Vorrink ... Een biografische Studie 1891–1940.* Amsterdam, 1986.

Wielenga, Friso. *West-Duitsland: partner uit noodzaak.* Utrecht, 1989.

Wijmans, Luuk. "De linkse stroming: Vleugelstrijd in de Nederlandse Sociaal-Democratie." In *Ideaal,* edited by Schaper. Pp. 43–57.

Wijne, Johan S. "Op weg naar de Partij van de Arbeid: Het beginsel van de SDAP van 1937 en het streven naar een democratisch-socialistische volkspartij." In *vierde jaarboek*, edited by Bank et al. Pp. 148–175.

Wilke, Manfred. *SED-Politik gegen die Realitäten: Verlauf und Funktion der Diskussion über die westdeutschen Gewerkschaften in SED und KPD/DKP 1961–1972*. Cologne, 1990.

Wilker, Lothar. *Die Sicherheitspolitik der SPD 1956–1966: Zwischen Wiedervereinigungs- und Bündnisorientierung*. Bonn-Bad Godesberg, 1977.

Williams, Philip M. *Crisis and Compromise: Politics in the Fourth Republic*. Hamden, CT, 1964.

———. *French Politics and Elections, 1951–1969*. Cambridge, 1970.

Willis, Frank. *France, Germany, and the New Europe, 1945–1967*. 2nd ed. Stanford, CA,1968.

Wilson, Frank. *The French Democratic Left, 1963–1969*. Stanford, CA, 1971.

Windmuller, John P. *Labor Relations in The Netherlands*. Ithaca, NY, 1969.

Winkler, Dörte, "Die amerikanische Sozialisierungspolitik in Deutschland, 1945–1948." In *Weichenstellungen*, edited by Winkler. Pp. 88–110.

Winkler, Heinrich August. *Arbeiter und Arbeiterbewegung in der Weimarer Republik 1918–1933*. Bonn, 1984–1990. 3 vols.

———. "Kurt Schumacher und die nationale Frage." *Frankfurter Allgemeine Zeitung*. (31 Oct. 1995).

———, ed. *Politische Weichenstellungen im Nachkriegsdeutschland 1945–1953*. Göttingen, 1979.

Winock, Michel. *La République se meurt*. Paris, 1978.

Wolff, Leon de. "Sociaal-democratie en neo-corporatisme." In *Eerste jaarboek*, edited by Bank et al. Pp. 41–71.

Wolfrum, Edgar. *Französische Besatzungspolitik und deutsche Sozialdemokratie: Politische Neuansätze in der "vergessenen Zone" bis zur Bildung des Südweststaates 1945–1952*. Düsseldorf, 1991.

———. *Krisenjahre und Aufbruchszeit: Alltag und Politik im französisch besetzten Baden 1945–1949*. Munich, 1996.

Wolinetz, Steven B. "The Dutch Labour Party: A Social Democratic Party in Transition." In *Parties*, edited by Paterson et al. Pp. 342–83.

———. *Party Re-alignment in the Netherlands*. Ph.D. Diss. Yale University, 1973.

Woltjer, Juriaan. *Recent Verleden: De Geschiedenis van Nederland in de Twintigste Eeuw* Amsterdam, 1992.

Wright, Gordon. *The Reshaping of French Democracy*. New York, 1948.

Ysmal, Colette. "Sur la Gauche socialiste." *Revue française de Science Politique*. 20 (1970), 991–1010.

Zeuner, Bodo. "Das Parteiensystem in der Grossen Koalition 1966–1969." In *Parteiensystem*, edited by Staritz, Pp. 174–93.

Ziebura, Gilbert. *Léon Blum et le Parti Socialiste*. Paris, 1967.

———. *Die deutsch-französischen Beziehungen seit 1945: Mythen und Realitäten*. Pfullingen, 1970.

———, ed. *Zur Geschichte und Problematik der Demokratie: Festgabe für Hans Herzfeld*. Berlin, 1958.

———. "Die Idee der Demokratie in der französischen Widerstandsbewegung." In *Demokratie*, edited by Ziebura. Pp. 355–73.

Zink, Harold. *The United States and Germany*. New York, 1957.

Zunneberg, Herman. *Willem Banning 1888–1971*. The Hague, 1988.

INDEX